Lecture Notes in Computer Science 4138

Commenced Publication in 1973
Founding and Former Series Editors:
Gerhard Goos, Juris Hartmanis, and Jan van Leeuwen

T0205257

Xiuzhen Cheng   Wei Li   Taieb Znati (Eds.)

Wireless Algorithms, Systems, and Applications

First International Conference, WASA 2006
Xi'an, China, August 15-17, 2006
Proceedings

 Springer

Volume Editors

Xiuzhen Cheng
The George Washington University
Department of Computer Science
801 22nd Street NW, Suite 704, Washington DC 20052, USA
E-mail: cheng@gwu.edu

Wei Li
The University of Toledo
Department of Electrical Engineering and Computer Science
2801 W. Bancroft St., Toledo, OH 43606-3390, USA
E-mail: wli@eecs.utoledo.edu

Taieb Znati
University of Pittsburgh
Computer Science Department
Pittsburgh, PA 15260, USA
E-mail: znati@cs.pitt.edu

Library of Congress Control Number: Applied for

CR Subject Classification (1998): F.1, F.2, D.1, D.2, D.4, C.2, C.4, H.4

LNCS Sublibrary: SL 1 – Theoretical Computer Science and General Issues

ISSN   0302-9743
ISBN-10   3-540-37189-3 Springer Berlin Heidelberg New York
ISBN-13   978-3-540-37189-2 Springer Berlin Heidelberg New York

Springer is a part of Springer Science+Business Media

springer.com

© Springer-Verlag Berlin Heidelberg 2006
Printed in Germany

Typesetting: Camera-ready by author, data conversion by Scientific Publishing Services, Chennai, India
Printed on acid-free paper   SPIN: 11814856   06/3142   5 4 3 2 1 0

Preface

The papers in this volume were presented at the First Annual International Conference on Wireless Algorithms, Systems, and Applications (WASA 2006), held on August 15-17, 2006, in Xi'an, China. The Program Committee selected 63 papers from a large number of submissions.

WASA 2006 was motivated by the recent advances in cutting-edge electronic and computer technologies that have paved the way for the proliferation of ubiquitous infrastructure and infrastructureless wireless networks. The objective of this conference was to address the research and development efforts of various issues in the area of algorithms, systems and applications for current and next-generation infrastructure and infrastructureless wireless networks. The conference was structured to provide a forum for researchers and practitioners, from the academic, industrial and governmental sectors, with a unique opportunity to discuss and express their views on the current trends, challenges, and state-of-the-art solutions addressing various issues related to current and next generation wireless networks.

WASA 2006 was the result of the hard work of a large group of renowned researchers from around the world. We would like to take this opportunity to thank all the Executive Committee members and the Technical Committee members. We would also like to express our gratitude towards our keynote speakers and panelists.

We would like to thank the Program Co-chairs, Xiuzhen Cheng of The George Washington University, Wei Li of The University of Toledo, and Taieb Znati of University of Pittsburgh, for their dedicated efforts towards the success of this conference. Our thanks are also due to the Finance Chair Xudong Hu of the Chinese Academy of Sciences, the Local Chair Jiangshe Zhang of Xi'an Jiaotong University, and the Publication Chair Fang Liu of The George Washington University.

Finally, we would like to express our special gratitude to our sponsors, The Chinese Academy of Sciences, The Operations Research Society of China, and Xi'an Jiaotong University, and the IEEE Technical Committee on Distributed Processing. Last, but not the least, we thank all the attendees for making this conference a success.

June 2006

Dingzhu Du and Wei Zhao
General Co-chairs
WASA 2006

Message from the Program Co-chairs

Welcome to the proceedings of the 2006 International Conference on Wireless Algorithms, System, and Applications (WASA 2006). This year's conference was the first conference in its series to address visionary approaches and future research directions dealing with effective and efficient state-of-the-art algorithm design and analysis, reliable and secure system development and implementations, experimental study and test bed validation, and new application exploration in wireless networks.

In just its first year, WASA received a large number of quality submissions from 19 countries. Each submission was assigned by the Program Co-chairs to obtain at least three reviews. Accepted papers represent state-of-the-art work in the area of algorithms, systems and applications for current and next-generation infrastructure and infrastructureless wireless networks, including mobility, localization, topology control, security, broadcast/multicast routing, data management, MAC, pervasive computing, modeling and system design. The conference was organized into 2 keynote sessions and 12 technical sessions. Also, we had a panel session with panellists invited from the National Science Foundation of the United States and academia. Two keynote speakers were invited from academia to provide a comprehensive and balanced view of a variety of issues engaged in wireless networking.

We are grateful to all those individuals whose dedicated work made WASA 2006 a successful and valuable conference. We would like to express our sincere gratitude to the TPC members for their excellent job in handling the review process, to all the panelists for their participation, and to the General Co-chairs Ding-Zhu Du and Wei Zhao for their support and hard work. We would also like to express our appreciation to all the authors for their contributions.

June 2006   Xiuzhen Cheng, Wei Li, and Taieb Znati
                                                           Program Co-chairs
                                                                WASA 2006

Organization

General Co-chairs

Dingzhu Du (University of Texas at Dallas, Xi'an Jiaotong University)
Wei Zhao (Texas A&M University, National Science Foundation, USA)

Program Co-chairs

Xiuzhen Cheng (The George Washington University, USA)
Wei Li (The University of Toledo, USA)
Taieb Znati (University of Pittsburgh, USA)

Finance Chair

Xudong Hu (Chinese Academy of Sciences, China)

Local Chair

Jiangshe Zhang (Xi'an Jiaotong University, China)

Publication Chair

Fang Liu (The George Washington University, USA)

Technical Committee Members

Dharma Agrawal (University of Cincinnati, USA)
Kemal Akkaya (Southern Illinois University Carbondale, USA)
Attahiru Alfa (University of Manitoba, Canada)
Jun Cai (University of Waterloo, Canada)
Feng Cao (Cisco Systems, USA)
Zhenfu Cao (Shanghai Jiaotong University, China)
Ionut Cardei (Florida Atlantic University, USA)
Mihaela Cardei (Florida Atlantic University, USA)
Han-Chieh Chao (National Ilan University, Taiwan)
Shigang Chen (University of Florida, USA)
Shu-Ching Chen (Florida International University, USA)
Songqing Chen (George Mason University, USA)

Yi Pan (Georgia State University, USA)
Symeon Papavassiliou (National Technical University of Athens, Greece)
Yi Qian (University of Puerto Rico at Mayaguez, Puerto Rico, USA)
Jian Ren (Michigan State University, USA)
Prasan Kumar Sahoo (Vanung University, Taiwan)
Kamil Sarac (University of Texas at Dallas, USA)
Wen-Zhan Song (Washington State University, USA)
Bo Sun (Lamar University, USA)
Willy Susilo (University of Wollongong, Australia)
My Thai (University of Texas at Dallas, USA)
Ali Tosun (University of Texas at San Antonio, USA)
Yu-Chee Tseng (National Chiao Tung University, Taiwan)
Cheng-Xiang Wang (Heriot-Watt University, UK)
Feng Wang (Seagate Inc., USA)
Huaxiong Wang (Macquarie University, Australia)
Haodong Wang (College of William and Mary, USA)
Bin Wei (AT&T Labs Research, USA)
Dapeng Oliver Wu (University of Florida, USA)
Jie Wu (Florida Atlantic University, USA)
Kui Wu (University of Victoria, Canada)
Shih-Lin Wu (Chang Gung University, Taiwan)
Ye Xia (University of Florida, USA)
Li Xie (Nanjing University, China)
Hui Xiong (Rutgers University, USA)
Cheng-Zhong Xu (Wayne State University, USA)
Zhen Xu (Beihang University, China)
Dong Xuan (Ohio State University, USA)
Guoliang Xue (Arizona State University, China)
Wei Yan (Peking University, China)
Kun Yang (University of Essex, UK)
Laurence T. Yang (St. Francis Xavier University, Canada)
Fan Ye (IBM Research, USA)
Qiang Ye (University of Prince Edward Island, Canada)
Mohamed Younis (University of Maryland Baltimore County, USA)
Gwo-Jong Yu (Aletheia University, Taiwan)
Qing-An Zeng (University of Cincinnati, USA)
Lisa Zhang (Bell Labs, USA)
Ning Zhang (University of Manchester, UK)
Wensheng Zhang (Iowa State University, USA)
Xi Zhang (Texas A&M University, USA)
Yan Zhang (National Inst. of Inf. and Comm. Tech., Singapore)
Ying Zhang (Palo Alto Research Center (PARC), USA)
Lian Zhao (Ryerson University, Canada)
Yiqiang Zhao (Carleton University, Canada)
Hao Zhu (Florida International University, USA)

Table of Contents

Session 3A: Data Management

Session 3B: Mobility, Localization and Topology Control

Session 4A: Performance Modeling and Analysis

Session 4B: MAC

Session 6A: Algorithm and System Design

Session 6B: Security

Session 7A: Broadcast/Multicast Routing

Session 7B: OFDM Networks

Session 8A: Algorithms and Protocols

Session 8B: Modeling and Algorithms

Application Oriented Networking (AON): Adding Intelligence to Next-Generation Internet Routers

Laxmi N. Bhuyan

Department of Computer Science and Engineering
University of California, Riverside

Abstract. Application Oriented Networking (AON) transforms the traditional network from pure packet-level routing to application-level processing by performing several customized computations at different nodes or routers. We study the operation of a Cisco AON system as a motivating example for our research.

A multimedia transcoding application, which dynamically transforms video streams to different output patterns to satisfy the bit rate and bandwidth requirements of a variety of clients, is considered in our research. We build an active router cluster for real MPEG stream transcoding service in our laboratory; and design, implement and evaluate various scheduling algorithms for the online transcoding operation. When transcoding operation is performed by multiple processors in the cluster, it produces out-of-order departure of media units and high jitter. We quantitatively define the QoS requirements for each media stream, and design a two-step QoS aware scheduling scheme, which is tested and compared with other algorithms.

Moving a packet from the network to the application level incurs large overhead due to PCI bottleneck and protocol stack in the operating system. Instead, we propose to move execution of the application to the network level by employing programmable network processors. We design and implement a web switch using Intel IXP 2400 network processor, and show its superiority compared to traditional Linux processing.

Biography

Laxmi Narayan Bhuyan is a professor of Computer Science and Engineering at the University of California, Riverside since January 2001. Prior to that he was a professor of Computer Science at Texas A&M University (1989-2000) and Program Director of the Computer System Architecture Program at the National Science Foundation (1998-2000). He has also worked as a consultant to Intel and HP Labs.

Dr. Bhuyan received his Ph.D. degree in Computer Engineering from Wayne State University in 1982. His current research interests are in the areas of network computing, multiprocessor architectures, router and web server architectures, parallel and distributed processing, and performance evaluation. He has published more than 150 papers in these areas in IEEE Transactions on Computers

X. Cheng, W. Li, and T. Znati (Eds.): WASA 2006, LNCS 4138, pp. 1–2, 2006.
© Springer-Verlag Berlin Heidelberg 2006

(TC), IEEE Transactions on Parallel and Distributed Systems (TPDS), Journal of Parallel and Distributed Computing (JPDC), and many refereed conference proceedings.

Dr. Bhuyan currently serves as the Editor-in-Chief of the IEEE Transactions on Parallel and Distributed Systems (TPDS). He is a past Editor of the IEEE TC, JPDC, and Parallel Computing Journal. His professional activities are too numerous to describe. To mention a few, he was the founding Program Committee Chairman of the HPCA in 1995, Program Chair of the IPDPS in 1996, General Chair of ADCOM-2001, and General Chair of HPCA-9 (2003). He was elected Chair of the IEEE Computer Society Technical Committee on Computer Architecture (TCCA) between 1995-1998.

Dr. Bhuyan is a Fellow of the IEEE, a Fellow of the ACM, a Fellow of the AAAS (American Association for the Advancement of Science), and a Fellow of the WIF (World Innovation Foundation). He has also been named as an ISI Highly Cited Researcher in Computer Science. He has received other awards such as Halliburton Professorship at Texas A&M University, and Senior Fellow of the Texas Engineering Experiment Station. He was also awarded the IEEE CS Outstanding Contribution Award in 1997.

Multi-channel Wireless Networks: Capacity, Protocols, and Experimentation

Nitin H. Vaidya

Department of Electrical and Computer Engineering,
and Coordinated Science Laboratory
University of Illinois at Urbana-Champaign

Abstract. Wireless technologies, such as IEEE 802.11, provide for multiple non-overlapping channels. Typical multi-hop wireless network configurations have only used a single channel for the network. The available network capacity can be increased by using multiple channels. However, the number of interfaces per node is expected to remain smaller than the number of channels, and therefore a single node cannot simultaneously use all the channels.

In this talk, we present the capacity of general multi-channel networks wherein the number of interfaces per node may be smaller than the number of channel. Under this scenario, we show that for a random network of n nodes, there is no capacity degradation even with only one interface per node, as long as the number of channels is less than $O(\log n)$.

Thus, in theory, multiple channels can improve network capacity significantly even with a small number of interfaces per node. However, in practice, many challenges have to be addressed before the capacity improvement can be realized. We present practical protocols for utilizing multiple channels that address many of these challenges. One set of protocols have been designed for the scenario where each node may have only one interface. Another set of protocols have been designed for the scenario where each node has multiple interfaces. We will present results from simulations that demonstrate the effectiveness of our proposed protocols in significantly increasing network capacity. The talk will also discuss our work on implementing selected protocols on an experimental testbed.

Biography

Nitin Vaidya received the Ph.D. from the University of Massachusetts at Amherst. He is presently an Associate Professor of Electrical and Computer Engineering at the University of Illinois at Urbana-Champaign (UIUC). He has held visiting positions at Microsoft Research, Sun Microsystems and the Indian Institute of Technology-Bombay. His current research is in wireless networking and mobile computing. He has co-authored papers that received awards at the ACM Mobi-Com and Personal Wireless Communications (PWC) conferences. Nitin's research has been funded by various agencies, including the National Science Foundation, DARPA, Motorola, Microsoft Research and Sun Microsystems. Nitin Vaidya is a

X. Cheng, W. Li, and T. Znati (Eds.): WASA 2006, LNCS 4138, pp. 3–4, 2006.
© Springer-Verlag Berlin Heidelberg 2006

recipient of a CAREER award from the National Science Foundation. Nitin has served on the committees of several conferences, including as program co-chair for 2003 ACM MobiCom and General Chair for 2001 ACM MobiHoc. He has served as an editor for several journals, and presently serves as the Editor-in-Chief for the IEEE Transactions on Mobile Computing. He is a senior member of the IEEE and a member of the ACM. For more information, please visit http://www.crhc.uiuc. edu/ nhv/.

A Priority Management Scheme for High Rate Wireless Personal Area Network

Jung-Hoon Song, Dong-Hoon Cho, and Ki-Jun Han

Department of Computer Engineering, Kyungpook National University, Korea
{pimpo, firecar}@netopia.knu.ac.kr, kjhan@bh.knu.ac.kr

Abstract. The High-Rate WPAN has been designed to provide a very high-speed short-range transmission capability with QoS provisions. However, the IEEE 802.15.3 standard does not specify the scheduling scheme. In this paper, we propose a priority management scheme for the IEEE 802.15.3 HR-WPAN, in which channel time allocations are scheduled, based on priority levels of data frames. We also analyze performance of management scheme by using an M/M/1 with priority queuing model. Our performance model has been validated via simulations.

1 Introduction

Recently, extensive research effort has been devoted to Wireless Personal Area Network (WPAN) which is promoted by the needs for wireless connectivity of high data rate, low cost, low complexity and low power consumption. WPAN enables short-range wireless ad hoc connectivity. Bluetooth has emerged as the first WPAN technology [1]. Because its data rate is less than 1 Mbps, it has a limited capability such that it is difficult to support bursty data or time-sensitive multimedia traffic [2]. The short-range applications in the near future are expected to support wireless transfer of multi-mega-byte multimedia files, high-quality streaming video and audio like MP3 in a very short time. These require high data rate and QoS provisions. The IEEE 802.15.3 task group is developing a new high-rate WPAN standard to provide communications between the multimedia-capable devices for real-time and large file transfer applications. The IEEE 802.15.3 standard was designed particularly for short-range communications among portable consumer electronic devices at high data rate up to 55Mbps [3].

In general, WPAN consists of several devices (DEVs). One of them should take the role of the piconet coordinator (PNC) in the piconet. If a DEV needs channel time on a regular basis, it asks the PNC for isochronous channel time. The PNC, upon receiving the channel time request command, allocates channel time for the DEV if the requested channel time is available [3]. The IEEE 802.15.3 standard defined a TDMA-based superframe structure which consists of three major parts: a beacon, an optional Contention Access Period (CAP) and a Channel Time Allocation Period (CTAP). The beacon frame transmitted by the PNC at the beginning of each superframe is used to set the timing allocations and broadcast management information for devices in the piconet. The CAP allows devices in the piconet to

X. Cheng, W. Li, and T. Znati (Eds.): WASA 2006, LNCS 4138, pp. 5–13, 2006.

transmit non-QoS asynchronous data and commands, during which Carrier Sense Multiple Access/Collision Avoidance (CSMA/CA) mechanism is used. The CTAP is composed of channel time allocations (CTAs), which are requested by the devices and allocated by the PNC according to the scheduling mechanism. However, the standard does not specify any special mechanism to efficiently allocate the channel time among competing source DEVs [4].

In this paper, we propose a priority management scheme for the IEEE 802.15.3 HR-WPAN, in which channel time allocations are scheduled based on priority levels of data frames depending on their QoS required by the higher layer entity. We also present its performance model by queuing analysis. Our performance model has been validated via simulations. The rest of this paper is organized as follows. The MAC protocol mechanism of 802.15.3 has been introduced in Section II. In Section III, we propose a priority management scheme and present the performance analysis of our scheme using a queuing model as well as simulation study. Finally, conclusions are made.

2   IEEE 802.15.3 MAC Protocol

The IEEE 802.15 is the standard that aims to deal with the physical and MAC layers of communications between devices in a WPAN. Fig.1 shows several components of an IEEE 802.15.3 piconet, which is a wireless ad hoc network. The piconet is distinguished from other types of wireless networks by its very short range. Basically, one of DEVs them is required to perform the role of PNC. The PNC, using beacon frames, provides the basic timing and allocates channel times to each DEV [3].

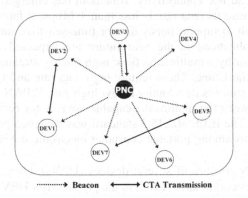

Fig. 1. Piconet topology

The access technique of the 802.15.3 MAC is based on the Time Division Multiple Access (TDMA) scheme whose basic framing structure is the superframe. The superframe is defined as the time that exists between two successive beacons as shown in Fig. 2. The superframe is divided into three periods; a beacon, CAP and

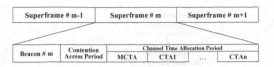

Fig. 2. IEEE 802.15.3 superframe structure

CTAP. Every superframe is composed of several frames, whose structure and length depend on the type of associated data. The elementary unit of a transmission is the slot and each frame is constituted by a different number of slots [5].

The beacon is needed for the management of the piconet synchronization. It is broadcast from the PNC during the Beacon period at the beginning of a superframe period. The beacon is used to set the channel time allocations and to communicate commands or asynchronous data if it is present in the superframe. The CAP uses CSMA/CA for the medium access. The contention in this period is based on the CSMA/CA technique which is a distributed access technique to offer fair opportunities to all the devices in the access to the channel [5]. The CTAP, on the other hand, uses a standard TDMA protocol where the DEVs have specified time windows. The CTAP, which is composed of CTAs including Management CTAs (MCTAs) are used for commands, isochronous streams and asynchronous connections [7]. The CTAP is the contention free period. If the CAP is distributed (in other words, all the devices are peer), the CTAP is centralized and is managed by the PNC. The PNC chooses the number of slots to be allocated in each data channel [5].

3 Priority Management Scheme

In the current version of 803.15.3 standard, the PNC does not consider priority level of data frame when allocating the CTA to them. Instead, the CTA is allocated simply in a "first come first serve" discipline. Members of piconet send the channel time request commands if they have data to transmit. Once there is channel time available, the PNC has to allocate the CTAs and remember that stream for every superframe until another channel time request for that stream is received from the source device. If there is no available channel time in the superframe, the PNC will reject the request with the Reason Code Field "unsuccessful" regardless of the QoS priority of that stream [4].

So, time-sensitive multimedia traffic such as high-quality streaming video and audio may be delayed or rejected when there is no available channel time in the superframe. In fact, all of the CTAs in the superframe will be allocated when the piconet becomes saturated in heavy traffic situation. Thus, in this case, even the highest priority traffic cannot be given any CTA.

In our scheduling scheme, a node sends the channel time request commands to transmit its data, which includes information about traffic priority level and the message size. If there is any channel time available in the next superframe, PNC is

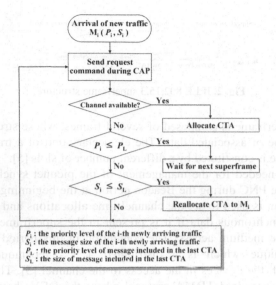

P_i : the priority level of the i-th newly arriving traffic
S_i : the message size of the i-th newly arriving traffic
P_L : the priority level of message included in the last CTA
S_L : the size of message included in the last CTA

Fig. 3. Our scheduling scheme

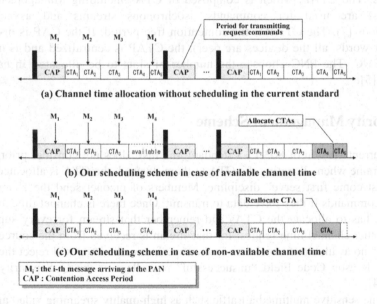

(a) Channel time allocation without scheduling in the current standard

(b) Our scheduling scheme in case of available channel time

(c) Our scheduling scheme in case of non-available channel time

M_i : the i-th message arriving at the PAN
CAP : Contention Access Period

Fig. 4. Channel time allocation

able to immediately allocate CTAs for the request command. In this case, CTAs are rearranged in the next superframe depending on the traffic priority level and the time of arrival at the MAC layer. If not, PNC should examine the priority level of the last CTA allocated in the current superframe as depicted in Fig. 3.

When the priority level of traffic is higher than that of message included in the last CTA, the last CTA will be reallocated to the newly arriving traffic in the following superframe as shown in Fig. 4(c). So, the higher priority traffic does not need to wait for idle channel provided that the last CTA is large enough to contain the new traffic. Otherwise, the traffic should wait until there is available channel time. Fig. 4 illustrates allocation of CTA with our priority management scheme.

4 Performance Evaluations

We evaluate performance of our priority management scheme by a queuing model M/M/1 with priority as illustrated in Fig 5 [8].

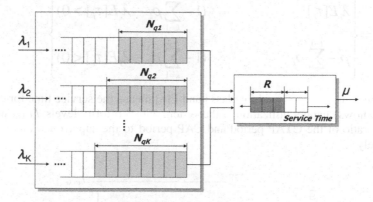

Fig. 5. M/M/1 queuing model with K priority levels

Assume that different classes of arrivals represent the different QoS priority streams requested by the device. We also assume that there are K classes of priority queues : Class 1 is the highest priority traffic, and class 2 is the second highest priority traffic, and class K means the lowest priority traffic. In addition, we assume that arrival events are mutually independent and each node has one type of traffic. Suppose that the channel time requests by 'node i' arrive at the PNC in a Poisson stream with a mean rate of λ_i.

It is also assumed that the server in queue system carries out a function associated for allocation of CTAs for the current transmission. Suppose that the service time is exponentially distributed with a mean value of $1/\mu$.

We first try to get an analytical model for the channel utilization for each class of priority traffic, denoted by ρ_i, by the type i node.

Since the total channel utilization should be less than 1, we have

$$\rho = \rho_1 + \rho_2 + \cdots + \rho_K + \rho_{CAP} \leq 1 \qquad (1)$$

where ρ_{CAP} means the ratio of the CAP period to the superframe duration.

In our scheme, the higher priority class is allocated the channel earlier, and then the lower priority class is later allocated the remaining channel. For instance, only the remainder of capacity left over the class 1 traffic will be available to class 2 traffic. Similarly, the PNC allocates the remainder of capacity to the class 4 traffic after class 1, 2, and 3 are allocated. So we have

$$\rho_1 = \lambda_1 E[\tau_1]$$

$$\rho_2 = \begin{cases} \lambda_2 E[\tau_2] & (1 - \rho_1 - \lambda_2 E[\tau_2] > 0) \\ \rho - \rho_1 & (1 - \rho_1 - \lambda_2 E[\tau_2] < 0) \end{cases}$$

$$\rho_3 = \begin{cases} \lambda_3 E[\tau_3] & (1 - \rho_1 - \rho_2 - \lambda_3 E[\tau_3] > 0) \\ \rho - \rho_1 - \rho_2 & (1 - \rho_1 - \rho_2 - \lambda_3 E[\tau_3] < 0) \end{cases}$$

$$\vdots$$

$$\rho_i = \begin{cases} \lambda_i E[\tau_i] & (1 - \sum_{k=1}^{i-1} \rho_k - \lambda_i E[\tau_i] > 0) \\ \rho - \sum_{k=1}^{i-1} \rho_k & (1 - \sum_{k=1}^{i-1} \rho_k - \lambda_i E[\tau_i] < 0) \end{cases} \tag{2}$$

where λ_i indicates offered load for class i and $E[\tau_i]$ means the service time for class i.

Fig. 6 shows channel utilization of the system with 3 priority levels. L_{CTAP} and L_{CAP} mean the ratio of the CTAP period and CAP period to the superframe duration (L_F), respectively.

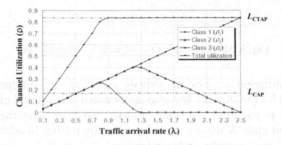

Fig. 6. Channel utilization

Consider the mean waiting time, denoted by $E[W_1]$, of the highest-priority traffic. If the PNC is requested allocation the highest priority traffic, it allocates channel time after the residual service time. The residual service time means the time that the highest priority request should wait for before it is reallocated CTA. The equation (3) and (5) give the mean waiting time in the first and second queues, respectively.

$$E[W_1] = E[R] + E[N_{q1}]E[\tau_1] = \frac{E[R]}{1 - \rho_1} \tag{3}$$

$$E[W_2] = E[R] + E[N_{q1}]E[\tau_1] + E[N_{q2}]E[\tau_2]$$
$$= E[R] + \rho_1 E[W_1] + \rho_2 E[W_2] \tag{4}$$

where $E[R]$, $E[N_{q1}]$, and $E[\tau_1]$ denote the average residual service time, the mean queue length of queue 1, and the mean service time of traffic with the highest priority class, respectively.

Solving for $E[W_2]$, we have

$$E[W_2] = \frac{E[R] + \rho_1 E[W_1]}{1 - \rho_2}$$

$$= \frac{E[R]}{(1 - \rho_1)(1 - \rho_2)}$$

(5)

where $E[N_{q2}]$, $E[\tau_2]$, and $E[R]$ mean the queue length of queue 2, the mean service time of traffic with the second highest priority class, and the residual service time of all types of traffic, respectively.

As shown in Fig 7, the traffic should wait for a certain amount of time before it is reallocated CTA. This waiting time consists of three components. First, the traffic needs to wait for the time of $E[W_{RQ}]$ on the average in the queue until the next superframe comes. Second, the traffic also has to wait for L_F to send request command during the CAP. Third, the traffic should wait for L_{CAP} to be transmitted.

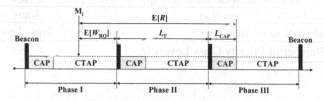

Fig. 7. Residual service time E[R]

From Fig. 7, we can get $E[R]$ by

$$E[R] = E[W_{RQ}] + L_F + L_{CAP}$$

$$= \frac{3 \times L_F}{2} + L_{CAP}$$

(6)

where $E[W_{RQ}]$ means the mean queuing delay before transmitting the request message and is given by $E[W_{RQ}] = \dfrac{L_F}{2}$

We finally get the mean waiting time for the class-i traffic

$$E[W_i] = \frac{E[R]}{(1 - \rho_1)(1 - \rho_2)\cdots(1 - \rho_i)}$$

$$= \frac{E[R]}{\displaystyle\prod_{j=1}^{i}(1 - \rho_j)} = \frac{\displaystyle\sum_{j=1}^{K}\lambda_j E[\tau_j^2]}{2\displaystyle\prod_{j=1}^{i}(1 - \rho_j)}$$

(7)

where λ is the total arrival rate $(\lambda = \lambda_1 + \lambda_2 + \cdots + \lambda_K)$.

We carry out simulation study to validate the performance model for the utilization and queuing delay. In the simulation, we consider three types of priority classes.

The network model for simulation consists of one PNC and three devices. Each device is assumed to be a Poisson traffic source with some priority level and the message size (including overhead) is exponentially distributed. Assume that the duration of the superframe is 30ms. The parameters used for simulation are listed in Table 1.

Fig. 8 shows the channel utilization for three different priority levels. This figure indicates that our analytical model is very accurate. In Fig. 8, we can see that the

Table 1. Simulation parameters

Attribute	Value
Channel Bit Rate	250 Mbps
Beacon + Contention Access Period (L_{CAP})	5ms
Channel Time Allocation Time (L_{CTAP})	25ms
Duration of Superframe (L_F)	30ms
The Mean Size of Message (μ)	1ms, 2ms
The Number of Priority Class Levels (K)	3 types

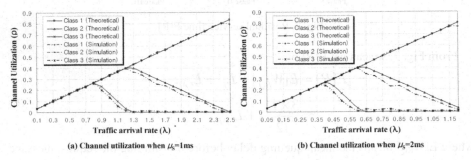

(a) Channel utilization when μ_S=1ms   (b) Channel utilization when μ_S=2ms

Fig. 8. Channel utilization

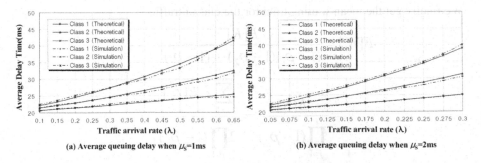

(a) Average queuing delay when μ_S=1ms   (b) Average queuing delay when μ_S=2ms

Fig. 9. Average queuing delay time

channel utilization of the high priority traffic increases linearly because it is not affected by the transmission of lower priority traffic. When channel becomes saturated, channel utilization of lower priority traffic begins to decrease linearly.

Fig. 9 depicts the average queuing delay time with our scheduling scheme. We can observe that the average delay time becomes shorter in proportion to priority class. This is because the higher priority traffic can be transmitted first.

5 Conclusions

In the IEEE 803.15.3 standard, the PNC does not consider priority level of data frame when allocating the CTA. So, QoS of multimedia traffic cannot be efficiently supported when there is no available channel time in the superframe. In this paper, a scheduling scheme has been suggested for the IEEE 802.15.3. We evaluate performance of our scheme by an M/M/1 queuing model with priority as well as simulation study. We show that our scheme can offer a satisfactory performance in terms of the queuing delay and utilization for the PAN with different QoS requirements.

References

[1] Specification of the Bluetooth System – Core vol. 1, v1.1, Available at www.bluetooth.com.

[2] J. Karaoguz, "High-Rate Wireless Personal Area Networks," *IEEE Communication Magazine*, vol. 39, no. 12, pp. 96-102, Dec. 2001.

[3] Seung Hyong Rhee, Kwangsue Chung, Yongsuk Kim, Wonyoung Yoon and Ki Soo Chang, "An Application-Aware MAC Scheme for IEEE 802.15.3 High-Rate WPAN," *Proc. of WCNC 2004*, vol. 2, pp. 1018-1023, March. 2004.

[4] Ranran Zeng and Geng-Sheng Kuo, "A Novel Scheduling Scheme and MAC Enhancements for IEEE 802.15.3 High-Rate WPAN," *Proc. of WCNC 2005*, vol. 4, pp. 2478-2483, March. 2005.

[5] Romano Fantacci, Daniele Tarchi and Gregorio Izzo, "Multimedia Traffic Management at MAC layer in IEEE 802.15.3a Personal Area Networks," *Proc. of Wireless Networks, Communications and Mobile Computing 2005 International Conference*, vol. 2, pp. 923-928, June 2005.

[6] IEEE 802.15 TG3, IEEE Standard for Information Technology – Telecommunications and Information Exchange Between Systems – Local and Metropolitan Area Networks – Specific Requirements Part 15.3 : Wireless Medium Access Control(MAC) and Physical Layer(PHY) Specifications for High Rate Wireless Personal Area Networks(WPANs), Sep. 2003.

[7] Xu Ningyi, Lou Dongjun and Zhou Zucheng, "Protocol accclerator design for IEEE 802.15.3 MAC implementation," *Proc. of the 5th International Symposium on Multi-Dimensional Mobile Communications and the 2004 Joint Conference of the 10th Asia-Pacific Conference*, vol. 1, pp. 189-192, Aug. 2004.

[8] Leon Garcia, *Probability and Random Processes for Electrical Engineering (Second Edition)*, Addison Wesley, 1994.

Connection Control by Virtual Admission in Wireless LAN Environment

Yen-Wen Chen[1], Yuan-Long Lee[2], and I-Hsuan Peng[1]

[1] Department of Communication Engineering
National Central University, Taiwan, ROC
ywchen@ce.ncu.edu.tw
[2] ZyXEL, Communications Corporation, Taiwan, ROC

Abstract. The traditional wireless technology confronted with some short-comings in practical use, such as insufficiency for bandwidth, and lack of guaranteed on Quality of Services (QoS). Both of the packet scheduling and connection admission control are the main consideration issues toward QoS networks. These two issues are mutually correlated. In this paper, we propose a measurement based with fake priority scheme for the control of connection admission in WLAN. As the concept of the virtual source and virtual MAC (VS/VMAC) is applied, the proposed scheme will not affect the transmission of existing traffic during traffic probing. The proposed scheme also provides a difference factor (D factor) for the compensation of the performance measured by VMAC. This factor is also applied to control the tightness of the policy of connection acceptance. The simulations results show that the proposed scheme can effectively manage the connection requests while maintaining QoS in WLAN.

Keywords: WLAN, Connection Admission Control, QoS.

1 Introduction

Recently, various kinds of wireless communication technologies, such as General Packet Radio Services (GPRS), Wireless Local Area Networks (WLAN), third Generation (3G) networks, etc., have been applied for internet access. Among them, WLAN is the most convenient one due to its high bandwidth and smooth integration with versatile application software. WLAN is basically a contention-based scheme, which is used in several data communication networks, for media access. And the GPRS and 3G architectures are more close to the approach of telecommunication networks. Although the contention-based approach has the advantage of flexible utilization of bandwidth, it suffers by the complexity of QoS management for various kinds of services. And the QoS management is an essential issue toward the provisioning of internet applications with various kinds of service demands. For example, some emerging services, such as voice and video, require real time QoS, while file transfer protocol (FTP) and e-mail services can tolerate delay. Therefore, the management of QoS is a very important issue in WLAN for the widely deployment of internet services.

X. Cheng, W. Li, and T. Znati (Eds.): WASA 2006, LNCS 4138, pp. 14–25, 2006.

From the network point of view, the management of QoS can be roughly divided into two aspects. One is the packet level management and the other one is the connection level management. The main consideration of packet level management is to schedule packets according to different priorities assignment [1, 2]. In addition to providing priority scheduling, the fairness and effectiveness for the usage of bandwidth [3, 4] are also issues of consequence, especially in the WLAN environment. Because valuable bandwidth will be wasted if the contention resolution algorithm applied in the scheduler is inefficient. The original media access control protocol of IEEE 802.11 (WLAN) was designed without considering QoS carefully. The IEEE 802.11e working group has proposed Enhanced Distributed Coordination Function (EDCF) to deal with this issue. EDCF introduces the concept of traffic categories. Each station has eight traffic categories with different priorities. Using EDCF, the Arbitration Inter-frame Space (AIFS) period is defined as a random waiting interval for a station to send its packet after the medium being idle. And this waiting interval is varied according to the corresponding traffic category. Thus, a higher-priority traffic category can have a shorter AIFS than that of a lower-priority traffic category. Instead of providing guaranteed QoS, EDCF supports a probabilistic priority mechanism to allocate bandwidth based on traffic categories.

The connection level management can also be regarded as the connection admission control (CAC) to regulate connection requests [5, 6]. CAC algorithm decides whether new connections can be allowed to enter the network according to the status and resource utilization of network. Ideally, a connection can only be accepted when its desired QoS can be satisfied and the quality of other connections will not be affected by its admission. A good CAC algorithm is to effectively allocate bandwidth so that the statistical gain of the number of accepted connections can be increased.

Both of packet level management and connection level management are highly correlated for the achievement of QoS. Status of resource utilization and quality of current connections perceived shall be considered in performing CAC. Packets generated by the accepted connections are forwarded according to the scheduling rules designed in the devices. Traditionally, routing and packet scheduling are the essence of internet, while CAC is not the main stream because of the connectionless characteristics of internet in its nature. However, if without CAC, it is impossible for a QoS scheduler to deal with unlimited traffic under finite network resources. Although several CAC algorithms [5, 6, 7, 8] were studied and proposed, most of them focus on the end-to-end fixed-wire connections. Seldom of them consider the changeable condition of performance in wireless transmission environment. As wireless has become one of the major ways in accessing internet, connection management of WLAN is a mandatory step toward end-to-end QoS. It shall also be noted that, instead of centralized control, the admission of connections is better performed in distributed self-control manner by each node, especially in the wireless mobile networks. And the connection admission control can also be performed after the authentication procedure in WLAN.

In this paper, the measurement based with fake priority scheme, named as virtual admission control (VAC) is proposed for the admission of connections in WLAN. The quality of transmission is measured passively, through the virtual source/virtual

MAC (VS/VMAC) concept described in [10, 11], so that the impact on the existing traffic can be minimized. The concept of the fake priority is adopted for the transmission of traffic with lower priority as probing. And the performance collected through VS/VMAC and the fake traffic is applied as the heuristic for admission control. This paper is organized as follows. In the following section, the VS/VMAC method is briefly described. We also examine the difference between VMAC and real MAC (RMAC) through simulations to illustrate the need of a difference factor. The proposed connection admission control scheme is described in Section 3. The simulations of the proposed scheme are shown and discussed in Section 4. Finally, conclusions are provided in the last section.

2   Virtual Source and Virtual MAC in WLAN

The concept of virtual source and virtual MAC was proposed in [10, 11] to measure traffic statistics for distributed access control. The behaviors of VS/VMAC are mostly like to the real MAC, including contention, backoff and drop mechanism, but there are some differences. First, packets are generated by VS virtually according to the desired traffic pattern and are then handled by VMAC for channel contention and transmission. However, in stead of sending packet to the medium, VMAC will not send packet out actually. Second, whether the "sent" packet suffers in collision is determined by checking the signal on the medium during the packet is sending. If the medium is busy during the packet transmission time, this packet is assumed to be collided (virtual collision) and the backoff procedure will start for retransmission and the packet is deferred.

The packet is assumed to be discarded if the retransmission limit reaches. The delay time of packets can also be measured by VMAC. Thus, VS/VMAC mechanism provides the estimation of channel status without loading the wireless medium. The statistics measured can be regarded as a kind of heuristic for packet scheduling. However, the measurement of VMAC may not be the same as the real MAC because no real packet is transmitted in VMAC, though VMAC is assumed to send out the packet in its operations. Consider that a station is performing VS/VMAC while another station (or the station itself) is sending a packet (RMAC) at the same time, then the station performing VS/VMAC will assume its sending to be fail and the packet is delayed, however, the packet sent by the station performing RMAC is successfully transmitted. It can be assumed that the number of active stations encountered by a mobile node with VS/VMAC during its measurement is at least greater than which of RMAC by 1. The reason is that VS is also treated as an active node from VMAC point of view and the possibility of collision detected by VMAC is higher than that occurred in RMAC. Therefore, the packet delay time measured by VMAC could be longer than which is measured by RMAC. In order to compare the difference of the measurement in delay time, a simulation is performed and depicted in Figure 1. It shows that the difference between VMAC and RMAC increases as the number of stations increases. The main reason is that the VS packet of a VMAC station has higher probability to encounter a collision with a packet sent by other station when the number of stations increases.

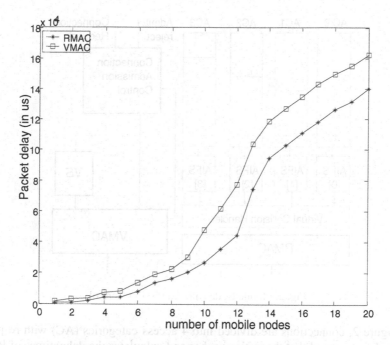

Fig. 1. Comparison between VMAC and RMAC

The difference of measurements between RMAC and VMAC not only depends on the number of active stations, but also correlates to the traffic behavior of the stations. As there is measurement difference between VMAC and RMAC, we propose a difference factor (which will be discussed in the next section) to compensate it. Hence the performance measured by VMAC can also be suitable to be applied as a heuristic to estimate the performance of sending a packet.

3 Virtual Admission Control Scheme

As mentioned in previous section, packets can be scheduled by referring to the performance measured through VS/VMAC. However, both of packet level and connection level management shall be considered together as cross layer design for the achievement of better QoS. By using the heuristic measured by VMAC, a control scheme at connection level, named virtual admission control, is proposed to regulate the connection requests. Basically, the virtual admission control scheme accepts the connection request virtually for a period of time and the actual decision of admission or rejection is made after some measurement during this period. Although there is a little delay for the establishment of a connection, this delay is tolerable when comparing to the delay time of real time packet. The virtually admitted connection is treated as either a VS or traffic with fake priority of this station. The actual admission decision of the proposed scheme mainly relies on the latest performance measured by RMAC and VMAC. The conceptual architecture of a station with the proposed admission control is shown in Figure 2.

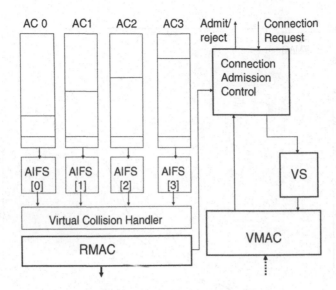

Fig. 2. Mobile Node with Admission Control

In Figure 2, connections are divided into 4 access categories (AC) with respect to 802.11e. It is assumed that the station probes and calculates the delay times of RMAC and VMAC (through VS mechanism) periodically. The process of connection admission control is performed by referring to the performance parameters measured by RMAC and VMAC. Theoretically, if more parameters are considered in CAC algorithm, the decision made by CAC may be more precise. However, the complexity of the algorithm will increase and it will not be practical in real applications. For simplicity, in this paper, we only consider the parameter of packet delay time as the main QoS parameter for connection admission control.

According to the simulation results depicted in Figure 1, there is measurement difference between RMAC and VMAC, therefore, the delay time measured by VMAC can be adjusted to be closer to that of RMAC. A difference factor, D, is defined in this paper to indicate the ratio between the delay time measured by RMAC (T_{D_R}) and VMAC (T_{D_V}). Thus,

$$D = T_{D\_R} / T_{D\_V} \qquad (1)$$

And the values of T_{D_R} and T_{D_V} are derived from the average delays measured by RMAC and VMAC within the latest time interval, respectively. As mentioned in previous section, T_{D_R} is smaller than T_{D_V}, therefore, the value of D ranges between 0 and 1. The adjusted delay time measured by VMAC, T_{A_DV}, can be obtained by multiplying T_{D_V} with D. Thus,

$$T_{A\_DV} = D * T_{D\_V} \qquad (2)$$

It is noted that the value of D is treated as the compensation factor between the delay measured by RMAC and VMAC. The adjusted virtual delay time T_{A_DV} may be larger or smaller than T_{D_R}. Then, in this paper, values of T_{D_R} and T_{A_DV} are applied as dual thresholds for the admission control. The detail procedure of the admission control by using these thresholds will be described latter. The selected value of D can be determined by the degree of tightness of the admission policy. Thus, if the value of D is selected to be larger than the actual compensation base, the value of T_{A_DV} may be greater than the delay estimated and will lead to a more conservative admission policy. It is noted that T_{A_DV} may also be smaller than T_{D_R} if the value of D is selected too small (i.e. too aggressive). For a connection request with desired delay tolerance, T_{req}, the proposed admission control algorithm will compare T_{req} with T_{D_R} and T_{A_DV}, respectively. There are three possible conditions for the above comparison. If T_{req} is greater than T_{D_R} and T_{A_DV}, it means that the required delay time can be satisfied and the connection will be admitted. If both of T_{D_R} and T_{A_DV} are greater than T_{req}, then it means the estimated delay time will be longer than the requirement and this connection will be rejected. And if T_{req} lies between T_{D_R} and T_{A_DV}, the judgment is on the margin and a further process, named as fake priority (FP) traffic measurement, is required. The concept of FP approach is to estimate the transmission performance without wasting network resource. The FP traffic measurement scheme upgrades existing traffic, whose priority is lower than the connection requested, to be the same as the connection for transmission and to measure its delay time during a short probing period. The delay time of the FP traffic is measured as T_{FP} for a period of probing time T_{probe}. The value of T_{prob} is regarded as the tolerable delay of the connection establishment. And the estimated delay time is calculated by the average of T_{FP} and the maximum of T_{D_R} and T_{A_DV} in a heuristic manner. This average delay time is compared with T_{req} for the decision of admission. The procedure of the proposed CAC algorithm is stated as follows.

Algorithm VAC

Step 1: if $(T_{D\_R} < T_{req}$ and $T_{A\_DV} < T_{req})$
          then admit;
Step 2: if $(T_{D\_R} > T_{req}$ and $T_{A\_DV} > T_{req})$
             then reject;

Step 3:
    if there exists traffic with lower priority
    of access category
        then
            upgrade this category as
            FP traffic to be the same as
            the connection and goto Step 4;
        else reject;
Step 4: Measure the delay time of FP traffic (T_{FP}) for T_{probe}

interval;
Step: 5:

$$if \ (T_{req} > (T_{FP} + Max(T_{D\_R}, T_{A\_DV})) / 2)$$

        then admit;
        else reject;
end VAC;

It is noted that above algorithm operates in a conservative mode because the connection will be rejected if there is no traffic with lower priority than this connection when the criteria of judgment is on the margin (step 3). The main reason is that if there is no traffic with lower priority than the new connection, it is suggested to reject the new connection so that the performance of existing connections can be maintained.

4 Experimental Results

In order to evaluate the performance of the proposed scheme, exhaustive simulations of 1 AP with multiple stations were performed. We assume that the channel is error-free and all of the stations are in the same BSS. The buffer of each station is assumed to be infinite (i.e. the packet will never be dropped due to buffer overflow). Each station has its own traffic generator to simulate the background and the on demand traffic. The on demand traffic of each station includes best effort, video, and voice traffic types. The session time, when a new request is admitted, is Poisson distributed with mean 2 minutes to emulate a voice call or a short video conference call. The tolerance time T_{prob} is defined as 1 second during the simulations. The channel rate is 11 Mbps and other parameters used in our simulation are listed in table 1. The number of stations is ranged from 1 to 20. We use the RTS/CTS mechanism to solve the hidden node problem. The collision will only occur when there are at least two stations choosing the same timeslot to send their packets after backoff procedure and will never occur during the transmitting. Characteristics of voice and video traffic are modeled as 32 Kbps and 200 Kbps CBR (constant bit rate), respectively. Best effort traffic has an infinite long traffic at 350 Kbps as the background traffic. The rate of voice and video are the same as adopted in [4].

Table 1. Simulation parameters

Slot time	20 us
SIFS	10 us
DIFS	50 us
PHY Header	192 us
AirPropagationTime	1 us
CWmin	31
CWmax	1023
RetryLimit	4
PacketSize	1500 bytes
Length of RTS	PHY Header+20 bytes
Length of CTS	PHY Header+14 bytes
Length of Ack	PHY Header+14 bytes

The simulation results are shown in Figures 3, 4, 5, and 6. Figures 3 and 4 depict the performance of packet delay time and Figures 5 and 6 show the simulation results of the blocking rate. We change the delay threshold of voice and video to examine the impact of the performance. In the following simulations, we use thresholds *thd*_voice and *thd*_video to represent the delay requirements of voice and video, respectively. For example, "*thd*_voice = 10ms" means that the delay tolerance of voice packet shall be no more than 10ms. From Figures 3 and 4, we found that the delay time for both of voice (VO) and video (VI) by using the proposed VAC can be restricted within the desired demands when comparing to that without connection admission control. Thus, the proposed scheme can effectively regulate the connection requests.

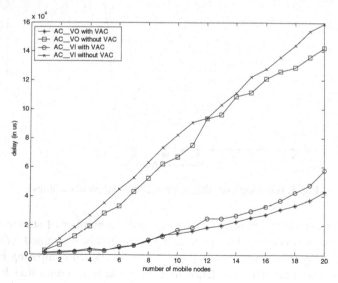

Fig. 3. Delay comparison of VAC and none-VAC (*thd*_voice =20ms, *thd*_video = 30ms)

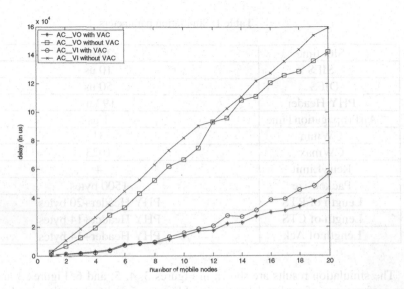

Fig. 4. Delay comparison of VAC and none-VAC (*thd*_voice =30ms, *thd*_video = 50ms)

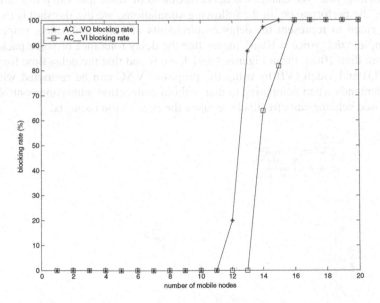

Fig. 5. Blocking rate (*thd*_voice = 20ms, *thd*_video = 30ms)

The relationships between the blocking rate and the number of stations are shown in Figures 5 and 6. It is noted that the blocking rates shall be examined with respect to the results of delay time illustrated in Figures 3 and 4. When comparing Figures 3, 5 and 4. 6, we can find that the delay time of packets is controlled by blocking connection requests. For example, in Figure 5, the blocking rates of voice and video

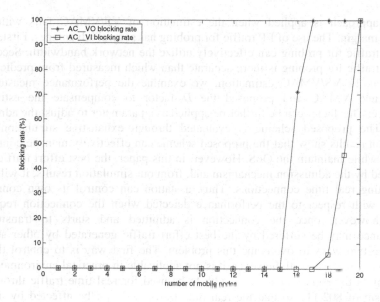

Fig. 6. Blocking rate (*thd*_voice = 30ms, *thd*_video = 50ms)

dramatically increase from 11 stations and 13 stations (and the blocking rates equal to 1 for 14 and 15 stations), respectively. And at the same number of stations, the average delay times of *thd*_voice and *thd*_video are 20ms and 30 ms, respectively, in Figure 3. The delay time of voice traffic is below 20 ms when the number of stations is less than 11 (and it is about 20 ms for 14 stations) and the delay time of video traffic is below 30 ms when the number of stations is less than 13 (and it is about 30ms for 15 stations), which satisfy the desired delay constraints. In Figure 6, the delay thresholds of voice and video are 30ms and 50ms, respectively, it has the same phenomenon when referring to Figure 4. It also notes that the delay time keeps increasing when the number of stations keeps increasing even when the voice and video connections are completely blocked (blocking rate equals to 1). The reason is that, when the number of stations exceeds its tolerable numbers, 14 and 15, although the voice and video connections are totally blocked, the best effort traffic still be generated by those stations as background traffic. Thus, those stations are with best effort traffic only. Since we do not control the best effort flow in this paper, those best effort traffic only stations still affect the performance of the voice and video traffic.

5 Conclusions

In this paper, we extend the VS/VMAC scheme to be used in connection admission control mechanism. The proposed self-governing control scheme, VAC, performs its admission control by using the heuristics of traffic probe and FP traffic. The main concept is that whenever there is a connection request, the station will estimate the current QoS parameter by using the VS/VMAC or current traffic stream with fake priority to determine whether the QoS can satisfy the requirements or not. The fake priority approach is applied when the estimation of VS/VMAC falls within the decision margin. The use of FP traffic for probing has several advantages. First, to use existing traffic for probing can effectively utilize the network bandwidth. Second, to use real traffic for probing is more accurate than which measured from prediction or estimation. In VS/VMAC estimation, we examine the performance measured by RMAC and VMAC and proposed the D factor to compensate the estimation difference. This factor can be further be applied as a parameter to adjust the admission policy. The proposed scheme is evaluated through exhaustive simulations. Our simulation results show that the proposed scheme can effectively manage connection requests while maintain the QoS. However, in this paper, the best effort traffic is not controlled by the admission mechanism and, from our simulation results, it will affect the existing real time connections. Thus, a station can control its own connection requests with respect to the performance detected when the connection request is issued, however, once the connection is admitted and starts to transmit, its performance may be suffered by the best effort traffic generated by other stations. There are two ways to overcome this problem. The first way is to control the best effort connections as well, however, it is not applicable in practical environment. The other way is to reserve some bandwidth to be used for real time traffic through the mechanism of 802.11e so that the real time traffic will not be affected by the best effort traffic. In this paper, we only consider the admission control of new connections within one BSS. However, in addition to providing new connection requests, an AP has to handle the handoff connections in mobile environment. Therefore, it is of interesting to consider the admission control by using the QoS-aware in a multiple AP environment for mobile stations.

Acknowledgements

This research was supported in part by the grants from National Science Council (NSC94-2213-E-008-036, and 93-2219-E-260-006), and National Center for High-performance Computing (NCHC).

References

1. H. Perros and K. Elsayed, "Call admission control schemes: A review," IEEE Commun. Mag., vol. 34, pp. 82-91, Nov. 1996.
2. J. Siwak, and I. Rubin, "Connection admission control for capacity-varying networks with stochastic capacity change times," IEEE/ACM Trans. On Networking, vol. 9, issue 3, pp. 351-360, June, 2001.
3. G. Bianchi, A. Capone, and C. Petrioli, "Throughput analysis of end-to-end measurement-based admission control in IP," in Proc. IEEE INFOCOM 2000, vol. 3, 2000, pp. 1461-1470.
4. L.-D. Chou, H,-J, Hsieh and J,-M, Chen, "Multicast with QoS support in heterogeneous wireless networks," Lecture Notes in Computer Science, vol. 3207, pp. 581-590, Aug. 2004.
5. http://www.research.avayalabs.com/techreport/ALR-2002-021-paper.pdf, "A New Admission Control Metric for VoIP Traffic in 802.11 Networks"

6. D. Pong and T. Moors, "*Call Admission Control for IEEE 802.11 Contention Access Mechanism*", Proc. Globecom 2003, Pages: 174-8, Dec. 1-5, 2003.
7. Gahng-Seop Ahn, Andrew T. Campbell, Andras Veres, Li-Hsiang Sun, "*SWAN: Service Differentiation in Stateless Wireless Ad Hoc Networks*", Proc. IEEE Infocom 2002, Jun. 2002.
8. http://www.merl.com/reports/docs/TR2003-122.pdf,"*A New Measurement- Based Admission Control Method for IEEE802.11*", Mitsubishi Electric Research Laboratory, 2003.
9. M.Visser and M.ElZarki, "*Voice and data transmission over an 802.11 wireless network*", Proceedings of PIMRC, Toronto, Canada, Sept. 1995.
10. Andras Veres, Andrew T. Campbell, Michael Barry, "*Supporting Service Differentiation in Wireless Packet Networks Using Distributed Control*", IEEE Journal on selected areas in communications, Vol.19, No.10, Pages: 2081-2093, Oct. 2001.
11. Barry, M., Campbell, A.T , A. Veres , "*Distributed Control Algorithms for Service Differentiation in Wireless Packet Networks*", IEEE Infocom 2001, Vol.1 , Pages:582-590, Apr. 2001.
12. T. Elbatt and A. Ephremides, "*Joint Scheduling and Power Control for Wireless Ad Hoc Networks,*" IEEE Trans. Wireless Communications, vol. 3, no. 1, Pages: 74-85, Jan., 2004.

A Scalable Port Forwarding
for P2P-Based Wi-Fi Applications

Ming-Wei Wu[1], Yennun Huang[2],
Ing-Yi Chen[3], Shyue-Kung Lu[4], and Sy-Yen Kuo[1]

[1] National Taiwan University, Taiwan
[2] AT&T Labs, Florham Park, NJ, USA
[3] National Taipei University of Technology, Taiwan
[4] Fu Jen Catholic University, Taiwan
benson@ee.ntu.edu.tw, yen@research.att.com,
ichen@ntut.edu.tw, sklu@ee.fju.edu.tw, sykuo@cc.ee.ntu.edu.tw

Abstract. A few killer applications that rocked the Internet community these years are peer-to-peer (P2P) file-sharing applications and VoIP (voice over Internet Protocol) telephony services. Unlike traditional client-and-server applications in which servers are services provider and by default should be public addressable, each peer in P2P networks can play both roles (client and server). However, legacy usage of the network address translation (NAT) module on most wireless access points (APs) causes new problems with emerging P2P communications especially in opposing APs (both peers of an Internet connection are behind AP) where each peer uses private Internet Protocol (IP) address and neither side has global visibility to each other. This article therefore examines such issue from three approaches, 1) leveraging the complexity of client application, 2) introducing additional intermediate gateways and protocols and 3) enhancing the wireless AP itself. Client-based solutions such as UDP/TCP hole-punching suffer from race condition while gateway-based solutions tend to incur overhead for interoperability and deployment. This paper proposes a scalable port forwarding (SPF) design for wireless AP, which introduces little or negligible time and space complexity, to significantly improve the connectivity and scalability of a conventional AP by 1) lessening the race condition of P2P traversals in opposing APs, 2) multiplexing the port numbers to exceed theoretical upper bound 65,535 and 3) allowing more servers to bind to a specific port.

Keywords: Wi-Fi, Access Point (AP), Peer-to-Peer (P2P), Port Forwarding, Network Address Translation (NAT).

1 Introduction

Thanks to the development of new networking technologies and paradigms, such as wireless metropolitan area networks (WMANs), wireless local area networks (WLANs), and wireless personal area networks (WPANs), during the past 25 years, wireless technologies have shown to be economic and feasible, especially the incredible penetration of the IEEE 802.11b WLAN standard, popularly known as

X. Cheng, W. Li, and T. Znati (Eds.): WASA 2006, LNCS 4138, pp. 26–37, 2006.
© Springer-Verlag Berlin Heidelberg 2006

Wi-Fi (wireless-fidelity). Wi-Fi hotspots have sprung up at varied places or even have grown into broader neighborhood "hot zones" by deploying one or several access points (APs) and allow its subscriber to access the Internet via these APs. Such nearly "anywhere, anytime" connectivity has brought innovative application and versatile services to the market. Two interesting segments are peer-to-peer (P2P) file-sharing (e.g. Gnutella/Napster/EDonkey/Bittorrent) and network telephony (e.g. Skype). In theory, whenever people with Wi-Fi phones have access to a hot spot, they might have little inclination to spend extra on a cell phone call. It could terrify the cellular carriers that have spent billions building their networks[1]. However, the feasibility of this scenario requires more efforts and extra works.

With the scarcity of IPv4 addresses, each AP is often equipped with a NAT (network address translation) module to associate public/private addressing and dynamically assign private IP address via DHCP (dynamic host configuration protocol) to its subscriber. The use of private IP address, which reduces Internet transparency, brings limitations for universal adopting of Internet applications. Since wireless AP shares one or several public routable IPv4 addresses to a pool of private addresses, it favors internal-initiated outgoing connections and denies external-initiated incoming connections. Such connection characteristics work fine in client-server communications because servers are by default public addressable. Private clients just need to initiate outbound connections to reach these public servers. However, with the popularity of running P2P-based applications over Wi-Fi networks, it is possible to have servers using private addresses and apparently these servers need extra workarounds to provide services smoothly. Depending on the deployment of wireless AP, there could be two scenarios of P2P traversals. The first one is *single AP* scenario where only one peer is behind an AP and mutual visibility therefore is reduced. Most existing P2P applications adopt a default practice called reverse connection (or push request) that works around easily.

Fig. 1 illustrates the steps in reverse connection. The originating peer (e.g. Node$_A$) sends the push request through an intermediate peer (e.g. Node$_B$), which relays it via an existing connection (e.g. Flow$_{cb}$), to the targeting peer (e.g. Node$_C$) inside the wireless AP. Upon receiving the push request, the targeting peer in return initiates an outbound connection (e.g. Flow$_{ca}$) directly to the originating peer.

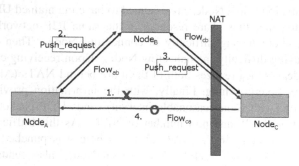

Fig. 1. Push-request (reversing the connection)

---

[1] Wi-Fi Phones Could Be Next Money-Saver In Telecom, http://www.informationweek.com/story/showArticle. jhtml?articleID=20300052.

The second scenario is *opposing APs* scenario where both peers are behind APs and their global visibilities are eliminated. This scenario is much more sophisticated to handle properly and had brought the attentions to many researchers. Aside from resolving P2P traversal problems, some people therefore argue NAT module as inevitable nightmares [1, 2] and in fact this is becoming a vicious cycle because scarce supply of IPv4 addresses prolongs NATs and wide use of NATs prolong the life of IPv4. While examining existing solutions for P2P traversals in opposing APs, it might also be interested to think what could be done to make private addressing more network-friendly.

The rest of this work is organized as follows. Section 2 examines existing solutions for P2P traversals in opposing APs and identifies their potential problems. Section 3 proposes a Scalable Port Forwarding (SPF) design that helps in resolving P2P traversals as well as raising the scalability of AP. The complexity and improvement of SPF are investigated in Section 4. Finally, we conclude the paper in Section 5.

2   Related Works

Two categories of solutions have been proposed to address P2P traversals in opposing APs: 1) the client-based solutions such as UDP and TCP hole punching [3] and 2) the gateway-based solutions such as JXTA [4], SOCKS5, UPnP [5], STUN [6] and TURN [7].

2.1   Client-Based Solutions

One characteristic of client applications is sophistication. Since P2P communications are blocked in opposing APs due to the lack of global visibility, a workaround named "hole-punching" is used to provide *temporal visibility*. A simpler example is shown in Fig. 2, which is the UDP hole-punching. This technique was first explored by Dan Kegel [8], mentioned in section 5.1 of RFC 3027 [9], and used in recent experimental Internet protocols [10, 11] as well as various proprietary protocols such as those for on-line gaming.

In Fig. 2, both $Node_A$ and $Node_C$ are assumed to have maintained UDP connections to $Node_B$ and together they share resource in the same P2P network. First, $Node_A$ informs $Node_B$ about having difficulty in connecting $Node_C$. Then $Node_C$ informs $Node_B$ about having difficulty in connecting $Node_A$. Upon receiving complaints from $Node_A$ and $Node_C$, $Node_B$ realizes both of them are behind NATs (APs) and informs them to perform hole-punching. Finally, with the information provided by $Node_B$, $Node_A$ repeatedly (with some reasonable interval) sends UDP packets designated to $FC_{IP}:FC_P$, which is the IP and port number of NAT_C. As this traffic passes through NAT_A, it creates an entry in the NAT table – a hole was punched that associates $FC_{IP}:FC_P$ with $A_{IP}:A_P$ and $FA_{IP}:FA_P$. Vice versa, $Node_C$ also sends UDP packets designated to $FA_{IP}:FA_P$. Since the UDP packets of each peer have created corresponding associations in both NATs, the connections can be resolved and established.

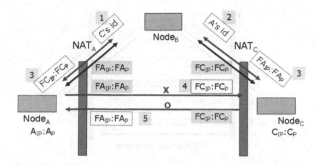

Fig. 2. Hole-punching for promiscuous UDP penetration

Extending the concept of propagating push request in reverse connection, UDP hole-punching leverages a public middleman to coordinate both sides in creating necessary NAT entries by UDP packets. For some non-promiscuous NAT, which is strict about who can send packets back in across the NAT, $Node_A$ and $Node_C$ would need to increment the port numbers such as FA_{p+1} and FC_{p+1}.

As UDP packets are sent repeatedly until the hole is punched (thus NAT association is created), such aggressive manner does not work on TCP traffic because TCP prohibits repeated connection attempts of same masqueraded port. When SYN packet arrives before the hole is being punched, NAT will return a RST (reset) packet, and the connection will fail. P2P Working Group has suggested the use of a little-known feature of TCP - the simultaneous open, which is slightly different from standard three-way handshake (SYN, SYN/ACK, and ACK). Fig. 3 shows how TCP hole-punching could be used in opposing APs situation. This technique was partially implemented in NatTrav [12] and extended in NUTSS [13] and NATBLASTER [14].

In Fig. 3, both $Node_A$ and $Node_C$ are assumed to have maintained TCP connections to $Node_B$ and together they share resource in the same P2P network. A reasonable RTT (round-trip time) between $Node_A$ and $Node_C$ are 50 ms.

Step 1 to 3 are identical to the UDP hole-punching scenario, except that the designated port numbers are incremented (FA_{p+1} and FC_{p+1}) since a port number cannot be reused in different TCP connections.

Then in step 4, before initiating the TCP simultaneous open, $Node_A$ first applies a UDP hole-punching to $Node_C$ so that $Node_C$ could send a time trigger to guarantee SYN requests always arrive after the NAT hole is punched. In this case, the SYN_C request needs to arrive after the hole is punched on NAT_A. After sending the UDP time trigger and waiting for a certain period of time (e.g. 10ms), $Node_C$ punches a hole on NAT_C to welcome the coming SYN_A request and hence a TCP connection for both sides is successfully established.

Unfortunately, both UDP/TCP hole-punching solutions suffer the race condition because there might be other sources competing the ports of a non-promiscuous NAT – the hole-punching technique is likely to work only when network traffic is not heavy.

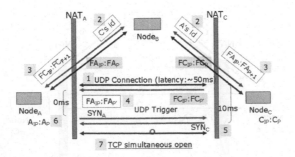

Fig. 3. Hole-punching for TCP penetration

2.2 Gateway-Based Solutions

The third party mentioned earlier in either UDP or TCP penetration is acting as a public addressable proxy. Depending on the add-on values of such intermediate proxy, it could be simply a relay (or router), for the two blocked peers, or an advanced relay (or rendezvous server) that provides a repository for advertisement information, such as that used by JXTA (pronounced *jux-ta*) to support peer discovery. JXTA is a P2P framework pioneered by Sun Microsystems that defines a set of six protocols that developers can handily use to build P2P applications. The advent of JXTA is welcoming because it is probably the first open standard that tries to unite different protocols, different architectures and different implementations in the P2P world. However, JXTA might be quite sophisticated for people seeking a *light-weight* solution for P2P traversals in opposing APs.

A SOCKS5 gateway can also act as an intermediate proxy fine, but it requires a SOCKS server and additional SOCKS support in the client application which would have interoperability and management overhead in practice.

Notably, the use of intermediate gateways for P2P traversals might in fact breaks the idea of direct P2P communication. Since these gateways are on behalf of the peers behind opposing APs, they are not just brokers, but form a triangle routing – they are part of the data path.

An up-and-coming protocol called Universal Plug-and-Play (UPnP) is defining an Internet Gateway Device (IGD) that allows client applications to transparently map, open, and close ports on the IGD/NAT. Such explicit signaling not only saves AP engineers from implementing various application-level gateways (ALG) but also let peers behind IGD/NAT to on-demand acquire their visibility. These UPnP-aware applications/stacks are promising and will be a must-have feature for all NAT-enabled devices in the near future.

RFC 3489, which is Simple Traversal of UDP through NAT (STUN), allows applications to discover the presence and types of NATs and firewalls between them and the public Internet. It defines a special STUN server in the public address space, which again is a middleman concept, to inform the STUN-enabled clients in the private address space of the necessary information for that particular session. This proposal has difficulty in applying to neither P2P applications since they do not generally support STUN nor non-promiscuous (or symmetric) NAT devices. Moreover, STUN does not address the need to support TCP based applications. As a matter of fact, Traversal Using Relay NAT (TURN), which is identical in syntax and general operation to STUN, is introduced to resolve the disadvantages of STUN. However, this solution comes at high cost to implement new protocol and new server.

Skype (an Internet telephony service based on P2P concept) uses a proprietary variation of STUN and TURN for NAT traversals [15] – Skype clients that are not behind NAT are utilized to proxy all the data for clients that are behind NAT. However, there are some security and efficiency concerns for this solution. One is that a Skype client outside the NAT does not know whose data is passing through his/her computer. Another is that it is using his/her bandwidth; after all, someone has to pay one way or another for Internet bandwidth necessary to proxy the voice stream.

3   A Scalable Port Forwarding for P2P Networks

As a matter of fact, UDP/TCP hole-punching is not a complete solution because it suffers from race condition when traversing through a busy AP. Let's assume the estimated load of an AP is 1 connection per second for home environment or 5~200 connections per second for SME (small-medium enterprise), then the expected deadline (timeout) for opposite peers to punch the hole on time would be 1000 ms or 20~200 ms respectively. A measurement study of P2P network [16] shows more than 80% of Gnutella users have large latency (>1000 ms). Therefore, the hole-punching solutions are very likely to fail in practice. The necessity of introducing a whole new framework or protocol for solving P2P communication in opposing APs is also questionable. Moreover, NAT itself could be a constraint for P2P applications to scale because it 1) limits the number of on-going connections to below 65,535 and 2) binds only one listening server per port. These two disadvantages not only limit the population of private peers but also prohibit multiple hosting of the same service. Imagine the case where only one Web server or Gnutella server could be established behind an AP. It might be okay for home users but would be infeasible for enterprise and ISP since they mat have hundred and thousands of users that demand service hosting. Therefore, this paper proposes a more general solution for P2P traversal in opposing APs that aims to improve the connectivity and scalability of a conventional AP by 1) lessening the race condition of P2P traversals in opposing APs, 2) multiplexing the port numbers to exceed theoretical upper bound 65,535 and 3) allowing more servers to bind to a specific port.

Given the three goals, we implement a scalable port forwarding (SPF) module that adds three enhancements to existing AP: 1) improving the data structure of the NAT translation table in maintaining six-tuples (source-destination socket pairs plus IP/port of AP) for conflict-checking, 2) reusing the port number for bidirectional traffic when necessary and 3) co-working with out-of-band signaling protocols such as Universal Plug-and-Play (UPnP) or Application-Level Gateway (ALG) for inbound traffic.

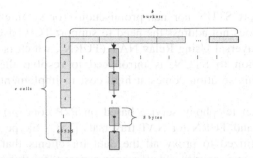

Fig. 4. Data structure of the enhanced translation table

Before exercising port reusing concept, SPF requires slight modifications to the data structure of a conventional NAT translation table so that the capacity of each NAT entry is increased meaning that more connections are stored and mapped per entry. Fig. 4 illustrates a modified NAT translation table with a fixed array of 65,535 cells, where the i-th cell represents the i-th port number of the NAT device. Each i-th cell contains one NAT hash table maintaining all connection mappings that are multiplexed to the i-th port number.

The main concept of SPF is simple: NAT should reuse its port number when necessary and whenever possible. Depending on the side that initiates the connection, SPF exercises port reusing in two approaches:

1. For outbound traffic where a private peer (acting as a client) is initiating outgoing connection, SPF should either 1) simply giving away a new port number as long as there are plenty of available ports or 2) reusing the port number when no connections are heading to the same destination IP and destination port.
2. For inbound traffic where a private peer (acting as a server) is waiting for incoming connections, SPF should co-work with out-of-band signaling protocols such as Universal Plug-and-Play (UPnP) or Application-Level Gateway (ALG) to determine in advance the source IP of all expected incoming connections and assign a wildcard value to any not-yet-know source port.

3.1 Conflict Resolution for Outbound Traffic

Since client applications often randomly select an unreserved local port to be used as an instance of the service, SPF takes two different actions for outbound traffic.

1. When the available NAT ports are still plenty or above certain threshold, SPF simply allocates port number incrementally or decrementally depending on the original implementation of NAT (Fig. 5)
2. When NAT is running out of available ports or below certain threshold, SPF would reuse a port number for better scalability (Fig. 6) and avoid destination conflict between connections (Fig. 7). With the six-tuples maintained in the translation table by SPF, NAT module is able to differentiate traffic targeting different destinations even when the port numbers are identical.

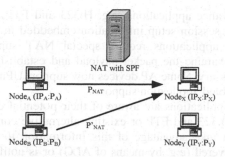

Fig. 5. Outbound traffic with plenty NAT ports available

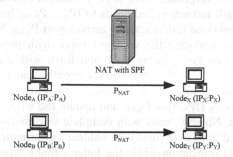

Fig. 6. Outbound traffic with few NAT ports available

```
function CheckConflict (IP_NAT,P_NATa,IP_source,P_source,IP_dest,P_dest) {
if (global_NAT[P_NATa]) { //P_NATa is occupied
/* a generic NAT hash function */
P_n=HASH_FN(IP_NAT,P_NATa,IP_source,P_source,IP_dest,P_dest);
/* a linear search for destination conflict */
if ConflictSearch (global_NAT[P_NATa][P_n],IP_dest,P_dest);
return true;  //there is a conflict
};
return false;   //there is no conflict
};
…
for (a=1024;a<=65535;a++) {
if CheckConflict(IP_NAT,P_NATa,IP_source,P_source,IP_dest,P_dest)
continue;
return P_NATa;
};
```

Fig. 7. Pseudo code snippets for port reusing

3.2 Conflict Resolution for Inbound Traffic

Since peers hosting some Internet services behind an AP only have private addresses, they are invisible to peers outside the AP. One common way to open a service port on the NAT module (of an AP) is to directly use port forwarding such that incoming traffic to certain ports on the AP is forwarded to specific internal hosts. Apparently, port forwarding is not feasible to peers that on-demand become servers during a session. There are advance applications (e.g. H.323 and FTP) that initiate a server (open a port) with the session setup information embedded in the packet's payload. These NAT-sensitive applications require special NAT supports such as ALG function in order to examine the packet payload and establish translation mapping beforehand when necessary. Some AP devices now support UPnP function in addition to numerous NAT-enabled application supports.

As these advance applications are aware of their potential clients (either through existing session like H.323 and FTP or existing alternative connection like Gnutella and Napter), SPF can take advantage of this information to scale. In Fig. 8, lets assume SPF has discovered (e.g. by means of ALG) or is notified (e.g. by means of UPnP) that $Node_A$ is expecting $Node_X$, it inserts a translation mapping that rewrites all incoming packets, which originates from IP_X:* (wildcard denotes port number P_X is *don't care* since it is still unknown) and heads to IP_{NAT}:P_{NAT}, be translated to IP_A:P_A. Later, when such IP_X inbound traffic actually arrives port P_{NAT}, SPF would update the translation mapping by replacing the wildcard value with now-available P_X value. Obviously, subsequent packets coming back and forth within the same connection between IP_A:P_A and IP_X:P_X could be translated correctly. Later on, SPF continues to offer wildcard insertion for subsequent incoming connections, for example $Node_A$ or $Node_B$ is expecting $Node_Y$ (IP_Y:*) at P_{NAT}, and update the wildcard when the inbound traffic actually arrives. Notably, rules with complete information should take higher precedence (be checked first) over rules with wildcard information because the former can provide immediate translation while the latter cannot. Since all six-tuples of a connection are known at the stage of receiving inbound traffic, reusing the port number on the SPF does not encounter any translation difficulty.

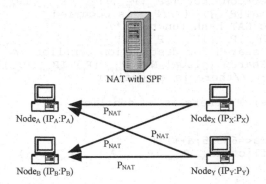

Fig. 8. Multiple inbound traffic heading to identical port

4   Discussion and Evaluation

4.1   Time and Space Complexity

The NAT module of a conventional AP uses a hash table to store the private-to-public translation mappings. Such hashing method provides access to stored records in constant time $O(1)$ or $O(n)$ when it needs to travel the linked list after evaluating the hash function (n represents the number of the private-to-public connections). Recalling

Fig. 4, the time complexity of SPF could be computed as: the constant time to point to the i-th cell of the fixed array plus the constant time to evaluate the hashing function and the linear time to traverse the linked list. This is a linear time complexity. As NAT module in practice is often embedded in the WAN edge gateway (AP), it requires high performance to introduce least transport delay. NAT module with time complexity $O(n)$ in real world implementation is measured to scale well [17].

For the space overhead, SPF covers a fixed array of c cells, a hash table of bucket size b and linked-lists to store n elements as shown in Fig. 4. Let s be the space required by an empty space (e.g. empty array cell) and S be the space required by a NAT entry. The space complexity of SPF is computed as follows:

Memory consumption of SPF:
= total empty space + total NAT entries
= $s(c+b+n)+S(n)$
= $sc+sb+sn+Sn$

Let's assume $s=2$ bytes, $c=65,535$ cells, $b=512$ buckets and $S=160$ bytes, then the translation table yields a space complexity of $162n+132094$ bytes or simply $162n$ neglecting the minor constant. In other words, 100,000 concurrent sessions consume about 16.2 MB, which is much lower than the minimum memory requirement of a typical edge gateway. Existing legacy NAT-enabled devices, therefore, can employ SPF module with little or negligible space overhead.

4.2 Improvement

Since SPF allows multiple bindings to every NAT port number, it increases the availability of port numbers on the AP. P2P applications that adopt UDP/TCP hole-punching solution in opposing APs therefore would have a better chance to succeed. As shown in Fig. 9, let's assume a possibility p=0.1 for any two connections heading towards an identical destination, then the permissible deadline (timeout) for competing the next NAT port is about 10 times longer than conventional AP that does not support SPF. With a permissive timeout of 2000ms, which satisfies the average latency of most P2P networks, UDP/TCP hole-punching is then able to catch its deadline when passing through NAT that implements SPF.

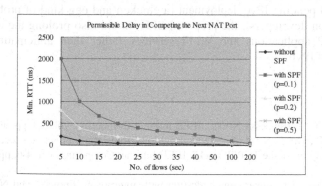

Fig. 9. Permissible timeout improved by SPF

As SPF binds more than one connection per port, it not only increases the degree of port multiplexing but also increases the scalability of NAT to serve more connections. The wildcard design of SPF helps an AP to permit multiple servers listening on the same port number, which is very beneficial to clients using private addresses. In addition, SPF also allows an AP (with sufficient computation power and memory capacity) to handle more than 65,535 connections. Table 1 summarizes the performances of a conventional NAT (w/o SPF) and an enhanced NAT (with SPF).

Table 1. The improvement of NAT performance before and after employing SPF

	NAT w/o SPF	NAT with SPF
Port scalability	Fair	High
	(less than 65,535)	(more than 65,535)
Port multiplexing	Low	High
	(one service per port)	(unlimited services per port)
Port availability	Low	High
	(race condition in busy server)	(next port is highly available)

5 Conclusions

As this paper has examined existing solutions for P2P traversals in opposing APs, they are either incomplete or too costly. Client-based solutions suffer from race condition and only work in light-weight traffic. UDP/TCP hole-punching therefore should co-work with the proposed SPF where client applications have better chance to punch the hole they requested. For gateway-based solutions, the idea of intermediate gateways could play a significance role in scaling up the P2P population. For example, a SPF-enabled AP device might want to integrate relay/rendezvous peer of JXTA as value-added services and eliminate the impact of a triangle routing. The scalability of such integrated AP is further improved by the proposed SPF.

In general, the proposed SPF not only could be transparently implemented because of negligible complexity but also significantly improves the connectivity and scalability of a wireless AP by 1) lessening the race condition of P2P traversals in opposing APs, 2) multiplexing the port numbers to exceed theoretical upper bound 65,535 and 3) allowing more servers to bind to a specific port. Given scarce IPv4 addresses and pending IPv6 deployment (a chicken and egg kind of problem for ISP and application developers), the proposed SPF should also prolong the useful life of IPv4 for P2P applications and Wi-Fi services rather than anticipating the wide deployment of IPv6.

References

1. J. D. Touch, "Those pesky NATs", IEEE Internet Computing, vol. 6-4, pp. 96, July 2002.
2. Shieh, S.-P., Ho, F.-S., et al., "Network address translators: effects on security protocols and applications in the TCP/IP stack", IEEE Internet Computing, vol. 4-6, pp. 42–49, Nov. 2000.
3. Bidirectional peer-to-peer communication with interposing firewalls and NATs, Peer-to-peer working group, Aug. 2001

4. Gong, L., "JXTA: a network programming environment", IEEE Internet Computing, vol. 5-3, pp. 88–95, May 2001.
5. B.A. Miller, and T. Nixon, "Home networking with Universal Plug and Play", IEEE Communications Magazine, vol. 39-12, pp. 104–109, Dec. 2001.
6. Rosenberg, J., Huitema, C., Mahy, R. and J. Weinberger, "STUN - Simple Traversal of UDP Through Network Address Translators", draft-ietf-midcom-stun-05 (work in progress), December 2002. Available at http://www.ietf.org/internet-drafts/draft-ietf-midcom-stun-05.txt
7. Rosenberg, J., Weinberger, J., Mahy, R., and Huitema, C., "Traversal Using Relay NAT (TURN)", draft-rosenberg-midcom-turn-02 (work in progress), October 2003. Available at http://www.jdrosen.net/papers/draft-rosenberg-midcom-turn-02.html
8. Kegel, D., NAT and peer-to-peer networking, July 1999, available at: http://alumnus.caltech.edu/~dank/peer-nat.html
9. Holdrege, M., and Srisuresh., P., Protocol complications with the IP network address translator, January 2001., RFC 3027.
10. Huitema. C., Teredo: Tunneling IPv6 over UDP through NATs, June 2004., Internet-Draft (available at http://www.dfn-pca.de/bibliothek/standards/ietf/none/internet-drafts/draft-huitema-v6ops-teredo-02.txt).
11. Rosenberg, J., Interactive connectivity establishment (ICE), October 2003., Internet-Draft (available at http://www.jdrosen.net/papers/draft-rosenberg-sipping-ice-00.html).
12. Eppinger., J. L., TCP connections for P2P apps: A software approach to solving the NAT problem., Technical Report CMU-ISRI-05-104, Carnegie Mellon University, January 2005.
13. Guha, S., Takeday, Y., and Francis, P., NUTSS: A SIP-based approach to UDP and TCP network connectivity., In ACM SIGCOMM 2004 Workshops, August 2004.
14. Biggadike, A., Ferullo, D., Wilson, G., and Adrian Perrig., NATBLASTER: Establishing TCP connections between hosts behind NATs., In ACM SIGCOMM Asia Workshop, Beijing, China, April 2005.
15. Baset, S. A., and Schulzrinne, H. An Analysis of the Skype Peer-to-Peer Internet Telephony Protocol. In Proceedings of the INFOCOM '06
16. Saroiu, S., Gummadi, P. K., and Gribble, S. D., "A Measurement Study of Peer-to-Peer File Sharing Systems", Proceedings of Multimedia Computing and Networking 2002 (MMCN'02), San Jose, CA, January 2002.
17. Lin, Y.-D., Wei, H.-Y., and Yu, S.-T. , "Building an Integrated Security Gateway: Mechanisms, Performance Evaluation, Implementation, and Research Issues", IEEE Communication Surveys and Tutorials, Vol.4, No.1, third quarter, 2002

An Adaptive Energy Saving Mechanism for the IEEE 802.15.4 LR-WPAN

Dong-Hoon Cho, Jung-Hoon Song, and Ki-Jun Han[*]

Department of Computer Engineering, Kyungpook National University, Korea
{firecar, pimpo}@netopia.knu.ac.kr, kjhan@bh.knu.ac.kr

Abstract. In this paper, an energy saving mechanism is proposed for the IEEE 802.15.4 Low-Rate Personal Area Network (LR-PAN). In the current version of IEEE 802.15.4 standard, each node can enter the sleep mode only during the inactive portion of superframe. In our scheme, the coordinator dynamically determines duty cycle and adjusts the interval of sleep mode by varying *BO* (Beacon Order) based on the arrival rate of packets in the network observed. Analytical results show that our scheme with a proper adjustment of *BO* can increase the average sleep time and shorten the energy consumption.

1 Introduction

The low rate wireless personal area networks will be used for a wide variety of applications with embedded devices, including home network, environmental monitoring and sensing. One of the most well-known on-going standards used in a Wireless Sensor Network (WSN) field is ZigBee. Since ZigBee uses IEEE 802.15.4 LR-WPAN as its PHY layer and MAC sub-layer, the LR-WPAN is expected to be widely used in WSN in accordance with ZigBee standardization. The IEEE 802.15.4 standard defines the physical (PHY) layer and medium access control (MAC) sub-layer specifications for low data rate (up to 250kbps@2450MHz) wireless connectivity. [6] In many applications that use the standard, the devices will be battery powered where their replacement or recharging in relatively short intervals is impractical; therefore the power consumption is of significant concern. The standard was developed with the limited power supply availability in mind. However, the physical implementation of the standard will require additional power management considerations that are beyond the scope of the standard. [1] The protocol has been developed to favor battery-powered devices. However, in certain applications some of these devices could potentially be mains powered. Battery-powered devices will require duty-cycling to reduce power consumption. These devices will spend most of their operational life in a sleep state; however, each device shall periodically listen to the RF channel in order to determine whether a message is pending. This mechanism allows the application designer to decide on the balance between battery consumption and message latency. Mains-powered devices have the option of listening to the RF channel continuously. So, the key concern in the LR-WPAN is energy consumption rather than the latency since it is undesirable to replace or recharge battery for the

---

[*] Corresponding author.

X. Cheng, W. Li, and T. Znati (Eds.): WASA 2006, LNCS 4138, pp. 38–46, 2006.
© Springer-Verlag Berlin Heidelberg 2006

devices. This is not the case in the general wireless networks where the basic concern is to provide high throughput and low latency since their device has either main powered and regularly rechargeable battery. The topology which is supported by LR-WPAN is star or peer-to-peer. In this paper, we consider only star topology in which communication is controlled by the network coordinator. The network coordinator transmits regular beacons for device synchronization and defines length of superframe by transmitting beacons periodically. A superframe is bounded by the transmission of a beacon frame and can have an active portion and inactive portion. The coordinator shall interact with its PAN only during the active portion of the superframe and may enter sleep mode during the inactive portion. Because of this periodic listen, nodes that do not join in transmission and reception must spend a lot of unnecessary energy during the active portion. [1]

In this paper, we propose an energy saving mechanism to solve this inefficiency problem. When the coordinator generates the next superframe, the value of *BO* determining the length of superframe is adjusted based on the current traffic state. At low traffic intensities the value of *BO* increases, which means that the length of superframe is increased. So, the sleep period becomes longer while the active period is maintained by a fixed length. This makes us obtain low duty cycle and reduce the needless energy consumption.

We present an overview of the IEEE 802.15.4 MAC protocol in Section 2. In the next section our algorithm is described. Section 4 describes our model for analytical and simulative evaluation. Finally, Section 5 includes some conclusions.

2 IEEE 802.15.4 MAC Protocol

The topology supported by LR-WPAN is a star or a peer-to-peer as illustrated in Figure 1.

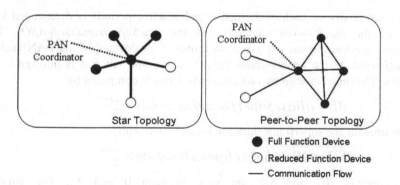

Fig. 1. Network topologies

In IEEE 802.15.4, with the star topology there are two communication methods: beacon mode and non-beacon mode. In beacon mode, communication is controlled by the network coordinator, which transmits regular beacons for device synchronization and network association control. The network coordinator defines the start and end of a superframe by transmitting a periodic beacon. The length of the beacon period and hence the duty cycle of the system can be defined by the user between certain limits as specified in the standard. [7]

In beacon mode, the superframe may consist of both an active and inactive period as shown in Figure 2. The active portion of the superframe, which contains 16 equally spaced slots, is composed of three parts: a beacon, a contention access period (CAP), and a contention free period (CFP). The beacon is transmitted without the use of CSMA at the start of slot 0 and the CAP commences immediately after the beacon. The coordinator only interacts with nodes during the active period and may sleep during the inactive period. There is a guaranteed timeslot (GTS) option in 802.15.4 to allow lower latency operation. There are a maximum of 7 of the 16 available timeslots that can be allocated to nodes, singly or combined. [7]

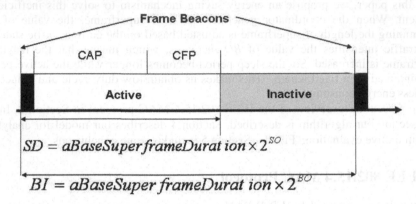

Fig. 2. Superframe structure of IEEE 802.15.4

The relative size of each of the active and inactive periods is determined by the values of the *macBeaconOrder(BO)* and the *macSuperframeOrder(SO)*. These parameters are transmitted via a beacon frame to all devices in the PAN such that each registered device knows about the duty cycle and when it is allowed to send messages. The time between two successive beacons is computed by

$$BI = aBaseSuperframeDuration \times 2^{BO} \tag{1}$$

And the time for the superframe duration is calculated with

$$SD = aBaseSuperframeDuration \times 2^{SO} \tag{2}$$

The parameters *BO* and *SO* can vary between 0 and 14. The parameter *aBaseSuperframeDuration* depends on the frequency range of operation. The 2.4GHz frequency range leads to *aBaseSuperframeDuration = 15.36ms*. [3] The duration of a superframe can not exceed a beacon interval because the range of both parameters is

$$0 \leq SO \leq BO \leq 14 \tag{3}$$

Knowing SD and BI allows conclusion about the duration of the inactive period in which the device can turn to sleep mode. Therefore, SO and BO are key parameters for potential energy savings. By changing the active and inactive portion via the parameters SO and BO, the WPAN can operate under low duty cycle to conserve energy.

A node wishing to send data to the personal area network (PAN) coordinator can understand the current superframe structure when receiving a beacon. If it has been allocated a guaranteed time slot (GTS), it sends its data during the contention free period (CFP) or it sends its data using CSMA-CA during the contention access period (CAP). For transferring data from the coordinator to the device, the device periodically listens to the network beacon and, if a message is pending in the pending list, transmits a MAC command requesting the data, using the slotted CSMA-CA.

If the node hears the beacon frames too frequently, it will consume the needless energy and thus shorten the overall life time of network. This inefficiency becomes more serious if the coordinator broadcasts the beacon frames when it does not have data to send to the device. In this paper, we propose an adaptive energy saving mechanism to solve this inefficiency problem.

3 An Adaptive Energy Saving Mechanism

As previously described, in the current version of IEEE 802.15.4 protocol, if the device always attempts to listen the beacon frame even when there is low traffic in the network, it will consume much energy. To improve this inefficiency problem in our scheme, if the node does not find its own address after checking the pending list in the beacon frame, it will be considered to be in the sleep-mode although it is in fact physically waked up. So, if the coordinator does not have data to send to the node, the interval of sleep mode is extended. Extending the length of sleep mode interval means increasing the value of BO by Eq (1). If the coordinator has data, it sets the value of BO to 0 as illustrated in Figure 3.

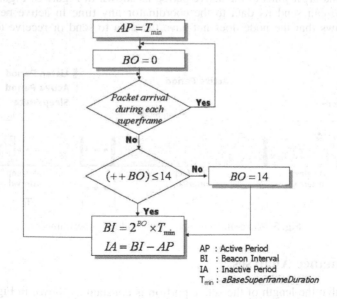

$$AP = T_{min}$$

$$BO = 0$$

Packet arrival during each superframe — **Yes**

No

$(++BO) \leq 14$ — **No** — $BO = 14$

Yes

$$BI = 2^{BO} \times T_{min}$$

$$IA = BI - AP$$

AP : Active Period
BI : Beacon Interval
IA : Inactive Period
T_{min} : aBaseSuperframeDuration

Fig. 3. Flow Chart of Mechanism

Figure 4 shows that the length of superframe is extended based on the value of *BO* which is determined by coordinator. For example, the coordinator shall determine the length of the next superframe based on the value of *BO* in the current surperframe. The coordinator increases the value of *BO* by one whenever it does not have data to send to the device. On the other hand, if the coordinator has data to send to the device, it resets the value of *BO* to 0.

At low traffic intensities the value of *BO* increases, which means that the length of superframe is increased. So, the sleep period becomes longer while the active period is maintained by a fixed length. This makes us obtain low duty cycle and reduce the needless energy consumption. As a result, our scheme can have low duty cycle and extend the battery life.

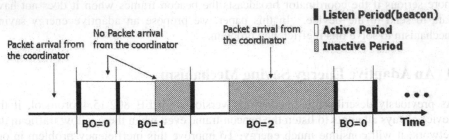

Fig. 4. Varying the length of superframe based on the value of *BO*

Figure 5 shows that the node commences the sleep mode if its own address is not included in the pending list (this means that it has no data to receive from the coordinator). In fact, if the node remains wake-up state when it does not need to join to active period, it must consume the unnecessary energy. If the node has data to send to the coordinator, it joins to the active period as shown in Figure 3. Figure 3 shows that the node can send its data to the coordinator any time in active period while Figure 4 shows that the node does not have the data to send or receive to/from the coordinator.

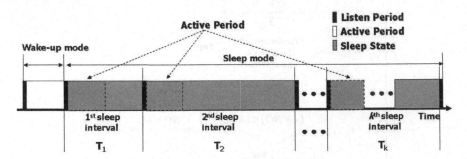

Fig. 5. Wake-up mode and sleep mode of superframe

4   Performance Analyses

We assume that the length of the active portion is constant as shown in Figure 2. We also assume that the listening time of the beacon frame has a fixed length. In addition, we assume that the frame arrival rate to the star network follows a Poisson distribution with a mean rate of λ (frames per unit time) because all nodes communicate through the coordinator of PAN. So, the coordinator can know traffic status in the network. Let T_k denote the length of the k-th sleep interval as illustrated in Figure 3. Let B denote the length of the listening time of the beacon frame.

Let n denote the number of BO's before the coordinator determines the length of superframe. The initial value of the sleep time interval is given by T_{min}, and the interval can increase up to T_{max}. If $BO = 0$ in Eq (1), $BI = T_{min} = aBaseSuperframeDuration$. If the coordinator does not have data by the k-th sleep interval as shown in Figure 3, we have

$$T_k = \begin{cases} 2^k \times T_{min}, & 0 \le k \le 13 \\ T_{max}, & 14 \le k < 15 \end{cases} \tag{4}$$

The 2.4GHz frequency range is assumed which leads to $aBaseSuperframeDuration = 15.36ms$. Therefore, $T_0 = aBaseSuperframeDuration = 15.36ms$. Let e_k denote the event where there is at least one frame arrival during the k-th sleep interval. Then, we have the probability of the event e_k by

$$P(e_k = true) = 1 - e^{-\lambda(T_k + B)} \tag{5}$$

From this, we can get the probability of the k-th sleep interval by

$$P(n = k) = P(e_k = true) \prod_{i=1}^{k-1} P(e_i = false) \tag{6}$$

$$= e^{-\lambda \sum_{i=1}^{k-1}(T_i + B)} \left(1 - e^{-\lambda(T_k + B)}\right)$$

So, the mean of the sleep interval is given by

$$E[n] = \sum_{k=1}^{\infty} kP(n = k) \tag{7}$$

$$= \sum_{k=1}^{\infty} ke^{-\lambda \sum_{i=1}^{k-1}(T_i + B)} - \sum_{k=1}^{\infty} ke^{-\lambda \sum_{i=1}^{k}(T_i + B)}$$

And we can obtain the mean of the sleep time by

$$E[T] = \sum_{k=1}^{\infty} P(n = k) \sum_{i=1}^{k} (T_i + B)$$

$$= \left(\sum_{k=1}^{\infty} e^{-\lambda \sum_{j=1}^{k-1}(T_j + B)} \sum_{i=1}^{k} (T_i + B) - \sum_{k=1}^{\infty} e^{-\lambda \sum_{j=1}^{k}(T_j + B)} \sum_{i=1}^{k} (T_i + B) \right) \tag{8}$$

Let E_S and E_B denote the energy consumption per unit time of sleep interval and the energy consumption to listen the beacon frame. Let EN_{sleep} denote the energy consumption during the sleep interval. Then we can get

$$EN_{sleep} = \sum_{k=1}^{\infty} P(n=k) \sum_{i=1}^{k} (T_i E_S + BE_B)$$

$$= \left(\sum_{k=1}^{\infty} e^{-\lambda \sum_{j=1}^{k-1}(T_j+B)} \sum_{i=1}^{k} (T_i E_S + BE_B) - \sum_{k=1}^{\infty} e^{-\lambda \sum_{j=1}^{k}(T_j+B)} \sum_{i=1}^{k} (T_i E_S + BE_B) \right) \quad (9)$$

Since we assume that the frame arrival rate follows a Poisson distribution with a mean rate of λ, the inter-frame arrival time follows an exponential distribution with a mean value of $1/\lambda$(unit time). The parameters used for performance evaluation are listed in Table 1.

Table 1. Parameters for performance evaluation

Symbol	Meaning	Value
PHY	Data Transmission Rate	250kbps
B	The length of beacon frame	20byte(constant)
SO	Superframe Order	0(constant)
BO	Beacon Order	0 ~ 14
T_{min}	The minimum time of superframe	variable
T_{max}	The maximum time of superframe	variable
E_S	Energy consumption of Sleep mode	$3uW$
E_L	Energy consumption of Listen mode	$30mW$

Figure 6 shows that the average number of sleep intervals obtained by Eq (7). Figure 6(a) shows the average number of sleep intervals as we vary T_{min}. We can see that a longer T_{min} produces a shorter number of sleep intervals. We can also see that the length of sleep interval is determined by the value of BO. In addition, this figure indicates that it is difficult for the value of BO to continuously increase because a packet arrival anytime resets it to 0. On the other hand, Figure 6(b) shows the average number of sleep intervals as we vary T_{max}. Figure 6(b) indicates that the length of sleep interval becomes shorter as T_{max} decreases. Therefore, the superframe is generated more frequently with a shorter T_{max}.

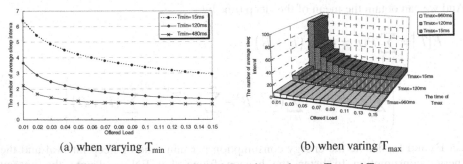

(a) when varying T_{min} (b) when varing T_{max}

Fig. 6. The average number of sleep intervals over T_{min} and T_{max}

Figure 7 shows that the average sleep time obtained by Eq (8). Since the length of superframe is determined based on the value of BO by Eq (1) and SO is given a fixed value, the interval of sleep mode will be extended when the length of superframe becomes longer. For example, the number of beacon frames heard when $T_{min}=15ms$ is six times greater than that when $T_{min}=960ms$ as shown in Figure 7(a). Thus, we can observe a longer sleep time when $T_{min}=960ms$. Figure 7(b) shows that the average sleep time increases as T_{max} increases at the same packet arrival rate. In other words, the sleep mode time becomes shorter as T_{max} decreases.

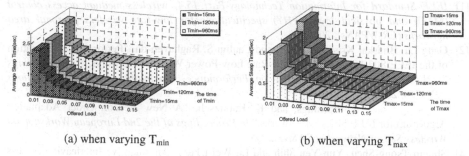

(a) when varying T_{min} (b) when varying T_{max}

Fig. 7. The average sleep time over T_{min} and T_{max}

Figure 8 shows that the average amount of energy consumption obtained by Eq (9). From Figure 8(a), we can see that a longer T_{min} offers a less energy consumption. This is because a longer T_{min} makes a longer sleep mode interval as shown in Figure 6(a). On the contrary, a shorter T_{min} produces a relatively shorter interval of sleep mode. As illustrated in Figure. 6(b), the number of sleep intervals increase as T_{max} decreases. The device listens the beacon frame more frequently as the number of sleep intervals increases. Therefore, we have to consume more energy with a small T_{max}.

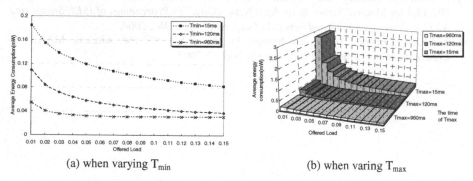

(a) when varying T_{min} (b) when varing T_{max}

Fig. 8. The amount of energy consumption over T_{min} and T_{max}

5 Conclusions

In this paper, we proposed an adaptive energy saving mechanism for the IEEE 802.15.4 by adjusting the length of superframe. The length of superframe is determined by BO (Beacon Order). The coordinator can adjust the length of the next frame based on the measurement of the packet arrival rate. The analytical results show that the average sleep time decreases as T_{max} decreases at the same packet arrival rate. On the other hand, we can observe that the average sleep time increases as T_{max} increases at the same packet arrival rate. As a result, our scheme with a proper selection of *BO* can significantly extend the overall lifetime of the network.

References

[1] *IEEE Standard for Information Technology-Part 15.4: wireless medium access control (MAC) and physical layer (PHY) specifications for low-rate wireless personal area networks (LR-WPANs). 2003.*

[2] Gang Lu, Bhaskar Krishnamachari, and Cauligi S. Raghaven-da, "Performance Evaluation of the IEEE 802.15.4 MAC for Low-Rate Low-Power Wireless Networks," *in Proceedings of IEEE International Conference on Performance, Computing, and Communications (IPCCC), 2004*

[3] M. Neugebauer, J. Ploennigs, and K. Kabitzsch, "A New Beacon Order Adaptation Algorithm for IEEE 802.15.4Networks," *in Proceedings of the 2nd European Workshop on Wireless Sensor Networks (EWSN), 2005.*

[4] Shiann-Tsong Sheu, Yun-Yen Shih and Lu-Wei Chen, "An Adaptive Interleaving Access Scheme (IAS) for IEEE 802.15.4 WPANs," *in Proceedings of IEEE Vehicular Technology Conference (VTC), 2005.*

[5] M. Neugebauer, J. Ploennigs, and K. Kabitzsch, "Performance evaluation of low rate WPANs for medical applications," *in Proceedings of IEEE International Conference on Military Communications Conference (MILCOM), 2004.*

[6] Daeyoung Kim, Minh-Long Pham, Yoonmee Doh, and Eunchang Choi, "Scheduling Support for Guaranteed Time Services in IEEE 802.15.4 Low Rate WPAN," *in Proceedings of IEEE International Conference on Embedded and Real-Time Computing Systems and Applications(RTCSA), 2005.*

[7] F. Nicholas, Timmons and William G. Scanlon, "Analysis of the Performance of IEEE 802.15.4 for Medical Sensor Body Area Networking," *in Proceedings of IEEE Sensor and Ad Hoc Communications and Networks Conference (SECON), 2004.*

[8] Y. Xiao, "Energy saving mechanism in the IEEE 802.16e wireless MAN," *in Communications Letters, IEEE; Volume 9, Issue 7, 2005.*

Traffic-Aware Power Control Algorithm for Low Rate WPAN

Younggoo Kwon

Konkuk University, 1 Hwayang-dong, Kwangjin-gu, Seoul, 143-701, Korea
ygkwon@konkuk.ac.kr

Abstract. Personal Area Networks (PANs) are expected to play an important role in future mobile ad-hoc wireless communications and information systems. It targets low data rate, low power consumption and low cost wireless networking, and offers device level wireless connectivity. In this paper, a traffic aware power control algorithm is proposed to achieve high energy efficiency and high performance in distributed networks by observing the beacon relaying characteristic of distributed wireless PANs. Through the various performance studies, the proposed algorithm shows significant performance improvements in wireless PANs[1].

1 Introduction

Wireless technology helps users to build up a network quickly, and supports them to set up a network anywhere and anytime regardless location limitations. Recently, wireless personal area networking technology attracts many researchers because of its huge potential for commercialization usages in near future. However, there are still many problems to solve for proper adaptation in real life. One of the main issues for wireless networks is the adaptive power saving technology under unexpected network traffic situations. In wireless PANs and sensor networks, the traffic is highly sporadic and does not necessarily follow any specific traffic pattern[1]-[3]. IEEE 802.15.4 is a new standard uniquely designed for low rate wireless PANs[4]-[6]. It targets low data rate, low power consumption and low cost wireless networking and offers device level wireless connectivity. In this paper, we propose the traffic-aware power control algorithm in beacon relayed distributed wireless PANs. We implemented beacon relayed distributed networks based on IEEE802.15.4 compatible platforms. By considering the beacon relay procedure of WPANs, the delay and power consumptions of each station are investigated through implementations and simulations for various operations. A traffic-aware power control algorithm in beacon relayed wireless PANs can improve the energy efficiency significantly with easy implementations. According to the traffic information, we dynamically change the length of the active and sleep period to support the traffic aware power control algorithm. We will investigate the operational characteristic of the IEEE 802.15.4 MAC protocol, and induce the energy efficient, traffic-aware power control algorithm in distributed wireless

---

[1] This work was supported by the faculty research fund of Konkuk University in 2006.

X. Cheng, W. Li, and T. Znati (Eds.): WASA 2006, LNCS 4138, pp. 47–56, 2006.
© Springer-Verlag Berlin Heidelberg 2006

PANs that provides significantly high performance. In beacon relayed distributed networks, the delay characteristic is important because the overheads come from beacon relay procedure are significant, which result in high power consumptions. The performance and operational difference between star topology and beacon relayed mesh networks are studied through the performance evaluations.

In the next section, we explain related research works. Then, the traffic-aware power control algorithm is shown in Section 3. The performance evaluations is given in Section 4. In the final section, we present the conclusions.

2 Related Works

For those power limited devices, we can trade off network performance with power efficiency by utilizing power saving mechanism that comes with IEEE 802.15.4. The IEEE 802.15.4 standard defines beacon enabled mode and super-frame structure for power saving purposes[4]. It can operate in either beacon enabled mode or beacon disabled mode. In beacon enabled mode, a network coordinator periodically broadcasts beacons so that other nodes in the network hear the beacons to synchronize to the superframe structure suggested by the coordinator. In beacon disabled mode, however, a network coordinator does not broadcast beacons except when other nodes request beacons for scanning or association purpose. In beacon enabled networks, a coordinator broadcasts beacons with superframe structure information recorded in the beacon. When other nodes in the network receive the beacon, they obtain the superframe information and start to synchronize to the coordinator's superframe structure. A superframe structure is defined by the network beacons. As shown in Figure 1, a network beacon marks the start of a superframe, while it also marks the end of previous superframe at the same time. A superframe generally consists of two parts - an active and an inactive part. The length of a superframe (beacon interval, BI) and its active part (superframe duration, SD) are determined by beacon order (BO) and superframe order (SO), respectively. BI can be calculated by using the equation

$$BI = aBaseSuperframeDuration \cdot 2^{BO} \tag{1}$$

and the time for superframe duration (SD) can be computed with

$$SD = aBaseSuperframeDuration \cdot 2^{SO} \tag{2}$$

The possible value for the two parameters BO and SO varies from 0 to 14 and must satisfy the following condition.

$$0 \leq SO \leq BO \leq 14 \tag{3}$$

Additionally, if both BO and SO are set to 15, IEEE 802.15.4 MAC will operate in beacon disabled mode. The length of inactive part can be determined by subtracting superframe duration from beacon interval. The active part is divided into 16 equally sized slots and has two periods - a contention access period (CAP) and an optional contention free period (CFP). During the CAP, IEEE

802.15.4 MAC utilizes slotted carrier sense multiple access with collision avoidance (CSMA-CA) mechanism for channel access. Following the CAP, CFP can be assigned for low latency applications or applications requiring specific data bandwidth. CFP may accommodate up to seven guaranteed time slots (GTSs), each of which may occupy one or more slots.

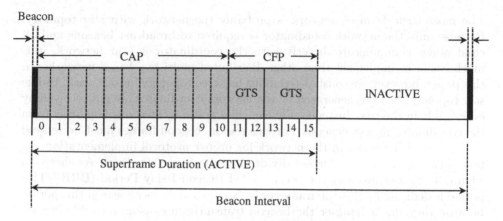

Fig. 1. An example of superframe structure

Ye et. al [8][9] proposed the S-MAC protocol that combines scheduling and contention with the aim of improving collision avoidance and scalability. The power saving is based on scheduling sleep/listen cycles between the neighbor stations. After the initial scheduling, synchronization packets are used to maintain the inter-station synchronization. When a station wants to use the channel, it has to contend for the medium. The scheme is very similar to 802.11 with physical and virtual carrier sense and RTS/CTS exchange to handle the hidden station problem. The overhearing control is achieved by putting to sleep all immediate neighbors of the sender and the receiver after receiving an RTS or CTS packet. The S-MAC operation and frame is divided into two periods; the active period and the sleep period. During the sleep period all stations that share the same schedule sleep and save energy. The sleep period is usually several times longer than the active period. Stations listen for a SYNC packet in every frame and the SYNC packet is transmitted by a device infrequently to achieve and maintain virtual clustering. Although S-MAC can reduce the idle listening time, it is not optimal due to a fixed interval of listening mode. Under the network traffic is very light, i.e., no stations have data traffic to send during the active listen period, all stations still have to be awake and waste their energies. If the traffic is very heavy with fixed active period, all stations can not handle properly the traffic because they have to sleep regardless the network traffic situations. This observation leads many researchers to propose new energy efficient sensor MAC protocols that allow the stations to go to active and sleep status considering the traffic information[1]-[3]. Though many algorithms are proposed in traffic-adaptive WSNs, most proposed algorithms have the complexity for announcing traffic information. Complex schedule-based protocols exhibit inherently higher delivery delays when compared to contention-based approaches, and they are not desirable considering the implementation aspect of view in wireless channels.

3   Traffic Aware Power Control Protocol

The most basic form of network is probably the network with star topology. Because only the network coordinator is required to broadcast beacons and all child nodes communicate directly with the coordinator in star network, it is much easier to implement than other distributed multi hop based networks. In this paper, however, we constructed multi hop tree topology for our work. Unlike star topology, beacons generated by the network coordinator are not received by every node in the tree. Instead, only the child nodes located one hop away from the coordinator receive beacons. For this reason, beacon frames must be relayed to the rest of the nodes in the network for proper protocol implementation. To relay beacons, we had to further divide the superframe structure. As shown in Figure 3, we assigned another period called Beacon Relay Period (BRP). This period is dedicated to beacon frames only. No other packets appear in this period because they might hamper the beacon transmission causing unstable beacon enabled tree network.

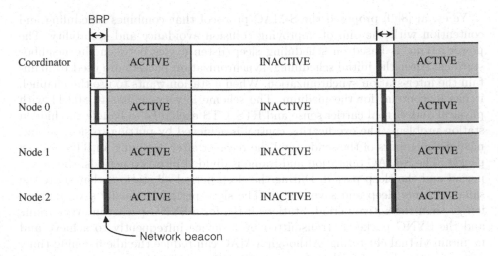

Fig. 2. Beacon Relay in Tree Network (Tree depth = 3)

A coordinator can determine whether to work in a beacon enabled mode, in which a superframe structure is used. The superframe is bounded by network beacons and divided into aNumSuperframeSlots equally sized slots. A coordinator sends out beacons periodically to synchronize the attached devices. A device attached to a coordinator operating in a beacon enabled mode can track the beacons to synchronize with the coordinator. In beacon relayed networks, all nodes synchronize after the beacon relay procedure. By using beacon information, they receive the superframe order, beacon order, active and inactive periods. With all these information, all nodes communicate with each other through distributed wireless networks.

The energy waste for idle listening is the biggest part compared with other collision and overhearing overheads. In the power saving mode a node wakes up periodically for a short time to check if any other node wants to transmit data to it. We designed traffic aware power control algorithm with the various circumstances under considerations by relaying beacons through networks in distributed manners. In high traffic situations, the active period of the medium increases by extending the active part in the superframe to deliver packets efficiently. In low traffic situations, the active part decreases, thereby increasing the inactive part for power saving. The beacon relay procedure is important because all other nodes depend on the information of the beacon delivered to them for exact synchronization. When the traffic is high enough, a transmitter of the node will be unable to process all the packets generated. In this case, the node has to buffer the incoming packets in its own TX queue until they get processed and sent. Therefore, we can assume the traffic loads at a given moment by monitoring the TX queue status. If the queue are occupied with many packets to send, the node immediately reports its current queue status by sending a special packet to the network coordinator. When a network coordinator receives this, it immediately maximizes the active period.

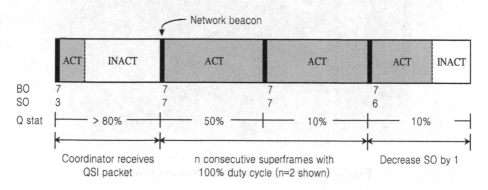

Fig. 3. Choosing superframe order in traffic aware MAC

Since the beacon relay procedure is implemented, the synchronization is very important factor for the network performance. We arranged the superframe size properly, so the beacon relay period does not affect much for the aggregate network performance because of its relatively small portion. That is, the period of the beacon relay period is much smaller compared with active and inactive periods. We set the network topology close enough with neighbor nodes, so that there is no missing beacons for performance evaluations. The start of active period and the ending of inactive period are set to equal for all nodes by calculating the beacon relay period for every node. If the network has heavy traffic, the superframe order will be set equal to that of beacon order. As the network load decreases, the superframe order decreases one by one until the queue status indicator reaches the minimum threshold value.

4 Performance Evaluation

We used Chipcon CC2420 Demonstration Board [11] (Figure 4) as our development platform, and additional parameters are shown on Table 1.

Figure 5 shows the tree network topology that we constructed for experiments. In a tree network, each node can transmit data packets only to its parent or one of its children. For example, node 6 (the source node) cannot transmit its packets directly to node 0 (the sink) even if node 0 is in the transmission range of node 6. The only way to transmit packets is to relay them along the intermediate nodes in the tree. Unlike one hop star network, beacon frames should also be relayed along the tree. While all the child nodes associated to the network coordinator receive beacon frames in one hop star network, child nodes in tree network only receive beacon frames from parents to which they are associated. Because of this, beacon relay is a prerequisite in tree network topology. That is, if any child node

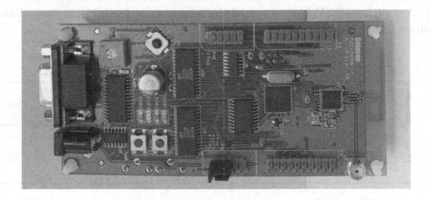

Fig. 4. Chipcon CC2420 demonstration board

Table 1. Parameters of Chipcon CC2420 Demonstration Board

Data rate	250Kbps
Symbol rate	62500 symbols/sec
1 symbol time	16 us
Data packet length	102 bytes
MAC header length	11 bytes
Power consumption (RX)	18.8 mA
Power consumption (TX)	14 mA
Power consumption (Idle)	0.426 mA

receives beacon frames from its parent, it must rebroadcast the received beacon frames for its child nodes.

As shown in Figure 5, a beacon frame generated from the network coordinator is relayed down to node 6. Regarding the traffic for the network, we generated 200 data packets (113 bytes each including MAC packet header) to be passed from their sources to their sinks for energy measurements. We changed the traffic load by varying the inter-arrival period of packets for checking the network throughput. In our experiments, the packet inter-arrival period varied from 0.1 to 3s. For the low rate wireless network, we also experimented with other inter-arrival periods longer than 3s.

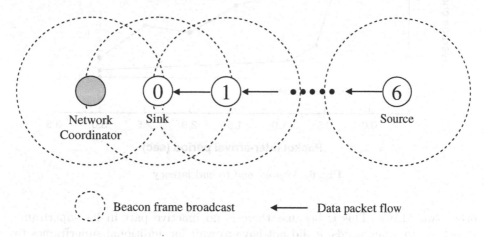

Network Coordinator   Sink

Source

⚬ Beacon frame broadcast   ← Data packet flow

Fig. 5. Network topology

Experiment results showed differences when compared to that of star topology in delay and power consumptions. That is, two network topologies differ greatly in terms of network beacon dissemination, and they resulted in differences in beacon transmission performance. While there was no delay occurred in star topology because all child nodes receive beacons from the coordinator simultaneously, tree topology generated some delay in receiving beacons because they had to be relayed from one node to the other. This delay, however, was very small. In fact, the most significant delay was generated from transmitting and receiving QSI packets. In star topology, QSI packets can reach network coordinator almost instantly because the coordinator is just one hop away. In tree topology, on the other hand, QSI packets must be relayed to the coordinator along the tree taking more time. This kept the network coordinator from dealing with high traffic situation more efficiently. As a result, each node in the tree network showed higher TX queue usage and this further led to more packet delay, and high energy consumption.

First, We have measured the average end to end latency of our network. Figure 8 shows each MAC's measured latency over the varying inter-arrival periods. The IEEE 802.15.4 MAC with 100% active period performed better than

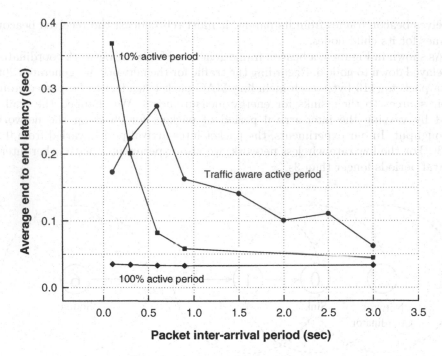

Fig. 6. Average end to end latency

other two MACs. This is because there is no inactive part in its superframe structure. In other words, it did not have to wait for additional superframes to finish the transmission of packets. If a packet is sent from the source node, it travels through intermediate nodes without waiting on the intermediate nodes. However, in case of IEEE 802.15.4 MAC with 10% active period, there is an inactive part in the superframe which hampers the data transmissions. For example, in Figure 5, if the source node sends a packet, it is received by node 5. Upon reception, node 5 relays the packet to node 4. When node 4 receives the packet, unfortunately, the active part is over. In this case, the packet must be buffered during the inactive part of the superframe. This causes packet delay and often leads to high end to end latency. For the traffic aware algorithm, it produced a bit unpredictable results, though average end to end latency generally decreased as the inter-arrival period becomes longer. This is due to the frequent superframe order (duration of active part) changes of the traffic aware MAC. In high active period conditions where the superframe order is high and packets have enough time to be transmitted, the end to end latency dramatically decreases. On the contrary, in low active period conditions where superframe order is in its smallest possible value, packets are more likely to be hold in the TX buffers of transmission thereby causing more delay. The end to end latency of the traffic aware MAC shown in Figure 6 resulted from the mixture of these conditions.

We have also measured total energy consumption by all seven nodes participated in packet transmission. Realizing power saving for the coordinator as well

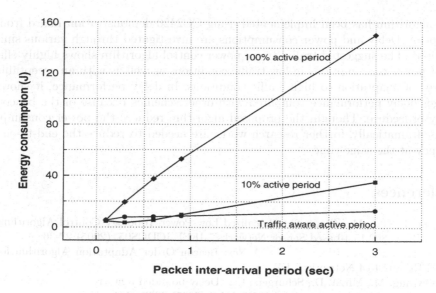

Fig. 7. Total energy consumption of the nodes

as for the sensors is the actual reason for the deployment of adaptive algorithm, the development of the beacon order is the key to power saving since a higher beacon order means less active phases and more opportunities for devices to sleep. We investigate the power consumption of the coordinator during the deployment of traffic aware power control algorithm. Figure 7 shows the measured total energy consumption over the distributed networks. IEEE 802.15.4 MAC with 100% active period consumed far more energy than 10% active period and traffic aware algorithm. When inter-arrival time was less than 1s, traffic aware algorithm performed similar to or a bit less than 10% active period MAC. However, traffic aware algorithm performed better as the inter-arrival period gets longer. When the inter-arrival period was longer than 1s, traffic aware algorithm consumed noticeably less energy than 802.15.4 MAC with 10% active period. The power consumption at 3s inter-arrival period of IEEE 802.15.4 MAC with 100% active period is close to 150J. All power consumptions increased when using beacon relaying networks compared with non beacon enabled networks. This means that the delay caused from relaying beacons affects the network performance. Depending on the application requirements the PAN user has to evaluate if the trade-offs due to the beacon order are adequate or not, and this will support the PAN user with adaptation according to the application requirements.

5   Conclusions

This paper proposed the traffic aware power control algorithm for beacon relayed distributed wireless PANs. We implemented the beacon relayed testbed platform which is based on IEEE 802.15.4 standards. Traffic aware power control algorithm has been implemented using CC2420 demonstration board from Chipcon. Delay and power consumptions are investigated through various simulations. The suggested traffic aware power control algorithm shows highly efficient power consumptions in low traffic conditions as well as with an acceptable degree of adaptation to high traffic conditions. In delay performance, it shows longer delay performance compared with other schemes because of the beacon relay procedure. Though, the proposed algorithm reduces the power consumptions dramatically, further research works are needed to reduce the end-to-end latency at the same time.

References

1. Ma, J., Gao, M., Zhang, Q.: "Localized Low-Power Topology Control Algorithms in IEEE 802.15.4-based Sensor Networks," IEEE ICDCS05, (2005) 27-36
2. Neugebauer, M., Plonnigs, J.: "A New Beacon Order Adaptation Algorithm for IEEE 802.15.4 Networks," EWSN05 (2005) 302-311
3. Owrang, M., Mirza, D., Schurgers, C.: "Delay-bounded adaptive power saving for ad hoc and sensor networks ," IEEE VTC (2005) 2337-2341
4. IEEE Std. 802.15.4-REVb-2005 edition, Wireless LAN Medium Access Control (MAC) and Physical Layer (PHY) Specification for Low-Rate Wireless Personal Area Networks.
5. Zheng, J., Lee, M. J.: A comprehensive performance study of IEEE 802.15.4. IEEE Press Book (2004)
6. Zheng, J., Lee, M. J.: "Will IEEE 802.15.4 make ubiquitous networking a reality? A discussion on a potential low power, low bit rate standard," Communications Magazine, IEEE **42** (2004) 140-146
7. Specification of the Bluetooth System. Available online: http://www. bluetooth.org/
8. Ye, W., Heidemann, J., Estrin, D.: An energy-efficient mac protocol for wireless sensor networks. IEEE INFOCOM, New York, NY (2002) 1567-1576
9. Ye, W., Heidemann, J., Estrin, D.: Medium Access Control With Coordinated Adaptive Sleeping for Wireless Sensor Networks. IEEE/ACM Trans. on Networking **12** (2004) 493-506
10. Tijs van Dam, Koen Langendoen: An Adaptive Energy-Efficient MAC Protocol for Wireless Sensor Networks in Proc. of 1st international conf. on Embeded networked sensor systems, Los Angeles, CA, USA (2003) 171-180
11. Chipcon CC2420 Demonstration Board Kit User Manual. Chipcon Corp., Oslo, Norway. Available online: http://www.chipcon.com/
12. Chipcon CC2420 RF Transceiver Data Sheet. Chipcon Corp., Oslo, Norway. Available online: http://www.chipcon.com/
13. AVR Microcontroller ATmega128L Reference Manual. Atmel Corp., San Jose, CA. Available online: http://www.atmel.com/
14. Singh, S., Raghavendra, C. S.: "PAMAS: Power aware multi-access protocol with signalling for ad hoc networks," ACM Comput. Commun. Rev. **28** (1998) 5-26
15. Huaming, L.; Jindong, T.: "An ultra-low-power medium access control protocol for body sensor network ," IEEE VTC (2005) 2342-2346

A Generic Software Partitioning Algorithm
for Pervasive Computing*

Songqiao Han, Shensheng Zhang, and Yong Zhang

Department of Computer Science and Engineering, Shanghai Jiaotong University
Shanghai 200240, P.R. China
{hansq, sszhang, zycs926}@sjtu.edu.cn

Abstract. The ever-changing context and resource limitation of mobile devices and wireless network are two challenges in the development of pervasive computing application. In this paper, we present a generic optimal partitioning algorithm of mobile applications which tries to overcome the two obstacles. The algorithm can reallocate the components of an application among machines for saving resources according to the environment variations. For each resource, we construct a corresponding cost graph, involving computation cost, communication cost and migration cost, in the foundation of the software architecture. Based on the network flow theory, we transform the cost graph into an equivalent flow network that can be optimally cut by well-known Max-flow Min-cut algorithm. As a generic algorithm, the proposed algorithm can be applied to save network bandwidth, time or energy. In addition, it can elegantly allocate the software components among the two machines so as to balance multiple resource consumptions. The simulation results demonstrate the validity and effectiveness of the proposed algorithm.

Keywords: Software partitioning, Algorithm, Pervasive computing.

1 Introduction

In a pervasive computing environment [1], people can take their pervasive devices anywhere, using them in various environments to access information and perform different tasks without the constraints of time and location. Over the last decade, although the mobile devices and wireless network have a dramatic development, the corresponding software that would make the vision of pervasive computing possible have not matured at the same rate. Two major obstacles that pervasive software meets are resource constraints of mobile devices and wireless network, and ever-changing environments. For example, a pervasive application may run over different wireless networks, such as GSM, 3G, WLAN, WiMax and Bluetooth, whose connectivity quality may highly vary over time. The resource constraint devices with different CPU processing speeds, memory capacities, screen sizes or battery capacities should provide users similar services using the same application. User requirements or preferences may change during different periods or at different locations. Therefore,

---

* This work was supported by grants 05SN07114 and 03DZ19320, all from the Shanghai Commission of Science and Technology.

X. Cheng, W. Li, and T. Znati (Eds.): WASA 2006, LNCS 4138, pp. 57–68, 2006.
© Springer-Verlag Berlin Heidelberg 2006

the traditional monolithic application and the static software allocation paradigms, such as client-server or remote execution, are obviously unsuitable for pervasive computing. Many researchers [2, 3] think that a promising solution is to exploit code mobility technology to provide pervasive applications the ability to move and reallocate themselves among machines at the runtime.

In this paper, we present an optimal partitioning algorithm of mobile applications. The algorithm can dynamically allocate the software components between the mobile device and the back server for saving resources according to the context variations. Based on the network flow theory, we reduce the problem of optimal software partition to an optimal bipartition problem of a corresponding flow network. Due to the consideration of the common features of different resource consumptions, the proposed algorithm can be applied to save network bandwidth, response time and energy consumption, respectively or simultaneously. For example, a visitor in a museum is watching some video clips about art pieces with his PDA. When the wireless network becomes congested, the scheduling algorithm may automatically reduce the amount of communication data over the network. Because there are so many people using the server that the media service has a relative long delay, the algorithm can reallocate some components between the PDA and the server to reduce response time. When the battery capacity of his PDA becomes scarce, the algorithm also reallocates the media player to save power.

The rest of this paper is organized as follows. Section 2 presents a generic partitioning algorithm. In Section 3, we propose three instances of the partitioning algorithm to save bandwidth, time and energy respectively. An instance of the partitioning algorithm for multiple resources optimization is presented in Section 4. Section 5 carries out some simulations and Section 6 discusses the related work. Finally, Section 7 concludes this paper.

2   Software Partitioning Algorithm

2.1   Cost Graph Construction

We assume that there are a resource-constraint mobile device, called client, and nearby resource-rich computer, called server, and both of them are connected by wireless network. For a distributed computing system, the occupation of network bandwidth mainly comes from transferring the date and moving components between different machines. Time consumption includes the computation time on different machines and the communication time over the network. Some researches [4, 5] demonstrate the energy of mobile device consumed mainly by three types of activities: computation on the mobile device, idleness of the mobile device and communication over wireless network. Although the server performs some tasks and the mobile device is idle, the mobile device also consume some power to keep some infrastructure services running, i.e. OS and communication interfaces. The energy consumption induced by the communication is almost directly proportional to the communication amount over wireless network. Communication amount is comprised of the amount of transferred data and the size of moving components among machines. In all, after analyzing the constitutions of different types of resource consumptions, we can abstract three classes of costs: computation cost, communication cost and migration cost, which constitutes the total consumption of each resource.

(1) Computation cost refers to the cost incurred by the computation procedure of the application, including computation costs on the client and server machines.

(2) Communication cost is induced by sending and receiving data between the components on different hosts. Compared with communication cost between different hosts, the local communication cost within a same host is trivial, thus ignored.

(3) Migration cost is incurred by moving components over wireless network. When the environment varies, dynamic component reallocation may lead to some components' migration among machines. In most of previous work, this class of cost is neglected.

For the component based software system, the next problem is to how to add three classes of costs to each component and connector in its software architecture so as to set up a general graph model of resource consumption.

The software architecture of an application can be represented by an undirected graph $G = (V, E)$ with vertex set V and edge set $E \subseteq V \times V$, where vertex v_i represents components c_i and edge e_{ij} or $e(c_i, c_j)$ indicates that component c_i interacts with component c_j. To standing for the three classes of costs, we add the vertex weight and edge weight to graph G, called cost graph. The weight of vertex v_i is represented by a triple set $(C_m(c_i), C_c(c_i), C_s(c_i))$, where $C_m(c_i)$ denotes migration cost of component c_i, $C_c(c_i)$ and $C_s(c_i)$ represent its computation cost on the client and server respectively. Note that if component c_i can't run on the client or server machine, then $C_c(c_i) = \infty$ or $C_s(c_i) = \infty$, and if it can't migrate between the two machines, then $C_m(c_i) = \infty$. The weight of edge e_{ij} is represented by $C_c(c_i, c_j)$ whose value is equal to communication cost between components c_i and c_j.

Therefore, the total resource consumption is equal to the sum of the following four values: (1) the sum of weight $C_c(c_i)$ of all components on the client; (2) the sum of weight $C_s(c_i)$ of all components on the server; (3) the sum of weight $C_c(c_i, c_j)$ of all edges connecting components on different machines; (4) the sum of weight $C_m(c_i)$ of all components moving between machines. As a result, the problem of minimizing the resource consumption is transformed into the optimal bipartition problem of the cost graph, subject to minimal cost Formula 1, where S_c and S_s are the sets of components on the client and server respectively, S_e is the set of all edges connecting the components on different machines, and S_m is the set of migrating components.

$$Min(\sum_{c_i \in S_c} C_c(c_i) + \sum_{c_j \in S_s} C_s(c_j) + \sum_{e(c_i, c_j) \in S_e} C_c(c_i, c_j) + \sum_{c_k \in S_m} C_m(c_k)) \tag{1}$$

2.2 Cost Graph Bipartition Algorithm

In graph theory, the max-flow min-cut theorem can find an optimal solution of the flow network bipartition problem. However, the constructed cost graph is not a flow network. In order to use the theorem, we try to transform a cost graph of an application into its flow network one of whose partitions corresponds to one of the application's allocations between the client and server machines.

Suppose that an application is comprised of four components, called a, b, c and d. We construct its cost graph $G = (V, E)$, including four vertices and five edges, as shown in Fig.1. Initially, component d locates on the client while other components, a, b and c, locate on the server. The weights of the vertices and edges are labeled beside them in Fig.1. Then the cost graph can be transformed into the corresponding flow network $G' = (V', E')$, as shown in Fig.2. The cost graph bipartition algorithm can be described as follows.

(1) Each node $v \in V$ in cost graph is transformed into a node $v' \in V'$ in flow network.
(2) For each undirected edge e_{ij} between node v_i and v_j in graph G, we add two edges e_{ij}' and e_{ji}' between node v_i' and v_j' in network G', and their capacities both are equal to the weight of e_{ij}.
(3) Add the node labeled S and T that represent the client and server machine, respectively, where S denotes the unique source node and T denotes the unique sink node in the flow network.
(4) For each node other than S and T, add an edge from S to that node and an edge from that node to T. The capacities of the newly added edges may be different due to the different initial locations of the component corresponding to the node. Let $cap(e)$ be the capacity of edge e, then the capacities of these edges in flow network can be obtained according to the following expressions.

Component c_i		$cap(e(S, c_i))$	$cap(e(c_i, T))$
Initial	Client	$C_s(c_i) + C_m(c_i)$	$C_c(c_i)$
Location	Server	$C_s(c_i)$	$C_c(c_i) + C_m(c_i)$

(5) Using the Max-flow Min-cut algorithm to cut network G', we can obtain two disjoint node sets V_s and V_t and $V' = V_s \cup V_t, S \in V_s, T \in V_t$. The components corresponding to the nodes other than S in V_s are allocated on the client and the components corresponding to the nodes other than T in V_t are allocated on the server.

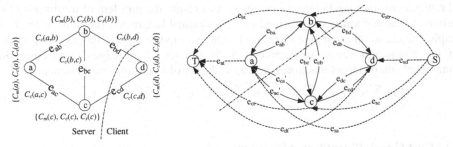

Fig. 1. Cost graph with node allocation   **Fig. 2.** Flow network transformed from cost graph

In network G', a cut edge is an edge (u, v) where $u \in V_s$ and $v \in V_t$. The cut set is the set of all cut edge in G'. In the Fig.2, the cut set denoted by the dashed dot line is $\{e_{db}', e_{cb}', e_{ca}', e_{sa}, e_{sb}, e_{cb}, e_{dt}\}$. The weight of a cut set is equal to the sum of the capacities of the edges in the cut set. Then the max-flow min-cut theorem[6] can be described as follows: *The value of a maximum flow in a flow network is equal to the weight of a minimum weight cut set of that network.*

Each cut set of the flow network partitions the nodes of the graph into two disjoint subsets, with S and T in distinct subsets. We associate a component assignment with each cut set such that if the cut set partitions a node into the subset containing S, then the corresponding component is assigned to client machine. Similarly, a node into the subset containing T, then the corresponding component is assigned to server machine. With this association of cut sets to component assignments, we can see that component assignments and cut sets of the flow network are in one-to-one correspondence. Therefore, we can use a maximum flow algorithm to find a minimum cost assignment according to Theorem 1.

Theorem 1. *The cost of a software assignment is equal to the weight of the corresponding cut set in the flow network G'.*

Proof. A component allocation incurs three types of costs: computation cost, communication cost and migration cost. The cut set corresponding to a component assignment contains two types of edges. One type of edge represents the cost of communication between the components locating on the different hosts. All communication costs contribute to the weight of the corresponding cut set, and all weights of the cut edges representing communication cost come from communication cost.

The second type of edge in the cut set is an edge from source node S to component node or from component node to sink node T. If a component locating initially the client machine and the new assignment places it on the server, the resource consumption induced by the component contains its computation cost on the server and migration cost from the client to server. In the flow network, the edge from S to the component must belong to the cut set. This edge carries the capacity equal to the sum of computation cost on the server and migration cost from the client to server. Moreover, no other edges incident to the component and belonging to this type of edge are included within the cut set. But if a component locates the same machine, such as the client, before and after new assignment, the resource consumption incurred by it only contains its computation cost on the client. In the flow network, the edge from the component node to T has a capacity equal to its computation cost on the client, and is only one cut edge connecting the component and node T. If a component locates initially the server machine, its case is similar to that of a component locating initially the client. Thus the weight of a cut set accounts for all costs due to its corresponding component allocation and no other costs contribute to the weight.

From Theorem 1, it is easy to infer the following corollary: *The minimum cost of component assignment is equal to the weight of a min-cut set or the value of max-flow in the flow network G'.* Based on the corollary, we use a minimum cut algorithm, such as Preflow-Push algorithm which has $O(N^3)$ time complexity where N is the number of components, to partition network G', thereby obtaining the optimal component allocation and minimal cost.

3 Software Partitioning for Single Objective

In the proposed algorithm, the term *cost* is an abstract concept, so it can be initialized into the consumption of any type of resource, such as network bandwidth usage, response time and energy consumption. To save one type of resource, we must first construct this cost graph of the type of resource.

(1) Saving bandwidth usage

Because of limited bandwidth, wireless communication is more expensive than wired communication. Also, when the connectivity of wireless network is weak, reducing communication amount over the network can obviously improve the service performance. Let $s(c_i)$ be the size of component c_i, and let $s(c_i, c_j)$ be the size of interaction data between components c_i and c_j. Both the interaction between the components on different hosts and component migration can increase the communication amount over the network. However, computation cost on the client and server do not occupy network bandwidth, so both computation costs should be equal to zero. The weights of components and edges in the cost graph of communication amount are shown in the second column in Table 1.

(2) Saving response time

Fast response of service is one of the important users concerns. Because computation, communication and migration of components all consume some times, the three costs should be equal to the values of computation time, communication time and migration time, respectively. Given an available network bandwidth b, let $t_c(c_i)$ and $t_s(c_i)$ be execution time of component c_i on the client and server, respectively. Besides network bandwidth, there are other factors, such as the distance and packet error, to impact the network conditions, further influence response time. So we introduce a network coefficient λ to reflect their influence on network conditions. The weights of components and edges in the cost graph of time are shown in the third column in Table 1.

(3) Saving energy

From the software perspective, the communication between different hosts, component's execution and migration all consume the energy of the client and server machines. Due to the battery powered of mobile devices, we focus on the energy consumption of the mobile client. Let p_i and p_c be power consumption rate when mobile device is idle and performs computation, respectively, and let p_t be the mean power consumption rate when transferring the data between the two machines. Then the weights of components and edges in the cost graph of energy are shown in the fourth column in Table 1.

Table 1. The weights of components and edges in the corresponding cost graphs

	Bandwidth	Time	Energy
$C_c(c_i, c_j)$	$s(c_i, c_j)$	$s(c_i, c_j)/\lambda b$	$s(c_i, c_j) \times p_t /\lambda b$
$C_m(c_i)$	$s(c_i)$	$s(c_i)/\lambda b$	$s(c_i) \times p_t /\lambda b$
$C_e(c_i)$	0	$t_c(c_i)$	$p_c \times t_c(c_i)$
$C_s(c_i)$	0	$t_s(c_i)$	$p_i \times t_c(c_i)$

For each optimization objective, after its cost graph is constructed, we can make use of the proposed partitioning algorithm to transform the cost graph to the corresponding flow network, and then employ the Min-cut algorithm to partition the application and obtain the optimal component allocation with regard to the single objective.

4   Software Partitioning for Multiple Objectives

Although reducing one type of resource consumption is useful in some cases, which is also the focus of most of previous researches in this area, it is practically more reasonable to conserve multiple resources at the same time in the most cases. So the term *cost* in our algorithm can also refer to the total consumption of multiple resources.

In order to reflect different importance of the resources for users, we use three weight coefficients: communication amount weight w_c, response time weight w_r and energy cost weight w_e, but the sum of these weights must be equal to 1. Because the three resource consumptions have different measurement units, we can not add directly them. Then we normalize the weights of nodes and edges in each cost graph. Specifically, for each cost graph, Let W be the sum of the weights of all components and edges except the nodes or edges with infinite weights, let V be a component set of an application and let E be its edge set, then

$$W = \sum_{e(c_i,c_j)\in E} C_c(c_i,c_j) + \sum_{c_i\in V} C_c(c_i) + \sum_{c_i\in V} C_s(c_i) + \sum_{c_i\in V} C_m(c_i) \tag{2}$$

Let W_c, W_r and W_e be the cost graph weights of communication amount, response time and energy, respectively.

$$\begin{cases} W_c = \sum_{e(c_i,c_j)\in E} s(c_i,c_j) + \sum_{c_i\in V} s(c_i) \\[2mm] W_r = \sum_{e(c_i,c_j)\in E} \frac{s(c_i,c_j)}{\lambda b} + \sum_{c_i\in V} t_c(c_i) + \sum_{c_i\in V} t_s(c_i) + \sum_{c_i\in V} \frac{s(c_i)}{\lambda b} \\[2mm] W_e = \sum_{e(c_i,c_j)\in E} \frac{s(c_i,c_j)\times p_t}{\lambda b} + \sum_{c_i\in V} p_c\times t_c(c_i) + \sum_{c_i\in V} p_i\times t_s(c_i) + \sum_{c_i\in V} \frac{s(c_i)\times p_t}{\lambda b} \end{cases} \tag{3}$$

Then the weights in the cost graph of the three resources are expressed in Equation 4 where the superscripts C, T and E of the costs represent the corresponding cost in the cost graph of communication, time and energy respectively. For example, $C_c^c(c_i,c_j)$ represents the communication cost $C_c(c_i,c_j)$ in the cost graph of communication amount.

Using the proposed algorithm, we can partition the cost graph of multiple resources to obtain the optimal component allocation for saving multiple resources at the same time.

$$\begin{cases} C_c(c_i,c_j) = \dfrac{C_c^c(c_i,c_j) \times w_c}{W_c} + \dfrac{C_c^R(c_i,c_j) \times w_r}{W_r} + \dfrac{C_c^E(c_i,c_j) \times w_e}{W_e} \\[2mm] C_m(c_i) = \dfrac{C_m^c(c_i) \times w_c}{W_c} + \dfrac{C_m^R(c_i) \times w_r}{W_r} + \dfrac{C_m^E(c_i) \times w_e}{W_e} \\[2mm] C_c(c_i) = \dfrac{C_c^c(c_i) \times w_c}{W_c} + \dfrac{C_c^R(c_i) \times w_r}{W_r} + \dfrac{C_c^E(c_i) \times w_e}{W_e} \\[2mm] C_s(c_i) = \dfrac{C_s^c(c_i) \times w_c}{W_c} + \dfrac{C_s^R(c_i) \times w_r}{W_r} + \dfrac{C_s^E(c_i) \times w_e}{W_e} \end{cases} \qquad (4)$$

5   Experiments and Simulations

We envision that there is a bus equipped with a server and wireless network. Some passengers get into the bus and continue to play an interactive war game with their PDAs. In order to save some resources, such as bandwidth, time and energy of the mobile devices, they can exploit three software allocation strategies: (1) Monolithic: the whole game runs on their PDAs; (2) Remote execution: most of components are offloaded to the server; (3) our algorithm: dynamically allocate the components between PDAs and the server.

We have developed the war game prototype using Java language. According to its software architecture, we construct its cost graph of communication amount, as shown in Fig.3 where a node represents a component and an edge represents the interaction of two connected components. The edge weight labeled on an edge indicates the communication amount between the two components within an execution cycle, notated by $N=1$.

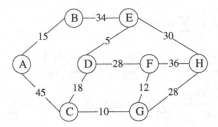

Fig. 3. The game's cost graph of communication amount

Table 2. Nodes' weights of the game

Nodes	A	B	C	D	E	F	G	H
$s(c_i)$ (kb)	450	220	360	120	100	150	80	200
$t_c(c_i)$ (s)	2	0.24	0.2	0.12	0.32	0.16	0.04	0.5
$t_s(c_i)$ (s)	0.5	0.06	0.05	0.03	0.08	0.04	0.01	∞

For each component c_i, we can use the profiling approach [7] to obtain its size $s(c_i)$, its execution times $t_c(c_i)$ and $t_s(c_i)$, as listed in Table 2. Suppose that all components of the game initially locate on the PDA. Given available network bandwidth b=100 kps, network coefficient λ = 0.8, the mean power consumption rates p_i=1.65w, p_c=2.4w, p_t=2.2w which are borrowed from Reference [4].

Based on the formulas in Table 1, we can construct the cost graphs of communication amount, response time and energy consumption, respectively. According to the proposed algorithm, we can transform the cost graphs into the corresponding flow networks. Because different passengers may spend different times playing the game in the bus, execution cycle N is a variable. Then the flow network of communication amount is shown in Fig.4.

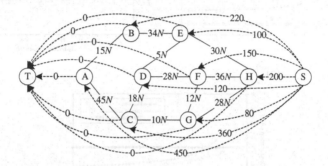

Fig. 4. The game's flow network of communication amount

If the game runs for N cycles, the average resource consumption per execution cycle $P = E/N$, where E refers to total resource consumption. We use the aforementioned three software allocation strategies for saving each resource when N increases in the step of 1. Fig.5.(a), (b) and (c) show the simulation results of saving communication amount, time and energy, respectively.

The monolithic application does not produce any communication amount, so its communication amount is zero, as shown in Fig.5.a. However it consumes a constant response time or energy no matter how N varies, so both the curve between response time and N, and the curve between energy consumption and N are horizontal lines, as shown in Fig.5.b and Fig.5.c.

In general, remote execution means merely allocate the necessary components on the client machine, and allocate others on the server machine. In the game, for example, the scheduling strategy of remote execution is to assign the UI Component H to the mobile device and other components to the server. Thus remote execution moves most of components from the client to the server, which induces a large amount of migration cost. With the increase of N, the weight of migration cost gradually decreases, so the total resource consumption decreases, as shown in Fig.5.

The proposed algorithm can dynamically partition the application according to different execution times. From Fig.5, we can reveal that our algorithm can save significantly more resources than remote execution when N is relatively small, while it saves a little more resources than remote execution when N is large. The reason is that a long execution time implies that migration cost per cycle is low. Since remote execution moves more components than our algorithm, the resource consumption of the former decreases faster than that of the latter with the increase of N. Table 3 shows that our algorithm can obtain different software allocations for saving time and energy when the game runs for different long times.

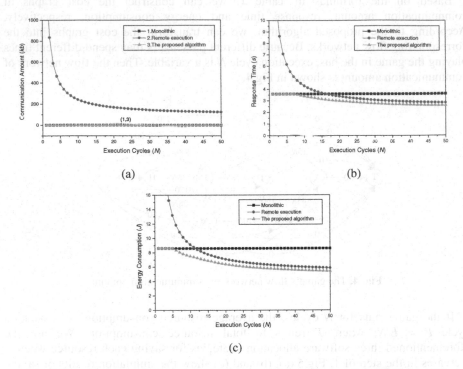

(a)   (b)

(c)

Fig. 5. Resource consumption comparisons among three software allocation strategies

Table 3. Software allocations for saving time or energy using the proposed algorithm

Time			Energy		
N	**Client**	**Sever**	**N**	**Client**	**Sever**
1~7	A,B,C,D,E,F,G,H	---	1~5	A,B,C,D,E,F,G,H	---
8~12	B,C,D,E,F,G,H	A	6~11	B,C,D,E,F,G,H	A
13~23	B,D,E,F,G,H	A,C	12~15	B,D,E,F,G,H	A,C
24~50	D,F,G,H	A,B,C,E	16~32	D,F,G,H	A,B,C,E
			33~50	F,G,H	A,B,C,D,E

In addition, we conduct more simulations under other network conditions, such as $b= 10kbs$, $b=1Mbs$ or $b=10Mbs$. The results of simulation show that our algorithm can always get better performance than other approaches, but it can save more resources in the bad or normal network condition than in the excellent network condition.

6 Related Work

In the traditional distributed computing, numerous researchers present lots of approaches to allocating an application on the multiple machines, but they mainly focus on balancing workload or improving performance. Close to our work, Harold [8] presented a multiprocessor scheduling algorithms based on the well-known Ford-Fulkerson theorem to assign the modules of a program among the processors so as to reduce its execution time. But his algorithm neglected the cost of module migration that may be important when dynamically assigning modules. Also, energy efficiency does not belong to the major research spectrum of the traditional distributed computing.

To save the energy of mobile devices, a few recent systems have explored how remote execution can reduce application energy usage. Rudenko et al [9] performed a series of remote process execution experiments to show the effectiveness of remote executions. Othman and Hailes [5] presented three simple algorithms to decides which jobs should be moved to remote machine. In contrast to our approach that optimally allocates components of an application between the two machines, they often allocate the whole application on the client or server machine. To minimize the energy consumption, Li et al [10,4] developed two elegant program partitioning approaches by using the branch-and-bound policy [10] and a Max-flow Min-cut algorithm [4] respectively. But their approaches are only static software allocation one. Chen et al [11] proposed adaptive execution strategy and adaptive compilation strategy to decide statically or dynamically where to compile a method, and how to execute it, to get better energy conservation. Compared with their work, our algorithm can not only guarantee to obtain the optimal software allocation, but also conserve network bandwidth, time and energy, respectively or simultaneously.

7 Conclusion

This paper presents a software partitioning algorithm applicable to the pervasive computing application. Using the component's mobility, the algorithm can reasonably reallocate the components between the mobile device and the server for resource conservation, which also makes possible for the resource constraint devices to operate the huge or complicated applications. Because the term *cost* in the proposed algorithm is an abstract concept so that it can be initialized into a type of concrete resource, the algorithm can be used to minimize the consumptions of network bandwidth, time and energy, respectively or simultaneously. The consideration of migration cost and the polynomial time complexity of our algorithm make possible the dynamic software allocation. Although the algorithm is applied merely in the field of pervasive computing in this paper, its abstraction and generality guarantee that it can also partition the mobile applications in other areas, such as grid, web services and sensor network. As future work, we plan to extend the proposed algorithm to accomplish the software partitioning and allocation on more than two machines by using the graph bipartition algorithm at multiple times.

References

1. M. Weiser. The computer for the 21st Century. Scientific American, 265(3): 66-75, 1991.
2. G. P. Picco. Understanding code mobility. In: Proceedings - International Conference on Software Engineering, Limerick, Ireland, pages 834, 2000.
3. R. Montanari Rebecca, E. Lupu, and C. Stefanelli. Policy-based dynamic reconfiguration of mobile-code applications. Computer, 37(7): 73-80, 2004.
4. L. Zhiyuan, W. Cheng, and X. Rong. Task Allocation for Distributed Multimedia Processing on Wirelessly Networked Handheld Devices. In: Proc. of 16th International Symposium on Parallel and Distributed Processing, 2002.
5. O. Mazliza and H. Stephen. Power conservation strategy for mobile computers using load sharing. SIGMOBILE Mob. Comput. Commun. Rev., 2(1): 44-51, 1998.
6. J. L. R. Ford, and D. R. Fulkerson, Flows in networks. Princeton: NJ:Princeton Univ. Press, 1962.
7. X. Feng, R. Ge, and K. W. Cameron. Power and energy profiling of scientific applications on distributed systems. In: Proceedings - 19th IEEE International Parallel and Distributed Processing Symposium, Denver, CO, United States, pages 34, 2005.
8. H. S. Stone. Multiprocessor scheduling with the aid of network flow algorithms. IEEE Transaction of Software Engineering, SE-3(1): 95-93, 1977.
9. A. Rudenko, P. Reiher, G. J. Popek, and G. H. Kuenning. Remote processing framework for portable computer power saving. In: Proc. of the ACM Symposium on Applied Computing, San Antonio, TX, USA, pages 365-372, 1999.
10. L. Zhiyuan, W. Cheng, and X. Rong. Computation offloading to save energy on handheld devices: a partition scheme. In: Proc. of international Conf. on Compilers, architecture, and synthesis for embedded systems, Atlanta, Georgia, USA, pages 238-246, 2001.
11. G. Chen, B.-T. Kang, M. Kandemir, N. Vijaykrishnan, M. J. Irwin, and R. Chandramouli. Studying energy trade offs in offloading computation/compilation in Java-enabled mobile devices. IEEE Transactions on Parallel and Distributed Systems, 15(9): 795-809, 2004.

A New Methodology of QoS Evaluation and Service Selection for Ubiquitous Computing*

Yong Zhang, ShenSheng Zhang, and SongQiao Han

Department of Computer Science and Engineering, Shanghai Jiao Tong University
No. 800, Dong Chuan Road, Shanghai, 200240, China
{zycs926, sszhang, hansq}@sjtu.edu.cn

Abstract. Ubiquitous Computing (UbiComp) has become a new computing model in computer systems. However, the characteristics of UbiComp, such as context-awareness, mobility and resource-limitedness, pose challenges for service infrastructure to provide effective service provision. In this paper, we present a suit of user-oriented models and methods that support dynamic Quality of Service (QoS) evaluation and adaptive service selection for UbiComp: 1) We propose a user-oriented QoS model with hierarchical structure to achieve scalability and flexibility; 2) An extended context model with time dimension is employed in QoS evaluation; 3) To capture the weights of quality criteria, we design a user preference model based on linguistic variable; 4) We also model QoS evaluation and service selection as the combination of first order logic inference and hierarchical fuzzy logic evaluation. A case study is presented to demonstrate the effectiveness of our approach.

1 Introduction

The dramatic evolution of microelectronics, wireless network and information services is delivering the technology to fulfill the vision of Ubiquitous Computing (UbiComp). Currently, many kinds of wireless networks (e.g 3G/HSDPA, WiFi and CDMA/GSM, etc.) are available almost everywhere. In the near future, the services will mainly be provided by third-party software vendors, commonly termed Value-Added Service Providers (VASPs), instead of traditional network operators and equipment vendors [1]. Moreover, VASPs will manage to deliver their information services to the mobile users. In particular, with the popularity of portable devices, the surging need of the user for accessing information services by his/her devices can be exploited as the potential of business applications.

However, unlike the desktop applications, not all services in UbiComp environments are suitable for the mobile users and the diverse devices. The context-awareness, mobility and resource-limitedness of Ubicomp pose challenges to service infrastructure for providing adaptive service provision [2], one of them being how to evaluate and select appropriate services for the users with diverse devices. There exists a gap between these services which require special executing environments, and mobile users with portable devices characterized with personalized preference,

---

* This work is funded by Shanghai Commission of Science and Technology and National Research Council of Canada / International Cooperation Project (05SN07114).

X. Cheng, W. Li, and T. Znati (Eds.): WASA 2006, LNCS 4138, pp. 69–80, 2006.

small screen size and limit battery life, etc. Moreover, compared with pervious computing systems, the UbComp applications center on the user, and information services should be delivered with more friendly interfaces and less distraction.

Adaptive Service Provision Framework (ASPF) is one of the most important parts in the joint project between Shanghai Jiao Tong University and Contec Innovation Inc., Canada [3]. In this paper, we present a suit of user-oriented models and methods that support dynamic Quality of Service (QoS) evaluation and adaptive service selection in ASPF. The goal is to generate a service set so that the set itself and its selecting process are a nice match for the context of the user and his/her devices, therefore most satisfying to the user. In our design, a service is implemented as the composition of service components, which is defined in a profile and published by VASPs [4]. Especially, the same type of services with different compositions of service components is looked as different services (e.g. text navigation and graphics navigation.). The dynamic service configuration is beyond the scope of this paper. To make it clear in this paper, we identify each pair of a mobile user and his/her portable device as a Mobile Peer (MP), denoted as (userid, deviceid), which is also abbreviated as MP_i, where i is an index number of the MP in a system. Userid and deviceid identify the mobile user and his/her device respectively.

The reminder of the paper is organized as follows: in section 2, we discuss key components associated with QoS evaluation including QoS model, context model, user preference model and service profile. Section 3 formalizes the process of service selection and fuzzy logic evaluation. Section 4 exemplifies our approach to service selection. In section 5, we discuss the related research. Finally, we come to the conclusion of this paper and discuss our future work.

2 QoS Evaluation

2.1 QoS Model

The quality criteria, derived from multimedia, telecommunication and Web-based applications, mainly involve jitter, reliability, interoperability and robustness, etc. Most of these applications employ a weighted utility function to compute utility values indicating the impact on service selection [5]. However, the same quality criteria are not applicable for UbiComp scenario in which the user is the core of computation. QoS model should focus on quality criteria associated with the user's context in people's perception. Moreover, the utility function can not deal with the situation which involves dominant criteria for QoS evaluation [6].

We explore the definition of QoS and propose a user-oriented concept of measurement for service selection in UbiComp, named as Degree of Service Satisfaction (DSS). DSS is an indicator which instructs the service to be delivered to satisfy a context-specific user. Most importantly, the value of DSS is the metric to service selection in our approach. We design the following DSS model that can produce a satisfactory result in our design:

1. DSS is quantified and measured by a real number between 0 and 1. The higher value of DSS means the higher degree of the service suitable for being delivered.

2. To achieve the scalability and flexibility, the DSS model is designed with a hierarchical structure. An example of the DSS model of our exhibition application is shown in Fig. 1. The model comprises such three sub-criteria as usability, device capability and network status. Furthermore, every sub-criterion contains leaf-criteria which involve delivered context (e.g. memory, bandwidth, location and color depth, etc).

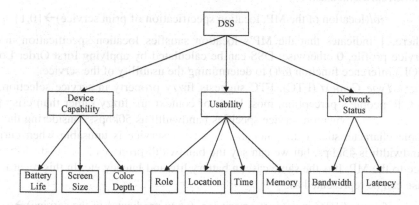

Fig. 1. Hierarchical DSS model

2.2 Context Model

As mentioned above, the context has an impact on service selection in UbiComp environments. Moreover, DSS model is built based on sub-criteria associated with a variety of context. To facilitate the QoS evaluation, we need a unified context representation. We extend the context predicate model in [7] with time dimension which enables the DSS model to promptly evaluate services when the context changes. The context model is denoted by a four-tuple as:

$$ContextCategory(Subject, Relater, Object, Time),$$

where:

- Subject: a subject name, e.g. a person or a room, etc;
- Object: the value of the subject's attribute associated with the relater;
- Relater: representing a relationship between subject and object. Usually, it may be a verb e.g. "enters", "stays" or "equals", etc;
- Time: the time point or duration at or in which the context information keeps true;
- ContextCategory: a name of context category, e.g. location and resource, etc.

For examples,

1. Location (John, enters, room 327, 14:30).
2. Resource (Battery Life of device1, equals, 80%, 17:00).

In ASPF, context collectors obtain the context from physical sensors (e.g. RFID readers) and documents (e.g. service and device profiles). The context interpreters produce high-level context by applying specific processing logics to the original context, e.g. mapping the signal of RFID reader to a room number.

We identify two types of context which influence service selection in different styles. We need to process them with different methods in computing DSS value:

1. *Boolean Type Context* (BTC). BTC refers to the type of context that does satisfy the service's requirement, or doesn't. For example, assuming that a print service will be usable if a MP locates in an area, the location of the MP is a BTC. The case can be represented as:

$$fol(\text{location of the MP, location specification of print service}) \rightarrow \{0,1\},$$

where, 1 indicates that the MP's location satisfies location specification in the service profile, 0 otherwise. DSS can be calculated by applying First Order Logic (FOL) inference function $fol()$ to determining the usability of the service.

2. *Fuzzy Type Context* (FTC). FTC suggests fuzzy property in service selection. In fact, in people's perception, most kinds of context are fuzzy rather than crisp [8]. Given that a navigation service specifies bandwidth as 50kbps, considering the unstable characteristic, it does not mean that the service is unusable when current bandwidth is 45kbps, but we can say the bandwidth proposes less satisfactory service to the MP. It is the same case in battery life and latency etc. In this regard, the case can be represented as:

$$fe(\text{ set of FTC in navigation service, fuzzy predicates of the service}) \rightarrow \alpha,$$

where $fe()$ is a function that executes fuzzy logic evaluation on all FTCs, $\alpha \in [0,1]$. The fuzzy predicates are the membership functions applied to the evaluation. In fact, the computation of DSS of a service requires applying hierarchical fuzzy evaluation on multiple grade levels (see Sect. 3.2).

Additionally, FTC needs to be pre-processed in order to facilitate producing fuzzy predicates and calculating DSS. According to their different quality characteristics, we adopt multiple quantitative methods to quantify them. Table.1 shows the quantification and normalization of color depth by second order model with saturated characteristic. We will not further describe these models that have presented in [9].

Table 1. Quantification of color depth

Color Depth	2	8	16	256	4096	65536
Value	0.10	0.21	0.40	0.69	0.95	1

2.3 Service Profile

ASPF utilizes XML to maintain a service profile that describes the service's requirement of quality criteria associated with the context. Fig.2 shows the partial listing of a service profile. Relational operators (e.g. "And", "Or" and "Not") for requirement composition enable VASPs to construct complex requirements associated with BTC. For example, as for a *btContext* of the service, "Usability" can be specified as:

$$Location=\text{"room 321" .and. } Role=\text{"everyone".} \tag{1}$$

In initial phase, ASPF utilizes context interpreters to process all service profiles for QoS evaluation. Every *btContext* will be translated into a FOL rule. For example, according to (1), the context interpreter can produce the rule as:

Rule: *If Location="room* 321" *.and. Role="everyone"*

then fol=1 else fol=0.

The context interpreter can also produce a hierarchical fuzzy logic evaluation tree: every *ftContext* is mapped to a sub-node, while every FTC is mapped to a leaf-node. Additionally, the context interpreter parses every FTC and produces a series of fuzzy predicates which are used to evaluate FTC on multiple grade levels. For example, suppose the FTC is specified as "Battery Life>50%" and there are three grade levels: Dissatisfactory (DSA), Satisfactory (SA) and Very Satisfactory (VSA), the corresponding fuzzy predicates may be *sigmf*(x,[0.2,35]), *gaussmf*(x,[20,50]) and *sigmf*(x,[0.2,65]). In general, these fuzzy predicates derive from the experiences in practical applications.

```
<service name="multimedia introduction">
   <btContext name="Usability">
      <Context> <name> Location </name>
         <Relation operator="Equal">room 324</Relation></Context>
      <Relation operator="And">
      <Context> <name> Role </name>
         <Relation operator="Equal">everyone</Relation></Context>
   </ btContext >
   ......
   <ftContext name="Device Capability">
      <Context> <name> Battery Life </name>
         <Relation operator="Great-Than">75</Relation></Context>
      ......
   </ftContext>
</service >
```

Fig. 2. A Service profile specified with XML

2.4 User Preference Model

To calculate the set of satisfying services to the user, we need an effective method to capture the user preference to quality criteria. Generally, the user preference to quality criteria is described in the user's profile and decides the weights of quality criteria in the fuzzy logic evaluation (see Sect. 3.2). However, it is difficult for a user to depict his/her preference in numeric scale precisely. The concept of linguistic variable is very useful in dealing with the situations which are too complex or too ill-defined to be reasonably described in the conventional quantitative expressions. The values of a linguistic variable are not numbers but words or sentences in a natural or artificial language [10].

To facilitate the expression of user preference to quality criteria with natural language, we define a set of linguistic terms as:

$T = \{t_1="$very unimportant$", t_2="$rather unimportant$", t_3="$important$", t_4="$rather important$", t_5="$very important$"\}$.

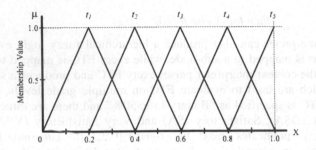

Fig. 3. Membership functions for linguistic terms

Such linguistic terms can be represented by triangular fuzzy numbers as shown in Fig.3. When a user assigns his/her preference with linguistic terms, the corresponding weights of quality criteria can be calculated as:

$$w = \mu(t_i) = \frac{\int x \cdot \mu_{t_i}(x) dx}{\int \mu_{t_i}(x) dx}, \quad i \in [1,5]. \tag{2}$$

The formula (2) provides the center of area that is covered by the fuzzy number to represent the transformation from the linguistic scale into the numeric scale. For example, if a user expresses his/her preference to battery life as $t_3 ="$important$"$, we can obtain the weight of battery life as:

$$w_{batterylife} = \frac{\int_{0.4}^{0.6} x \cdot (5x-2) + \int_{0.6}^{0.8} x \cdot (4-5x)}{\int_{0.4}^{0.6} (5x-2) + \int_{0.6}^{0.8} (4-5x)} = 0.5995.$$

3   Service Selection

3.1   Process of Service Selection

The goal of service selection is to calculate the values of QoS and select appropriate services, which can not only meet the resource constraints, but also achieve the high QoS value. The service selection can be denoted as:

$$\Re : S \times MPS \rightarrow RS ,$$

where, $S = \{s_1, s_2, ..., s_m\}$ is the set of initial services, m is the number of the services. $MPS = \{MP_1, MP_2, ..., MP_n\}$ is the set of MPs, n is the number of MPs in a system. $RS = \{S' | S' \subseteq S\}$ is the collection of all subsets of S .

For each MP_j ($j \in [1,n]$), the process of service selection can be formalized through two steps.

Step1: Calculating the DSS values of the services:

$$DSS(S, MP_j) = (DSS(s_1, MP_j), DSS(s_2, MP_j), ..., DSS(s_m, MP_j)) \; and \tag{3}$$

$$DSS(s_i, MP_j) = DSS_{BTC}(s_i, MP_j) \cdot DSS_{FTC}(s_i, MP_j), i \in [1,m], j \in [1,n]. \tag{4}$$

Where:

1. $DSS_{BTC}()$ is used to check the resource constraints by comparing the values of BTCs with the corresponding requirements of s_i depicted in the service profile as:

$$DSS_{BTC}(s_i, MP_j) = \prod_{r \in R, p \in P} fol(r, p) \; and \; fol : R \times P \to \{0,1\},$$

where, P is the set of FOL predicates of s_i. R is the set of current BTCs associated with MP_j, which acts as resource constraints. The FOL inference function $fol()$ has been discussed in Sect. 2.2.

2. $DSS_{FTC}() = fe()$ is responsible for calculating the DSS value of FTCs, which aggregates the evaluation on all FTCs associated with MP_j. Compared with FOL inference function $fol()$, fuzzy logic evaluation $fe()$ is more complex. We will introduce it in Sect. 3.2.

Step 2: Calculating the final set of services:

$$\Re(S, MP_j) = \Box DSS(S, MP_j) \Box_\lambda = \{s_i \in S \mid DSS(s_i, MP_j) \geq \lambda \; and \; \lambda \in (0,1)\},$$

where, λ denotes a threshold value of DSS for getting the cut set of the services. In general, λ can be obtained from the experiences in practical applications. In this stage, we can compute $\Re(S, MP_j)$ by an optimal strategy:

$$Let \; LS_{MP_j} = \{s_i \in S \mid DSS_{BTC}(s_i, MP_j) = 1\}. \tag{5}$$

Firstly, we calculate $DSS_{BTC}(s_i, MP_j)$. Then, according to the formula (3), (4) and (5), we only calculate:

$$\Re(LS_{MP_j}, MP_j) = \Box DSS(LS_{MP_j}, MP_j) \Box_\lambda = \Box DSS_{FTC}(LS_{MP_j}, MP_j) \Box_\lambda.$$

3.2 Process of Fuzzy Logic Evaluation

The function $fe()$ applies hierarchical fuzzy logic evaluation to calculating DSS value based on current FTCs, fuzzy predicates and their weights that suggest the user's preference to quality criteria. It firstly calculates each sub-criterion's DSS value based on leaf-criteria which the sub-criterion contains, then calculates the DSS value of the service depending on all sub-criteria. We describe the process of calculation as follows:

1. Defining the set of grade levels for evaluation: $G=\{g_1, g_2,..., g_n\}$, where n represents the number of grade levels.
2. Initializing fuzzy evaluation tree according to the service profile: the set of sub-criterion (sf) can be represented as $SF=\{sf_1, sf_2,..., sf_m\}$, where m represents the number of sub-criteria; Then, each sf can be denotes as $sf_i=\{lf_1, lf_2,..., lf_l\}$, where l represents the number of leaf-criterion (lf) of sf_i, and each lf is associated with the corresponding FTC.
3. As discussed in Sect. 2.3, the context interpreter has created a set of fuzzy predicates of each lf, which can be denoted as: $FP=\{fp_1, fp_2,..., fp_l\}$ and $fp_k=\{ fp_{k,1}, fp_{k,2},..., fp_{k,n}\}$. Here, fp_k is the set of fuzzy predicates for lf_k on the grade levels and $fp_{k,j}$ is a fuzzy predicate that acts as a evaluator of lf_k on the ith grade level, $i \in [1, m]$ and $k \in [1, l]$.
4. Calculating fuzzy matrix R_i which represents fuzzy relationship in terms of degree of service satisfaction between sf_i and grade levels:

$$R_i = (R_{i,1}, R_{i,2},..., R_{i,l})^T \text{ and } R_{i,k} = (r_{k,1}, r_{k,2},..., r_{k,n}),$$

where, $r_{k,j}=fp_{k,j}(c_k)$ denotes the evaluation of lf_k of sf_i on the jth grade level for the service. c_k is a quantified FTC associated with lf_k, which is delivered by the context interpreter, $i \in [1, m]$, $j \in [1, n]$ and $k \in [1, l]$.
5. Calculating the DSS value of sf_i of the service based on all lfs and their weights:

$$dsf_i = wlf_i \circ R_i = (b_{i,1}, b_{i,2},..., b_{i,n}),$$

where, $b_{i,j} = \sum_{k=1}^{l} w_{i,k} r_{k,j}$ and $j \in [1,n]$. Moreover, $0 \le w_{i,k} \le 1$ and $\sum_{k=1}^{l} w_{i,k} = 1$. Based on the user preference model, the weight vector wlf_i can be obtained from the user's preference to leaf-criteria in sf_i, which is described in the user's profile (see Sect. 2.4).
6. Analogously, we can calculate the DSS value of other sfs. Let $R=(dsf_1, dsf_2,..., dsf_m)^T$ and weight vector $wsf=(w_1, w_2,..., w_m)$, we calculate the DSS value of the service:

$$dss = wsf \circ R = (w_1, w_2,..., w_m) \cdot (dsf_1, dsf_2,..., dsf_m)^T = (d_1, d_2,..., d_n),$$

where, $d_j = \sum_{i=1}^{m} w_i b_{i,j}$ and $j \in [1,n]$. Similar to wlf_i, wsf shows a user's preference to sub-criteria in the service. Actually, dss is the DSS value of the service represented by a vector of the evaluation on grade levels.
7. To be consistent with the DSS model described in Sect. 2.1, dss is transformed as follows:

$$DSS = dss \times V = (d_1, d_2,..., d_n) \cdot (v_1, v_2,..., v_n)^T = \sum_{j=1}^{n} d_j v_j,$$

where v_i is a score assigned to ith grade level. Moreover, $0 < v_j \le 1$ and $\sum_{j=1}^{n} v_j = 1$.

4 Case Study

In this section, we exemplify a process of service selection and show how to utilize our approach to compute the set of satisfying services for MPs. We assume that there are five services in an exhibition application, and the system has obtained the information of these services by parsing the service profiles specified in Table 2. The mobile devices in the scenario are a Nokia 3100 cell phone and an Asus Pocket PC MYPAL 716A. So in this example, there are two mobile users equipped with their portable devices:

MP_1 =(mobile-user0, Nokia 3100);

MP_2 =(mobile-user1, Asus Mypal 716A).

The context information of MPs is listed in Table 3. Firstly, we apply FOL to validating the usability of current services according to the BTC of MPs, due to:

fol(Role of MP_1, Role specification of video monitor)=0;

fol(Location of MP_2, Location specification of multimedia introduction)=0;

fol(Memory of MP_1, Memory specification of video monitor)=0;

fol(Memory of MP_1, Memory specification of multimedia introduction)=0.

Then, we can obtain the refined service sets:

LS_{MP1} = { text navigation, text introduction };

LS_{MP2} = { text navigation, video monitor, text introduction }.

Table 2. Service profiles

DSS Criteria		text navigation	text-introduction	video monitor	multimedia introduction
Usability	Role	EO	EO	ST	EO
	Time	CU/OT, ST/AT	CU/OT, ST/AT	AT	CU/OT, ST/AT
	Location	EW	EW	EW	room 324
Device Capability	Memory(KB)	80	200	1000	2000
	BatteryLife(%)	>25	>40	>50	>75
	ScreenSize(pl)	128*64	128*96	128*160	240*320
	ColorDepth	8	16	4096	65536
Network Status	Bandwidth(Kbps)	56	384	1000	2000
	Latency(ms)	1500	1500	800	200

Everyone—EO Everywhere—EW CU—Common User ST—Staff OT—Opening Time AT—All Time

Table 3. Delivered context information of MPs

MPs	BTC Information			
	Role	Time	Location	Memory
MP_1	common user	opening time	Room 324	450KB
MP_2	staff	opening time	Room 345	10MB

MPs	FTC Information				
	BatteryLife	ColorDepth	ScreenSize	Bandwidth	Latency
MP_1	60%	4096	128*128	40.2Kbps	1000ms
MP_2	80%	65536	240*320	5Mbps	250ms

Table 4. Computational results of DSS for MPs

Service Name	DSA(w_1=0.1)		SA(w_2=0.35)		VSA(w_3=0.55)		DSS	
	MP_1	MP_2	MP_1	MP_2	MP_1	MP_2	MP_1	MP_2
text navigation	0.25	0	0.10	0	0.75	1	0.47	0.55
text introduction	0.25	0	0.03	0.07	0.75	0.99	0.45	0.58
video monitor	0	0	0	0.14	0	0.99	0	0.60
multimedia introduction	0	0	0	0	0	0	0	0

Provided that we adopt three grade levels: G={DSA, SA, VSA} and corresponding weight set W ={0.1, 0.35, 0.55}, the weights of all criteria associated with devices capability and network parameter are set to average value. On these assumptions, we can calculate the DSS of services shown in Table 4. If we set $\lambda = 0.4$ as a threshold value, then the final set of services we obtained are:

$\Re(S, MP_1) = \{$ text navigation, text introduction$\}$ $_{\lambda=0.4}$,

$\Re(S, MP_2) = \{$ text navigation, video monitor, text introduction$\}$ $_{\lambda=0.4}$.

5 Related Work

Our work discussed in this paper relates to several research domains involving representation and processing context information, service selection and QoS model. In this section, we discuss the related work in these domains.

In fact, the research of context information representation and processing has been conducted for a decade, since Schilit first proposed the concept of context in [11]. Ranganathan et al. described the context as context predicate in Conchat system [7]. The behaviors of system can be adapted to the variation of context by binding system action with the specific context. In [12], Chen et al. represented context ontology by OWL in order to share and reuse the knowledge of context among applications. Jani et al. adopted fuzzy logic to represent sensed information [8]. They implemented the adaptation of various applications and user interfaces for portable devices utilizing fuzzy control. Unlike previous research, we firstly classify the context by their characteristics, and then respectively apply FOL and fuzzy logic method to operating QoS evaluation on the context.

QoS model has been widely discussed in multimedia and Web-based applications by numerous researchers [5, 13]. These work depended on the collection of generic non-functional quality criteria associated with network, communication (e.g. jitter, reliability and availability etc.) and service execution such as delay, security and cost, etc. In [14], Liu et al. proposed an extended QoS model which contains such domain-specific criteria as transaction, compensation and penalty rates for business model. Maximlien et al. developed a dynamic service selection via an agent framework coupled with QoS ontology [15]. In the ontology, they defined several quality aspects deviated from distributed system (e.g. interoperability, stability and integrity, etc.).

Their work greatly inspired us to propose a hierarchical QoS model that includes user-oriented quality criteria such as battery life, memory, latency, etc. The criteria are used to measure whether the services are suitable for being delivered to the resource-constrained devices and whether the services are satisfying to the mobile user. Furthermore, the QoS model can classify context and employ different methods to compute the value of QoS which acts as metric to service selection.

Recently, much research has been made on service selection in Web services. In [4], Moor et al. designed an algorithm of web service selection including three sub-processes: syntactic discovery, semantic matching and pragmatic interpretation. But the algorithm concerned static functional factors. Moreover, the service selection is in the design phase rather than runtime. In [15], Maximilien et al. proposed an agent-based web service selection framework which can dynamically operate selection depending on QoS attributes, and the service specification. However, these studies based on WSDL and UDDI require powerful computational capability and rich resource. That is not applicable for resource-constrained UbiComp environments. In this paper, we designed and implemented a user-oriented, dynamic QoS evaluation and service selection for UbiComp.

6 Conclusion and Future Work

To tackle the problems introduced by context-awareness, mobility and resource-limitedness, the service provision for UbiComp must be capable of dynamic QoS evaluation and adaptive service selection. In this paper, we have described a suit of models and methods applied in the components of QoS evaluation and service selection in ASPF. Besides the hierarchical QoS model and extended context model for service provision, we also have designed the user preference model based on linguistic variable to calculate the weights of quality criteria. In particular, we have modeled QoS evaluation and service selection as the combination of FOL inference and fuzzy logic evaluation. We have demonstrated an example of service selection that confirms the validity of our approach.

The future work will be done towards the improvement and extension of ASPF. To implement a disturbed service provision framework that can automatically deliver services to mobile users among a large area, e.g. multiple exhibitions of a city even a nation, the research on the ontology of service and context is absolutely necessary. Furthermore, integrated with mobile agent technology, ASPF enable UbiComp systems to provide seamless service provision for mobile users during the shift of service domains.

References

1. Zhu, F., Mutka, M. W., and Ni, L. M.: Service Discovery in Pervasive Computing Environments. IEEE Pervasive Computing, Vol. 4, (2005) 81-90
2. Houssos, N., Alonistioti, A., Merakos, L., Mohyeldin, E., Dillinger, M., Fahrmair, M., and Schoenmakers, M.: Advanced Adaptability and Profile Management Framework for the Support of Flexible Mobile Service Provision. IEEE Wireless Communications, Vol. 10, (2003) 52-61
3. Project of Adaptive Service Provision Framework. http://hornet.sjtu.edu.cn

4. De Moor, A. and Van Den Heuvel, W.-J.: Web Service Selection in Virtual Communities. Proceedings of the Hawaii International Conference on System Sciences,Vol. 37. Big Island, HI., United States, (2004) 3105-3114

5. Chalmers, D. and Sloman, M.: A Survey of Quality of Service in Mobile Computing Environments. IEEE Communications Surveys, (Second Quarter,1999) 2-10

6. Elfatatry, A.: Service-Oriented Software: A Negotiation Perspective. Ph.D. dissertation,University of Manchester Institute of Science and Technology, Manchester, U.K, (2002)

7. Ranganathan, A., Campbell, R. H., Ravi, A., and Mahajan, A.: ConChat: A Context-Aware Chat Program IEEE Pervasive Computing, Vol. 1, (2002) 51-57

8. Mantyjarvi, J. and Seppanen, T.: Adapting applications in handheld devices using fuzzy context information. Interacting with Computers, Vol. 15, (2003) 521-538

9. Lum, W. Y. and Lau, F. C. M.: User-Centric Content Negotiation for Effective Adaptation Service in Mobile Computing. IEEE Transactions on Software Engineering, Vol. 29, (2003) 1100-1111

10. Zimmermann, H. J.: Fuzzy Set Theory and its Applications. The second ed. Kluwer Academic Publishers,Dordrecht, (1991)

11. Schilit, B., Adams, N., and Want, R.: Context-aware computing applications. Mobile Computing Systems and Applications - Workshop Proceedings. Santa Cruz, CA, USA, (1995) 85-90

12. Chen, H., Finin, T., and Joshi, A.: An ontology for context-aware pervasive computing environments. Knowledge Engineering Review, Vol. 18, (2003) 197-207

13. Menasce, D. A.: QoS Issues in Web Services. IEEE Internet Computing, Vol. 6, (2002)

14. Liu, Y., Ngu, A. H. H., and Zeng, L.: QoS computation and policing in dynamic web service selection. 13th International World Wide Web Conference Proceedings, WWW2004. New York, NY, United States, (2004) 798-805

15. Maximilien, E. M. and Singh, M. P.: A framework and ontology for dynamic web services selection. IEEE Internet Computing, Vol. 8, (2004) 84-93

An Enhanced Energy Saving Scheme in Mobile Broadband Wireless Access Systems*

Junfeng Xiao, Shihong Zou, Biao Ren, and Shiduan Cheng

State Key Laboratory of Networking and Switching Technology,
Beijing University of Posts and Telecommunications,
100876 Beijing, China
{xiaojf, zoush, renb, chsd}@bupt.edu.cn

Abstract. Excessive listening operations in sleep-mode will waste a lot of energy and shorten the lifetime of Mobile Station (MS) in Mobile Broadband Wireless Access (MBWA) systems. In this paper, we propose an enhanced energy saving scheme to overcome this problem. An embedded Markov chain model is adopted to analyze the enhanced energy saving scheme analytically. At the same time, a closed-form expression of the average energy consumption in the sleep-mode for the suggested scheme is presented. We evaluate and validate the suggested scheme via analytical results and simulation results. Extensive simulation results illustrate that the proposed scheme can obtain better effects of energy conservation to minimize MS power usage and to extend the lifetime of MS effectively.

Keywords: Mobile Broadband Wireless Access System, IEEE 802.16e, Energy Conservation, Sleep-model.

1 Introduction

Energy is a scarce resource in wireless networks because wireless devices are expected with limited battery power [1]. So for wireless networks to be applied popularly, it is critical to design energy efficient techniques maximizing wireless device's lifetime. Although energy efficient design in hardware has been extensively studied [2], significant additional energy saving still can be obtained by incorporating energy efficient strategies into the design of Medium Access Control (MAC) protocol. This paper focuses on the improvement of Energy Saving Mechanism (ESM) in IEEE 802.16e [3, 4] MAC layer.

To fill the gap between very high data rate wireless local area networks and very high mobility cellular systems, the emerging IEEE 802.16e standard enhances the original standard with mobility so that Mobile Stations (MSs) can move during services. Mobility of MSs implies that energy saving becomes an issue so that lifetime of MS can be extended before re-charging. The IEEE 802.16e protocol proposes the ESM, a sleep-mode operation, to save the energy. Yang Xiao [5] analytically modeled the ESM and

---

* This work was supported by the Research Fund of National Nature Science (Grant No.90204003, Grant No. 60402012), the National Basic Research Program of China (Grant No. 2003CB314806).

X. Cheng, W. Li, and T. Znati (Eds.): WASA 2006, LNCS 4138, pp. 81–92, 2006.
© Springer-Verlag Berlin Heidelberg 2006

validated the model with simulations. Jun-Bae Seo *et al.* [6] investigated the queuing behavior of the sleep mode operation in IEEE 802.16e for conserving the power of a MS in terms of the dropping probability and the mean waiting times of the queue of Base Station (BS). The ESM requires that the initial-sleep window is the minimum sleep interval in each sleep-mode operation. This will result in excessive listening operations, which consume more energy, when traffic is low. Neung-Hyung Lee *et al.* [7] proposed a sleep mode interval control algorithm that considers downlink traffic pattern and terminal mobility to maximize energy-efficiency.

In this paper, we propose an Enhanced Energy Saving Scheme (EESS) for IEEE 802.16e Mobile Broadband Wireless Access (MBWA) systems to overcome this problem and promote the energy conserving effect. We apply the embedded Markov chain to analyze our suggested energy saving scheme. We denote the suggested scheme as EESS. By simulation results, we compare the effects of energy conservation, the average listening number, the average sleep lengths of MS and the MAC Service Data Unit (SDUs) delays between the EESS and the ESM.

The rest of this paper is organized as follows. In Section 2, the sleep-mode operation for the energy saving in the IEEE 802.16e standard is introduced. In Section 3, a Markov model for the enhanced energy saving scheme (EESS) is presented. We provide a performance evaluation for the suggested scheme via analytical results and validated with simulations in Section 4. Meanwhile, the performance between the original mechanism ESM and the enhanced one EESS are compared. Finally, we draw conclusions in Section 5.

2 Overview of Sleep Mode in IEEE 802.16e

In the IEEE 802.16e standard, there are three types of Power Saving Classes recommended for connections of Unsolicited Grant Service (UGS), Real Time Variable Rate (RT-VR), Non-Real Time Variable Rate (NRT-VR) and Best Effort (BE) type. As in [5, 6], only the power saving class for connections of BE, NRT-VR type is considered in this paper. In the scenario, a MS has two modes: wake-mode and sleep-mode, shown in Fig.1. Before entering the sleep mode, the MS in the wake-mode sends the sleep request message to the BS and waits for BS's approval before goes to sleep. After receiving the sleep response message which notifies the sleep request of the MS approval, the MS enters the sleep-mode. The sleep request message includes some parameters as follows: initial sleep window (or interval), listening interval and so on. The sleep response message includes some parameters, such as the start time of sleep-mode, the minimum sleep interval T_{min}, the maximum sleep interval T_{max} and the listening interval are presented in units of MAC frames. Such a procedure should be negotiated beforehand between the MS and the BS. The MS gets sleep for an interval, and then temporarily wakes up a short interval, called listening interval, to listen the traffic indication message broadcasted from the BS, and the message includes information about MSs to whom the BS has SDUs waited. If there are SDUs for the MS, the MS goes to wakeup mode. Otherwise, the MS is still in the sleep-mode and continues sleep for another interval. The MS keeps performing the above procedure until it goes to the wake-mode. We call the procedure from entering sleep-mode to exit sleep-mode as one sleep-mode operation in a MS, shown in Fig.1. In the IEEE

802.16e, T_{min} is used as the initial sleep interval when a MS enters the sleep-mode. Then each sleep interval is doubled ($2^j T_{min}$), until T_{max} is reached, and then the sleep interval keeps T_{max}, where j denotes the jth sleep interval. During each sleep interval, a MS can turn off its transmitter and receiver unit in order to conserve the energy. Furthermore, the MS can terminate the sleep-mode if there is an out-going SDU, mostly because of the user's manual interaction [5]. For more detailed operation of the sleep mode, refer to [3, 4].

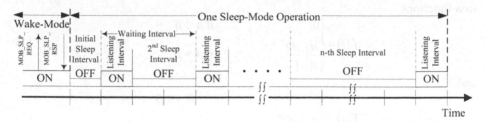

Fig. 1. Sleep mode operation in IEEE 802.16e

3 Analytical Models

According to above description, we can find that the minimum sleep interval is always used as the initial sleep interval when a MS enters sleep-mode every time. It is obvious that there are a lot of listening intervals in sleep-mode when the traffic is low. These listening operations consume much energy and shorten the lifetime of MS before re-charging. Therefore, we propose an enhanced energy saving scheme, namely EESS, to minimize MS power usage and extend the lifetime of MS.

3.1 The Enhanced Energy Saving Scheme

Differing from ESM, the initial sleep interval is not the minimum sleep interval T_{min} in EESS. A MS uses half of the last sleep interval when it exits from the previous sleep-mode operation as the initial sleep interval in next sleep-mode operation. When the initial sleep interval is less than T_{min} the initial sleep interval should be equal to T_{min}. BS can be informed of the initial sleep interval of MS in the sleep request message sent by a MS. After the initial sleep interval, the MS temporarily wakes up a short interval to listen the traffic indication message. If there are SDUs for the MS, the MS goes to wake-mode, and the half of the last sleep interval of the previous sleep-mode operation is used as the initial sleep interval in next sleep-mode operation. Otherwise, the MS is still in the sleep-mode and the sleep interval is doubled. When traffic is low, the inter-SDU arrival interval is large and EESS can effectively decrease the number of listening intervals in one sleep-mode operation.

The main idea of EESS is to reduce the listening operation as few as possible while to monitor the arrival of SDUs effectively. There is no any change needed in IEEE 802.16e standard for EESS. We only set the 'initial-sleep window' field of MOP_SLP_REQ message as half of the last sleep interval of the previous sleep-mode operation. The EESS algorithm can be well kept the compatibility with the IEEE 802.16e standard.

3.2 Embedded Markov Model for EESS

In [5, 6], it is assumed that the SDU, dedicated for a MS, arrival process from network to a BS follows a Poisson process. In fact, however, the traditional traffic-generating models, like the Poisson packet arrival, are bursty over very limited timescales, real world traffic seems to be self-similar [8, 9], i.e., long-range dependent. Thus, we assume the inter-SDU arrival time follows a Pareto distribution with shape parameter α and location parameter β (α, $\beta>0$), and with density and distribution functions

$$f(t)=\begin{cases}0, & \text{if } t \le \beta \\ \dfrac{\alpha}{\beta}\left(\dfrac{\beta}{t}\right)^{\alpha+1}, & \text{if } t > \beta\end{cases} \tag{1}$$

and

$$F(t)=\begin{cases}0, & \text{if } t \le \beta \\ 1-\left(\dfrac{\beta}{t}\right)^{\alpha}, & \text{if } t > \beta\end{cases} \tag{2}$$

respectively, and a mean value

$$E[t]=\alpha\beta/(\alpha-1)=1/\lambda \tag{3}$$

where λ is the SDU arrival rate. If $\alpha\le2$, then the distribution has infinite variance, and if $\alpha\le1$, it has infinite mean and variance. In addition, we assume that the listening interval is a fixed length, during which period the BS sends traffic indication message broadcasted. We define a waiting interval which is denoted by W_i to be a sum of a sleep interval and a listening interval as follows.

$$W_i=T_i+T_L=2^iT_{min}+T_L \quad 1\le i\le N_{max} \tag{4}$$

where $N_{max}=\log_2(T_{max}/T_{min})$. Because half of the last sleep interval is used as the initial sleep interval. There are N_{max} cases for the initial state. Let I_j denote the initial sleep interval. It is expressed as follows.

$$I_j=T_j=2^jT_{min}. \quad 0\le j\le N_{max}-1 \tag{5}$$

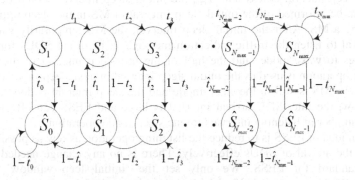

Fig. 2. State transition model of MS

Let S_i ($1 \leq i \leq N_{max}$) denote the state that a MS is on a waiting interval W_i. Meanwhile, let $\hat{S}_j$ denote the state that a MS is on an initial sleep interval I_j. So we can describe the states of a MS, which is in the sleep-mode, and the state transitions by using an embedded Markov chain, shown in Fig.2. The transition probability from S_i to S_{i+1}, which is denoted by t_i, is the probability that there is no SDU arrived during a waiting interval W_i. It is expressed as

$$\Pr(S_{i+1} \mid S_i) = t_i = \left(\frac{\beta}{W_i}\right)^{\alpha}, \ 1 \leq i \leq N_{max} \tag{6}$$

The transition probability from $\hat{S}_j$ to S_{j+1}, which is denoted by $\hat{t}_j$, is the probability that there is no SDU arrived during the initial interval I_j. It is expressed as

$$\Pr(S_{j+1} \mid \hat{S}_j) = \hat{t}_j = \left(\frac{\beta}{I_j}\right)^{\alpha}, \ 0 \leq j \leq N_{max}-1 \tag{7}$$

The transition probability from S_i to $\hat{S}_{i-1}$ is the probability that there are some SDUs arrived during a waiting interval W_i and the initial sleep interval of MS is I_{i-1} in next sleep-mode operation. It is expressed as

$$\Pr(\hat{S}_{i-1} \mid S_i) = 1 - t_i = 1 - \left(\frac{\beta}{W_i}\right)^{\alpha}, \ 1 \leq i \leq N_{max} \tag{8}$$

The transition probability from $\hat{S}_j$ to $\hat{S}_{j-1}$ is the probability that there are some SDUs arrived during an initial sleep interval I_j and the initial sleep interval of MS is I_{j-1} in next sleep-mode operation. It is expressed as

$$\Pr(\hat{S}_{j-1} \mid \hat{S}_j) = 1 - \hat{t}_j = 1 - \left(\frac{\beta}{I_j}\right)^{\alpha}, \ 1 \leq j \leq N_{max}-1 \tag{9}$$

Note that during the listening interval following the initial sleep interval, a serving BS only informs a MS of the arriving SDUs in the initial sleep interval. Furthermore, all the transition probabilities between other states are zero. According to Fig.2, the transition matrix P can be expressed as shown in (10).

In this paper, we use the notation $E[\cdot]$ to stand the mean/average function. We define T_s as the sleep length experienced by a MS before it goes to the wake-mode. In order to calculate $E[T_s]$, the average sleep length of MS, we model the state transitions between initial sleep intervals as a Markov chain, shown in Fig. 3. Let SI_j denote the state that the initial sleep interval is $2^j T_{min}$ ($0 \leq j \leq N_{max}-1$). The transition probability from SI_i to SI_j, which is denoted by φ_{ij}, is the probability that the initial sleep interval of current sleep-mode is I_i and that of next sleep-mode is I_j. According to Fig. 3 and equation (10), we can obtain that

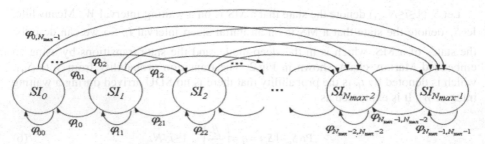

Fig. 3. State transition model of initial sleep interval

$$P=\begin{array}{c|cccccccccccc}
& \hat{S}_0 & \hat{S}_1 & \hat{S}_2 & \cdots & \hat{S}_{N_{max}-2} & \hat{S}_{N_{max}-1} & S_1 & S_2 & S_3 & \cdots & S_{N_{max}-1} & S_{N_{max}} \\
\hline
\hat{S}_0 & 1-\hat{t}_0 & 0 & 0 & \cdots & 0 & 0 & \hat{t}_0 & 0 & 0 & \cdots & 0 & 0 \\
\hat{S}_1 & 1-\hat{t}_1 & 0 & 0 & \cdots & 0 & 0 & 0 & \hat{t}_1 & 0 & \cdots & 0 & 0 \\
\hat{S}_2 & 0 & 1-\hat{t}_2 & 0 & \cdots & 0 & 0 & 0 & 0 & \hat{t}_2 & \cdots & 0 & 0 \\
\vdots & \vdots & \vdots & \vdots & \ddots & \vdots & \vdots & \vdots & \vdots & \vdots & \ddots & \vdots & \vdots \\
\hat{S}_{N_{max}-1} & 0 & 0 & 0 & \cdots & 1-\hat{t}_{N_{max}-1} & 0 & 0 & 0 & 0 & \cdots & 0 & \hat{t}_{N_{max}-1} \\
S_1 & 1-t_1 & 0 & 0 & \cdots & 0 & 0 & 0 & t_1 & 0 & \cdots & 0 & 0 \\
S_2 & 0 & 1-t_2 & 0 & \cdots & 0 & 0 & 0 & 0 & t_2 & \cdots & 0 & 0 \\
\vdots & \vdots & \vdots & \vdots & \ddots & \vdots & \vdots & \vdots & \vdots & \vdots & \ddots & \vdots & \vdots \\
S_{N_{max}-1} & 0 & 0 & 0 & \cdots & 0 & 1-t_{N_{max}-1} & 0 & 0 & 0 & 0 & 0 & t_{N_{max}-1} \\
S_{N_{max}} & 0 & 0 & 0 & \cdots & 0 & 0 & 1-t_{N_{max}} & 0 & 0 & 0 & 0 & t_{N_{max}}
\end{array} \qquad (10)$$

$$\varphi_{ij}=\Pr\left(SI_j\mid SI_i\right)=\begin{cases}1-\hat{t}_i, & j=i-1 \\ \hat{t}_i\left(1-t_{j+1}\right), & j=i \\ \hat{t}_i t_{i+1}\cdots t_j\left(1-t_{j+1}\right), & i<j\le N_{max}-2 \\ \hat{t}_i t_{i+1}\cdots t_{N_{max}-1}, & j=N_{max}-1 \\ 0, & \text{others}\end{cases} \qquad (11)$$

where $1\le i\le N_{max}-2$. When $i=0$, the transition probability from SI_0 to other states is expressed as

$$\varphi_{0j}=\Pr\left(SI_j\mid SI_0\right)=\begin{cases}1-\hat{t}_0 t_1, & j=0 \\ \hat{t}_0 t_1 t_2\cdots t_j\left(1-t_{j+1}\right), & 1\le j\le N_{max}-2 \\ \hat{t}_0 t_1 t_2\cdots t_{N_{max}-1}, & j=N_{max}-1\end{cases} \qquad (12)$$

As a result, the state transition matrix Φ of initial sleep intervals can be expressed as

$$\Phi=\begin{pmatrix}
\varphi_{00} & \varphi_{01} & \varphi_{02} & \cdots & \varphi_{0,N_{max}-2} & \varphi_{0,N_{max}-1} \\
\varphi_{10} & \varphi_{11} & \varphi_{12} & \cdots & \varphi_{1,N_{max}-2} & \varphi_{1,N_{max}-1} \\
0 & \varphi_{21} & \varphi_{22} & \cdots & \varphi_{2,N_{max}-2} & \varphi_{2,N_{max}-1} \\
\vdots & \vdots & \vdots & \ddots & \vdots & \vdots \\
0 & 0 & 0 & \cdots & \varphi_{N_{max}-2,N_{max}-2} & \varphi_{N_{max}-2,N_{max}-1} \\
0 & 0 & 0 & \cdots & \varphi_{N_{max}-1,N_{max}-2} & \varphi_{N_{max}-1,N_{max}-1}
\end{pmatrix} \qquad (13)$$

Let $\bar{\pi} = \left\{ \pi_{SI_0}, \pi_{SI_1}, \cdots, \pi_{SI_{N_{max}-1}} \right\}$ be the steady-state probability. With $\bar{\pi} = \bar{\pi} * \Phi$ we can obtain each steady-state probability as

$$\pi_{SI_j} = \frac{\hat{t}_0 \prod\limits_{k=1}^{j} t_k}{\prod\limits_{k=1}^{j}\left(1-\hat{t}_k\right)} \pi_0, \qquad 1 \le j \le N_{max}-1 \tag{14}$$

Using the normalized condition $\sum\limits_{k=0}^{N_{max}-1} \pi_{SI_k} = 1$, π_{SI_0} is obtained by

$$\pi_{SI_0} = \frac{1}{1 + \sum\limits_{k=1}^{N_{max}-1} \dfrac{\hat{t}_0 \prod\limits_{i=1}^{k} t_i}{\prod\limits_{i=1}^{k}\left(1-\hat{t}_i\right)}} \tag{15}$$

When the initial sleep interval is I_j the average sleep length of MS is

$$
\begin{aligned}
E[T_s \mid SI_j] &= \sum\limits_{l=1}^{\infty}\left(\Pr\{\text{no arriving SDU in } l \text{ successive sleep intervals}\} \cdot \sum\limits_{k=j}^{l+j} T_k \right) \\
&= \sum\limits_{l=1}^{\infty}\left(\Pr\{\text{no arriving SDU in } l \text{ successive sleep intervals}\} \cdot \sum\limits_{k=j}^{l+j} 2^k T_{min} \right) \\
&= \sum\limits_{m=j+2}^{N_{max}-1}\left[\left(\sum\limits_{i=j}^{m} 2^i T_{min}\right)\hat{t}_j\left(1-t_m\right)\prod\limits_{k=1}^{m-1} t_k\right] + 2^j T_{min}\left(1-\hat{t}_j\right) + 3(j+1)T_{min}\hat{t}_j\left(1-t_{j+1}\right) + \left(\sum\limits_{i=j}^{N_{max}} 2^i T_{min} + 2^{N_{max}} T_{min}\sum\limits_{k=1}^{\infty} k\right)\hat{t}_j\prod\limits_{i=j+1}^{N_{max}} t_i
\end{aligned}
\tag{16}
$$

Therefore, according to the full probability formula, we can obtain the average sleep length of MS as follows.

$$E[T_s] = \sum\limits_{j=0}^{N_{max}-1} \Pr\{SI_j\} * E[T_s \mid SI_j] = \sum\limits_{j=0}^{N_{max}-1} \pi_{SI_j} E[T_s \mid SI_j] \tag{17}$$

Let E_S and E_L denote the energy consumption units per unit of time in the sleep interval and the listening interval, respectively. Adopting the same idea as calculating $E[T_s]$, when the initial sleep interval is I_j, the average energy consumption of MS in the sleep-mode is

$$
\begin{aligned}
E[\text{Energy} \mid SI_j] &= \sum\limits_{l=1}^{\infty}\left(\Pr\{\text{no arriving SDU in } l \text{ successive sleep intervals}\} \cdot \sum\limits_{k=j}^{l+j}\left(T_k E_S + T_k E_L\right) \right) \\
&= E[T_s \mid SI_j]\cdot E_S + \left[\hat{t}_j\left(1-t_{1+j}\right) + \sum\limits_{m=j+1}^{N_{max}-1}\prod\limits_{k=1}^{m}\hat{t}_j t_k\left(1-t_{m+1}\right)\right]\cdot T_L \cdot E_L
\end{aligned}
\tag{18}
$$

Therefore, according to the full probability formula, we can obtain the average energy consumption in the sleep mode as follows.

$$
\begin{aligned}
E[\text{Energy}] &= \sum\limits_{j=0}^{N_{max}-1} \Pr\{SI_j\}\cdot E[\text{Energy} \mid SI_j] = \sum\limits_{j=0}^{N_{max}-1} \pi_{SI_j} E[\text{Energy} \mid SI_j] \\
&= \sum\limits_{j=0}^{N_{max}-1} \pi_{SI_j}\left\{ E[T_s \mid SI_j]E_S + \left[\hat{t}_j\left(1-t_{1+j}\right) + \sum\limits_{m=j+1}^{N_{max}-1}\prod\limits_{k=1}^{m}\hat{t}_j t_k\left(1-t_{m+1}\right)\right]T_L E_L \right\}
\end{aligned}
\tag{19}
$$

4 Performance Evaluation and Comparison

We evaluate the EESS scheme with analytical results and validate the results by simulations. Meanwhile, we compare the effects of energy conservation, the average listening number $E[n]$, the average sleep lengths of MS and the average delays of MAC SDU between the EESS and the ESM. In this paper, let $E[D]$ denote the average SDU delay from the time when the SDU arrives at the MAC layer of BS to the time it is listened by the MS.

4.1 Simulation Validation

We conduct simulations to validate analytical results for EESS. The parameters for the simulation are the same as [5] except the SDU arrival process. They are listed as follows: $T_L=1$ (unit time), $T_{min}=1$ (unit time), $T_{max}=1024$ (unit time), $E_S=1$ and $E_L=10$. At the meantime, an OFDMA frame length, the basic unit time, is 5ms. As [8], the burstiness of each traffic source is controlled by α which is set to 1.3 in the simulation. Thus, β can be derived as $((\alpha-1)/\alpha\lambda)$. The simulation is achieved via Matlab tools and results are obtained via averaging values from 10 different runs with different seeds. Fig. 4 shows both simulation results and analytical results of $E[T_S]$ over the SDU (or packet) arrival rate λ. As illustrated in the figure, the simulation results match analytical results pretty well.

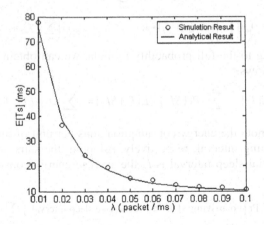

Fig. 4. Simulation results vs. analytical results

4.2 EESS vs. ESM

Fig. 5 shows the percentage of energy saved by EESS, compared to ESM, with different values of T_{min} when $T_{max}=1024$. The larger percentage means that EESS saves more energy than ESM. From this figure, we can see that the percentage of energy saved by EESS increases as λ decreases. In addition, it can be seen that the effect of energy saved by EESS is better than ESM when the value of T_{min} is smaller under the same λ. If the value of T_{min} is large, EESS works better or gives the same performance of ESM. $T_{min}=1$ is only considered in following evaluations and comparisons.

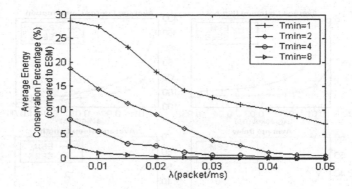

Fig. 5. Average energy conservation percentage (T_{max}=1024)

Fig. 6, Fig. 7 and Fig. 8 compare performance metrics of EESS with ones of ESM over λ when T_{max}=4, 16 and 1024 respectively. From these figures, we see that performance difference between two schemes becomes smaller as the T_{max} decreases. It's obvious that performance metrics of EESS are the same as ones of ESM when T_{max}=2 since the initial sleep interval of EESS is always equal to T_{min}. When T_{max} is larger than 2, EESS experiences less average listening number $E[n]$ and consumes less energy than ESM. The average listening number difference of EESS and ESM is very distinct when T_{max}=1024. In this case, the average listening number of EESS is always kept nearby 2. In addition, the average SDU delay difference of EESS and ESM decreases as T_{max} value decreases. In these figures, the performance difference of EESS and ESM shortens as λ rises. It's reasonable that EESS has the same performance as ESM when λ is high.

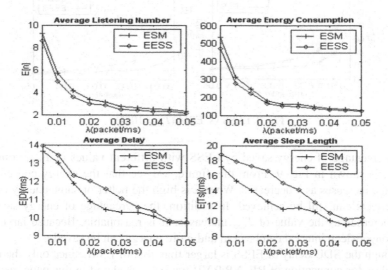

Fig. 6. EESS vs. ESM (T_{max}=4)

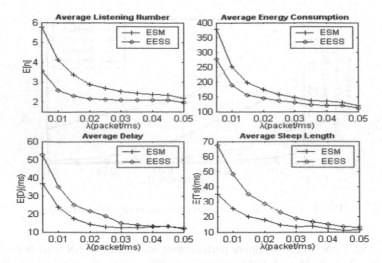

Fig. 7. EESS vs. ESM (T_{max}=16)

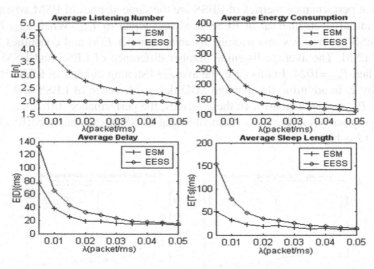

Fig. 8. EESS vs. ESM (T_{max}=1024)

The percentage of energy saved by EESS with different values of T_{max}, compared to ESM, is shown in Fig. 9. From this figure, we see that the energy conservation percentage increases as λ decreases. When λ is high the better or same energy conservation effects can still be achieved. In addition, the percentage of energy saved by EESS increases as the value of T_{max} increases. It is reasonable. Because larger T_{max} means longer sleep interval can be used and more energy can be saved.

Although the SDU delay of EESS is larger than that of ESM, since only the power saving class for connection of BE, NRT-VR type is considered in this paper as [8, 9],

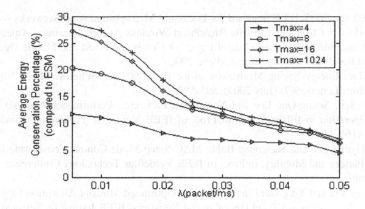

Fig. 9. Average energy conservation percentage ($T_{min}=1$)

a little increase of SDU delay is acceptable and tolerable for these connections. According to above analysis, we can get that EESS with appropriate T_{min} and T_{max} can obtain better effects of energy conservation than ESM while not compromise the performance of BE and NRT-VR connections.

5 Conclusion

In this paper, we proposed an enhanced energy saving scheme for the emerging IEEE 802.16e MBWA system. Differing from ESM, EESS uses half of the last sleep interval when it exits from the previous sleep-mode operation as the initial sleep interval in next sleep-mode operation. We apply an embedded Markov chain model to analyze our suggested energy saving mechanism. A closed-form expression of the average energy consumption in the sleep-mode for the enhanced energy saving scheme is presented. We evaluate the suggested scheme via analytical results and validate it with simulation results. Meanwhile, extensive simulation results show that the proposed mechanism with appropriate T_{min} and T_{max} can reduce the listening operation and obtain better effects of energy conservation than ESM to minimize MS power usage and to extend the lifetime of MS effectively.

References

1. Shihong Zou, Haitao Wu and Shiduan Cheng: Adaptive Power Saving Mechanisms for DCF in IEEE 802.11, Mobile Networks and Applications. 10 (2005) 763-770
2. A. Chandrakasan and R.W. Brodersen: Low Power Digital CMOS Design, Kluwer Academic Publishers, Norwell, MA, (1995)
3. IEEE 802.16e/D6-2005: Draft IEEE Standard for Local and Metropolitan Area Networks --- Part 16: Air Interface for Fixed and Mobile Broadband Wireless Access Systems – Amendment for Physical and Medium Access Control Layer for Combined Fixed and Mobile Operation in Licensed Bands, (Feb., 2004)

4. IEEE 802.16e-2005: IEEE Standard for Local and Metropolitan Area Networks --- Part 16: Air Interface for Fixed and Mobile Broadband Wireless Access Systems – Amendment 2: Physical and Medium Access Control Layer for Combined Fixed and Mobile Operation in Licensed Bands and Corrigendum 1, (Feb., 2006)
5. Yang Xiao: Energy Saving Mechanism in the IEEE 802.16e Wireless MAN, IEEE Communications Letters, 9(7) (July 2005), 595-597
6. Jun-Bae Seo, Seung-Que Lee and Nam-Hoon Park etc.: Performance Analysis of Sleep Mode Operation in IEEE802.16e, in Proc. of IEEE Vehicular Technology Conference, 2 (2004), 1169-1173
7. Neung-Hyung Lee and Saewoong Bahk: MAC Sleep Mode Control Considering Downlink Traffic Pattern and Mobility, in Proc. of IEEE Vehicular Technology Conference, 3(2005), 2076-2080
8. Wei-Ming Yin and Ying Dar Lin: Statistically Optimized Minislot Allocation for Initial and Collision Resolution in Hybrid Fiber Coaxial Networks, IEEE Journal on Selected Areas in Communications, 18(9) (2000), 1764-1773
9. V. Paxson and S. Floyd: Wide area traffic: The failure of Poisson modeling, IEEE/ACM Trans. Networking, 3 (1995), 226-244

Energy Aware Multimedia Messaging Services Across Networks and Across Devices for Mobile Users

Bin Wei[1] and Lin Zhong[2]

[1] AT&T Labs-Research, Florham Park, NJ 07920
bw@research.att.com
[2] Rice University, Houston, TX 77005
lzhong@rice.edu

Abstract. The extensive coverage of wireless networks brings tremendous opportunities for messaging services to satisfy the demands of accessing multimedia and time-critical information from mobile users. This trend makes energy efficiency an increasing challenge on mobile devices. In this paper, we propose a novel solution toward meeting this challenge. We explore communications utilities along both "cross-network" and "cross-device" dimensions for managing multimedia messaging services. Along the cross-network dimension, we consider the multitude of networking capabilities at a mobile terminal and select the most energy-efficient communication medium to maintain the connectivity or accomplish data transfer. Along the cross-device dimension, we consider the multitude of user interface devices by which mobile users can further improve overall energy efficiency in consuming multimedia messages. In this writing, we discuss our method as a position paper. Related experiments were performed and results are presented to justify our approach.

Keywords: energy aware, energy efficiency, and multimedia messaging system.

1 Introduction

In the world of wireless communications, there is always a concern of energy consumption to sustain network connectivity and accomplish data transfer, especially for emerging messaging services, which may generate data and push it to mobile devices at any time. This always-on requirement poses a great challenge on managing energy consumption on mobile devices.

Traditionally, mobile devices are managed by some specific service associated with a distinct network. For example, a mobile phone can only operate in the cellular network that it is designed for and enabled by the network carrier. A PDA (Personal Digital Assistant) device, which is a handheld device for easy access of personal information, may be able to connect to a data-oriented communication wireless network, such as WiFi. Today, mobile users desire to break through the separations of these communications mechanisms. These expectations ask for device convergence and service integration. Since the convergence results in more wireless communication requirements, energy efficiency becomes even more critical on mobile devices.

X. Cheng, W. Li, and T. Znati (Eds.): WASA 2006, LNCS 4138, pp. 93–103, 2006.

On the other hand, small special-purposed electronic gadgets, which have long battery life, are constantly coming out to the market. These devices not only have more user preferred functions, such as a built-in MP3 player in a wrist watch, they are also able to connect to other nearby devices, forming a personalized network. A wrist watch may be used to display real-time stock market information through other mobile devices. It may also be used as a secondary user interface for communication management to a PDA which consumes much more power than a watch.

By taking into account these advances on networks and mobile devices, we propose an energy management methodology for multimedia messaging communications to mobile users by exploring the communication utilities along both "cross-network" and "cross-device" dimensions. Along the "cross-network" dimension, we consider the inter-relationship between networks. Along this dimension, while multiple wireless networks co-exist and each was originally developed based on certain technologies, unified control schemes are emerging for integrated or blended services on top of different access networks. A unified control provides the possibility of selecting an energy-efficient channel among several available ones for wireless communications. Along the "cross-device" dimension, we mean that mobile users may interact with connected multiple mobile devices for data access to minimize energy consumption. For example, a mobile user can choose to retrieve data via a wrist-worn device instead of a mobile phone in the pocket.

In this paper, we describe our work that actively selects the best communication and interaction resources to achieve both the goals of messaging services and energy efficiency. Our proposed method includes:

- The network connection of a mobile device is primarily maintained through the low-power medium among all its available networks.
- Messaging services to a mobile device always considers the available low-power network first.
- Supplemental data can be transferred semi-automatically by allowing a user to select a preferred network for transferring data.
- More mobile devices can be used in a hierarchy to further reduce energy consumptions for retrieving and displaying messages.

Fig. 1 is a high-level diagram, illustrating our approach for energy efficient wireless communications by exploring both cross-network and cross-device dimensions.

We would like to emphasize that the paper is to present our method for energy efficient communications in multiple dimensions. Although we have components, the whole system is not completely integrated yet. Thus, performance data concerning the overall system behavior is not available. We made related experiments with current environments to justify our ideas and present them in the paper.

In the rest of the paper, we discuss our energy efficiency studies along the cross-network dimension with performance data we collected in our experiments. In Section 3, we present our work on exploring energy aware multimedia communications along the cross-device dimension, by utilizing a device hierarchy with an example of a wrist-worn secondary interface for mobile devices to retrieve multimedia messages in an energy-efficient way. We discuss related work in Section 4 and conclude in Section 5.

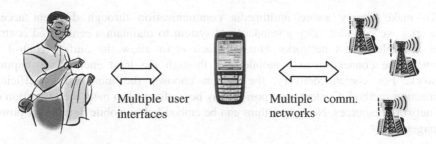

Fig. 1. Energy-aware multimedia messaging service by considering multiple access networks on the right and a hierarchical mobile device structure on the left

2 Energy Aware Multimedia Communications Across Networks

In this section, we first take a look at typical multimedia messaging systems and the emerging trend of unified control for supporting applications across networks. We then present performance data from our current experiments.

2.1 Alert Messaging Services

With the proliferation of information, many messaging services [1,2,3] are developed to alert users by filtering and extracting information segments according to user's interests. These systems normally consist of a content network where information is acquired from various sources. The original content is then processed, extracted, and indexed. Alerting messages are constructed according to the user's interest profile and delivered to the user. Depending on the device that a user selects, alerting messages may need to be repurposed in order to fit content to the target device. Fig. 2 is a simplified diagram of a typical alert messaging system that supports mobile users.

As users request more on connectivity and mobility, we begin to see the convergence of networks in Telecommunications Industry. Standardized systems are also emerging [4, 5].

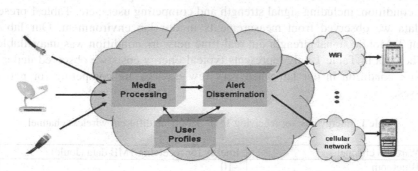

Fig. 2. A block diagram of an alerting system

To make energy aware multimedia communication through different access networks, we consider using a standardized system to maintain a centralized control over multiple access networks. Our approach is to allow the unified control to maintain the connection to a mobile user through the least energy consumption network. For content delivery, the system chooses the most energy efficient connection method. Content repurposing may be performed to meet the restriction of the network resources. New algorithms can be embedded in mobile devices for power management.

2.2 Performance

We conducted some experiments relating to the issues along the cross-network dimension and report some of the measurement data here.

Power Consumption

We obtained power consumption of an Audiovox SMT5600 Smartphone by measuring the voltage drop cross a 100m• sense resistor embedded in the battery VDD output with a USB-1608FS module from *Measurement Computing* [6]. We employed a differential measurement approach similar to that used in [7] to obtain the power consumption during the process of downloading a video clip through GPRS. We found GPRS power consumption can be as high as 1.6W, depending on the network condition. The energy cost of downloading a 70 second video clip (696KB) is around 100 Joules. Note that the battery capacity is about 15000 Joules and every watt increase in power can lead to more than 10°C surface temperature increase [8] in the phone. This indicates that multimedia communications impose a great challenge toward mobile device battery lifetime and thermal management.

The energy cost to transfer a certain amount of data depends on the wireless technology and network condition. Network technologies differ in their coverage, data rate, and network association cost; network condition refers to the number of competing users, signal strength, and achievable data rate. Table 1 shows our measurement of energy cost on an I-Mate K-Jam Pocket PC phone [9], which has Bluetooth, WiFi, and GPRS/EDGE. Note that energy cost depends on network condition, including signal strength and competing users, etc. Table 1 presents the data we observed from measurements in our lab environment. Our lab has decent T-Mobile signal strength but real-time network condition was unavailable to us. The data in Table 1 only represents typical energy costs we observed under the network condition in our lab when very few devices are competing for network accesses.

Table 1. Energy cost for receiving 1MB data from different wireless channel

Wireless channel	Energy for receiving 1MB data (Joule)
Bluetooth	~10
802.11b (WiFi)	~3-10
GPRS/EDGE (T-Mobile)	~115

Table 1 clearly demonstrates that different wireless interfaces differ drastically in energy cost for receiving data. More importantly, the availability and energy efficiency change when the user moves around. For example, 802.11b takes about 3 Joules for receiving 1MB data when signal strength is good to support 10Mbps data rate; it takes about 10 Joules when signal strength can also support 1Mbps data rate. Ideally, a mobile device should dynamically select the most energy-efficient available interface. In addition to the energy cost of receiving data, different wireless interfaces also differ significantly in power overhead for maintaining connectivity and establishing connection. In our measurement with the I-Mate K-Jam phone, GSM/GPRS costs about 25mW to stay connected. However, 802.11b consumes about 300mW during idle time and consumes about 5 Joules to get connected when the device WiFi is in the "Battery Optimized" configuration. Our power traces indicate that the wireless interface spends most of the time in the power-saving mode when configured with the "Battery Optimized" option. These data suggest that while GPRS/EDGE is more energy-efficient in maintaining connectivity, WiFi is much more efficient in receiving large amount of data. Their strengths complement each other and offer new opportunities [10].

2.3 Discussion

The energy cost for a mobile device to transfer (similarly for receiving) M bits of data through a wireless channel, E, can be calculated as:

$$E = Ena + Ebit * M \qquad (1)$$

Ena is the overhead for setting up a connection and $Ebit$ is the energy consumption per bit. Both Ena and $Ebit$ depend on the wireless technology, network condition and the mobile device. For a given wireless technology, Ena and $Ebit$ can often be estimated for a given device, if the network condition is also known. Therefore, in order to choose the most energy-efficient channel, both networks and devices need to know the network condition for available channels in an energy-efficient and timely fashion. Unfortunately, this is not well supported with even the state-of-the-art wireless technologies. For example, most wireless technologies do not provide the achievable data rate for a new user. In 802.11 (WiFi) networks, the energy overhead for mobile devices to stay associated is very high, as indicated in our measurement. Current wireless technologies do not yet provide adequate support for a centralized control and mobile devices to select the most energy-efficient wireless channel for multimedia messaging services. However, since a wireless network infrastructure normally already know the network conditions, it just needs to provide such information to the centralized control system and also broadcast the information to associated mobile devices. For example, an 802.11 access point broadcasts traffic indication map (TIM) to associated mobile devices so that the latter know when there are incoming packets. Network condition can be broadcast along with TIM with a very small overhead.

It is worth noting that a wireless medium can be more energy efficient when transferring a large amount of data while less energy efficient otherwise. For example,

802.11 can be more efficient when M is large, because it has a small *Ebit* but large *Ena*. On the other hand, GPRS is more energy efficient when transferring sporadic data, such as control packets. A natural energy-efficient configuration is to use GPRS to stay connected and select 802.11 to transfer intensive data when needed.

3 Utilizing Device Hierarchy in Multimedia Message Delivery

In Section 2, we discussed how to choose the most energy-efficient wireless channel from IMS for wireless data transfer. Given the most energy-efficient wireless channel, we address, in this Section, how a mobile user can retrieve a multimedia message in an energy efficient fashion, with a hierarchy of interfacing devices.

3.1 Motivation

Table 2 shows the energy cost in an Audiovox SMT5600 Smartphone for the process of downloading a multimedia message, which contains a 70 second video clip. It also shows repurposed versions when text and animated key-frames are used from the same content. The exact energy cost may vary, depending on network conditions and the way that the user interacts with the device. "Downloading Energy" is the energy consumption of downloading a complete message. There are two situations: automatic fetching and manual downloading. Manual downloading incurs extra energy cost in the display, because the display typically remains on when the user waits. "Consuming Energy" is the energy cost for the user to access the message, which is mostly related to display. We use a typical reading rate of 300 words per minute [11] for consuming a text message; for animated key-frames, we assume that four key-frame images are consumed with 4 seconds/shot; we assume that video is consumed in the same duration of its play time with built-in speakers on.

Table 2. Energy cost by downloading and consuming different message formats

Message Format		Text	Key-Frames	Video
Size (Byte)		140	10K	696K
Downloading Energy (Joule)	Automatic	~0.03	~1.2	~80
	Manual	~0.08	~1.7	~114
Consuming Energy (Joule)		~5	~10	~48

According to Table 2, the energy cost of obtaining a video clip message is extremely high. 90 such messages will exhaust the Audiovox Smartphone. The energy costs of different media formats differ significantly. Manual downloading costs more than 40% more energy due to the use of the display. "Consuming Energy" dominates when the message is delivered as text or key-frames. These insights motivate us to design a vertical hierarchy in message delivery for better battery lifetime and usability, as will be addressed next.

3.2 Hierarchical Message Content

For an alerting service, a mobile end-user needs to download the whole message even if he/she wants to see a portion of it. This all-or-none messaging style can potentially waste a huge amount of energy on mobile devices. To address this issue, we can provide multiple formats for the same content and allow users to choose and obtain information progressively, beginning with text messages that consume very little energy. Thus, every clip extracted for a user is transcoded into a few more formats: a small number of key-frames and low and high quality of video that can be played on the mobile device. Each format of the message is then loaded onto a web server so that it can be retrieved with a unique URL through standard Internet protocols. The server also generates a priority score for the message by matching it with the user interest profile. The server then prepares a text message and delivers it to the user through SMS service. The SMS message, which has a limitation of 140 bytes, provides the user with brief information about the content, the URLs for more detailed content, message priority, and lifetime. More detailed information can be requested following the SMS, forming a hierarchy of content deliveries.

3.3 Battery-Aware Message Fetching

SMS messages can always be automatically retrieved due to their very low energy cost. Upon receiving a SMS message, the mobile device can analyze the data to obtain basic information of the message, and determine whether the key-frame or the video part of the message should be fetched before notifying the user. The decision will be based on battery information, energy cost of fetching rich formatted content, and the message priority. Battery-aware message fetching will not only minimize more than 40% overhead due to user-engaged downloading but also minimize interruption to the user.

3.4 Hierarchical User Notification

Many media alerting systems notify their mobile users with a message in an interruptive fashion. For example, a mobile device makes a sound upon arrival of a message, We incorporated a Microsoft CacheWatch [12] as a secondary display. The CacheWatch can connect with a Bluetooth-capable mobile device, which is called the *host*. The watch serves as a low-power remote display for the host. It can display a message notification in a non-interruptive and persistent fashion. Moreover, it takes user input through three series of touch sensors. The user can retrieve the text version of the message and instruct the mobile device to download a richer version of the content, without directly operating the personal mobile device, thus avoiding use of the power-hungry display on the host during the download process.

The CacheWatch, however, incurs energy consumption in the Bluetooth interface. To minimize Bluetooth energy consumption, the watch disconnects from the host after each communication. Every time they are connected, the host notifies the watch when to reconnect. While saving energy in Bluetooth, it can introduce delays in message notification: when the host receives a message, it has to wait until the next connection to send the message notification to the CacheWatch. Such delays can be

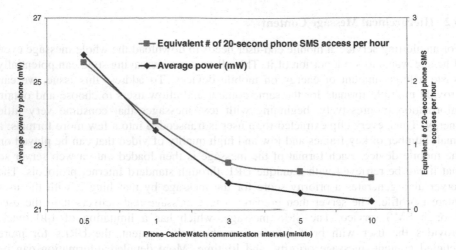

Fig. 3. Justifying Bluetooth energy overhead for phone-CacheWatch communication

reduced and are often tolerable with multimedia content delivery. On the other hand, we have to make sure the energy cost due to Bluetooth will be justified by energy savings through the use of the CacheWatch. Assuming a user takes 20 seconds to consume a text message on the Audiovox Smartphone, Fig. 3 gives the average Audiovox Smartphone power consumption when the phone synchronizes with the watch based on different phone-CacheWatch communication intervals. It also shows that the numbers of 20-second phone accesses per hour that will lead to the same average phone power consumption. The figure shows that when the synchronization interval is 10 minutes, the watch will save energy for the phone if it reduces one text message access to the phone in every two hours.

With these design considerations, we present an overview of the new system next.

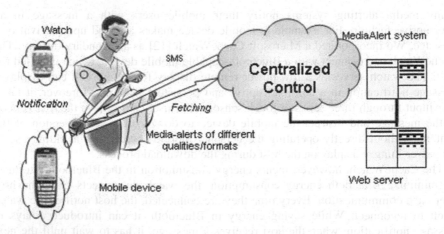

Fig. 4. Justifying Bluetooth energy overhead for phone-CacheWatch communication

3.5 A Hierarchical Device System

Fig. 4 presents an overall view of a cross-device system, SMERT. SMERT is based on a media alert system with a web server for message retrieval and with the capability of generating multiple versions to support the content hierarchy. Such an augmentation reuses most of the original infrastructure illustrated in Fig. 2. Indeed, most of the additional functions can be implemented as software installed on mobile devices. In our prototype system, mobile users sign up for SMERT service and specify their device and interest profiles. They also download and install software for progressive content delivery, battery-aware fetching and notification. Users may choose to wear the watch, although the service works even without it.

4 Related Work

Utilizing a low-energy channel to wake up or turn off a high-energy channel has been shown an effective way to conserve energy in battery powered communication devices [13, 14]. An example of this approach can be found in "Wake on Wireless (WoW)", proposed by Shih et. al. [13]. WoW is to reduce idle power by shutting down WiFi wireless network interface card of a mobile device when the device is not being used. The device is powered only when an incoming call through a secondary radio with low-energy out-of-band signaling is received. Pragmatically, the low-energy channel provides a remote control to turn on and off the communication system on the device before real wireless communication takes place. However, this requires a dual radio system deployed in the same network. Our approach takes the advantage of the unified control architecture for the control across networks and the multiple network accessibility of a mobile device, without the need of deploying a dedicated secondary out-of-band mechanism as a low-energy control channel for the high-energy communication channel. With the initial message, the user can then determine whether to access more detailed information through other, possibly more power-consumed channels.

Multi-hop wireless networking has also been studies extensively. In [15], the authors propose an application-aware link layer protocol to reduce energy for the operation of multi-hop networks. Based on the concept of Message Ferrying (MS), the authors of [16] present a power management framework, in which nodes switch their power management models, depending on the knowledge of ferry location. Saving energy by trading off data delivery delay is an important issue in multi-hop wireless networks. The hierarchical structure of multiple mobile devices we have proposed is for single user environment, where devices are reachable to and managed by the same person.

Related studies also include power management with application support or with consideration of all the mobile devices. In [17], the authors describe the design and implementation of an innovative transport protocol capable of significantly reducing the power usage of the communication device. In [18], the authors propose power management techniques addressing mobile host communications that encompass all components of a mobile host in an effort to optimize total energy consumption. These studies focus on single network environment. Our power saving scheme involves multiple networks and crossing the networks requires a unified control scheme with content repurposing support.

5 Conclusion

We described a methodology to achieve energy-efficient communications by seeking solutions in both "cross-network" and "cross-device" dimensions. Along the cross-network dimension, we proposed an energy management technique based on a unified control scheme on multiple access networks. We discussed the technical challenges with performance data. Along the cross-device dimension, we presented a hierarchical device structure to save energy for content delivery and to minimize the interruptions to the user. We demonstrated this approach with an implemented system.

Although our cross-network and cross-device techniques can be utilized together, they can be considered as orthogonal approaches. We can develop and improve techniques in each dimension separately. However, combining them enable us to achieve better results.

Acknowledgments. The authors would like to thank Rittwik Jana at AT&T Labs-Research for the discussion of the paper. The authors would also like to thank Ahmad Rahmati from Rice University for collecting the power data for the I-Mate K-Jam Pocket PC. Comments from the reviewers provided helpful information for the revision of the paper.

References

1. B. Wei, B. Renger, R. Chen, R. Jana, H. Huang, L. Begeja, D. Gibbon, Z. Liu, and B. Shahraray., "MediaAlert: a broadcast video monitoring and alerting system for mobile users," in *Proc. USENIX/ACM MobiSys*, June 2005.
2. Google Alert, http://www.googlealert.com
3. Yahoo Alert, http://help.yahoo.com/help/alerts/
4. Conzalo Camarillo and Miguel A. Garcia-Martin, The 3G IP Multimedia Subsystem (IMS): Merging the Internet and the Cellular Worlds, John Willey & Sons, 2004.
5. 3GPP IMS, http://www.3gpp.org/ftp/Specs/html-info/22228-CRs.htm.
6. Measurement Computing™: http://www.measurementcomputing.com
7. Lin Zhong and Niraj K. Jha, "Energy efficiency of handheld computer interfaces: Limits, characterization, and practice," in *Proc. USENIX/ACM MobiSys*, June, 2005.
8. Bert Haskell, Portable Electronics Product Design and Development, McGraw-Hill Professional, 2004.
9. I-Mate K-JAM Pocket PC phone: http://www.clubimate.com/t-DETAILS_KJAM.aspx
10. Ahmad Rahmati, "Extending the interfacing capability of mobile systems with a wireless body-area network," ELEC599 Research Project Report, Dept. of ECE, Rice University, May, 2006.
11. R. P. Carver, Reading Rate: A Review of Research and Theory, Academic Press, Inc., San Diego, CA, 1990.
12. Lin Zhong, Mike Sinclair, and Ray Bittner, "A Phone-Centered Body Sensor Network Platform: Cost, Energy Efficiency & User Interface," in Proc. IEEE Int. Wkshp. Body Sensor Network, Apr. 2006.
13. E. Shih, P. Bahl, and M.J.Sinclair, Wake on Wireless: An Event Driven Engergy Saving Strategy for Battery Operated Devices, In Proceedings of the 8th Annual International Conference on Mobile Computing and Networking, pp. 160-171. 2002.

14. Carla F. Chiasserini and Ramesh Rao, Combining Paging with Dynamic Power management, In IEEE INFOCOM 2001, pages 12-19, April 2001.
15. A. Harris, C. Sengul, R. Kravets and P. Ratanchandani, Energy-Efficient Transmission Policies for Multimedia in multi-hop Wireless Networks, the 6th IFIP IEEE International Conference on Mobile and Wireless Communication Networks, MWCN, 2004.
16. H. Jun, W. Zhao, M. Ammar, E. Zegura and C. Lee, Trading Latency for Energy in Wireless Ad Hoc Networks Using Message Ferrying, the 3rd International Conference on Pervasive Computing and Communications Workshops, 2005.
17. Robin Kravets and P. Krishnan, Application-Driven Power management for mobile Communication, MobiCom 1998.
18. R. Kravets, K. Schwan, and Ken Calvert, Power-Aware Communication for Mobile Computers, the 6th International Workshop on Mobile Multimedia Communication, November 1999.

Dynamic Bandwidth Allocation in IEEE 802.16

Weiwei Wang[1], Zihua Guo[2], Xuemin (Sherman) Shen[3], Changjia Chen[1], and Jun Cai[3]

[1] Beijing Jiaotong University, Beijing, China
[2] Lenovo Corporate Research, Beijing, China
[3] Department of Electrical and Computer Engineering,
University of Waterloo, Ontario, Canada

Abstract. IEEE 802.16 has gained significant research attention because of its broadband wireless services over a large coverage area. Bandwidth allocation plays very important role at the link layer of IEEE 802.16. In this paper, by considering the Automatic Repeat reQuest (ARQ) scheme for an erroneous wireless channel, a dynamic bandwidth allocation algorithm for downlink traffic in a multiuser environment is proposed and a detailed analysis is performed. Simulation results show that the proposed algorithm significantly improves the delay performance of the Service Data Unit (SDU) which consists of multiple Protocol Data Units (PDUs), and ensures the fairness among different users.

1 Introduction

IEEE 802.16, also known as WiMax (Worldwide Interoperability for Microwave Access), provides broadband wireless services over a large coverage area. It includes Fix Broadband Wireless Access (FBWA) and Mobile BWA (MBWA). In 2004 and 2005, IEEE 802.16d and 802.16e are ratified for FBWA and MBWA, respectively, which define the medium access control (MAC) and physical (PHY) layers. In MAC, the standards define two air-interfaces: Point-to-Multi-Point (PMP) and Mesh. In PMP, two Subscriber Stations (SSs) can only communicate with each other through the Basic Station (BS), while in Mesh, two SSs can communicate directly. TDD (Time Division Duplexing) and FDD (Frequency Division Duplexing) are both supported.

WiMax has gained lots of interest from both industry and academia after its appearance. In TDD mode for PMP, each frame is divided into two subframes: Downlink (DL) and Uplink (UL). The duration of DL/UL and the bandwidth allocation in DL/UL are determined by BS according to the QoS (Quality of Service) requirements of each flow. However, the scheduling algorithm is not specified in the standards. As a result, it has become one of the hottest research topics. A scheduling scheme for uplink is proposed in [1], where DL and UL subframes have the equal duration. Another uplink scheduling scheme for VoIP services is presented in [2] by considering the characteristics of voice data. Both of them focus on the bandwidth allocation of the UL subframe. In [3], a framework is provided for scheduling different types of service flows in both uplink and downlink. The bandwidth of DL/UL is allocated dynamically in PMP mode and the fairness among different flows becomes the main target. However, there is no consideration of the delivery delay of SDU. In this paper, we propose a novel

X. Cheng, W. Li, and T. Znati (Eds.): WASA 2006, LNCS 4138, pp. 104–114, 2006.

dynamic bandwidth allocation algorithm for the DL traffic in PMP mode by considering ARQ in an erroneous channel. The objective is to provide a fair bandwidth sharing and reduce the delivery delay of SDU, which consists of multiple PDUs.

The rest of this paper is organized as follows. Section II gives the brief introduction of IEEE 802.16 MAC. In Section III, the proposed adaptive bandwidth allocation algorithm is presented in detail. Section IV analyzes performance of the proposed algorithm. Numerical results are given in Section V, followed by the conclusions in Section VI.

2 IEEE 802.16 MAC

In IEEE 802.16, several PHYs are defined, such as Single Carrier (SC) and Orthogonal Frequency Division Multiplexing (OFDM). The frame structure varies with different PHYs and duplexing modes. In this paper, we focus on the OFDM frame structure with TDD mode in PMP , as shown in Fig.1. The DL subframe consists of a preamble, Frame Control Header (FCH), and a number of data bursts. The FCH specifies the burst profile and the duration of one or more DL bursts that immediately follow the FCH. The burst profile specifies the coding algorithm, code rate and modulation level used for data transmission. The DL-MAP, UL-MAP, DL Channel Descriptor (DCD), UL Channel Descriptor (UCD), and other broadcast messages are transmitted after the FCH and describe the remainder of the frame. The rest of the DL subframe is the data burst to individual SSs. The data frame from upper layer, which is called SDU, is partitioned into ARQ blocks, and several ARQ blocks are encapsulated into one or multiple PDUs. The details of other components in Fig. 1 can be found in [4].

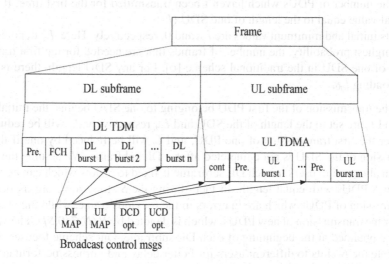

Fig. 1. OFDM frame structure with TDD in PMP

In order to provide a reliable wireless link, ARQ schemes are introduced in IEEE 802.16 MAC. In a typical ARQ with Selective Acknowledgement (ARQ-SA) scheme, the error information of the transmitted DL packets is reported in the subsequent UL subframe and the erroneous packets will then be retransmitted in the following DL subframe.

There are many research works for the uplink scheduling, but few for the downlink one. In [5], Weighted Round Robin (WRR) is proposed for the downlink scheduling. It allocates the bandwidth according to the QoS requirements of each service flow. Thus, for the service flows belonging to the same QoS class, the allocated bandwidth to each flow in DL is fixed. We term such scheduler as the *traditional scheme* in this paper. We will demonstrate that this scheme is by no means the best solution in terms of delay. On the other hand, ARQ scheme does play important role on the delay performance. Based on the analysis in [6], it is found that under a typical ARQ-SA scheme, the delivery delay of SDU is primarily determined by the first transmission of all its PDUs, and such delay can be reduced significantly with the increase of the allocated bandwidth (BW). As a result, when multiple users compete for the BW, it should be dynamically allocated according to the buffered SDU status to improve the delay performance. Therefore, bandwidth allocation algorithms should consider the following two key features:

- the SDU delay instead of an individual PDU delay.
- the effects of the ARQ scheme on the scheduling.

3   Bandwidth Allocation Algorithm

We first define some useful parameters for SDU:

- L_p: the number of PDUs which haven't been transmitted for the first time. It has an initial value equal to the length of one SDU (L);
- L_f: its initial and minimum values are L_{f0} and 0, respectively. Here, L_{f0} denotes, with the highest probability, the number of frames that are needed for the first transmission of one SDU in the traditional scheme [6]. For any SDU length, there is a corresponding L_{f0}.

When the transmission of the first PDU belonging to one SDU begins, the initial value of L_p and L_f are set to the length of the SDU and L_{f0}, respectively. L_p will be reduced by one after the first transmission of one PDU, and L_f will be reduced by one if the first transmission of the SDU is not completed after a DL subframe. We assume the whole duration allocated to users in each DL subframe is fixed to S slots which can be used to transmit S PDUs with equal length. In fact, during the S slots, some are used for the retransmission of PDUs which are in errors in the previous frame, while the others are used for the transmission of new PDUs, which is denoted by N ($N \in [0,S]$). The value of N can be obtained at the beginning of each DL subframe. Our scheme focuses on how to allocate the N slots to different users for better delay and fairness performance. We define a two-level priority for each user given in (1) and (2):

$$P_1 : L_f \tag{1}$$

$$P_2 : \min(L_p, N) \tag{2}$$

That means, when allocating BW, we first consider L_f for priority determination. If some users have the same L_f, we will further consider $\min(L_p, N)$. Note that, in each priority level, the smaller the value, the higher the priority.

Without loss of generality, we consider a two-user scenario (userA and userB) to illustrate the algorithm, and it can be extended directly to more users' scenario. Each user has a sender queue at the BS. The lengths of SDU from userA and userB are assumed to be L_A and L_B, respectively. At the beginning of the i-th frame, the corresponding parameters of userA and userB are denoted by $(L_{p_A}^i, L_{f_A}^i, L_{p_B}^i, L_{f_B}^i)$. We set the initial values as $(N, L_{pA}, L_{fA}, L_{pB}, L_{fB}) = (N^i, L_{p_A}^i, L_{f_A}^i, L_{p_B}^i, L_{f_B}^i)$, which will be used for the bandwidth allocation in our algorithm. In initial values, N^i means the number of slots which can be used for the first transmission of new PDUs in the i-th DL subframe. We can get the two-level priority of each user by (1) and (2), denoted as $(P_A^1, P_A^2, P_B^1, P_B^2)$. Finally, we denote L_{sA} and L_{sB} the number of slots allocated to userA and userB, respectively, in the frame, and the initial values of them are zero. Our algorithm follows two steps:

Step 1. It is used for a BW pre-allocation to each user. We sort the users by ascending order based on the two-level priority and allocate the BW to the user with the highest priority as:

$$(A, B) =$$

$$\begin{cases} (\min(L_{p_A}, N), 0) & \text{if} \quad \begin{pmatrix} P_A^1 < P_B^1 \\ \text{or} \quad (P_A^1 = P_B^1, P_A^2 < P_B^2) \end{pmatrix} \\ (0, \min(L_{p_B}, N)) & \text{if} \quad \begin{pmatrix} P_B^1 < P_A^1 \\ \text{or} \quad (P_A^1 = P_B^1, P_B^2 < P_A^2) \end{pmatrix} \\ (\min(L_{p_A}, N), 0) & \\ \text{or} \quad (0, \min(L_{p_B}, N)) & \text{if} \quad P_A^1 = P_B^1, P_B^2 = P_A^2 \end{cases} \tag{3}$$

where A and B are the allocated bandwidth to userA and userB, respectively.

Step 2. Step 1 is for bandwidth pre-allocation. This step is to update the involved parameters. In other words, in step1, some slots have been allocated to each user. The parameters are updated for next iteration pre-allocation as

$$
\begin{cases}
N = N - A - B \\
L_{sA} = L_{sA} + A \\
L_{sB} = L_{sB} + B
\end{cases}
\tag{4}
$$

(L_{pA}, L_{fA}) should be updated by

$$
(L_{p_A}, L_{f_A}) =
\begin{cases}
(L_{P_A} - A, \ \max (L_{f_A} - 1, 0)) & \text{if } A < L_{p_A} \\
(L_A, \ L_{f_{A0}}) & \text{if } A = L_{p_A}
\end{cases}
\tag{5}
$$

In (5), if the allocated bandwidth is smaller than the left PDUs of the SDU at the head of userA's sender buffer, the number of the left PDUs after this pre-allocation is L_{pA} -A, and L_{fA} is reduced by one till zero; if the first transmission of the left PDUs which belong to the SDU at the head of userA's sender buffer can be finished at this allocation, L_{pA} and L_{fA} are updated to the length (L_A) and L_{fA0} of next SDU, respectively. Likewise, (L_{pB}, L_{fB}) is updated in the similar way.

> **input parameters :**
>
> $L_{sA} = 0 \ L_{sB} = 0 \ (N^i, L_{p_A}^i, L_{f_A}^i, L_{p_B}^i, L_{f_B}^i)$
>
> **set** $(N, L_{p_A}, L_{f_A}, L_{p_B}, L_{f_B}) = (N^i, L_{p_A}^i, L_{f_A}^i, L_{p_B}^i, L_{f_B}^i)$
>
> **while**$(N > 0)$
>
> > **using** (1) **and** (2)
> >
> > > **get the two-level priority of two users :**
> > > $(P_A^1, P_A^2, P_B^1, P_B^2)$
> >
> > **using** (3)
> >
> > > **pre-allocate bandwidth for two users :**
> > > (A, B)
> >
> > **using** (4) **and** (5)
> >
> > > **refresh** $(N, L_{sA}, L_{sB}, L_{p_A}, L_{f_A}, L_{p_B}, L_{f_B})$
>
> **end while**
>
> **output parameters :** $L_{sA} \ L_{sB}$
>
> **using** (6)
>
> > **get** $(L_{p_A}^{i+1}, L_{f_A}^{i+1}, L_{p_B}^{i+1}, L_{f_B}^{i+1})$

Fig. 2. Pseudo-code of proposed scheme

After updating the parameters, we can recalculate the two-level priority of each user. Then steps 1 and 2 can be repeated until all N^i slots have been allocated. Finally, L_{sA} and L_{sB} are the final allocated BW for the first transmission of the new PDUs of userA and userB, respectively, in the current DL subframe.

After the transmission of the i-th frame, $(L_{p_A}^i, L_{f_A}^i, L_{p_B}^i, L_{f_B}^i)$ is updated to

$(L_{p_A}^{i+1}, L_{f_A}^{i+1}, L_{p_B}^{i+1}, L_{f_B}^{i+1})$ which will be used for the allocation in the $(i+1)$-th frame:

$$(L_{p_A}^{i+1}, L_{f_A}^{i+1}) =$$

$$\begin{cases} (L_{p_A}^i - L_{sA}, \max (L_{f_A}^i - 1, 0)) & \text{if } L_{sA} < L_{p_A}^i \\ (L_A, L_{f_{A0}}) & \text{if } L_{sA} \ge L_{p_A}^i, \text{mod } (L_{sA} - L_{p_A}^i, L_A) = 0 \\ (L_A - \text{mod } (L_{sA} - L_{p_A}^i, L_A), \max (L_{f_{A0}} - 1, 0)) \\ \qquad \text{if } L_{sA} > L_{p_A}^i, \text{mod } (L_{sA} - L_{p_A}^i, L_A) \ne 0 \end{cases} \qquad (6)$$

$mod(c, C)$ means the remainder of c being divided by C. From (6), we can see that if the allocated bandwidth is not enough for the first transmission of the left PDU of the SDU,

$L_{p_A}^{i+1}$ is updated to the left PDUs after the i-th frame and $L_{f_A}^{i+1}$ is reduced by one till

zero. If the first transmission of a SDU is just finished at the end of the i-th frame,

$L_{p_A}^{i+1}$ and $L_{f_A}^{i+1}$ are updated to the initial values. The third condition in (6) means

the first transmission of a SDU is started at this frame but not finished. Similarly, we can update the parameters of userB.

Based on above description of the algorithm, the pseudo-code of our algorithm is shown in Fig.2.

4 Performance Analysis

The time spent by the first transmission of all PDUs of one SDU determines the delivery delay of SDU, and this duration is equivalent to the number of frames (l) spent by the first transmission of the whole PDUs. Therefore, the distribution of l is an important metric for the SDU delivery delay. In the following, we try to get the distribution of l for the proposed algorithm.

Let state variable $X(i)$ ($X(i) \in E$) be defined as $(N, L_{pA}, L_{fA}, L_{pB}, L_{fB})$ at the beginning of the i-th frame, where E is the set of all possible values of $X(i)$ (how to obtain E is given in Appendix). Let $P(X_2|X_1)$ denote the one-step transition probability from state $X_1 = (N_1, L_{pA1}, L_{fA1}, L_{pB1}, L_{fB1})$ at the beginning of the i-th frame to state $X_2 = (N_2, L_{pA2}, L_{fA2}, L_{pB2}, L_{fB2})$ at the beginning of the $(i+1)$-th frame. $(L_{pA2}, L_{fA2}, L_{pB2}, L_{fB2})$ in the $(i+1)$-th frame can be determined by X_1, and the number of slots (N_2) used for the first transmission of PDUs in the $(i+1)$-th frame is independent of X_1. Then, the transition probability can be calculated by:

$$P(X_2 \mid X_1) = P((L_{pA2}, L_{fA2}, L_{pB2}, L_{fB2}) \mid X_1) P(N_2) \tag{7}$$

where $P(N_2)$ is the probability of S-N_2 error packets among S packets. Due to the random choosing in (3), we may get one or multiple different $(L_{pA2}, L_{fA2}, L_{pB2}, L_{fB2})$ when the input parameters (see Fig.2) is X_1. By assuming each $(L_{pA2}, L_{fA2}, L_{pB2}, L_{fB2})$ is obtained by m ways and each way has n_k ($k \in [1,m]$) random choosing,

$$P((L_{pA2}, L_{fA2}, L_{pB2}, L_{fB2}) \mid X_1) = \sum_{k=1}^{m} 0.5^{n_k} \tag{8}$$

Assume each PDU has an independent error probability of p,

$$P(N_2) = \binom{S}{N_2} p^{S-N_2} (1-p)^{N_2} \tag{9}$$

Combining (7)-(9), we can get the transition probability matrix (**P**) of $X(i)$ with all possible values in **E**. Let the steady-state probability of $X(i)$ be $\Pi = (\pi_1, \cdots, \pi_e)$, where e is the number of elements in **E**, $\pi_j = P(X^j)$, and X^j means the jth element of **E**.

Vector Π can be obtained by solving the following linear equations of a Markov chain:

$$\begin{cases} \Pi * P = \Pi \\ \sum_{j=1}^{e} \pi_j = 1 \end{cases} \tag{10}$$

Therefore, we have:

$$P(Ls_{A1}, Ls_{B1}, X_1) = P(Ls_{A1}, Ls_{B1} \mid X_1) P(X_1) \tag{11}$$

Under the condition of X_1, we can get $(Lp_{A2}, Lf_{A2}, Lp_{B2}, Lf_{B2})$ and (Ls_{A1}, Ls_{B1}). Then, $P(Ls_{A1}, Ls_{B1} \mid X_1)$ can be calculated by(8).

We use userA as an example to get the distribution of the number of frames, $(P(l_A=k), k \in [1,\infty])$, which are required for the first transmission of a complete SDU for userA. Let Y_1 denote (Ls_{A1}, Ls_{B1}, X_1) in i-th frame, and Y_2 denote (Ls_{A2}, Ls_{B2}, X_2) in $(i+1)$-th frame. The set of all possible values of Y_1, which indicates that the first transmission of the SDU can be finished in one frame for userA is denoted as F_{A1}. So, $P(l_A=1)$ can be obtained by using (11)

$$P(l_A = 1) = \sum_{F_{A1}} P(Y_1) \tag{12}$$

In order to obtain $P(l_A{=}2)$, we have

$$
\begin{aligned}
&P(Y_2, Y_1)\\
&= P(Y_2 \mid Y_1)P(Y_1)\\
&= P(Ls_{A2}, Ls_{B2} \mid X_2, Y_1)P(X \, 2 \mid Y_1)P(Y_1)\\
&= P(Ls_{A2}, Ls_{B2} \mid X_2)P(X_2 \mid Y_1)P(Y_1)\\
&= P(Ls_{A2}, Ls_{B2} \mid X_2)\binom{S}{N_2} p^{S-N_2}(1-p)^{N_2} P(Y_1)
\end{aligned} \tag{13}
$$

Because L_{sA2} and L_{sB2} are just determined by X_2, $P(L_{sA2},L_{sB2}|X_2,Y_1)$ is equal to $P(L_{sA2},L_{sB2}|X_2)$ which can be computed using the same approach as that of $P(L_{sA1},L_{sB1}|X_1)$. With respect to $P(X_2|Y_1)$, $(Lp_{A2},Lf_{A2},Lp_{B2},Lf_{B2})$ are determined by Y_1 so that $P(X_2|Y_1)$ only depends on the number of slots which are used for the first transmission of PDUs in the $(i+1)$-th frame, i.e.,

$$P(X_2 \mid Y_1) = \binom{S}{N_2} p^{S-N_2}(1-p)^{N_2} \tag{14}$$

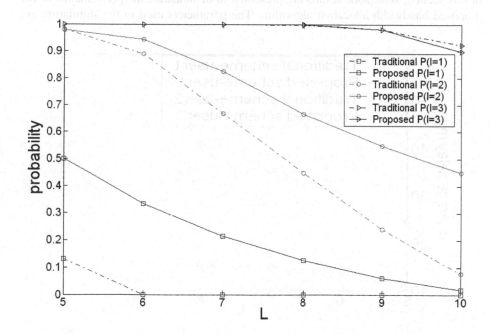

Fig. 3. Probability comparison

Assume $\mathbf{F_{A2}}$ is the set of all possible values of (Y_2, Y_1), which indicates the first transmission of one SDU for userA can be finished in two frames. Then, $P(l_A=2)$ can be calculated by:

$$P(l_A = 2) = \sum_{F_{A2}} P(Y_2, Y_1) \qquad (15)$$

Similarly, we can get $(P(l_A=k), k \in [1,\infty])$.

Fig. 3 shows some numerical results based on our analysis. Total 10 slots are allocated to both userA and userB in each DL subframe. UserA and userB have the same data rate. For the traditional scheme, each user can transmit 5 PDUs in each DL subframe. The results of the traditional scheme denoted by dotted line are obtained by using the similar way as our analysis except with the fixed BW allocation. In Fig.3, the probability of finishing the first transmission of SDU in one, two and three frames under different SDU lengths are compared. It can be seen that $P(l_A=1)$ and $P(l_A=2)$ in our algorithm are much higher than the traditional scheme, while $P(l_A=3)$ almost reaches 100% for both schemes. This implies that, in our algorithm, the first transmission of whole PDUs will be finished in one or two frames in most cases. The numerical results also indicate that the delay of SDU can be significantly decreased.

5   Simulation Results

In this section, simulation results are presented to demonstrate the performance of the proposed bandwidth allocation algorithm. The parameters used in the simulation are

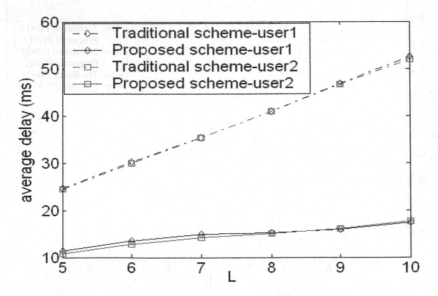

Fig. 4. Delay comparison (equal BW)

as follows. N_{FFT} =256 is the number of OFDM FFT points, N_{SD} =192 is the subcarriers used for data transmission, and p =0.1 is the PDU error rate. The length of each user's SDU varies from 5 to10 PDUs. Each frame has duration T_{frame} =10ms and each slot has duration T_{slot} =685us for the transmission of one PDU with 1200 bytes. T_{DL_head}=1ms is the time duration spent by transmitting control messages (i.e. preamble, FCH, DL-MAP, UL-MAP. etc) and other users' data in DL subframe. The simulation duration is 100s, and 10 slots in each DL subframe are used for users' data.

In Fig. 4, five users are simulated but only the average SDU delay of user1 and user2 are presented. Similar results are obtained for other users. We assume the bandwidth requirement of all users is equal. Thus, each user is allocated 2 slots under the traditional scheme. In this figure, the X-axis denotes the length of SDU. It can be seen that the SDU delay with our algorithm is decreased significantly. In addition, the equal bandwidth allocation in the traditional scheme implies the fairness among users in terms of delay. By comparing the delay performance between two users, we can find that our algorithm has the similar fairness performance as that of the traditional scheme.

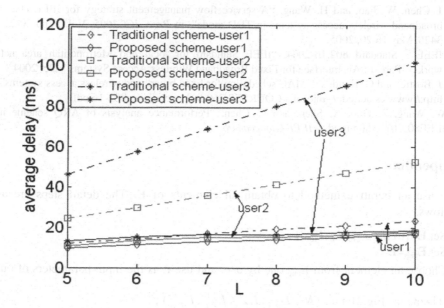

Fig. 5. Delay comparison (unequal BW)

Note that our algorithm is not only applicable to the equal average BW requirement among users, but also to the case with different BW requirements. Fig. 5 gives the delay performance comparison for 5 users. The average required BWs for user1 to user5 are 5, 2, 1, 1 and 1, respectively. From the figure, the delay of SDU for our scheme is also decreased significantly. Moreover, it can be seen that the fewer the bandwidth required, the more the delay is decreased in our algorithm.

6 Conclusions

In this paper, a dynamic bandwidth allocation algorithm for the downlink traffic scheduling in IEEE 802.16 has been proposed. A detailed analysis on delay performance has been carried out. The analytical and simulation results have shown that the proposed algorithm can greatly reduce the delivery delay of SDUs while keeping the fairness among different users. A more complete simulation based on ns-2 simulator is under way.

References

1. K. Wongthavarawat, and A. Ganz, "Packet scheduling for QoS support in IEEE 802.16 broadband wireless access systems", *International Journal of Communication Systems*, Vol. 16, pp. 81-96, Feb. 2003.
2. H. Lee, T. Kwon, and D-H Cho, "An enhanced uplink scheduling algorithm based on voice activity for VoIP services in IEEE 802.16d/e system", *IEEE Commun. Letters*, Vol. 9, No. 8, pp. 691-693, Aug. 2005.
3. J. Chen, W. Jiao, and H. Wang, "A service flow management strategy for IEEE 802.16 broadband wireless access systems in TDD mode", in *Proc. ICC2005*, Vol. 5, pp. 3422 - 3426, May 16-20, 2005.
4. IEEE™ Standard 802.16-2004, "IEEE Standard for local and Metropolitan area networks---Part 16: Air Interface for Fixed Broadband Wireless Access Systems", Oct 2004.
5. J. Bostic, and G. Kandus, " MAC scheduling for fixed broadband wireless access systems". http://www.cs.ucr.edu/~michalis/COURSES/260-03/papers/janez802-16.pdf.
6 W. Wang, Z. Guo, X. Shen, and C. Chen, "Performance analysis of ARQ scheme in IEEE802.16", submitted to *IEEE Globecom06*.

Appendix

We use an iterative method to obtain all elements of **E**. The detail steps are as follows.

1. Set $\mathbf{E}=\{(S, L_A, L_{fA0}, L_B, L_{fB0})\}$
2. Set $\mathbf{E}_{tmp}=\mathbf{E}$
3. Choose an element from $\mathbf{E}_{tmp}$ one by one, and use it as the input parameters of our scheme (as Fig.2), i.e., $(N^i, L_{p_A}^i, L_{f_A}^i, L_{p_B}^i, L_{f_B}^i)$;

4. The possible output parameters, i.e., $(L_{p_A}^{i+1}, L_{f_A}^{i+1}, L_{p_B}^{i+1}, L_{f_B}^{i+1})$, with each possible value of $N^{i+1} (N^{i+1} \in [0,S])$ are $(N^{i+1}, L_{p_A}^{i+1}, L_{f_A}^{i+1}, L_{p_B}^{i+1}, L_{f_B}^{i+1})$. Those that are not appeared in **E** are put into **E** as the new elements;
5. Repeat steps 3 and 4 until all elements in $\mathbf{E}_{tmp}$ are chosen;
6. If the updated **E** is not equal to $\mathbf{E}_{tmp}$, go back to step2; otherwise, stop.

A Memory Efficient Algorithm for Packet Classification

Zhen Xu[1], Jun Sun[2], and Jun Zhang[1]

[1] School of Electronic and Information Engineering, Beihang Univeristy
[2] Chinese Academy of Space Technology

Abstract. In order to provide more value added services, the Internet needs to classify packets into flows for different treatment. High performance packet classification algorithms for large classifiers and edge classifiers are highly demanded.

In this paper, we will describe a new algorithm for packet classification that makes use of bits distribution features. It is a high level classification method. It always takes the bits from every dimension into account, instead of constraining the search process in some of the dimensions at every stage. The experiments provide the evidence that it has outstanding performance even for large edge classifiers. It is also scalable to IPv6.

Keywords: Packet Classification, Routing, Hash table.

1 Introduction

Due to the emergence of some advanced complex services, such as DiffServ and InterServ, Internet routers need to classify the packets into flows according to some rules [1,2,4,6]. The rules in a classifier are arranged in order of priority and have an associated action (such as drop, forward, and place in queue etc.). A packet must be classified to the first (highest priority) rule that matches the packet [3]. As the demand for packet classification is increasing, the size of a classifier grows fast. Meanwhile, the packet processing time also needs to keep up with the rapid increasing fiber link speed to provide good QoS. These two trends combine to put pressure on router vendors. Heuristic algorithms are needed to meet the increasing demand [7,8,9].

In general, the existing packet classification algorithms can be classified into trie-based algorithms, range-based algorithms, and hash-based algorithms. Some of them may have an outstanding performance both in memory access and in storage requirement. But most of them are designed for backbone and small classifiers. Nowadays, packet classification issue is becoming more important at edge routers. In this paper, a novel packet classification that can be applied for large classifiers at the edge will be introduced.

All the rules in a multi-dimensional classifier can be regarded as a list of one-dimensional mask-based binary strings. The lengths of all the strings are the same. In the strings, the bits defined as 0 or 1 are what we are interested in, while others defined as * (not masked) are what we are not interested in. The packet classification problem is transformed to an extended one-dimensional matching problem. The main advantage of this concept is that the one-dimensional search algorithm is much simpler.

In designing the new algorithm, firstly, we create a hash function to represent the bits distribution features of all the rules. All the rules can be assigned into a set of hash buckets based on their distinct distribution features. Those collision rules may not have the

X. Cheng, W. Li, and T. Znati (Eds.): WASA 2006, LNCS 4138, pp. 115–126, 2006.

same prefix or they are not confined to some narrow ranges in some specific dimensions. It has better performance when it operates for edge routers. Secondly, this proposed algorithm also tries to build a global optimal search trie in each bucket by inspecting some most significant bit positions. The search path is directed by the bits chosen over all the dimensions at each step. Branching terminates when the number of the remaining collision rules in a node is smaller than the pre-defined maximum value. Thirdly, in the leaves of the search trie, a matching process to the rules is needed until the highest priority matching is found. Hardware-based search can speed up the procedure.

Our algorithm is unique in the sense that it always tries to reach a high-level optimal solution at each step, other than concentrating on some consecutive bits in a specific dimension. It provides a comparable average performance. It also performs well for large classifiers and edge classifiers.

2   The Structure of the Proposed Algorithm

The proposed algorithm is composed of three layers: hash table lookup, dynamic search trie lookup and small search set lookup.

2.1   Hash Table

I   Definition of the hash function. This proposed hash function is based on the bits distribution. In other words, it can reflect how 1's (or 0's) spread in the sequences.

(a)   Definitions of Sum1 and Sum2. Let $a_1a_2a_3...a_{|a|}$ express a binary sequence α, where $|\alpha|$ is the width of α and a_i is either 0 or 1. Assuming that $EL(EL \leq |\alpha|)$ bits are extracted beginning from the leftmost bit in α. We assign a weight to each bit of the extracted string $a_1a_2a_3...a_{EL}$. The bit on the left (higher position) has higher weight than the bit on the right (lower position). The maximum weight MW ($MW \geq EL$) is assigned to a_1. The minimum weight $MW - EL + 1$ is assigned to a_{EL}. The difference of weights between any two adjacent bits is 1.

Let $Sum1(\alpha, EL) = \sum_{i=1}^{EL} a_i$. The value of $Sum1(\alpha, EL)$ represents the number of 1s that occur in the extracted bits. Let $Sum2(\alpha, EL, MW) = \sum_{i=1}^{EL} a_i(MW - i + 1)$. The value of $Sum2(\alpha, EL, MW)$ reflects the distribution of all the 1s in the extracted bits. The combined values, $(Sum1, Sum2)$, can represent the the bits distribution of a binary sequence.

The proposed hash function is a more to one function. There will be collisions in some hash buckets. When EL and MW are fixed, some sequences are mapped into such a set of hash values $(h, Sum2)$, where $Sum1$ takes the fixed value h and all the possible values $Sum2$ can take are a set of consecutive positive integers.

For any two pairs of hash values, $(Sum1_1, Sum2_1)$ and $(Sum1_2, Sum2_2)$, $(Sum1_1, Sum2_1)$ is said to be smaller than $(Sum1_2, Sum2_2)$, if either of the two following conditions is satisfied: $(Sum1_1 \leq Sum1_2)$ or $(Sum2_1 < Sum2_2$, when $Sum1_1 = Sum1_2)$.

(b)   Sum1 and Sum2 of a prefix. Assuming that P is a prefix, and its prefix length is PL. Let EL bits be extracted beginning from the leftmost of P for calculations. Then P is assigned to one or several hash buckets with respect to different values of EL.

- If $EL \leq PL$, then both $Sum1(P,EL)$ are $Sum2(P,EL,MW)$ are definite values. P is assigned into one hash bucket.
- If $EL > PL$, then the hash process is more complicated. The prefix P is expanded into 2^{EL-PL} EL-bit long prefixes, named P_1, P_2, ..., $P_{2^{EL-PL}}$, in which $P_1 = P \oplus 00...00$, $P_2 = P \oplus 00...01$ and $P_{2^{EL-PL}} = P \oplus 11...11$. Each expanding prefix is mapped into a hash bucket $(Sum1, Sum2)$ and some of them may share one bucket.

P is duplicated into a set of hash values $(Sum1, Sum2)$. Let $ExpandSet$ denote the size of the duplication set. $ExpandSet = \frac{1}{6}(EL-PL)[(EL-PL)^2+5]+1$, which is controlled by the value of $EL-PL$.

(c) *$Sum1s$ and $Sum2s$ in a multi-dimensional classifier.* Let $P = (D_1; D_2,...,D_n)$ be the abbreviation for the $n-$fields of a packet. EL_i bits are extracted sequentially from each field for calculation, respectively. Let $MW = MAX(EL_1, EL_2, ..., EL_n)$.

$Sum1(P) = \sum_{i=1}^{n} Sum1(D_i, EL_i)$ and $Sum2(P) = \sum_{i=1}^{n} Sum2(D_i, EL_i, MW)$

When EL_i is longer than the prefix length of any field, the rule will be mapped into multiple pairs of hash values, which causes the expansion.

A larger weight always makes a bigger contribution to $Sum2$ calculation. In order to allow the contributions of all fields to $Sum2$ in equilibrium, the same maximum weights are assigned to all the fields.

In general, we can extract an arbitrary number of the bits from each field. When determining the widths of the extracted bits for hash calculations, we need to examine the bits in each field first, in order to make sure that the width of the extracted bits is not smaller than most lengths of prefixes of the rules to avoid storage explosion.

II Data Structure

A complete hash lookup process is composed of one $Sum1$ table lookup and one $Sum2$ table lookup. Each entry in the $Sum1$ table is a corresponding index value of the $Sum2$ table. A definite $Sum1$ value, as a hash key, can index into the $Sum1$ Table directly. Each entry in the $Sum2$ table denotes a pointer to a search trie. All the entries are sorted with respect to the pairs of hash values, $(Sum1, Sum2)$, in an increasing order.

As we know, when $Sum1$ is fixed, say $Sum1 = i$, there are a set of hash values that can be expressed as $(i, *)$, where $*$ means a set of consecutive values of $Sum2$. Therefore, information of entry i in the $Sum1$ table is composed of two components: P_i and B_i, where $P_0 = 0$; $B_i = Min(Sum2)|_{Sum1=i}$; $P_i = P_{i-1} + (Max(Sum2)|_{Sum1=i-1} - B_{i-1}+1), i >$

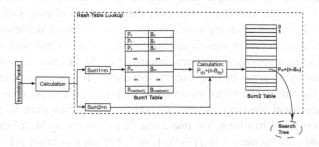

Fig. 1. Hash Lookup Flow Chart

0. P_i is the index of the pair of hash values (i, $Min(Sum2)|_{Sum1=i}$) located in the $Sum2$ table. No hash value overlap in $Sum2$ table.

If there is an incoming packet, then the pair of hash values (m, n) is achieved after calculation,. First, it is indexed into the mth entry in the $Sum1$ table and fetches P_m and B_m. Then, it is indexed into the $(P_m + (n - B_m))^{th}$ entry in the $Sum2$ table to get the pointer to a specific search trie. Figure 1 describes how the entire hash lookup performs.

2.2   Search Trie

After the hash table lookup, the number of the collision rules, N_k, in each hash bucket narrows down rapidly. Let $LEAFSIZE$ be predefined as the maximum size of a final small set (bucket size). When N_k is larger than $LEAFSIZE$, an optimal search trie is needed. The branching decision is made by inspecting some most significant bit positions at each step until the number of the collision rules contained in any leaf is no more than $LEAFSIZE$.

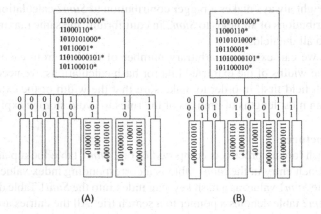

Fig. 2. Comparison of Different Bit Selection Methods

As shown in Fig. 2, there is a set of sequences falling into the hash bucket ($Sum1 = 4$, $Sum2 = 24$), where both EL and MW are 9. (A) illustrates a result when using the first 3 bits of the sequences in building a search tire. (B) gives us a result when selecting the other 3 bits in building a search trie. Not only does the ratio of empty children nodes reduce, but also the maximum number of the rules in a child node decreases.

How to determine the most significant bits is a key step in building a search trie. A similar bit selection approach has been discussed in [5]. All the rules in a classifier can be expressed by an array of long binary sequences. The length of the array, N, is the number of the rules. The width of array, M, depends on the dimensions. In IPv4, if it is a 2-dimensional classifier (Source IP address and Destination IP address), the width of the array is 64-bits long. We use a matrix $E(N$ rows by M columns) to stand for the array, and each element $E(i, j)$ is 0, 1, or *. For each column $j (1 \leq j \leq M)$, 3 quantities, $Q_{0,j}$, $Q_{1,j}$ and $Q_{*,j}$ are defined as follows: $Q_{v,j} = \sum_{i=1}^{N} (E(i, j) == v)$, where

v could be 0, 1, or *. In short, $Num_{v,j}$ is the total number of rows whose j^{th} column is v. Furthermore, $D_j = |Q_{0,j} - Q_{1,j}|$,

We also denote the smallest and the largest values of D_j among all the columns of E by D_{min} and D_{max}, respectively. $Q_{*,min}$ and $Q_{*,max}$ are defined to express the smallest and the largest values of $Q_{*,j}$ among all the columns of E.

$$Preference[j] = \frac{D_j - D_{min}}{D_{max} - D_{min}} + \frac{Q_{*,j} - Q_{*,min}}{Q_{*,max} - Q_{*,min}};$$

The $Preference[j]$ is the combination function of D_j and $Q_{*,j}$. The smaller value of D_j means that it may lead to a more equal amount of rules into child nodes of the next level. Hence, in order to maximize the benefit of branching, both the values of $Q_{*,j}$ and D_j should be minimized.

Assume that the number of the rules in a classifier is N. After the hash table lookup procedure, the number of rules in hash bucket k will be decreased to $N_k(N_k \ll N)$. Only when N_k is larger than $LEAFSIZE$, it is required to build a multi-way search trie. The ideal branching is the one that not only keeps the depth of the search trie lower, but it also allows the number of the rules in each leaf to be close to $LEAFSIZE$.

Let $MAXBITS$ be a pre-defined value to denote the maximum number of the significant bits that can be chosen at a node. We define $NBits = min(\overline{\log_2 \frac{N_k}{LEAFSIZE}}, MAXBITS)$, where the notation $\overline{a}$ denotes the nearest integer to a. $NBits$ bit positions with the smallest $Preferences$ are selected at a node.

2.3 Small Set

The basic unit in the proposed algorithm is the leaf node of the search trie. Every leaf node contains a small set of rules and has the following properties. Firstly, it contains a small pre-defined maximum number ($LEAFSIZE$) of rules; typical sizes of it are 8, 16, 32. Secondly, the rules are similar in that there is a set of bit positions such that all the rules in it are consistent. Since the number of the rules in such a set is small, many techniques can be used to search in it efficiently. Linear search and binary search are two examples. Since the set of rules is very small, the search can be easily sped up by the pipelined or parallel solution.

3 An Example

Table 1 is a simple 2-dimensional classifier with 12 entries. We define $EL_1 = EL_2 = MW = 2$. The $Sum1$ Table has 5 entries and the $Sum2$ Table has 9 entries, as shown in Fig. 3. The 12 rules are divided into 8 hash buckets. We also define $LEAFSIZE = 1$ and $MAXBITS = 2$. An optimal search trie is built in each hash bucket if it contains more than one rule. Figure 3 also illustrates the classification process of the proposed algorithm when an incoming packet is (11011, 10110).

4 Performance Analysis

The performance of the proposed algorithm will be discussed in this section. The algorithm is applied in two types of classifiers: 2-dimensional classifiers, which are composed of two fields: IP Source Address Prefix and IP Destination Address Prefix; and

Table 1. A small two-dimensional classifier

No.	Field 1	Field 2	No.	Field 1	Field 2
1	00*	00*	7	10*	01*
2	00*	111*	8	10*	111*
3	000*	100*	9	101*	001*
4	001*	100*	10	101*	100*
5	010*	001*	11	11*	110*
6	011*	01*	12	110*	1011*

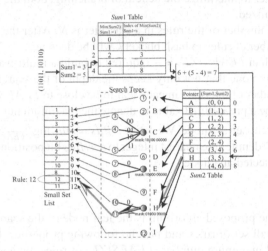

Fig. 3. An Example for 2-Dimensional Packet Classification

5-dimensional classifiers, which are composed of five fields: Source IP address, Destination IP address, Protocol, Source Port, and Destination Port. These classifiers are generated based on the base prefixes from the Mae-east, Mae-west, Aads and Paix.

4.1 Performance for 2-Dimensional Packet Classification

Hash table lookup and search trie lookup are two major lookup steps in this proposed algorithm. We will analyze the performance of (*Sum1*, *Sum2*) hash function first (We call it and its hash table as SUMs function and SUMs table for short.). Then the total system performance combined with search tries will be discussed next.

(a) The features of the SUMs Table. This proposed new heuristic packet classification algorithm has a similar basic structure to the algorithm proposed in [5], which also organizes the search space into 3 layers, JUMP table, search trie, and filter bucket. The JUMP table is built with respect to the JUMP function, in which the first a_i bits are concatenated from each field to form a $2^{\Sigma_i a_i}$ long JUMP table.

Let "*a* by *b*" express extracting the first *a* bits and the first *b* bits from the prefixes in field 1 and field 2, respectively. The bits increment pattern is from "3 by 4", "4 by 4", "4 by 5", ... to "16 by 16". Since the size of the JUMP table explodes with the increase of *a* and *b*, *a* and *b* are confined to be no more than 10.

The SUMs table is composed of a *Sum*1 table and a *Sum*2 table. The *Sum*1 table is very small. The incremental growth of the *Sum*1 table is only two entries, when the number of the extracted bits is increased by 1 in each field. It is much more stable and shorter, compared with the incremental growth of the *Sum*2 table. What we discuss here will be concentrated on the *Sum*2 table only.

Figure 4 describes the lengths of the SUMs table and the JUMP table of a 2-dimensional classifier. The SUMs table is smaller and more stable, compared with the JUMP table, proposed in [5]. When the first 16 bits are extracted from each field to build a hash table, the SUMs table contains no more than 4K entries, while the JUMP table contains 1G entries. The length of the JUMP table even can be larger than 4K when both a and b are only 6. Assume that Ex bits are extracted from each field to build the hash table. Once the number of the extracted bits from each field is increased to $Ex+1$, then the incremental growth of the SUMs(Sum2) table is $2(Ex^2+Ex+1)$, which is a quadratic function, while the incremental growth of the JUMP table is $3(2^{Ex})$, which is an exponentially increasing function. Therefore, SUMs function makes it possible to extract more bits to generate a hash table, to reduce the collision in each bucket.

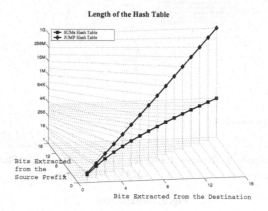

Fig. 4. Length of the Hash Table

The merits derived from Sums function can be summarized into the following three aspects. Firstly, the SUMs table only consumes a very small amount of memory. Even when 16 bits are extracted in each field, it costs no more than 16K bytes, which is small enough to be stored in cache (or on-chip SRAM memory). It is helpful to speed up the hash lookups.

Secondly, if the width of the extracted bits is larger than a Destination/Source prefix length in any field, then the duplication size when using SUMs function is much smaller than using JUMP hash. For example, assuming that the prefixes of a rule in both fields expand 8 bits, then the rule will be duplicated into 353 buckets according to the SUMs function, while the duplication is 2^{16} when using JUMP function.

Thirdly, it can overcome the unbalanced prefix distribution problem. If the prefixes are not uniformly distributed, it will result in a big variance in the collisions in every hash bucket as compared to the JUMP table. The colliding rules in one SUMs hash

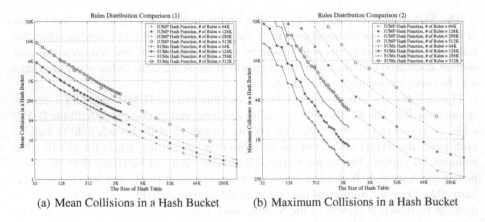

(a) Mean Collisions in a Hash Bucket   (b) Maximum Collisions in a Hash Bucket

Fig. 5. Collisions

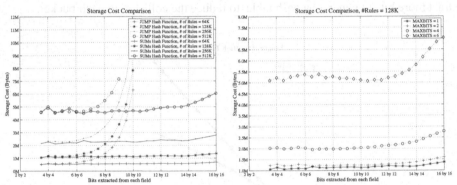

(a) Storage Cost Comparison Between Using (b) Comparison of the Storage Cost When
Different Hash Functions   *MAXBITS* Varies

Fig. 6. Storage cost

bucket may not share a common prefix in any dimension. Figure 5(a) and Figure 5(b) compare the collisions in each hash bucket between SUMs tables and JUMP tables. The horizontal axis denotes the length of the hash table. Each marked point in the graph is the experiment results in terms of the the extracted bits "*a* by *b*". The comparison can evaluate the performances of the hash functions when the lengths of (SUMs/JUMP) hash tables are almost the same. It shows that the mean collisions in the SUMs hash bucket is slightly higher than that of the JUMP hash table in Fig. 5(a). The reason is that when the lengths of the (SUMs/JUMP) tables are almost the same, the bits used to build the SUMs table are more than the bits used to build the JUMP table, which causes the higher probability of bit expansion. However, the maximum collisions in a SUMs hash bucket is much smaller than that in a JUMP hash bucket in Fig. 5(b).

(b) The performance of the total system
This proposed heuristic packet classification algorithm based on bit characteristics is a memory saver. The storage cost has three resources: hash table, search trie and small

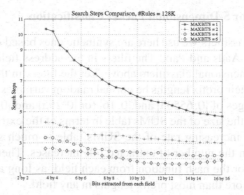

Fig. 7. Comparison of the Search Steps When *MAXBITS* Varies

sets. When using SUMs hash function, the length of the hash table can not exceed 4K. Search tries and small sets are the main contributors to storage cost. Figure 6(a) compares the storage consumptions between using distinct hash functions. The horizontal axis denotes the bits extracting strategy from both fields. The storage cost of using SUMs funcion is much steadier when the number of the extracted bits varies. When "12 by 12" is used for the SUMs table, its total storage cost is comparable to the cost of using "6 by 6" for the JUMP table.

Figure 6(b) evaluates the storage consumption when *MAXBITS* varies. For each individual curve, its slope climbs up rapidly once the extracted bits are more than "12 by 12". While investigating all the curves, we can find that the storage cost increases with the growth of *MAXBITS*. The main increase of the storage cost is resulted from the nodes consumed in the search tries. Although *MAXBITS* is very big, the number of branches is also limited by the parameter *PreBound*. Actually, many nodes can not reach $2^{MAXBITS}$ children nodes, however each node consumes more storage, which is wasteful. There is still some potential to improve it.

When the length of the hash table is fixed, let us examine the mean search steps till reaching a final small set in the search trie for random traffics. Figure 7 verifies that the search steps vary with the parameter *MAXBITS* when using the SUMs function. If *MAXBITS* is larger than 1, the mean search steps are reduced sharply, however, the reducing rate decreases with the growth of *MAXBITS*.

We can draw the conclusion that the multi-way search trie is beneficial to the search performance. But when *MAXBITS* is larger than 4, it will not reduce the search steps significantly, while the storage cost bursts. It is not worth choosing a very big *MAXBITS*. That let *MAXBITS* be 4 is ideal respect to our experimental case.

Wildcard rules are the main contributors toward storage explosion. If a dimension contains a large percentage of wildcard rules, it is better to separate them out, to build an additional 1-dimensional table to avoid the storage explosion.

In summary, the algorithm of packet classification using bits characteristics performs well for large 2-dimensional classifiers, no matter whether the prefix distribution is balanced or not, as long as the percentage of wildcard rules is not too big.

4.2   Performance for 5-Dimensional Packet Classification

The 5-dimensional classifiers we use here are synthetic ones based on the prefixes from Mae-east, Mae-west, Aads and Paix. The filters in the address fields are randomly selected from the 2-dimensional classifiers above. Let the filters in the port fields (or the protocol fields) and their prefix lengths be normal random variables. They are randomly selected from the ranges of $[0, 65535]$ and $[0, 16]$ (or $[0, 255]$ and $[0, 8]$) respectively.

First, we examine the size of the SUMs table in terms of the extracted bits from each field. In Table 2, the increasing rate of the SUMs table is much steadier than that of the JUMP table when the number of extracted bits increases. Therefore, it is possible to extract more bits for the hash function from each field, as long as the number of the extracted bits is no more than most prefix lengths in any field.

Table 2. hash table size

Extracted bits from each field					Length of the SUMs Table	Length of the JUMP Table
Source Address	Dest. Address	Protocol	Source Port	Dest. Port		
4	4	4	0	0	103	4K
4	4	0	4	4	177	16K
8	8	8	4	4	1333	1G
8	8	8	8	8	2141	256G
10	10	8	4	4	2045	...
16	16	8	4	4	6037	...
16	16	8	8	8	7613	...

Next, we will examine how the rules are distributed into the hash buckets. In our experiments, the filters in the Port fields and Protocol field are artificial normally distributed random variables. The mean and the standard deviation of the filters in the Port fields are 32767 and 3000. The mean and the standard deviation of the prefixes of the filters in the Port fields are 10 and 2. The mean and the standard deviation of the filters in the Protocol field are 127 and 30. All the protocols are 8 bit long.

Table 3. subentries distribution using SUMs hash function (# of Rules = 256K)

Extracted bits from each field					Mean Collisions	Max Collisions
Source Address	Dest. Address	Protocol	Source Port	Dest. Port		
8	8	0	4	4	583	4446
8	8	8	4	4	428	3301
8	8	8	8	8	440	3927
10	10	8	4	4	296	2287
16	16	8	4	4	144	1094

From Table 3, it is obvious that the performance of the hash function depends on the extracted bits. The collision in a hash bucket declines with the increasing of the extracted bits in any field. However, in any field, when the number of the extracted bits

Table 4. algorithm performance (# of rules = 128K, $MAXBITS$ = 4, $LEAFSIZE$ = 16) (in bytes)

Extracted bits from each field					Storage Cost	Mean Bits Examined	Mean Search Steps
Sour. Addr.	Des. Addr.	Protl	Sour. Pt	Des. Pt			
8	8	0	4	4	2.10MB	4.82	2.39
8	8	8	4	4	2.22MB	4.78	2.41
8	8	8	8	8	3.59MB	4.83	2.41
10	10	8	4	4	2.31MB	4.33	2.20
10	10	8	8	8	3.93MB	4.63	2.35
16	16	8	4	4	3.28MB	3.87	1.87

is not longer than most prefixes, it will result in storage explosion in the hash process. For example, when the number of the extracted bits in the Port fields is increased to 8 from 4, and the number of the bits extracted from other fields are fixed, either the mean collision or the maximum collision in the buckets increases, which is the opposite of what we expected. The reason is that the number of the rules whose port prefix lengths are smaller than 4 is no more than 11%, according to Chebyshev's inequality, while there are many port prefix lengths smaller than 8. Therefore, examining the sequences in each field first to find a set of suitable number of extracted bits is a key in our approach.

Table 4 describes the experiment performance results of 128K classifiers. It shows that after the hash process, only a few most significant bits are needed to be inspected to reach the final small set. The SUMs hash function makes a big contribution in the new approach. It is suitable for higher dimensional classifiers. The best bits extracting strategy is " 10, 10, 8, 4, 4", considering the combination of the storage cost and search performance.

5 Summary

In this paper, we presented a new packet classification algorithm, which is designed for big classifiers and is suitable for edge classifiers. Our approach combines three lookup processes: a heuristic hash lookup, a novel multi-way dynamic search trie lookup and a lookup through a small rule set. This architecture construction is motivated by practical observation, aimed at finding the best matching rule by traversing an optimal search path. It is an efficient way to take advantage of the bit characteristics of all the rules.

Through experiments with a large number of classifiers, we demonstrated that our approach constrained the maximum collision in each hash bucket effectively. It possesses advanced capabilities in fast search and small storage requirement. It is also scalable to multidimensional classifier and to IPv6. When the wildcards reach an upper bound, it is necessary to separate out those rules with wildcards. Then a full size system and a few reduced size systems are needed to operate in parallel to find the best matching rule.

Acknowledgment

This work was supported by the NSFC (No.10377005), the Aviation Science Foundation of China (No.02F51070) and the Aerospace Support Technology Foundation of China. The authors also would like to thank Prof. Yiqiang Zhao and Prof. Ioannis Lambadaris for his valuable comments.

References

1. P. Gupta and N. McKeown, *Packet classification using hierarchical intelligent cuttings*, in *Proc. of Hot Interconnects*, 1999.
2. P. Gupta and N. McKeown, *Packet Classification on Multiple Fields*, in *Proc. of Sigcomm, Computer Communication Review*, 1999.
3. F. Baboescu, S. Singh, and G. Varghese, *Packet classification for core routers: Is there an alternative to CAMs?* in *Proc.of INFOCOM*, 2003.
4. S. Singh, F. Baboescu, G. Varghese, and J. Wang, *Packet Classification Using Multidimensional Cutting*, in *Proc. of ACM Sigcomm*, 2003.
5. T. Woo, *A modular approach to packet classification: Algorithms and results*, in *Proc. of INFOCOM*, 2000.
6. D. Stiliadis and T. V. Lakshman, *High-speed policy-based packet forwarding using efficient multi-dimensional range matching*, in *Proc. of ACM Sigcomm*, 1998.
7. J. V. Lunteren and T. Engbersen, *Fast and Scalable Packet Classification*, in *IEEE Journal on Selected Areas in Communications*, May, 2003.
8. V.Srinivasan, S.Suri, G. Varghese and M. Waldvogel, *Fast and Scalable Layer for Switching*, in *Proc. of ACM Sigcomm*, September, 1998.
9. A. Feldman and S. Muthukrishnan, *Tradeoffs for Packet Classification*, in *Proc. of INFOCOM*, 2000.
10. Zhen Xu, *Efficient Table Algorithms for the Next Generation IP Networks*, Ph.D Thesis, 2005.

Energy-Efficient Multi-query Optimization over Large-Scale Sensor Networks*

Lei Xie, Lijun Chen, Sanglu Lu, Li Xie, and Daoxu Chen

State Key Laboratory of Novel Software Technology
NJU-POLYU Cooperative Laboratory for Wireless Sensor Network
Nanjing University, Nanjing, China

Abstract. Currently much research work has been done to attempt to efficiently conserve the energy consumption for sensor networks, recently a database approach to programming sensor networks has gained much attention from the sensor network research area. In this paper we developed an optimized multi-query processing paradigm for aggregate queries, we proposed an equivalence class based merging algorithm for in-network merging of partial aggregate values of multi-queries, and an adaptive fusion degree based routing scheme as a cross-layer designing technique. Our optimized multi-query processing paradigm efficiently takes advantage of the work sharing mechanism by sharing common aggregate values among multiple queries to fully reduce the communication cost for sensor networks, thus extending the life time of sensor networks. The experimental evaluation shows that our optimization paradigm can efficiently result in dramatic energy savings, compared to previous work.

1 Introduction

Due to advances in wireless communication, embedded computing and low cost design of sensors, large scale networks consisting of sensor nodes equipped with the capacity of sensing , computing, and communicating have widely emerged in many of the related application regions. Such applications include environmental data collection, security monitoring, and target tracking, etc. Such networks have resource constraints on communication, computation and energy consumption. Due to these properties, recently a database approach [7][10][13] has been introduced to program nodes in sensor networks to effectively utilize the character of "in network processing" to efficiently reduce the energy consumption of sensor networks. The sensor nodes are programmed through declarative queries in a variant of SQL, in this way the sensor nodes can actively collect the correlated sensor data user specified, effectively do some filtering, aggregating, caching works in network before they're sent to the end users, energy is efficiently saved using this approach. In the above scenario, the sensor network is usually shared by many users and they typically impose multiple queries over sensor network at

* This work is partially supported by the National Basic Research Program of China (973) under Grant No.2002CB312002, the National Natural Science Foundation of China under Grant No.60573132.

X. Cheng, W. Li, and T. Znati (Eds.): WASA 2006, LNCS 4138, pp. 127–139, 2006.
© Springer-Verlag Berlin Heidelberg 2006

the base station during a time range, and it's likely that many users pose similar queries such that these queries can be processed in an optimized approach to share intermediate results so as to efficiently save the total energy consumption. Current proposals for query processing over sensor networks haven't considered the multi-query processing and optimization issues, the TinyDB system [8][10] supports multiple queries running simultaneously on a single device, but very little processing is shared between the execution of those queries. In this paper, we target the optimization problem for multi-query processing over sensor networks. The contributions of this paper can be summarized as follows:

- We analyse the optimization problems for multi query processing over sensor networks.
- We propose an equivalence class based data merging algorithm for multiple aggregation query processing over sensor network.
- We propose an adaptive, fusion degree based routing scheme for multiple aggregation query processing over sensor network.

The rest of the paper is organized as follows. Section 2 gives some background and motivation for multi-query processing. In Section 3, we do analysis on the multi-query optimization problem, present our merging algorithm and adaptive routing mechanism for multiple aggregation query processing. Experimental results and performance evaluation are shown in Section 4. In Section 5 we introduce the related work and we end with a conclusion in Section 6.

2   General Architecture for Multiple Query Processing

In sensor networks, queries are initiated by users at the base station, dissemination begins with a broadcast of queries from the root of the network, as each node hears the queries, it must decide whether some of the queries apply locally or need to be broadcast to its children in the routing tree. Once queries have been disseminated and optimized, each sensor node starts executing the correlated queries during every epoch: first, nodes sleep for most of an epoch; then they wake, sample sensors and apply operators to data generated locally and received from neighbors, then deliver results to their parent. This architecture is generally for the continuous query scenarios, it is utilized for applications such as environment data collection, because when the queries are disseminated through out the network, the query execution and data propagation phase are running for quite a long time compared with the query dissemination phase. The most general kind of queries utilized for environment monitoring over sensor networks is the aggregation queries [11]. The aggregation queries are proposed to request the sensor network to continuously report the aggregate value of some specified regions(usually represented as bounding boxes), so it allows local aggregation at every level of the routing tree, using data aggregation we are able to locally combine the same class of values into one value. In general, in network aggregation can reduce communication cost and power consumption by pushing part of the computation into sensor networks.   General processing paradigms for multiple aggregation queries can be divided into two classes:

– **Naive multi-query processing approach:** The base station simply collects all raw sensor readings from the tree based network, and does data aggregation work for each aggregate query at the base station.
– **Power aware query processing without optimization:** The base station processes each aggregation query separately using the single power aware processing technique utilized by TinyDB.

Such above two methods do have some deficiencies in multiple query processing. The naive approach simply doesn't consider in network aggregation, as a result the communication cost is quite huge for the sensor networks, this approach is obviously not energy efficient. The latter query processing approach without optimization supports multiple queries running simultaneously on sensor network, however, it doesn't consider work sharing among multiple queries, sensor data acquisition, local computing and transmission load haven't been well cooperated among queries to suppress overlapped operations. So in order to energy efficiently process these multiple aggregate queries over sensor networks, a new paradigm considering multi-query optimization should be developed. In the next section we will do some analysis on the optimization problem and propose our optimized paradigm for multi-query processing.

3 Multi-query Optimization

3.1 Optimization Problem Analysis

The problem of multi-query optimization has been studied in several research areas such as relational database systems and data stream processing, for the sensor network, optimization for multi-query processing is motivated by adequately sharing acquisition of sensor readings, data transmission, and in-network processing capacity. The optimization goal we eventually want to achieve is: energy efficient, simple and adaptive. Energy efficient means to efficiently reduce the resource consumption especially the communication cost through work sharing among the queries; Simple means the optimization algorithm for the processing should be computationally simple enough to implement over the sensor network. The adaptive property means to adaptively modify the optimization scheme with the runtime observations of query patterns.

For the optimization issue over the multiple aggregate queries, since the aggregate queries are always depicted as to request the aggregate values of those bounding boxes over the tree based network topology, the optimization scheme can be motivated by sharing the sensor reading and data transmissions among different queries if the query regions of different queries overlap. Therefore, energy can be efficiently conserved by sharing the partial aggregate results of common regions among different queries.

We consider a set of aggregate queries Q= $\{Q_1, Q_2, \ldots, Q_n\}$ over regions R= $\{R_1, R_2, \ldots, R_n\}$, we assume that all the queries have the same type of aggregation functions, and for the sake of simplicity, we assume multiple queries run as a batch and all queries have the same sampling rate. Figure 1 depicts an example of multiple query processing scenario. The most general method for the work sharing optimization for multiple queries is to divide the intersected aggregation regions (bounding box) into many separated groups, and calculate the aggregate values for each separated groups using the "group by" processing technique introduced in TAG. For example in Figure 1, the 3 overlapped bounding boxes can be divided into 4 separated groups: $G_1 = R_1 \cap R_2, G_2 = R_1 - (R_1 \cap R_2), G_3 = R_2 - (R_1 \cap R_2), G_4 = R_3$. This approach can effectively share the common partial aggregate results among different queries to avoid the redundant data acquisition and transmission load, however when the number of aggregate queries increases, the number of divided separated groups can grow into a quite huge number, so the total communication cost may become too high for the network to bear. To solve this problem, Niki Trigoni [1] proposed an optimal algorithm using linear reduction and a hybrid algorithm to reduce the number of the separated groups divided from the query bounding boxes, however their algorithm is too computation complicated to implement on the sensor nodes which always have low local-processing ability. Faith Emekci [2] proposed an appropriate paradigm to process multiple aggregate queries. In their paradigm they classify edges in the query tree which intersect with the query bounding boxes into two types: the incoming edge and the outgoing edge. The incoming edge is the edge which intersects with the query bounding box R_i and the ending node is inside the query region and the starting node is outside the query region; The outgoing edge is the edge which intersects with the query bounding box R_i and the starting node is inside the query region and the ending node is outside the query region. For example, in Figure 1, e_3, e_5, e_6, e_7 are the incoming edges and e_1, e_2, e_4, e_7 are the outgoing edges. During the phase of multi-query execution, the partial aggregate results are calculated in the network, the starting nodes of the incoming or outgoing edges should inform their parents to pass their partial aggregate values to the base station. In order to answer the aggregate query Q_i, their paradigm use the following formula to compute the final answer at the base station:

$$V_Q = \sum_{i=1}^{n_{out}} V_i - \sum_{j=1}^{n_{in}} V_j \tag{1}$$

In the above formula, n_{out}/n_{in} is the number of the outgoing/incoming edges of the bounding box for query Q_i, and V_i/V_j is the partial aggregate value for the outgoing/incoming edge of the bounding box for query Q_i. In their paradigm they see the bounding box as a black box, we can get the aggregate value of the bounding box simply by subtracting the sum of the incoming partial aggregate values from the sum of the outgoing partial aggregate values. This approach can efficiently reduce the total communication cost than the former solution using separated groups, utilizing the sharing work of partial aggregate values. However this paradigm doesn't consider further partial aggregate data merging in network and utilizes the simple routing construction scheme that is not adaptive to the multiple query processing. Our optimized paradigm is build upon the above paradigm introduced by Faith Emekci, and we propose two optimization approaches for multiple aggregation query processing.

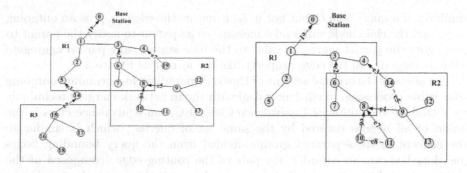

Fig. 1. Multi-Aggregation Query Process- **Fig. 2.** The candidate path selecting issue
ing

3.2 Equivalence Class Based Data Merging Algorithm

Emekci's paradigm requires the sensor nodes to send to their parent nodes only
their partial aggregate values and the incoming/outgoing edge partial aggregate
values from their sub-trees, all the base station receives are the incoming/outgoing
partial aggregate values, this approach can be efficient in some way, but if we investigate further into this multiple query processing paradigm, we can find that we
can further merge the partial aggregate value at the intermediate nodes instead of
the base station. For example in Figure 1, the partial aggregate value of e_5 and e_6
can be merged at node 8, and their merged partial value can be further merged at
node 1 with the partial aggregate value of e_3, but the partial aggregate value of e_7
can not be easily further merged because it's both the incoming edge of Q_1 and the
outgoing edge of Q_2, so we need an appropriate criterion to decide whether further
merging work can de done with the partial aggregate values at local sensor nodes
in a distributed way. We can construct the in-network merging algorithm based on
the equivalence class method.

Packet Header	Incoming/Outgoing Tag	Query Id	Data Fileds

Fig. 3. The Original Packet Format

Packet Headers	Start EC Id	End EC Id	Partial Aggregate Values

Fig. 4. The EC based Packet Format

Equivalence Class Method. After the multiple aggregate queries are disseminated to the sensor network, every sensor node sends its query list lp to its
children n, which consists of all queries involving the parent node. Then each
node compares the query list of its parent with its own query list, if a query Q_i
is in l_p but not in l_n ,it means the edge $\langle n, p \rangle$ is a incoming edge of query Q_i ,

similarly, if a query is in l_n but not in l_p, it means the edge $\langle n, p \rangle$ is an outgoing edge, and the child node will send a message to its parent to notify the parent to propagate the partial aggregate value to the base station, any partial aggregate value is tagged with the edge property like the format as Figure 3.

The above is the original scheme of Emekci's paradigm for incoming/outgoing edge value processing, to efficiently deal with the in network merging technique, we introduce the notion of Equivalence Class (EC), an equivalence class is the union of all regions covered by the same set of queries., which is similar to the concept of the separated groups divided from the query bounding boxes mentioned above. So consider any pair of the routing edge (composed of the child node and its corresponding parent node), so if the two nodes are in the same EC, that means the edge is just a common edge that's neither an incoming nor outgoing edge; if the two nodes fall into two different ECs, that means at least an incoming edge or outgoing edges exists between the two nodes. For example if two nodes fall into two different ECs with parent node in $EC_1\{Q_1,Q_2,Q_3\}$ and the child node in $EC_2\{Q_2,Q_3,Q_4\}$,that means there exists one incoming edge for Q_1 and one outgoing edge for Q_4, so if we utilize the original query based packet format, we need to send 2 packets for each edge with the same partial value, when we use the merging technique the intermediate nodes can merge those packets with the same incoming/outgoing tag and the same query id, it is true this scheme can reduce the transmission load in network, however, this processing scheme based on queries doesn't investigate deeply into the work sharing mechanism, multiple copies of the same partial results are sent with different tags and query ids. We propose our equivalence class based merging scheme to ensure the same partial aggregate value has to be sent only once and the intermediate nodes can still do some merging work in network.

EC Based Merging Paradigm for Partial Values. We propose the EC based packet format as Figure 4, it contains the start node's EC id and the end node's EC id, so if the pair of parent and child nodes in the routing tree fall into two equivalence classes, the child node only have to send one copy of the partial aggregate data compared with the multiple copies sent in Emekci's paradigm with the original query based packet format. The equivalence class identity can be simply expressed as the binary expression of the query list, where it contains n bits (n is the maximum number of queries the sensor network can support), the ith bit is set to 1 when Q_i is in the node's local query list, otherwise it is set to 0. So in this approach each sensor node can get its EC id in a simple, distributed way after the queries are disseminated to each node. When we eventually get the partial aggregate values at the base station, we can revert the EC based partial aggregate values into the query based partial aggregate values utilizing Algorithm 1.

After the processing procedure provided by Algorithm 1, we can use Formula 1 to compute the final aggregate answer for each query. So we present our EC based merging processing flow as follows:

1. First, the multiple queries are disseminated to all the sensor nodes in the sensor network, forming a tree based routing structure, each sensor node gets its according query list and compute out its EC ID locally, expressed as binary bits.

Algorithm 1. Revert the EC based partial aggregate values into the query based partial aggregate values

---

Input:
PAV: the EC based partial aggregate values
SID: the edge's starting node's equivalence class id, expressed as binary bits
EID: the edge's ending node's equivalence class id, expressed as binary bits
Procedure:
//The following $\oplus$,AND are bit-wise Boolean operators for the binary values SID and EID
Common ID= SID$\oplus$ EID
// Incoming ID contains those queries which have incoming edges partial aggregate value belongs to.
Incoming ID=EID AND Common ID
// Outgoing ID contains those queries which have outgoing edges partial aggregate value belongs to.
Outgoing ID=SID AND Common ID
End Procedure
Output:
return Incoming ID and Outgoing ID

---

2. Then, each node gets its parent's EC ID and compares it with its local EC ID, if they are in the different EC, the child node need to inform the parent node to pass its partial aggregate value to the base station and tag the partial aggregate value with the Start EC Id and the End EC Id.

3. When the local node receives from all its children the partial aggregate values, if its query list is not null, it aggregates its local sensor reading to the partial aggregate values, then it does the merging work according to the Start EC Id and the End EC Id for the tagged partial aggregate values, after the merging work, the partial aggregate values are relayed to its parent node.

4. When the tagged partial aggregate values are eventually sent to the base station, it uses Algorithm 1 to revert the EC based partial aggregate values into the query based partial aggregate values, and uses Formula 1 to compute the final aggregate answer for each query.

3.3   Adaptive Fusion Degree Based Routing Scheme

The original paradigm of Emekci's work only considers a general routing scheme to support the multiple aggregate query processing, however, the multiple aggregate query processing sometimes cannot be well supported by this general routing scheme. For example, in Figure 2, note that node 9 may have 2 candidate parents that is node 8 and node 14, according to the general routing scheme, node 9 selects the path e_4 as it routing path, this choice would make node 9 to send an additional partial aggregate value for the incoming edge for Q_1 compared to the alternative choice of e_5, the same issue also happens with the node 11 with the two candidate path e_7 and e_8. So we need to find an adaptive routing scheme to efficiently support the multiple query processing by effectively reducing the transmission load for incoming/outgoing edges.

Fusion Degree Method. The ultimate goal we want to achieve is to efficiently reduce the total transmission load so as to meet the energy efficiency criterion. To design a routing scheme based on the above paradigm for multi-query processing, we should reduce the in-network transmission load of incoming/outgoing edge partial aggregate values to the best of our ability. We construct our adaptive routing scheme based on the fusion degree method.

Considering the condition where there exists a local node j and its candidate parent nodes, the current node gets the candidate parent nodes' query lists $ql_1, ql_2, \ldots, ql_i, \ldots ql_n$ and its local query list ql_j, we define query vector, similarity degree, difference degree and fusion degree of two nodes as follows:

Definition 1. Query vector: The query vector of node j is define as vector $q_j = (w_{1,j}, w_{2,j}, \ldots, w_{n,j})$ where n is the maximum number of queries the sensor network can support, the weight $w_{i,j}$ is a binary value which is set to 1 when Q_i is involved in the local query list and set to 0 otherwise.

Definition 2. Similarity Degree: The similarity degree evaluates the degree of similarity of query tasks between the current node i and its candidate parent node p, this correlation can be quantified by the cosine of the angle between these two nodes' query vectors. That is,

$$sim(\overrightarrow{q_i}, \overrightarrow{q_p}) = \frac{\overrightarrow{q_i} \bullet \overrightarrow{q_p}}{|\overrightarrow{q_i}| \times |\overrightarrow{q_p}|} = \frac{\sum_{t=1}^{n}(w_{t,i} \times w_{t,p})}{\sqrt{\sum_{t=1}^{n} w_{t,i}^2} \times \sqrt{\sum_{t=1}^{n} w_{t,p}^2}} \quad (2)$$

Definition 3. Difference Degree: The difference degree evaluates the degree of difference of query tasks between the current node i and its candidate parent node p, this correlation can also be quantified as following format:

$$diff(\overrightarrow{q_i}, \overrightarrow{q_p}) = \frac{|\overrightarrow{q_i} - \overrightarrow{q_i} And \overrightarrow{q_p}| + |\overrightarrow{q_p} - \overrightarrow{q_i} And \overrightarrow{q_p}|}{n}$$

$$= \frac{\sum_{t=1}^{n}(w_{t,i} - w_{t,i} \times w_{t,p}) + \sum_{t=1}^{n}(w_{t,i} - w_{t,i} \times w_{t,p})}{n} \quad (3)$$

The *And* operator in the definition above is defined similar to the And operator in binary bit computing because the query vector actually can be understood as a sequence of binary bits. The difference degree is actually the quotient of the count of distinct query tasks between the two nodes divided by the maximum number of query tasks for normalization.

Definition 4. Fusion Degree: The fusion degree is the integrated evaluation of both similarity degree and difference degree, so it is in the format as follows:

$$fd(\overrightarrow{q_i}, \overrightarrow{q_p}) = \frac{sim(\overrightarrow{q_i}, \overrightarrow{q_p})}{diff(\overrightarrow{q_i}, \overrightarrow{q_p})} \quad (4)$$

The difference degree depicts the additional transmission loads for the incoming/outgoing edges, so the lower difference degree is, the better choice is made for the candidate parent, the difference degree makes the current node prefer to select those candidate nodes which incur less transmission load of additional incoming/outgoing edges so as to reduce communication cost and make energy consumption efficient. The similarity degree describes the degree of similarity of the query tasks between the current node and its candidate parent, the similarity degree is an efficient complement of the difference degree. The effects of the similarity degree is to make the current node to negatively suppress the edges to those candidates which have no query tasks at all, this method can make the path construction only involve those task-active nodes to the best ability, so we can make the nodes which currently have no tasks to have enough sleeping chance to be ready for the coming new queries, and at the same time, we can make the aggregation tree more convergent to be convenient for the merging work mentioned above to perform early near the sensor sources. So we utilize fusion degree, the integrated evaluation as a guideline to instruct our optimized routing path construction, both the similarity degree and the difference degree are normalized to the region [0, 1], in order to prevent the similarity degree and the difference degree to have zero value to impact the effective criterion of the fusion degree, we modified the calculation of fusion degree as following format:

$$fd(\overrightarrow{q_i}, \overrightarrow{q_p}) = \frac{sim(\overrightarrow{q_i}, \overrightarrow{q_p}) + \frac{1}{n}}{diff(\overrightarrow{q_i}, \overrightarrow{q_p}) + \frac{1}{n}} \tag{5}$$

In the above formula n is the maximum number of queries the sensor network can support.

Adaptive Fusion Degree Based Routing Scheme. We use the fusion degree to guide our optimized routing path construction, this routing path construction technique is called the cross layer designing, we construct our routing paradigm with the application specific information from multi-queries to make good use of the work sharing mechanism so as to efficiently reduce the communication cost to achieve our energy efficient designing goal. Our adaptive fusion degree based routing scheme can be divided into three phases shown as follows.

Diffusion based query propagation. We do the multi-query propagation based on the paradigm of direct diffusion[4], while queries are flooded into sensor network, the query message records the number of hops taken, this allows a node to discover the minimum number of hops to the base station, called the node's height, so during the query flooding, the gradients are established in each node. While the current node receives the neighbor node's height information, it negatively discards the height that is more than its current minimum heights. The current node sees the neighbor nodes which bring the minimum heights for it as the candidate parent nodes, in this gradient based construction approach, we can effectively avoid the loop formation, then the local node increases its height by one and broadcast it to its neighbors. At the end of this diffusion based query propagation, each node get its local query list and has one or more candidate parent nodes which have less hop counts to the base station.

Path probing and construction. After the topology is formed and candidate paths for each sensor node are fixed on, each node makes path probing by require its candidate parent nodes to send the query vectors to it, then the current node calculates the fusion degree between each candidate parent and itself, the current node then selects the candidate which has the largest fusion degree with itself, and send a routing message to the winner candidate to inform it of the path construction. After this phase, each node has a record of its parent node and a list of its children nodes, the tree based routing structure for the sensor network is completely constructed.

Routing structure maintenance. While the application query patterns changes with the time, new queries will come and some old queries will go, the routing structure will be timely updated and reconstructed to adapt to the current multi-query processing patterns.

4   Experimental Evaluation

In this section we measure the communication cost of our proposed algorithms described above using a home-grown simulator. We show the benefits of our proposed algorithms with some contrasting multi-query processing techniques.

4.1   Experimental Setup

In order to show the effectiveness of our proposed multi-query processing technique, we compare it with the multi-query processing techniques: *Naive multi-query processing approach (NMP)*; *Power aware query processing without optimization (MPWO)*. Both of the above approaches are introduced in Section2, and we further compare our multi-query processing technique with the following multi-query processing techniques: *Bounding-box paradigm for multi-query processing (BMP)*, this is just the multi-query processing paradigm proposed by Emekci which we have introduced in detail in Section 3.1, that is also the original paradigm which our optimized processing approach are based on., and we will compare the experiment results of the above multi-query processing mechanisms with our *Query-based partial aggregate value merging work (QBM)* and *EC based partial aggregate value merging paradigm (ECM)*, and we will compare our proposed *Adaptive Fusion Degree based Routing Scheme (AFD)* with the general scheme used in the original paradigm, we will then further compare with our *Hybrid AFD & ECM approach* to show the efficiency for energy conservation of our proposed algorithms. In our experiment we conducted a set of random SUM queries over a 40*40 grid and varied the total number of queries from 10 to 70. We assume all the queries in the network have the same frequency. Given N queries, the query set consists of $N/5$ queries over 5*5, $N/5$ queries over 10*10, $N/5$ queries over 15*15, $N/5$ queries over 20*20, $N/5$ queries over 25*25. To make the measurements of communication cost realistic, we consider a packet size of 34 bytes (similar to the size of TOS_MSG used in TinyOS) that consists of a 5-byte header and a 29-byte payload.

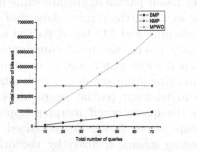

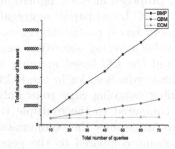

(a) Experiment results of multi-query pro-(b) Experiment results of merging algorithm
cessing paradigm

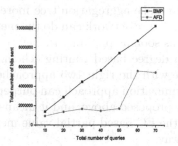

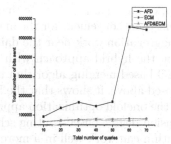

(c) Experiment results of routing construc-(d) Experiment results of hybrid algorithm
tion algorithm

Fig. 5. Adaptive Fusion Degree based Routing Scheme

4.2   Experimental Results Analysis

The experimental results are shown in Figure 5(a)~5(d), which show that our
proposed multi-query processing techniques significantly outperform the other
approaches in different points of views. In Figure 5(a), the compared results
show that the original bounding box paradigm which our optimized processing approaches are based on saves the communication cost by one order of a
magnitude compared to the naive multi-query approach, the power-aware query
processing without work sharing becomes so inefficient that even the naive approach outperforms it when the number of query grows. It is because that in
power-aware query processing without work sharing scheme, a tree is built for
each single query, and a sensor node may send its readings multiple times if it's
involved in multiple queries, but the naive approach only sends its raw sensor
reading once. The bounding box approach utilizes the work sharing mechanism
to share the sensor readings and the common partial results, it only has to transmit the incoming/outgoing partial values to the base station, so the bounding
box processing approach which our optimized approaches are based on outperforms the two above general multi-query processing approaches. In Figure 5(b),
it shows the compared results of the original bounding box approach and two

of our proposed merging algorithms: query based partial aggregate value merging and EC based partial aggregate value merging, the results show that both the query based partial aggregate value merging and EC based partial aggregate value merging algorithm can efficiently reduce the total communication cost and the EC based merging algorithm is more significant in communication cost reduction, for in the EC based merging approach nodes with multiple incoming/outgoing edge roles only have to transmit partial aggregate values once compared to the multiple times in the query based merging approach. Figure 5(c) shows the communication costs of our fusion degree based routing scheme compared to the general routing scheme utilized by the original paradigm, it shows that our approach can efficiently reduce the transmission load for we utilized the fusion degree to support the cross-layer design work of routing scheme, in this way we can fully reduce the incoming/outing edges in the network and we adjust the routing scheme to make aggregation tree more convergent to be convenient for the merging work so the network can do the merging and aggregation work near the data sources as soon as possible. In Figure 5(d), we use the hybrid approach with the fusion degree based routing scheme and the EC based merging algorithm to compare with the right two approaches we proposed above, it shows that the hybrid optimization approach can outperform both the onefold optimization approaches we proposed above, and it means that the fusion degree based routing scheme and the EC based partial value merging algorithm can work well in a more efficient way.

5   Related Work

Query processing over sensor networks has been extensively exploited for several recent years, several research groups have focused on query processing especially for data aggregation as an efficient way of reducing energy consumption. The impact of data aggregation for sensor network is fully analyzed in literature [11]. The TinyDB Project at UC Berkley investigates query processing techniques for sensor networks [5][10], the TAG approach [3] is proposed to efficiently process aggregation queries for sensor network and an acquisitional approach [8] is proposed to schedule the frequency and timing of data sampling. The Cougar Project [6] introduces the push and pull based view selection mechanism [9] for multi-query processing and proposed an aggregation tree selection scheme [12]. Our study differs from most previous works in that we consider multi-query processing optimization for sensor network.

6   Conclusions

In this paper we introduced the concept of multiple query processing over sensor networks, and we analyzed the deficiency of current multi-query processing approaches, then we proposed our optimized multi-query processing paradigm over sensor networks by sharing the readings and communication of common sensors among different queries, we proposed two multi-query optimization technique:

the equivalence class based data merging algorithm and adaptive fusion degree based routing scheme. Our experimental results show that our multi-query optimization paradigm can reduce the number of messages dramatically.

References

1. Niki Trigoni, Yong Yao, Alan J. Demers, Johannes Gehrke, Rajmohan Rajaraman: Multi-query Optimization for Sensor Networks. DCOSS 2005: 307-321
2. Fatih Emekci, Hailing Yu, Divyakant Agrawal, Amr El Abbadi Energy-Conscious Data Aggregation Over Large-Scale Sensor Networks
3. Samuel Madden, Michael J. Franklin, Joseph M. Hellerstein, and Wei Hong. TAG: A Tiny AGgregation Service for Ad-Hoc Sensor Networks. In OSDI, 2002.
4. Chalermek Intanagonwiwat, Ramesh Govindan, and Deborah Estrin. Directed diffusion: A scalable and robust communication paradigm for sensor networks. In Mobi-COM, Boston, MA, August 2000.
5. Samuel Madden and Michael J. Franklin. Fjording the stream: An architechture for queries over streaming sensor data. In ICDE, 2002.
6. Y. Yao and J. Gehrke. The cougar approach to in-network query processing in sensor networks. In SIGMOD Record, September 2002.
7. Yong Yao and Johannes Gehrke. Query processing in sensor networks. In Proceedings of the First Biennial Conference on Innovative Data Systems Research (CIDR), 2003.
8. Samuel Madden, Michael J. Franklin, Joseph M. Hellerstein, Wei Hong: TinyDB: an acquisitional query processing system for sensor networks. ACM Trans. Database Syst. 30(1): 122-173 (2005)
9. Niki Trigoni, Yong Yao, Alan J. Demers, Johannes Gehrke, Rajmohan Rajaraman: Hybrid Push-Pull Query Processing for Sensor Networks. GI Jahrestagung (2) 2004: 370-374
10. Madden S. The Design and Evaluation of a Query Processing Architecture for Sensor Networks. Ph. D Thesis, UC Berkeley, Fall 2003
11. Bhaskar Krishnamachari, Deborah Estrin, Stephen B. Wicker: The Impact of Data Aggregation in Wireless Sensor Networks. ICDCS Workshops 2002: 575-578
12. Alan J. Demers, Johannes Gehrke,Rajmohan Rajaraman, Agathoniki Trigoni, Yong Yao: The Cougar Project: a work-in-progress report. SIGMOD Record 32(4): 53-59 (2003)
13. Johannes Gehrke ,Samuel Madden Query Processing in Sensor Networks Sensor and Actuator Networks

On the Design of Soft-Decision Fusion Rule for Coding Approach in Wireless Sensor Networks*

Tsang-Yi Wang[1], Po-Ning Chen[2], Yunghsiang S. Han[3], and Yung-Ti Wang[3]

[1] Institute of Communications Engineering
National Sun Yat-sen University Kaohsiung, Taiwan 545, R.O.C
tcwang@mail.nsysu.edu.tw
[2] Department of Communications Engineering
National Chiao-Tung University Hsinchu, Taiwan 300, R.O.C
qponing@mail.nctu.edu.tw
[3] Graduate Institute of Communication Engineering
National Taipei University Sanhsia, Taipei, Taiwan 237, R.O.C
yshan@mail.ntpu.edu.tw

Abstract. In this work, two soft-decision fusion rules, which are respectively named the maximum *a priori* (MAP) and the suboptimal minimum Euclidean distance (MED) fusion rules, are designed based on a given employed sensor code and associated local classification. Their performance comparison with the distributed classification fusion using soft-decision decoding (DCSD) proposed in an earlier work is also performed. Simulations show that when the number of faulty sensors is small, the MAP fusion rule remains the best at either low sensor observation signal-to-noise ratios (OSNRs) or low communication channel signal-to-noise ratios (CSNRs), and yet, the DCSD fusion rule gives the best performance at middle to high OSNRs and high CSNRs. However, when the number of faulty sensor nodes grows large, the least complex MED fusion rule outperforms the MAP fusion rule at high OSNRs and high CSNRs.

1 Introduction

One of the general emerging visions for future applications is to deploy a large number of self-sustained wireless sensors to perform, e.g., environmental monitoring, battle field surveillance and health care maintenance. These wireless sensor nodes are typically battery-powered and made by economical techniques, and hence are vulnerable if they are employed in a harsh environment [1]. This makes energy efficiency and fault-tolerance capability becoming critical design factors in wireless sensor networks (WSNs). Another factor that distinguishes a WSN from other communication networks is that its end goal is to draw a

---

* This work was supported in part by Research Center of Wireless Network and Multimedia Communication under "Aim for Top University Plan" project of NSYSU and Ministry of Education, Taiwan and by the NSC of Taiwan, R.O.C., under grant NSC 94-2213-E-305-001.

X. Cheng, W. Li, and T. Znati (Eds.): WASA 2006, LNCS 4138, pp. 140–150, 2006.
© Springer-Verlag Berlin Heidelberg 2006

discrete decision out of several possible events of interest, but not to convey information. For these reasons, research on collaborative signal processing, and in particular, collaborative detection and classification has been studied extensively in WSNs [2,3,4,5].

In order to achieve the desired robustness against sensor faults under limited energy support, a distributed classification fusion using error correcting codes (DCFECC) has been proposed to be used in WSNs [6]. In the DCFECC approach, the fusion center makes multi-hypotheses decision by receiving only one-bit information from each sensor to minimize the local energy consumption. As contrary to the hard decision decoding used in the DCFECC approach, a soft-decision DCSD approach was later proposed in [7]. It is suggested by the investigation on the DCSD approach in [7] that employing soft-decision can markedly enhance the fault-tolerance capability of the same code in WSNs. This motivates our further investigation on the design of soft-decision-based fusion rules in this work.

Three soft-decision fusion rules are investigated in this paper: The maximum *a priori* (MAP) fusion rule, the minimum Euclidean distance (MED) fusion rule, and the previously proposed DCSD fusion rule. It is obvious that the MAP fusion rule provides the best classification performance if no sensor nodes are faulty. However, when some faulty sensors do not follow the local classification rules that are mutually pre-agreed between the fusion center and the local sensors, the MAP fusion rule is expected to degrade considerably since among the three soft-decision fusion rules considered, it is the one that mostly trusts the local classification. Therefore, the DCSD and the MED, although suboptimal in performance at a fault-free situation, may be more robust, if several sensor faults are present. Our simulations do match our anticipation. Details will be given subsequently.

The paper is organized as follows. The distributed classification problem is described in the next section. The MAP and the MED fusion rules, as well as the DCSD fusion rule, are introduced in Section 3. Simulations on these soft-decision fusion rules are presented and remarked in Section 4. Conclusion is given in Section 5

2   System Model

Fig. 1 depicts a parallel fusion structure in which a number of sensors respectively make sensor measurements $z = \{z_j\}_{j=1}^N$ given that one of the M hypotheses is true, where N is the number of sensors. The sensor measurement $\{z_j\}_{j=1}^N$ are conditionally independent given each hypothesis. Each sensor makes a preliminary decision $x = \{x_j\}_{j=1}^N$, where $x_j \in \{-1, 1\}$, about the true hypothesis uncooperatively according to a pre-specified local classification rule, and sends the result to the fusion center. The received vector $y = \{y_j\}_{j=1}^N$ may be subject to transmission errors due to the incorporation of link fading and interference. It is assumed that given $\{x_j\}_{j=1}^N$, $\{y_j\}_{j=1}^N$ are independent across sensors given each hypothesis. Also assume equal prior on the M hypotheses. Denote by $h_{\ell|i}^{(j)}$ the

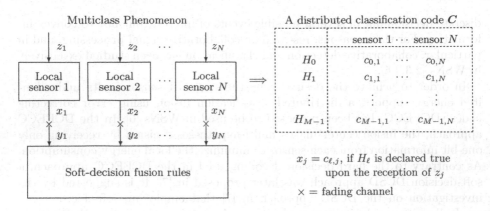

Fig. 1. System model for a WSN with distributed classification code

probability of classifying measurement z_j to H_ℓ given that the true hypothesis is H_i.

In the coded distributed detection system considered, a $M \times N$ binary distributed classification code C is designed in advance. This code can be obtained based on the misclassification error criterion as used in [6] or by the efficient code search algorithm proposed in [8,9]. In the code matrix, each row is associated with one hypothesis, and forms the codeword corresponding to this hypothesis. Specifically, the ℓth codeword in C is given by $c_\ell \triangleq (c_{\ell,1}, c_{\ell,2}, \ldots, c_{\ell,N})$, where $c_{\ell,j} \in \{0, 1\}$. On the other hand, the column vector in C provides the local binary output according to the classified hypothesis at the respective sensor. Thus, if the jth sensor makes a local classification in favor of hypothesis H_ℓ, it will transmit a binary decision whose value equals $(-1)^{c_{\ell,j}}$. As a result of the above setting,

$$\Pr\{x_j = -1 | H_i\} = \sum_{\ell=0}^{M-1} c_{\ell,j} h_{\ell|i}^{(j)}, \tag{1}$$

and

$$\Pr\{x_j = 1 | H_i\} = 1 - \Pr\{x_j = -1 | H_i\} = \sum_{\ell=0}^{M-1} (1 - c_{\ell,j}) h_{\ell|i}^{(j)}. \tag{2}$$

The communication channel between sensors and fusion center is assumed flat fading due to the assumption of very low bit rate. Perfect phase coherence is also assumed since the transmission range is usually small in most WSNs. Therefore, y_j can be expressed as

$$y_j = \alpha_j x_j \sqrt{E_b} + n_j, \tag{3}$$

where α_j is the attenuation factor that models the fading channel, E_b is the energy per channel bit, and n_j is a noise sample from a white Gaussian process with single-sided power spectral density N_0. Our objective then becomes to investigate the robustness of the fusion rules given the local classification rules associated with the employed code C.

3   Soft-Decision Fusion Rules

3.1   MAP Fusion Rule

The MAP fusion rule makes the decision in favor of H_i if $\Pr(H_i|\boldsymbol{y})$ is maximal for $0 \leq i \leq M - 1$. It can be derived as

$$
\begin{aligned}
i &= \arg \max_{0 \leq \ell \leq M-1} \Pr(H_\ell|\boldsymbol{y}) \\
&= \arg \max_{0 \leq \ell \leq M-1} \Pr(\boldsymbol{y}|H_\ell) & (4) \\
&= \arg \max_{0 \leq \ell \leq M-1} \sum_{\boldsymbol{x} \in \{-1,1\}^N} \Pr(\boldsymbol{x}, \boldsymbol{y}|H_\ell) \\
&= \arg \max_{0 \leq \ell \leq M-1} \sum_{\boldsymbol{x} \in \{-1,1\}^N} \Pr(\boldsymbol{x}|H_\ell) \Pr(\boldsymbol{y}|\boldsymbol{x}, H_\ell) \\
&= \arg \max_{0 \leq \ell \leq M-1} \sum_{\boldsymbol{x} \in \{-1,1\}^N} \Pr(\boldsymbol{x}|H_\ell) \Pr(\boldsymbol{y}|\boldsymbol{x}) \\
&= \arg \max_{0 \leq \ell \leq M-1} \sum_{\boldsymbol{x} \in \{-1,1\}^N} \left(\prod_{j=1}^{N} \Pr(x_j|H_\ell) \right) \Pr(\boldsymbol{y}|\boldsymbol{x}) & (5) \\
&= \arg \max_{0 \leq \ell \leq M-1} \sum_{\boldsymbol{x} \in \{-1,1\}^N} \left(\prod_{j=1}^{N} \Pr(x_j|H_\ell) \Pr(y_j|x_j) \right) & (6) \\
&= \arg \max_{0 \leq \ell \leq M-1} \sum_{j=1}^{N} \log \left(\sum_{x_j \in \{-1,1\}} \Pr(x_j|H_\ell) \Pr(y_j|x_j) \right) & (7)
\end{aligned}
$$

where (4) follows from the assumption of equally likely hypotheses, (5) is valid since the local measurements are assumed spatially conditionally independent given each hypothesis and x_j is determined uncooperatively across sensors, and (6) follows from the assumption of spatially independent communication channel statistics between local sensors and the fusion center. Notably, $\Pr(x_j|H_\ell)$ and $\Pr(y_j|x_j)$ in (7) are given by (1), (2) and (3).

3.2   DCSD Fusion Rule

For a given binary code C, the DCSD fusion rule proposed in [7] chooses H_i as the final decision, if

$$
\begin{aligned}
i &= \arg \max_{0 \leq \ell \leq M-1} \sum_{j=1}^{N} \log \left(\sum_{x_j \in \{-1,1\}} g(x_j|s = c_{\ell,j}) \Pr(y_j|x_j) \right) \\
&= \arg \min_{0 \leq \ell \leq M-1} \sum_{j=1}^{N} (\phi_j - (-1)^{c_{\ell,j}})^2,
\end{aligned}
$$

where ϕ_j is the bit log-likelihood ratio defined as

Table 1. The code obtained by the pruned exhaustive search algorithm

H_0	1	1	1	1	1	0	0	0	0	0
H_1	1	1	1	1	1	1	1	1	1	1
H_2	0	0	0	0	0	1	1	1	1	1
H_3	0	0	0	0	0	0	0	0	0	0

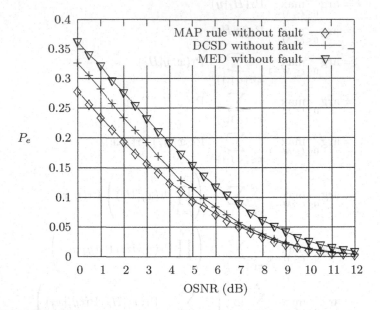

Fig. 2. Performance of the MAP rule, the DCSD rule, and the MED rule at CSNR=5 dB in fault-free situation

$$\phi_j \triangleq \log \frac{\sum_{x_j \in \{-1,1\}} \Pr(y_j|x_j) \cdot g(x_j|s=0)}{\sum_{x_j \in \{-1,1\}} \Pr(y_j|x_j) \cdot g(x_j|s=1)},$$

and

$$g(x_j|s) \equiv \frac{\sum_{\ell=0}^{M-1} \mathbf{1}\{c_{\ell,j}=s\} \cdot \Pr(x_j|H_\ell)}{\sum_{k=0}^{M-1} \mathbf{1}\{c_{k,j}=s\}},$$

and $\mathbf{1}\{\cdot\}$ is the indicator function. Since the DCSD fusion rule is not equivalent to the MAP fusion rule, it is suboptimal when there are no faulty sensors.

3.3 MED Fusion Rule

The DCSD fusion rule can be treated as averaging $\Pr(x_j|H_\ell)$ with respect to the adopted code. The MED fusion rule however is originated from an observation that the local classification is in general accurate. This observation can be mathematically termed as $\Pr\{x_j = (-1)^{c_{\ell,j}}|H_\ell\} \gg \Pr\{x_j \neq (-1)^{c_{\ell,j}}|H_\ell\}$, which immediately implies the approximation that $\Pr\{x_j = (-1)^{c_{\ell,j}}|H_\ell\} \approx 1$ and $\Pr\{x_j \neq (-1)^{c_{\ell,j}}|H_\ell\} \approx 0$. Taking this approximation to (7), we obtain:

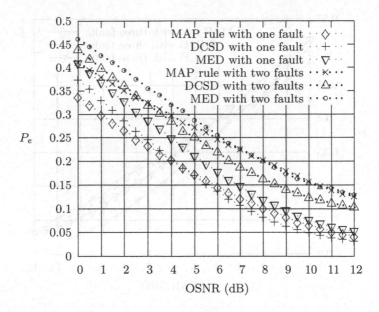

Fig. 3. Performance of the MAP rule, the DCSD rule, and the MED rule at CSNR=5 dB when one or two sensors suffer stuck-at fault

$$i = \arg \max_{0 \le \ell \le M-1} \sum_{j=1}^{N} \log \left(\sum_{x_j \in \{-1,1\}} \Pr(x_j|H_\ell) \Pr(y_j|x_j) \right)$$

$$\approx \arg \max_{0 \le \ell \le M-1} \sum_{j=1}^{N} \log \left[\Pr(y_j|x_j = (-1)^{c_{\ell,j}}) \right]$$

$$= \arg \min_{0 \le \ell \le M-1} \sum_{j=1}^{N} (\varphi_j - (-1)^{c_{\ell,j}})^2,$$

where

$$\varphi_j = \log \frac{\Pr(y_j|x_j = 1)}{\Pr(y_j|x_j = -1)}.$$

4   Simulation on Robustness

In this section, we study the performance of the three aforementioned fusion rules through simulations. Both fault-free (without stuck-at faults) and faulty situations (sensors in the presence of stuck-at faults) are simulated. The hypothesis number M and the sensor number N are four and ten, respectively. We further assume that all sensor measurements have the same distribution given each hypothesis, and are randomly drawn from a unit-variance Gaussian distribution with means 0, V, $2V$ and $3V$ corresponding to hypotheses H_0, H_1, H_2 and

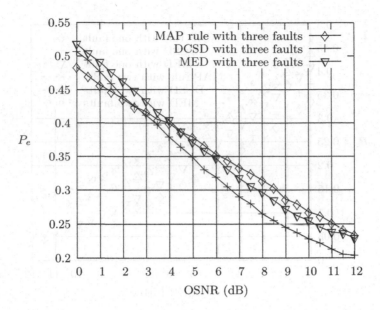

Fig. 4. Performance of the MAP rule, the DCSD rule, and the MED rule at CSNR=5 dB when three sensors are faulty

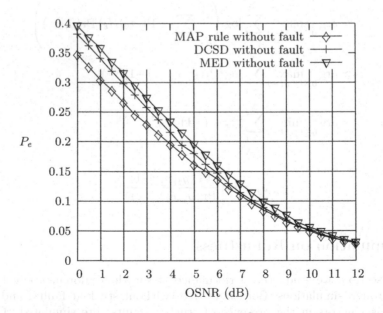

Fig. 5. Performance of the MAP rule, the DCSD rule, and the MED rule at CSNR=0 dB in fault-free situation

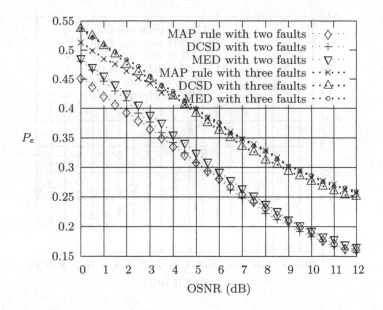

Fig. 6. Performance of the MAP rule, the DCSD rule, and the MED rule at CSNR=0 dB when two or three sensors are faulty

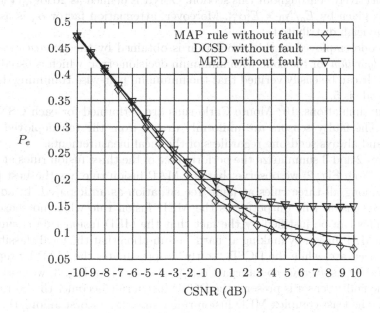

Fig. 7. Performance of the MAP rule, the DCSD rule, and the MED rule at OSNR=5 dB in fault-free situation

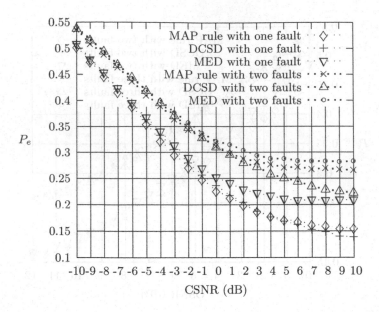

Fig. 8. Performance of the MAP rule, the DCSD rule, and the MED rule at OSNR=5 dB when one or two sensors are faulty

H_3, respectively. Throughout this section, OSNR is defined as $20 \log_{10}(V)$, while CSNR is given by $E_b/N_0 \times E[\alpha_j^2]$. Moreover, attenuation factor α_j is assumed to be Rayleigh distributed.

The code employed in this simulation is obtained by the *pruned exhaustive search algorithm* for the code with minimum decision error, which is listed in Table 1 [8]. It can be easily verified that the minimum pair-wise Hamming distance in this code is 5.

In our simulations, 10^5 Monte Carlo runs are performed for each OSNR and CSNR. The faulty sensors are uniformly drawn from the ten deployed sensor nodes, and always send one regardless of the local measurements.

Figures 2 and 3 summarize the performance of the three fusion rules at CSNR = 5 dB. From Fig. 2, we observe that the MAP fusion rule has the best performance among all three rules at fault-free situation as anticipated. In addition, the DCSD fusion rule outperforms the MED fusion rule when no sensors are faulty. This can be justified by the fact that the MED fusion rule is simplified from the MAP fusion by making a "hard" assumption that the local classification is 100% accurate, while the DCSD "softly" approximates the MAP by replacing $\Pr(x_j|H_\ell)$ by its average counterpart $g(x_j|s = c_{\ell,j})$. From Fig. 3, we notice that when one faulty sensor is present, the DCSD fusion rule becomes the best at high OSNRs. The least complex MED fusion rule remains the worst among the three. Hence, we remark that at high OSNRs, the DCSD replacement $g(x_j|s = c_{\ell,j})$ is sufficient to compensate the impact due to the faulty sensor. When two faulty nodes are present, the robustness of the DCSD fusion rule extends to middle to high OSNRs.

Figure 4 presents the simulated performance when the number of faulty nodes further increases to 3. It can be seen that the least complex MED fusion rule becomes better than the MAP fusion rule at high OSNRs. This figure also shows that the DCSD fusion rule still possesses the best fault-tolerance capability at most simulated OSNRs.

Repeating the simulations with fault-free case, two faulty nodes, and three faulty nodes as in Figs. 2, 3 and 4 but fixing CSNR at 0 dB, we result Figs. 5 and 6. Figures 5 and 6 indicate that the DCSD fusion rule still provides the best performance at faulty situation at high OSNRs, but the OSNR range at which the DCSD performs the best decreases.

Figures 7 and 8 presents the simulation results corresponding to the situation when OSNR is fixed at 5 dB, and CSNR ranges from −10 dB to 10 dB. We observe from these two figures that the MAP fusion rule provides the best performance at low CSNRs either in the anticipated fault-free situation or in the sensor-faulty situation. The DCSD approach however performs the best at high CSNRs.

5   Conclusion

In this paper, we introduce two soft-decision fusion rules, and compare their robustness with the previously proposed DCSD fusion by simulations. We conclude our simulations that i) the MAP fusion rule gives the best performance in fault-free situation as well as at low OSNRs or low CSNRs; ii) the DCSD fusion rule has a better fault-tolerance capability at middle to high OSNRs and at high CSNRs; iii) the MED fusion rule, although least complex, can perform better than the MAP fusion rule only when the number of faulty nodes is large, but is always worse than the DCSD fusion rule. These results can serve as a guide when the determination of suitable fusion rules for coding approach in wireless sensor networks is necessary.

References

1. Akyildiz, I.F., Su, W., Sankarasubramaniam, Y., Cayirci, E.: A survey on sensor networks. IEEE Communications Magazine (2002) 102–114
2. Dan, L., Wong, K.D., Yu, H.H., Sayeed, A.M.: Detection, classification, and tracking of targets. IEEE Signal Processing Magazine 19 (2002) 17–29
3. Wang, H., Elson, J., Girod, L., Estrin, D., Yao, K.: Target classification and localization in habitat monitoring. In: IEEE International Conference on Acoustics, Speech, and Signal Processing (ICASSP 2003), Hong Kong, China. (2003)
4. Aldosari, S.A., Moura, J.M.F.: Detection in decentralized sensor networks. In: IEEE International Conference on Accoustics, Speech, and Signal Processing, Montreal, Canada (2004)
5. Chamberland, J.F., Veeravalli, V.V.: Asymptotic results for decentralized detection in power constrained wireless sensor networks. IEEE Journal of Selected Areas in Communications 22(6) (2004) 1007–1015

6. Wang, T.Y., Han, Y.S., Varshney, P.K., Chen, P.N.: Distributed fault-tolerant classification in wireless sensor networks. IEEE Journal of Selected Areas in Communications **23**(4) (2005) 724–734
7. Wang, T.Y., Han, Y.S., Chen, B., Varshney, P.K.: A combined decision fusion and channel coding scheme for distributed fault-tolerant classification in wireless sensor networks. IEEE Trans. Wireless Commun. **5**(7) (2006)
8. Pai, H.T., Han, Y.S., Sung, J.T.: Two-dimensional coded classification schemes in wireless sensor networks. submitted to IEEE Trans. on Wireless Commun. (2006)
9. Chen, P.N., Wang, T.Y., Han, Y.S., Varshney, P.K., Yao, C.: Performance analysis and code design for minimum hamming distance fusion in wireless sensor networks. submitted to IEEE Trans. Inform. Theory (2005)

Reliable and Real-Time Data Gathering in Multi-hop Linear Wireless Sensor Networks

Haibo Zhang[1], Hong Shen[1], and Hui Tian[2]

[1] Graduate School of Information Science
Japan Advanced Institute of Science and Technology
1-1, Asahidai, Nomi, Ishikawa 923-1211, Japan
{haibo, shen}@jaist.ac.jp
[2] Department of Computing and Mathematics
Manchester Metropolitan University
Oxford Road, Manchester, M1 5GD, UK
H.Tian@mmu.ac.uk

Abstract. Data gathering is a critical operation in wireless sensor networks for extracting useful information from the operating environment. In this paper, we study the problem of data gathering in multi-hop linear sensor networks. We employ a simple model based on random channel access scheme to tackle the high degree of channel contention and high probability of packet collision induced by bursty traffic. In our model, each node optimally attempts a transmission, and our goal is to tune the attempt probability for each sensor node with the objective to minimize the data gathering duration on condition that each link can provide guaranteed per-hop packet delivery reliability. We formulate this problem as an optimization problem and propose a distributed solution which relies on only two hop neighbors information. Based on this model, a simple and scalable protocol RADG (Random Access Data Gathering) is designed. Simulation results show that our algorithm has fast convergence speed. Moreover, RADG is robust to link error in essence and particularly suitable to monitor environments with high degree of interference.

1 Introduction

Consider wireless sensor networks (WSNs) deployed in a region to monitor the environment, for instance, networks for habitat sensing [1], healthcare monitoring [2][3] and target tracking[4]. An important task for such scenarios is data gathering, where each sensor must periodically report its sensed data to the base station (BS). In many applications, the sensed data from different locations is expected to be transported to the BS with high reliability and low latency.

In WSNs, the distance between a node and the BS may exceed its transmission range. Relaying packets by intermediate nodes needs to be performed and data gathering must be operated in a multi-hop fashion. During data gathering, the large burst of data packets generated in such a short period will lead to high degree of channel contention and high probability of packet collision. The situation is further exacerbated by the fact that packet is delivered over

X. Cheng, W. Li, and T. Znati (Eds.): WASA 2006, LNCS 4138, pp. 151–162, 2006.
© Springer-Verlag Berlin Heidelberg 2006

multi-hop routes. Consequently, the packet loss rate is very serious during data gathering. For example, in [5], the authors observed that around 50% packets are lost for most events in Lites with the default radio stack of TinyOS. Hence, the high-volume bursty traffic poses special challenges for reliable and real-time data gathering.

To improve packet delivery reliability, control frames such as RTS/CTS and ACK are usually exployed. However, such control packets can improve system performance only for large data frames. But in most data gathering WSNs, the packet generated by the sensor is usually small. The message may contain only several bits data besides the header. In [6], the authors observed that the total percentage of bandwidth invested on control packets accounts for nearly 46%, which implies that these control packets have further increased the channel contention and caused more data loss.

Random access schemes are seen as better solutions to bursty packet networks [7], and there are two advantages for exploring random access scheme to perform data gathering task.

- It is simple and no additional control frame is used for channel reservation. Therefore, channel utilization may be greatly improved.
- It has low delay (under light load) for bursty traffic. It is well known that the random access channel throughput increases initially with increasing aggregate traffic generation rate[8].

In this paper, we explore the random channel access scheme to tackle the problem of reliable and real-time data gathering for multi-hop wireless sensor networks. This work continues our previous work in [10] where a novel model based on random channel access scheme was proposed to explore the trade-off between reliability and latency for data gathering. In that model, we simply assumed that all the nodes have the same *attempt probability* [9] and designed centralized algorithm to compute the optimal attempt probability for data gathering operation. In this paper, we insist that it will be more suitable for each node to have its own attempt probability. First because maintaining the same attempt probability at every sensor is difficult. More importantly, different sensors may need different attempt probability to counter the local inhomogeneities in the node placement.

The *attempt probability* is a critical parameter for random access schemes. Improper attempt probability may lead to high probability of packet collision and too much delay. Some work has been done on tuning the attempt probability for random access wireless networks. Two iterative, decentralized algorithms were presented in [11] to compute the global optimal rates for the problem of max-min fair rate allocation in ALOHA networks. In [12], the authors view the problem of optimizing the node attempt probability as a non-cooperative game and show the existence of a Nash equilibrium giving an optimal channel access rate for each node. However, all these approaches try to optimize the performance of individual node, such as maximizing the throughput or obtaining fairness. In data gathering, each sensor node is not independent, and all the sensors must work in a cooperative manner. Therefore, the approaches mentioned above are not suitable to solve our problem.

In this paper, our goal is to compute the optimal attempt probability for each sensor node so that the data gathering duration can be minimized on condition that each link in the data gathering structure can provide guaranteed hop-by-hop delivery reliability. We design a fully distributed algorithm to solve this problem.

The remainder of this paper is organized as follows. In section II, we describe our model and formulate the problem as an optimization problem. Section III describes the distributed solution for linear networks. In section IV, we present the protocol RADG. We evaluate our algorithm and protocol by simulations in section V. Finally, we conclude in section VI.

2   Model and Problem Formulation

2.1   System Model

In our model, we make the following assumptions about the wireless sensor network.

- **Node Model:** All sensors are equipped with the same radio transceiver that enables the sensor to transmit/receive over distance of R. Each sensor node is assumed to be static and distinguishable by a unique identifier.
- **Antenna Model:** Each node can transmit and receive on a common carrier frequency using omnidirectional antennas.
- **Channel Access Model:** Time is slotted and nodes are synchronized on time slots. At each time slot, a node can be in two states: active and sleep. If node v_i is in active state, it decides to transmit a packet with probability α_i and decides to receive with probability $(1 - \alpha_i)$.
- **Collision Model:** Collisions occur if a node simultaneously receives transmissions from two or more of its neighbors. In our model, we assume that all colliding packets will be lost.

We model the network as a graph $G = (V, L)$, where $V = (v_1, v_2, ..., v_n)$ is the set of sensor nodes, and L is the set of wireless links. There is a link between v_i and v_j if the distance between them is less than the transmission range R. We further assume that there is only one BS in the network, and all the data generated by the sensor nodes should be reported to the BS during data gathering. For each node v_i, we define its first hop neighborhood set as

$$N_1(i) = \{v_j \in V \backslash \{v_i\} : L(i, j) \in L\}$$

Also let $N_2(i)$ be the second hop neighbor set of node v_i.

$$N_2(i) = \{v_k \in V \backslash N_1(i) \backslash \{v_i\} : \exists v_m \in N_1(i), v_k \in N_1(m)\}$$

2.2 Problem Formulation

To collect sensed data in WSN, all the nodes must operate in a cooperative manner. Each node should optimally attempt a transmission, which means that a node should neither be too aggressive in attempting a transmission (thereby risking a collision) nor be too conservative so as to miss the chance of successful transmission. The model employed in this paper is similar to that in [10] except that each node v_i has a different attempt probability α_i.

Given any node v_i, let $P_L(i, j)$ be the probability that node v_i can successfully transmit a packet to node v_j in any time slot t, then

$$P_L(i, j) = \alpha_i(1 - \alpha_j) \prod_{k \in N_1(j) \backslash \{v_i\}} (1 - \alpha_k) \tag{1}$$

It is obvious that the transmission from node v_i to node v_j is successful if and only if node v_i is in transmit state, while node v_j and all its one hop neighbors except v_i are in non-transmit states at this time slot.

Let $S_{i,j}$ denote the number of time slots allocated to v_i for delivering its packet to v_j. $C_{i,j}$ denotes the number of collision-free time slots among $S_{i,j}$ time slots, then the probability that at least one transmission is successful during the $S_{i,j}$ time slots, denoted by $P_L(i, j, S_{i,j})$, can be computed by the following equation.

$$P_L(i, j, S_{i,j}) = P(C_{i,j} \geq 1) = 1 - P(C_{i,j} = 0)$$
$$= 1 - [1 - \alpha_i(1 - \alpha_j) \prod_{k \in N_1(j) \backslash \{v_i\}} (1 - \alpha_k)]^{S_{i,j}} \tag{2}$$

$P_L(i, j, S_{i,j})$ is called the *per-hop delivery reliability* (PHDR) in our model. Given threshold $\tau(i, j)$ for $P_L(i, j, S_{i,j})$, $S_{i,j}$ can be computed by the following equation.

$$S_{i,j} = \lceil \frac{\log(1 - \tau(i, j))}{\log[1 - \alpha_i(1 - \alpha_j) \prod_{k \in N_1(j) \backslash \{v_i\}} (1 - \alpha_k)]} \rceil \tag{3}$$

Let $P(i)$ be the path from node v_i to the BS, and $E(i)$ be the set of links on $P(i)$. $L(i)$ is defined as the latency for delivering a packet from node v_i to the BS on condition that each link in $E(i)$ can provide predefined PHDR.

$$L(i) = \sum_{(k,j) \in E(i)} S_{k,j} \tag{4}$$

In this paper, we study the multi-hop linear sensor networks. Assume that the BS is placed at one end of the network. The sensor nodes are randomly placed as long as connectivity of the network is ensured. For ease of analysis, we assume that each node v_i except the BS and the last node v_n has only two one hop neighbors: v_{i-1} and v_{i+1} (an example is given in Fig.1). Hence, all the packets must be delivered along the unique path during data gathering.

Denote by T the minimal duration for data gathering, obviously, the last node has the maximum latency. Thus, $T = \max_{v_i \in V} L(i) = L(n)$. Our goal is to

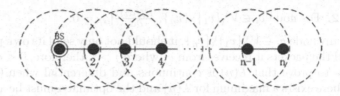

Fig. 1. A linear network composed of n sensor nodes

compute the optimal attempt probability for each node that can minimize the duration of data gathering while providing guaranteed PHDR. Hence, we aim to solve the following optimization problem.

$$Minmize \quad L(n) = \sum_{j=1}^{n-1} S_{j+1,j}$$

$$s.t. \ P_L(k, k-1, S_{k,k-1}) \geq \tau(k, k-1) \ 1 < k \leq n$$

$$0 \leq \alpha_i \leq 1, \quad v_i \in V \tag{5}$$

Where $\tau(k, k-1)$ is the user specified threshold for $P_L(k, k-1, S_{k,k-1})$.

3 Distributed Attempt Probability Computation

Denote by α the vector of α_i, $\alpha = (\alpha_1, \alpha_2, ..., \alpha_n)$. We propose a fully distributed algorithm for computing the optimal attempt probability for each node in linear networks, which relies on only two hop local information.

Lemma 1. For linear networks, α_i will only influence $S_{i,i-1}$, $S_{i+1,i}$ and $S_{i+2,i+1}$.

Proof. Since node v_i has at most two one hop neighbors: v_{i-1} and v_{i+1}, i.e., $v_i \in N_1(i-1)$ and $v_i \in N_1(i+1)$. From Eq. 3, $S_{i,j}$ only depends on $\alpha_k, k \in \{j\} \bigcup N_1(j)$. Therefore, α_i will only influence $Link(i, i-1)$, $Link(i+1, i)$ and $Link(i+2, i+1)$. ♮

Definition 1. $f(\alpha_i)$ is defined as the aggregated latency for the links α_i influences.

$$f(\alpha_i) = \begin{cases} S_{2,1} + S_{3,2} & i = 1 \\ S_{i,i-1} + S_{i+1,i} + S_{i+2,i+1} & 1 < i < n-1 \\ S_{n,n-1} + S_{n-1,n-2} & i = n-1 \\ S_{n,n-1} & i = n \end{cases} \tag{6}$$

Let α_i^* denote the optimal attempt probability of node v_i, then,

Theorem 1. $\alpha_1^* = 0, \alpha_n^* = 1$.

Proof. From Eq.3 and Eq.6, $L(n)$ increases as α_1 decreases. While for node v_n, $L(n)$ decreases as α_n increases. Hence, $\alpha_1^* = 0, \alpha_n^* = 1$. Consider the data gathering scenario, the theorem is also correct because v_1 is the BS and it only needs to receive packets, while v_n is the last node in the line network and it only needs to send its packet and no need to receive any packet. ♮

Theorem 2. For node $v_i \in V \backslash \{v_1\} \backslash \{v_n\}$, $\frac{\partial f(\alpha_i)}{\partial \alpha_i} |_{\alpha_i^*} = 0$.

Proof. For any node $v_i \in V \backslash \{v_1\} \backslash \{v_n\}$, it should not only send its own packet but also forward the packets it receives from v_j where $j > i$, therefore, $0 < \alpha_i^* < 1$.

It is easy to prove that $L(n)$ is continuous and differential when $0 < \alpha_i < 1$, therefore, there exists a maximum for $L(n)$ and the optimal α must be an extreme point of $L(n)$. According to the extremum existence theorem for continuous and differential multi-variable functions, $\frac{\partial L(n)}{\partial \alpha_i} |_{\alpha_i^*} = 0, 1 < i < n$. From Lemma 1 and definition 4, $\frac{\partial L(\alpha)}{\partial \alpha_i} = \frac{\partial f(\alpha_i)}{\partial \alpha_i}, 1 < i < n$. Hence, the theorem is proved. ♮

In the following, we first describe the local data structure maintained at each node, the message communication between the nodes and the attempt probability update procedure performed at each node. Then, we present the distributed attempt probability tuning algorithm.

Local Data Structure: To compute $S_{i,j}$, node v_i needs to know $\alpha_k, k \in N_1(j)$. From Lemma 1, α_i influences at most three links, therefore, each node only need to store the attempt probability of its one-hop and two hop neighbors. In our algorithm, each sensor node, v_i, maintains a simple local data structure, $<PNtab>$, which records $\alpha_j, j \in \{i\} \bigcup N_1(i) \bigcup N_2(i)$.

Communication: To maintain $<PNtab>$, at each time slot, if node v_i is in transmit state, it broadcasts $<PNtab>$ to its one hop neighbors. Otherwise, if node v_i is in receive state, it listens and receives the $<PNtab>$ message from its one hop neighbors. Once node v_i has successfully received a $<PNtab>$ message, it checks the message and performs one of the following actions.

1. If v_i receives a $<PNtab>$ message from v_{i-1}, v_i only needs to update α_{i-1} and α_{i-2} with the corresponding values in the received $<PNtab>$.
2. If v_i receives a $<PNtab>$ message from v_{i+1}, v_i only needs to update α_{i+1} and α_{i+2} with the corresponding value in the received $<PNtab>$.

We illustrate the procedure by an example. For instance, if v_3 receives a $<PNtab>$ message from v_2, v_3 only needs to replace α_1 and α_2 with the corresponding values in the received $<PNtab>$. Although α_4 may also exist in the received $<PNtab>$, it may be outdated and v_3 can get the latest α_4 from the $<PNtab>$ broadcasted by v_4. The case is the same when v_3 receives a $<PNtab>$ from v_4.

Computation: For each intermediate node v_i, we use an iterative scheme to tune α_i. According to Lemma 1, α_i only influences a few links, and it is easy to prove that $f(\alpha_i)$ is a strict concave function of α_i. Therefore, there is an optimal α_i', $\frac{\partial f(\alpha_i)}{\partial \alpha_i} |_{\alpha_i'} = 0$ that minimizes $f(\alpha_i)$. From Theorem 2, $\frac{\partial L(\alpha)}{\partial \alpha_i} = \frac{\partial f(\alpha_i)}{\partial \alpha_i}, 1 < i < n$. The main idea of our scheme is to iteratively adjust the attempt probability, so that each adjustment locally minimizes the objective function. Finally, this interactive local optimization is expected to lead to a global optimal solution. Thus, once the $<PNtab>$ stored in node v_i has been changed, v_i simply updates its attempt probability α_i with α_i' that minimizes $f(\alpha_i)$.

Now, we give the distributed algorithm for computing the attempt probability for each node in linear networks.

Algorithm1. Tune α for Linear Network(node u)

1: Initialize α_u and $\bar{\alpha}_u$;
2: state=GenerateState($\bar{\alpha}_u$);
3: If state=*Transmit* then
4:      broadcast(u,$<PNtab>$);
5: If state=*Receive* then
6:      If SuccessReceive(u-1,$<PNtab>$);
7:          UpdatePNtab($\alpha_{u-2}, \alpha_{u-1}$);
8:      If SuccessReceive(u+1,$<PNtab>$);
9:          UpdatePNtab($\alpha_{u+1}, \alpha_{u+2}$);
10:     $\alpha_u = \alpha'_u$, where $\frac{\partial f(\alpha_i)}{\partial \alpha_i}|_{\alpha'_u} = 0$;

---

4   Random Access Data Gathering Protocol (RADG)

In this section, a simple and scalable protocol RADG is designed based on our model for gathering data in multi-hop linear sensor networks. In RADG, both data combination and aggregated acknowledge are exploited to increase channel utilization and to reduce packet collision.

4.1   Data Combination at Relay Nodes

In many applications of wireless sensor networks, the data packet generated by sensors is small. Therefore, data combination may be particular useful to improve data delivery reliability and alleviate packet congestion and collision. In RADG, we assume each intermediate node can encapsulate the data it generates or receives into one packet. Each node v_i maintains a data queue Q_i, and the queue structure is shown in Fig.2. For each element in Q_i, we call it a data unit.

Fig. 2. Data queue maintained at node v_i

At any time slot, if node v_i successfully receives a packet from v_{i+1}, it first checks whether the data units in the received packet are duplicates of previously received ones. To achieve this, each node v_i maintains a dynamic array $R(i)$, which records the nodeID from which it has received the sensed data during one data gathering cycle. For each data unit in the received packet, if the nodeID has appeared in $R(i)$, it just discards this data unit, otherwise it inserts the data unit into Q_i and adds the nodeID to $R(i)$. After all data units have been processed, node v_i encapsulates all data units in Q_i together with the header into one packet, denoted by P, and replaces the original packet in the node buffer. When the node enters into transmit state, it just simply broadcasts packet P.

4.2 Transmission and Timer Aggregated Acknowledgement

During data gathering, packets may be lost due to collision and the lost packets need to be retransmitted to ensure the data gathering reliability. Many protocols use explicit acknowledgments (ACKs) mechanism to deal with this problem. However, wireless links are error-prone and ACKs may also be lost. Moreover, the additional ACK frames may exacerbate the severity of traffic. To reduce packets collision and improve throughput, we explore two mechanisms to tackle this problem in RADG.

1. *Transmission Timer* (TT): Each data unit in the data queue has a TT (also see Fig.2). When a data unit is received by node v_i for the first time, TT for this data unit is initiated with 0. In each slot, TT is increased by one. The number of time slots allotted to v_i to ensure a packet can be successfully received by node v_{i-1} with predefined reliability is $S_{i,i-1}$, which is also called the lifetime of the data unit for its existence in the data queue. Therefore, if TT is larger than $S_{i,i-1}$, node v_i just drops the data unit. This mechanism will ensure that each data unit can be delivered with predefined per-hop reliability.
2. *Aggregated Acknowledge*(AAck): When encapsulating packet, the set $R(i)$ is also attached. When node v_i receives a packet from v_{i-1}, for any data unit in Q_i, it is discarded if its nodeID is in $R(i-1)$, which implies that it has been received by node v_{i-1}. The advantage of this mechanism is that it doesn't use additional ACK frames, so it will not exacerbate the degree of channel congestion and packets collision.

For these two mechanisms, the size of packet will not be large although data combination is employed.

5 Simulation Results and Analysis

5.1 Algorithm Convergence

The algorithm was simulated over a linear network of 12 nodes. In our simulations, all the links along the data delivery path from the last node to the BS were set with the same PHDR. Therefore, the attempt probability for each node is independent on PHDR. Table 1 lists the attempt probability for each node computed by the algorithm, and Table 2 gives $S_{i,j}$ and T for the links under different PHDR.

In simulation, each node v_i used a fixed attempt probability $\bar{\alpha}_i$ since each node needs to broadcast the $<PNtab>$ to its neighbors, and all the links are expected to have fair throughput to fasten the convergence speed of the algorithm. In [10], we consider the attempt probability computation problem for one hop networks on the assumption that each node has the same attempt probability. We proved that the $S_{j,i}$ is minimized only when $\alpha = \frac{1}{n+1}$, where n is the number of neighbors of node v_i. Therefore, in our simulation, we simply set $\bar{\alpha}_i$ with $\frac{1}{|N_1(i)|+1}$.

Table 1. Attempt probability for each node

Node	α_1	α_2	α_3	α_4	α_5	α_6	α_7	α_8	α_9	α_{10}	α_{11}	α_{12}
Value	0	0.269	0.285	0.325	0.336	0.342	0.355	0.360	0.374	0.410	0.556	1

Table 2. $S_{i,j}$ and T with different PHDR

$S_{i,j}$	$S_{2,1}$	$S_{3,2}$	$S_{4,3}$	$S_{5,4}$	$S_{6,5}$	$S_{7,6}$	$S_{8,7}$	$S_{9,8}$	$S_{10,9}$	$S_{11,10}$	$S_{12,11}$	T
$\tau=0.85$	7	9	11	11	12	12	12	12	11	9	7	113
$\tau=0.90$	8	10	12	13	14	14	15	14	12	10	8	130
$\tau=0.95$	10	13	16	17	18	18	19	18	17	13	10	169
$\tau=0.98$	13	17	21	22	23	24	25	24	22	17	13	221

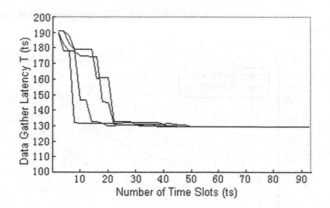

Fig. 3. Convergence speed of algorithm 1

Since the algorithm is based on random channel access, it is difficult to give a theoretical upper bound on the number of iterations. Fig.3 plots the convergence speed for four runs. The threshold for PHDR is 90%, and the initial value for each α_i is 0.5. The simulation results clearly indicate that our algorithm has a fast convergence speed.

5.2 Reliability and Latency Tradeoffs

We first evaluate the data gathering reliability by tuning PHDR. Since our model is based on random channel access, we use average packet delivery ratio(APDR) as the evaluation metric for data gathering reliability. APDR is defined as the average percentage of received packets (n_{succ}) compared with the total number of nodes n. In this simulation, we simply used the same PHDR for each link and we compare the simulation results with the theoretical average delivery reliability(TADR). Fig.4 gives the APDR and TADR obtained by increasing PHDR step by step. The simulation results were obtained by 5000 runs with the same configuration. Due to the employment of the Transmission Timer and the Aggregated Acknowledge schemes, APDR is a little larger than TADR.

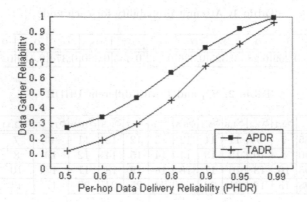

Fig. 4. Average packet delivery ratio(APDR) with different guaranteed per-link packet delivery probability

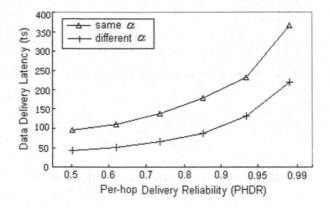

Fig. 5. Data gather latency T with different guaranteed PHDR

To compare with the algorithm proposed in [10], we investigate two run-time scenarios. In the first scenario, all the sensor nodes are assigned with the same attempt probability computed by the algorithm proposed in [10]. In the second scenario, each node has a different attempt probability, which is computed by the algorithms proposed in this paper. Fig. 5 depicts the comparison of the data gathering duration T in these two scenarios. It can be observed that the data gathering duration T has been greatly decreased when each node is assigned with different attempt probability.

By analyzing Fig.4 together with Fig.5, the tradeoff between reliability and latency is clear, and different applications can select different tradeoff between them. For example, the improvement of APDR is only 5.7% when we change PHDR from 0.95 to 0.99, but the latency has been prolonged by more than 100 time slots. For some applications that require both high packet delivery reliability and low latency, fixing PHDR with 0.95 may be more suitable.

5.3   Robustness to Link Error

In our model, we assume that packets collision is the key factor for data loss for data gathering in random access wireless sensor networks. However, in real-time scenarios, packets may also be lost due to link error caused by environmental interference. To understand the protocol behaviors in the presence of link errors, we conduct a series of simulations under different link error rate. Fig.6 shows the data gathering reliability under different link error rate when PHDR=0.99. When each link is imposed on 30% error rate, which implies that the environmental interference is very serious, APDR drops only 3.2% compared with the case that there is no channel errors.

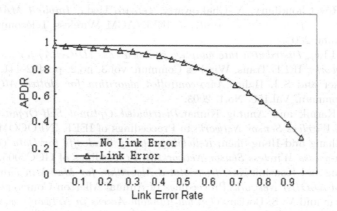

Fig. 6. Data gather reliability under different link error rate, PHDR=0.99

6   Conclusion

The high volume bursty traffic has posed special challenges for reliable and real-time data gathering in WSNs. In this paper, we employ random access schemes to tackle the problem of high degree channel contention and high probability of packet collision induced by bursty traffic. We formulate the attempt probability computation problem as an optimization problem and proposed a fully distributed algorithm to solve it for linear networks. Based on the model, we design a simple and scalable protocol RADG. Simulation results show that our algorithm has fast convergence speed. Moreover, RADG is robust to link error in essence and particularly suitable to monitor environments with high degree of interference.

Acknowledgement

This work is supported by the 21st Century Center of Excellence Program in JAIST on "Verifiable and Evolvable e-Society".

References

1. Alan Mainwaring, Joseph Polastre, Robert Szewczyk, David Culler, John Anderson, *Wireless Sensor Networks for Habitat Monitoring*,In Proceedings of WSNA02.
2. Einstein Lubrin, Elaine Lawrence, Karla Felix Navarro,*Wireless Remote Healthcare Monitoring with Motes*,In Proceedings of ICMB'05.
3. Nicolas Chevrollier, Nada Golmie, *On the Use of Wireless Network Technologies in Healthcare Environments*, IEEE Workshop on Applications and Services in Wireless Networks,2005.
4. Kirill Mechitov and Sameer Sundresh,*Cooperative Tracking with Binary-Detection Sensor Networks*.In Proceedings of ACM Sensys 03.
5. Hongwei Zhang, Anish Arora, etc. *Reliable Bursty Convergecast in Wireless Sensor Networks*, In Proceedings of MobiHoc'05.
6. Romit Roy Choudhury, A. Chakravarty, Tetsuro Ueda, *Implicit MAC Acknowledgment: An Improvement to 802.11*. IEEE/ACM Wireless Telecommunications Symposium, 2005.
7. H.Yin, H.Liu, *Distributed rate adaptive packet access (DRAPA) for multicell wireless networks*, IEEE Trans. Wireless Commun, vol.3, no.2, pp.432-441, 2004.
8. J.H.Sarker and S.J. Halme.*Auto-controlled algorithm for slotted AlOHA*, IEEE Proc. Commun, Val.150, No.1, 2003.
9. Aditya Karnik and Anurag Kumar.*Distributed Optimal Self-Organisation in a Class of Wireless Sensor Networks*,In Proceedings of IEEE INFOCOM2004.
10. Haibo Zhang and Hong Shen, *Reliability-latency Tradeoffs for Data Gathering in Random-access Wireless Sensor Networks*,In Proceedings of GCC2005.
11. Xin Wang and Koushik Kar, *Distribtuted Algorithm for Max-Min Fair Rate Allocation in ALOHA Networks*,Proceedings of Annual Allerton Conference 2004.
12. E. Altman and V. S. Borkar, *Optimal Random Access in Networks with Two-Way Traffic*, In Proceedings of PIMRC 2004.

Path Selection of Reliable Data Delivery in Wireless Sensor Networks

Liao Xiangke, Li Shanshan, Zhu Peidong, Peng Shaoliang, Cheng Weifang,
and Dong Dezhun

School of Computer, National University of Defense Technology, ChangSha, China, 410073
{xkliao, shanshanli, pdzhu, slpeng, wfangch, dong}@ nudt.edu.cn

Abstract. Multipath is a sought-after mechanism to achieve reliability along the error-prone channel in wireless sensor networks. However, its benefits are not easily explored because the critical energy constraints and the multipath interference. In this paper, we first prove that finding several disjoint paths with minimum energy consumption is an NP-complete problem, then give the near-optimal solution on how to choose path based on the accurate energy model. Furthermore, we make use of the multi-frequency characteristic of CC2420 radio and propose IEMM-FA to minimize interference and energy consumption of multiple paths. Simulation results verify its performance.

1 Introduction

Wireless sensor networks are a distributed, self-organization solution to provide sensing and computing in various environments where conventional networks are impractical. However, reliability in wireless sensor networks is an intractable issue due to the limited power and computing capability of little sensors [1][2]. Furthermore, sensors are often deployed unattended in inhospitable environments. Energy-efficiency is very critical. There is loss of network coverage when some sources can no longer send packets to the sink because all the available paths have failed. Therefore, efficiently handling losses in wireless environments assumes central importance. Besides, various factors, like interference, multi-path effect and collision, also lead to heavy loss rates on wireless links [3]. It's necessary to study how reliability can be guaranteed in such an error prone environment.

There are two well-known ways to achieve reliability on multi-hop paths: multipath and retransmission [3-6]. The essence of these techniques is to achieve reliability by adding redundancy to data transmission. Retransmission computes the expected number of transmissions. This technique is used when reliable delivery with low communication overhead is more important than latency in delivery. Multipath routing allows the establishment of multiple paths between source and destination, which provides an easy mechanism to increase the likelihood of reliable data delivery by sending multiple copies of data along different paths. By introducing such redundancy, the system can compensate for data losses caused by local channel error. Multipath routing does not require retransmission so the latency in data delivery is significantly lower. Hence this approach would be better if latency in data delivery is a more important factor than communication overhead. Since applications that need high reliability also demand real time at the same time, we use multipath as a basis to

X. Cheng, W. Li, and T. Znati (Eds.): WASA 2006, LNCS 4138, pp. 163–174, 2006.

introduce reliability here. A detailed investigation of the feasibility and performance implications of schemes using retransmission will be carried on in our future work.

This paper addresses the issue of path selection in multipath routing in an energy-efficient way. We find out that finding the optimal energy-efficient disjoint paths to achieve *desired reliability* r is an NP complete problem in a given network. Based on the accurate energy consumption model of sensor, this problem can be easily relaxed to find some near-optimal solutions. However, multipath ability may be discounted by path interference so that not only we cannot attain the desired reliability, but also energy isn't effectively utilized. In this paper, we make use of the multi-frequency characteristic of CC2420 radio and propose an Interference-and-Energy Minimum Multipath Frequency Assignment (IEMM-FA) method to construct practical near optimal multiple paths.

The rest of this paper is organized as follows. In Section 2, we briefly describe some related work. The energy model and some suggestion on transmission hop based on this model are showed in Section 3. Section 4 first proves the NP complete path selection problem by expressed in integer program, and illustrates how to find the near-optimal solution, then proposes a method with minimum interference and energy consumption (IEMM-FA). Several simulations described in Section 5 verify the obtained theoretical results. The paper ends with conclusion.

2 Related Work

There are several notions related to the reliability: coverage and deployment problem, information accuracy problem and reliable data delivery problem [1]. Coverage and deployment problem studies whether the area of interest sufficiently and moderately covered by sensor nodes; Information accuracy problem is concerned about delivering various sensor readings or improve the signal-to-noise ratio to enhance information accuracy; The last one is our focus in this paper which explores how to transport information reliably over multiple hops towards special sink. The discussion of the other two issues is beyond the scope of this paper.

In [4], multiple paths from source to sink are used in diffusion routing framework [5] to quickly recover from path failure. The multiple paths provided by such protocols could be used for sending multiple copies of each packet. [6] proposes a lightweight end-to-end protocol called ReInForM to deliver packets at desired reliability. Memory less nature of ReInForM is suitable for memory constrained sensor nodes. EAR [7] balances the dissipation of energy among the nodes on all path and try to minimize the total energy consumption, but it use braided multipath that leads to much conflict and long delay. [8] aims at prolonging the network lifetime and preserving network coverage and makes its path selection decision based on the activity field in its route reply message. [3] addresses how to achieve reliability using retransmission in minimum energy consumption. All these works use inaccurate energy model and thus haven't considered the total energy consumption of all selected paths.

[9] points out the packets on one path can interfere with the packets on another path. This is called the route-coupling problem. However it just gives some analysis and expands the capabilities of reactive routing by decomposing available route into link states to reconstruct shorter and more diverse ARP route. [10] presents a routing scheme for on-demand construction of multiple non-interfering paths by controlling

the relative distance between different paths. But in this scheme the hops of two paths differ quite often which result in unbalanced energy consumption. The situation would be worse in sparse networks. In this paper, we will take advantage of the multi-frequency characteristic of CC2420 radio to reduce path interference.

3 Hop Analysis

3.1 Energy Model

Traditional opinion often assumed that a reduction of the transmitting (or radiated) energy yields a proportional reduction of total energy consumption. Energy consuming will increase e exponentially with the increase of transmission distance. So much work has been done on controlling the hop distance for energy efficiency [11, 12] or analyzing systematic cost based on this energy model [13,14]. Actually, even without taking into account reception energy, this is not true for any practical power amplifier. In general, all transceiver energy components are summarized as:

$$E(Joule) = \theta + \alpha d^n \qquad (1)$$

Where θ is a distance-independent term that accounts for the local oscillators overhead, α represents the amplifier factor, d is the transmission distance, n could be a number between 2 and 4. The distance-independent part θ dominates the energy consumption [15,16]. Some measurement presented in [15] shows that for the MicaZ and Mica2 hardware, the total power consumption is almost independent of the transmit power. The fraction of power actually transmitted ranges from less than 0.1 percent at the lowest power setting to 1.4 percent for MicaZ and 14 percent for Mica2 at their respective highest output power levels. Therefore, short-hop routing does not yield any substantial energy benefit if more distant relay node can be reached with sufficient reliability. Table 1 illustrates the Atheros 2004 tri-mod chipset [17] energy model based on the manufacturers' data sheet. It verifies again that attenuation energy increases exponentially by the transmission distance, θ dominates the path loss and So if a more distant relay node can be reached with sufficient reliability, short-hop routing does not yield any energy benefit. therefore, causes the total power consumption to remain constant as transmission distance increases. Clearly, reducing the output power does very little to save energy, and the receive power consumption is as high as the transmit power consumption (θ).

Table 1. Energy consumption parameters for Atheros 2004 tri-mod chipset [17]

Mode	Max Output Power, αd^n (dBm)	Total Power Consumption (W)	θ (Watt)	$n_{min} \times \alpha d^n$ (Watt)
802.11a	+14	1.85 / 1.20	2.987	0.0625
802.11b	+21	1.75 / 1.29	2.727	0.3125
802.11c	+14	1.82 / 1.40	3.157	0.0625

3.2 Distinguished Long Hops

Short-hop routing has gained a lot of support, and its proponents mainly produce two arguments: reduced energy consumption and less signal interference. Actually, both arguments stem from a simplified analysis based on inaccurate channel models and neglects delay, end-to-end reliability, bias power consumption and routing overhead. [16] sheds light on this issue by listing many reasons why should we choose long-hop routing. As discussed in section 3.1, reducing output power does very little to save energy, hence we should choose long hop as long as packets can be delivered with sufficient reliability. Furthermore, since packet errors or bit errors accumulate (the end-to-end reliability is the product of the link reception probabilities), the reliability of short-hop path would be worse compared to long hop. According to [18], SIR (signal-to-noise) does not depend on absolute power levels. So increasing all transmit power levels does not have a negative impact on any packet reception probability. As far as delay is concerned, while a mean delay constraint can simply be broken down to individual links, the superlinear growth of the guaranteed delay with the number of hops in the case of hard delay constraints enforces the use of fewer (i.e. longer) hops [16]. Besides, the control traffic for routing and route maintenance is proportional to the number of nodes in the route. Also, the probability of a route break due to energy depletion and node failure clearly increases with the number of nodes involved, as well as the memory requirements for the routing tables. To sum up, routing as far as possible is a very competitive strategy in many cases. In section 4, we will select path based on this long-hop standpoint.

4 Path Selection

4.1 System Model

In our network model, each network node is assumed to be equipped with an omnidirectional antenna. A wireless network is modeled as a directed graph $G = (V,E)$, where V is the set of nodes and E is the set of directed links. Each node has a maximum transmission power of $P_{\max}$. Each directed link (i,j) has a non-negative weight (i,j), which is computed from equation (2). 2θ includes the reception power.

$$weight(i, j) = 2\theta + \alpha d_{i,j}^{\,n} \tag{2}$$

$d_{i,j}$ denotes the distance between node i and node j. Data is transmitted from source s to a destination t. If node i is closer to t than j and is within the transmission range of node j (with the maximum transmission power), there is a directed link (i,j) between node i and node j.

Each link (i,j) has a loss rate e(i,j), which is the probability that a transmission over link (i,j) fails. For simplicity, we assume that each link has equal loss rate, denoted by **er**. In order to compensate for this loss rate, we should choose multipath from s to t to achieve the desired reliability **R**. Out of many possible designs for multipath routing protocols, there exist two distinct mechanisms: *disjoint* and *braided* [4]. Disjoint multipath routing tries to construct a number of alternate paths that are node disjoint with the primary path, and each other. These alternate paths are thus unaffected by failures on the primary path, but could potentially be less desirable (e.g., maybe have longer length) than the primary path and therefore expend more energy than that on the primary path. Braided multipath routing relaxes the requirement for node disjointness. Alternate paths in a braid are partially disjoint from the primary path, not completely node-disjoint. But braided path are interfered with each other due to some share nodes and therefore affected by failures on the primary path. Furthermore, since one node can only receive one packet at the same time, the delivery delay of braided path will be much longer. Since applications that need high reliability also demand real time, we choose disjoint multipath mechanism.

4.2 Problem Statement

We refer to the general problem of finding several disjoint paths with minimum energy consumption, to achieve desired reliability **R**. Assume that P is the set of all possible paths which is composed of a set of conjointly link, more formally:

$$\forall p = (e_1, e_2, ..., e_k) \in P : head(e_1) = s \wedge end(e_k) = t \wedge end(e_i) = head(e_{i+1})$$

Where $i = 1, 2, ...k - 1$ and $e_1, e_2, ..., e_k \in E$

head(e) and end(e) represent the start and end of link e respectively. We define the total energy consumption **C** to be the sum of cost of the selected paths. An optimal solution can be found using an integer program with linear constraints. The integer program will use the following variables: let x_p, $x_{e,p}$, $x_{v,p}$ be boolean variables indicate whether path p is selected, whether link e is included in path p and whether node v is included in path p respectively (1 means yes), c_p and r_p indicate the cost and reliability of path p. The integer program computes the minimum energy consumption (3) subject to the constraint (4)-(8):

Objective: Minimum C   (3)

Constraints:

$$x_{v,p_i} + x_{v,p_j} \leq 1, \quad \forall v \in V - \{s, t\} \text{ and } p_i, p_j \in P, i \neq j \tag{4}$$

$$r_p = \coprod_{x_{e,p}=1} (1 - er), \quad \forall e \in E \text{ and } p \in P \tag{5}$$

$$1 - \coprod_{x_p=1} (1 - r_p) = R, \quad \forall p \in P \tag{6}$$

$$c_p = \sum_{x_{e,p}=1} weigh(head(e), end(e)), \quad \forall e \in E \text{ and } p \in P \tag{7}$$

$$C = \sum_{x_p=1} c_p, \quad \forall p \in P \tag{8}$$

Constraint (4) enforces no shared nodes in different path, constraints (5) and (6) enforce that the redundant multipath will compensate for the channel loss rate and data will be delivered to **t** in the probability **R**.constraints (7) and (8) ensure that the accumulated cost of all selected path to be **C**. Finally, for the integer program, all variables are required to take non-negative integer values.Integer program problem can be easily proved to be NP complete by reducing to 0-1 program, here we do not discuss it in detail. In the foliing section, we will examine how to find the near-optimal algorithm.

4.3 Finding Near-Optimal Solution

Based on the discussion in section 3, the distance-independent part θ dominates the transmission energy consumption, thus the less nodes take part in routing, the less the energy consumption. Therefore, in order to find the optimal result of the problem discussed in section 4.3, each node should use its maximum transmission power $Power_{max}$ to find its next hop neighbor. By this way, the problem can be relaxed to that we only need to find disjoint paths with the least hops, maybe they are not optimal, but the difference resulted from the different hop length (d) can be neglected due to the domination of θ. We assume that the network is densely deployed, the appropriate neighbors are located around the edges of the neighborhood. To be noticed, the neighborhood should be limited to some range that the probability of packet successfully delivery is not lower than some threshold, since wireless propagation suffers severe attenuation [19].

To achieve this, each node could only choose next hop neighbors whose received power $Power_r$ satisfies some condition, such as equation (9):

$$Power_r \geq Power_1 \; \& \; Power_r \leq Power_2 \tag{9}$$

This ensure each node choose long hop. The distances correspond to $Power_1$ and $Power_2$ are d_1 and d_2 which is shown in figure 1. Assume that some low-rate interests (also in $Power_{max}$) have been flooded throughout the network and each node contains the relative distance between itself and its neighbor. Each node knows its shortest hop number to sink. So the source node could estimate the average hop number **h** of the multipath from its multiple appropriate neighbors to sink (In general, **h** is equal to the least hops from source to sink, in sparse network, several copies could be delivered along the same path). Then the path number **N** can be computed by equation (10). Actually, we just add two constraints (11) and (12) to the NP complete problem. The problem can be relaxed since the distance-dependent part is neglectable compared to θ. However, this relaxation is not enough because there is much interference among different paths that will cause failures of data transmission and thus waste energy. In section 4.4, we are concentrated on the construction of practical multipath with minimum energy and interference based on this relaxation.

Fig. 1. Each node finds its next hop neighbor in the range of (d_1, d_2)

$$N = \frac{\log(1 - R)}{\log(1 - (1 - er)^h)} \tag{10}$$

$$\sum x_{e,p} = h, \ \forall e \in E \text{ and } p \in P \tag{11}$$

$$\sum x_p = N, \ \forall p \in P \tag{12}$$

4.4 Constructing Interference-and-Energy Minimum Multipath

Since we try to choose paths with the least hops, the spacing between different paths may be close, thus the transmission ability will be discounted by the route-coupling [9] problem. This interference hinders multipath from taking effect and energy consumption could not be saved. Therefore, we should build multiple paths with as little interference as possible.

We are enlightened by the fresh MAC protocol MMSN proposed in [20], which takes advantage of multi-frequency to use dynamic frequency assignment to minimize interference. The current WSN hardware, such as Micaz and Telos that use CC2420 radio, already provide multiple frequencies. Here we do not use frequency assignment in MAC layer (a little more complicated), but propose a new method IEMM-FA to assign frequency statically to different region around sink, based on which interference-and-energy minimum multipath can be easily constructed. Assume there are k available different frequencies, sensor node is aware of its location information. We divide the network into multiple rings around sink, and each ring has a spacing of d_1. Each ring is also divided into k sub-rings as showed in figure 2 and different frequencies are allocated to these k sub-rings in the decreasing order. The spacing of the sub-ring closer to sink should be larger than that further to sink in one ring in order to guarantee there are approximately the same number of nodes in each sub-ring. Node knows which sub-ring it belongs to based on its location and uses the corresponding frequency to transmit and receive packets. Since d_1 is the appropriate hop length (with enough length and delivery probability), then nodes in the i th ($1 \le i \le k$) sub-ring of the j th ($j > 1$) ring could transmit data to nodes in the i th sub-ring of the $j-1$ th ring simultaneity without interference. Actually, this technique divides nodes that contend for the same channel into k part, then the contention is reduced to one kth after channel assignment.

Multiple paths could be constructed in the following way: source node first computes the needed paths by equation (10). Then allocate the first hop of these paths to the k sub-rings adjacent to the sub-ring it located (If too many paths are needed, multiple copies will delivered along the same path since the path may not be the physical path). Except for the first hop, nodes in path will choose the next hop neighbor in the same sub-ring of the adjacent ring that is closer to sink. In order to construct disjoint paths, a node selected for one path is labeled and rejects the request for another path. Different nodes in the same sub-ring should choose the next hop neighbor that are not near from each other in order to reduce interference caused by contention for the same channel.

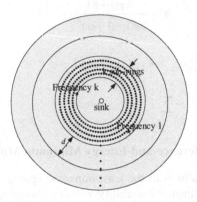

Fig. 2. Ordering frequency assignment in each ring around sink

There are some exceptions that IEMM-FA cannot find path in some frequency since space of each sub-ring is limited and distance between adjacent sub-rings is long. In this case, source will reallocate these paths to frequency that least used. Actually, IEMM-FA will be regressed to single frequency case in sparse network, however, since spacing between paths is wider in sparse network (interference is little) so multi-frequency is unnecessary. Here we only consider the densely deployment for simplicity.

The superiority of IEMM-FA is obvious. It can reduce the interference between different paths as much as possible but do not need much extra cost. Furthermore, since all paths use hop as long as possible (Although the first hop is the exception, the increase of energy consumption caused by which is just a little), the constructing result is satisfying which can be seen in section 5.

5   Evaluation

We have performed several simulations in order to verify the theoretical results. Our goal is to get a better understanding on how well IEMM-FA works relative to the optimal result of the minimum energy multiple disjoint paths constructing problem. Besides, the performance of the conflict avoidance of IEMM-FA is also examined.

We analyze a 1200 nodes network, dispersed uniformly in a square area 500m*500m. We set d_1 50m to be the appropriate transmission range in $Power_{max}$ (For simplicity, the range keeps 50m under different channel error rate in our simulations). There are five available frequencies in total. Source is located in the lower left zone and sink is adjusted for different simulation (For example, sink is adjusted to meet different hop number from source to sink).

5.1 Energy Consumption and Attained Reliability

We first give some analytical bounds on this NP complete problem. We try to find the lowest bound on the total energy consumption. Let I_E be the optimal result, for the N path satisfying the constrains, I_E is the sum of the energy consumption of these

$$I_E = c_{p_1} + c_{p_2} + \cdots + c_{p_N} \tag{13}$$

N paths, then I_E satisfies the following bounds:

$$I_E \geq N * (h * 2\theta) \tag{14}$$

In this section, we will make some comparisons with this lowest bound. For simplicity, we neglect the distance-dependent part of the energy consumption and only consider the hop number, that is, the number of θ needed for transmission. The sink is located near the centre of the area, where the Euclid distance between source and sink is 270m, that is to say source are located in the second sub-ring of the sixth ring around sink.

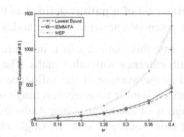

Fig. 3. Energy consumption under different channel error rate

The first simulation examines the energy consumption of IEMM-FA under different channel error rate (Figure 3). The desired reliability is 0.8. Except that compared with the lowest bound of I_E, we also give the energy consumption of traditional multipath routing (we use the method in [4] to construct several shortest paths), for short, MSP. In MSP, nodes find their neighborhood only with $0.5 * Power_{max}$. From this figure we can see that although the first hop of IEMM-FA may not be the longest hop (which result in more hops), the energy consumption of

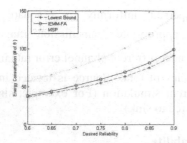 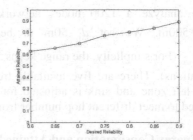

Fig. 4. Energy consumption under different desired reliability

Fig. 5. Retained reliability of IEMM-FA under different reliability

IEMM-FA approaches to the lowest bound of the optimal value. While MSP only uses $0.5 * Power_{max}$ to locate nodes' neighborhood so that more hops are needed, which result in much more energy consumption.

Figure 4 shows the energy consumption under different desired reliability. The channel error rate is 20%. With the increase of desired reliability, the more number of paths are needed to compensate for the channel loss. We can see the satisfying result of IEMM-FA again that long-hop routing can save much communication energy consumption. Figure 5 illustrates the corresponding attained reliability of IEMM-FA. Since neighborhood is effectively controlled so that each hop can guarantee certain degree of reliability, which helps IEMM-FA to guarantee the desired reliability.

5.2 Interference Avoidance

In this section, we examine the interference avoidance performance of IEMM-FA. First we define a performance metric in evaluation.

Definition 1. Influence factor (η) of a path is defined as the total number of nodes in other paths that may have potential interference with nodes in this path.

If η of one path is 0, we say this path doesn't interfere with any other paths. Otherwise, this path has **η-interference** with other paths. The average influence factor of multiple paths is defined as the average of the influence factor of each path. The interference range of two paths is double transmission range of sensor.

Figure 6 gives the average η of multipath when multi-frequency is used and not under different hop number from source to sink. In single channel case, we also use

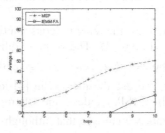

Fig. 6. Average Influence Factor under Different Hop Number

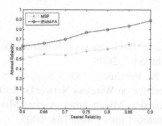

Fig. 7. Attained Reliability of IEMM-FA vs. MSP (in $Power_{max}$)

MSP to construct multiple shortest paths, but here MSP uses $Power_{max}$ to locate the neighborhood of nodes. In this figure, the superiority of IEMM-FA is obvious since at least five paths can delivery data simultaneously without interference. Since the spacing between different paths in **dense** network is close, MSP has much potential interference in data transmission. The result is alike for different channel error rates and desired reliability. We don't explicitly discuss it here because of space reason.

Interference influences delay and throughput since one has to wait if other paths that interfere with it are transmitting data. In worst case, the total throughput of two paths is less than that of one path. Here we haven't examined these effect since our focus is the reliable data delivery, we want to see how interference influences reliability. We assume that there is a MAC layer retransmission mechanism, node will retry after a random back-off if it finds the channel is busy. But data will be deleted after three trials. Figure 7 gives the attained reliability of IEMM-FA vs. MSP (in $Power_{max}$) under different desired reliability. The location of source and sink and the channel error rate are the same with those in figure 5. We can see that the attained reliability of MSP is not satisfying due to much interference among multipath. Sometimes when path number is increased, the retained reliability even decreased, which can be seen when desired reliability is 0.7 and 0.9.

6 Conclusion

Multipath routing can provide load balancing, loss compensation, lower frequency of route inquiries and congestion avoidance. These benefits make multipath routing appear to be an ideal routing approach for the error prone sensor networks. However, these benefits are not easily explored because the critical energy constraints and the multipath interference. We have proposed an energy-and-interference minimum multipath constructing method IEMM-FA based on the accurate energy model to alleviate this problem. Our future work will continue to extend the research of path selection and focus on how to effectively deal with congestion and interactional routing of multiple sources from the whole network perspective.

Acknowledgement

This work is supported by the National High-Tech Research, Development Program of China (Grant No. 2005AA121570, 2002AA1Z2101 and 2003AA1Z2060) and Granted Project 51415040205KG0151.

References

[1] Andreas Willig, Holger Karl. "Data Transport Reliability in Wireless Sensor Networks---A survey of Issues and Solutions", 2005.

[2] Dazhi Chen and Pramod K. Varshney. " QoS Support in Wireless Sensor Networks:A survey",Internatioal Conference on Wireless Networks, 2004.

[3] Qunfeng Dong, Suman Banerjee, Micah Adler, Archan Misra."Minimum Energy Reliable Path Using Unreliable Wireless Links". MobiHoc 2005.

[4] D.Ganesan, R.Govindan,S.Shenker,andD.Estrin," Highly-resilient, energy-efficient Multi path routing in wireless sensor networks",In Mobile Computing and Communications Review(MC2R) Vol 1.,No.2,2002.

[5] C.Intanagonwiwat, R.Govindan, and D.Estrin, "Directed diffusion:a scalable and robust communication paradigm for sensor networks", In MOBICOM,pages 56-57,2000.

[6] B. Deb, S. Bhatnagar and B. Nath , "ReInForm: Reliable Information Forwarding using Multiple Paths in Sensor Networks", Proc. of IEEE LCN, 2003.

[7] SHAH, R.C., et. al., "Energy Aware Routing for Low Energy Ad Hoc Sensor Networks", IEEE Wireless Commun. Networking Conf., vol. 1, pp. 350–355, March 2002.

[8] V. Ponduru, B. Mukherjee, and D. Ghosal," A Distributed Coverage-Preserving Multipath Routing Protocol in Wireless Sensor Networks", Technical Report, Department of Computer Science, University of California, Davis, March 2004.

[9] Pearlman, M. R., Haas, Z. J., Sholander, P., und Tabrizi, S. S." On the impact of alternate path routing for load balancing in mobile ad hoc networks". MobiHOC 2003.

[10] Thiemo Voigt, Adam Dunkels, Torsten Braun. "On-demand Construction of Non-interfering Multiple Paths in Wireless Sensor Networks".Informatik 2005.

[11] L.C. Zhong, "The impact of the transmission power level", technical document, http://bwrc.eecs.berkeley.edu/People/Grad Students/czhong/restricted/phase2.pdf, J 2003.

[12] L.C. Zhong, J.M. Rabaey and A. Wolisz, "An integrated data-link energy model for wireless sensor networks", ICC 2004, Paris, France, June 20-24, 2004.

[13] Bhaskar Krishnamachari, Yasser Mourtada, and Stephen Wicker. "The Energy-Robustness Tradeoff for Routing in Wireless Sensor Networks", Autonomous Network Research Group (ANRG) Technical Report TR02-001, 2002.

[14] Vivek Mhatre, Catherine Rosenberg, "Design guidelines for wireless sensor networks: communication, clustering and aggregation", Ad Hoc Network (2004), p45-63.

[15] MIN, R., et. al., "Top Five Myths about the Energy Consumption of Wireless Communication", Mobile Comput. and Commun. Review, vol. 1, Num. 2, 2003.

[16] Martin Haenggi, Daniele Puccinelli, "Routing in Ad Hoc Networks: A Case for Long Hops", IEEE Communication Magazine, October, 2005.

[17] MEHTA, S., et al., A CMOS Dual-Band Tri-Mode Chipset for IEEE 802.11a/b/g Wireless LAN, 2003 IEEE Radio Frequency Integrated Circuits (RFIC)Symposium, pp. 427–430, June 2003.

[18] Martin Haenggi. "Twelve Reasons not to Route over Many Short Hops", IEEE VTC' 04 , pp. 48-59.

[19] G. S. Lauer. *Packet Radio Routing*, chapter 11, pages 351–396. Prentice Hall, 1995.

[20] Gang zhou, Chengdu Huang, He Tian, et al. "MMSN: Multi-Frequency Media AccessControl for Wireless Sensor Networks". INFOCOM 2006.

An Efficient and Robust Routing Protocol for Data Aggregation

Xiwei Zhao[1], Kami (Sam) Makki[2], and Niki Pissinou[1]

[1] Telecommunication & Information Technology Institute,
Florida International University, Miami, FL 33174, USA
[2] Department of Electrical Engineering & Computer Science,
University of Toledo, Toledo, OH 43606
xzhao001@fiu.edu, kmakki@eng.utoledo.edu, pissinou@fiu.edu

Abstract. Wireless Sensor Network (WSN), which is free from infrastructure, greatly enhances our capability of observing physical world. However, WSN's independent and un-attended usages, which are generally supposed to be advantages, also limit its power supply and life expectancy. As a result, energy efficiency is a critical issue for any WSN implementation. In-network processing (a process of data local convergence and aggregation) which intends to minify data volume locally can greatly reduce the energy consumption of data delivery over long distance to the sink. However, open problems are still remain, such as, how to carry out in-network processing, and how to combine routing scheme to the sink (corresponding to the long distance delivery) with in-network processing. For any WSN application, a pre-assumption is vital that there must be a physical signal field (e.g. a field of sensing signal) that bridge physical event to sensors, otherwise WSN can not work. Moreover, the physical signal field can be used for data local convergence. Our proposed algorithm exploits the gradient direction of the physical signal field. Along the gradient direction of the physical signal field, sensory data at sensors will also converge to local extremes of the physical signal field. In addition, this routing scheme for in-network process requires zero overhead, because the physical signal field exists naturally. The proposed schemes are simple to be implemented, and details of the implementation are discussed. Simulation shows that the schemes are robust, adaptable, and reliable to variation of physical events.

Keywords: Wireless sensor network, in-network processing, in-network aggregation, routing of in-network processing, self-organization in ad hoc network, applications for ad hoc network.

1 Introduction

In recent years, developments of micro-electronics promote application of WSN. On the other hand, no matter how powerful the battery embedded in sensor nodes is, WSN's independent and un-attend usages destine that their power supply will be expired in some time and the sensor node will die finally. Thus, energy efficiency is always a critical issue for WSN implementation.

It's widely accepted that Network can be treated as Database [1], and so is Wireless Sensor Network. Furthermore, all applications of WSN are data-central. Thus, many

X. Cheng, W. Li, and T. Znati (Eds.): WASA 2006, LNCS 4138, pp. 175–186, 2006.

techniques of database, such as data filtering and data aggregation, can also be employed by WSN. Thus, delivering all sensory data to the sink would not be necessary. Instead, those semantic-related data should be aggregated locally, and only those high-level data (or aggregated data) are needed to be transmitted to the sink. The whole process for aggregation is called in-network processing [2]. In-network processing can reduce the traffic load of long distance delivery, and thus save the power and bandwidth resources of WSN.

The semantic-related data must converge to some nodes first before aggregation. However, semantic-related doesn't mean location-related and vice versa. If two sensor nodes are far away from each other with semantic-related data, in-network processing would not be necessary because the delivery cost for aggregation is expensive. In other words, only those location-related nodes with semantic-related data can benefit from in-network processing.

The goal of any application is to monitor some physical phenomenon among the region. On the other hand, the physical phenomenon should distribute among the region. Only in this way, some sensor nodes could sense the phenomenon at its location, and the sensory data corresponds to the intensity of the phenomenon at that location. Among the region, the intensity of the phenomenon constructs a physical signal field. In fact, this physical signal field is prerequisite for us to monitor the physical phenomenon by WSN. In this paper, the physical signal field of the phenomenon would be exploited for sensors clustering and data converging. Following the Cost-field routing [3][4], the algorithm we proposed here makes the semantic-related data converge to the local extremes of the physical signal field. As no node is predefined as the header of the cluster and all nodes are same, the proposed algorithm enhances the robustness of WSN. In addition, this routing scheme for in-network process requires zero overhead, because the physical signal field exists naturally.

In section 2, related work are summarized. In section 3, we analyze the physical signal field of physical phenomenon in detail. The algorithm is presented in section 4. In section 5, we discuss the performance of the algorithm and do simulation. In section 6, the conclusion is drawn.

2 Related Work

In [5], the data-centric property of WSN applications is discussed, so is the framework of in-network processing. In their scheme, query diffuses among the region of one cluster (directed diffusion). Nodes are activated by the query, and begin to collect related data. The related data will be delivered along the reverse path of the query, and aggregated at intermediate nodes when data pass by. In [6], the energy costs and delay of in-network processing are investigated regarding to the node density. Three suboptimal routing schemes of in-network processing are proposed. The first one is named "Center at Nearest Source (CNS)". In this scheme, the cluster header is the node that is nearest the sink. The data aggregation is conducted at the cluster header. The second one is "Shortest Paths Tree (SPT)", in which shortest path tree from the sink to source nodes is used. In addition, the data aggregation can be conducted along the path when data meet at junction nodes. The third one, which is called "Greedy Incremental Tree (GIT)", is an iterative scheme. At the beginning, the GIT is just the shortest path between the sink and the nearest source. At next step, the nearest source to the current tree is connected to the tree by the shortest path. The whole process would stop when all source nodes are connected to the tree. For all those three schemes, the routing paths must be constructed before data delivery.

The throughput of in-network processing is investigated in [7]. All nodes are sorted by its function. Each node has different computing capability, and each link has different transmitting cost. The proposed algorithm is decentralized, for each node makes its own decision by the knowledge of itself and its neighbors. Data packets are enhanced to be agent-based in [8], and the routing path to the sink is decided by agent-based packets themselves along their way. Whenever a packet arrives at a node, it will ask the node to select its next step based on the current information, such as energy remaining of the node and communication cost of next step. In [9], nodes are still clustered by the location, and the cluster headers are predefined. However, the efficiency of the proposed scheme is discussed in the case that the sink moves.

From the summary above, the routing path can be determined hop by hop. Some schemes explore the possibility of aggregating data along the routing path to the sink. In this way, when a data packet meets another data packet at a node on its routing way, both packets will be aggregated at that node. Some solutions even group the nodes by the branches of routing path tree toward the sink.

In [10], two schemes are proposed with the goal of energy efficiency. The nodes are clustered along the path toward the sink. In addition, the data sampling are not only triggered by the time, but also by the variation of sensed signal. Following the sampling strategy, an idle scheme of sensor nodes can be induced. The same idea can also be found in [11] and [12]. LTP (local target protocol) [13] is based on gradient routing, but the data could detour concave holes of WSN. Just as normal gradient routing, search phase of LPT finds out the node which is closer to the terminal, and direct transmission phase sends the data out. On the other hand, when no node can be found during the search phase and the data hasn't arrived the terminal, backtrack phase is incurred, and the data packet is sent back to the node where it came from.

Training protocol is an innovative scheme for nodes clustering [14]. Among 2-dimension area, two nodes would be selected to initiate a training process. Each of those two nodes broadcasts the message among the whole network, and constructs the cost-field around itself. Thus, every node has two cost values which can be used as coordinates of its location. Those nodes with similar coordinates can be grouped to form a cluster; furthermore, the distance to the sink can even be calculated by coordinates. In [15], the local clusters are associated with the physical events, and are bounded by the signal amplitude that sensor has. The threshold is given in advance, and the boundary of the cluster is identified by the node whose signal amplitude is less than the threshold. Cluster leader is elected within the boundary, and the leader should be the node with highest signal amplitude within the cluster.

Above all, Routing scheme of in-network process is always considered within the cluster which is instinctively location-aware. Thus, any routing schemes within the cluster are fit for in-network processing. On the other hand, physical events are always location aware. If routing scheme is associated with physical events, the routing scheme can be location aware directly, and we don't need to take care of the issues of node clustering and the header election any more.

2.1 Gradient Routing and Beyond

In 2000, Dr. Robert D. Poor proposed his Gradient Routing in Ad hoc (GRAd) network [3]. The distinguished aspect of Ad hoc network is its ad hoc, in other words, none of the node know others without hearing something. Thus, on-demand routing, which follows the rule that "if you wish to be spoken to, you must speak first", is an obvious choice for the message delivery. GRAd belongs to on-demand routing, in addition, it assume that all links of the network are symmetrical. In [4], gradient routing is extended to WSN which is also a kind of Ad hoc network. Similar to the previous work, the scheme GRAdient Broadcast (GRAB) constructs and maintains the field of cost value, and each sensor can get gradient direction by probing its neighbor nodes. In the scheme of GRAB, a band of the routing paths are used for the data delivery. Morcover, the width of the band can also be controlled.

According to GRAB, each node can measure the cost of transmitting data to the neighbor. The sink propagates advertisement (ADV) packets by which one data item, cost value, could be distributed and changed hop by hop. The cost value of all nodes together with their location forms the cost field. If we let height denotes the cost value of each point among the region, the whole field forms a funnel in 3-D space.

When a packet is sent from a node, it should include the cost value of that node. All its neighbors whose cost values are smaller than that of packet may forward the packet (Be aware that the cost value included in packets should be changed hop by hop). In this way, more than one delivery path exist, and all of those paths construct a band path to the sink. GRAB even introduce a mechanism to control the width of the bind. An interesting concept of "CoS" (Center of Stimulus) is also proposed in GRAB. In their words: any stimulus would create a field of sensing signal strength and more than one node (maybe tens of hundreds) may detect the stimulus, if each of those nodes sends a report, then resources will be wasted heavily. Thus, an election is necessary among those nodes that detect the same stimulus, and only one node would be selected to send the report to the sink. This node is called "CoS". The election of CoS based on the field of sensing signal strength, and only the node with the strongest signal generates a report. This node is CoS. However, as the paper focus on presenting the scheme of "GRAB", which is about the routing algorithm from sources to the sink, the discussion of in-network processing is simplified to be CoS election.

2.2 In-Network Processing

Regarding to energy efficiency, sensory data should be aggregated locally which is called in-network processing. Commonly, sensory data in WSN are semantics-related. This makes a large room for in-networking aggregation. On the other hand, source nodes may distribute among WSN: some of them may close to each other; others may far away from each other. It's obvious that only those sources that close to each other need to be clustered together for in-network processing.

Most schemes cluster nodes of WSN no matter if it's a source. Some schemes separate the whole region by square patches, and each patch corresponds to a cluster. One node of each cluster acts as cluster header. The cluster header can be elected from nodes of the cluster, or be predefined. Some schemes cluster the nodes by the routing path to the sink. For example of the shortest routing path tree, branches are used for clustering. Thus, nodes that locate on the same branch are in the same cluster. In this way, in-network aggregation can be conducted along the data routing path. In this scheme, sensory data that is far from the sink can pass by the source that is near the sink if they are at same branch. The aggregation can also be conducted hop by hop.

There are still some schemes that cluster sources based on sensing signal strength field. To find out the boundary of physical phenomenon, some schemes set the minimum threshold of sensed signal strength. The cluster header is elected by the sensed signal and the strongest one is selected [15]. Just as discussed above, in GRAB, CoS election is also to find out the cluster header from sources and only the data of Cos is sent to the sink.

3 Physical Phenomenon

For any physical phenomenon, the sensing signal must exist, otherwise how can we sense the phenomenon? Let's have an example: a group of people distribute in an area and act as sensors, and now an object moves toward the area just as a physical phenomenon emerges. Somebody see the object coming, somebody see a black dot moving, and somebody see nothing. When the object goes into the area, more people see the object clearly, but there are still some people who stand far away from the object can't see it

Now, we describe the example in another way: there is a sight field around the object and the field intensity of any specific point is associated with the distance from the point to the object. Thus, if a person stands at a point that is much closer to the object, the field intensity is higher and he will see the object clearly. And if another person stands at a point which is a little bit far from the object, the field intensity is lower and he will see the object vaguely. By the distance to the object increasing, the field intensity decreases and the image of the object which is sensed by the people will be smaller and vaguer and finally disappear.

We expand the example above in a general way that any physical event has a field around itself, and sensor would generate data based on the field intensity. In the following discussion, we will call it "the physical signal field". The physical signal field is the way that bridges physical event to sensor nodes. Without the physical signal field, there would be no signal sensed by the sensor, then how can we know that whether the physical event happened or not? Moreover, how can we make sensors or WSN work? It's true that physical event is always companied by a physical signal field. However, there are still some facts need to be clarified.

First, it's not necessary that the physical event should always be surrounded by its physical signal field. Furthermore, the location where the event occurs can be different from where its physical signal field locates. In such case, how to identify the location where the event truly occurs is another issue of how to understand data gathered from WSN. Second, the physical signal fields that caused by different events can be overlapped. Thus, still let the strength of sensed signal be the height at each location, the shape of the physical signal field can even look like mountains spanning among the region.

The physical signal field can also be used for routing, just as the cost-field routing does. As shown in the picture above, along the valley and saddle, the region can also be separated into small patches, corresponding to the cluster of WSN. Along the direction of field intensity increasing, data can be converged to each peak of mountains, and then aggregated at the peaks.

4 Algorithm

At each node of sensor network, routing algorithm should be split into two parts. One is for delivering message to the sink, and the other is for in-network process. Corresponding to those two parts, all messages are assigned with two tags. One is "in-network process" (INP); the other is "sink routing" (SR). We assume that the part of routing to sinks is given. (In fact, the routing algorithm can be Reverse Path Forwarding, Cost-Field Based Forwarding, Geographical Forwarding, etc.) Here, only the part of in-network process routing is present. For this part of algorithm, two subroutines need to be executed separately and simultaneously at each node. Those two are written in pseudo codes which is following the structure of C language.

The first subroutine is used to identify the tag of the message. When the node received a message, it should check the tag of that message first. If the tag is INP, then the message is put into the buffer; if not, its tag must be SR, then the message would be delivered to the sink based on the sink routing scheme (We assume that algorithm of routing to sinks is given,). If the message is generated by the node itself, the message will be tagged INP, and put into buffer.

The Pseudo Codes for the First Program

```
if (message is generated at the node)
{
        add the title INP to the message
        put the message into the buffer
}
else if (message is received from other nodes)
{
        check the title of the message
        if (the title is INP)
```

```
        {
            put the message into the buffer
        }
        else if (the title is SR)
        {
            send the message toward sink
        }
    }
}
```

The second subroutine is used to probe its neighbors periodically, and send message out. When a predefined timer is run out, all messages in the buffer are aggregated. The aggregated message can be one message, or can be several messages. Anyway, we will treat it as one unit no matter how many messages it is. Next we should assign tag to the aggregated message. If the node is at a local peak of the physical signal field, the aggregated message should be tagged "SR", and delivered by the given sink routing algorithm. Otherwise, the tag is "INP", and the aggregated message is sent along the gradient direction of the physical signal field toward the local peak.

The Pseudo Codes for the Second Program

```
    while (the pre-defined timer is run out)
    {
        pack messages in the buffer together (aggregation)
        let Val= data sensed by the sensor
        probe Val of neighbor nodes
        if (exist nodes with Val larger than Val of itself)
        {
            title the packed message with INP
            select the node with largest Val
            send the packed message to this node
        }
        else
        {
            title the packed message with SR
            send packed message toward sink
        }
        empty the buffer
        reset the timer
    }
```

5 Simulation and Analysis

To investigate the performance of the proposed scheme, many aspects need to be evaluated: such as energy efficient, the variation of the physical signal field, and the cases that some nodes may die. Contrast to all other clustering scheme, our scheme reduce the overhead greatly, such as energy cost for electing cluster header and constructing routing tree within the cluster. In addition, the scheme is robust even if some nodes die, and flexible to the variation of the physical signal field.

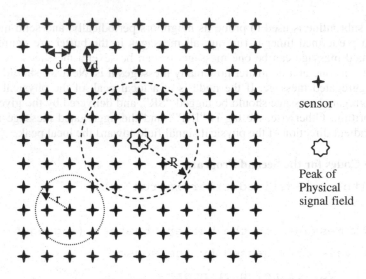

sensor

Peak of
Physical
signal field

Fig. 1. Sensors on uniform square grid

Considering an area, in which nodes are arranged on a uniform square grid, the distance between each pair of neighbor nodes is "d". The transmitting radius of each node is "r". To simplify the analysis, only one peak is set in the physical signal field. The physical signal field covers a round area with radius "R", and the field intensity decreases by the distance to the peak increasing.

Of course, "r" should be larger than "d", otherwise no link exists but a bunch of isolated nodes. Let "E" be the energy cost of each hop transmission per message, and the data are only aggregated at the field peak. The entire energy consumption of in-network processing should be

$$= \sum_{i=1}^{\lfloor R/r \rfloor} \pi \left[(i \cdot r)^2 - (i-1)^2 \cdot r^2 \right] \cdot 1/d^2 \cdot i \cdot E + \pi (R^2 - \lfloor R/r \rfloor^2 \cdot r^2) \cdot 1/d^2 \cdot \lceil R/r \rceil \cdot E$$

$$= \pi \cdot \frac{1}{d^2} E \cdot r^2 \lceil R/r \rceil \cdot \left\{ R^2/r^2 - \frac{1}{6} \lfloor R/r \rfloor - \frac{1}{3} \lfloor R/r \rfloor^2 \right\}$$

in which $\lceil R/r \rceil$ is the ceiling of R/r; $\lfloor R/r \rfloor$ is the floor of R/r, and the node density is $1/d^2$.

From the expression above, the energy consumption for in-network processing is direct proportion to the node density. In addition, the consumption will increase when

R/r increases. If R is smaller than r, the total average energy cost of in-network processing equals to ER^2/d^2. When some nodes die and the node density decrease, d would increase. However, the upper bound of d is r. If d equals to r, the energy cost is $\pi E\lceil R/r \rceil \{R^2/r^2 - \lfloor R/r \rfloor/6 - \lfloor R/r \rfloor^2/3\}$, and then the ratio of R/r is the only factor of energy cost

The simulation is on a square area 400m X 400m, and sensor nodes are arranged on a uniform square grid with d equal to 12m, 16m and 20m. For each case, the node intensity equals to 1/144; 1/256; 1/400. The transmitting radius r of each node is 25m. The physical signal field covers a round area which radius can be varied from 10m to 100m. We locate the peak of the field at the center of the area.

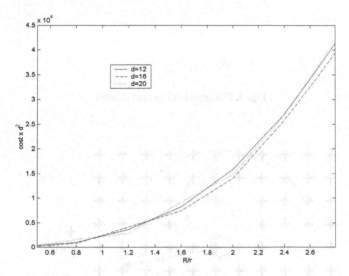

Fig. 2. Communication cost per node

From the figure 2, we can see that three curves overlap together, which infers that average communication cost of each node is direct proportion to the node density.

Let d and r be fixed, then if R/r is too large, the performance of the algorithm will get worse. From the figure 3, we can see that the communication cost will increase even through the increment of the physical signal field area is considered. As we have r fixed, so if R is too large, the average communication cost of each node will also increase.

In some cases, several neighbor nodes die, and a hole may emerge in WSN. For those holes with convex boundary, our algorithm could even make packets detour the hole for in-network processing. Even for some holes with concave boundary that can't be detoured, according to our algorithm, original cluster will break up into 2 or more small cluster, and the data are gathered to the local peaks. Just as figure shown below, besides the peak of physical signal field, sensor A will act as another local peak. All nodes inside the field will split into two clusters.

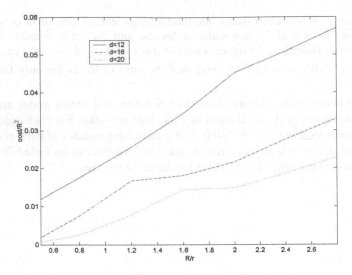

Fig. 3. Communication cost density

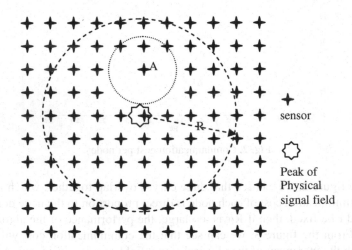

Fig. 4. Concave hole in WSN

In fact, those concave holes are much common, and they can also prevent from making the cluster too large even through R is large. From the figure 5, 1000 sensor nodes are distributed among the area of 400m X 400m. The node intensity should be 1/160 which corresponds to d equals to 12.65m, and we can see concave hole are much common. In such case, even through only one large physical signal field exists, sensor nodes can still be clustered into several small groups.

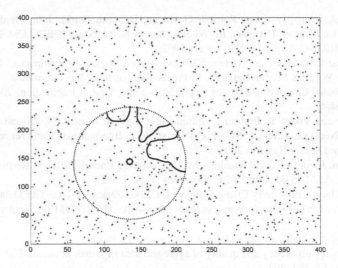

Fig. 5. Concave hole with random distribution

6 Conclusion and Future Work

From the analysis above, our scheme is robust and reliable. However, there are still two cases we need to discuss even more. One is that several neighbor nodes have same intensity value of the physical signal field, or in other words, the physical signal field is flat around the area of those nodes. In such case, we should introduce some idling scheme to let part of those nodes sleeping. The other case is that one cluster covers too large area and too many sensor nodes are included, just as we analyzed above, the performance of the scheme may get worse.

In fact, if we adopt cost-field routing scheme for each sensor forwarding its data to the sink, then each sensor should have two scale values. One is the cost value to the sink, and the other is intensity value of the physical signal field. Those two values can also be used as coordinate of each sensor, and in this way, sensor nodes can also be divided into several clusters according to their coordinates, and such clustering scheme is obvious location aware.

References

1. Wai Fu Fung, David Sun, Johannes Gehrke. COUGAR: the network is the database. SIGMOD Conference 2002: 621.
2. John Heidemann, Fabio Silva, Chalermek Intanagonwiwat. Building Efficient Wireless Sensor Network with Low-Level Naming. In Proceedings of the 18th ACM symposium on Operating systems principles 2001.
3. R. Poor. Gradient Routing in Ad Hoc Network.
   http://www.media.mit.edu/pia/Research/ESP/texts/poorieeepaper.pdf 2000.
4. F. Ye, G. Zhong, S. Lu, and L. Zhang. GRAdient Broadcast: A Robust Data Delivery Protocol for Large Scale Sensor Network. ACM Wireless Network (WINET), 11(2), March 2005.

5. Chalermek Intanagonwiwat, Ramesh Govindan, Deborah Estrin, John Heidemann, and Fabio Silva. Directed Diffusion for Wireless Sensor Networking. IEEE/ACM TRANS. ON NETWORKING, VOL. 11, NO. 1, Feb. 2003

6. 6. Bhaskar Krishnamachari, Deborah Estrin, Stephen Wicker. The Impact of Data Aggregation in Wireless Sensor Network. In Proceedings of the 22nd International Conference on Distributed Computing Systems Pages: 575 - 578   Year of Publication: 2002 ISBN:0-7695-1588-6

7. Bo Hong and Viktor K. Prasanna. Optimizing a Class of In-network Processing Applications in Networked Sensor Systems. The 1st IEEE International Conference on Mobile Ad-hoc and Sensor Systems 2004

8. Long Gan, Jiming Liu, and Xiaolong Jin. Agent-Based Energy Efficient Routing in Sensor Network. AAMAS'04, July 19-23, 2004. New York, USA.

9. Fan Ye, Haiyun Luo, Jerry Cheng, Songwu Lu, Lixia Zhang. A Two-Tier Data Dissemination Model for Large-scale Wireless Sensor Network. MOBICOM'02, September 23–28, 2002, Atlanta, Georgia, USA.

10. Mohamed A. Sharaf, Jonathan Beaver, Alexandros Labrinidis, Panos K. Chrysanthis. Balancing energy efficiency and quality of aggregate data in sensor network. The VLDB Journal (2004) 13: 384–403.

11. Jonathan Beaver, Mohamed A. Sharaf,Alexandros Labrinidis, Panos K. Chrysanthis. Location-Aware Routing for Data Aggregation in Sensor Network. In Proceedings of Geo Sensor NetworkWorkhop, 2003.

12. Jonathan Beaver, Mohamed A. Sharaf, Alexandros Labrinidis, Panos K. Chrysanthis. Power-Aware In-Network Query Processing for Sensor Data. In Proceedings of the 3rd ACM MobiDE Workhop, 2003.

13. Ioannis Chatzigiannakis, Sotiris Nikoletseas and Paul Spirakis. Efficient and Robust Protocols for Local Detection and Propagation in Smart Dust Network. Mobile Network and Applications 10, 133–149, 2005

14. A. Wadaa, S. Olariu and L. Wilson. Training a Wireless Sensor Network. Mobile Network and Applications Feb.2005 Volume 10 Issue 1-2.

15. Qing Fang, Feng Zhao, Leonidas Guibas. Lightweight Sensing and Communication Protocols for Target Enumeration and Aggregation. MobiHoc '03, June 1-3, 2003, Annapolis, Maryland, USA

An Area-Based Vertical Motion Estimation on Heterogeneous Wireless Networks

Ing-Chau Chang[1], Ching-Hsiang Wang[2], and Lin-Huang Chang[2]

[1] Department of Computer Science and Information Engineering, National Changhua
University of Education, Changhua, Taiwan, R.O.C
icchang@cc.ncue.edu.tw
[2] Graduate Institute of Networking and Communication Engineering, ChaoYang University of
Technology, Wufeng County, Taichung, Taiwan, R.O.C
shang@yles.tcc.edu.tw, lchang@cyut.edu.tw

Abstract. In this paper, we will propose an *area-based vertical motion estimation* (AVME) scheme to efficiently and accurately predict target wireless networks and corresponding target cells for the next handoff of the mobile node (MN) on the increasingly prevalent heterogeneous wireless network environment which consisting of several different wireless networks such as wireless LAN (WLAN), third generation cellular network (3G), etc. We adopt the *back propagation neural network* (BPN) model in this AVME scheme to generate mobility patterns of MNs by training the BPN model with historical handoff information of these MNs. By using the IBM City Simulator [1] to create the city plan and motions of all MNs, simulation results show that our AVME scheme on heterogeneous wireless networks can achieve higher level of predication accuracy for next handoff than traditional cell-based prediction scheme does on a single wireless network, but with less resources and computations.

1 Introduction

Future communication environment will be composed of different types of heterogeneous wireless networks, where the mobile node (MN) will be equipped with several wireless network interfaces. In this kind of heterogeneous wireless network, as shown in Figure 1, different sizes of wireless cells, which belong to different wireless networks, may coexist in the same space. Depending on characteristics of these cells, they can be divided into three types, i.e., the macro-cell, such as GSM and 3G, micro-cell, such as IEEE 802.11a/b WLAN, and pico-cell, such as Bluetooth, networks. If the MN moves from one cell to another in the same wireless network, we can detect signal strengths of these cells in the cell boundary, where signals of neighboring cells overlap, for the traditional horizontal handoff. However, under heterogeneous wireless networks, different types of cells are deployed to cover the same geographical area to form a complex layout pattern, for example, micro-cell *B, C, D, E, F, G, H* and *I* can overlap with macro-cell *A*, as shown in Figure 1. For macro-cell *A*, the MN may hand over to macro-cell *J* in its cell boundary of the macro-cell network or a micro-cell at any location within *A* if this micro-cell provides more resources to satisfy MN's requirements such as user preference, quality of service (QoS), etc. This kind of handoff which occurs among different kinds of wireless network cells is called as *vertical handoff* [2].

X. Cheng, W. Li, and T. Znati (Eds.): WASA 2006, LNCS 4138, pp. 187–198, 2006.

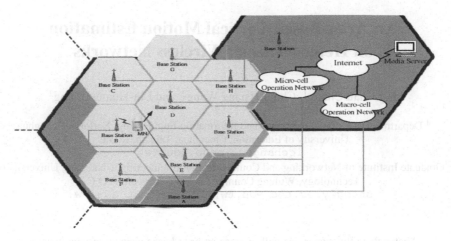

Fig. 1. Architecture of heterogeneous wireless networks

Researchers have found lots of challenges for vertical handoff in this envisioned heterogeneous wireless environment. Zhang [3] proposed a connection manager to handle two vertical handoff scenarios, one is the handoff from WWAN to WLAN and the other from WLAN to WWAN. The objective of the former is to improve QoS by handing over to WLAN with the traditional physical and MAC layer sensing approaches and that of the latter is for the MN to stay in the WLAN as long as possible with their accurate FFT-based decay detection method before WLAN link breaks. However, this work assumes the WLAN is optional such that the vertical handoff is triggered by extensions of traditional WLAN signal detection approaches, without considering various metrics described above. McNair [4] argued any handoff process operation was a three-stage process that includes handoff decision, radio link transfer, and channel assignment. Opposite to the Zhang's work, it contains the proposed vertical handoff decision policy which is based on the specific cost function to simultaneously evaluate various metrics for vertical handoff. However, this work did not mention when to trigger the vertical handoff decision policy and two latter stages for achieving seamless vertical handoff with required QoS.

For maintaining multimedia QoS during MN's handoff, lots of researchers worked on the location management issue for a single wireless network to choose the minimal number of neighboring cells for resource reservation when the MN moves [4]. Hwang proposed the direction-based motion prediction scheme to predict future motion direction of MN [5]. Soh used the global positioning system (GPS) to know MN's current location [6]. Misic proposed the event-based approach to predict possible target cells for next handoff by referring to MN's current location, motion direction, etc. and found that the number of target cells were reduced as the MN moves toward the cell boundary [7]. Based on the theory of mobility pattern, Yu proposed to train the *back propagation neural network* (BPN) with MNs' important motion characteristics such as current location, velocity, direction, etc. as input parameters and then to generate handoff possibilities to all target cells as output values of this converged BPN [8]. However, these methods were only applicable to the traditional single wireless network where horizontal handoffs occur in the hexagonal cell boundary and cannot be directly used on heterogeneous wireless networks where vertical handoffs may happen at any position within the cell, which is overlapped with different types of cells.

Based on motion histories of the MN over heterogeneous wireless networks, we will propose an *area-based vertical motion estimation (AVME)* algorithm in this paper. AVME first automatically generates the heterogeneous cell layout, i.e., *resource map and corresponding areas*, of the current cell of the MN for vertical handoff by detecting wireless signals from base stations (BS) of heterogeneous cells, then uses historical handoff data of each area to train the BPN for building mobility patterns of MNs, and finally uses the trained BPN to predict possible areas which consists of target networks and corresponding target cells for resource reservation of next handoff efficiently and accurately. This paper is organized as follows. In section 2, details of the AVME approach will be described. Simulation environment, parameters, results and discussions will be shown in section 3. Section 4 will conclude this paper.

2 Area-Based Vertical Motion Estimation (AVME)

The flow of AVME consists of three phases. The first two phases are preprocesses before AVME works for prediction as the MN moves. The first phase is to discover neighboring cells for each cell in different wireless networks and generate the corresponding *external* and *internal resource maps* before the BPN training. The second phase uses historical handoff data of each area to train the BPN network, according to topology information in the external resource map. Finally, our AVME enters the third phase to predict next possible areas with the trained BPN network, if the MN is leaving its current cell, i.e., executing an *external handoff*. However, if the MN requests to change its QoS requirements inside its current cell, AVME will find whether any cell of different wireless networks can provide better QoS than the current cell. This kind of handoff is called the *internal handoff* in this paper. By referring to resource maps, AVME selects possible target cells from areas with high BPN prediction possibilities, i.e., *AP values*. Cells which cannot support MN's requirements like moving speed, QoS, cost, etc., should be filtered out from these target cells. Those remaining cells will be sorted to form candidate cells for efficient resource reservations.We will focus on flows before candidate cell selection for the external handoff.

2.1 Wireless Resource Map Discovery and Demarcation of Handoff Area

For executing area-based vertical motion estimation (AVME) to guarantee multimedia QoS during MN's vertical handoff, the first phase of AVME needs to automatically build the wireless resource map, which was first proposed by Ohta with manual configuration [9], that records which cells exist and how they overlap with each other in the space by analyzing locations where MN can receive signals, such as beacons, of these cells. There are two kinds of wireless resource maps. One is the external resource map which records all neighboring cells in the boundary of a specific cell and the other is the internal resource map which records all cells inside a cell. The former is used when the MN leaves its current cell boundary and, maybe vertically, hands over to a neighboring cell for continuing the connection and the latter is for the MN to vertically hand over to other kinds of cells to achieve better QoS or reduce communication costs within its current cell. In Figure 2, cell *1, 4, 6, 7, 8, 9* and *0* are all belong to the same macro-cell network; cell *2, 3* and *5* are micro-cells in the boundary of macro-cell *0*. In the resource map, each record is represented as the form of (Net_i, $Cell_j$, $\theta_{min}(Cell_j)$, $\theta_{max}(Cell_j)$), where Net_i is the wireless network identifier, $Cell_j$ is the wireless cell identifier, $\theta_{min}(Cell_j)$ and $\theta_{max}(Cell_j)$ are the minimal and maximal angles, where MN can receive signals of $Cell_j$, between the current cell and the neighboring cell *j*.

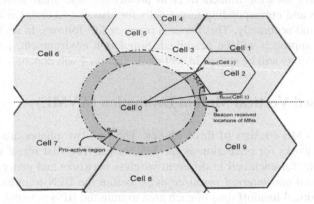

Fig. 2. External Resource Map of cell *0*

In the following, we will describe how to set up size of the *pro-active region* (PR) and demarcate neighboring cells of the external resource map into handoff areas, which is shown in Figure 3. For reducing numbers of predicted target cells and raising prediction accuracy of vertical handoff, our AVME will be triggered only when the MN enters the pre-defined pro-active region of the current cell. Because different kinds of cells have different sizes and support different maximal motion velocities, the width of the PR for cell *i*, i.e., $D^i_{Pro-active}$ in Equation 1, must be larger than the maximal motion distance, which is the product of the maximal velocity ($\overline{V}$) of the MN and the fixed time duration (τ) for the BS to monitor possible handoff, and the pre-defined PR width, which is the product of the radius (R^i) and percentage of the PR width over the cell radius (δ^i) of cell *i*. Accordingly, the minimal distance, i.e., R^i_{out}, from the BS to the edge of the PR of cell *i* is calculate by Equation 2.

$$D^i_{Pro-active} = max(\overline{V} \times \tau, R^i \times \delta^i), \ 0 \le \delta \le 1 \tag{1}$$

$$R^i_{out} = R^i \times (1 - \delta^i) \tag{2}$$

AVME then divides external space into sectors of handoff areas with an angle θ from the BS of the cell. According to the distance between the BS and PR (R_{out}) and the maximal motion distance ($\overline{V} \times \tau$), the value of θ is calculated by Equation 3, which is shown in Figure 3. Numbers of handoff area (N) can be easily calculated by Equation 4. These handoff areas are called Area $1, 2,..., N$, respectively. The range of each area is represented by its minimal angle, $\theta_{min}(Area_i)$, and maximal angle, $\theta_{max}(Area_i)$. The space inside PR of the current cell is called as Area 0. In Figure 4, we list the algorithm to decide which external cells belong to each handoff area by comparing the maximal and minimal angles of them, which are recorded in the external resource map. Depending on the value of θ and the layout of external resource map, a handoff area may contain several different kinds of cells or a cell may span over numbers of areas. For example, in Figure 5, handoff area 3 contains macro-cell 1 and micro-cell 2 and 3; macro-cell 1 and micro-cell 2 belong to both area 2 and 3; area 0 consists of internal cells, ICell $1, 2$ and 3.

$$\theta = 2 \times ATan(\frac{\overline{V} \times \tau}{R_{out}})$$
(3)

Number of handoff area (N)= $360°/\theta$
(4)

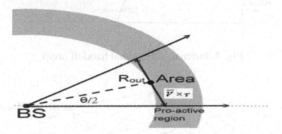

Fig. 3. Demarcation of pro-active region and handoff area

```
for (i=1; i<=N; i++) {//each External handoff Area i
    for each External cell j{
        if ( θmax(Areai) ≥ θmin(Cellj) and θmax(Cellj) ≥ θmin(Areai) )
            add Cellj into Areai ;
}}
```

Fig. 4. The algorithm to deduce external cells to handoff areas

2.2 BPN Neural Network Training

After establishing of wireless resource maps, our AVME feeds historical handoff information into the BPN neural network for training in the second phase. Whenever the MN enters the PR, its current BS continues to monitor and record its location information every τ units of time until it vertically hands over to a neighboring cell. For increasing prediction accuracy of vertical handoffs when the MN leaves its current cell, AVME first analyzes historical vertical handoff information of MNs to find their mobility patterns. These historical information consists of the ID of destination handoff area where the vertical handoff actually occurs, and a series of four location information, including the distance (D_{MN}) and angle (θ_{MN}) between the MN's hand-off location and the BS, the average velocity (V_{MN}) and motion direction angle ($\theta_{V(m)}$) during one τ units of time, from the MN enters the PR till the handoff. AVME proposes to train a three-layer back propagation neural network (BPN), which is shown in Figure 6 and consists of the input, hidden and output layers, with four historical information (D_{MN}, θ_{MN}, V_{MN} and $\theta_{V(m)}$) as input values to the input layer and hand-off possibilities of all areas as output values of this BPN. Note that the hidden layer is composed of 10×10 nodes and the output transfer function is *logsig*.

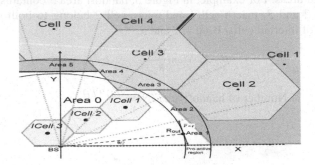

Fig. 5. Internal and external handoff areas

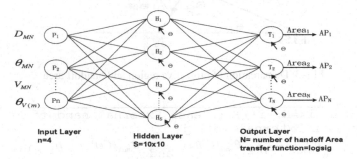

Fig. 6. The BPN architecture adapted by AVME

2.3 Target Cells Prediction Using BPN Neural Network

After the training process of BPN is completed, AVME can use this BPN in the third phase to predict the destination handoff area of the MN whenever the MN enters the PR. The input layer of BPN accepts four values of the MN, which are monitored at the first τ units of time after the MN enters the PR, and its output layer finally generates N output values (AP_i) for N handoff areas. If the normalized AP value of any handoff area is larger than the pre-defined threshold value T, all external cells belonging to this handoff area, which are recorded in the external resource map in the resource discovery process, will be selected as target cells for next vertical handoff. If a cell span over several neighboring handoff areas and APs values of these areas are larger than T, it would be selected as a target cell more than once. These redundant

```
if ( D_MN > R^i_Out ){ //••Pro-active region
  for each handoff Area i {
    AP_i is the normalized BPN output value for Area i;
    if ( AP_i > threshold T) {
      for each external cell j in this Area i
        select cell j as an external target cell;
}}}
drop redundant external target cells;
```

Fig. 7. External target cells selection algorithm

target cells should be dropped before the candidate cell selection process. The external target cell selection algorithm is listed in Figure 7.

3 Simulations

3.1 Simulation Environments

In our simulation, we generate motion information of MNs by City Simulator [1] of IBM alphaWorks project according to parameter values and their distribution functions in Table 1. This simulation is executed on a city map of 6000×6000 square meters. As shown in Figure 8, this map consists of straight crossroads, buildings along roads, a dark river in the right side, a green grassland in the most right side, etc. As progress of the simulation, locations of MNs will be changed and shown as small white points on this city map. On this city map, two wireless networks, with 9 macro-cells and 25 micro-cells respectively, provide network connections by two different wireless signals. The radius of the macro-cell, i.e., the large blue circle in Figure 9, is 800 meters, and that of the micro-cell, i.e., the small red circle, is 400 meters. All these cells are formed the hexagonal layout.

Table 1. Simulation parameters for City Simulator

Simulation parameters	Parameter values
Minimal Interval for the MN to change its motion velocity and direction	τ =5 secs
Initial velocity of MN	Normal distribution with a mean of 2 KM/h and a variance of $1(KM/h)^2$
Velocity variation of MN	Uniform distribution with dV=[-0.5, 0.5]kM/h
Initial direction of MN	Uniform distribution with angle Q=[-π, π]
Direction variation of MN	Uniform distribution with dQ=[-0.2π, 0.2π]
Duration of MN's connection	Normal distribution with the mean of 600 secs and the variance of 200 secs

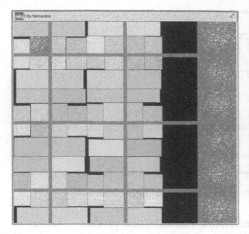

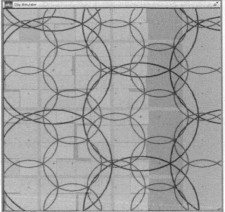

Fig. 8. The city map for City Simulator   **Fig. 9.** Cell layouts on the city map

In this simulation, we will compare prediction accuracies of the traditional cell-based and our area-based schemes to prove that our area-based scheme can achieve higher level of prediction accuracies but with much less system resources and computation times. These two schemes are described below.

Traditional Cell-Based Scheme
This traditional scheme is used on a single wireless network to predict the same kind of cells for horizontal handoff. In this paper, we extend this cell-based scheme by using a BPN for each wireless network to predict target handoff cells on each network, according to the location information of the MN. They are called as the "*cell-based-macro*" and "*cell-based-micro*" schemes in this paper, respectively. For extending these traditional schemes for vertical handoffs in heterogeneous wireless networks, we must first allocate two copies of system resources and spend twice of time and computation efforts to train these two BPN networks. Then depending on the type of MN's current cell, we can predict target micro-cells or macro-cells from the same network of the current cell by using the cell-based-micro or cell-based-macro BPN network respectively. Finally, we have to include all cells of another wireless network, which are overlapped with each target micro-cell or macro-cell by referring to the external resource map, to generate all target cells for candidate cell selection. However, with this approach, the higher the number of different wireless networks is, the more system resources and computation efforts for all BPN networks consume. In this paper, these two cell-based schemes are considered as reference values of prediction accuracies for our proposed area-based AVME on vertical handoff of heterogeneous wireless networks. We will show that the area-based AVME achieves at least the same, and even higher, level of prediction accuracy for target cells as the cell-based-macro and cell-based-micro schemes do in the following, which means it can be used as an efficient approach for mobility management in heterogeneous wireless networks with less consumed resources and computation efforts. We define Equation 5 to calculate the *prediction accuracy* (A_i^c) for neighboring cell i with two cell-based schemes as the ratio of total number of actual handoffs to cell i over that predicted by

their corresponding BPN for all M MNs over N_k^c predictions, where $AP_{i,j,k}^c$ is the normalized AP value of the j-th prediction of cell i for MN k in the cell-based scheme.

$$A_i^c = \frac{\text{total number of actual handoff to cell}_i}{\text{total number of predicted handoff to cell}_i}$$

$$= \text{total number of actual handoff to cell}_i \Big/ \sum_{k=1}^{M} \sum_{j=1}^{N_k^c} AP_{i,j,k}^c \tag{5}$$

Proposed Area-Based Scheme

After the AVME target cell prediction and selection process as described above, all possible target cells in handoff areas with their AP values larger than the threshold are found. We select the final candidate handoff cell from all target cells with equal possibilities and then continue executing AVME on this cell. Comparing to traditional cell-based schemes, this area-based scheme consumes less computation time and system resources only with one BPN network. If the area-based scheme can achieve at least the same level of prediction accuracy as the cell-based ones, it is efficient to be adopted for vertical motion estimation in heterogeneous wireless networks. We define Equation 6 to calculate the prediction accuracy (A_i^a) of neighboring area i for the area-based scheme as the ratio of number of actual handoffs to area i over that predicted by the AVME for all M MNs over N_k^a predictions, where $AP_{i,j,k}^a$ is the AP value of the j-th prediction of area i for MN k in the area-based scheme.

$$A_i^a = \frac{\text{total number of actual handoff to area}_i}{\text{total number of predicted handoff to area}_i}$$

$$= \text{total number of actual handoff to area}_i \Big/ \sum_{k=1}^{M} \sum_{j=1}^{N_k^a} AP_{i,j,k}^a \tag{6}$$

We execute City Simulator three times with 5000, 10000 and 20000 MNs for 100 cycles respectively. The timestamp and location information, i.e., the distance (D_{MN}) and angle (θ_{MN}) between the MN's location and the BS, the average velocity (V_{MN}) and motion direction angle ($\theta_{V(m)}$), of these MNs at each cycle are recorded and considered as inputs of BPN to generate N output values (AP) for N handoff areas or cells. We will compare prediction accuracies of cell-based and area-based schemes with four different percentages (10%, 40%, 70%, 100%) of information for training BPN and remaining information (90%, 60%, 30%, 100%) for prediction. Note that the upper bound of prediction accuracy is generated by applying 100% of information for both training and prediction of BPN. Three area-based schemes, i.e., 6, 12 and 18 neighboring areas, are simulated. For reducing the time spent on training the large amount of MN information and increasing accuracy for BPN prediction, we will first pre-process all information to locate specific data, which are recorded when handoffs are executed at boundaries of cells, and then trace back to gather related information about trajectories of MNs in proactive regions. Depending on   distances (D_{MN}) and angles (θ_{MN}) of these trajectory data, they are classified into corresponding cells for the cell-based scheme and into corresponding areas for the area-based scheme by referring to the wireless resource map. Finally, we choose the first 10%, 40%, 70% and 100% of classified data of each cell/area for training BPN respectively. In opposition to simply choosing the first 10%, 40%, 70% and 100% of original data for training some cells/areas only, our approach can train as much cells/areas as possible to increase prediction accuracy.

After sorting AP values of six neighboring cells generated by BPN with the descending order for cell-based-macro and cell-based-micro schemes, we will calculate prediction accuracies of them by Equation 5. For the area-based scheme, BPN will generate AP values of all 6/12/18 areas. In order to compare prediction accuracies of 12/18 area-based schemes with cell-based-macro and cell-based-micro ones, we will sum up AP values of every two or three areas, starting from the X axis, into six values and then sort them with the descending order. In practice, MN can hand over to a neighboring macro(micro)-cell/area only, which means that the handoff probability to this cell/area is 1 and probabilities to other five cells/areas are 0. However, BPN predictions can not generate such kind of definite and ideal outcomes in most cases. We propose to compare *average mean square errors* (AMSE) of the cell-based-macro, cell-based-micro, and 6/12/18 area-based schemes by first measuring the *mean square error* (MSE) between practical and predicted handoff probabilities for every handoff in all N_k handoffs of MN k and then averaging MSEs over all handoffs of M MNs with Equation 7, where $X_{i,j,k}$ are results after sorting $AP^a_{i,j,k} / AP^c_{i,j,k}$ of the j-th handoff prediction for MN k with the descending order, which means $X_{1,j,k}$ is the highest value and $X_{6,j,k}$ is the lowest one among all six $AP^a_{i,j,k} / AP^c_{i,j,k}$ values.

$$\text{AMSE} = \sum_{k=1}^{M} \sum_{j=1}^{N_k} \sqrt{(X_{1,j,k}-1)^2 + (X_{2,j,k}-0)^2 + (X_{3,j,k}-0)^2 + (X_{4,j,k}-0)^2 + (X_{5,j,k}-0)^2 + (X_{6,j,k}-0)^2} \Bigg/ \sum_{k=1}^{M} N_k \qquad (7)$$

3.2 Simulation Results

With 5000, 10000 and 20000 MNs, we can observe results for 10%, 40% and 70% of data for training in Figure 10, 11 and 12, respectively. (1) Because radius of the macro-cell (800m) is twice of that of the micro-cell (400m), the region occupied by a macro-cell is four times of that of a micro-cell. Further, due to the majority of MNs move along roads or buildings on the city map of City Simulator, handoffs of MNs with the cell-based-macro scheme are more concentrated on fewer neighboring cells than those with the cell-based-micro scheme. Consequently, the cell-based-macro scheme, which is denoted as "*Macro-cell*" in these figures, achieves smaller AMSE values than the cell-based-micro one, which is denoted as "*Micro-cell*". (2) Because the MN with the 6-area scheme can hand over to both kinds of micro-cells and macro-cells, AMSE values of the 6-area scheme fall between those of the cell-based-macro and cell-based-micro schemes, which only consisting of one kind of cells. (3) Since area-based schemes with number of areas larger than six provide more classes for BPN to predict, the prediction accuracy of each area will raise. This will lead to the

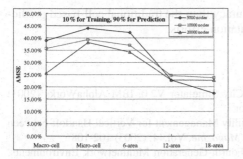
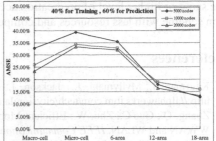

Fig. 10. AMSE values with 10% for training and 90% for prediction

Fig. 11. AMSE values with 40% for training and 60% for prediction

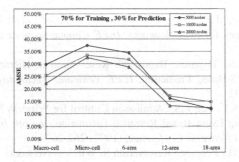

Fig. 12. AMSE values with 70% for training and 30% for prediction

fact that AMSE values of the six areas after combining every two or three neighboring areas with the 12-area and 18-area schemes are lower than those of traditional cell-based-macro, cell-based-micro and 6-area schemes. (4) Under the same training percentage, the more the number of MNs is, the more handoff data are available for BPN training. For most of cases in these simulations, AMSE values of 20000 MNs are the lowest ones and those of 5000 MNs are the highest ones, no matter the training percentage is. However, if there are not sufficient handoff data to train the BPN network, BPN prediction accuracies and AMSE values may be lower than those of 12-area or 18-area schemes with 5000 MNs in these figures. Consequently, the area-based scheme achieves high availability and prediction accuracy on the envisioned heterogeneous wireless network environment.

4 Conclusion

In this paper, we propose an AVME scheme to efficiently and accurately predict target cells on heterogeneous wireless networks for the next handoff of MN by first discovering the wireless resource map, demarcating handoff areas and finally training the BPN model to generate mobility patterns of MNs in advance. We also show in simulations that our AVME scheme on heterogeneous wireless networks can achieve the same or higher level of predication accuracy than the traditional cell-based prediction scheme with less resources and computation efforts.

References

1. Kaufman, J., Myllymaki, J., Jackson, J.: City Simulator V2.0, IBM AlphaWorks (2001) http://alphaworks.ibm.com/tech/citysimulator
2. Zhang, Q., Guo C., Zhu, W.: Efficient Mobility Management for Vertical Handoff between WWAN and WLAN, *IEEE Communication Magazine*, Vol.44. (2003) 102-108
3. McNair, J., Zhu, F.: Vertical Handoffs in Fourth-Generation Multinetwork Environments, *IEEE Wireless Communications*, (2004) 8-15
4. Misra, A., Das, S., Dutta, A., McAuley, A., Das, S.K.: IDMP-based Fast Handoffs and Paging in IP-based 4G Mobile Network, *IEEE Communications Magazine*, Vol. 40. (2002) 138-145
5. Hwang, H.W., Chang, M.F., Tseng, C.C.: A Direction-Based Location Update Scheme with a Line-Paging Strategy for PCS Networks, *IEEE Communications Letters*, Vol. 4. (2000) 149 -151
6. Soh, W.S., Kim, H.S.: Dynamic Bandwidth Reservation in Hierarchical Wireless ATM Networks using GPS-Based Prediction, *IEEE Vehicular Technology Conference (VTC)*, Vol.1. (1999) 528-532
7. Misic, J., Chanson, S.T., Lai, F.S.: Admission Control for Wireless Networks with Heterogeneous Traffic using Event Based Resource Estimation, *the 6th International Computer Communications and Networks Conference*, (1997) 262-269
8. Yu, W.W.H., He, C.H.: Resource Reservation in Wireless Networks Based on Pattern Recognition, *IEEE International Joint Conference on Neural Network (IJCNN'01)*, Vol. 3. (2001) 2264-2269
9. Ohta, K., Yoshikawa, T., Nakagawa, T., Isoda, Y., Kurakake, S., Sugimura, T.: Seamless Service Handoff for Ubiquitous Mobile Multimedia, *IEEE PCM*, (2002) 9-16

A Density Control Algorithm for Surveillance Sensor Networks

Yang Shen[1], Xianglan Yin[1], Hua Chen[1], Wangdong Qi[1], and Hao Dai[2]

[1] Institute of Command Automation, PLA Univ.of Sci. &Tech., Nanjing 210007, China
[2] Chinese Electronic equipment and System Engineering Corporation,
Beijing 100039, China
{sy95414@hotmail.com, sy197610@163.com}

Abstract. Density control is a key technique in dense sensor networks for prolonging network's lifetime while providing sufficient sensing coverage. In this paper we present a new density control algorithm called ESSC(Enhanced Sponsored Sector Coverage) based on the SSC(Sponsored Sector Coverage) proposed by Tian Di. ESSC algorithm takes note of the deficiency of the SSC algorithm and modifies the model of SSC to minimize the active node number. Analysis and experimental results show that ESSC can use up to 15%~25% fewer active nodes than SSC while promising the performance of the network surveillance.

Keywords: SSC, ESSC, Sponsored Sector, Coverage.

1 Introduction

With the rapid development of MEMS(micro-electro-mechanism system) and SOC(system on chip) the micro-sensors with ability of sensing, computing and communicating can be used for various applications (e.g., environment monitoring and predicting, structure state surveillance, military reconnaissance, intrude detection and evaluation of beating effect)[1][2][3][4]. Since the sensors have limited battery life and are deployed in remote areas or dangerous battlefield, it is infeasible to recharge the batteries on tens of thousands of them. Once energy is used up, sensors can not work any more. To prolong the network lifetime, we always deploy more nodes than needed which alternate between working state and sleeping state. In this network, the node density is very high(up to 20 nodes/m$^{3[5]}$). If all the nodes are in working state, the system performance will be affected in several ways. For one, much energy will be wasted (power consumptions in transmission, reception and sleep mode are 60mW, 12mW and 0.03mW[6]). When some event happens, many sensors will be trigged and send a lot of packets. That will result in excessive interference, cause collision in MAC layer and reduce the traffic carrying capacity. Hence we propose density control technique to mitigate the above effect on sensor network by limiting the density level.

Xu et al. present GAF[7] (Geographical Adaptive Fidelity algorithm). In this work the monitored area is divided into many grids. Within each grid only one node stays up and the rest go to sleep. Cerpa and Estrin present ASCENT[8] (Adaptive Self-Configuring sEnsor Networks Topologies), in which each node measures the number of active neighbors and the per-link data loss rate then decides whether to sleep or

X. Cheng, W. Li, and T. Znati (Eds.): WASA 2006, LNCS 4138, pp. 199–205, 2006.

keep awake. Ye et al. present PEAS[6][9] (Probing Environment and Adaptive Sleeping), a probing-based distributed density control algorithm. In this algorithm each node checks if there exist any active neighbor nodes around itself by probing when it occasionally wakes up. If there exist active neighbor nodes, probing node will sleep again. Otherwise it will start to work.

Tian et al. devise SSC[10] (Sponsored Sector Coverage) which is based on the model of Sponsored Sector and judges if its coverage area is completely covered by the neighbors' coverage areas. If it does, the node will go to sleep to save energy. GAF, ASCENT and PEAS do not take into account the complete coverage problem. When a node takes off itself "blind points" maybe appear in the network. SSC algorithm is based on the complete coverage. But it only considers the neighbor nodes which are at a distance of Rs (sensing range) and not consider the neighbor nodes which are at a distance of 2Rs. That increases the number of active nodes, some of which are covered completely by other nodes and may be turned off. Thus a lot of energy is wasted. In this paper a new density control algorithm called ESSC(Enhanced Sponsored Sector Coverage) is presented. The new method based on the model of enhanced sponsored sector turns off the redundant active nodes so as to save energy.

The rest of paper is organized as follows. In Section 2 we introduce the basic principles of SSC and its deficiency. In Section 3 we propose the ESSC algorithm. Simulation results are present in Section 4. Finally we conclude the paper in Section 5.

2 SSC Algorithm

2.1 Introduction

Some definitions and theorems are presented in following:

Sensing area $S(i)$ ——the sensing area of node i is a circle centered at this node with radius Rs. That is to say any node which locates in the circle can be sensed by node i.
Neighbor set $N(i)$ — — the neighbor set of node i is defined as: $N(i) = \{ j \mid j \in s(i), j \neq i \}$.

Sponsored Sector $S_{j \to i}$ ——Suppose nodes i and j are neighbors and sensing areas $S(i)$ and $S(j)$ are intersected at point P_1 and P_2. As illustrated in Figure 1, the sector bounded by radius N_1P_1 , N_2P_2 and inner arc P_1P_2 is defined as the sponsored sector by node j and node i, and is denoted as $S_{j \to i}$.

Lemma 1——if $\bigcup_{j \in N(i)} S_{j \to i} \supseteq S(i)$, then $\bigcup_{j \in N(i)} (S(i) \cap S(j)) \supseteq S(i)$.

In SSC each node in the network autonomously and periodically makes decisions on whether to turn on or turn off itself only using local neighbor information. A node decides to turn it off when it discovers that its neighbors can help it to monitor its whole sensing area. As illustrated in Figure 2, the sponsored sectors of node 0, node 1 and node 3 are $S_{1 \to 0}, S_{2 \to 0}, S_{3 \to 0}$. According to Lemma 1 the sensing area of node 0 is completely covered and it can switch to sleeping state.

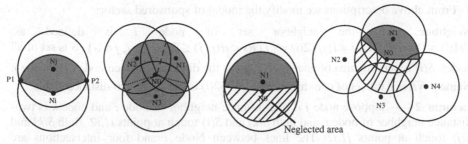

Fig. 1. $S_{j\to i}$ **Fig. 2.** $\bigcup_{j\in N(i)} S_{j\to i} \supseteq S(i)$ **Fig. 3.** Neglected area   **Fig. 4.** Deficiency of SSC

2.2 Deficiency of SSC

It is easy to deduce that the range of the sponsored sector angle defined in Neighbor N(i) is $[120°,180°)$. By calculating we know the 10%~50% of the sensing area of one node is covered by neighbor nodes. Namely at most half of sensing area is covered if only considering sponsored sector. In Figure 3, when two nodes are very close the sensing area of node 0 is almost covered by sensing area of node 1. But the area of sponsored sector calculated from SSC algorithm accounts for only about 50% of the sensing area of node 0. In Figure 4 the node 0 is actually covered by its neighbor nodes but the union of sponsored sectors calculated from SSC algorithm is less than 360 degree. So node 0 has to work. The reason is only neighbors at a distance of Rs (called one-distance neighbor) are considered in SSC algorithm and neighbors at a distance of 2Rs (called two-distance neighbor) are ignored. The result is many nodes have to work even if they are actually covered by other nodes completely. That wastes amount of energy.

3 ESSC Algorithm

According to [12] the locations of nodes randomly deployed can be modeled by a stationary two-dimensional Possion point process. It has two following characteristics: (1) The density of the Possion point process is λ. The number of nodes located in an area A of region S, N(A), follows a Possion distribution of parameter $\lambda \| A \|$, where $\| A \|$ represents the some area of the region;

$$P(N(A) = k) = \frac{e^{-\lambda\|A\|}(\lambda \| A \|)^k}{k!} \tag{1}$$

(2) Given n nodes in area A, the locations of nodes are uniformly and independently distributed in the area A.

From above definition we can know the expectation of the number of the nodes in area A is $\lambda \| A \|$. Thus the number of one-distance nodes of one node is $\lambda\pi Rs^2$ and the number of two-distance nodes of it is $4\lambda\pi Rs^2$. The number of two-distance nodes is larger than number of one-distance nodes. Even if a node is not covered completely by its one-distance nodes it may be covered by its two-distance nodes with high probability.

From above descriptions we modify the model of sponsored sector:

Neighbor set——the neighbor set of node i is defined as: $N1(i) = \{ j \mid j \in S(i), j \neq i \}, N2(i) = \{ j \mid Rs < d(i, j) \leq 2Rs, j \neq i, j \in S \}$, S is set of all nodes. $S(i)$ is sensing area of node i. $d(i, j)$ is the distance between node i and node j. Namely $N1(i)$ is the set of one-distance nodes. $N2(i)$ is the set of two-distance nodes.

Lemma 2——Suppose node j is one-distance neighbor of node i and node k is two-distance neighbor of node i, and both $S(k)$ and $S(i)$ touch at points $i1,i2$. Both $S(k)$ and $S(j)$ touch at points $j1,j2$. The lines between Node i and four intersections are L_{i1}, L_{i2}, L_{j1}, L_{j2}. Then the sector between the lines which are two middle ones of the four lines and $S(i)$ is the covered area defined as $S_{j,k \to i}$, as illustrated in Figure 5.

Sponsored sector——Composed of two parts, one is the sector between node and its one-distance neighbors, as illustrated in Figure 1, $S_{j \to i}$. The other is $S_{j,k \to i}$.

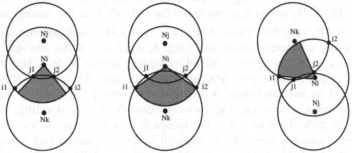

(a)choosing Lj1 and Lj2 (b)choosing Li1 and Li2 (c) choosing Li1 and Lj2

Fig. 5. $S_{j,k \to i}$

Lemma 3 — — if $\bigcup\limits_{j \in N1(i)} S_{j \to i} \bigcup\limits_{j \in N1(i), k \in N2(i)} S_{j,k \to i} \supseteq S(i)$, then $\bigcup\limits_{j \in N1(i)} (S(i) \cap S(j)) \bigcup\limits_{j \in N1(i), k \in N2(i)} S_{j,k \to i} \supseteq S(i)$. Lemma 3 can be deduced directly from Lemma in [11].

ESSC algorithm is based on the new model of sponsored sector. Active nodes judge whether their sensing area is covered completely by active one-distance neighbors and two-distance neighbors. If the sensing area is covered completely the node turns off itself so that energy can be saved.

4 Simulation Results

To evaluate the proposed design of ESSC, we make following assumptions: (1) the sensing area of each node is a circle with the same radius; (2) the communication radius is at least twice as large as sensing radius. So the network is connected from the Lemma 1 in [11]; (3) locations of nodes is random in region which follow Possion Distribution; (4) Each nodes knows its location and locations of all neighbors at a distance of 2Rs.

We conducted a simulation study in a 100×100 region. Initially all the nodes are in working state. If a node switches to sleeping state after completing ESSC algorithm, its neighbors do not see the node when they make decision whether they should go to sleep. To calculate the coverage degree of network, we divide network into 1×1 cells, if the center of a cell is within the sensing area of a working node, then we think the cell is covered by the node. The performance metrics of interest are: (1) number of active nodes, defined as the number of active nodes after completing the algorithm; (2) average coverage degree D, i.e. each point of network can be monitored by at least D

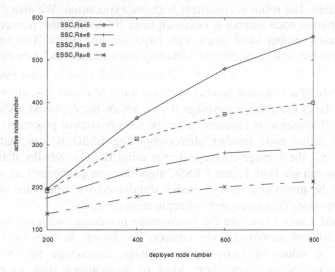

Fig. 6. Deployed node num vs active node number

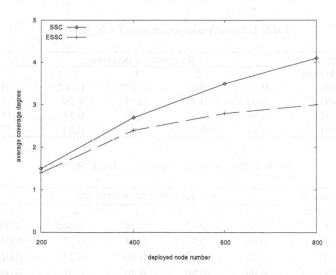

Fig. 7. Deployed node number vs average coverage degree(Rs=5)

active nodes. The metric reflects the monitoring quality for network; (3) Ks-coverage percentage, defined as the percentage of the deployed area that can be monitored by at least Ks active nodes. The metric reflects the monitoring quality for network.

The deployed node number are 200, 400, 600, 800 respectively. We try two different sensing radius: 5 and 8. Each data point reported below is an average of 20 simulation runs unless specified. Figure 6 shows the result of deployed node number versus the active node number. From Figure 6 we can see that the saving of active nodes by ESSC against SSC goes up to about 15%~25% when the sensing range is fixed. This is due to two-distance neighbor nodes of current node that are used in ESSC algorithm. The result is consistent with our expectation. We also discover that when the deployed node number is increased from 200 to 800, the increasing trend of the active node number slow down with large sensing radius. The reason is the number of current node's neighbors including one-distance and two-distance is in proportion to $\lambda * Rs^2$. As illustrated in Figure 6, with large sensing range of 8 the increasing trend of active node number slow down in ESSC and SSC algorithms.

Figure 7 shows the average coverage degree versus the deployed node number in the network. The metric is measured after the density control process is completed. Because the active node number after completing ESSC is less than that after completing SSC, the average coverage degree using ESSC is smaller than that using SSC. Also we can see from Figure 7 ESSC algorithm can guarantee that some area of the network be monitored by 2~3 nodes simultaneously when the node density reaches some value. This meets most of application demands.

Table 1 and Table 2 compare the Ks-coverage percentage achieved by ESSC and SSC with different deployed node number. As shown in two Tables, for two algorithms, the values of 1-coverage percentage, 2-coverage percentage and 3-coverage percentage are very close. Most of applications such as environment monitoring, structure state monitoring, tracking of mobile vehicles and so on only

Table 1. Ks-coverage percentage of SSC (Rs=5)

Deployed node num	Ks-coverage percentage				
	1	2	3	4	5
200	0.77	0.43	0.175	0.062	0.012
400	0.92	0.77	0.53	0.29	0.11
600	0.98	0.91	0.76	0.51	0.25
800	0.99	0.96	0.86	0.65	0.37

Table 2. Ks-coverage percentage of ESSC(Rs=5)

Deployed node num	Ks-coverage percentage				
	1	2	3	4	5
200	0.75	0.42	0.16	0.045	0.009
400	0.94	0.75	0.44	0.15	0.04
600	0.98	0.85	0.60	0.23	0.07
800	0.99	0.90	0.70	0.27	0.09

need 1~3 nodes to complete task. So 1~3 nodes suffice for these applications. When Ks is larger than 3 Ks-coverage percentage achieved by ESSC is smaller than that achieved by SSC apparently. This is because ESSC turns off redundancy nodes to save energy and at the same time the possibility of more active nodes monitoring an area is reduced. But most applications do not need so many nodes to monitor an object. ESSC can meet requirements of most of applications.

5 Conclusion

In this paper we propose a new density control algorithm ESSC based on model of enhanced sponsored sector. ESSC is fully localized and turns off the active nodes that are covered completely by other nodes and guarantees the monitoring performance. Simulations show that ESSC outperforms the SSC algorithm with respect to the number of active nodes needed (decreasing 15%~25%), and meet requirements of most of applications in the performance of Ks-coverage percentage and average coverage degree.

References

1. IF Akyildiz, W Su, Y Sankarasubramaniam and E Cayirci . Wireless Sensor Networks: A Survey, Computer Networks. 2002.
2. D Estrin, R Govindan, J S Heidemann, and S Kumar . Next century challenges: Scalable coordination in sensor networks. Proceeding of ACM MobiCom99.
3. J M Kahn, R H Katz and K S J Pister . Next century challenges: Mobile networking for "smart dust". Proceeding of ACM MobiCom99.
4. A Mainwaring, J Polastre, R Szewczyk and D Culler. Wireless sensor networks for habitat monitoring. First ACM International Workshop on Wireless Workshop in Wireless Sensor Networks and Applications (WSNA 2002).
5. E Shih, S Cho, N Ickes, R Min, A Sinha, A Wang and A Chandrakasan. Physical layer driven protocol and algorithm design for energy-efficient wireless sensor networks. Proceeding of ACM MobiCom01.
6. F Ye, G Zhong, S Lu and L Zhang. Peas: A robust energy conserving protocol for long-lived sensor networks. The 23nd International Conference on Distributed Computing Systems (ICDCS).
7. Y Xu, J Heidemann and D Estrin. Geography-informed energy conservation for ad-hoc routing. Proceeding of ACM MOBICOM01.
8. A Cerpa and D Estrin. Ascent: Adaptive self-configuring sensor networks topologies. Proceeding of Infocom 02.
9. F Ye, G Zhong, S Lu and L Zhang. Energy efficient robust sensing coverage in large sensor networks. Technical report, UCLA.
10. D Tian and N D Georganas. A coverage-preserving node scheduling scheme for large wireless sensor networks. First ACM International Workshop on Wireless Sensor Networks and Applications.
11. H. Zhang and J. Hou . Maintaining Sensing Coverage and Connectivity in Large Sensor Networks. MobiCom 03.
12. L Benyuan and T Don. A Study of the Coverage of Large-scale Sensor Networks. The First IEEE International Conference on Mobile Ad-hoc and Sensor System. 2004.

Adaptive Weighted Clustering for Large Scale Mobile Ad Hoc Networking Systems

Tinku Rasheed[1], Usman Javaid[1], Laurent Reynaud[1], and Khaldoun Al Agha[2]

[1] France Telecom R&D, 2 Avenue Pierre Marzin, 22307 Lannion, France
{tinku.mohamedrasheed, usman.javaid,
laurent.reynaud}@francetelecom.com
[2] LRI, University of Paris XI, 91405 Orsay, France
alagha@lri.fr

Abstract. Constructing stable and reliable weight-based clusters which can provide faster convergence rates and performance results for dynamic routing is a challenging task in mobile ad hoc networks. In this paper, we propose an adaptive framework for weight estimation and dissemination which considers decisive node properties in determining a node's suitability for becoming clusterheads and employs adaptive cluster radius and dynamic network constraints as a weight dissemination criterion. It is observed that the proposed algorithm is suitable for scalable ad hoc networks and is adaptable for any cluster formation decisions based on weighted or cost metric approaches. We present a cluster formation and maintenance algorithm that forms well distributed clusters and performs adaptive control to increase the cluster life time so as to optimize routing efficiency. The simulation results corroborate that this protocol is the best suited scheme for adaptive stable clustering and control overhead reduction in large scale mobile ad hoc networks.

Keywords: Clusters, ad hoc networks, protocols, weight metric and performance analysis.

1 Introduction

The rapid proliferation of wireless devices has influenced the potential growth of mobile networking applications which lead to an augmentation in wireless ad hoc networking scenarios, particularly interesting for network operators. Routing of information has been an important concern in ad hoc networks owing to the intrinsic dynamics of the network topology. A large amount of work has been devoted over the past few years to designing scalable routing protocols for mobile ad hoc networks [1]. Creating and maintaining distributed network structures like dominating sets, clusters, spanning graphs etc has been the agreed upon solution for organizing the network so as to enable efficient and reliable communication and cooperation between nodes in a large scale topology and among those clustering is the most familiar approach. Clustering provides for efficient radio resources allocation, location and energy management, and routing and backbone formation in ad hoc mobile wireless networks and is an effective method for tackling the scalability issues pertinent to this networking domain.

Clustering in self organized networks is the phenomenon of partitioning the network by dynamically grouping geographically closer nodes into clusters, identified by

X. Cheng, W. Li, and T. Znati (Eds.): WASA 2006, LNCS 4138, pp. 206–216, 2006.
© Springer-Verlag Berlin Heidelberg 2006

their clusterheads and linked to each other by border nodes. Many prevalent clustering algorithms are based on heuristic approaches for clusterhead election and cluster formation [2][3] since the problem of choosing optimal clusterheads is NP-complete. However, these heuristic algorithms do not consider the quality and the suitability of the mobile node elected to be a clusterhead. In an ad hoc network, where the nodes are mobile and the topology is dynamic, the effect of node behavior is greatly exaggerated. Consequently, the aforementioned clustering algorithms do not form reliable clusters and invites frequent cluster re-organizations.

Clustering solutions in [4][5][6] considers different node characteristics and perceives different weights as a priority criterion in electing clusterheads. The clustering algorithm in [7] considers an associativity-based criterion in choosing clusterheads. However, these techniques are not satisfactorily applicable to all ad hoc networking scenarios. Certain scenarios demands clustering based on mobility of nodes, but certain other scenarios may form better clusters based on energy information or density of nodes. Thus, they are not the best algorithms to be employed for ad hoc clustering. WCA algorithm, a combined weight metric based clustering approach presented in [8] and the clustering heuristic presented in [9] form single-hop clusters and demonstrates the use of multiple node properties like the ideal node-degree, transmission power, link changes, mobility and the battery power of the nodes in performing clustering. Limiting cluster dimensions to single hop clusters are not effective solutions to achieve absolute scalability for large scale networking environments. The cluster sizes formed should be variable and adaptive depending on the networking scenarios in consideration. In [2], k-hop clusters are formed based on weight factor estimations, but they employ flooding mechanisms for weight metric dissemination. This can create unnecessary overhead during cluster formation. Many of these protocols do not have efficient weight metric updation policies thereby raising the difficulties in cluster re-organization and maintenance.

In this paper, we present the Stable Clustering Algorithm (SCA), an adaptive, robust and constraint aware heuristic clustering algorithm for heterogeneous wireless networks applicable to any level of network scalability and density. It employs distributed cluster organization and produces stable clusters with controlled cluster sizes adaptive to the network scenarios making the algorithm an ideal choice for large scale manager-controlled ad hoc networking systems. The clusterhead election is based on a weight estimation and dissemination approach which reduces the cluster formation overhead and elects the best possible set of clusterheads to manage the network topology. Adaptive policies are used for cluster maintenance to increase cluster lifetime and to reduce frequent cluster reorganizations.

The paper is organized as follows. Sec. 2 describes the details of the SCA algorithm. Sec. 3 provides the performance evaluation results. Conclusion and perspectives are depicted in sec. 4.

2 SCA Clustering Algorithm

2.1 Network Representation and Clustering Assumptions

We consider a reinforced ad hoc networking scenario, described in [10] as the basis for the application of our clustering algorithm. In such networks, a special entity, or network controller, is defined as part of the reinforced topology, which is a specific wireless device or a global mechanism having a total view of the network topology that can provide critical information to network nodes. The SCA algorithm profits from the controller in getting vital information about cluster sizes and network property selection.

According to our approach, the requirements for clustering has two general implications: firstly, from a macroscopic point of view, clustering of mobile nodes are controlled based on generic parameters like network size and density and secondly, from a microscopic level, clustering is mastered by specific node properties like mobility, transmission power, bandwidth, load, connectivity etc. This approach can provide better stability to the partitioned network and will form more reliable clusters for a dynamic networking environment. The clusters are named as C_i and identified by their clusterheads (CH) and the nodes at cluster peripheries, having cross-cluster connectivity are identified as border nodes, BN. The rest of the nodes are classified as cluster members. From a routing protocol point of view, any routing strategy can be adopted depending on protocol considerations, be it a hybrid routing prototype using a combination of proactive and reactive routing information or a hierarchical routing protocol. In the case of applying hierarchical routing, the clustering process will have to be recursively repeated to form a multi-level logical cluster topology [11]. We also do not put in place any hypotheses on the role of clusterheads in data exchange.

For introducing macroscopic control on clustering, we use a parameter termed as cluster radius, r which is defined as the maximum number of direct hops between a clusterhead node and nodes at the cluster periphery. This dynamic parameter determines the dimensions of the clusters formed by the algorithm and serves as an input (from network controller) for the cluster formation process. It is a good metric to directly control the clustering process and enables the formation of well distributed clusters. In high group mobility environments, largely dense scenarios and for shorter network scopes, smaller values of r are preferred whereas in stable and large scale scenarios, larger clusters and hence increasing values of r maybe adopted. By default, the value of r is set as two. An upper bound is defined for r depending on overall network size and the challenges in maintaining the topology and is generally set to be less than or equal to three [2]. The cluster radius parameter plays a major role in weight dissemination as will be explained in the following sub-sections.

Each node discovers the neighborhood information using periodic exchange of HELLO messages. The nodes maintain neighbour tables that are frequently updated based on the reception of the HELLO messages from adjacent nodes. At each node, the algorithm has four main stages of operation. Firstly, each node calculates its weight metric according to the weight estimation framework. Then, based on the value of cluster radius, the local weight dissemination process is carried out. Once the weight dissemination process is effectuated and the nodes have a weighted view of their neighborhood, the cluster organization and election of CH and BN nodes can be performed thereby forming the physical clusters. The cluster maintenance constitutes the final stage of algorithm operation. Each step of algorithm operation is briefly described in the following sub sections.

2.2 Weight Estimation Method

The property of a node is defined as some characteristic that directly or indirectly influences the rate of control messages generated by the associated clustering protocol. These properties or metrics, for example, the mobility of the node, density and connectivity degree, transmission power and energy consumption rate can determine the adequacy of nodes to be clusterheads. This suitability for becoming clusterheads is decided by a generalized combined weight metric approach that will take into account the different node properties. The weight metric could also be an attribute of a single property or constraint, but a generalized vision is always interesting since ad hoc networks exist in different scenarios and that clustering can be based on different priority properties largely depending on the communication scenarios and environment. The suitable properties can be selected according to the weightage factor attributed to each parameter for the intended scenarios. The node with the highest/lowest weight in its neighborhood can be chosen as the clusterhead. A unified framework of weight calculation is introduced in [2] where the weight is defined as:

$$W_N[P(n)] = w_1 P_1 + w_2 P_2 + ... + w_n P_n \tag{1}$$

where W_N is the combined weight for node N for n properties, w is the weightage factor, and the scalar product $w_i P_i$ represents the weighted property depending on the application or network scenarios. In [8], the authors adopt the same idea for weight estimation and in [9], the authors propose an ILP based weight estimation method inline with the above framework. The main disadvantage of applying such methods is in determining the independent role of the different properties in establishing the suitability of nodes to be clusterheads. Also, using LP solutions are more costly and also do not reflect the real nature of dynamic mobile networks since the LP calculations are performed in static environment. Otherwise stated, the framework does not explain the critical fact that the best choice of clusterhead is attributed to which corresponding property. Thus, the estimated weight may not directly reflect the actual node conditions.

We propose the node weight estimation method that is based on the general expression of weight calculation given above, but considering the cost incurred for clustering. We assume that each node has a cost $C(N)$ associated to it in becoming a clusterhead, a border node or a cluster member. This cost is calculated with respect to the different node properties and is an indirect measure of the potential overheads and cluster re-organizations. Therefore, we can quantitatively assess each property separately and the contribution it gives to the weighted equation. The overall weight of the mobile node is determined by considering the inverse of the total cost at the node to be in a cluster. The total clustering cost for a node for each property i, can be computed as

$$C(N(i)) = C_i(N_{CH}) + C_i(N_{BN}) + C_i(N_{CM}) \tag{2}$$

where $C(N_{CH})$, $C(N_{BN})$ and $C(N_{CM})$ are the costs of a node N to be clusterhead, border node or cluster member respectively. These associated cost attributes are determined for each property P_i and the total sum indicated the overall clustering cost of the mobile node. The determined total costs are then processed using the cost-gradient for each property which linearizes the parameter according to system needs. The cost gradient is analogous to weightage factor and determines the utility of the metric or property in the overall clustering cost of a node. Thus, the total weight at a node can be estimated as

$$W_N = \frac{1}{\sum_P g_P C(N)}$$

(3)

where g_P is the cost-gradient for property P. The optimal value for the cost-gradient product is one and hence for the optimally suited node for becoming clusterhead, the maximum weight can reach infinity.

The weight metric is periodically updated at each node depending on the dynamicity of the network topology. In the proposed weight estimation framework, we consider all the decisive network properties and metrics into account and assume that the choice of properties will be decided by the network controller.

2.3 Weight Dissemination

The second step of the algorithm is a method of disseminating the estimated weight values of nodes in its r-hop neighborhood. Apart from classical dissemination algorithms like ideal dissemination, flooding or gossiping [12] and the weight metric flooding adopted in existing k-hop clustering algorithms; we introduce a novel technique for weight metric dissemination which is performed completely as a local process using the neighbour discovery HELLO messages. At each node, our method works as follows.

Algorithm. Weight Metric Estimation and Dissemination

a. Retrieve the values of r and the desired properties (from the network controller)

b. Identify neighbors using HELLO messages and update neighbour table

c. Estimate weight and store as $H(W_N, N)$ where W_N is the node weight and N is the node ID.

d. Transmit $H(W_N, N)$ to neighbors using HELLO.

e. Determine if H is received from all the neighbors

f. Calculate High_H, the highest weighted node in its 1-hop neighborhood including itself and replace as $H(W_N, N)$. Now, the node will have information of the highest weighted in its 1-hop neighborhood

g. Decrement r. if $r > 0$, Transmit new $H(W_N, N)$ to neighbors using HELLO

h. Determine if new H is received from all neighbors

i. Repeat step f. Now, the node will have information of the highest weighted node in its $2 - $ hop neighborhood

j. Decrement r. if $r > 0$, repeat (d – f). Terminate at $r = 0$

Once the algorithm has performed r runs of local iterations using the HELLO messages, each node in the network will have information about the highest weighted node in its r-hop neighborhood. The synchronization between nodes for the algorithm is not required since the node verifies (step e) for weight information of neighboring nodes using the neighbour table updates and after a pre-defined wait period, eliminates nodes from the neighbour list from whom the node have not received the weight updates. This method of weight information dissemination is much more efficient than other existing methods and allows the formation of larger clusters bounded by r.

2.4 Cluster Organization

After the nodes have obtained a weighted view of the neighboring topology, thanks to the weight dissemination process; we move to the cluster organization step which is a distributed process. We do not adopt a greedy approach of cluster formation where the largest weighted node advertises to other neighboring nodes to join their clusters. The objective is to form nearly equal sized and distributed clusters with self-decided cluster admissions. The nodes in the cluster can have three different roles: Clusterhead (CH), Border Node (BN) or Cluster Member (CM). The clusterhead election and cluster formation is carried out initially and the border node assignment is performed as the next step. The important cluster organization messages are as follows.

Cluster Organization at Node, N

a. If node, N gets its own identity as largest weighted, it elects itself as clusterhead, discards all further messages (except for $CH(m)$ message, step d) and then broadcasts $Join\_Cluster$ message to neighboring nodes. This refrain is to avoid the convergence of the algorithm into a greedy heuristic.

b. If node, N received a $Join\_Cluster$ message, it registers the message and waits for all $Join\_Cluster$ messages. If there are multiple messages, choose the lower weighted node as clusterhead and sends a $Cluster\_Accept$ message to the source node.

c. If node N consecutively elects the same node, N' as the largest weighted node during the r iterations, N chooses N' as clusterhead, and unicasts $CH(m)$ to N'. Then, the node broadcasts My_CH message to neighbors at $(r-1)$ hops (this step is applied only if $r > 1$).

d. If N gets $CH(m)$ message, the node will update its status as clusterhead. In most of the cases, N will be the node which is the largest weighted

e. If N gets My_CH message, registers the message. Compares with other received My_CH messages and selects the lowest weighted node to be clusterhead and sends the $Cluster\_Accept$ message.

f. If N does not receive any message and it is not a clusterhead node, broadcasts a $No\_Cluster$ message to the neighboring nodes.

The clusterhead will keep information of all the nodes in its cluster in a cluster table. Initially, all nodes are marked as CM in the table. The nodes at the periphery which has cross cluster connectivity with the adjacent clusters will advertise a BN message to its clusterhead. The clusterhead node updates the cluster table by associating BN status to these nodes. More information can be exploited by the clusterhead in terms of the cluster orientation and related to cluster neighborhood information, but since those are more appropriate to the chosen routing protocol, the options are kept open.

2.5 Cluster Maintenance

The cluster life time and period of cluster reorganization largely depends on the cluster maintenance mechanisms associated to the clustering protocol. We defined two distinct types of operations for cluster maintenance: the weight threshold property and the node movements.

Weight Threshold Criterion

The weight of nodes changes frequently according to the network environment. Even if the weight of the clusterhead node diminishes compared to that of the cluster members, the node will continue to be the clusterhead until the CH node's weight reaches or goes below a threshold value, δ. As the node weight reaches its threshold value, the CH node sends a life_down message to the CM nodes in the immediate neighborhood and relieves of its clusterhead status. Then, a local cluster re-organization is performed with the cluster members evoking the clustering algorithm.

Node Movements

The node movements can be in the form of node joining or node leaving a cluster. These operations will have only local effects on the clustered topology if the moving node is a CM node. If the leaving node is CH node, the cluster reorganization has to be performed for the nodes in the cluster by evoking the clustering algorithm. The transition to the new cluster will be faster, thanks to the periodic weight metric estimation carried out at the nodes. If BN nodes are leaving the cluster, the intermediate node will inform the CH node and CH will update its cluster table.

3 Performance Analysis

Extensive simulations using OPNET simulator were carried out to study the performances of the proposed clustering mechanism and to compare them with some existing clustering solutions. We choose WCA [8] and Lowest-ID [1] protocols in an attempt to compare the performance of our strategy. The parameters considered for evaluation are the cluster stability and also the cluster dimensions. We consider mobility and node density as the weight metric parameters. The cost gradient is chosen giving equal weightage to both the weight parameters. The node density, for weight metric estimation is measured as the ratio of local connectivity scores at each mobile node. The algorithm was simulated for cluster radius values of $r = 1 \& 2$. The nodes move using a random ad-hoc mobility model [5] with a constant speed chosen uniformly between zero and a maximum speed, which is here taken as 15m/s and the direction was uniformly distributed over $(0,2\pi)$. The pause time takes a value that is exponentially distributed with mean 30 seconds. The HELLO message interval is set to 3 seconds. The transmission range of each mobile node is set to 70 m. Each scenario was run for a 900 simulated seconds.

3.1 Stability Analysis

The stability of the clustering algorithm is assessed by analyzing the CH changeovers and the CH change ratio with respect to node count, average node density, average node speed and induced mobility. CH change over is the number of times each mobile node either attempts to become a CH or gives up its role as CH whereas CH change ratio is the ratio of the number of nodes that change their clusterhead to the total number of nodes in the network.

The fig. 1 shows the frequency of CH changes by the mobile nodes, and hence a measure of stability associated with each clustering algorithm as a function of increasing number of nodes. (The lower the frequency of CH changes, the more stable the cluster is).

The average node density is kept nearly constant in order to understand the proper effect of increasing network nodes. The number of nodes is varied from 200 to 1000 for different simulation scenarios of area, 600x600 m2 to 1400x1400 m2. The average number of CH changes, which occurred every 3 minutes, is seen to be lower in the case of our clustering algorithm. The cluster stability shows comparable results when varying the cluster radius with increasing number of nodes.

The cluster stability as a function of increasing average node density is shown in fig. 2. Here, the simulation area is kept constant at 1000x1000m2 and density of nodes is increased. The cluster stability is lower when there is lower node-density which maybe due to the fact that there is a transient instability due to node mobility and lesser node degree.

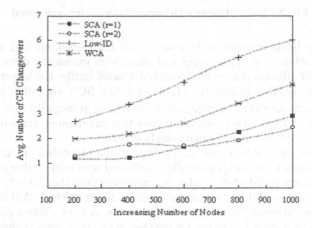

Fig. 1. Cluster Stability with respect to increasing node count. The Cluster Stability is measured as the average number of CH changeovers.

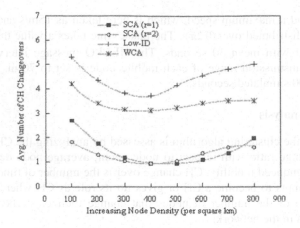

Fig. 2. Cluster Stability with respect to increasing node density

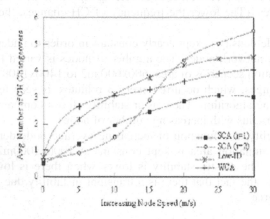

Fig. 3. Cluster Stability with respect to increasing node speed

The stability increases with node count in all the algorithms and at a moderate level, the algorithms converges faster and then, with increasing density, clustering stability is again affected due to the increased control traffic and larger convergence time. Although, mobility affects the cluster stability, SCA algorithm performs well for $r = 1$. When cluster radius is increased, there is a steep instability for average node speed greater than 15m/s. This anomaly proves that maintaining multi-hop clusters in a largely dynamic environment is increasingly difficult.

Fig. 3 shows the stability and scalability of the algorithm in terms of node-mobility. The pause time is exponentially distributed with mean value of 30 seconds, while the maximum speed of the nodes are increased from 0 to 30 m/s. The number of nodes was fixed as 500 in a simulation area of 1000x1000m2. Although, mobility affects the cluster stability, SCA algorithm performs well for . When cluster radius is increased, there is a steep instability for average node speed greater than 15m/s. This anomaly proves that maintaining multi-hop clusters in a largely dynamic environment is increasingly difficult.

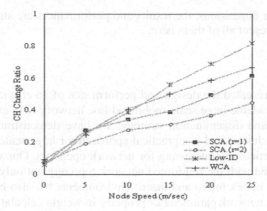

Fig. 4. CH Change ratio with respect to node – speed

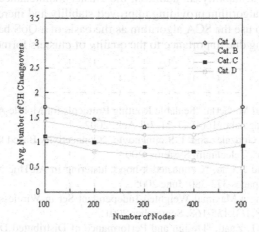

Fig. 5. Clustering scenarios for reinforced ad hoc stability analysis

The clusterhead change ratio is measured in fig. 4 based on a similar scenario adopted earlier. The metric directly relates to the node movements and brings forward the effect of maintenance operation in a cluster algorithm. As the node speed increases, the clusterhead change ratios also increase, and SCA algorithm outperforms the other clustering mechanisms, thanks to its adaptive maintenance policies.

Fig.5. demonstrates the analysis of the clustering algorithm in reinforced ad hoc scenarios (sec II). There are four scenarios that are simulated for cluster radius, $r = 2$. In category A, there are 20% static nodes, 30% semi-mobile nodes (0-3m/s), 50% fully mobile nodes (0-15m/s). In categories B, C and D, the percentage of static nodes are incremented by 10 and percentage of fully mobile nodes are decremented by 10 keeping the percentage of semi-mobile nodes constant. The stability of the clustering algorithm increases with the addition of static nodes into the network. Also, since the weight parameter under consideration is mobility and density, the clustering algorithm produces excellent performance results in the dynamic environment under consideration. Notice that the parameter setting or weight metrics and for the analysis are just for demonstrations. We have carried our other settings to analyse the reliability, robustness and cluster dimensions, the results and performances are stable, due to space limit, we can not present all of them here.

4 Conclusions

In this paper, we presented the design and performance of an efficient stable clustering algorithm for scalable large scale mobile ad hoc networks. By employing a novel weight estimation and dissemination strategy, we have demonstrated that the algorithm forms stable clusters and is a practical approach for large scale ad hoc networking applications particularly interesting for network operators. Our weight estimation framework combined with the reinforced network topology not only provides a complete picture of the node's micro and macro environments but also helps in determining the role of each network parameter or property in weight calculation. The adaptive cluster organization scheme makes the SCA protocol an appropriate mechanism for any level of network scalability. In addition, the cluster maintenance schemes add to the robustness of the algorithm providing improved stability and increasing the cluster lifetime. We intend to use the SCA algorithm as the basis of a QoS based Hierarchical routing protocol giving due importance to the quality of clusters formed.

References

1. X. Hong, K. Xu and M. Gerla, "Scalable Routing Protocols for Mobile Ad Hoc Networks", IEEE Networks Magazine, 16(4):11-21, Jul-Aug, 2002.
2. F. G. Nocetti, J. S. Gonzalez and I. Stojmenovic, "Connectivity Based k-hop Clustering in Wireless Networks", Telecomm. Systems, 2003.
3. S. Yang, J. Wu and J. Cao, "Connected k-hop Clustering in Ad Hoc Networks", In Proceedings of ICCP, pages 373-380, June 2005.
4. S. Basagni "Finding a Maximal Weighted Independent Set in Wireless Networks", Telecomm. Systems. 18(1/3):155-168, September 2001.
5. B. McDonald and T. Znati, "Design and Performance of Distributed Dynamic Clustering Algorithm for Multimode Routing in Wireless Ad Hoc Networks", Sim: Trans. of the Society of CS&MI, Vol. 78, 2002.
6. Younis and S. Fahmy, "HEED: A Hybrid, Energy-Efficient, Distributed Clustering Approach for Ad Hoc Sensor Networks", IEEE Trans. on Mobile Computing, vol. 3, pp. 366-279, Oct-Dec, 2004.
7. S. Sivavakeesar and G. Pavlou,"Scalable Location Services for Hierarchically Organized Mobile Ad Hoc Networks", in Proceedings of ACM Mobihoc, Illinois, USA, 2005.
8. M. Chatterjee et al, "WCA: A Weighted Clustering Algorithm for Mobile Ad Hoc Networks" Journal of Cluster Computing, V. 5/2, April, 2002.
9. B. Lâtré et al.,"A Heterogeneity Based Clustering Heuristic for Mobile Ad Hoc Networks" in Proc. ICC, Paris 2004. pp. 3728 – 3733.
10. L. Reynaud and J. Meddour "An Open Architecture that Manages Quality of Service within Ad Hoc Networks", in Proc. IEEE IWWAN, 2004.
11. E. M. Royer, "Hierarchical Routing in Ad Hoc Mobile Networks", Wireless Communications & Mobile Computing, pp. 515 – 532, 2002.
12. W. Rabiner et al.,"Adaptive Protocols for Information Dissemination in Wireless Sensor Networks" In Proceedings of. ACM Mobicom 1999.

An Interference Free Cluster-Based TDMA Protocol for Wireless Sensor Networks*

Gong Haigang[1], Liu Ming[2], Wang Xiaomin[1], Chen Lijun[2], and Xie Li[2]

[1] School of Computer Science and Engineering,
University of Electronic Science and Technology of China, P.R. China
[2] Department of Computer Science and Technology, Nanjing University

Abstract. In this paper, we propose IFCT protocol, an Interference Free Cluster-based TDMA protocol for wireless sensor network. IFCT protocol employs two schedules to avoid transmission interference. The first schedule assigns different frame number to neighboring clusters so that neighboring clusters could collect their member's data during different frames, avoiding inter-cluster interference. The second schedule allocates different slots to cluster members and they sending their data to their respectively cluster heads during different slots to avoid intra-cluster interference. Simulation results show that IFCT performs better than HEED, which is a clustering protocol based on TDMA. In addition, IFCT is more practical than HEED which uses CDMA code to avoid inter-cluster interference for deploying large-scale wireless sensor networks.

1 Introduction

A wireless sensor network (WSN) is a distributed system comprised of a large number of extremely small, low-cost and battery-powered sensors equipped with low-power radio, which can be used to collect useful information (i.e. temperature, humidity) from a variety of environment. WSNs have been envisioned to have a wide range of applications in both military as well as civilian domains [1][2] such as battlefield surveillance, machine failure diagnosis, and chemical detection.

Since sensor nodes powered by battery are often left unattended after deployment, e.g., in hostile or hash environments, making it difficult to replace their batteries, the protocols running on WSNs must be energy efficient. According to D. Estrin [2], the radio component of sensor nodes consumes most of nodes' energy. Moreover, medium access control (MAC) protocol directly controls the activity of nodes' radio. So, medium access is a major consumer of sensor energy and MAC protocol must be energy efficient to achieve longer network lifetime.

A lot of MAC protocols have been studied in recent years and could be categorized into two classes: schedule-based and contention-based (S-MAC [3]). In schedule-based MAC protocol, TDMA is an important approach that is inherently collision free and avoids unnecessary idle listening, which are two major sources of energy consumption. For the inherently property of energy conserving, TDMA protocols have been recently attracted significant attention for many applications [4-6]. However, TDMA has poor scalability. Cluster-based protocols such as LEACH [7] and HEED [8] are more scalable than traditional TDMA protocol. But cluster-based

---

* This work is partially supported by the National Natural Science Foundation of China under Grant No. 60573132.

X. Cheng, W. Li, and T. Znati (Eds.): WASA 2006, LNCS 4138, pp. 217–227, 2006.

protocol introduces inter-cluster interference, resulting in cluster's transmission interfering with neighboring clusters. As shown in Fig. 1, shadowed node C is a member of cluster head A and is also covered by cluster head B. While node D sends data to cluster head B, if node C transmits to A simultaneously, the reception of B will be interfered with the signal from C. And the packet sent by D is corrupted and energy dissipated for transmitting and receiving is consumed unnecessarily.

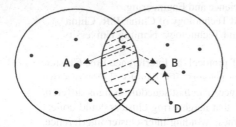

Fig. 1. Inter-cluster interference   **Fig. 2.** Clustering and routing tree of ICFT

To avoid inter-cluster interference, LEACH and HEED then exploits Direct Sequence Spread Spectrum (DS-SS) code, a CDMA-like scheme so that cluster heads can filter the code belongs to other clusters among multiple received signals and decode the signal sent from their members. The approach taken by Sonia et al. [9] uses different frequencies (FDMA) in different clusters to transmit so as to avoid inter-cluster interference. However, either FDMA or CDMA needs to extend the function of sensor's hardware, which complicates the hardware design and increases node's hardware costs. The increase of hardware cost is undoubtedly uneconomical especially for large-scale wireless sensor network. Therefore, the goal of our ICFT protocol is to avoid inter-cluster interference and improve energy utilization efficiency with a reasonable TDMA schedule in a wireless sensor network in which nodes operates only on a single frequency.

The main idea of ICFT is that neighboring cluster heads collect their member's data during different TDMA frames to avoid inter-cluster interference. As in Fig. 1, cluster head A gathers the data during the first TDMA frame and cluster head B collects the data during the second TDMA frame, avoiding the transmission collision that appears when A and B gather the data at the same time.

The rest of the paper is organized as follows. Section 2 states system models. Section 3 describes our ICFT protocol in detail. Section 4 discusses the simulation results. Finally, Section 5 concludes the paper and presents future research directions.

2 System Models

2.1 Network Model

Assume that N nodes are dispersed in a square $M \times M$ field randomly, and the follow assumptions hold:

1) The only base station sits at a fixed location outside the field.
2) All nodes have same capabilities and data fusion is capable.
3) Nodes are left unattended after deployment and nodes are stationary.

2.2 Radio Model

We use the same radio model in [7] for the radio hardware energy dissipation where the transmitter dissipates energy to run the radio electronics and the power amplifier, and the receiver dissipates energy to run the radio electronics. To transmit a k-bit message a distance d, the radio expends energy as (1).

$$E_{Tx} = \begin{cases} k * E_{elec} + k * e_{fs} d^2, & d < d_0 \\ k * E_{elec} + k * e_{amp} d^4, & d \geq d_0 \end{cases} \tag{1}$$

And to receive this message, the radio expends energy as (2)

$$E_{Rx} = k * E_{elec} \tag{2}$$

E_{elec}, the electronics energy, depends on factors such as the digital coding, modulation, and filtering of the signal before it is sent to the transmit amplifier. And the amplifier energy, $e_{fs} d^2$ or $e_{amp} d^4$, depends on the distance to the receiver.

In addition, data fusion is capable of reducing the amount of data to deliver. E_{DA} denotes the energy consumed by data fusion. For example, Aggregating L k-bit signals into a single representative k-bit signal consumes energy $L * E_{DA} * k$.

3 ICFT Protocol Design

Like HEED, the operation of ICFT is divided into rounds. Each round begins with a set-up phase, followed by a working phase. In the set-up phase, clusters are organized and the routing tree is constructed among the cluster heads after clustering. For example, nodes are grouped into 9 clusters as shown in Fig. 2 and 9 cluster heads are organized into a routing tree. Then there is time synchronization for the network. In the working phase, data are gathered from the nodes to base station. At first, members send their monitored data to their cluster heads. Then cluster heads aggregate the data and send it to their parent in the routing tree, i.e. cluster head E send to cluster head B and cluster head G send to D (in Fig. 2). Until the data is transmitted to the root of the routing tree, the root A then sends all the aggregated data to the base station.

As shown in Fig. 3, $T_{cluster}$, T_{tree} and T_{SYNC} represent the time for clustering, constructing tree and time synchronization respectively. T_{data} is the time for data gathering in a round. Clustering scheme and tree building algorithm are described in our previous work [10]. In this paper, we mainly discuss the working phase of ICFT.

Data gathering (working phase) consists of a two level TDMA schedules (TLTS) and K super-frames. A super-frame consists of N_f frames, which comprise m time slots. The goal of TLTS is to assign different frames to neighboring clusters so as to avoid inter-cluster interference and to allocate slots to cluster members to avoid collision within clusters. TLTS includes two phases: inter-cluster TDMA schedule and intra-cluster TDMA schedule.

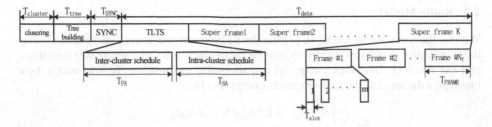

Fig. 3. Frame structure of ICFT

3.1 Inter-cluster Schedule

The task of inter-cluster schedule is to assign different frames to neighboring clusters. Then neighboring cluster heads could gather their members' data during different time, avoiding the inter-cluster interference. Frame assignment is analogous to coloring problem in graph theory [11] and frequency allocation in cellular communication [9]. Define frame assignment problem as follows:

Given a connected graph $G = (V, E)$, V is set of cluster heads, $E = \{(u,v) \mid u, v \in V\}$, edge *(u, v)* means u is adjacent to v. If $\forall (u,v) \in E$, then $u.frame\# \neq v.frame\#$。

FA (Frame Assignment) algorithm is described in Fig. 4. Each cluster head maintains CH_{nb}, a set of its one-hop neighboring cluster heads. n_i is the number of cluster heads that haven't been assigned frame and t should be long enough to receive messages from neighbors. In step i, a cluster head (CH) broadcasts a *RESERVATION* message with probability $1/n_i+1$ and becomes competing CH (line 5~10). *RESERVATION* message includes the CH's *ID* and an unused frame number (frame #). After time t, if it doesn't receive any other *RESERVATION* message, meaning no neighbors subscribe frame number in this step, it will broadcast a *CONFIRM* message to confirm its reservation (line 17~20). After receiving this *CONFIRM* message, its neighbors should label the reserved frame number used and delete the CH from its CH_{nb} (line 23). If it receives other *RESERVATION* message, meaning its neighbors subscribe frame number at the same time, collision happens if they reserve the same frame number. The competing CH that has max *ID* would be the winner of that frame number and the losers will book the frame number in the next step until all cluster heads have got their frame number. As in Fig. 2, the number in parenthesis is the frame number assigned to the corresponding cluster head.

Parameter N_f influences the performance of the protocol. A large N_f introduces long delay and a small N_f leads to frame assignment collision that neighboring cluster heads get same frame number. $N_f = D+1$ meets the requirement to assign different frame number to neighboring clusters according to Grable[11], where D is the max number of neighboring cluster heads. However, N_f can be far fewer than $D+1$ for that cluster heads that are not adjacent can use the same frame number. Fig. 5 shows two frame assignment schemes ($D=7$). Fig. 5a assigns 8 frames to 8 neighboring clusters. In fact, 4 frames are enough as shown in Fig. 5b.

```
1.  GotFrame = FALSE
2.  REPEAT:
3.       n = |CH_nb|; contending = FALSE;
4.       p = 1 / (n+1)
5.       IF (random (0,1) <= p)
6.           my_frame# = SELECT frame# different
                                  from my neighbors
7.               RESERVATION.ID = my_ID;
8.               RESERVATION. frame# = my_frame#
9.           BROADCAST (RESERVATION)
10.          contending = TRUE

11.      WAIT t

12.      IF ( contending )
13.          IF (received RESERVATION)
14.              IF (my_ID > RESERVATION. ID AND
                      my_frame# = RESERVATION. frame#)
15.                  contending = FALSE
16.              ELSE
17.                  CONFIRM. ID = my_ID ;
18.                  CONFIRM.frame# = my_frame#
19.              BROADCAST( CONFIRM )
20.              GotFrame = TRUE

21.      WAIT t

22.      IF( received CONFIRM)
23.          CH_nb = CH_nb - CONFIRM.ID

23. UNTIL (GotFrame)
```

Fig. 4. Frame assignment algorithm

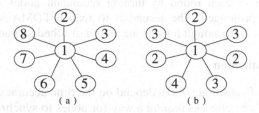

Fig. 5. Two frame assignment schemes

3.2 Intra-cluster Schedule and Coverage

Intra-cluster schedule is similar to the traditional TDMA schedule in HEED but with a more field of frame number in the schedule packet. The field of frame number tells cluster members during which frame their cluster heads collect the data and the field of slot tells them during which slot of that frame they should be active and send data to cluster heads.

The number of cluster members decides the length of schedule packet. Assume N nodes are randomly deployed in a $M \times M$ field A. Then the average number of cluster members is $N \cdot \pi R^2 / M^2$, where R is cluster radius. The higher node density, the more cluster members and the longer the length of schedule packet that leads to more energy consumption for transmitting and receiving the packet. The more cluster members, the longer frame time, leading to longer delay. In fact, sensors are usually deployed densely (high up to 20nodes $/m^3$ [2]). In such a high-density network with energy-constrained sensors, it is neither necessary nor desirable to have all nodes work at the same time. In [12], authors think it is hard to guarantee full coverage for a given randomly deployment area even if all sensors are on-duty and small sensing holes are not likely to influence the effectiveness of sensor networks and are acceptable for most application scenarios. So we introduce the idea of intra-cluster coverage discussed in our previous work [10]. Intra-cluster coverage means that only a subset of cluster members should be active if these nodes cover the most of sensing field. Based on [10], cluster heads randomly choose m nodes according to (3).

$$P_{cover} = \sum_{i=1}^{m} C_m^i \left(\frac{r}{R}\right)^{2i} \left(1 - \frac{r^2}{R^2}\right)^{m-i},$$ (3)

where P_{cover} is the expected coverage ratio of sensing field determined by applications, and r is sensing radius. After cluster heads choosing active node, they broadcast the schedule packet. Cluster members go to be active if they find their *ID* in the packet. Otherwise, they become to be asleep. For example, distributing 2000 nodes in a 200×200m^2 field, $r = 12$m, $R = 30$m, then the average number of cluster members is 120 or so. With intra-cluster coverage, if $P_{cover} = 99\%$ which means 99% of sensing field is expected to be monitored, 27 members should be active in each cluster. If $P_{cover} = 95\%$, only 16 nodes should be active.

Therefore, using intra-cluster coverage has two advantages. The first is to preserve energy consumption in each round by turning redundant nodes' radio off so that network lifetime is prolonged. The second is to reduce TDMA schedule overhead when node density is high enough for that the length of schedule packet is invariable.

3.3 Time Synchronization

Many applications of sensor networks depend on the time accuracy kept by nodes in the network. So sensor networks require a way for nodes to synchronize their clocks to a global time. Moreover, time synchronization is indispensable in the implementation of the commonly used medium access control protocols such as TDMA. Time synchronization problem has been studied over years in Internet. Well known synchronization schemes include GPS and the Network Time Protocol (NTP [13]). However, the time synchronization requirements differ drastically in the context of sensor networks. For example, scalability and energy efficiency are two major concerns in sensor network due to the characteristics of sensor networks.

There have been several time synchronization protocols for wireless sensor networks in recent years such as Reference Broadcast (RBS [14]) and Timing-Protocol for Sensor Networks (TPSN [15]). In RBS scheme, the nodes periodically send beacon messages to their neighbors using the network's physical layer broadcast. Recipients use the message's arrival timestamp as point of reference for comparing their clocks. However, the RBS scheme is effective only for a small cluster of nodes lying in a neighborhood. TPSN protocol is level-based time synchronization, which is more scalable than RBS. In TPSN, a hierarchical topology is created first, assigning each node a level in the hierarchy. Then, each node synchronizes itself to a node belonging to exactly one level above in the hierarchy. Eventually all nodes in the network synchronize their clocks to a reference node.

In our ICFT protocol, the cluster heads are organized into a routing tree as shown in Fig. 2. The tree structure could be viewed as a hierarchical topology, e. g., the level of the root cluster head A is 1 and the level of A's child such as B, C, D is 2, and so on. So TPSN could be incorporated into ICFT after the routing tree has been constructed among the cluster heads. When the time is synchronized among the cluster heads using TPSN, the cluster heads synchronize with their respective cluster members using simple local synchronization technique. Obviously, time synchronization introduces extra energy overhead especially in large hierarchical topology. The time to resynchronization (a round time) should be long enough to reduce the synchronization overhead, which is determined by the synchronization accuracy and clock drift of nodes.

3.4 FA Algorithm Analysis

Lemma 1. FA algorithm terminates in O (D) steps, where D is the max number of neighboring cluster heads.

Proof. Assume FA algorithm terminates in L steps. At the beginning, a cluster head has n_1 neighboring cluster heads to compete for frame number. After $L-1$ steps, n_1 cluster heads should reserve their frame number successfully. Then the last cluster head gets its frame number in the last step.

In step i, n_i+1 cluster heads compete for frame number. The probability to subscribe the frame number is $p_i = 1/(n_i + 1)$, where n_i is the number of neighbors that have not got frame number in the previous i-1 steps. Then the probability of only one cluster head reserving frame number successfully is

$$P_i = p_i (1 - p_i)^{n_i}, \tag{4}$$

The number of cluster heads reserving frame number successfully is $N_i \geq (n_i + 1) \cdot P_i$。 After $L-1$ steps, the number of cluster heads reserving frame number successfully is

$$n_1 = \sum_{i=1}^{L-1} N_i \geq \sum_{i=1}^{L-1} (n_i + 1) \cdot P_i = \sum_{i=1}^{L-1} (1 - \frac{1}{d_i + 1})^{n_i}, \tag{5}$$

Note that $(1 - \dfrac{1}{n_i + 1})^{n_i} \geq e^{-\frac{n_i}{n_i+1}} \geq e^{-1}$, then

$$n_1 \geq (L-1) \cdot e^{-1}, \tag{6}$$

Thus we have

$$L \leq n_1 \cdot e + 1 \leq D \cdot e + 1, \tag{7}$$

In the worst case, algorithm will terminate in $D \cdot e + 1$ steps, i.e. O (D).

4 Performance Evaluation

4.1 Simulation Setup and Parameters

We implemented ICFT protocol and HEED in the ns-2 network simulator with the wireless extension. Assuming 300 nodes dispersed in 200×200m^2 field, the simulation parameters are shown in Table 1. Data transmission rate is set to 115.2 kps, the same as that in TR1000 [16] transceiver equipment on MICA motes [17] when using ASK modulation. Then it spends 7ms or so transmitting 100 bytes data and T_{slot} is set to 8ms. The P_{cover} is set to 95% and 16 active nodes ($m=16$) are enough to ensure 95% intra-cluster coverage. Then the frame time T_{frame} is $m \times T_{slot}=128$ms. To HEED, the frame time is variable with the number of cluster members.

Table 1. Simulation parameters

Parameters	Value
Sense radius (r)	12m
Cluster radius (R)	30m
E_{elec}	50nJ/bit
e_{amp}	0.0013pJ/bit/m^4
e_{fs}	10pJ/bit/m^2
E_{da}	5nJ/bit
Initial Energy	2.0J
P_{cover}	95%
m	6
$T_{cluster}$	400ms
T_{tree}	200ms
T_{sync}	300ms
T_{slot}	8ms
$T_{collect}$	200ms
T_{round}	300s
T_{frame}	128ms
T_{SF}	968ms
T_{FA}	50ms

4.2   The Setting of N_f

Fig. 6 plots the relationship between the number of clusters that have been assigned same frame number and N_f under different monitoring fields. The less the N_f, the more opportunity that same frame number is assigned to neighboring clusters, which increases the number of clusters that have same frame number and leads to inter-cluster interference severely. Fig. 7 shows the relationship between the energy wastage due to frame number collision and N_f under different monitoring areas. The larger the area is, the more the number of clusters, which causes more inter-cluster collision and energy wastage. With the increasing of N_f, the probability of assigning different frame number to neighboring clusters increases too. As seen from the figures, almost all neighboring clusters can get different frame number when N_f is greater than 5. Consequently, we set N_f to 6 in the following simulations and the following results are sampled when simulation runs 1000s.

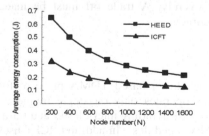
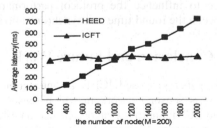

Fig. 6. Percentage of collided clusters .vs N_f **Fig. 7.** Energy wasted due to collision .vs N_f

4.3   Simulation Results

We choose 3 metrics to evaluate the performance of ICFT.

1) Energy consumption: the average energy consumption per node.
2) Latency: the average end-to-end delay of all nodes.
3) Energy efficiency: the throughput achieved by per unit energy.

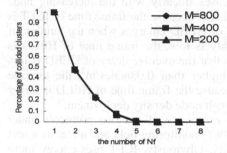
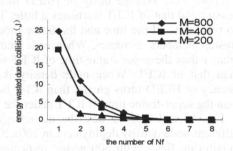

Fig. 8. Average energy consumption   **Fig. 9.** Average packet latency

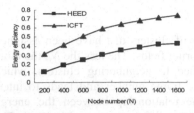

Fig. 10. Energy efficiency vs. *N*

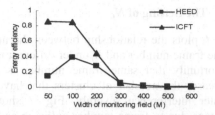

Fig. 11. Energy efficiency vs. *M*

Fig. 8 shows the average energy consumption per node under different node density deployment. Due to the intra-cluster coverage, ICFT has less active nodes to collect data than HEED. In each round, there always some nodes go to sleep in ICFT. So the average energy consumption of ICFT is lower than HEED.

Fig. 9 shows the average packet latency under different node density deployment. Similarly, the average delay of HEED increases linearly with the increasing node density and that of ICFT fluctuates a little. This is because the frame time of ICFT is 16 time slots all the time and the frame time of HEED enlarges when the number of cluster members increases. When node density is low, the frame time of HEED is greater than the super-frame time of ICFT so that the average delay of HEED is less than that of ICFT. When node density is higher than $0.03nodes/m^2$, the average latency of HEED turns greater than ICFT because the frame time of HEED is larger than the super-frame time of ICFT under the high node density deployment.

Fig. 10 and Fig. 11 describe the energy efficiency of the two protocols under different node density deployment in $200 \times 200m^2$ monitoring field and under different monitoring fields with 500 nodes, respectively. Obviously, ICFT uses energy more efficient than HEED as seen from Fig. 10. The energy efficiency of ICFT is almost twice than HEED. However, as shown in Fig. 11, with the enlargement of the monitoring fields, the energy efficiency of ICFT is decreased rapidly. The reason is that when the monitoring field is large, the number of clusters in network increases, which increases the size of the routing tree increases, too. So the synchronization overhead that is linear to the size of the routing tree increases drastically. More energy is dissipated for time synchronization and then the energy efficiency decreases. To improve the energy efficiency under large monitoring area, we must enlarge the time of a round to decrease the frequency of time synchronization. But the round time is limited by the synchronization accuracy. If the round time is too long, network will be unsynchronized. If the round time is small, the synchronization overhead will be very large to influence the protocol performance severely. A trade off must be made between the round time and synchronization accuracy.

5   Conclusion and Future Work

This paper proposed ICFT, an interference free cluster-based TDMA protocol for wireless sensor network in which sensor nodes operates only on single frequency radio. ICFT improves energy utilization efficiency by avoiding inter-cluster and intra-cluster transmission interference with two TDMA schedules. In addition, ICFT uses intra-cluster coverage to reduce the packet delay. Simulation results show that ICFT has better performance than HEED and is more practical than HEED which needs special hardware.

In the future work, we'll try to make a trade off between the time for a round and synchronization accuracy under large monitoring field. In addition, we aim to implement ICFT on a Mote-based sensor network platform and evaluate its performance through real experiments.

References

[1] I. F. Akyildiz, W. Su, Y. Sankarasubramaniam, and E. Cayirci, "Wireless sensor networks: a survey", *Computer Networks*, Vol. 38, pp. 393-422, March 2002.

[2] D. Estrin and R. Govindan, J. Heidemann, and S. Kumar, "Next century challenges: scalable coordination in sensor networks", in *Proc. of MobiCOM '99*, August 1999.

[3] W. Ye, J. Heidenmann, and D. Estrin, "An Energy-Efficient MAC Protocol for Wireless Sensor Networks", *In Proceedings of IEEE INFOCOM*, New York, NY, June 2002.

[4] K. Arisha, et al. "Energy-aware TDMA-based MAC for sensor networks", *In IEEE Workshop on Integrated Management of Power Aware Communications, Computing and NeTworking(IMPACCT 2002)*, New York City, NY, May 2002.

[5] S. Kulkarni, et al. "TDMA service for sensor networks", *In 24th Int. Conf. on Distributed Computing Systems (ICDCS04), ADSN workshop*, pp. 604-609, Tokyo, Japan, March 2004.

[6] G. Pei and C. Chien, "Lower power TDMA in large wireless sensor networks", in *Military Communications Conference (MILCOM 2001)*, volume 1, pp. 347-351, Vienna, VA, Oct. 2001.

[7] W. R. Heinzelman, et al. "An Application -Specific Protocol Architecture for Wireless Microsensor Networks", *IEEE Transactions on Wireless Communications,* vol. 1, no. 4, Oct. 2002.

[8] O. Yonis, et al. "HEED: A Hybrid, Energy-Efficient, Distributed Clustering Approach for Ad-hoc Sensor Networks", *IEEE Transactions on Mobile Computing*, volume 3, issue 4, Oct-Dec, 2004.

[9] S. Waharte, et al. "Performance comparison of distributed frequency assignment algorithms for wireless sensor networks", *In Proceedings of the IFIP International Conference on Network Control and Engineering (Net-Con'2004)*, Palma de Mallorca, Spain, November 2004.

[10] LIU Ming, et al. "A Distributed Energy-Efficient data Gathering and aggregation Protocol for Wireless sensor networks", in *Journal of Software*, January, 2006.

[11] D. A. Grable, et al. "Fast distributed algorithms for brooks-vizing colourings", in *ACM-SIAM Symposium on Discrete Algorithms*, 1998, pp. 473-480.

[12] Y. Gao, K. Wu, and F. Li, "Analysis on the redundancy of wireless sensor networks," in *Proceedings of WSNA 03*, September 2003, San Diego, CA.

[13] D. Mills, Network Time Protocol (Version 3) Specification,Implementation and Analysis, from *http://www.faqs.org/ftp/rfc/rfc1305.pdf*.

[14] J. Elson, L. Girod, and D. Estrin, "Fine-Grained Network Time Synchronization using Reference Broadcasts", *in Proceedings of the Fifth Symposium on Operating Systems Design and Implementation (OSDI 2002)*, Bo, December 2002.

[15] S. Ganeriwal, R. Kumar, and M.B. Srivastava, "Timing-Sync Protocol for Sensor Networks", *in Proc. of SenSys'03*, Los Angeles, California, USA, October 2003.

[16] RF Monolithics. http:// www. rfm. com/, *ASH Transceiver TR1000 Data Sheet.*

[17] J. Hill, R. Szewczyk, A. Woo, S. Hollar, D. E. Culler, and K. Pister, "System architecture directions for network sensors", in *Proceedings of the International Conference on Architectural Support for Programming Languages and Operating Systems (ASPLOS)*, November 2000.

Integrated Multi-layer Registration Combining SIP with Mobile IP Schemes

Lin-huang Chang [1], Jui-jen Lo[1], Chih-Yu Hsu[1,2], and Ing-chau Chang[3]

[1] Graduate Institute of Networking and Communication Eng.
ChaoYang University of Technology, Taichung, R.O.C.
lchang@cyut.edu.tw
[2] Chung Shan Medical University, Taiwan, R.O.C.
[3] Department of Computer Science and Information Eng.
National Chunghua Univ. of Education, Chunghua, R.O.C.

Abstract. Mobile communications will be the major applications of next-generation Internet. The users may access the mobile services using handheld devices anywhere and anytime. Therefore, mobility management will play a significant role in providing mobile multimedia services. Both MIP and SIP have been proposed to solve the IP mobility issues. For the multimedia application such as VoIP, SIP has been studied and widely deployed recently. To process various data with both MIP and SIP protocols, it is necessary to design an efficient multi-layer registration scheme for mobility management and multimedia services. In this paper, we propose an integrated scheme to improve the registration efficiency for mobile nodes carrying out both MIP and SIP protocols. The number of registration message as well as the registration delay will be reduced by using the proposed integrated multi-layer registration scheme.

Keywords: Mobile IP, SIP, mobility management, multi-layer registration.

1 Introduction

In the recent years, the wireless communication network has been popular for most people. Under the various network environments, novel wireless network technologies has emerged and developed rapidly. For example, IEEE 802.11 and 802.16 are used in Local Area Network (LAN) and Metropolitan Area Network (MAN), respectively; Bluetooth is used in transmission through short distance for personal devices; telecommunications including 2.5 generation and the third generation are used for Wide Area Network (WAN).

Different designs and applications for these technologies may result in dissimilar performance and efficiency. The personal devices are designed as pocket-sized mobile handhelds, with which people can carry to anywhere and at anytime when they need certain network service. In view of mobility management, the network developing organizations have designed lots of wireless network protocols or standards. Among these protocols or standards, Mobile IP (MIP) [1], which allows transparent routing of IP datagrams to mobile nodes in the Internet, is one of the most popular protocols.

X. Cheng, W. Li, and T. Znati (Eds.): WASA 2006, LNCS 4138, pp. 228–239, 2006.

Another important trend over the past few years is the Voice over IP (VoIP) service. The voice data being transmitted over a packet network will encounter some problems. The first one is the out-of-order problem in the packet network. Secondly, the traditional voice is based on the circuit-switch network which means some bandwidth would be dedicated from one end all the way to the other end during the communication even the period with no voice data transmission. The drawback for such circumstance will be the waste of the network bandwidth. The Internet Engineering Task Force (IETF) sets up many protocols for the VoIP to compensate for these problems such as Media Gateway Control Protocol (MGCP) [2] and Session Initiation Protocol (SIP) [3]. Among these protocols, SIP has become the mainstream for VoIP signaling recently. The SIP operates at the application layer and handles all aspects of signaling such as call forwarding, conference call (via multicast) and media capability negotiation (via Session Description Protocol, SDP). Because the communication procedure of SIP is much easier than that of the other VoIP standards, such as H.323 [4, 5], SIP is more convenient for users in applications. On the other hand, because SIP can also support user mobility, the SIP-based mobility management has become one of the interesting issues.

The research in [6] discussed opportune moment of using MIP and SIP. They pointed out that there are different features for these two protocols. If one mobile node (MN) wants to transmit real-time packets, such as using VoIP, it would communicate with the other node using SIP. On the other hand, for non real-time data transmission, such as FTP and HTTP, generally the MN would apply MIP for mobility management. Based on these situations, researches [7] proposed a multilayered mobility management scheme for auto-configured wireless IP networks. Although they integrated the MIP and SIP to transmit different time-sensitive messages, they did not consider the issue regarding dual registration to the home agent (HA) and SIP server with integration. That is, when an MN roams to a foreign network (FN), it needs to register with HA and SIP server respectively. This will enlarge the set-up signaling delay for real-time applications, especially for VoIP service.

In order to enhance the registration efficiency for dual registration, we propose the integration of the registration phase combining SIP with MIP schemes. Our design will reduce the number of registration messages as well as overall signaling delay and consequently enhance the registration performance.

This paper is organized as follows. In section 2, we will discuss briefly the mobility management procedures of both MIP and SIP schemes. The proposed scheme will be described completely in section 3 which is followed by the performance analysis of the proposed scheme in section 4. In section 4, we will also provide the comparison of simulated results among our design with MIP and SIP schemes. Finally, we will conduct a conclusion for this research.

2 Background and Related Work

In this article, we emphasize on the integration of MIP and SIP. For this reason, we will briefly describe the MIP and SIP schemes with registration procedures, and then discuss some of the possible problems as well as related researches.

2.1 Mobile IP

Mobile IP architecture is mainly composed of MN, Correspondent Node (CN), HA and Foreign Agent (FA). When an MN roams to an FN, the MN will acquire a provisional IP called Care-of-Address (CoA) by sending the solicitation message to or receiving the advertisement from the FA. After the acquirement of the CoA, the MN will inform its HA located at HN through the registration procedure. The HA will bind the CoA to the MN's home address (HoA).

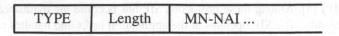

Fig. 1. The MN NAI extension format

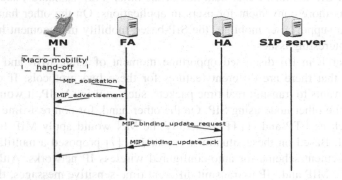

Fig. 2. MIP registration procedure

However, this process may cause a problem for the unfixed IP address allocation in the HN. For example, if an MN's HoA is allocated by the HA using Dynamic Host Configuration Protocol (DHCP) [8], it may not provide HA the same HoA to identify the MN. To solve this problem, the MIP employs the Network Address Identifier (NAI) [9] extension header, as shown in Figure 1, to identify the MN. The detailed description of the NAI extension header is referred to [10]. The MIP registration procedure is shown in Figure 2. Upon registering to the HA, the MN needs to obtain the CoA through the solicitation and advertisement processes. The detailed discussion about the process delay will be presented in section 4.

2.2 Session Initiation Protocol (SIP)

SIP is an IETF standardized protocol for establishing, manipulating and tearing down an interactive user session that involves multimedia parts such as audio, video, instant message, or other real-time data communications. Although H.322 was designed early than SIP for VoIP signaling, SIP has played a major role in VoIP applications and even replaces H.323 currently due to its simplicity and flexibility.

The research in [11] has used SIP to proceed with the mobility management. When an MN roams to a foreign network, it will obtain an IP address from the DHCP server first. The MN will then notify its register server to re-register or to re-invite the CN for transmitting message. The SIP registration procedure is shown in Figure 3. The simplified SIP registration message format is shown in Figure 4.

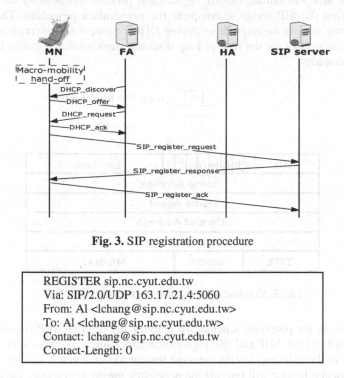

Fig. 3. SIP registration procedure

```
REGISTER sip.nc.cyut.edu.tw
Via: SIP/2.0/UDP 163.17.21.4:5060
From: Al <lchang@sip.nc.cyut.edu.tw>
To: Al <lchang@sip.nc.cyut.edu.tw>
Contact: lchang@sip.nc.cyut.edu.tw
Contact-Length: 0
```

Fig. 4. SIP registration message

In this paper, the major concern is to reduce the registration delay with procedures accommodated to both MIP and SIP schemes. For MIP scheme, the registration process provides a more efficient procedure than that of the SIP mobility management in acquiring an IP address while roaming into an FN [12]. However, for the applications using SIP as signaling and MIP as mobility management, the complete registration procedures will be complicated and time consuming. Therefore, we will propose an efficient registration procedure combining SIP with MIP schemes. The integration of registration procedure can be accomplished by piggybacking the SIP registration messages through the MIP registration process, which will be discussed in the next section.

3 The Proposed Scheme

In this section we will describe the detailed procedures of our proposed scheme—the MN registers to the SIP server through its FA and HA by using the MIP registration message. First, we assume that the MN is able to employ both MIP and SIP as mobility management. If an MN, implemented with SIP-based mobility management, roams into an FN, it will apply the DHCP to acquire a new IP address. Completing the DHCP process will take four transmission messages traveling from the MN, located at FN, to the DHCP server, located at SIP server domain. After obtaining the IP address, the MN will initiate the SIP registration process followed by the responded signaling from the SIP server to complete the registration procedure. This scenario with four transmission message flows during DHCP process will increase the handoff delay time, especially for the case of long distance transmission between the FN and SIP server domain.

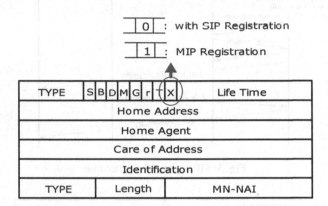

Fig. 5. Modified MIP Registration Message with NAI

Therefore, in the proposed scheme, we employ the original MIP registration message to complete both MIP and SIP registration procedures. We also apply the extension header in the MIP registration message format to our scheme, as shown in Figure 5. This extension header will provide the necessary message to reduce the registration process. On behalf of the MN, the FA in our scheme will register to the SIP server. Furthermore, if the SIP server is located at the same domain as HA, the HA in our scheme will register to the SIP server on behalf of the MN.

As recommended by IETF's request for comments (RFC) [13], the SIP request-URI should be unique and identical to the NAI whose format is similar to the e-mail style. Because the MIP provides the NAI extension capability therefore the FA or HA, which stands for the MN, could register to the SIP server by employing the NAI extension header. Furthermore, the NAI option header is originally designed for the HA to identify the MN when the MN's HoA is not available. That means, one way for the MN without a fixed HoA to authenticate itself to the HA as well as FA while being away from the HN is to apply this NAI option header. A message containing the MN NAI extension in the registration request may set the home address field to zero to request for an assigned HoA.

In order to register to the SIP server smoothly, the FA or HA on behalf of the MN in our proposed scheme will employ the third-part registration mechanism described in SIP protocol [3]. As recommended, the SIP registration, standing for a particular address-of-record, can be completed through the authorized third-party registration. In our proposed scheme, we will utilize the "x" flag in the MIP registration message to fulfill this registration as shown in Figure 5. The "x" flag in the registration field, being set to zero, originally is not used and is ignored on reception. When the "x" flag is set to one, the FA or HA will stand for the MN to register to the SIP server.

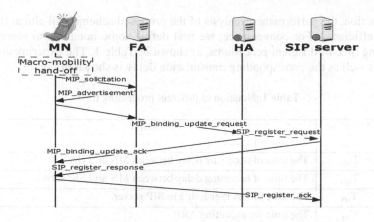

Fig. 6. Registration procedure with MIP and SIP

When an MN leaves its home network and moves into a foreign network, it will acquire a CoA through the advertisement message of the FA. For simplicity, we discuss the following analysis of our proposed scheme when the HA and SIP server are located in the same domain. In this case, the HA on behalf of MN will perform the registration to SIP server. The MN will send a registration request with NAI extension header through FA to its HA after realizing that it is away from home. Upon receiving the registration request, the HA decides whether it will proceed the SIP registration. The registration procedure combined SIP with MIP is shown in Figure 6. The detailed registration steps are described as follows:

Step1. When an MN moves to the FN from its HN, it will acquire a CoA through the advertisement sent from the FA or the solicitation sent by the MN itself.

Step2. The MN will send a registration request to its HA which contains the NAI extension header with the acquired CoA.

Step3. Upon receiving the registration request, the HA will update its binding table followed by sending a registration response to the MN to complete the procedure of the MIP registration phase.

Step4. In the mean while, the HA will exam the "x" flag bit. If it is set to one, the HA should proceed the SIP registration on behalf of the MN. The HA will utilize the NAI field message to deploy the third-party registration.

Step5. The HA on behalf of the MN will register to the SIP server with the NAI message.

Step6. Upon receiving the registration message sent from the HA, the SIP server will response with a message "200 OK" to the MN.

This proposed procedure therefore will provide a mechanism for the MN to complete both the MIP and SIP registration with the assistant of the third-party, HA. The next section will conduct the performance analysis of our proposed scheme. The comparison among different schemes will also be presented.

4   Performance Analysis

In this section, the performance analysis of the proposed scheme will aim at the transmission efficiency. For convenience, we first define some notations to represent the processing time of different procedures, as shown in Table 1. The experimental architecture as well as the corresponding transmission delay is shown in Figure 7.

Table 1. Notation of different processing time

Notation	Definition
T_{MF}	The time of accessing delay between MN and FA
T_{MH}	The time of accessing delay between MN and HA
T_{MS}	The time of accessing delay between MN and SIP server
T_{HS}	The time of HA registering to SIP server.
T_{arp}	The time for executing ARP
T_{mip}	The time for a simple MIP registration
T_{sip}	The time for a simple SIP registration

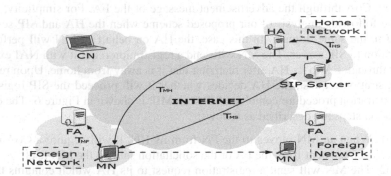

Fig. 7. Experimental Architecture

4.1   Transmission Delay

From the discussion above, we could set $T_{MH} \approx T_{HS}$. On the other hand, the access delay from MN to HA is larger than the delay from MN to FA while the MN being away from home. Thus, $T_{MF} < T_{MH}$ is expected.

For MIP registration procedure, as shown in Figure 2, the solicitation and advertisement messages for discovering and initiating the connection will take one round–trip transmission between the MN and the FA, denoted as $2T_{MF}$. After the initiation, when the MN sends a registration message to the HA, the HA will return a registration reply. To complete the registration procedure, the MN needs one round-trip transmission time between the MN and the HA, denoted as $2T_{MH}$. Therefore, the transmission time of MIP registration can be expressed as equation (1).

$$T_{mip} = 2T_{MF} + 2T_{MH} . \tag{1}$$

For SIP registration procedure, as shown in Figure 3, the time for an MN to conduct a DHCP discovery as well as request and then to acquire an IP will take two round-trip transmissions between the MN and the DHCP server, denoted as $4T_{MF}$. While acquiring an IP through the DHCP procedure, the MN will employ the duplicate address detection (DAD)[14] to ensure that the acquired IP is not used by others. Under such circumstance, the MN will perform the address resolution protocol (ARP) which takes T_{arp}. After all these processes, the MN will register to the SIP server. To complete the registration, it needs three message transmission delay between the MN and the SIP server, denoted as $3T_{MH}$. Therefore, the transmission time of registration can be expressed as equation (2).

$$T_{sip} = 4T_{MF} + T_{arp} + 3T_{MH} . \tag{2}$$

When both MIP and SIP mobility management protocols exist simultaneously in the network, an MN, which supports both schemes, will need to register to them individually. The total time consuming for the registration procedures will be the summation of equations (1) and (2), denoted as

$$T_{mip\_sip} = 6T_{MF} + T_{arp} + 5T_{MH} . \tag{3}$$

The total time consumption for our integrated registration procedure, however, can be expressed as equation (4) which is followed by the explanation below.

$$T_{ours} = 2T_{MF} + 4T_{MH} + T_{HS}. \tag{4}$$

Because the MN employs the MIP registration procedure, it only takes $2T_{MF}$ to acquire an IP. Then, the MN sends a registration message to its HA followed by a registration response by the HA. In the mean while, the HA on behalf of the MN will register to the SIP server. The SIP server will then respond a message to the MN. The time consumed for this registration process will be $4T_{MH}$. The transmission delay within the local network under such circumstance is ignored due to the relatively high bandwidth and short transmission distance. On the other hand, the processing time for the HA to register to the SIP server, T_{HS}, can be assumed to be 2 ms according to [15]. It is reasonable to take T_{HS} as 2ms because HA and SIP server are located in the same domain and connected via high speed wired lines.

We conduct the numerical analysis of our proposed integrated scheme according to the equations described above. If an MN accesses a foreign network through the wireless connection, the access delay time can be assumed to be 10ms and T_{MH} would be a variable according to the research in [12]. The analysis on the other hand does not take T_{arp} into account for all different registration schemes because its value is about 1-3 seconds which will become the dominant factor for all result. This was also discussed in [12] and the T_{arp} could be replaced by the time delay through Dynamic Rapid and Configuration Protocol (DRCP) [16].

Based on the proposed scheme, we conduct the following two numerical analyses. First of all, we calculate the total registration delay (including MIP and SIP registrations) while an MN roaming into different FNs. Different FNs result in different distances from FN to HN, meaning different transmission delay from FA to HA. Different FNs may also result in different access speed at FN, meaning different wireless link delay at FN. Under such circumstance, it implies that different T_{MH} will be conducted for the numerical analyses according to the equations described early. Figure 8 shows the results of the total registration delay while an MN being away from HN with different distances from FN to HN. Different T_{MH}, ranged from 15ms to 50ms, due to the transmission times from different FAs to the HA are carried out in Figure 8. The proposed scheme is compared with MIP registration followed by SIP registration.

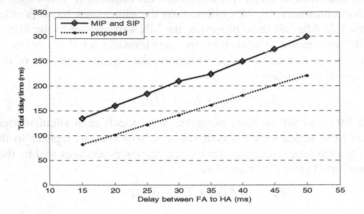

Fig. 8. The total process delay with different T_{MH} at foreign network

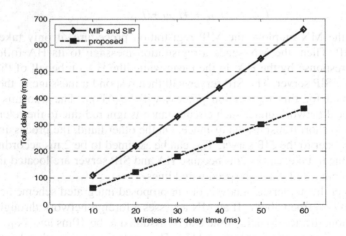

Fig. 9. The total process delay with different wireless link delays at foreign network

On the other hand, Figure 9 represents the results of the total registration time with different wireless link delays at FN. For example, the direct sequence rating scaling (implying the transmission speed) for IEEE 802.11b can be 1, 2, 5.5 or 11 Mbps. This numerical analysis is carried out for different wireless link delays at FN from 10ms to 60ms.

Both Figures 8 and 9 conclude that our proposed algorithm, compared with the existed MIP and SIP while an MN is away from home, provides an efficient registration scheme in terms of total registration delay.

The second numerical analysis calculates the total registration delay when the MN moves back to the HN. Thus, Equations (1) to (4) can be modified as follows, respectively,

$$T_{mip} = 4T_{MH}.$$ (5)

$$T_{sip} = 7T_{MH} + T_{arp}.$$ (6)

$$T_{mip\_sip} = 11T_{MH} + T_{arp}.$$ (7)

$$T_{ours} = 6T_{MH} + T_{HS}.$$ (8)

Under such situation, different access speed at HN, meaning different wireless link delay at HN will affect the total registration delay. Figure 10 shows the results of the total registration delay with different wireless link delay from 10ms to 60ms at HN based on Equations (5) to (8). Besides our scheme and MIP/SIP registration processes, the solo MIP and SIP registration delays are also shown in Figure 10 for reference.

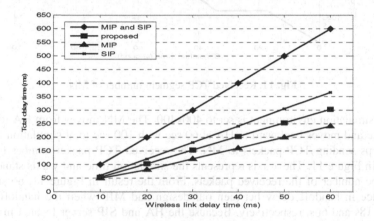

Fig. 10. The total process delay with different wireless link delays at HN

From Figure 10 we can see that our proposed algorithm is not only superior to the existed MIP and SIP schemes in terms of efficient registration but also better than the solo SIP registration. The reason for slightly higher delay with solo SIP registration than our scheme is because SIP registration deploys the DHCP to acquire IP address which takes 2 round trip wireless transmissions. These results in relative raise of the total registration delay for solo SIP registration compared with our design when the wireless link delay increases. This is because the effect of the wireless link delay becomes the dominated factor under such scenario.

Figures 8 to 10 conclude that our proposed scheme not only integrates the registration message flow for both MIP and SIP protocols, but also reduces the total registration delay efficiently. The outstanding performance and efficient registration of our proposed scheme is sustained for different distances between MN and HN as well as different wireless line access delays.

4.2 Throughput

We employ the network simulation-2 (ns2) to simulate the influence of the received packets on MN handoff. We compare our design with solo MIP handoff. The reason to conduct this simulation is to evaluate the packet loss of handoff for our design which takes additional SIP registration process via MIP registration procedure.

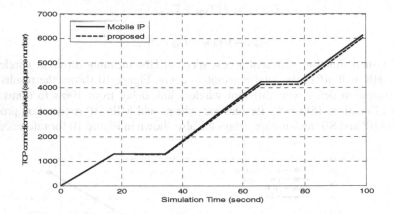

Fig. 11. Received TCP segment number of MN

The simulation environment is set to 400x400. The MN moves from HA toward FA at 15 sec and moves backward to HA at 60 sec with 100 sec total simulation time. The CN keeps sending TCP packets to MN. The received TCP packet number for MN is shown in Figure 11. The x axis represents the simulation time and y axis stands for the sequence number of the received packets. From the result in Figure 11, no significant difference in handoff delay between our design and MIP when the handoff starts at around 18s and 66s, respectively. Because the HA and SIP server located in the same domain, the delay for both MIP and SIP registration is minimized by using our proposed scheme. Therefore, the received packets for our design maintains about the same amount as that of MIP. However, our scheme accomplished both MIP and SIP registrations simply with integration and reduced the total registration delay effectively.

5 Conclusions

To carry out multi-layer mobility management using MIP and SIP protocols, an MN needs to process them separately. In this research, we have proposed an integrated multi-layer registration scheme combining SIP with MIP for mobility management as well as multimedia applications. The designed scheme effectively reduces the transmission message flows and the overall registration delay.

More tuning in transmission delay parameters for our proposed scheme is under studied and analyzed. For the micro mobility using both MIP and SIP, different registration mechanisms to achieve better performance in terms of registration delay, message flow and bottleneck issue will also be studied for the further research.

Acknowledgement

The authors would like to thank the support from National Science Council of Republic of China, under contract number NSC 93-2622-E-324-011-CC3.

References

1. C. Perkins, "IP Mobility Support for IPv4," RFC 3344, Aug 2003.
2. F. Andreasen, B. Foster.," Media Gateway Control Protocol (MGCP) V. 1.0," RFC 3435, Jan 2003.
3. J. Rosenberg, H. Schulzrinne, G. Camarillo, A. Johnston, J. Peterson, R. Sparks, M. Handley, E. Schooler, "SIP: Session Initiation Protocol," RFC 3261, Jun 2002.
4. ITU-T Recommendation H.323 (07/03), Packet-based multimedia communications systems, 2003.
5. OpenH323 Resources. (http://www.openh323.org).
6. Jin-Woo Jung, Hyun-Kook Kahng, Ranganathan Mudumbai, Doug Montgomery "Performance Evaluation of Two Layered Mobility Management using Mobile IP and Session Initiation Protocol", Proceedings of IEEE GLOBECOM 2003.
7. K.D. Wong, A. Dutta, J. Burns, R. Jain, K.Young, H. Schulzrinne, "A multilayered mobility management scheme for auto-configured wireless IP networks," IEEE Wireless Communications, Vol 10 , Issue 5 , Oct 2003.
8. R. Droms, "Dynamic Host Configuration Protocol," RFC 2131, IETF,March 1997.
9. B. Aboba, M. Beadles, "The Network Access Identifier," RFC 2486, Jan 1999
10. P. Calhoun, C. Perkins, "Mobile IP Network Address Identifier Extension," RFC 2794, Mar. 2000.
11. Elin Wedlund, "Mobility support using SIP," ACM international workshop on Wireless mobile multimedia, 1999.
12. T.T. Kwon, M. Gerla, and S. Das, "Mobility management for VoIP service: Mobile IP vs. SIP," IEEE Wireless Communications, Vol 9 , Issue 5 , Oct 2002.
13. J. Rosenberg, H. Schulzrinne, P. Kyzivat, "Caller Preference for the Session Initiation Protocol (SIP)", IETF RFC 3841, Auguest 2004.
14. S. Thomson, Bellcore, T. Narten, IBM, "IPv6 Stateless Address Autoconfiguration," RFC 2462, Aug 2003.
15. E. Hernandez and A. Helal, "Examining Mobile-IP Performance in Rapidly Mobile Environments: The Case of a Commuter Train," 26th Annual IEEE Conf. Local Comp. Net., Nov. 2001.
16. A. McAuley, D. Chee, J. Chiang, S. Das, K. Manousakis, R. Morera, L. Wong and K. Young, "Automatic Configuration and Reconfiguration in Dynamic Networks," Army Science Conf. 2002, Dec. 2002.

ELS: Energy-Aware Some-for-Some Location Service for Ad Hoc Mobile Networks

Abdelouahid Derhab[1], Nadjib Badache[2], Karim Tari[2], and Sihem Sami[2]

[1] Basic software laboratory, CERIST, Rue des 3 frères Aissou, Ben-Aknoun,
BP 143 Algiers, 16030 Algeria
[2] LSI, USTHB, BP 32 El-Alia Bab-Ezzouar, 16111, Algiers, Algeria

Abstract. In this paper, we propose a new location service for Ad hoc mobile networks. The network area is divided into non-overlapping zones. Using a hash function, a node identifier is mapped to a set of zones, in which the location information of the node are stored. We also propose a location information distribution scheme that achieves low rate of outdated location information. Using cross-layer design, the service can tolerate servers mobility and failure, and last for a long time period. Simulation Results show that the proposed location service experiences low overhead and high location information availability and accuracy.

1 Introduction

A mobile ad hoc network is a collection of mobile nodes forming a temporary network without any form of centralized administration or predefined infrastructure. Each node acts both as a host and a router. Due to mobility, the network topology changes frequently, which makes the design of a scalable and robust routing protocol with low message overhead one of the challenging tasks in such a network.

In recent years, location-awareness is increasingly becoming an important feature of routing protocols and applications. Position-based routing protocols [3,11,9,7,13,18] use the geographic position of nodes available from positioning systems such as GPS [8] or other type of positioning service [1,4,2] to forward data packets. In contrast with topology-based category, they do not need to keep global states for routing data packets. To enable position-based routing, a node must be able to discover the location of the node whom it wants to communicate with. Thus, they have the advantage to scale to a larger number of nodes. Location information are provided by a so-called location service. The use of location services extends to other location-aware applications, e.g., location tracking and navigation, geocasting, or a tour guide that can provide location-dependent information to tourists (such as map, traffic, and site information). The effort needed to search for tourism information can be significantly reduced with the help of positioning.

The role of a location service is to map the ID of a node to its geographical position. Each location service performs two basic operations: the *location update* and the *location query*. The location update is responsible for distributing

X. Cheng, W. Li, and T. Znati (Eds.): WASA 2006, LNCS 4138, pp. 240–251, 2006.
© Springer-Verlag Berlin Heidelberg 2006

information about the current location of a given node D to a set of nodes called *location servers*. If a node S wants to know the location of node D, it sends a location query message to one of the location servers of node D.

When designing a location service, the following basic questions need to be considered: (1) When should a node update its location information? (2) to whom should a node send its position information? and (3) how should a node find the appropriate servers to query for a location. Ad hoc networks characteristics impose different challenges on designing location services. First, dynamic topology leads that there is no static relation between a node and its location. To distribute location information to a set of servers, the location service utilizes a routing protocol, but the routing protocol requires the location information of these servers in first place, which results in a functional deadlock. Second, the location service must incur low overhead in order that the servers do not drain out their batteries quickly. Third, network partitioning would make the location servers unreachable to some nodes, and hence it considerably decreases the availability and the accuracy of location information.

According to Mauve classification [15], the location services are classified according to how many nodes host the service (i.e., *some* or *all* nodes). Furthermore, each location server may maintain the position of *some* specific nodes or *all* nodes of the network. Thus, the four possible combinations are as follows: some-for-some, some-for-all, all-for-some, and all-for-all.

In this paper, our original contributions are the following. First, we propose a location information distribution scheme that achieves a lower cost than the quorum scheme. The proposed scheme is more likely to provide high location information availability and accuracy. Second, we combine the flat hashing-based approach and the proposed scheme to construct an efficient some-for-some location service. Third, we propose a cross-layer framework that helps the service to estimate when a server will run out of battery power or leave its zone. In doing so, the server will seamlessly replicate its stored location information on an alternative node before it disappears from its actual zone, and hence the service lifetime is increased. Fourth, according to application requirements, position information are provided with different levels of accuracy.

The rest of the paper is organized as follows: In Section 2, we present an overview of the system framework. A detailed description of the location service is presented in Section 3. Section 4 presents simulation results. Finally, Section 5 concludes the paper.

2   System Framework

The architecture of the proposed system framework shown in Fig. 1 consists of four layers: the application layer, the middleware layer, the routing layer and the mac layer. As part of the framework, the routing and the mac layers provide an estimation of the residual node lifetime and the available bandwidth respectively.

When a location-aware application such as the tour guide wants to obtain the position of a certain node D, it contacts the location service. This latter will

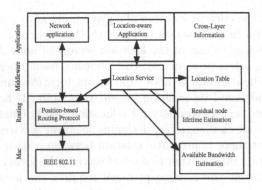

Fig. 1. System framework

check if such a position is available in its own location table. If so, it will directly respond to the application. Otherwise, it will demand the position-based routing protocol to find one of the location servers of D. The forwarding decision at each node is based on the destinations position and the position of the neighboring nodes. Typically, the packet is forwarded to a neighbor that is closer to the destination than the forwarding node itself, thus making progress toward the destination. In order to inform all neighbors within transmission range about its own position, a node transmits beacons at regular intervals. The location servers should respond with the current location of D. On the other hand, when a node S wants to communicate with a node D, it first contacts the routing protocol, which in turn contacts the location service. The location servers of D should respond with an approximative location information, i.e., the geographic area where D is located. In the cross-layer information, the routing layer estimates the residual battery lifetime by recording the different packets that pass through it. It can be used to determine the time at which the location information table will be replicated onto another node, in order to maintain location information availability for a long time period. The available bandwidth estimation provided by the mac layer is used to derive an upper-bound on the replication time.

3   Energy-Aware Some-for-Some Location Service

3.1   Basic Idea

The quorum based location services [10,12,6,14] can be configured to operate as a some-for-some approach. Update and query operations are performed on a subset of servers called a write quorum and a read quorum respectively. Using a such construction, we can avoid flooding the network, thus avoid wasting mobile nodes battery power. Furthermore, the load of each location server can be reduced by evenly distributing the load among the servers.

These subsets are designed such that each read quorum for a node intersects the write quorum for any other node. An important aspect of quorum-based position services is the following trade-off: the larger the quorum sets, the higher the cost for position updates and queries, but also the larger the number of nodes in the intersection of two quorums, which improves resilience against unreachable location servers. Ad hoc networks are subject to frequent network partitioning, link and node failures. In such environments, quorum systems may suffer from low availability in the face of node failures or unreachable nodes. Update and query operations may be performed at non-intersecting quorums, which may disable the quorum system, since the intersection property of that system is not guaranteed. To alleviate the problem of query failures, a set of heuristics is used in selecting servers for update and queries, by maintaining a list of servers that are unreachable [10].

The fundamental property of the quorum system states that "each read quorum must overlap with any write quorum". A location information can be written to or read from any randomly chosen quorum. Thus, the quorum systems are only efficient in an environment where the relation between a datum and a node is not considered. The location information are shared private, i.e., they are updated by a unique node (single-writer), and queried by the other nodes (multiple-reader). The existence of one-to-one relation between nodes and their positions, allows us to relax the intersection property and propose a new construction that maps each node i to a fixed subset of nodes, FS_i. To illustrate the advantage of the proposed construction, let us consider an example of a quorum system $A = \{\{1, 2, 3\}, \{1, 4, 5\}, \{2, 4, 6\}, \{3, 5, 6\}\}$. In this example, only one member is in the intersection of any pair of quorums. The absence of a single node makes the system inefficient. On the other hand, if we apply the proposed construction to the system A, and consider that the fixed subsets are the quorums of A, (i) we can get the same cost since update and query operations are performed on subsets with the same size, and (ii) the correct information is more likely to be provided since the probability that all nodes of a specific subset are unreachable is lower than that of the quorum construction.

The proposed construction is simple and more resilient to node failure and network partitioning than the quorum systems. However, such static membership may result in low data availability and accuracy, because nodes drain out of power very quickly. Thus, the disadvantages of quorum system still remains. To deal with the static feature of the proposed construction, we define the fixed subset FS as a set geographic zones. In each zone, a node is dynamically selected as a location server.

3.2   Area Partitioning

The area covered by the ad hoc network is partitioned into G square zones of equal-sizes. All of these zones have well-known identifiers (IDs) distributed over the range $[0, \cdots, G - 1]$. We assume that there exists a static function f that maps a node's ID into a specific zone. Formally, $f(\text{node ID}) \rightarrow \text{zone ID}$. This many-to-one mapping is also known by all nodes in the network. Figure 2 shows the partitioning scheme. The respective zones' identifier are shown in the upper-left corner of each zone. Each node is assigned a fixed subset consisting of α

Algorithm 1. The fixed subset construction for node A

1: $FS_A = \emptyset$;
2: $k := 0$;
3: **for** $j = 1$ to α **do**
4:    $FS_A = FS_A \cup \{f(id(A) + k)\}$;
5:    $k := k + \lceil \frac{G}{\alpha} \rceil$;
6: **end for**

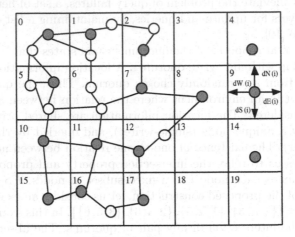

Fig. 2. Area partitioned according to a flat-based approach

zones, where α is a system parameter upper-bounded by G. The construction of the fixed subset for a node A is presented in Algorithm 1, where U_A denotes the set of zones' identifier. An example of a function f is: $f(ID) = (ID\%G)$. For $k = 0$, nodes that return the same value of $f()$ are assigned to the same fixed subset.

3.3   Location Server Selection

In the flat-based location services [19,17,5], a well-known hash function is used to map each node's identifier to a home region. All nodes in the home region maintain the location information for the node and reply to queries for that node. A major disadvantage of this design is the single fixed home region. Absence of a server from the region makes the service carries out complex actions like storing the location information in the neighboring regions.

Unlike the other flat-based location services, a unique node from the zone is selected as a location server. We propose the *stability of a node* as a metric for the location server selection criterion. The metric predicts the time period during which the node will remain in its zone. It is based on the residual battery power and the current positions of the node. A node disappears from its zone either: (i) if it moves out of its current zone, or (ii) or it drains out of its energy power. Each node i estimates its stability as follows: First, it calculates the rate of its battery power depletion R_i for every time period $\triangle T$, then it estimates, as shown in equation 1, the residual time before it runs out of energy power such that E_i denotes i's residual battery power.

$$Tpow_i = \frac{E_i}{\max(R_i)}(s) \tag{1}$$

Second, it calculates the remaining time before it moves out of its current zone, $Tmob_i$.

$$Tmob_i = \frac{\min(dN(i), dS(i), dE(i), dW(i))}{Vmax_i} \tag{2}$$

Where $dN(i)$, $dS(i)$, $dE(i)$, and $dw(i)$ are the distances that separate node i from the north, south, east, west sides of its current zone, and $Vmax_i$ is the node i's maximum velocity. The respective distances are depicted in Fig. 2. Equation 2 derives a conservative estimate on $Tmob_i$. It assumes that the node is moving toward the nearest side. Finally, the stability of node i ξ_i is given by the following equation.

$$\xi_i = \min(Tpow_i, Tmob_i) \tag{3}$$

Initially, the node with the highest value of stability will be selected as the location server of its zone. Ties are broken by comparing node identifiers.

The fixed subsets construction, the flat-based approach, and the location server selection procedure leads to the creation of G servers. We assume that $G < n$. Each server node stores the location information of $(\frac{\alpha \times n}{G})$ nodes. As $(\frac{\alpha}{G}) < 1$, the proposed location service can be classified as a some-for-some approach.

3.4   Service Operations

Nodes perform two types of operations: *update* and *query*. Each operation has its corresponding response, *ack* for update and *reply* for query. Each operation is transformed into a message. Each location server holds a location table, which records for each stored node the following fields: (1) its id, (2) the zone id where that node is in, (3) its exact location, and (4) its tiemstamp(i.e. the latest update time known by the location server).

Location Update. When a node i moves out of its current zone and into a new one, it sends an *update* message toward the center of each zone $\in FS_i$. The update packet contains the following information:

$< src\ id,\ seq,\ src\ region,\ target\ region,\ new\ region,\ new\ position,\ new\ timestamp >$.

The pair (*src id, seq*) denotes the source node and the sequence number of the packet. It uniquely identifies the update packet. *src region* is the id of the source node's zone and *target region* is the server node's zone. *new region* and *new position* is the node's new region and new position respectively. The update packet includes the id of its new zone and the new timestamp. the new timestamp is obtained by increasing the current timestamp by one.

When the packet reaches a node in the target zone, two cases can occur. If that node has a cached route to the location server, the packet is immediately routed toward the server. Otherwise, a route discovery packet is broadcasted in the zone to find a route to the location server. Upon receiving the update packet, the location server sends back an ack packet to the source node.

Location Query. According to users and applications requirements, query packets can be sent with two levels of accuracy: high, and low:

- *High accuracy:* The exact position of the requested node is needed by the location-aware applications.
- *Low accuracy:* It is required by position-based routing protocols, that aims to deliver data packets to destination nodes, and not to know the exact location of those nodes.

A source node S wishing to obtain the position of a node D, sends a query packet toward the center of each zone $\in FS_D$. The query packet contains the following information: $< src\ id,\ seq,\ src\ region,\ target\ region,\ queried\ id,\ accuracy >$.

queried id is the id of the node whose location is being queried. *accuracy* indicates the accuracy level required.

A node inside a target zone which receives the query packet, either it uses a cached route to the location server or it broadcasts a route discovery packet to all nodes within the zone so that a route toward the location server is established, and then it routes the packet to the server.

Upon receiving the query packet, the location server will first check the *accuracy* field of the packet. If the accuracy required is low, it sends back to S a reply packet containing D's zone along with the timestamp. Node S chooses among the reply packets that of the largest timestamp (i.e., the most recent location information). If the accuracy field is high, the location server will send the query packet to the target node D. D sends back a reply packet containing D's location to node S. Any further query packets with the same source node and sequence number will be discarded by node D.

3.5   Unreachable Zones

If a node i fails to contact the server of a certain zone, it considers that the zone is unreachable. A zone is called unreachable if either it is empty or the location server in that zone is unreachable due to network partitioning. To avoid unnecessary message overhead, each node keeps a set, called the *Unreachable zone list (UZL)*. This latter includes the zones' ID which are unreachable. When a given zone is declared as unreachable, it will be added to *Unreachable zone list* for a period of time T. During that period, update and query packets are sent to $FS_i - UZL_i$. After the expiration of T, the zone in question will be removed from that set.

3.6   Handling Mobility and Failure of Location Servers

When a location server becomes no longer available, queries that arrive between the time that the server is unavailable and the next updates from nodes whose locations are stored at the server will fail. To address this issue, the location server node that is about to cross the boundary of its zone or it is about to run out of battery power, has to replicate the location information table onto a new node before it leaves the zone or it dies. The service replication is triggered when the following constraint is verified: $(\xi_i - \Delta T) < time\ of\ replication\ process$. Let us consider that D denotes the size of location information table to be replicated and transmitted over an end–to–end wireless connection with an available bandwidth of B bits/s. The replication process needs $(\frac{D}{B})$ seconds in order to be achieved. The old server i and the new server j must fulfill the following requirements: (1) $(\xi_i(t) - \Delta T) < (\frac{D}{B})$ and (2) $\xi_j(t)$ is the maximum among the nodes of its zone.

The problem that can occur when tracking the residual lifetime of a node in its zone, is its disappearance during the interval Δt. No warning is generated until the next period. By that time, the server may be already disappeared or not enough time is left to carry out the replication process. To efficiently track the node in its zone, the following property must hold true $\Delta t < \max\left(\frac{1}{Vmax_i}, \frac{1}{\max(R_i)}\right)$. This technique ensure any-time service availability as long as the zone is not empty.

4   Simulation Results

In this section, we study the performance of the proposed service using GloMoSim simulator [21]. The entire region is a square with 2000 m. All nodes have a transmission range of 250 m. They move according the waypoint mobility model. In this model, a node randomly selects a location and moves toward it with a constant speed uniformly distributed between zero and a maximum speed $V_{max} = 7\ m/s$, then it stays stationary during a pause time of 1 second before moving to a new random location. Initially, each mobile node has a battery capacity of 400 joules. We have implemented three location services, which are (1) the quorum-based location service with unreachable node list and hybrid construction [10] that uses AODV routing protocol [16], (2) DLM [20], and (3) our proposed energy-aware location service (ELS). We have also implemented GPSR [9] with perimeter as a routing protocol. Nodes periodically initiate queries with different levels to random destinations. The following metrics are evaluated for the location service protocols:

1. *Update cost:* The total number of hops traversed by update packets.
2. *Query cost:* The total number of hops traversed by query packets.
3. *Availability:* It indicates the ability to access location information when needed. If N_s denotes the number of successful attempts to access a location information, and N_a is the total number of attempts. The availability is defined to be: $\frac{N_s}{N_a}$.
4. *Accuracy:* If N_q denotes the number of query operations. and N_o the number of outdated values returned by those queries. The accuracy is defined to be: $\frac{(N_q - N_o)}{N_q}$.
5. *Service lifetime:* The time until all the location servers run out of power.

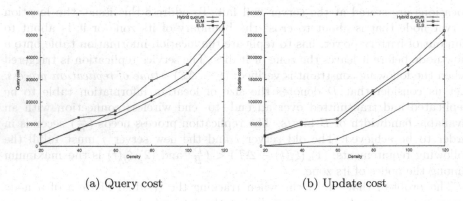

(a) Query cost   (b) Update cost

Fig. 3. Overhead cost

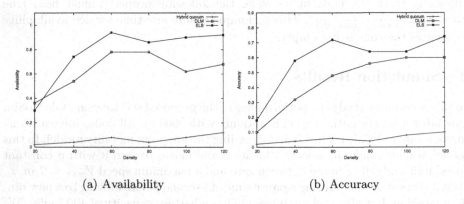

(a) Availability   (b) Accuracy

Fig. 4. Service reliability

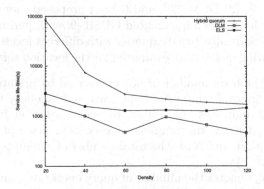

Fig. 5. Service life-time

All of our simulations are conducted without any data traffic, which discard the factors affecting node lifetime, and hence allows us to better judge the performance of services. To study the performance of the service for network scalability, we have varied the total number of nodes in the network.

Figure 3(a) and figure 3(b) show the location query cost and the location update cost respectively. Hybrid quorum has the best results. However, these results are misleading because as topology changes frequently, more nodes will be added to the set of *unreachable nodes* and hence, *query* and *update* packets will be sent to a fewer number of nodes. The quorum construction fails to efficiently spread the location information in the network. In contrast to hybrid quorum, the targets of query and update packets in DLM and ELS do not consist of moving nodes but of regions with fixed positions making the scheme more robust to node mobility. ELS performs better than DLM since packets are routed directly toward the target zones. In DLM packets must follow the defined hierarchical order, which results that packets take long routes in terms of number of hops.

Figure 4(a) and figure 4(b) show the availability and accuracy of the three location services. Availability and accuracy increase as density increase in all services, because the network gets more connected, and hence nodes are likely to successfully deliver their query and update packets to the target location servers. ELS shows the best rates of availability and accuracy. This is due to the fact that packets are sent toward location servers locating in different zones. A node can obtain location information of a queried node following the response of one server. Second, as we will see in Fig. 5, ELS lasts for a long time period because the servers replicates their location tables onto a new node before they leave their zones or run out of power. So, the location information is more likely to be available and be correct. In contrast to ELS, DLM must access a chain of location servers in a certain order. If any single server in this chain is unreachable, the query operation fails. Moreover, a server in DLM does not hand over the location information to another server before it leaves its region, and does not handle the depletion of node's power, which increase the probability of query failures.

Figure 5 shows the service lifetime experienced by the location services. Hybrid quorum has the best results. However, these results are misleading since as we have seen in Fig. 3, hybrid quorum does not efficiently spread location information in the network, and as topology changes, more nodes will be added to the set of unreachable nodes resulting in less messages generation. ELS performs better than DLM because the location servers replicate their location tables onto a new elected location server before they disappear from their zones, which considerably increases the lifetime of ELS.

5   Conclusion

In this paper, we have presented the Energy-aware Some-for-some Location Service (ELS). ELS combines a simple location information distribution scheme and a flat-based hash function to select zones where location information will be stored. ELS is suitable for different application requirements. Updates and query packets are sent toward fixed zones, which permits to avoid tracking the location servers when they change their zones or die. A new server is elected when the current server is about to leave the zone or run out of power. This technique significantly increases the service lifetime. The simulation results show the effectiveness of the proposed scheme. The proposed location service experiences high location information availability and accuracy, high service lifetime and it incurs low cost.

References

1. S. apkun, M. Hamdi, and J. Hubaux. Gps-free positioning in mobile ad-hoc networks. In *Proceedings of the 34th Hawaii International Conference on System Sciences*, 2001.
2. S. apkun, M. Hamdi, and J. P. Hubaux. Gps-free positioning in mobile ad-hoc networks. *Cluster Computing Journal*, 5(2), April 2002.
3. S. Basagni, I. Chlamtac, V.R. Syrotiuk, and B.A. Woodward. A distance routing effect algorithm for mobility (dream). In *Proceedings of the ACM/IEEE International Conference on Mobile Computing and Networking (MOBICOM)*, pages 76–84, 1998.
4. N. Bulusu, J. Heidemann, and D. Estrin. Gps-less low-cost outdoor localization for very small devices. *IEEE Personal Communications*, 7(5):28–34, October 2000.
5. Saumitra M. Das, Himabindu Pucha, and Charlie Hu. Performance comparison of scalable location services for geographic ad hoc routing. In *Proceedings of IEEE INFOCOM 2005*, March 2005.
6. Zygmunt J. Haas and Ben Liang. Ad hoc mobility management with uniform quorum systems. *IEEE/ACM Transactions on Networking*, 7(2):228–240, 1999.
7. R. Jain, A. Puri, and R. Sengupta. Geographical routing using partial information for wireless ad hoc networks. *IEEE Personal Communications*, pages 48–57, February 2001.
8. E. Kaplan. *Understanding GPS*. Artech House, Norwood, MA, 1996.
9. B. Karp and H. T. Kung. Gpsr: Greedy perimeter stateless routing for wireless networks. In *Proceedings of the ACM/IEEE International Conference on Mobile Computing and Networking (MOBICOM)*, pages 243–254, 2000.
10. Goutham Karumanchi, Srinivasan Muralidharan, and Ravi Prakash. Information dissemination in partitionable mobile ad hoc networks. In *Symposium on Reliable Distributed Systems*, pages 4–13, 1999.
11. Y. Ko and N.H. Vaidya. Location-aided routing (lar) in mobile ad hoc networks. In *Proceedings of the ACM/IEEE International Conference on Mobile Computing and Networking (MOBICOM)*, pages 66–75, 1998.
12. Hyunyoung Lee, Jennifer L. Welch, and Nitin H. Vaidya. Location tracking with quorums in mobile ad hoc networks. *Ad Hoc Networks, Elsevier Science*, 1(4):371–381, November 2003.
13. W.-H. Liao, Y.-C. Tseng, and J.-P. Sheu. Grid: a fully location-aware routing protocol for mobile ad hoc networks. *Telecommunication Systems*, 18:6184, 2001.
14. Dahlia Malkhi, Michael K. Reiter, Avishai Wool, and Rebecca N. Wright. Probabilistic quorum systems. *Information and Computation*, 170(2):184–206, 2001.
15. M. Mauve, J. Widmer, and H. Hartenstein. A survey on position-based routing in mobile ad hoc networks. *IEEE Network*, 15(6):30–39, November/December 2001.

16. C. E. Perkins and E. M.Royer. Ad hoc on demand distance vector (aodv) algorithm. In *Proceedings of 2nd IEEE Workshop on Mobile Computing Systems and Applications (WMCSA'99)*, pages 90–100, February 1999.
17. I. Stojmenovic. Home agent based location update and destination search schemes in ad hoc wireless networks. Technical Report TR-99-10, University of Ottawa, September 1999.
18. I. Stojmenovic and X. Lin. Loop-free hybrid single-path/flooding routing algorithms with guaranteed delivery for wireless network. *IEEE Transactions on Parallel and Distributed Systems*, 12, 2001.
19. S.-C. Woo and S. Singh. Scalable routing protocol for ad hoc networks. *ACM Wireless Networks*, 7(5):513–529, September 2001.
20. Y. Xue, B. Li, and K. Nahrstedt. A scalable location management scheme in mobile ad-hoc networks. In *Proceedings of the IEEE Conference on Local Computer Networks (LCN2001)*, Tampa, Florida, November 2001.
21. X. Zeng, R. Bagrodia, and M. Gerla. Glomosim: A library for parallel simulation of large-scale wireless networks. In *Workshop on Parallel and Distributed Simulation*, pages 154–161, 1998.

Throughput Capacity of UWB Ad-Hoc Networks with Infrastructure Support

Fan Zhang and Xiaoyun Kang

Dept. of Electronics and Information Engineering
Huazhong University of Science and Technology
Wuhan, 430074, P.R. China
fzhang9@gmail.com, acerHust_2006@smail.hust.edu.cn

Abstract. To provide scalable capacity of wireless ad-hoc networks, we employ a joint approach of both Ultra-Wide-Band (UWB) radio and hybrid architecture (ad-hoc network with infrastructure support). By using the AP(access point)-assisted percolation model, and utilizing sufficiently wide bandwidth under per-link power constraint, we find the asymptotic per-node throughput capacity of a UWB hybrid network in a unit disk area, as a function of the number of randomly distributed nodes, the number of randomly distributed AP, and the path loss exponent. This result shows an asymptotically significant factor of improvement in capacity by deploying AP, compared to the recent result for UWB pure ad-hoc network. An extension of the result in the more general D-dimensional space is also obtained.

Keywords: Wireless Networks, Ad-Hoc Networks, Ultra-Wide-Band (UWB), Throughput Capacity, Information Theory, Scalability.

1 Introduction

The capacity of wireless networks, which is fundamentally limited by interferences at the shared media, has recently attracted much research interest. Ad-hoc networking uses peer-to-peer cooperation to increase network capacity, to expand wireless coverage, and to enhance connection reliability, with applications from wireless Internet to sensor networks. Critical to fulfill such promise is rigorous investigation on the achievable capacity as well as scalable techniques to increase capacity, despite the immaturity of network information theory as compared to Shannon's classic result.

The seminal work [1] proved that in a wireless ad-hoc network with n nodes randomly placed on a plane and each source randomly choosing a destination, assuming a limited number of simultaneous transmissions, the per-node throughput decreases asymptotically as $O(1/\sqrt{n \log n})$, where the $\{O, \Omega, \Theta, o, \omega\}$ notations follow Knuth's convention. This inspired many subsequent researches [2][3][4].

For the power-constrained UWB case where bandwidth restriction is relaxed, assuming power and rate adaptation, the capacity bound presented in [8] is $\tilde{\Theta}(n^{(\alpha-1)/2})$, where $\alpha > 1$ is the path loss exponent, and the notation $\tilde{\Theta}(f(n))$ represents ignoring logarithmic factors in the asymptotic order. Its capacity is further

X. Cheng, W. Li, and T. Znati (Eds.): WASA 2006, LNCS 4138, pp. 252–263, 2006.

analyzed in [9] by percolation model, which is a statistical physics tool to analyze the stochastic behavior of wireless network [11][12][13], to be $\Theta(n^{(\alpha-1)/2})$.

As another approach to increase capacity, hybrid network is ad-hoc network with the support of wire-line infrastructure such as access points (AP). Its capacity gain [5][6][7][10] is asymptotically significant when $m = \Omega(\sqrt{n})$, where m is the number of randomly distributed APs.

In this paper, we investigate how the combination of UWB and hybrid network can improve the capacity of wireless ad-hoc network. In Section 2, we discuss the model that we've used for our analysis. In Section 3, we explore the scaling law of UWB hybrid ad-hoc networks as well as simulation results. An extension to the D-dimensional space is discussed in Section 4. Finally, we conclude in Section 5.

2 Analysis Framework

2.1 Network Model

Assume that there are n static nodes and $m = n^d$ stationary AP randomly i.i.d. according to Poisson point process on a unit planar disk, where the exponent $d = \log_n m$, and usually $0 < d < 1$. We denote $X_i, i = 1, 2, ..., n$ as node i as well as its position. As for sensor (or actuator) network, node Y acts as the sink (or source) node for all X_i nodes' traffic. Since this unit area is a dense network model, a simple scaling can be conducted for an extended network model as shown in [12].

Each node randomly picks a destination node for its own traffic.
All nodes' antennas are omni-directional with only one shared wireless channel.
At inter-AP links, sufficiently large rates are available.

2.2 Protocol Model

It has been shown in [8] that, when the frequency bandwidth B of a UWB link from X_i to X_j is sufficiently large, the Shannon capacity

$$r_{ij} = \lim_{B \to \infty} B \log(1 + W_{ij} g_{ij} / (N_0 B))$$
$$= W_{ij} g_{ij} / N_0 \tag{1}$$

is independent of B, where W_{ij} is the transmitted power, N_0 is the noise figure, and

$$g_{ij} = |X_i - X_j|^{-\alpha} \tag{2}$$

is the path loss, with $\alpha > 1$ being the path loss exponent.

The transmission from X_i is successfully received by the receiver X_j only if

$$|X_k - X_j| \geq (1 + \Delta) |X_i - X_j|, \tag{3}$$

for every node $k \neq i$. Here $\Delta > 0$ models a guard zone around the receiver.

2.3 Performance Metric

The per-node throughput capacity is the transmission rate of the link over a source-destination pair, given all links have an equal transmission rate.

As has been shown in [8], the throughput capacity maximization problem translates into finding the minimum power routing for each source-destination pair, under the relaxed power constraint that the total power does not exceed n times the per-node power constraints. Let $R_i = [X_{i_1}, X_{i_2}, \cdots, X_{i_K}]$ denote the minimum power route for a given i-th source-destination pair, and $r_i(n)$ denote the achieved throughput on route R_i, then from (1), the minimum power on this route is

$$W(R_i) = N_0 r_i(n) Q_i , \tag{4}$$

where

$$Q_i \; \square \; \sum_{k=1}^{K-1} |X_{i_k} - X_{i_{k+1}}|^\alpha , \tag{5}$$

is the power rate, ignoring the near-field effect [11] as density $n \to \infty$. So, the minimum total power rate over all routes in the wireless network is

$$\sum_i W(R_i) = N_0 \sum_i r_i(n) Q_i = N_0 r(n) \sum_i Q_i , \tag{6}$$

since all source-destination pairs have an equal rate from the capacity metric assumed. Note that because the minimum power route is used for both ad-hoc type of traffic and for sensor network type of traffic, for asymptotic analysis, the same order of growth in uplink and downlink capacity applies.

2.4 AP-Assisted Percolation Model

We extend the percolation model in [9][12] into a percolation model with infrastructure support, as shown in Fig. 1, where the unit disk has a hierarchical geometry: Voronoi cell is the tessellation for AP at a macroscopic level, and hexagon-based percolation is the inter-connection for nodes at microscopic level.

Each sub-disk is centered at each AP with an area of $1/m$. In a general case, the sub-disks might overlap, or some area in the unit disk is not covered by any AP disk. Thus, the sub-disk is then re-shaped into polygon in Voronoi tessellation. If the APs are distributed in a spatially regular pattern, a Voronoi cell degenerates into a baseline case of purely macro-hexagon (as shown in Fig. 1 to the right), i.e., a hierarchy of hexagons. Given one Poisson distribution of APs with density m and the other independent Poisson distribution of nodes with density n in the unit disk area, the throughput achieved in the general case would be asymptotically the same as the throughput achieved in the baseline case of regular deployment of APs. So, the following analysis focuses on the baseline case only for simplicity.

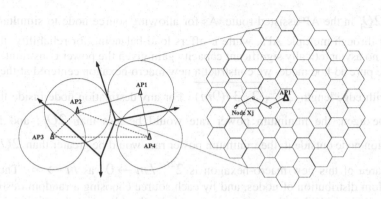

Fig. 1. The AP-assisted percolation model, where a hierarchy of Voronoi cells (polygons) centered at the AP, and hexagons centered at the nodes are shown

At the macroscopic level, each macro-hexagon spans an area of $1/m$ with an edge length $\sqrt{2\sqrt{3}/(9m)}$, and contains $n/m = n^{1-d}$ nodes by the central limit theorem with high probability (w.h.p.) as $n^{1-d} \to \infty$.

At the microscopic level, the unit disk is divided into n/c hexagonal grids each with area of c/n, where $0 < c < 1$ is a constant independent of n. Each hexagonal grid has an area of c/n, and therefore an edge length of $\sqrt{2\sqrt{3}c/(9n)} = \sqrt{c'/n}$, where $c' \square 2\sqrt{3}c/9$.

A grid is said to be open if there is at least one Poisson point inside it (depicted with a small circle inside the grid), and closed otherwise. Two grids are said to be adjacent if they share an edge or a vertex. So, a grid is adjacent up to 6 other grids. A list of adjacent nodes forms a path, which is open if all the grids on the path are open.

3 Capacity Improvement with Infrastructure

3.1 Upper Bound of Capacity

Theorem 1. With high probability (w.h.p.), the per-node throughput capacity of the UWB hybrid network assumed in Section II is

$$r(n) = O(n^{(\alpha+d-1)/2}). \tag{7}$$

Proof. Since each node has both the pure ad-hoc route and the AP-assisted route, we first identify which contribution to the total capacity is more significant.

In the AP-assisted route, a source node can reach its destination by at most 2 ad-hoc sub-routes: one sub-route from the source node to the source AP, inside the source macro-hexagon; and the other from the destination AP to the destination node. Denote Q_1 as the minimum power rate at each sub-route, so we have a total power rate of $2Q_1$ in the AP-assisted route. As for allowing source node to simultaneously transmit through multiple APs, while it offers load-balancing for reliability, it would achieve no asymptotically significant capacity gain given the power constraint.

In the pure ad-hoc mode, we construct a new macro-hexagon centered at the source node, with edge length $2^{1/\alpha}\sqrt{2\sqrt{3}/(9m)}$. For any destination node inside this new macro-hexagon, the minimum power rate would be less than $2Q_1$; and for any destination node outside it, the minimum power rate would be greater than $2Q_1$.

The area of this new macro-hexagon is $2^{2/\alpha}/m \to 0$, as $m \to \infty$. Thus from the random distribution of nodes, and by each source choosing a random destination, we only need to calculate the contribution made by the AP-assisted capacity.

As in Fig. 1, for an AP, there is a first circle of 6 neighboring hexagons, a second circle of 12 hexagons at 2 hexagons' distance to the AP, and so on. So, the number of hexagons within δ hexagons' distance to the AP is $1 + \sum_{j=1}^{\delta} 6j = 3\delta^2 + 3\delta + 1$. We minimize power rate of each node by redistributing all the $n/m = n^{1-d}$ nodes of the macro-hexagon into these $3\delta^2 + 3\delta + 1$ grids, such that every grid contains one node at the center. Solving $3\delta^2 + 3\delta + 1 = n^{1-d}$ yields the number of hops

$$\delta = \sqrt{n^{1-d}/3 - 1/12} - 1/2. \tag{8}$$

And since each hop length is $\sqrt{3c'/n}$, the total power rate of the n^{1-d} nodes is

$$\sum_{i=1}^{n^{1-d}} Q_i = \sum_{k=1}^{\delta} 6k \cdot k(\sqrt{3c'/n})^\alpha$$
$$= 2(n^{1-d} - 1)\sqrt{n^{1-d}/3 - 1/12}(3c'/n)^{\alpha/2}/3. \tag{9}$$
$$= \Theta(n^{(3-3d-\alpha)/2})$$

From (6), we obtain

$$r(n) = \frac{\sum_i W(R_i)}{N_0 \sum_i Q_i}$$
$$= O(\frac{n^{1-d}W_0}{N_0 n^{(3-3d-\alpha)/2}}). \tag{10}$$
$$= O(n^{(\alpha+d-1)/2})$$

In practical deployment, the ratio between the range of an AP to that of a typical user node might be greater than 1. Assume all APs has a same constant radiation range of R, where $0 < R \le \sqrt{2/(3\sqrt{3}m)}$. Here, without loss of generality in an asymptotic sense, we choose to use a value of $R = 1/\sqrt{3m}$. So, each AP spans a region of grids within $\delta_0 = R/(\sqrt{3/nc'})$ hops' reach to the AP.

Furthermore, we assume that each AP supports a maximum allowable number, λ, of concurrent links. So, for sufficiently large n, we have

$$\delta_1 = \min(\delta_0, \sqrt{\lambda/3}) \atop = \sqrt{\lambda/3} \tag{11}$$

This is independent of n. Thus,

$$\sum_{i=1}^{n^{1-d}} Q_i = (\sum_{k=\delta_1+1}^{\delta} 6k \cdot (k-\delta_1) + \sum_{i=1}^{\delta_1} 6k \cdot k^\alpha)(\sqrt{3}c'/\sqrt{n})^\alpha \atop = \Theta(n^{(3-3d-\alpha)/2}) \tag{12}$$

Therefore, Theorem 1 still holds.

3.2 Lower Bound of Capacity

Theorem 2. W.h.p., the per-node throughput capacity of the UWB hybrid network assumed in Section II is

$$r(n) = \Omega\left(n^{(\alpha+d-1)/2}\right). \tag{13}$$

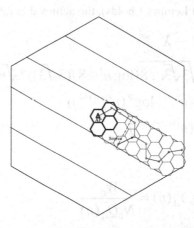

Fig. 2. The macro-hexagon is divided into trapezoids. A highway, i.e., an open-path route crossing of one trapezoid from left to right, is shown.

Proof. As shown in Fig. 2, we divide the macro-hexagon of area $1/m$ into trapezoids (including one at the center) with equal height of $\sqrt{3\sqrt{3}c/(8n)}\log n'$, and different lengths of up to $\sqrt{8/(3\sqrt{3}m)}$, where

$$n' \triangleq \sqrt{n/(cm)} = \sqrt{n^{1-d}/c} \quad. \tag{14}$$

So, the number of trapezoids in a macro-hexagon is $\sqrt{2/(\sqrt{3}m)}/(\sqrt{3\sqrt{3}c/8n}\log n') = 4n'/(3\log n')$. Each trapezoid has $n'' \times \log n'$ grids in the bond percolation model, where $n'' \leq n'$. With the exact proof in [12] (Theorem 1), the following lemma holds.

Lemma 1. (Theorem 1 in [12]) If c is sufficiently large, there exists a constant $\beta = \beta(c)$ such that w.h.p. there are $\beta \log m$ disjoint open paths that cross each trapezoid from left to right.

Denote "highway" [12] as disjoint open paths route crossing of one trapezoid from left to right. From Lemma 1, there are βm highways in the macro-hexagon. Due to rotational symmetry, the same result also holds true for both of two sets of trapezoids that are at $\pi/3$ and $-\pi/3$ angles from the set of trapezoids in Fig. 2, and the existence of these highways in trapezoids of different angles are mutually independent.

Denote the distance between a source node and one randomly chosen high-way path as the minimum distance between the source node and any node along the high-way. So, this distance is bounded by the sum of height of the trapezoid and the grid diagonal length $\sqrt{3\sqrt{3}c/(8n)}\log n' + \sqrt{8\sqrt{3}c/(9n)}$.

Thus, w.h.p. (such that Lemma 1 holds), the achievable rate at the this link is

$$\begin{aligned}
Q_{i1}(n) &= |X_i - X_{i_1}|^\alpha \\
&\leq (\sqrt{3\sqrt{3}c/8}(\log n' + 8/(3\sqrt{3}))/\sqrt{n})^\alpha \\
&= O(n^{-\alpha/2}\log^\alpha(n^{(1-d)/2})) \\
&= O(n^{(1-\alpha-d)/2})
\end{aligned} \tag{15}$$

So, we have

$$\begin{aligned}
r_{i1}(n) &= \frac{W_0}{N_0 Q_{i1}(n)} \\
&= \Omega(n^{(\alpha+d-1)/2})
\end{aligned} \tag{16}$$

By symmetry between the first link from source node to source highway, and the final link from destination highway to destination node, the two links are of same asymptotic throughput capacity. So we next investigate the highway link.

Every node in the highway will need to relay traffic to its next hop node, with a distance of at most $4\sqrt{2\sqrt{3}c/(9n)}$. Thus each node on the highway can support a transmission rate of $\dfrac{W_0}{N_0|X_{i_1}-X_{i_2}|^\alpha} = \Omega(\dfrac{W_0}{N_0(4\sqrt{2\sqrt{3}c/(9n)})^\alpha}) = \Omega(n^{\alpha/2})$.

Each of the $\beta n'$ highways serves the traffic from $(n/m)/(\beta n') = \sqrt{cn^{1-d}}/\beta$ nodes. So, one highway can support a per-node throughput capacity of

$$r_{i2}(n) = \frac{\Omega(n^{\alpha/2})}{cn^{(1-d)/2}/\beta}.$$

$$= \Omega(n^{(\alpha+d-1)/2})$$

(17)

From (16) and (17), we have $r(n) = \min(r_{i_1}(n), r_{i_2}(n)) = \Omega(n^{(\alpha+d-1)/2})$.

3.3 Result

Combining the upper and lower bounds, we proved the exact asymptotic order.

Theorem 3. W.h.p., the per-node throughput capacity of the UWB hybrid network assumed in Section II is

$$r(n) = \Theta(n^{(\alpha+d-1)/2}).$$

(18)

This shows an asymptotic factor of $n^{d/2}$ improvement in capacity by deploying AP, compared to the recent result [9] of $\Theta(n^{(\alpha-1)/2})$ for UWB pure ad-hoc network. Also, the contribution due to UWB is evident in the $\Theta(n^{(\alpha-1/2)})$ over the $\Theta(n^{-1/2})$ for narrow-band ad-hoc networks [1].

For simulation of UWB hybrid ad-hoc network, we generated random network topology a unit square such as the case shown in Fig. 3, and applied the following values: $W_0 = 0.01(mW)$, $N_0 = KT$, $K = 1.38 \times 10^{-23}(Joul/K)$, $T = 300(K)$. The per-node throughput as a function of network density (the number of nodes in a unit) is shown in Fig. 4, where Fig. 4(a-d) represents the case of $d = 0, 0.25, 0.5, 1$ respectively, and for each case, $\alpha = 2, 3, 4$ is shown. Minimum power routing is used for the random network. The results show the asymptotic order of growth as a function of α and d in the random network.

As a relaxation of assumption, the range can be extended to $0 \le d \le 1$, i.e., the order of growth is continuous at these two margin points. At $d = 0$, the contribution

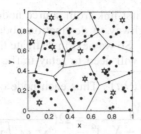

Fig. 3. A simulated network, n=100 (nodes shown in *dots*) and m=10 (APs shown in *stars*)

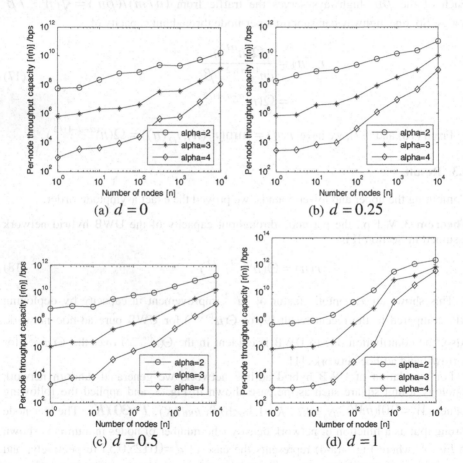

(a) $d = 0$

(b) $d = 0.25$

(c) $d = 0.5$

(d) $d = 1$

Fig. 4. Simulation results of per-node throughput capacity of UWB hybrid network

by AP is asymptotically insignificant and the above result is the same as [9]. At $d = 1$, where the ratio of n/m is upper bounded by some constant (which was the assumption in [4], where the result of $r(n) = \Theta(1)$ was obtained for non-UWB wireless networks), $r(n) = \Theta(n^{\alpha/2})$ for UWB networks is obtained.

4 Discussion

The above derivation assumes 2-dimensional unit disk area. For UWB which is applicable for in-building or indoor communications, a complex 3-dimensional environment needs to be addressed. The capacity of a 3-dimensional wireless ad-hoc network without specific UWB or hybrid network model was investigated in [14].

Let D denote the dimension of the "smart space", then the unit space is divided into n/c hexagonal grids each with edge length of $(c/n)^{1/D}$, where c is a constant independent of n. For the upper bound, the maximum number of hops is

$$\delta = \Theta((n/m)^{1/D}) = \Theta(n^{(1-d)/D}) . \tag{19}$$

and the minimum total power rate

$$\sum_{i=1}^{n^{1-d}} Q_i = \Theta(\sum_{k=1}^{\delta} i^{D-1} \cdot i(c'/n)^{\alpha/D}) = \Theta(n^{((1-d)(D+1)-\alpha)/D}) . \tag{20}$$

Therefore, w.h.p.,

$$r(n) = O(\frac{n^{1-d}W_0}{N_0 n^{((1-d)(D+1)-\alpha)/D}}) = O(n^{(\alpha+d-1)/D}) . \tag{21}$$

For the lower bound, the achievable rate from source X_i to the source highway is

$$
\begin{aligned}
r(n) &= \frac{W_0}{N_0 |X_i - X_{i_1}|^\alpha} \\
&\geq \frac{W_0}{N_0} (\frac{n^{1/D}}{(c\log(n/m)^{1/D} + c'')})^\alpha , \\
&= \Omega(n^{(\alpha+d-1)/D})
\end{aligned}
\tag{22}
$$

where c'' is a constant. At the highway link, each node can support a rate of

$$\frac{W_0}{N_0 |X_{i_1} - X_{i_2}|^\alpha} = \Omega(\frac{W_0}{N_0 n^{-\alpha/D}}) = \Omega(n^{\alpha/D}) . \tag{23}$$

Denote $n' \triangleq (n/(cm))^{1/D} = (n^{1-d}/c)^{1/D}$. Since each of the $\beta n'^{D-1}$ highway serves the traffic generated by $(n/m)/(\beta n'^{D-1}) = (cn^{1-d})^{1/D}/\beta$ nodes, one highway can support a per-node throughput capacity of

$$r_{i2}(n) = \frac{\Omega(n^{\alpha/D})}{(cn^{1-d})^{1/D}/\beta} = \Omega(n^{(\alpha+d-1)/D}) .$$
(24)

Thus, we have proved the following result.

Theorem 4. W.h.p., the per-node throughput capacity of the UWB hybrid network assumed in Section II but with a dimension of D is

$$r(n) = \Theta(n^{(\alpha+d-1)/D}) .$$
(25)

5 Conclusion

In this paper we have shown how the support of infrastructure can alleviate the intrinsic scalability limitations in the capacity of wireless ad-hoc networks. The derivation of the asymptotic capacity bounds for UWB hybrid ad-hoc network shows a theoretical characteristic of ad-hoc network. The result is applicable to realistic UWB hybrid deployment scenario for the upcoming new generation of mobile communications as well as large-scale sensor network.

As a final note, we view that a more rigorous information theoretic analysis with detailed physical layer characteristics of UWB is still an open problem and subject to future research.

Acknowledgments. The authors would like to thank the anonymous reviewers for their helpful comments.

References

1. P. Gupta, P. R. Kumar: The capacity of wireless networks. IEEE Transactions on Information Theory, vol. 46, (2000) 388–404.
2. S. Toumpis, and A.J. Goldsmith: Capacity Regions for Wireless Ad Hoc Networks. IEEE Transactions on Wireless Communications, vol. 2, (2003) 736–748.
3. L. L. Xie, and P. R. Kumar: A Network Information Theory for Wireless Communication: Scaling Laws and Optimal Operation. IEEE Transactions on Information Theory, vol. 50, (2004) 748–767.
4. M. Franceschetti, O. Dousse, D. N. C. Tse et al.: Closing the gap in the capacity of random wireless networks. in Proc. IEEE ISIT, (2004) 439–439.
5. B. Liu, Z. Liu, and D. Towsley: On the capacity of hybrid wireless networks. in Proc. IEEE INFOCOM, (2003) 1543–1552.
6. U. C. Kozat, L. Tassiulas: Throughput capacity of random ad hoc networks with infrastructure support. in Proc. ACM MOBICOM, (2003) 55–65.
7. S. Toumpis: Capacity bounds for three types of wireless networks: Asymmetric, cluster and hybrid. in Proc. ACM MOBIHOC, (2004) 133–144.
8. R. Negi, A. Rajeswaran: Capacity of power constrained ad-hoc networks. in Proc. IEEE INFOCOM, (2004) 453–463.

9. H. Zhang, J.C. Zhou: Capacity of Wireless Ad-hoc Networks under Ultra Wide Band with Power Constraint. in Proc. IEEE INFOCOM, (2005) 123–133.
10. A. Zemlianov, G. Veciana: Capacity of Ad Hoc Wireless Networks with Infrastructure Support. IEEE Journal on Selected Areas in Communications, vol. 23, (2005) 657–667.
11. I. Glauche, W. Krause, R. Sollacher, M. Greiner: Continuum percolation of wireless ad hoc communication networks. Physica A, vol. 325, (2003) 577–600.
12. M. Franceschetti, O. Dousse, D. Tse, P. Thiran: On the throughput capacity of random wireless networks. IEEE Transactions on Information Theory, (2004).
13. O. Dousse, M. Franceschetti, P. Thiran: Information theoretic bounds on the throughput scaling of wireless relay networks. in Proc. IEEE INFOCOM, (2005) 2670–2678.
14. P. Gupta, P. R. Kumar: Internets in the sky: The capacity of three dimensional wireless networks. Communications in Information and Systems, (2001) 33–49.

Performance of Tomlinson-Harashima Precoding over Spatially Correlated MIMO Channels

Anjian Li, Chongxiu Yu, Zhuo Chen, and Dongmei Fang

School of Electronic Engineering, Beijing University of Posts and Telecommunications
Beijing, P.R.C.
li_an_jian@yahoo.com.cn

Abstract. In this paper, the performance of Tomlinson-Harashima precoding (TH-precoding) algorithm is studied over spatially correlated multiple input multiple output (MIMO) channels. The symbol error rate (SER) is also presented by theoretical derivation and Monte-Carlo simulations. It is shown that the performance of TH-precoding is better than the classical V-BLAST algorithm. It is mainly due to the cancellation of error propagation. The comparison between TH-precoding with sub-channel ordering and one without sub-channel ordering is also investigated.

Keywords: Tomlinson-Harashima precoding, MIMO, V-BLAST.

1 Introduction

High data rates in fast and reliable wireless wideband access has led to extensive research on multiple antenna systems. The use of multiple transmit and receive antennas can be exploited to significantly increase the channel capacity. Pioneering work by E. Telatar [1] and J. Foschini [2] ignited much interest in this area by predicting remarkable spectral efficiencies for wireless systems with multiple antennas when the channel exhibits rich scattering and its variations can be accurately tracked. These initial works result an explosion of research activity to characterize the theoretical and practical issues associated with MIMO wireless channels [3]-[7].

Many detection algorithms are studied to recover the superposited transmitted signals in MIMO systems, including maximum likelihood detection (MLD), V-BLAST, linear equalization, decision feedback equalization (DFE), sphere decoding (SD), lattice reduction-aided detection, subspace lattice reduction-aided detection *et.al.*.In contrast to the detection methods, we can also apply transmit precoding to the signal transmission. It means pre-equalization in transmitter to facilitate detection at the receiver. Among these precoding schemes, TH-precoding is a typical one to improve the system performance.

TH-precoding is a nonlinear precoding scheme, which is firstly proposed by Tomlinson [8] and Harashima [9] for intersymbol interference (ISI) mitigation, was extended to the MIMO precoding [10].The main idea behind TH-precoding is to move the decision feedback equalization (DFE) structure to the transmitter. Because the interference of the transmitted symbols is known to the transmitter, it can overcome the frequent problem of error propagation of DFE.

X. Cheng, W. Li, and T. Znati (Eds.): WASA 2006, LNCS 4138, pp. 264–270, 2006.

In this letter, we firstly describe the TH-precoding algorithm in Section II. Then, the spatially correlated Rayleigh channel model is presented in Section III. In Section IV, the performance of TH-precoding is theoretically analyzed and evaluated by Monte-Carlo simulation. Conclusions are followed in section V.

2 Tomlinson-Harashima Precoding

As shown in Fig.1, TH precoding is a nonlinear pre-equalization technique which moves the feedback part of decision feedback equalization to the transmitter.

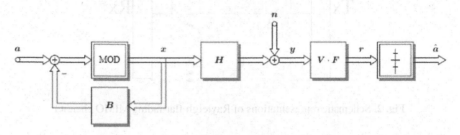

Fig. 1. Tomlinson-Harashima precoding in MIMO channels

Since linear pre-equalization would boost transmit power, especially used on channels which have deep spectral nulls in the pass band, a modulo operator is introduced to avoid this problem. The operation is defined by

$$M(x) = x - \left\lfloor \frac{\mathrm{Re}(x)}{\kappa} + \frac{1}{2} \right\rfloor \kappa - \left\lfloor \frac{\mathrm{Im}(x)}{\kappa} + \frac{1}{2} \right\rfloor \kappa \tag{1}$$

The modulo constant κ is chosen according the signal modulation constellations. Re(x), Im(x) is the real part and imaginary part of x respectively.

The implementation of this algorithm is described as follows [10]:

(1) Get the estimated channel matrix H_c from receiver. This is available, especially in symmetric time-division-duplex systems and slow fading environment, where the uplink channel is the reciprocal of the downlink one.

(2) Channel matrix factorization. By a modified Cholesky factorization [11], we can calculate the lower triangular matrix S. Then, the feedforward filter F is calculated by $H_c \times inv(S)$.

(3) V is a diagonal matrix to make the decision convenient. It makes unit gain to signal transmission.

$$V = diag(\frac{1}{s_{11}}, \frac{1}{s_{22}}, ..., \frac{1}{s_{n_T} s_{n_T}}) \tag{2}$$

(4) The construction of feedback matrix B. By B=C-I (I: identity matrix), the feedback matrix is constructed to a strictly lower left triangular matrix. This ensures a causal loop for successive decisions and interference cancellation.

3 Correlated MIMO Channel Model

Fig.2 shows a MIMO channel model with Rayleigh flat-fading channel.

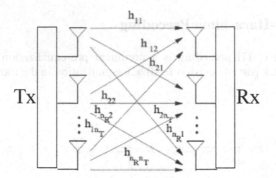

Fig. 2. Schematic representations of Rayleigh flat-fading MIMO channel

It can be described by a $n_R \times n_T$ channel matrix H which is represented in this form

$$H = \begin{bmatrix} h_1 & h_2 & \dots & h_i & \dots & h_{n_R} \end{bmatrix}^T \qquad (3)$$

where $h_i, i = 1, 2, \dots, n_R$ is given by

$$h_i = \begin{bmatrix} h_{i1} & h_{i2} & \dots & h_{in_T} \end{bmatrix} \qquad (4)$$

Where h_{ij} represents the base band complex attenuation from j-th transmitter to i-th receiver. It is of the i.i.d., complex, zero mean, unit variance Gaussian distribution:

$$h_{ij} = Normal(0, 1/\sqrt{2}) + \sqrt{-1} \cdot Normal(0, 1/\sqrt{2}) \qquad (5)$$

Then the correlated channel can be constructed by [12]

$$H_c = K_R^{1/2} H K_T^{1/2} \qquad (6)$$

Where K_R K_T are the $n_R \times n_R$ receive covariance matrix and $n_T \times n_T$ transmit covariance matrix respectively. Here we assume the antenna spacing is one wavelength. The superscript "1/2" denotes Cholesky decomposition.

The system can be represented as

$$r = H_c x + n \qquad (7)$$

Where $r = \begin{bmatrix} r_1 & r_2 & \dots & r_{n_R} \end{bmatrix}^T$ is the receiver vector, $n = \begin{bmatrix} n_1 & n_2 & \dots & n_{n_R} \end{bmatrix}^T$ is the mutually independent AWGN noise, i.e. $E\begin{bmatrix} nn^H \end{bmatrix} = \sigma_n^2 I$. σ_n^2 is the noise variance.

Given a particular channel realization H_c, the average SNR over the antennas, i.e., the ratio of total receiver power to total noise power is:

$$SNR \triangleq \varepsilon_{H_c} \left\{ \varepsilon_x \left\{ trace(H_c xx^H H_c^H) \right\} \middle/ (n_R \cdot \sigma_n^2) \right\}$$

$$= \varepsilon_{H_c} \left\{ \frac{\sigma_x^2}{n_R \sigma_n^2} \sum_{i=1}^{n_T} \sum_{j=1}^{n_R} |h_{ij}|^2 \right\} == \frac{n_R \sigma_x^2}{\sigma_n^2} \qquad (8)$$

Where σ_x^2 is the transmitted symbol power.

Usually, the power efficiency is expressed in terms of the average received energy per information bit ε_b divided by the one-sided noise power spectral density N_0.

For complex-valued signaling it is related to the signal-to-noise ratio by

$$\frac{\varepsilon_b}{N_0} = SNR \frac{n_R}{n_T R_m} = \frac{n_R \sigma_x^2}{R_m \sigma_n^2} \qquad (9)$$

Here R_m denotes the average number of information bits per channel symbols. $R_m = \log_2 M$.

4   Simulation and Performance Analysis

In this section, we will firstly evaluate the TH-precoding performance through Monte-Carlo simulation. Then, we derive the analytical average symbol error rate (SER) of TH-precoding. Finally, some analysis and discussion are shown.

We assume $n_R = n_T = 4$ .The channel matrix is constructed following the description in part III. The channel state information (CSI) is perfectly known by transmitter. Channel symbol in 4 antennas are all un-coded 16QAM modulated ($R_m = 2$). The antenna spacing is one wavelength.

For comparison, the theoretical SER curve of 16QAM in AWGN channel [13] and 16QAM in correlated Rayleigh flat-fading channel in equation (10) are also included. The deviation of the latter is in Appendix A. In general, the accurate form of SER in equation (10) is not found. Therefore, we can only calculate the approximated closed solutions by numerical analysis.

$$SER = \int_0^\infty 4 \left(1 - \frac{1}{\sqrt{M}}\right) Q\left(\sqrt{\frac{3}{M-1} \frac{\varepsilon_b}{N_0}}\right) \prod_{i=1}^{n_T} \prod_{j=1}^{n_R} \left[\frac{1}{[\Gamma(n_R n_T + 1)]^{-n_R n_T}} \frac{\frac{\varepsilon_b}{N_0}}{\left(\frac{\varepsilon_b}{N_0}\right)^{-n_R n_T}} \frac{e^{(-\frac{\frac{\varepsilon_b}{N_0}}{\rho_i \cdot \sigma_j})}}{\frac{\varepsilon_b}{N_0} \cdot \rho_i \cdot \sigma_j} \right] d(\frac{\varepsilon_b}{N_0}) \qquad (10)$$

Fig.3 illustrates the simulation results for SER of TH-precoding system. From the results, we can see that TH-precoding with sub-channel ordering (V-BLAST like detection) [14] offers significant gains (about 4.5dB with SER=10^{-1}). Even without optional ordering, the performance of TH-precoding is also better than that of V-BLAST. This is mainly due to the error propagation in the DFE structure of BLAST, while in TH-precoding this interference is pre-avoided by the algorithm.

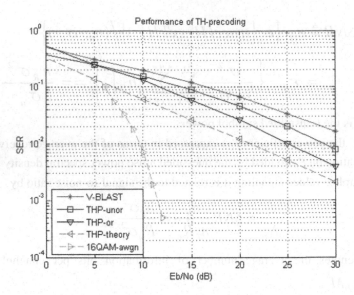

Fig. 3. Symbol error rate of V-BLAST, TH-precoding without subchannel ordering, TH-precoding with subchannel ordering, TH-precoding theoretical results and 16QAM in AWGN channel

Noticeable, from equation (1) the channel symbols using TH-precoding are no longer taken from the signal constellation but the modified one. This leads to a somewhat increased transmit power, quantified by the precoding loss, which for square QAM constellation calculates to M/ (M-1) [10]. When M is big, this influence can be neglected.

5   Conclusions

By employing Tomlinson-Harashima precoding (TH-precoding) algorithm in spatially correlated MIMO system, we find that the performance of TH-precoding is better than the classical V-BLAST algorithm. The performance of TH-precoding with sub-channel ordering is also better than the one without sub-channel ordering. We also present the symbol error rate (SER) theoretically in this transmission environment and verify it through Monte-Carlo simulations.

References

1. I.E.,Telatar: Capacity of multi-antenna Gaussian channels. Euro. Trans. Telecommun., Vol. 10, No. 6, pp. 585-595, Nov.1999.
2. M.J.Gans and G.J.Foschini: On the limits of wireless communications in a fading environment when using multiple antennas, Wireless Personal Commun., Vol. 6, No. 3, pp. 311-335, 1998.
3. J.B.Andersen: Array gain and capacity for known random channels with multiple element arrays at both ends, IEEE J. Select. Areas Commun., Vol. 18, No. 11, pp. 2172-2178, Nov.2002.

4. M.Bengtsson: From single link MIMO to multi-user MIMO, IEEE International Conference on Acoustics, Speech, and Signal Processing, Vol. 4, pp. 697-700, May.2004.
5. A.J.Paulraj, D. A. Gore, R. U. Nabar and H. Bolcskei: An overview of MIMO communications - a key to gigabit wireless, Proceedings of the IEEE, Vol. 92, No. 2, pp. 198-218, Feb.2004.
6. G. L. Stuber, J. R. Barry, S. W. McLaughlin, Ye Li and M. A. Ingram, T. G. Pratt: Broadband MIMO-OFDM wireless communications, Proceedings of the IEEE, Vol. 92, No. 2, pp. 271-294, Feb.2004.
7. D. Shiu, P. J. Smith and D. Gesbert: From theory to practice: An overview of MIMO space time coded wireless systems, IEEE J. Select. Areas Commun , Vol. 21, No. 3, pp. 281-302, Apr.2005.
8. M.Tomlinson: New automatic equalizers employing modulo arithmetic, Electronics Letters, Vol. 7, pp. 138-139, Mar.1971.
9. H.Harashima and H.Miyakawa: Matched-transmission technique for channels with intersymbol interference, IEEE Trans. On Commun., Vol. 20, No. 4, pp. 774-780, Aug.1972.
10. R.Fisher, C. Windpassinger, A.Lampe and J. Huber: Space-time Transmission using Tomlinson-Harashima Precoding, Proc.4th.Intern.ITG Conference on Source and Channel Coding, pp. 139-147, Jan.2002.
11. G.Golub and C. Van Loan: Matrix Computations, the Johns Hopkins University Press, Baltimore, 1996.
12. H.Bolcskei, D.Gesbert and A.J.Paulraj: On the capacity of OFDM-based multi-antenna systems, Proc. IEEE int. Conf. Acoust. Speech Sig Proc., Vol. 5, pp. 2569-2572, Jun.2000.
13. J.G.Proakis, Digital Communications, McGraw-Hill, 4th. 2002.
14. P.W.Wolniansky, G.J.Roschini, G.D.Golden and R.A.Valenzuela:V-BLAST:an architecture for realizing very high data rates over the rich-scattering wireless channel, Pro.1998 Int. Symp. Sig. Sys. Elect. Pisa,Italy, Sep.1998.

Appendix: Derivation of Equation(10)

The error probability of the MIMO system is completely determined by the probability distribution of SNR , i.e. the probability density function (pdf) of the SNR .Let us denote it as $p(\frac{\varepsilon_b}{N_0})$. In this system, we use 16QAM modulation. By averaging the symbol error probability [13] over $p(\frac{\varepsilon_b}{N_0})$ as:

$$SER = \int_0^\infty 4\left(1-\frac{1}{\sqrt{M}}\right)Q\left(\sqrt{\frac{3}{M-1}\cdot\frac{\varepsilon_b}{N_0}}\right)p(\frac{\varepsilon_b}{N_0})d(\frac{\varepsilon_b}{N_0}) \tag{11}$$

$$p(\frac{\varepsilon_b}{N_0}) = \int_{-\infty}^\infty \phi(z)e^{jz\frac{\varepsilon_b}{N_0}}dz \tag{12}$$

$$\phi(z) = \int_{-\infty}^{+\infty} \frac{1}{\det(I_{n_T\times n_R} + j\cdot z\cdot(\xi)\cdot\frac{\varepsilon_b}{N_0}} = \prod_{i=1}^{n_T}\prod_{j=1}^{n_R}\frac{1}{1+j\cdot z\cdot\frac{\varepsilon_b}{N_0}\cdot\rho_i\cdot\sigma_j/n_R/n_T} \tag{13}$$

Where $\xi = z \cdot (K_T^T \otimes K_R) / n_R / n_T$.

ρ_i, σ_j are the eigenvalues of K_T, K_R respectively. Then,

$$p(\frac{\mathcal{E}_b}{N_0}) = \int_{-\infty}^{\infty} \phi(z) e^{jz\frac{\mathcal{E}_b}{N_0}} dz = \int_{-\infty}^{\infty} \prod_{i=1}^{n_T} \prod_{j=1}^{n_R} \frac{1}{1 + j \cdot z \cdot \frac{\mathcal{E}_b}{N_0} \cdot \rho_i \cdot \sigma_j / n_R / n_T} e^{j\frac{\mathcal{E}_b}{N_0} \cdot z} dz \tag{14}$$

Assume

$$\eta = p(\frac{\mathcal{E}_b}{N_0}) = \prod_{i-1}^{n_T} \prod_{j-1}^{n_R} \int_{-\infty}^{\infty} \frac{1}{1 + j \cdot z \cdot \frac{\mathcal{E}_b}{N_0} \cdot \rho_i \cdot \sigma_j / n_R / n_T} e^{j\frac{\mathcal{E}_b}{N_0} \cdot z} dz \tag{15}$$

$$t = j \cdot \frac{\mathcal{E}_b}{N_0} \cdot \rho_i \cdot \sigma_j / n_R / n_T, w = j \cdot \frac{\mathcal{E}_b}{N_0} \tag{16}$$

Then,

$$\eta = \prod_{i=1}^{n_T} \prod_{j=1}^{n_R} \int_{-\infty}^{\infty} \frac{1}{1 + t \cdot z} e^{w \cdot z} dz = \prod_{i=1}^{n_T} \prod_{j=1}^{n_R} \left\{ \left[-\frac{1}{t} e^{(\frac{-w}{t})} Ei(1, -wz - \frac{w}{t}) \right]_{z=-\infty}^{z=\infty} \right\} \tag{17}$$

Where Ei is the classical exponential integral extended by analytic contribution to the entire complex plane, i.e. $Ei(1, -wz - \frac{w}{t}) = \Gamma(0, -wz - \frac{w}{t})$ .Combining t, w and equation (17), we can get

$$\eta = \prod_{i=1}^{n_T} \prod_{j=1}^{n_R} \left[\frac{1}{[\Gamma(n_R n_T + 1)]^{-n_R n_T}} \cdot \frac{\frac{\mathcal{E}_b}{N_0}}{(\frac{\mathcal{E}_b}{N_0})^{-n_R n_T} \frac{\mathcal{E}_b}{N_0} \cdot \rho_i \cdot \sigma_j} e^{(-\frac{\frac{\mathcal{E}_b}{N_0}}{\rho_i \cdot \sigma_j})} \right] \tag{18}$$

Then,

$$SER = \int_0^\infty 4 \left(1 - \frac{1}{\sqrt{M}} \right) Q \left(\sqrt{\frac{3}{M-1} \cdot \frac{\mathcal{E}_b}{N_0}} \right) p(\frac{\mathcal{E}_b}{N_0}) d(\frac{\mathcal{E}_b}{N_0})$$

$$= \int_0^\infty 4 \left(1 - \frac{1}{\sqrt{M}} \right) Q \left(\sqrt{\frac{3}{M-1} \frac{\mathcal{E}_b}{N_0}} \right) \prod_{i=1}^{n_T} \prod_{j=1}^{n_R} \left[\frac{1}{[\Gamma(n_R n_T + 1)]^{-n_R n_T}} \frac{\frac{\mathcal{E}_b}{N_0}}{(\frac{\mathcal{E}_b}{N_0})^{-n_R n_T} \frac{\mathcal{E}_b}{N_0} \cdot \rho_i \cdot \sigma_j} e^{(-\frac{\frac{\mathcal{E}_b}{N_0}}{\rho_i \cdot \sigma_j})} \right] d(\frac{\mathcal{E}_b}{N_0}) \tag{19}$$

Upper Bound on Operational Lifetime of Ultra Wide Band Sensor Network

Juan Xu[1], Yongfa Hong[1,2], Changjun Jiang[1], and Lin Chen[1]

[1] School of Electronics and Information Engineering,
Tongji University, Shanghai 201804, China
jxujuan@mail.tongji.edu.cn
[2] College of Information Science and Technology,
Shandong University of Science and Technology, Qingdao 266510, China

Abstract. The asymptotic upper bound on operational lifetime of time hopping ultra wide band (TH-UWB) wireless sensor network is derived using percolation theory arguments. The operational lifetime is defined as the maximum number of times the task of delivering certain data to the sink node can be repeated before some node runs out of energy under an initial energy of each sensor node is given. It is shown that for such a static TH-UWB sensor network, which sensor nodes are distributed in a square $[0, \sqrt{S}] \times [0, \sqrt{S}]$ according to a Poisson point process of intensity n and each sensor node transmitting R bits data packet to the sink node, the upper bound on the operational lifetime is $O\left(R^{-1} S^{-\alpha/2} n^{(\alpha-1)/2}\right)$, where α is the path loss exponent. The upper bound shows the operational lifetime increases with node density n/S, thus the large-scale dense TH-UWB wireless sensor network is preferable.

1 Introduction

Recent developments in wireless technology have excited extensive research in wireless sensor networks. It can be implemented in a variety of applications, such as military, inventory tracking, consumer electronics, or fault detection [1]. These applications demand long lifetime, low cost and small size, but sensor nodes rely on limited energy resources such as a battery, and furthermore, replenishing energy via replacing batteries on up to tens of thousands of nodes is infeasible. Hence, the network lifetime becomes a critical concern in the design of wireless sensor networks under energy constraint. Recently there have been reported many routing algorithms for the network lifetime maximization, which dealt mainly with the energy efficiency [2], [3].

Ultra wide band (UWB) is a highly promising physical layer technology for wireless sensor networks due to its unique characteristics such as low power transmission, low cost and low complexity transceiver circuitry, unlicensed but masked spectrum availability, precise location capability, resilient to Rayleigh fading from multipath interference. It is considered in this paper the most common version of UWB based on the transmission of very short (picosecond) pulses emitted in periodic sequences, in an impulse radio fashion. Time hopping (TH) codes which introduce a variable delay on each transmitted pulse are used [4].

X. Cheng, W. Li, and T. Znati (Eds.): WASA 2006, LNCS 4138, pp. 271–282, 2006.
© Springer-Verlag Berlin Heidelberg 2006

While upper bounds on lifetime have been derived for various wireless sensor networks [5], [6], [7], to the best of our knowledge, the upper bound on lifetime of TH-UWB sensor network using percolation theory arguments is not available in the literature.

In this paper we are to explore the upper bound on operational lifetime of TH-UWB sensor network in theory, which is defined as follows: given an initial energy at each sensor node, the operational lifetime is the maximum number of times the task of delivering certain data to the sink node can be repeated before some node runs out of energy. The upper bound on operational lifetime obtained in this paper follows from a natural application of percolation theory techniques [8], [9], and this percolation theory has mainly been proposed in the past to study connectivity of wireless networks [10], [11], [12].

Our motivation for doing so is two-fold. First, studies on the asymptotic behavior of the operational lifetime with respect to the network size and node density provide insights pertinent to the network scalability and feasibility of deploying large-scale wireless sensor networks. Second, the results with respect to the operational lifetime offers important guidance to research on the network management issues such as topology control, MAC and routing, especially when it comes to the performance evaluation of proposed protocols.

The remainder of this paper is organized as follows. Section 2 presents system model, and the SINR and link's Shannon capacity of TH-UWB is given in Section 3. The upper bound on the operational lifetime of TH-UWB wireless sensor networks using percolation theory arguments is derived in Section 4. Finally, Section 5 concludes the paper.

2 System Model

We consider a random wireless sensor network composed of n static sensor nodes and one sink node, placing sensor nodes according to a Poisson point process of intensity n over a square $[0, \sqrt{S}] \times [0, \sqrt{S}]$, where S is the area of square and it is a constant. Each sensor node sends its acquired data to the sink node located at the center of the sensor field. The n sensor nodes communicate over wireless channels, and relay traffic each other.

Let N_i denote the node and its position. Let $P_{ti} \geq 0$ be the transmitting power of node N_i to transmit to its chosen receiver N_j, and let $P_{rj} \geq 0$ be the receiving power of node N_j. Let $E_i \geq 0$ be initial energy level of node N_i. For simplicity assuming that it is a homogenous network, i.e. $P_{ti} = P_t, P_{rj} = P_r, \forall i, j \in \{1, 2, \cdots, n\}$.

The objective of this paper is to bound the operational lifetime $LT(n)$ of TH-UWB wireless sensor network by a function of n. Since the underlying network is random, so is the operational lifetime. The operational lifetime bound is derived to be certain functions with high probability $(w.h.p.)$, i.e., with probability approaching one as the number of nodes n goes to infinity. Specifically, if there exist deterministic constants $c > 0$ such that

$$\lim_{n \to \infty} \Pr(LT(n) = cf(n) \; is \; feasible) < 1 \; , \tag{1}$$

we say that the operational lifetime $LT(n)$ is upper bounded by $O(f(n))$.

3 SINR and Link's Shannon Capacity of TH-UWB

Suppose that all physical links are point-to-point. Each link is assumed to support a data rate corresponding to the Shannon capacity of that link.

Consider n nodes, binary pulse position modulation, and additive white Gaussian noise (AWGN). The Gaussian noise power spectral density is η. Supposing that the signal power decreases in proportion to the α order of the distance between the transmitter and receiver, and $\alpha \ge 2$, is the distance loss exponent. And for simplicity assuming that near field effects is neglected in this paper. The signal-to-interference and noise ratio (SINR) at the receiver N_j is the ratio of received power by the total interference perceived by the receiver including the ambient AWGN noise and the transmissions of other links that occur at the same time. For TH-UWB, a receiver does not capture the full power of an interferer, but just a fraction that depends on the correlation of the spreading sequences of the sender and the interferer. The total noise at a receiver can thus be modeled as the sum of the ambient noise and the total interference multiplied by the orthogonality factor. Thus, SINR can be written as below.

$$SINR = P_t h_{ij} / (\eta W + \sum_{k=1}^{M} a_k P_t h_{kj}) \; , \tag{2}$$

where P_t is the transmitting power of sensor node; h_{ij} is the signal power attenuation for the useful data packet, $h_{ij} = |N_i - N_j|^{-\alpha}$, and the distance $|N_i - N_j|$ is defined as the length of the segment connecting N_i and N_j on the square; h_{kj} is the power attenuation for the k-th colliding packet; W is the signal bandwidth corresponding to the rate used to transmit the useful data packet; M is the number of colliding data packet, supposing M nodes transmit data simultaneously; a_k is the orthogonality factor. For homogeneous network, assuming that $a_k = a$, $\forall k \in \{1, 2, \cdots, n\}$.

The first term ηW of the denominator of SINR represents the ambient AWGN noise power, and the second term represents multiuser interference (MUI). If bandwidth is so large that the ambient AWGN noise power is markedly more than the MUI, then the MUI can be negligible with respect to the ambient AWGN noise. Accordingly, SINR can be simplified as below.

$$SINR = P_t h_{ij} / (\eta W) \; . \tag{3}$$

According to Shannon capacity formula, each link's Shannon capacity C_{ij} is

$$C_{ij} = \lim_{W \to \infty} W \log(1 + P_t h_{ij} / (\eta W)) = P_t h_{ij} / \eta \; . \tag{4}$$

4 Upper Bound on Operational Lifetime

Suppose that every time each sensor node sends a packet with equal length which contains R bits data to the sink node. Because the initial energy of each sensor node is constrained, the coupling of the various routes complicates the upper bound on the operational lifetime analysis. Hence, the upper bound is derived under a relaxed assumption that the total energy constraint of all the nodes is nE_0, instead of that each node energy constraint E_0, i.e.

$$\sum_{i=1}^{n} E_i = nE_0 , \tag{5}$$

instead of $E_i = E_0, \forall i \in \{1,2,\cdots,n\}$.

This is sufficient because the upper bound under a more relaxed assumption is clearly an upper bound under a more restricted assumption.

In order to obtain the upper bound on the operational lifetime, the expected total energy required by all the n routes over the ensemble of graphs is bounded by the total available energy nE_0. Therefore, by symmetry, the expected energy of each route is bounded by E_0 as

$$E_0 \geq E\{E_{tot}(n)\}LT(n) , \tag{6}$$

where $LT(n)$ is the operational lifetime of TH-UWB sensor network; $E_{tot}(n)$ is the total energy consumption along the routing of source sink pair. In the following we will give the lower bound on $E_{tot}(n)$.

4.1 Total Energy Consumption

Radios of sensor nodes typically have four power levels corresponding to the following states: transmitting, receiving, listening, and sleeping. Typically, the power required to listen is about the same as the power to transmit and receive. The sleep power is usually one to four orders of magnitude less.

In order to let the energy consumption as small as possible, assuming if a sensor is not engaged in transmitting or receiving, it will keep sleep. Therefore, in this paper we only consider the consumed energy in the state of transmitting and receiving. We ignore the energy dissipation in the sleeping state, because it is much smaller than the transmitting and receiving energy dissipation.

Thus, the energy consumption of node N_i transmitting R bits data to its neighbor N_j is

$$E_{ij} = E_{ti} + E_{rj} = P_t \times R / C_{ij} + P_r \times R / C_{ij} , \tag{7}$$

where E_{ti} and E_{rj} represent energy consumption for the i-th node transmission and j-th node reception respectively.

Supposing that sensor node N_s wants to send R bits data to the sink node N_o using multihop fashion, the medial relay node N_i need send R bits data to its neighbor N_{i+1}. The energy consumption $E_{i,i+1}$ which includes the transmission energy consumption of node N_i and the reception energy consumption of its neighbor N_{i+1} can be written as follows.

$$E_{i,i+1} = P_{ti} R / C_{i,i+1} + P_{r,i+1} R / C_{i,i+1}$$
$$= P_t R\eta / (P_t h_{i,i+1}) + P_r R\eta / (P_t h_{i,i+1}) \ .$$
$$= (1 + P_r / P_t) R\eta |N_i - N_{i+1}|^\alpha$$
(8)

Because minimizing the energy consumption of a route for each source sink pair is equivalent to minimizing the average energy consumption of all nodes. Let R_y denote the minimum energy consumption route for a given source-sink pair y, i.e., $R_y = [N_{y1}, N_{y2}, \cdots, N_{yi}, N_{y,i+1}, \cdots, N_{yX}]$. Therefore, the total energy consumption $E_{y,tot}(n)$ which source node N_s sends R bits packet to the sink node N_o along the route R_y is as below.

$$E_{y,tot}(n) = \sum_{i=1}^{X} E_{i,i+1} = \sum_{i=1}^{X} \left((1 + P_r / P_t) R\eta |N_{yi} - N_{y,i+1}|^\alpha \right),$$
(9)

where X is the number of nodes along the route R_y of source sink pair in TH-UWB sensor network, $N_{y1} = N_s$, and $N_{y,X+1} = N_o$. Note that in most applications the sink node is energy unconstrained, but for simplicity, the receiving energy dissipation of sink node is included in Eq. (9). In addition, the energy consumption of retransmission due to failure of communication is neglected.

In order to obtain the $E_{y,tot}(n)$ along the routing R_y, we should first get energy index D_y which is defined

$$D_y := \sum_{i=1}^{X} |N_{yi} - N_{y,i+1}|^\alpha \ .$$
(10)

Let d_y denote the distance between the source node N_s and sink node N_o, i.e.,

$$d_y = |N_s - N_o| = |N_{y1} - N_{y,X+1}| \ .$$
(11)

Then the lower bound on D_y and the total energy consumption $E_{y,tot}(n)$ will be derived, where the site percolation model will be used.

4.2 Construction of the Site Percolation Model

The square of area S will be divided into grids of edge length $t_1 \sqrt{S} / \sqrt{n}$ as depicted in Fig. 1, where t_1 is a constant, with respect to n. And in the sequel, t_2, t_3, t_4 are all constants. As the mean number of nodes per grid is t_1^2, by adjusting the constant t_1, we can adjust the probability that a grid contains at least one node:

$$P \text{ (a grid contains at least one node)} / 1 - P \text{ (a grid contains zero}$$
$$\text{node)} / 1 - e^{-t_1^2} := p \ .$$
(12)

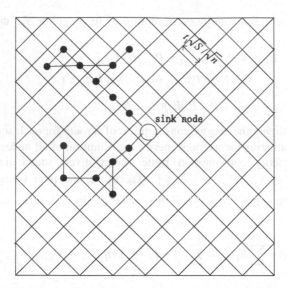

Fig. 1. Construction of the site percolation model. We assume each grid open, if there is at least a Poisson point inside it, closed otherwise. An open grid is denoted with a solid circle in it. The sink node is denoted with a hollow circle which lies at the center of the square. The dashed lines show all the possible open chains.

A grid is said to be open if it contains at least one node, and closed otherwise. Two grids are said to be adjacent if they share an edge or a vertex. Any grid is thus adjacent to eight other grids. For notational convenience in the following, we use (i) a chain to refer to a list of grids such that any two neighboring grids in the list are adjacent; and (ii) a route to refer to a list of wireless sensor nodes that are actually used to transport packets from the source node to the sink node. By convention in graph theory, we assume a chain does not include any grid twice, except that its first grid may be the same as the last grid. A chain is said to be open if all the grids on the chain are open, and a chain is said to be close if all the grids on the chain are closed.

If there is an open chain in the percolation model from the grid where the source node is located to the grid where the sink node is located, then a route can be formed from the source node to the sink node by picking one node from each grid on the chain. Every hop on this path is bounded from above by $2\sqrt{2S}t_1/\sqrt{n}$. On the other hand, if there is no such an open chain in the percolation model, then in any route from the source node to the sink node, at least one hop is of length at least $t_1\sqrt{S}/\sqrt{n}$ because there is at least one close grid in the chain.

Fig.2 illustrates the relation between a closed grid and a line segment of length at least $t_1\sqrt{S}/\sqrt{n}$ on a link of the minimum energy consumption route. Without loss of generality, we can assume a link crosses a closed grid at the two opposite edges or two adjacent edges. If a link crosses a closed grid at the two opposite edges (as in the

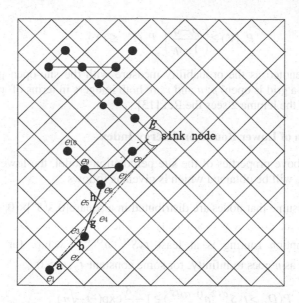

Fig. 2. Illustration of the relation between a closed grid and a line segment of length at least $t_1 \sqrt{S} / \sqrt{n}$

grid e_2), the line segment ab on the link that is contained by the grid have length at least $t_1 \sqrt{S} / \sqrt{n}$. If a link crosses a closed grid at the two adjacent edges (as in the grid e_4), the line segment $gh\psi$has length at least $t_1 \sqrt{S} / \sqrt{n}$. If a link intersects more than one grid on the chain, similar analysis can be performed.

Two important properties of the site percolation model will be used in the following, we formally state in the lemma below.

Lemma 1. Let p be the probability that a grid is open in the site percolation model we have defined (Eq. (12)). Then the probability that there exists an open chain of length u starting from a source node in terms of grids is upper bounded by

$$P(N(u) \geq 1) \leq \frac{8}{7}(7p)^u , \tag{13}$$

where $N(u)$ is the number of open chains of length u starting from a given source node.

Its proof sees the Ref.[13].

If we choose $p < 1/7$ and the distance (in terms of grids) between the source node and the sink node goes to infinity, then w.h.p. there is no open path between them.

Lemma 2. Let V be the event that there exists an open path of length u starting from a given source and F_V the minimum number of grids that need to be turned open from closed in order for the event V to take place. Then for any $0 < q < p < 1$, we have

$$P_p(V) \geq \left(\frac{p-q}{1-q}\right)^r P_q(F_V \leq r) , \tag{14}$$

where P_p is denoted as the probability measure with the site-open probability (the probability that a grid is open) p; u and r are both integers in terms of grids.

The proof of the lemma 2 sees the Ref.[13].

4.3 Derivation of Lower Bound on Energy Index

Based on the above properties of the site percolation model, the lower bound on the energy index D_y will be obtained which is given as follows.

Theorem 1. Assume that nodes are distributed in a square$[0, \sqrt{S}] \times [0, \sqrt{S}]$ according to a Poisson point process with intensity n. The energy index D_y of the minimum energy consumption routing is at least $t_2 S^{\alpha/2} n^{(1-\alpha)/2}$ w.h.p. for some constant $t_2 > 0$. That is, as n goes to infinity, for some constant $t_2, t_3 > 0$,

$$P(D_y > t_2 S^{\alpha/2} n^{(1-\alpha)/2}) \geq 1 - \frac{8}{7} \exp(-t_3 \sqrt{n}) . \tag{15}$$

Proof. For any route between the source node and the sink node, we can construct a chain in the site percolation model by including all the grids that intersect with the route. The chain can be further trimmed into a chain which contains the minimum number of closed grids by removing unnecessary grids (see an illustration in Fig. 3).

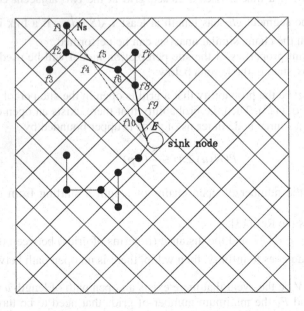

Fig. 3. Illustration of the formation of minimum number of closed grids by removing unnecessary grids

In Fig. 3, the bold lines show a route from source node N_s to sink node N_o. We can construct a chain that is composed of grids that intersect with the route: $[f_1, f_2, f_4, f_5, f_6, f_8, f_9, f_{10}, E]$. Some of the grids can be removed from the chain. For example, f_9 can be removed because f_8 and f_{10} are connected. Similarly, f_4 or f_5 can be removed. There are multiple ways of trimming the path. Among all the trimmed paths, we pick as T^* the one that contains the minimum number of closed grids. In the above example, the path $[f_1, f_2, f_4, f_6, f_8, f_{10}, E]$ contains minimum number (which is one in this case) of closed grids.

We denote T^* as an optimally trimmed chain that contains the minimum number of closed grids. Note that the distance between the source node N_s and sink node N_o pair in terms of grids is at least $u := d_y /(\sqrt{2S}t_1 / \sqrt{n}) = d_y \sqrt{n} /(\sqrt{2S}t_1)$. This implies the path length of T^* is at least u. Applying Lemma 2, the bound on the probability that the optimally trimmed chain T^* contains at most $t_4 \sqrt{n}$ closed grids can be obtained, where t_4 is a constant yet to be determined.

Let V denote the event that there is an open chain of length u starting from the source, and F_V the minimum number of closed grids that need to be turned into open in order for event V to take place. If the trimmed path T^* contains at most $t_4 \sqrt{n}$ closed grids, then by Lemma 2, we have

$$P_p(V) \ge P_q(F_V \le t_4 \sqrt{n}) \left(\frac{p-q}{1-q} \right)^{t_4 \sqrt{n}}. \tag{16}$$

By Lemma 1,

$$P_p(V) \le \frac{8}{7}(7p)^u = \frac{8}{7}(7p)^{d_y \sqrt{n}/(\sqrt{2S}t_1)}. \tag{17}$$

We can choose t_1 such that $p = 1 - e^{-t_1^2} < 1/7$. After fixing t_1 and p, because $0 < p < 1$, we can choose $k > 1/p$ and $q = \frac{kp-1}{k-1} < p$. Now plugging the equation of q and Eq.(17) into Eq.(16), we have

$$P_q(F_V \le t_4 \sqrt{n}) \le P_p(V) \left(\frac{p-q}{1-q} \right)^{-t_4 \sqrt{n}}$$

$$\le \frac{8}{7}(7p)^{d_y \sqrt{n}/(\sqrt{2S}t_1)} \times k^{t_4 \sqrt{n}}, \tag{18}$$

$$= \frac{8}{7} \exp\left(\sqrt{n} \left(\frac{d_y \log(7p)}{\sqrt{2S}t_1} + t_4 \log k \right) \right)$$

where $k = \dfrac{1-q}{p-q}$.

If we choose $0 < t_4 < -\dfrac{d_y \log(7p)}{\sqrt{2S}t_1 \log k}$, we obtain

$$P_q(F_V \le t_4\sqrt{n}) \le \frac{8}{7}\exp(-t_3\sqrt{n}) \to 0 \qquad (19)$$

as $n \to \infty$, where $t_3 = -\left(\dfrac{d_y \log(7p)}{\sqrt{2S}t_1} + t_4 \log k\right) > 0$.

Hence, if we choose the grid size $t_0\sqrt{S}/\sqrt{n}$ such that P (a grid contains at least one node)$/1 - e^{-t_0^2} = q$, where t_0 is a constant with respect to n, then the optimally trimmed path T^* contains more than $t_4\sqrt{n}$ closed grids with probability at least $p' = 1 - \dfrac{8}{7}\exp(-t_3\sqrt{n})$.

It is easy to see that for each closed grid on T^*, there is one line segment completely contained in a link on the route with length at least $t_0\sqrt{S}/\sqrt{n}$ (See the illustration in Fig. 2). In addition, if a link on the route intersects with j closed grids on T^*, the link has length at least $jt_0\sqrt{S}/\sqrt{n}$. To derive the lower bound of the energy index D_y of the minimum energy consumption route, we can assume each link only intersects at most one grid in T^*. Thus the route contains at least $t_4\sqrt{n}$ links each with length at least $t_0\sqrt{S}/\sqrt{n}$ with probability at least p'. Hence the energy index D_y of the route R_y is at least $t_4\sqrt{n} \times \left(t_0\sqrt{S}/\sqrt{n}\right)^\alpha = t_4 t_0^\alpha S^{\alpha/2} n^{(1-\alpha)/2}$ with probability at least p'. Let $t_2 = t_4 t_0^\alpha$, we obtain

$$P(D_y > t_2 S^{\alpha/2} n^{(1-\alpha)/2}) \ge (p' = 1 - \frac{8}{7}\exp(-t_3\sqrt{n})) \ . \qquad (20)$$

4.4 Upper Bound on Operational Lifetime

Based on the result of energy index D_y which is given in theorem 1, we can obtain the total energy consumption along the routing R_y w.h.p.

$$E_{y,tot}(n) = (1 + P_r/P_t)R\eta \bullet \sum_{i=1}^{X}\left(\left|N_{yi} - N_{y,i+1}\right|^\alpha\right) = (1 + P_r/P_t)R\eta \bullet D_y$$

$$\ge (1 + P_r/P_t)R\eta t_2 S^{\alpha/2} n^{(1-\alpha)/2} \qquad (21)$$

According to Eq.(6), we obtain the operational lifetime of TH-UWB sensor network w.h.p.

$$LT(n) \le \frac{E_0}{E\{E_{y,tot}(n)\}} \le E_0\left((1 + P_r / P_t)R\eta\right)^{-1} t_2 S^{-\alpha/2} n^{(\alpha-1)/2}. \tag{22}$$

This proves the upper bound on operational lifetime is

$$LT_{upp}(n) = O\left(E_0\left((1 + P_r / P_t)R\eta\right)^{-1} S^{-\alpha/2} n^{(\alpha-1)/2}\right). \tag{23}$$

Obviously, if the node density n/S is increased, the upper bound on operational lifetime $LT_{upp}(n)$ will be increased. Thus, in order to increase the operational lifetime, the large-scale dense TH-UWB wireless sensor network is preferable.

We must point out that the upper bound on the operational lifetime of TH-UWB wireless sensor network which is derived above allowing arbitrary communication strategies and assuming only the power decay law in the propagation medium.

5 Conclusion

In this paper, we study the asymptotic upper bound on the operational lifetime of TH-UWB wireless sensor network using the percolation theory. It is shown that for such a static TH-UWB sensor network, which sensor nodes are distributed in a square $[0, \sqrt{S}] \times [0, \sqrt{S}]$ according to a Poisson point process of intensity n and each sensor node transmitting R bits data packet to the sink node, the upper bound on the operational lifetime is $O\left(E_0\left((1 + P_r / P_t)R\eta\right)^{-1} S^{-\alpha/2} n^{(\alpha-1)/2}\right)$. The upper bound demonstrates that the operational lifetime increases with node density n/S, thus in order to increase the operational lifetime, the large-scale dense TH-UWB wireless sensor network is preferable. And decreasing the number of bits R contained in each packet as small as possible will also be beneficial to prolong the operational lifetime of TH-UWB sensor network.

Acknowledgment

This work is partially supported by National Natural Science Foundation (Grant No. 90612006, No. 60534060), Shanghai Science & Technology Research Plan (Grant No.05JC14063, No.04XD14016, No.05DZ15004) and International Cooperation Project.

References

1. Akyildiz, I. F., Su, W., Sankarasubramaniam, Y., and Cayirci, E.: A Survey on Sensor Networks. IEEE Communication Magazines, vol.40. (2002) 102–114
2. Chang, J.-H., and Tassiulas, L.: Energy Conserving Routing in Wireless Adhoc Networks. in Proceedings IEEE INFOCOM'2000, Tel Aviv, Isreal (2000) 22–31
3. Li, Q., Aslam, J., and Rus, D.: Online Power-aware Routing in Wireless Adhoc Networks. in Proceedings ACM MOBICOM'2001, Rome, Italy (2001) 97–107
4. Win, M., and Scholtz, R.: Ultra-wide Bandwidth Time-hopping Spread-spectrum Impulse Radio for Wireless Multiple-access Communications. IEEE Transactions on Communications, vol.48. (2000) 679–691

5. Bhardwaj, M., Garnett, T., and Chandrakasan, A.: Upper Bounds on the Lifetime of Sensor Networks. in Proc 2001 IEEE International Conference on Communications (2001) 785–790
6. Bhardwaj, M., and Chandrakasan, A.: Bounding the Lifetime of Sensor Networks via Optimal Role Assignments. in Proceedings INFOCOM 2002(2002)1587–1596
7. Zhang, H., and Hou, J.: On Deriving the Upper Bound of Lifetime for Large Sensor Networks. in Proceedings MobiHoc (2004) 121–132
8. Grimmett, G.: Percolation. Second edition, Springer Verlag (1999)
9. Meester, R., and Roy, R.: Continuum Percolation. Cambridge University Press (1996)
10. Booth, L., Bruck, J., Franceschetti, M., and Meester, R.: Covering Algorithms, Continuum Percolation, and the Geometry of Wireless Network. Annals of Applied Probability, Vol. 13(2003) 722–731
11. Dousse, O., Baccelli, F., and Thiran, P.: Impact of Interferences on Connectivity of Ad Hoc Networks. ACM/IEEE Transactions on Networking, Vol. 13 (2005) 425–436
12. Franceschetti, M., Booth, L., Cook, M., Meester, R., and Bruck, J.: Continuum Percolation with Unreliable and Spread out Connections. Journal of Statistical Physics, Vol. 118 (2005) 721–734
13. Zhang, H., and Hou, J.: Capacity of Wireless Ad-hoc Networks under Ultra Wide Band with Power Constraint. in Proceedings INFOCOM 2005(2005) 455–465

Single-Actor Selection Algorithms
for Wireless Sensor and Actor Networks

ZhenYang Xu[1], GuangSheng Zhang[1], Jie Qin[2], and WenHua Dou[1]

[1] Computer Institute, National University of Defense Technology,
Changsha Hunan, 410073, China
[2] School of information Science and Engineering, Henan University of Technology,
Zhengzhou Henan, 450052, China
xuzy_sun@sina.com, gszhang@nudt.edu.cn, qinjie0160@yahoo.com.cn,
douwh@vip.sina.com

Abstract. Wireless sensor and actor networks (WSANs) are composed of a large number of sensors and a small number of (mobile) resource-rich actors. Sensors gather information about the physical phenomenon, while actors take decisions and then perform appropriate actions upon the environment. Due to many actors, an important problem appears: which sensor(s) communicate with which actor(s). In this paper, a linear programming of single-actor selection for event-driven data model is put forward from event reliability and time constraints for WSANs. Then some approximate algorithms, such as MECT (Minimum Energy Cost Tree) and MPLCT (Minimum Path Length Cost Tree), are addressed from path length and energy aspects respectively. Since those approximate solutions need the whole state, and can't adapt to WSANs, so a distributed approximate algorithm HBMECT (Hop-Bound and Minimum Energy Cost Tree) is proposed from both energy and delay. In the performance evaluation, those algorithms are compared from average number of hops and energy consumption.

Keywords: Wireless Sensor and Actor Networks, Real-Time Communications, Energy Efficiency, Hop-Bound.

1 Introduction

In the wireless sensor networks (WSNs), sensor nodes, which are passive elements sensing from the environment, have limited energy, processing and wireless communication capabilities, and sink nodes are far from sensors nodes around event area. So it spends more time for sink nodes receiving reading from sensor nodes, which makes it difficult to realize real-time requirement for WSNs. In the wireless sensor and actor networks (WSANs), there are a small number of actor nodes as well as a large number of sensor nodes. Those actor nodes, which are active elements acting on the environment, have higher processing and communication capabilities, less constrained energy resources (longer battery life or constant power source). Compared with sink nodes, actor nodes are closer to sensor nodes around the event area, so the delay of data delivery is shorter, and the real-time requirements of the applications are met easily. There are many potential applications of WSANs, such as

X. Cheng, W. Li, and T. Znati (Eds.): WASA 2006, LNCS 4138, pp. 283–294, 2006.
© Springer-Verlag Berlin Heidelberg 2006

battlefield surveillance and microclimate control in buildings, nuclear, biological and chemical attack detection, industrial control, home automation and environmental monitoring [1] [2].

Fig 1 shows single-actor and multi-actor models in WSANs. In the single-actor model, sensor readings may be sent only to one actor node. In this way, if the actor has enough capability to perform the action, it can immediately perform the action, especially for single-actor task. This implies that in the model latency between sensing and acting may be low as well as there may be no needed for actor–actor coordination [1]. Even if one actor is not sufficient for the required action, that actor can publish the announcement message to other actors. After it receives responses from other actors, it selects one or some of the available actors and lets it/them perform the action. In the multi-actor model, multiple actors can also receive the information about the sensed event. In the model, actor–actor coordination is always necessary; on the one hand each actor receiving sensor data has some partial information about the overall event, on the other hand it can avoid many actors making repetitive and redundant action decisions to the same event. So the model may cause high network load as well as high latency.

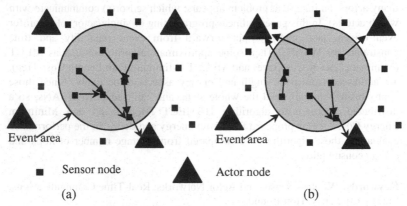

Fig. 1. (a) Single-actor vs. (b) Multi-actor

In wireless networks, leader election [18] [19] [20] is a useful building block, and used for key distribution, routing coordination, sensor coordination and general control. Leader election problem is to eventually elect a unique leader from a set of homogeneous nodes according to the nodes' metrics, such as remaining energy, average distance to other nodes or computation capability. Different from leader election, single-actor problem is that one actor is selected by sensor nodes in event area via sensor-sensor coordination, and that the sensors' energy is also important besides the actors' metrics.

In the paper [3], a distributed coordination framework for WSANs is proposed. It considers multi-actor single task model mainly, and involves multi-actor selection algorithm. Some real-time and energy-efficient routing [4] [5] [6] are concerned. In multi-sink networks, more consideration is paid to Multi-sink position [7], placement of integration points between the wireless and wired network [14], minimum energy data gathering problem with multiple sinks [15], and data acquisition with voronoi clusters [16]. But the single-actor selection problems have not been presented.

In this paper, we investigate schemes to efficiently select single actor of the event-driven data model [21] in WSANs. Our key contributions are:

- We formulate the single-actor selection problem from event reliability and time constraints for event-driven model. Our algorithm aims to minimize the total energy consumption of the network at the premise of meeting the requirements of real-time and event reliability.
- We put forward approximate algorithms from different aspects: MECT (Minimum Energy Cost Tree), MPLCT (Minimum Path Length Cost Tree), and HBMECT (Hop-Bounded and Minimum Energy Cost Tree). We compare those algorithms from average number of hops and energy consumption through simulation.

The remainder of this paper is organized as follows. In Section 2, we propose the assumption and network model used in the paper. In section 3, we state the single-actor selection problem and propose an integer linear programming, while in section 4 we propose some approximate algorithms. In section 5 detailed comparative performance evaluation and simulation results are presented. Finally, we draw the main conclusions in Section 6.

2 Assumption and Network Model

2.1 Assumption

In the paper, we assume as follows:

Each sensor node is aware of: i) its position, as the sensor node can be equipped with a GPS receiver, or the position can be determined by means of localization techniques [8], [9], or the position can be provided by localization server [10]; ii) the position of its neighbors, as every node periodically sends its position to its neighbors; iii) the position of the actors, as each actor periodically beacons its position in the sensor field; iv) the network is synchronized by means of one of the existing synchronization protocols [11].

Sensors have the same capability such as communication range, energy, and sensing range.

Sensors and actors are immobile.

The presuppositions are used in the distributed approximate algorithm HBMECT mainly.

2.2 Network Model

The network of sensor and actor nodes is represented as a graph G (V, E), where V is a finite set of sensors and actors (vertexes) in a finite-dimension terrain, with $N=|V|$, and E is the set of links (edges) among nodes, $e_{ij} \in E$ iff nodes i and j are within each other's transmission range. Let A represent the set of actors, with $N_A=|A|$. Let S represent the set of sensors, with $N_S=|S|$. We refer to an actor that is collecting traffic from one or more sources as a collector. Let $S1$ be the set of traffic sources, with

$N_{SI}=|SI|$. This set represents the sensor nodes that detect the event, i.e. the sensors residing in the event area. It is obvious, $N=N_A+N_S$, $V=S\cup A$, $SI\subseteq S$, and $S\cap A=\phi$.

3   Linear Programming Problem of Selection Algorithm

As we know, there are many factors influencing on single-actor selection, such as distance, energy and timing, and some objective functions are contradictive. For example, a sensor may relay a packet more possible to the neighbor node with the most forward within radius, which may consume more energy; while a sensor is likely to select the neighbor node with the nearest distance to relay a packet, which may increase time delay. Therefore to find the 'best' actor for the sensors reside event area, we must consider integral factors influencing selection algorithm, such as distance, energy or timing issues.

Two pre-defined latency bound B and event reliability r for sensor-actor communications are introduced to character real-time and reliability requirements respectively from the paper [3].

Definition 1. The **latency bound** B is the maximum allowed time between the instant when the physical features of the event are sampled by the sensors and the instant when the actor receives a data packet describing these event features.

A data packet that does not meet the latency bound B when it is received by an actor is said to be expired and thus unreliable. Similarly, a data packet received within the latency bound is said to be unexpired and thus reliable.

Definition 2. The **event reliability** r is the ratio of reliable data packets over all the packets received in a decision interval.   The event reliability threshold r_{th} is the minimum event reliability required by the application.

The lack of reliability is the difference $(r_{th}-r)$ between the required event reliability threshold r_{th} and the observed event reliability r at a given time. A negative lack of reliability indicates reliability above the required threshold and is also referred to as an excess of reliability.

The multi-constraint problem of single-actor selection is to find minimum cost tree from all the sensors that reside in the event area to the selected actor, at the premise of meeting the requirements of real-time and event reliability.

- e_{ij} is a binary variable representing a link, that equals 1 iff nodes i and j are within each other's communication range;

- c_{ij} is the cost of the link between nodes i and j,

- x_{ij}^k is a binary variable that equals 1 iff link (i, j) is part of the tree associated with actor k;

- $f_{ij}^{s,k}$ is a binary variable that equals 1 iff node s sends data to actor k and link (i, j) is in the path from source s to actor k;

- $l^{s,k}$ is a binary variable that equals 1 iff sensor s sends data to actor k;

- p_{ij} is the propagation delay associated with link (i, j), defined as d_{ij}/v, where v is the signal propagation speed;

-$\tilde{d}$ is a parameter that accounts for the average sum of processing, queuing, and access delay at each sensor node;

- B is the latency bound on each source-actor flow;

- r and r_{th} are the event reliability and the required event reliability threshold, respectively;

-$b^{s,k}$ is a binary variable that equals 1 iff the connection between source s and actor k is not compliant with the latency bound, i.e., the end-to-end delay is higher than the latency bound B;

- Q is the number of non-compliant sources.

The multi-constraint problem of single-actor selection can be cast as follows:

$$\text{Given: } c_{ij}, e_{ij}, p_{ij}, v, \tilde{d}, B, r_{th}. \tag{1}$$

$$\text{Find: } x_{ij}^k, f_{ij}^{s,k}, r. \tag{2}$$

$$Min \sum_{k \in A} \sum_{(i,j) \in E} x_{ij}^k \circ c_{ij} \tag{3}$$

Subject to:

$$\sum_{j \in V} (f_{sj}^{s,k} - f_{js}^{s,k}) = l^{s,k}. \qquad \forall s \in S1, \forall k \in A. \tag{4}$$

$$\sum_{j \in V} (f_{jk}^{s,k} - f_{kj}^{s,k}) = l^{s,k}. \qquad \forall s \in S1, \forall k \in A. \tag{5}$$

$$\sum_{j \in V, \, j \notin S \cup A} (f_{ij}^{s,k} - f_{ji}^{s,k}) = 0. \qquad \forall i \in V, i \notin S1 \cup A. \tag{6}$$

$$l^{s1,k} = l^{s2,k} \qquad \forall s1, s2 \in S, \forall k \in A. \tag{7}$$

$$\sum_{k \in A} l^{s,k} = 1. \qquad \forall s \in S. \tag{8}$$

$$f_{ij}^{s,k} \le e_{ij}. \qquad \forall s \in S, \forall k \in A, \forall i,j \in V. \tag{9}$$

$$f_{ij}^{s,k} \le l^{s,k}. \qquad \forall s \in S, \forall k \in A, \forall i,j \in V. \tag{10}$$

$$f_{ij}^{s,k} \le x_{ij}^k. \qquad \forall s \in S, \forall k \in A, \forall i,j \in V. \tag{11}$$

$$\varepsilon \circ \left[\sum_{(i,j) \in E} f_{ij}^{s,k} \circ D_{ij} - B \right] \le b^{s,k}. \qquad \forall s \in S1, \forall k \in A. \tag{12}$$

$$Q = \sum_{k \in A} \sum_{s \in S1} b^{s,k}. \qquad r = \frac{|S| - Q}{|S|} \ge r_{th}. \tag{13}$$

The objective function in (3) minimizes the overall energy consumption. Constraints (4-6) express conservation of flows, i.e. each source generates a flow, which is collected by an actor. In particular, constraint (4) guarantees that a source node generates a flow on the tree of the selected actor, and only on that one; while non-source nodes do not generate any flow. Constraint (5) requires that only one actor collect flows generated by each source. Constraint (6) imposes that the balance between incoming and outgoing flows is null for non-source and non-actor nodes. Constraint (7, 8) imposes that each source sends data to exactly one actor, and the same actor. Constraint (9) ensures that flows are created on links between adjacent nodes (i.e., that are within transmission range of each other). Constraint (10) ensures that all flow variables from a source to a particular actor are zero unless that actor is selected by the source. Constraint (11) forces all flows from different sources directed towards the same actor to be aggregated in the tree associated with that actor.

Constraint (12) requires that the binary variable $b^{s,k}$ be equal to 1 always and only when the flow between source s and actor k violates the latency bound B. Note that the small positive coefficient ε is needed to scale the value of the difference between the delay and the delay bound to make it smaller than 1. In (13), Q is defined as the number of non-compliant sources and the reliability r is constrained to be over the required threshold.

Integer linear programming belongs to a class of problems known as NP-hard [17]. It is difficult to solve ILP even with the ILP solver such as cplex [8]. So we put forward some approximate algorithms in the following section.

4 Approximate Algorithms

4.1 Minimum Cost Tree (MCT) Selection Algorithms

Minimum Path Length Cost Tree (MPLCT). Real-time requirement of the applications is a key factor of WSANs. So the time, from sensors sensing event to actors receiving data, should be shorten as soon as possible. The shorter the path between the event area and the selected actor is, the earlier the actor gets information. In MPLCT, sensors try to find an actor so that the minimum path length from the sensors in the event area to that actor can be constructed and thus event information can be transmitted in a short latency. It is intuitive that MPLCT minimizes the number of hops in the path and the distance traveled by the packet, and makes the delay low.

Minimum Energy Cost Tree (MECT). Energy constraint of the sensors is also a key factor of WSANs. Once sensors are deployed, their energy could not be recharged. So the energy consumption of sensors effect the lifetime of the WSANs. In MECT, sensors try to find an actor so that the minimum energy path from the sensors in the event area to that actor can be constructed and thus event information can be transmitted in an energy efficient way. Every connection in the tree will be established depending on the energy cost measurement of that link. Using these connections, minimum energy paths from every sensor node to the selected actor node are constructed. The collection of these paths forms the minimum energy tree of single-actor. In this tree, we guarantee that each data packet reaches to the selected node with the overall minimum energy dissipation caused at the sensor nodes.

Linear programming of the minimum cost tree. MECT and MPLCT are the sub-problems of the minimum cost tree, and different in cost function only. So we set up a linear programming for the minimum cost tree only.

Before describing the objective function and the conditions for the single-actor selection algorithm, we first introduce the following notations.

- e_{ij} is a binary variable representing a link, that equals 1 iff nodes i and j are within each other's communication range;

- c_{ij} is the cost of the link between nodes i and j, i.e. energy cost function $c_{ij} = \kappa d_{ij}^{\alpha} + \tau$ [12] (where α is the path loss exponent with the range between 2 and 5, d_{ij} represents the distance between nodes i and j, and κ, $\tau \in \mathfrak{R}$ are real numbers), or path length cost function $c_{ij} = d_{ij}$.

- f_{ij} is an integral variable representing data across the link between nodes i and j.

- h_i is a binary variable representing actor i, that equals 1 iff actor i is selected as a collector.

The minimum cost tree problem of selecting a single-actor can be described as:

$$\text{Given: } c_{ij}, e_{ij.} \tag{14}$$

$$\text{Find: } h_i, f_{ij.} \tag{15}$$

$$\text{minimize} \sum_{j \in V} \sum_{i \in N} f_{ij} \bullet c_{ij} \tag{16}$$

Subject to:

$$\sum_{j \in V} f_{ij} - \sum_{j \in V} f_{ji} = 1. \qquad \forall i \in S1. \tag{17}$$

$$\sum_{j \in V} f_{ij} = 0. \qquad \forall i \in A. \tag{18}$$

$$\sum_{j \in V} f_{ji} = |S1| \bullet h_i. \qquad \forall i \in A. \tag{19}$$

$$\sum_{j \in V} f_{ij} - \sum_{j \in V} f_{ji} = 0. \qquad \forall i \in S - S1. \tag{20}$$

$$f_{ij} = 0. \qquad \forall e_{ij} = 0, i, j \in V. \tag{21}$$

$$0 \leq f_{ij} \leq |S1|. \qquad \forall i, j \in V. \tag{22}$$

$$\sum_{j \in A} h_j = 1. \qquad h_j \in \{0,1\}, \forall j \in A. \tag{23}$$

The objective function (16) minimizes the total cost between the sensors in event area and one actor. If we define c_{ij} as the energy consumption of the link (i, j), the objective function (16) is the objective of the minimum energy cost tree. If we defined c_{ij} as the path length of the link (i, j), the function (16) is the objective of the minimum path length cost tree. Constraints (17-20) express conservation of flows. Constraints (19, 23) require that only one actor is selected and receives all data flow from the sources.

This shortest-cost-paths problem is proved to have a polynomial complexity [13]. Shortest paths from one (source) node to all other nodes on a network are normally referred to as one-to-all shortest paths. Shortest paths from one node to a subset of the nodes are defined as one-to-some shortest paths, while those paths from every node to every node are called all-to-all shortest paths [14]. Our single-actor selection problem can be considered as the transpose of the one-to-some shortest path, since not all sensors are in the event area. A recent study by Zhan and Noon [15] suggested that the best approach for solving the one-to-some shortest path is Dijkstra's algorithm.

4.2 A Hop-Bounded and Minimum Energy Cost Tree Algorithm (HBMECT)

MECT and MPLCT are the approximate algorithms of the multi-constraint selection problem from energy and delay respectively. In the paragraph, we put forward a Hop-Bounded and Minimum Energy Cost Tree algorithm (HBMECT) for single-actor selection problem. In HBMECT, sensors try to find an actor so that at the premise of hop-bounded constraint, the minimum energy path from the sensors in the event area to that actor can be constructed and thus event information can be transmitted in an energy efficient way.

An actor with the nearest distance to the center of event area will be a collector of the event in HBMECT. The shorter the distance between the center of event area and the selected actor is, the faster the actor may take appropriate action. Moreover, if all the actors have same action range, it is more possible that the event area is fully covered by the closest actor's action range; Even if the different actor has different action range, the actor is closer to the actors whose action range cover the event area, which is help to decrease time-delay of action. So in the approximate algorithm, the actor that is nearest to the center of event area is selected as sensors' collector, and then the sensors residing in the event area delivery the packets to the selected actor via geographic routing.

When a sensor senses an event, it calculates the coordinate of the event source with multi-lateration localization technologies [9] by one hop information exchange. Then the sensor computes the distance between the event source and each actor, and selects the actor, whose distance is smallest, as its collector.

To meet the hop-bounded threshold H (H is the hops bound on each source-actor flow), we alter geographic routing algorithm for ensuring that each hop length of a packet traveled is more than the distance D_{sd}/H, where D_{sd} is the distance between source node s and the selected actor d. the pseudonym code for routing algorithm is shown in Fig. 2.

```
Each source sends a packet to the selected actor d.
for each sensor i received a packet from the node u do
   if the actor d is neighbor node then
         sends the packet to the node d
   else
      begin
            computes D_id the distance to the actor d and
remaining hops H_i=H_u-1 (if u is a source node, H_u=H)
            if there are neighbor node set T in the circle
with the center actor d and the radius (H_i-1)*D_sd/H then
            selects the neighbor node j, which satisfy D_jd<D_id
and D_ij<D_ik, ∀k∈T, k≠j, as own relay node,
      else
            selects the neighbor node j, which is nearest to
destination node d, as own relay node
      end
```

Fig. 2. Pseudonym code for routing algorithm

5 Performance Evaluation

Before evaluating the performance of the algorithms, we introduce two metrics:

Average energy per packet. This metric represents the average energy consumed in the network for transmitting and relaying a data packet until the actor successfully receives it.

Average number of hops. with perfect MAC and time synchronization, average number of hops reflects the time by the packets traveled. The smaller average hops are, the shorter the delay of data delivery is.

All approximate algorithms were implemented in Matlab [16]. We consider two different simulation scenarios. In each scenario, there is a square area of 100mX100m, and a circle event area with centre coordinate (50, 50) and radius 20m. Four actors are randomly placed at 10mX10m area in the four different corner of the deploy area. In scenario 1: we vary sensors nodes with the number ranging in [50,200], step 25. In scenario 2: 150 sensors nodes are randomly deployed. We vary hop-bounded threshold from 3 to 10 hops for the HBMECT algorithm. The simulation parameters are chosen to be τ=50nJ/bit, κ=100pJ/bit/mα, α=4. Each data packet is 525 bytes. The transmission range of sensors is set to 25m. For different setup in each scenario, we simulate at least 100 times, all figures in the section report over 90 percent confidence intervals.

In scenario 1, the study focuses on sensor density effect on different algorithm. Fig 3 (a-b) show that average number of hops of each source-actor pair for MECT are most, are 9 when the number of sensors is more than 100, but the average energy per packet is less than that of other algorithms. The average number of hops is smallest for MPLCT, and less than 3 hops in MECT at least. It leads to paths with lower delay (lower number of hops and straight towards the destination); however, since this is paid with a higher energy consumption, the average energy per packet of MPLCT is

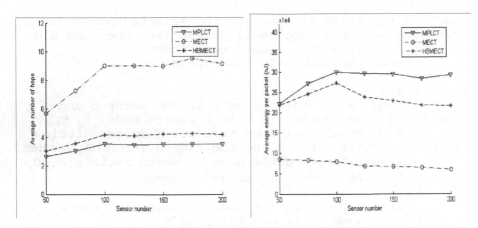

Fig. 3. Scenario 1. (a) Sensor density vs. Average number of hops (b) Sensor density vs. Average energy per packet.

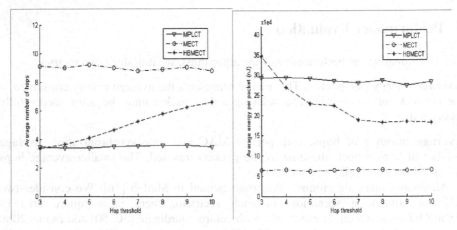

Fig. 4. Scenario 2. (a) Hop threshold vs. Average number of hops (b) Hop threshold vs. Average energy per packet.

most. Since the hop-bound threshold is 4 in HBMECT, the average number of hops is almost less than 4, and the average energy per packet is between the value of MPLCT and MECT.

In scenario 2, the study focuses on hop-bounded threshold effect on approximate algorithm. To contrast the approximate algorithm conveniently, we also list the corresponding metrics of MPLCT and MECT. Fig 4 (a-b) shows, for HBMECT, as hop threshold increases, the average energy per packet drops slowly. When hop threshold is 3, the average energy per packet in HBMECT is more than that in MPLCT. It is since different algorithms may select different actors. HBMECT reduces average energy per packet at the premise that the real-time requirements are met via setting hop threshold.

6 Conclusion

In the paper, we presented a single-actor selection problem, and formulated it as an Integer Linear Programming. We also proposed some approximate algorithms, such as MECT, MPLCT and HBMECT. MECT and MPLCT are centralized algorithms, and aim to low energy consumption and low delay respectively. HBMECT is a distributed algorithm, and can meet different real-time and energy-efficient requirements of the applications via setting the hop threshold.

In the future, we plan to perfect the HBMECT from avoiding 'void area' and contention based MAC. Moreover, bandwidth constraints, variable link capacity and nodes' remaining energy aren't considered in the HBMECT, so single-actor selection problem with capacity-bounded and a single-actor framework for WSANs are our future works.

References

1. F. Akyildiz and I. H. Kasimoglu, "Wireless sensor and actor networks: Research challenges," Ad Hoc Networks (Elsevier), vol. 2, no. 4, pp. 351–367,October 2004.
2. I.F. Akyildiz, W. Su, Y. Sankarasubramaniam, E. Cayirci, "Wireless sensor networks: a survey", Computer Networks (Elsevier) Journal 38 (4) (2002) 393–422.
3. T. Melodia, D. Pompili, V. C. Gungor and Ian F. Akyildiz, "A Distributed Coordination Framework for Wireless Sensor and Actor Networks", MobiHoc'05, May 25–27, 2005, Urbana-Champaign, Illinois, USA.
4. T. He, J. Stankovic, C. Lu, and T. Abdelzaher, "SPEED: A real-time routing protocol for sensor networks," in Proceedings of IEEE ICDCS, Providence,RI, USA, May 2003, pp. 46–55.
5. E. Felemban, C.G. Lee, E. Ekici, R. Boder, and S. Vural, "Probabilistic QoS Guarantee in Reliability and Timeliness Domains in Wireless Sensor Networks," in Proceedings of IEEE INFOCOM 2005, Miami, FL, USA, Mar. 2005.
6. K. Akkaya, M. Younis, "An Energy-Aware QoS Routing Protocol for Wireless Sensor Networks", Proc. of the IEEE Workshop on Mobile and Wireless Networks (MWN 2003), Providence, RI, May 2003.
7. Haeyong Kim, Yongho Seok, Nakjung Choi,Yanghee Choi, and Taekyoung Kwon "Optimal Multi-sink Positioning and Energy-efficient Routing in Wireless Sensor Networks" in ICOIN 2005, Jeju Island, Korea, January 31- February 2, 2005, Proceedings.
8. T. He, C. Huang, B. Blum, J. Stankovic, and T. Abdelzaher, "Range-Free Localization Schemes for Large Scale Sensor Networks," in Proceedings of Mobicom, 2003.
9. Andreas Savvides, Chih-Chieh Han, and Mani B. Strivastava, "Dynamic fine-grained localization in ad hoc networks of sensors," In Proc. Of. ACM Mobicom, 2001.
10. Jinyang Li, J. Jannotti, D. S. J. De Couto, D. R. Karger, and R. Morris "A Scalable Location Service for Geographic Ad Hoc Routing," in Proc. of. ACM MobiCom, August 2000.
11. B. Sundararaman, U. Buy, and A. Kshemkalyani, "Clock synchronization for wireless sensor networks: a survey," Ad Hoc Networks (Elsevier), vol. 3, no. 3, pp. 281–323, May 2005.
12. W. Heinzelman, A. Chandrakasan, and H. Balakrishnan, "An application-specific protocol architecture for wireless microsensor networks," IEEE Transactions on Wireless Communications, vol. 1, no. 4, pp. 660–670, Oct. 2002.

13. S. Chen, "Routing Support for providing guaranteed End-To-End Quality of Service," Ph.D. Thesis Dissertation, University of Illinois at Urbana-Champaign, 1999.
14. F. Zhan, "Three Fastest Shortest Path Algorithms on Real Road Networks: Data Structures and Procedures," Journal of Geographic Information and Decision Analysis, 1(1), 1998.
15. M. H. Hung and J. J. Divoky, "A Computational Study of Efficient Shortest Path Algorithms," Computers & Operations Research, Vol. 15, pp. 567-576, 1988.
16. Matlab. http://www.mathworks.com
17. GAREY, M. R., and JOHNSON, D. S. "Computers and Intractability: A guide to the theory of NP completeness". W. H. Freeman and Company, 1979
18. Stefan Dulman, Paul Havinga,Johann Hurink. "WAVE LEADER ELECTION PROTOCOL FOR WIRELESS SENSOR NETWORKS", Proceedings of the 3rd International Symposium on Mobile Multimedia Systems & Applications, pp. 43 – 50, 2002.
19. Navneet Malpani, Jennifer L. Welch, Nitin Vaidya, "Leader Election Algorithms for Mobile Ad Hoc Networks", Fourth International Workshop on Discrete Algorithms and Methods for Mobile Computing and Communications, pp. 96-103, 2000.
20. Sudarshan Vasudevan, Jim Kurose, Don Towsley, "Design and Analysis of a Leader Election Algorithm for Mobile Ad Hoc Networks", Proceedings of the 12th IEEE International Conference on Network Protocols (ICNP'04).
21. S. Tilak, N. Abu-Ghazaleh and W. Heinzelman, "A taxonomy of wireless micro-sensor network communication models", ACM Mobile Computing and Communication Review (MC2R), June 2002.

A Genetic Algorithm on Multi-sensor Networks Lifetime Optimization

Yantao Pan, Wei Peng, and Xicheng Lu

School of Computer, National University of Defense Technology, Changsha, P.R. China
pytmail@126.com

Abstract. Since data communications consume the most energy of sensor networks, it is reasonable to take efficient traffic balancing to prolong the lifetime. In addition, the traffic aggregation is a main characteristic that distinguish sensor networks from others e.g. Internet and MANET. Therefore, an optimal traffic distribution will maximize the network lifetime. Furthermore, sensor networks are generally developed for special applications. If different sensor networks deployed in the same region can cooperate with each other in data transmission, their lifetimes can be improved remarkably. In this paper, we propose a genetic algorithm to achieve optimal traffic distribution on multi-sensor networks and show its efficiency by experiments.

Keywords: Sensor Networks, Lifetime Optimization, and Genetic Algorithm.

1 Introduction

Wireless sensor networks provide us a new way to cognize environments around. However, scarce energy limits its actual distribution. The energy storage of a sensor node is highly constrained. Replacing a large amount of nodes' batteries is almost infeasible, since they may be deployed randomly in harsh or hostile areas. One of the key challenges of sensor networks is therefore to maximize the lifetime.

The lifetime of a sensor network is usually regarded as the period of the time from its deployment to the network partition when there is a node that cannot send its data to its sinks. Some existing works focus on this problem. Bhardwaj et al. provide bounds on the lifetime [1] [2]. The literature [3] presents a modeling framework based on probability distributions of the node densities, link costs and data rates over the sensing field. The literature [4] also provides a mathematical analysis for the lifetime of a sensor network. These works [1-4] investigate the upper bounds or expected value of the maximum lifetime. In [5] and [6], Chang et al. provide a heuristic algorithm. But it performs arbitrarily badly in the worst case [7]. In the literature [8], another heuristic approach is presented, but the running time of it has a bad scalability to the network size [9]. In [10], a tree-based approximate algorithm is presented to reduce the running time and achieve better scalability in terms of network size. These works [5-10] present heuristic algorithms to maximize the lifetimes approximately.

However, these works cannot deal with the energy consumed by receiving data. In literature [11], the powers of RX and TX units are about 12 mW and 15 mW. The DEC Roamabout radio [12] consumes 5.76W during transmission, 2.88W during

X. Cheng, W. Li, and T. Znati (Eds.): WASA 2006, LNCS 4138, pp. 295–306, 2006.
© Springer-Verlag Berlin Heidelberg 2006

reception. The radio unit in [13] consumes $15W$ while transmission and $11W$ while receiving. The energies consumed by Mote [14] to send and receive a packet are 20 nAh and 8 nAh. Therefore, this energy consumption should not be ignored in most cases. Different from above approaches, we make use of genetic algorithm to exploit this lifetime optimization problem. Genetic computation is a general method in solving complex optimization problems. With this method, we could consider conditions more complex and actual than those in the exiting works.

The rest of this paper is organized as follows. In section 2, the problem is formulated. We propose a basic edition of our approach in section 3 and then perfect it in section 4. In section 5, we evaluate the performance of the approach. Finally in section 6, some concluding remarks are made.

2 Problem Statement and Formulation

A multi-sensor network in consideration is modeled as a connected simple directed graph $G(V, A)$, where V is the set of all nodes and A is the set of all directed links (u, v) where $u, v \in V$. Let N_u be the set of neighbors of node u under its maximum transmission power level. We assume that link (u, v) exists if and only if $v \in N_u$. Let each node u have an initial energy E_u. Let $w(u)$ and $p(u)$ be the data-generating rate and the residual energy of node u. Assume that the energies required by node u to send and receive an information unit to and from its neighbor v are $q(u, v)_s$ and $q(u, v)_r$. For each sensor network, there are a source set X and a sink set Y. Regarding the data flow between each pair (X, Y) as a kind of commodity, we have a commodity set $Z = \left\{ z_i \mid z_i = (X_i, Y_i), X_i, Y_i \in V, X_i \cap Y_i = \varnothing \right\}$.

Definition-1. A Multi-SensorNet is defined to be a multi-commodity transportation network with the form of $N^s = (G, p, q, Z)$.

Definition-2. Let $N^s = (G, p, q, Z)$ be a Multi-SensorNet. Suppose $f(a): A \mapsto \overline{\mathbb{R}^-}$ is a function. f is defined to be a transmission scheme of N^s, if $\sum_{v \in V} f(x, v) - \sum_{v \in V} f(v, x) = w(x), \forall x \in X$ and $\sum_{u \in V} f(v, u) = \sum_{u \in V} f(u, v), \forall v \in V \setminus (X \cup Y)$ for $\forall (X, Y) \in Z$.

$$T_u \triangleq \frac{p(u)}{\sum_{v \in V} f(v, u) \cdot q(v, u)_r + \sum_{v \in V} f(u, v) \cdot q(u, v)_s}, \forall u \in V \text{ is the lifetime of node } u.$$

$T \triangleq \min_{u \in V}(T_u)$ is the lifetime of N^s under the transmission scheme f. If there is no transmission scheme f' and its corresponding lifetime T' so as to $T' > T$, f is an optimal transmission scheme and T is the maximum lifetime denoted by T^*.

The problem is stated as follows. Given a Multi-SensorNet $N^s = (G, p, q, Z)$, ask for the optimal transmission scheme and its maximum lifetime T^*. In this paper, we regard f as a flow velocity assignment scheme. And then, the lifetime optimization problem can be regarded as a flow velocity assignment optimization problem.

3 A Basic Genetic Algorithm

3.1 Genetic Coding

Since the lifetime optimization problem can be modeled as a flow velocity assignment optimization problem, we take paths with unit flow velocity as coding objects. The main advantage of this method is that an individual will not violate the nodes' energy constraints, and we do not need to add punishment to fitness evaluation.

Consider a Multi-SensorNet. Its maximum lifetime is T^*. In the period of the whole lifetime, a node u generates $w(u) \cdot T^*$ packets. Suppose a node must receive or send a unit packet a time. A node is deemed to be died, if its residual energy is not enough to send or receive a packet. Therefore, node u can take $w(u) \cdot T^*$ paths at most to balance its original data flow. The traffic that transits a unit path in the whole lifetime is equal to the size of a unit packet. That is to say, a source node could take any path from such a path set to send a unit packet a time. A Multi-SensorNet is expected to achieve the maximum lifetime under an optimal flow velocity assignment.

However, it is difficult to estimate the maximum lifetime T^*. If its estimation d is smaller than T^*, the number of the paths is smaller than that of the total packets. Therefore, we have to assign a flow more than a unit packet to each path. In addition, the flow on each path is usually not integral times of a unit packet. This contradicts the given assumption that a node receives or sends a packet a time. A calculated lifetime can not be achieved in fact. If d is greater than T^*. The original flow of a source will be distributed overly to more paths than what is needed. Therefore, the flow assigned to each path is smaller than a unit packet. This contradicts the given assumption too.

Considering these difficulties, we might as well regard the data generated by a source as a continued flow. In sequence, a node can receive or send data if only its residual energy hasn't dropped to zero. Therefore, the parameter d is not an estimation of T^* any longer. It denotes a precision on which the original flows of sources are divided and distributed to paths. That is, it controls the number of paths that a node can take to balance its original data flow. If a node has a data-generating rate $w(u)$, the number of paths it could take is $\lfloor w(u) \cdot d \rfloor$, where $\lfloor w(u) \cdot d \rfloor$ is the greatest integer no more than $w(u) \cdot d$. While d increases, a node can balance its original data flow to more paths, and the network is expected to live for a longer time.

Here are the details of our genetic coding. An individual that is denoted by $I \triangleq \{C_x\}_{x \in X_i, z_i \in Z}$ is a set of chromosomes, where X_i is a set of source nodes. A chromosome $C_x \triangleq \{Path_{x-y} | (x, y) \in z_i, z_i \in Z\}$ is a set of unit paths from source x to any of its sinks. We take such unit paths as genes. Because there are different amount of data that is generated in the period of the lifetime by different sources, the corresponding chromosomes contain different number of paths.

3.2 Initial Population Generator

The average fitness of an initial population affects greatly on the performance of a genetic algorithm. In our approach, we use two generators for different purposes.

The first one generates individuals by taking random source-sink paths as genes. This is the most basic method. We take advantage of its randomicity to achieve high community diversity. However, the main disadvantage of this method is that the fitness of a random generated individual may be every low. This disadvantage will bring more bad effects on the performance of our approach when d is set to a great value. This phenomenon can be well explained as follows. Consider a population that is generated randomly under certain population size and precision. Suppose this population size offers sufficient community diversity under this precision. However, when the precision increases, the same population size maybe cannot offer the same community diversity. This is because the number of genes increases with the precision, and the population size seems to be smaller contrastively.

We might take two methods to deal with this difficulty. The first is to use a greater population size. However, this method is not always effective. In section 4, we will show that the basic algorithm obtains little improvement with the increase in population size, when precision is great. This is because the algorithm complexity depends on the population size greatly. The second method is to generate an initial population with high fitness to improve the performance under great precisions and small population sizes. This comes to the second generator.

The basic idea of the second generator is to take use of a last population under a smaller precision to generate an initial population under a greater precision. As mentioned before, a precision sets a limit to the number of paths, on which a node can balance its original data flow. We use a small precision as a tight limit at the beginning. Each node takes a few paths and a small population size is enough to offer sufficient community diversity. Then we loose this limit step by step. A node may divide its original flow velocity into more pieces and distribute them to more paths basing on their earlier assignments. In this way, we get a high fitness initial population, and a small population size works well even under a great precision.

3.3 Fitness Evaluation and Genetic Operations

The fitness of individuals only depends on their maximum lifetimes. We do not need to consider punishment function.

CROSSOVER_PROB and *CROSSOVER_NUM* are two parameters used in the crossover operation. *CROSSOVER_PROB* is a probability ranging from 0.00 to 1.00. It determines how many individuals will take part in the crossover operation. Each individual has a probability to participate the crossover operation, which depends on its fitness. An individual with greater fitness has more chance than others. *CROSSOVER_NUM* is a natural number. It determines how many points the corresponding chromosomes of two individuals will crossover in.

The crossover operation includes two steps. The first step is to choose individuals according to parameter *CROSSOVER_PROB* and individuals' fitness. The second step is to crossover two individuals at each chromosome. The crossover of two chromosomes is taken at multi points. The points are chosen randomly from the gene sequence and number of points depends on *CROSSOVER_NUM*. For example, if 3, 5 and 8 are chosen to be crossover points from the whole chromosome length 12, the gene segments 0~2 and 5~7 of the two chromosomes will be exchanged, but the other segments 3~4 and 8~12 are remained at their original chromosomes.

There are two parameters *MUTATION_PROB* and *MUTATION_PERCENT* in the mutation operation. *MUTATION_PROB* is a probability ranging from 0.00 to 1.00. It determines how many individuals will take part in the mutation operation. The chance of each individual to be chosen depends on its fitness. The smaller the fitness is, the greater the chance is. *MUTATION_PERCENT* is a number ranging from 0.00 to 1.00. It determines how many percents of genes should be changed in each chromosome of an individual. The mutation operation includes two steps. The first step is to choose individuals according to *MUTATION_PROB* and individuals' fitness. The second step is to choose genes randomly according to *MUTATION_PERCENT* and replace them with new generated genes.

3.4 Parameters Selection

We take following numeric experiments to determine the values of main parameters. Consider a simple Multi-SensorNet shown in Fig. 1.1. The number in the upper part of a node is the sequence number. The numbers in the under part are the data-generating rate and the initial energy. The energy consumed by sending or receiving an information unit is marked on arcs. Fig.1.2 shows an ideal transmission schedule of this network, which is termed 'ideal solution'. The optimal flow velocity assignments are plotted on arcs in the form of "source node # flow velocity". The lifetime of each node are shown in Table 1. The first node to 'die-out' is 3. The maximum lifetime of this network is 1.8 approximatively.

Table 1. The lifetime of each node under an ideal transmission schedule

Node	0	1	2	3	4
Lifetime	3.000000	1.800000018	1.800000077	1.799999856	1.818182

Table 2 shows the lifetime as functions of parameters. The lifetime achieves 1.799571 when *MUTATION_PERCENT*=0.15, 1.800000 when *MUTATION_PROB*=0.95, 1.797857 when *CROSSOVER_PROB*=0.40, and 1.800000 again when *CROSSOVER_NUM*=4.

Table 2. The lifetime as functions of *MUTATION_PERCENT, MUTATION_PROB, CROSS-OVER_PROB* and *CROSSOVER_NUM*

Values	0.00/1	0.25/2	0.50/3	0.75/4	0.95/5
MUTATION_PERCENT	1.684000	1.797857	1.794429	1.798286	1.794857
MUTATION_PROB	1.778369	1.792714	1.797429	1.800000	1.800000
CROSSOVER_PROB	1.586058	1.788571	1.797857	1.797143	1.796429
CROSSOVER_NUM	1.786270	1.795714	1.799286	1.800000	1.800000

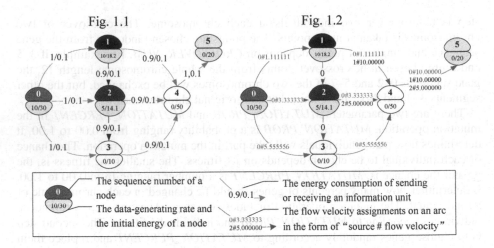

Fig. 1. A 6-node 1-sink Multi-SensorNet and one of its ideal solutions

From these numeric experiments, we get a set of parameter values: *MUTATION_PERCENT* = 0.15; *MUTATION_PROB* = 0.95; *CROSSOVER_PROB* = 0.40; *CROSSOVER_NUM* = 4. In the reset of this paper, this is a basic configuration that is taken by experiments.

4 An Improvement with Precision Vector

Now, let's consider a Multi-SensorNet shown in Fig. 2.1. Node 0, 1 and 2 take node 6 as their sink. Node 3 and 4 take node 7 as their sink. An ideal solution is plotted in Fig.2.2. The lifetime of each node is shown in Table 3. The maximum lifetime of the network is 1.113468.

Table 3. The lifetime of nodes in the ideal solution

Node	0	1	2	3
Lifetime	1.338458	1.113468	1.113468	1.397984
Node	4	5	6	7
Lifetime	1.113468	1.236226	1.724138	6.666667

Firstly, we attempt to achieve 1.113 by the basic algorithm. We set *PRECISION* =10 and increase *POPULATION_SIZE*. The results are shown in Table 4. The parameter *GENERATION_NUM* denotes the time of genetic manipulations.

We find that the lifetime increases scarcely while *POPULATION_SIZE* rises from 100 to 600. This phenomenon can be explained as follows. For a node e.g. 0, the flow velocity that is assigned to a path is $w(0)/\lfloor w(0) \cdot d \rfloor = 0.1$, when *PRECISION*=10. On arc $(0,1)$ and $(0,2)$, the adjustment granularity of flow velocity is 0.10 at least. However, the basic algorithm cannot achieve 1.113 under such a great granularity.

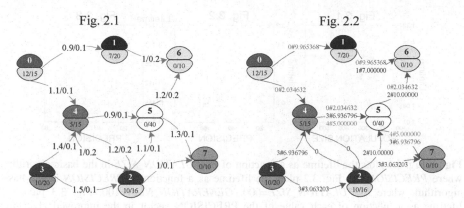

Fig. 2. An 8-node 2-sink Multi-SensorNet and one of its ideal solutions

Table 4. The lifetime as a function of *POPULATION_SIZE* (*GENERATION_NUM*=100)

POPULATION_SIZE	100	150	200	250	300
Lifetime	1.078167	1.102688	1.101322	1.109570	1.111111
POPULATION_SIZE	400	450	500	550	600
Lifetime	1.111111	1.104362	1.111111	1.111111	1.111111

Therefore, we must set *PRECISION* to a greater value to get a better result. Table 5 shows the lifetime as a function of *PRECISION*, which increases from 10 to 80. *POPULATION_SIZE*=600. *GENERATION_NUM*=100. Note that the lifetime decreases while *PRECISION* increases. The reason has been analyzed in section 3.2.

Table 5. Lifetime as a function of *PRECISION* (*POPULATION_SIZE*=600)

PRECISION	10	30	50	60	70	80
Lifetime	1.111111	1.038287	0.914599	0.894988	0.853593	0.847009

In order to improve the basic algorithm's performance under a great *PRECISION*, we propose an improved algorithm that is called GAMSN. As mentioned before, its basic idea is to use a last population under a smaller *PRECISION* to generate an initial population under a greater *PRECISION*. In this way, the calculation under a greater *PRECISION* could benefit from the one under a smaller *PRECISION*. Table 6 shows a result of GAMSN, where *POPULATION_SIZE* = 400.

This improved algorithm achieves 1.113173. As shown in Table 7, the flow velocity assignments are very close to those in the ideal solution shown in Fig. 2.2.

Table 6. The lifetime under each value of the *PRECISION* vector

PRECISION	5	10	20	40	80
GENERATION_NUM	100	50	50	50	100
Lifetime	1.111111	1.111111	1.111111	1.112811	1.113173

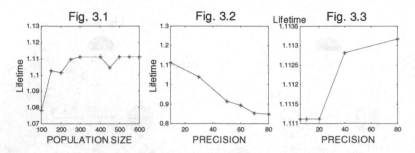

Fig. 3. Fig. 3.1 plots the lifetime as a function of *POPULATION_SIZE* in the basic algorithm, where *PRECISION*=10. Fig. 3.2 plots the lifetime as a function of *PRECISION* in the basic algorithm, where *POPULATION_SIZE*=600, *GENERATION_NUM*=100. Fig. 3.3 plots the lifetime as a function of each value of the PRECISION vector in the improved algorithm GAMSN, while *POPULATION_SIZE*=400.

Table 7. The flow velocity assignments to each arc (ideal solution VS GAMSN)

Arcs	Idea solution	Best solution
(0,1)	9.965368	9.962500
(0,4)	2.034632	2.037500
(2,5)	10.00000	10.00000
(2,7)	3.063203	3.062500
(3,2)	3.063203	3.062500
(3,4)	6.936796	6.937500
(4,5)	13.971428	13.975000
Lifetime	1.113468	1.113173

5 Performance Evaluation

The basic algorithm has a complexity of *PANSMG* . *P* is the maximum *PRECISION*. *A* is the maximum data-generating rate. *N* is the *POPULATION_SIZE*. *S* is the number of the sources. *M* is the number of the arcs. *G* is the *GENERATION_NUM*.

FA(1,50,50) in [6] is a flow augmentation algorithm. The authors announce that it has a probability of 100% to achieve a solution that is not less than 90% of the maximum lifetime, when the augmentation step size λ =0.001. However, as to the Multi-SensorNet shown in Fig. 2.1, FA(1,50,50) only achieves 1.112801 (λ = 0.001) and 1.112867 (λ = 0.0001). Contrastively, GAMSN achieves 1.113173.

Additional, we compare GAMSN with FA(1,50,50) on random networks. We generate seven Multi-SensorNets, which has 20, 30, 50, 60, 80, 100 and 120 nodes being distributed randomly in a 10×10 square area. To each network, 2~8 nodes are selected to be sinks. An initial energy (chosen from 200 to 500 randomly) and a data-generating rate (chosen from 5 to 12 randomly) are assigned to each node. The energy needed to receiving or sending an information unit is assigned to each link according to its length. The maximum value of the *PRECISION* vector is set to be 3.2.

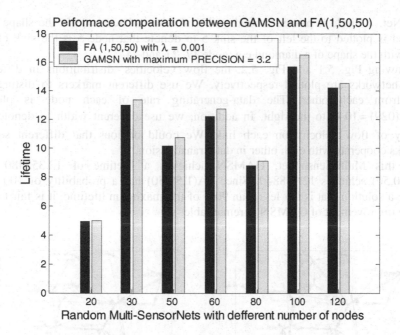

Fig. 4. Performance of GAMSN comparing with FA

Table 8. The lifetime of GAMSN comparing with FA on random Multi-SensorNets

Multi-SensorNet	FA(1,50,50)	GAMSN	Improvement (%)
20nodes(2sinks)	4.895738	4.947670	1.0608
30nodes(3sinks)	12.978840	13.355480	2.9020
50nodes(8sinks)	10.143168	10.709813	5.5865
60nodes(4sinks)	12.159179	12.730590	4.6994
80nodes(8sinks)	8.738673	9.101068	4.1470
100nodes(8sinks)	15.672667	16.506536	5.3205
120nodes(8sinks)	14.196439	14.504745	2.1717
Average	11.254957	11.693700	3.8982

Consequently, each source might take 16 to 38 paths to balance its original traffic in GAMSN. The augmentation step size λ is set to be 0.001 and each source could take 1000 paths in FA consequently. In fact, this comparison is not fair. However, GAMSN outperforms FA in this comparison. The results are plotted in Fig. 4.

The details of flow velocities' distributions on the 30-node Multi-SensorNet are given in Fig. 5. The figures in the left column plot the results of GAMSN, and the figures in the right column plot the results of FA(1,50,50).

Firstly, the flow velocities' distributions of all sensor networks are plotted in Fig. 5.1 and Fig. 5.2. A number in the form of "T(node sequence)=lifetime" is plotted to the right of each node. Node 5, 9, and 21 are the three sinks in the 30-node Multi-

SensorNet. A circle is plotted around each sink. An isolated node in the shape of a diamond is plotted to the left of the sink 5 to denote that node 5 is the sink of the nodes with the shape of a diamond e.g. node 17, 21 and 24.

Following Fig. 5.1 and Fig. 5.2, the flow velocities' distributions in different sensor networks are plotted respectively. We use different markers to distinguish them from each other. The data-generating rate of each node is plotted as Data(029) = 10.40 to the right. In addition, we use different width to denote the quantity of flow velocity on each link. We could obvious that different sensor networks cooperate with each other in data transmission.

For this Multi-SensorNet, GAMSN achieves a lifetime of 13.355480 and FA(1,50,50) achieves 12.978840. Since FA(1,50,50) has a probability of 100% to achieve a solution that is not less than 90% of the maximum lifetime, it is fair to say that the improvement of GAMSN is remarkable.

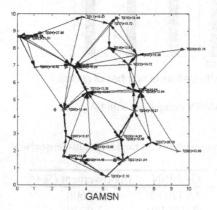

Fig. 5.1. The flow velocities' distributions on all sensor networks

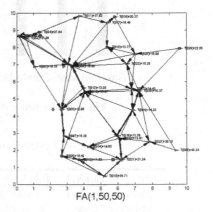

Fig. 5.2. The flow velocities' distributions on all sensor networks

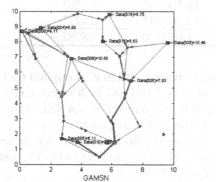

Fig. 5.3. The flow velocities' distributions on sensor network 1

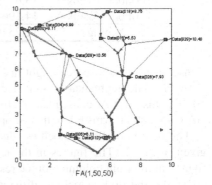

Fig. 5.4. The flow velocities' distributions on sensor network 1

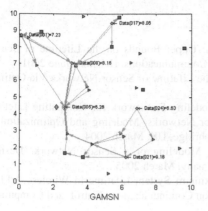

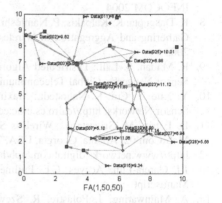

Fig. 5.5. The flow velocities' distributions on sensor network 2

Fig. 5.6. The flow velocities' distributions on sensor network 2

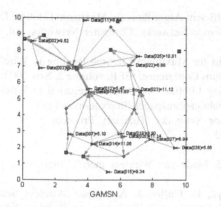

Fig. 5.7. The flow velocities' distributions on sensor network 3

Fig. 5.8. The flow velocities' distributions on sensor network 3

Fig. 5. The distribution of flow velocities on the 30-node Multi-SensorNet

6 Conclusion

In this paper, we propose a genetic algorithm to solve the lifetime optimization problem in multi sensor networks. Different from previous works, we take the energy consumed by receiving data into account. Experiments show our approach performs well.

After finding out a transmission schedule, we are aware of the flow velocities' distributions on each link. Therefore, we could schedule the nodes to send and receive data synchronously such that they can go to sleep instead of listening while there is nothing to transmit. We take this as our future work . And it is also the reason why we have not take energy consumption of listening into account in this paper.

References

1. M. Bhardwaj, A. Chandrakasan, T. Garnett.: Upper Bounds on the Lifetime of Sensor Networks. IEEE International Conference on Communications, Helsinki, June 2001
2. M. Bhardwaj, A. Chandrakasan.: Bounding the Lifetime of Sensor Networks Via Optimal Role Assignments. IEEE INFOCOM'2002
3. E. J. Duarte-Melo, M. Liu, A. Misra.: A Modeling Framework for Computing Lifetime and Information Capacity in Wireless Sensor Networks. Modeling and Optimization in Mobile, Ad Hoc and Wireless Networks, Cambridge, UK, March 2004
4. Vivek Rai, Rabi N. Mahapatra.: Lifetime Modeling of a Sensor Network. Design, Automation and Test in Europe, Munich, Germany, March 2005
5. J.-H. Chang, L. Tassiulas.: Routing for Maximum System Lifetime in Wireless Ad-hoc Networks. 37th Annual Allerton Conference on Communication, Control, and Computing, Monticello, IL, September 1999
6. J.-H. Chang, L. Tassiulas.: Energy conserving routing in wireless ad-hoc networks. IEEE INFOCOM'2000
7. Sankar, Z. Liu.: Maximum Lifetime Routing in Wireless Ad-hoc Networks. INFOCOM'2004
8. K. Dasgupta, K. Kalpakis, P. Namjoshi.: Efficient Algorithms for Maximum Lifetime Data Gathering and Aggregation in Wireless Sensor Networks. Computer Networks, vol. 42, 2003
9. R. Madan, S. Lall.: Distributed Algorithms for Maximum Lifetime Routing in Wireless Sensor Networks. Global Telecommunications Conference, IEEE, volume 2, Nov 2004
10. Y. Xue, Y, Cui, K. Nahrstedt.: Maximizing Lifetime for Data Aggregation in Wireless Sensor Networks. http://cairo.cs.uiuc.edu/publications/paper-files/xue-monet.pdf
11. D. Estrin, M. Srivastava.: Wireless Sensor Networks (Tutorial). Proceedings of ACM MobiCom'02, Atlanta, Georgia, USA, 2002
12. http://www.networks.digital.com/npb/html
13. J.J. Garcia-Luna-Aceves, C.L. Fullmer, E. Madruga.: Wireless mobile internetworking. Manuscript
14. A. Mainwaring, J. Polastre, R. Szewczyk, D. Culler, J. Anderson.: Wireless Sensor Networks for Habitat Monitoring. ACM International Workshop on Wireless Sensor Networks and Applications, 2002
15. G. Winter, J. Periaux, M. Galan.: Genetic Algorithms in Engineering and Computer Science. Published by JOHN WILEY & SON Ltd, 1995
16. L. Darrell Whitley, Michael D. Vose.: Foundations of Genetic Algorithms Volume 3. Published by Morgan Kaufmann Publishers Inc, 1995

A Power Efficient MAC Protocol for IEEE 802.11 Multihop Ad Hoc Networks

Hung-Jui Wu, Kuochen Wang*, and Lung-Sheng Lee

Department of Computer Science
National Chiao Tung University
Hsinchu, 300, Taiwan, ROC
kwang@cs.nctu.edu.tw

Abstract. In this paper, we propose a power efficient MAC protocol (PEMP) for IEEE 802.11 *multihop* ad hoc networks. Most of related work targeted at *single hop* ad hoc networks. In PEMP, when a node intends to transmit data, it will piggyback a data profile, which includes data size, on ATIM* and ATIM-ACK*. ATIM* and ATIM-ACK* are ATIM and ATIM-ACK with piggybacked data profiles, respectively. In this way, senders and receivers can inform their neighbor nodes of their data profiles. Then, each node calculates its transmission priority according to the collected data profiles. Based on transmission priorities, PEMP can schedule a better transmission sequence to reduce power consumption. By decreasing the idle time in the active state and adjusting the ATIM window dynamically based on network conditions, the power consumption of PEMP is 20% and 10% ~ 30% less than that of DPSM and IEEE 802.11 PSM, respectively. PEMP is applicable to multihop ad hoc networks and can achieve a good tradeoff between power consumption, throughput and delay.

Keywords: IEEE 802.11, MAC protocol, multihop ad hoc network, power efficient.

1 Introduction

Rapid development of wireless digital communication technologies makes it possible to have information accessible anywhere, at any time, and at any device. Among these wireless technologies, IEEE 802.11 [1] [2] plays an important role. The IEEE 802.11 MAC consists of two components: PCF (Point Coordination Function) and DCF (Distributed Coordination Function). PCF is a centralized MAC protocol that supports collision free and time bounded services, and an access point uses it to control all transmissions. DCF is a random access scheme, which is based on the *carrier sense multiple access with collision avoidance* (CSMA/CA), and thus works even without an access point. The above mentioned characteristic makes DCF popular for ad hoc networks. Ad hoc networks are dynamic, distributed and self-organizing networks. No access point is needed. So they are suitable for constructing temporary networks for

* This work was supported by the NCTU EECS-MediaTek Research Center under Grant Q583 and by the National Science Council under Grant NSC94-2213-E-009-043.

X. Cheng, W. Li, and T. Znati (Eds.): WASA 2006, LNCS 4138, pp. 307–318, 2006.
© Springer-Verlag Berlin Heidelberg 2006

special situations, such as battlefields, temporary conferences, natural resources monitoring, entertainments, and etc. However, mobile hosts have considerable usage limitations that result from limited battery capacity. To extend battery lifetime, minimization of power consumption in the network interface has become an essential issue.

Solutions addressing the power-saving issue in the IEEE 802.11 MAC layer can generally be classified to two major categories: *power control* and *power management*. Power control reduces the power level of a transmission to achieve reduced power consumption while maintaining the transmission success rate and network connectivity. In this paper, we focus on power management issues. Wireless interfaces support active, sleep and completely power-off states. The active state contains three physical states: transmitting, receiving, and idle. In the MAC layer, the IEEE 802.11 standard supports two power modes: active mode and power saving mode. In the active mode, a node is active and is ready to transmit or receive data at any time. In the power saving mode, a node only needs to wake up periodically. In Section 2, we will describe detailed operations of the power saving mode.

When to switch the power mode is an interesting problem. On-demand power management [3] determines power saving mode or active mode based on traffic load. In [4] it dynamically adjusts the ATIM window size according to observed network conditions. In [5], it focuses on wireless sensor networks, and it proposed nodes to sleep periodically, virtual and physical carrier sense to avoid collisions, and nodes to fragment long messages into small fragments to reduce the high cost of retransmitting long messages. Considering the IEEE 802.11 power saving mode, the ATIM (Ad Hoc Traffic Indication Map) window size will affect network performance and power efficiency. In [6] it assumed that mobility is unpredictable and no clock synchronization exists. It proposed three protocols to determine when a node will wake up to receive packets asynchronously. For single hop ad hoc networks, in [7], it schedules a transmission sequence based on ATIM announcements to remove contention overhead. Similarly, in [8] it schedules a transmission after the ATIM window and also adjust the ATIM window dynamically to adapt to the traffic status. TRACE [9] was designed for real-time voice packets in single hop broadcast networks. In TRACE, nodes predetermine the transmissions based on the receiver-based listening cluster and schedule the transmissions to improve energy efficiency.

Power management in *multihop* ad hoc networks is a difficult problem [6]. First, a multihop ad hoc network is a distributed network, and access points do not exist. Secondly, a node can be a data source, a destination or an intermediate node, and the node will play different roles with time. Thirdly, it is difficult to get information of nodes in entire networks compared to single-hop ad hoc networks. In the paper, we will assume that time is divided into beacon intervals that begin and end approximately at the same time at all nodes [8]. We focus on power management in the power saving mode of *multihop* ad hoc networks and propose a power efficient MAC protocol (PEMP) that integrates the information exchange method, the QoS method and the ATIM window adjustment to achieve a better trade-off between power consumption, throughput and delay.

2 Existing Approaches

IEEE 802.11 WLANs support two power modes: *active* and *power-saving* modes. The protocols for infrastructure networks and ad hoc networks are different. We briefly review the main operation of the power saving mode in an IEEE 802.11 ad hoc network. In the power saving mode, all nodes are connected synchronously by waking up periodically to listen beacon messages. The length of a beacon interval and the size of an ATIM window are known by all nodes. The ATIM window that nodes wake up is a small interval at the beginning of the beacon interval. If a node acquires the medium, it will send an ATIM frame to the desired-destination node based on the CSMA/CA access scheme. The ATIM frame is announced inside the ATIM window. If the desired-destination node receives the ATIM frame, it will reply with an ATIM-ACK frame and stay active to receive data in the rest of the beacon interval. However, the ATIM frames need not be acknowledged for buffered broadcast data. After the ATIM window, the buffered data should be sent based on the CSMA/CA access scheme. If a node fails to send its ATIM frame in the current ATIM window, it should retransmit the ATIM frame in the next ATIM window. If a node does not send or receive any ATIM frame during the ATIM window, it will switch to the sleep mode to decrease power consumption until the next beacon interval begins.

Fig. 1 shows an example. Initially, all nodes wake up at the beginning of the beacon interval. Since all nodes did not send or receive any ATIM frames in the first beacon interval, all nodes will switch to the sleep state. In the ATIM window of the next beacon interval, node A has a packet destined for node B and similarly node C has a packet destined for node D. Therefore, nodes A and C, respectively, sent ATIM frames to nodes B and D based on the CSMA/CA access scheme and both successfully received the ATIM-ACKs. After the ATIM window finishes, nodes A and C tried to transmit buffered data to nodes B and D, respectively, based on the CSMA/CA access scheme.

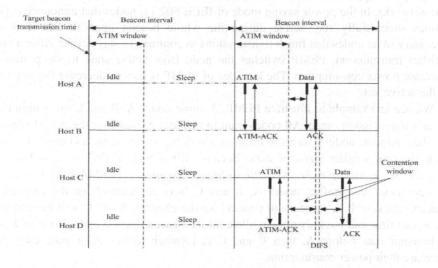

Fig. 1. Power saving mechanism for DCF in IEEE 802.11 [1][2]

In the dynamic power saving mechanism (DPSM) [4], each node independently chooses an ATIM window size based on observed network conditions. This might result in each node using a different ATIM window size. To adjust the ATIM window size, five rules needed to be followed. First, a node checks its buffer data to see if the ATIM window is big enough to announce ATIM frames. Otherwise, the node increases the ATIM window size. Secondly, if ATIM-ACK has not been received after exceeding the retry limit, the transmitted packet is "marked" and will be tried to transmit in the next beacon interval. When a node receives a marked packet, the node will increase its ATIM window size to the next higher level. Thirdly, each node piggybacks its own ATIM window size on all transmitted packets. A node will increase its ATIM window size if it overhears a ATIM window size that is much larger than its own ATIM window size. Fourthly, as long as a node is active, it will accept the ATIM message not only during the ATIM window but also in the rest of the beacon interval. Finally, a node will decrease the ATIM window size slowly. By adjusting the ATIM window dynamically according to network load, a node can decrease unnecessary power consumption and improve network throughput. The size of an ATIM window in IEEE 802.11 significantly affects the throughput and the amount of energy saving. Thus, a fixed ATIM window cannot perform well all the time. A node can dynamically adapt its ATIM window size according to observed network conditions to achieve a better trade-off between power consumption and throughput.

3 Design Approaches

3.1 Basic Idea

We propose a power efficient MAC protocol (PEMP) for IEEE 802.11 multihop ad hoc networks. In the power saving mode of IEEE 802.11, nodes that announce ATIM frames successfully stay active during the whole beacon interval. But it is not necessary to let nodes that finish transmissions to continue to stay active. After a node finishes transmission, PEMP switches the node from active state to sleep state to decrease power consumption. The key idea of PEMP is how to decrease the idle time in the active state.

We use an example to illustrate PEMP. Assume nodes A, B and C are within each other's transmission range. All nodes want to transmit packet after the ATIM window finishes. Assume node A wants to transmit a very big size of data, and nodes B and C both transmit smaller sizes of data. Because IEEE 802.11 DCF is based on the *Carrier Sense Multiple Access with Collision Avoidance* (CSMA/CA) to support asynchronous data traffic, nodes A, B and C have to contend for the channel to transmit packets. If A succeeds to contend for the channel, B and C will have to wait for a long time and possibly remain idle until the beacon interval ends. If we let B and C transmit data before A, then B and C can switch to the sleep state early and decrease their power consumption.

In single hop ad hoc networks, each node can communicate with each other directly. Each node can receive transmission announcements, such as ATIM and ATIM-ACK, from other nodes. Each node can schedule a better transmission sequence easily by listening to network traffic. However, for a multihop ad hoc network, it is difficult to schedule a good transmission sequence because a node can not hear the transmissions of those nodes that are not within its transmission range. In multihop ad hoc networks, we can schedule a better transmission sequence by information exchange and QoS methods.

3.2 Information Exchange Method

For information exchange, we modify the operation flow of ATIM announcement in the original IEEE 802.11 power saving mode. In PEMP, the information exchange can be divided into two steps, as illustrated in Fig. 2. In the first step, when node A has a packet destined for node B in the IEEE 802.11 power saving mode, node A broadcasts an ATIM* to neighbor nodes, including B , C and E. ATIM* is an ATIM with a piggybacked data profile, which includes data size. In the second step, B will retrieve a data profile from ATIM* if B succeeds to receive the ATIM*. B piggybacks its data profile on the ATIM-ACK* and broadcasts the ATIM-ACK* to its single hop neighbor nodes, including A, C and D. ATIM-ACK* is an ATIM-ACK with a piggybacked data profile. By broadcasting the ATIM* and ATIM-ACK* to neighbor nodes, nodes that are within single hop distance from the sender or the receiver may obtain the data profile. The reason why nodes don't flood the entire network with ATIM* and ATIM-ACK* is that flooding will consume too much energy and bandwidth.

3.3 QoS Method

In PEMP, each node employs prioritized contention based on the Enhanced Distributed Channel Access (EDCA), as defined in the 802.11e [10]. Each transmission queue has a different arbitration interframe space (AIFS) and different contention window (CW) limits (maximum CW (CW_{max}) and the minimum CW (CW_{min})). After the ATIM window, nodes that want to transmit data or want to receive data will awake. Each node that intends to transmit data will calculate its priority according to the collected data profiles, which include data-related information, such as data sizes. Nodes will adjust their CW limits and AIFS. It can be expected that the smaller AIFS a node has, the higher priority it can have. Similar arguments apply to the CW limits. IEEE 802.11e suggests the use of different AIFS and different CW limits according to different ACs (Access Categories). Table 1 shows the parameters for CW_{max}, CW_{min} and AIFS for each AC. The value of AIFS is determined by the following equation (1) [10]:

$$AIFS = AIFSN \times aSlotTime + SIFS \tag{1}$$

where the value of $AIFSN$ (AIFS number) is an integer greater than zero and is dependent on each AC and $aSlotTime$ is the length of a slot.

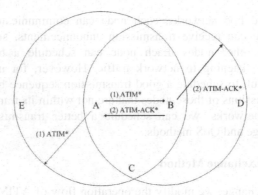

Fig. 2. The exchange of ATIM* and ATIM-ACK* between nodes A and B

Table 1. The default EDCA parameters [10]

AC	CW_{min}	CW_{max}	AIFSN
AC_BK	aCW_{min}	aCW_{max}	7
AC_BE	aCW_{min}	aCW_{max}	3
AC_VI	$\dfrac{aCW_{min}+1}{2}-1$	aCW_{min}	2
AC_VO	$\dfrac{aCW_{min}+1}{4}-1$	$\dfrac{aCW_{min}+1}{2}-1$	2

3.4 Calculating Transmission Priority

In this section, we describe how a node obtains its transmission priority. After the ATIM window, a node calculates *data_sum*, *Mean* and *Var* (variance) according to the following formulas:

$$data\_sum_{host} = \sum_{i=1}^{n} data_i \qquad (2)$$

$$Mean = \frac{1}{host\_count} \sum_{i=1}^{host\_count} data\_sum_i \qquad (3)$$

$$Var = \frac{1}{host\_count} \sum_{i=1}^{host\_count} (data\_sum_i - Mean)^2 \qquad (4)$$

where *data_sum*$_{host}$ is the total data size of the node. *Host_count* is the number of neighboring nodes with buffered data. *Mean* is the average of all *data_sum*'s received. *Var* is the variance of all *data_sum*'s received. AC can be AC_BK (background), AC_BE (best effort), AC_VI (video) or AC_VO (voice) [10]. The results of calculation will be related to an AC, as follows:

AC_BK = {data_sum$_{host}$ $\geqq$ Mean and (data_sum$_{host}$ $-$ Mean)^2 $\geqq$ Var }
AC_BE = {data_sum$_{host}$ $\geqq$ Mean and (data_sum$_{host}$ $-$ Mean)^2 $<$ Var }
AC_VI = {data_sum$_{host}$ $<$ Mean and (data_sum$_{host}$ $-$ Mean)^2 $<$ Var }
AC_VO = { data_sum$_{host}$ $<$ Mean and (data_sum$_{host}$ $-$ Mean)^2 $\geqq$ Var }

At the end of the ATIM window, nodes will contend for the medium for transmission. By employing the QoS method, the priorities of nodes that have smaller data destined for other nodes will be increased. In this way, higher priority nodes have less waiting time to transmit data.

The activities in the beacon interval of PEMP are shown in Fig. 3, which is based on the topology in Fig. 2. Assume node A has a packet destined for node B and node C has a packet destined for node B. Node A broadcasts an ATIM* frame to its single-hop neighbors, like B and C. When B succeeds to receive the ATIM* frame, B replies an ATIM-ACK* frame to its single-hop neighbors, like A, C and D. By the above steps, A and B complete the information exchange and announcement. For the transmission of C to B, similar steps are followed. After the ATIM window, all nodes calculate their priorities according to the received data profiles and then determine their AIFS and CW limits. Assume node A succeeds to contend for the channel according to its transmission priority. After its transmission finishes, node A switches to the sleep state to decrease power consumption.

3.5 Avoiding Starvation

If nodes that have succeeded to transfer ATIM frames do not finish sending the entire data in the beacon interval, they will retransmit ATIM frames in the next beacon interval. In PEMP, it is possible that a low priority node may fail to transmit the entire data after several beacon intervals and result in high delay. With buffered data increasing, it may be hard for a low priority node to succeed to contend for the medium. In other words, it may cause starvation for low priority nodes. To avoid starvation, each node records its buffer delay. The buffer delay is expressed in terms of number of beacon intervals passed. The *bc* maintains the count of beacon intervals passed for the buffered data. After completing a beacon interval, each node increases its *bc* of buffered data by one. We set an *up-bc* as the upper limit of the number of beacon intervals passed. If a node has buffered data with *bc* higher than *up-bc*, the node's AC will be switched to AC_VO until *bc* is smaller than *up-bc*. By increasing the priority for those nodes with long buffer delays, starvation can be avoided.

3.6 Adjusting ATIM Window Size Dynamically

According to [4], the ATIM window has a great effect on energy efficiency and performance. If the ATIM window is too large, nodes will not get chance to transmit data and increase power consumption. On the contrary, if the ATIM window is too small, only a few nodes can send ATIMs successfully. In PEMP, the ATIM window size is also adjusted dynamically based on network conditions.

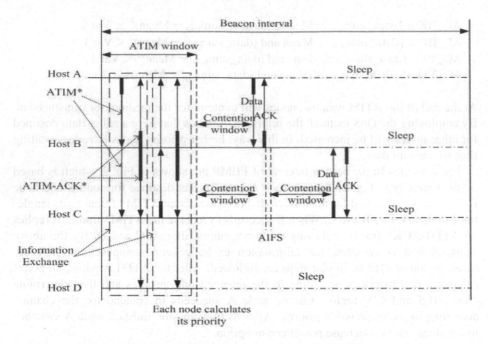

Fig. 3. Activities in the beacon interval of PEMP

4 Simulation Results and Discussion

4.1 Simulation Model

For evaluation, we used *ns-2* [11] with the CMU wireless extension [12]. Simulation parameters are showed in Table 2 [8][13][15]. Nodes are randomly placed in an area of 1000 by 1000 square meters. The transmission rate of each node is 2 *Mbits/sec*. The transmission range is 250 meters. The routing protocol is DSR (Dynamic Source Routing) [14].The length of a beacon interval is 100 *ms*. Total number of flows is half of the number of nodes [13]. We set the upper limit of the number of beacon interval passed *(up-bc)* to three. Each node generated variable-rate traffic according to the exponential on-off traffic model. The packet size is randomly selected between 256 and 1024 bytes. We use the same energy model as that in [8][15]. The power consumption for switching between active and sleep states is negligible and not considered here. Nodes do not run out of energy during the simulation. We have three performance metrics: *power consumption (J/sec/node)*, *aggregate throughput (Kbytes/sec)* and *average end to end delay (msec)*. We simulated PEMP, DPSM and PSM. We define PSM(*T*) as power saving mode, and *T* represents the size of an ATIM window. In PSM simulations, we changed the ATIM window size between 5 *ms* and 30 *ms*. Note that nodes in PSM continue to stay active after finishing transmissions. But for fair comparison in our experiments PSM will allow a node to switch to the sleep state after finishing its transmissions.

Table 2. Simulation parameters

Simulation configuration	Area	1000 m × 1000 m
	Bandwidth	2 Mbps
	Range	250 m
	Routing protocol	DSR
	Beacon interval	100 ms
	Number of nodes	20, 40
	Up-bc	3
Traffic configuration	Traffic rate	Exponential
	Packet size	256 ~ 1024 bytes
Energy model	Transmit	420 + 1.9 × frame size(μJ)
	Receive	330 + 0.42 × frame size(μJ)
	Idle	808 mw
	Sleep	27 mw

4.2 Simulation Results and Discussion

Fig. 4 and Fig. 5 show the power consumption ($J/sec/node$) under 20 and 40 nodes, respectively. When the number of nodes increases, the power consumption becomes large. Power consumption of PSM increases approximately linear with T (ATIM window size) as T increases from 5 ms to 30 ms. That is, if the ATIM is longer in PSM, nodes will consume more power according to Fig. 4 and Fig. 5. Comparing to PSM and DPSM, PEMP can decrease unnecessary idle time in the active state by using the information exchange and QoS methods. The power consumption of PEMP is 10% ~ 30% less than that of PSM with T between 5 ms and 30 ms. The power consumption of PEMP is 20% less than that of DPSM.

Fig. 6 and Fig. 7 illustrate the aggregate throughput (Kbytes/sec) among PEMP, DPSM and PSM under 20 and 40 nodes, respectively. If the ATIM is too small in PSM, time is inadequate to announce the ATIM. In the simulation results, the aggregate throughput degrades when the ATIM window size decreases. PSM with ATIM window size of 5 ms may suffer severe degradation in throughput. In Fig. 6 and Fig. 7, we observe that for PSM the ATIM window of about 20 ms achieves the best throughput. DPSM can achieve higher throughput by choosing a suitable ATIM window. We observe that the aggregate throughput of PEMP is 0.5% less than that of DPSM.

The average end to end delay is shown in Fig. 8 and Fig. 9 under 20 and 40 nodes, respectively. The average end to end delay is computed by summarizing the end to end delay of all the connection flows and averaging it. We can see that a smaller ATIM size cause a larger end to end delay. This is because using a small ATIM window size it will not have sufficient time to announce the ATIM. When a node fails to send its ATIM frame in the current ATIM window, it retransmits ATIM frames in the next ATIM window, which results in long end to end delay. PEMP has 6% longer end to end delay than DPSM.

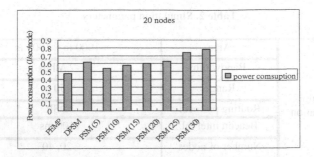

Fig. 4. Power consumption comparison under in 20 nodes

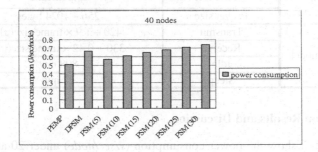

Fig. 5. Power consumption comparison under 40 nodes

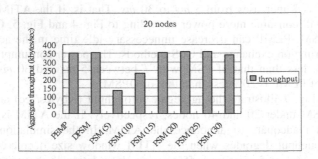

Fig. 6. Aggregate throughput comparison under 20 nodes

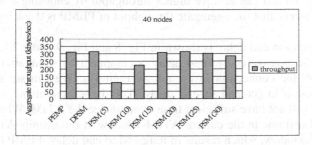

Fig. 7. Aggregate throughput comparison under 40 nodes

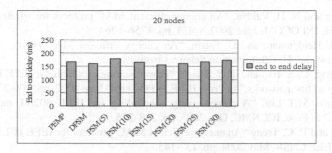

Fig. 8. End to end delay comparison under 20 nodes

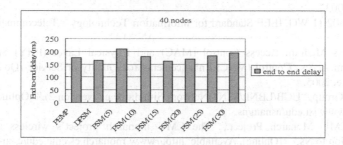

Fig. 9. End to end delay comparison under 40 nodes

5 Conclusions

A simple and power efficient MAC protocol (PEMP) for multihop ad hoc networks has been presented in this paper. We decrease the idle time in the active state and adjust the ATIM window dynamically based on network conditions. The power consumption is reduced by using the proposed information exchange and QoS methods. In addition, starvation avoidance has also been addressed by raising a node's transmission priority if necessary. As multihop ad hoc networks are getting popular, it is important to have a power efficient MAC protocol for extending the battery life of wireless nodes. Simulation results have shown that the proposed PEMP can achieve 20% less power consumption with penalty of 6% longer end to end delay and 0.5% less aggregate throughput than DPSM. In summary, PEMP is applicable to multihop ad hoc networks and can achieve a good tradeoff between power consumption, throughput and delay.

References

1. IEEE Std 802.11b, IEEE Standard for Wireless LAN Medium Access Control (MAC) and Physical Layer Specifications: Higher-Speed Physical Extension in the 2.4 GHz Band, 1999.
2. IEEE Std 802.11a, IEEE Standard for Wireless LAN Medium Access Control (MAC) and Physical Layer Specifications: Higher-Speed Physical Extension in the 5 GHz Band, 1999.
3. R. Zheng and R. Kravets, "On-demand power management for ad hoc networks," in Proc. IEEE INFOCOM, Apr. 2003, vol. 1, pp. 481-491.

4. E. S. Jung and N. H. Vaidya, "An energy efficient MAC protocol for wireless LANs," in Proc. IEEE INFOCOM, June 2002, vol. 3, pp. 1756-1764.
5. W. Ye, J. Heidemann, and D. Estrin, "An energy efficient MAC protocol for wireless sensor network," USC/Information Sciences Institute.
6. Y.-C. Tseng; C.-S. Hsu and T.-Y. Hsieh, "Power-saving protocols for IEEE 802.11-based multi-hop ad hoc networks," in Proc. IEEE INFOCOM, June 2002, pp. 200-209.
7. M. Liu and M.T Liu, "A power-saving scheduling for IEEE 802.11 mobile ad hoc networks," in Proc. ICCNMC, Oct. 2003, pp. 238-245.
8. S.-L. Wu and P.-C. Tseng "An energy efficient MAC protocol for IEEE 802.11 WLANs," in Proc. IEEE CNSR, May 2004, pp. 137-145.
9. B. Tavli and W.B. Heinzelman, "TRACE: time reservation using adaptive control for energy efficiency," IEEE Journal on Selected Areas in Communications, pp. 1506-1515, Dec. 2003.
10. IEEE 802.11 WG, IEEE Standard for Information Technology – Telecommunications and Information Exchange between Systems – LAN/MAN Specific Requirements - Part 11: Wireless Medium Access Control (MAC) and Physical Layer (PHY) Specifications: Medium Access Control (MAC) Enhancements for Quality of Service (QoS), IEEE Std. 802.11e, 2005.
11. VINT Group, "UCB/LBNL/VINT Network Simulator ns (version 2)." [Online]. Available: http://www.isi.edu/nsnam/ns.
12. The CMU Monarch Project., "The CMU monarch project's wireless and mobility extension to Ns," [Online]. Available: http://www.monarch.cs.cmu.edu/cmu-ns.html.
13. E.S. Jung and N.H. Vaidya, "A power saving MAC protocol for wireless networks," Tech. Rep., July 2002, [Online]. Available: http://www.crhc.uiuc.edu/~nhv/papers/npsm_tech.pdf.
14. D.B. Johnson and D.A. Maltz, "Dynamic source routing in ad hoc wireless networks" draft-ietf-manet-dsr-04.txt, 2001.
15. L.M. Feeney. "An energy consumption model for performance analysis of routing protocol for mobile ad hoc networks," ACM/Kluwer Mobile Networks and Applications, Vol. 6, No. 3, pp. 239-249, 2001.

A Novel Energy-Aware TDMA Scheduling Algorithm for Wireless Sensor Networks

Jianlin Mao[1,2], Xing Wu[3], Zhiming Wu[1], and Siping Wang[1]

[1] Department of Automation, Shanghai Jiao Tong University
Shanghai, China 200240
{jlmao, ziminwu, wangsiping}@sjtu.edu.cn
[2] School of Information Engineering and Automation
Kunming University of Science and Technology
Kunming, Yunnan Province, China 650093
[3] School of Mechanical and Electrical Engineering
Kunming University of Science and Technology
Kunming, Yunnan Province, China 650093
km_wx@yahoo.com

Abstract. In wireless sensor networks, time division multiple access (TDMA) -based MAC can eliminate collisions, hence save energy and guarantee a bounded delay. However, the slot scheduling problem in TDMA is an NP problem. To minimized the total slots needed by a set of data collection tasks and saving the energy consumed on switching between the active and sleep states, a novel particle swarm optimization (PSO)-based scheduling algorithm called PSOSA is proposed in TDMA sensor networks. This algorithm can take full advantage of the searching ability of PSO, which is powerful for solving NP problems. Simulation results show that PSOSA requires less slots and energy to finish a set of data collection tasks. Moreover, compare with coloring algorithms, PSOSA have more flexibility to deal with a multi-objective optimization problem.

1 Introduction

Wireless sensors networks have become popular recently across a diverse research community due to their potential usage in defense, commercial, and scientific applications. In such networks, sensors are units with sensing, processing, and wireless networking capability, which can automatically collect the information and report the results to an access point.

In sensor networks, as the sensors are usually battery-powered, saving energy becomes an essential problem. Moreover, time constraint would be considered in some time-critical applications. Both these two objectives can be dealt with in the medium access control (MAC) layer of network. While different medium access methods result in different time and energy efficiency. Among the current MAC protocols, including contention based access and contention free access, TDMA is a suitable access method for wireless sensor networks. First, TDMA

X. Cheng, W. Li, and T. Znati (Eds.): WASA 2006, LNCS 4138, pp. 319–328, 2006.

can save energy by eliminating collisions, avoiding idle listening and make sensors enter into inactive states when they are idle. Secondly, as a collision-free access method, TDMA can bound the delays of packets and guarantee reliable communication.

However, assigning time slots to each sensor to finish a couple of data collection tasks is an NP-complete problem[11], additionally the energy constraint makes the problem more difficult to resolve. Therefore, in sensor networks, the main challenge of TDMA scheduling is how to allocate time slots to sensors so that the consumed energy and the total slots are minimum.

In this paper, we propose a new scheme for the above problem in sensor networks. we introduce an evolutionary algorithm called Particle Swarm Optimization(PSO) into this problem. Through setting up a mapping between the problem and the method reasonably, we define the problem space and searching space, followed which we use PSO algorithm to search the desired scheduling solutions. The main contribution of this paper is that our scheme is capable of handling problems with multiple objectives or constraints, such kind of problem is common in wireless sensor networks.

The reminder of the paper is organized as follows: Section 2 describes the related works. The problem statement are introduced in section 3. Section 4 describes standard PSO algorithm and how to apply it to TDMA scheduling problem. In section 5, the computational results are given. Some concluding remarks are made in section 6.

2   Related Work

In this section, we discuss the related work on TDMA-based MAC protocols in sensor networks from energy and time aspects.

Some researchers have discussed the energy saving problem [1][2][3][4] for TDMA scheduling. Pei et al.[1] adopt an energy-saving method which is to shut down the radio when nodes are idle. Li et al. [2] design a MAC protocol in clustered network to reduce the idle listening and collision, hence to reduce the energy consumption. Jolly et al. [3] discuss both transmission energy and active/inactive state transition energy at sensor nodes, they use Tabu search to get a best scheduling at the cluster head. Cui et al. [4] present a joint convex optimization problem across routing, MAC, and link layers, where the transmission energy and the circuit processing energy are considered, they solve the problem through relaxation methods.

Many researches focus on the time performance of TDMA scheduling. Some[5][6] are discussed under peer-to-peer sensor networks with random data flows, however, these solutions would result in a large delay[9][10][11] for data collection, because they do not consider the sequence of task execution. To those many-to-one sensor networks, Wang et al.[8] show that convergecast scheduling problem is NP-hard. Using a pipeline method, Florens et al. [7] and Gandham et al. [9] propose a centralized algorithm and distributed algorithm for convergecast respectively. To reduce the total time to finish a set of transmission tasks, Ergen et al. [11] proposed two centralized algorithms and one distributed algorithms, which are all based on coloring algorithm in graph theory. These researches does not directly discuss the energy consumption of sensor nodes.

Compare with the previous works, at the energy aspect, we consider the energy consumed in active/inactive state transition of nodes, which is inspired by reference[3], however, we use a different optimization algorithm. Different from other TDMA scheduling methods in many-to-one sensor networks, we take both the time and the energy performance into consideration.

3 Problem Statement

3.1 Network Model and Scheduling Model

A sensor network can be represented by a graph $G=(V,E)$, where V is the set of all sensors in the network and $E \subset V \times V$ is the set of communication links between a pair of nodes. There is one access point (AP) in V. All traffic generated at sensors is destined for AP, which means that a routing tree would be generated.

The distance $d(i,j)$ between nodes i and j is defined as the minimum number of edges to go from one to the other. An interference matrix $C_{N \times N}$ is then given, where if $d(i,j) <= 2$, $C_{ij} = 1$; else $C_{ij} = 0$. In other words, i and j can transmit at the same time if the communication distance $d(i,j)$ is greater than 2.

In TDMA scheduling problem, time is split into equal intervals called timeslots. A basic principle of TDMA scheduling is to assign these time slots to nodes so that collisions would not happen when they are transmitting packets.

In sensor networks, as the data collected by sensors are flowing toward AP, the TDMA scheduling problem may be formulated as followed. There is a set of N packets generated by sensors which plan to transmit to AP over the routing tree. Each process that a packet flow to AP from its source node is called a task. According to the corresponding route, each task consists of a sequence of transmission actions which is called subtasks. The TDMA problem is thus to determine a sequence of the subtasks and the corresponding slots so that collisions would not happen, and some criteria are minimized, which is described in the next section.

In addition, as settings in many centralized algorithms[10][11], our assumption is that the data collection tasks are known at the access point before scheduling, and the access point schedules the node transmissions and announces this schedule to the nodes by broadcast.

3.2 Optimization Objective Description

Two optimization objectives are considered in this paper. The first one is to minimize the energy consumption, the other is to shorten the number of total slots which is define as a collection of time slots that is needed to finish a set of tasks.

In order to save energy, a common idea is just to switch off the radio when it is neither transmitting nor receiving. However, frequently turning off/on the radio also waste large amounts of power[12][3], especially when the packet is small. Hence, we take this part of energy into account, which is ignored in many TDMA researches. According to [12], the energy consumption formula of a network is listed as follows:

$$EC = \Sigma_{i=1}^{N}[P_i^{tx} * (t_i^{tx} + t_i^{s-tx}) + P_i^{rx} * (t_i^{rx} + t_i^{s-rx})]$$

where N denotes the number of nodes in the network, $P_i^{tx/rx}$ is the power consumption of transmitter/receiver at node i. $t_i^{tx/rx}$ is the total work time of the transmitter/receiver at node i. $t_i^{s-tx/rx}$ is the total transition time consumed between the sleep and active states.

As another performance metric, the number of total slots should be as small as possible, which can help to finish more tasks in the same time.

To an optimization problem with multiple objectives, a common way is to transform it to a mono-objective problem by combining those objectives into a weighted sum. Thus the weighted sum of the above objectives is taken as the objective function of our TDMA scheduling algorithm, as follows:

$$minimize \quad F(s) = \omega * MaxSlots + (1 - \omega) * EC \tag{1}$$

where $MaxSlots$ is the total slots of the schedule, EC is the total energy consumption of the network under a schedule s, ω is a tradeoff factor between these two objectives.

4   Particle Swarm Optimization-Based Scheduling Algorithm (PSOSA)

4.1   Standard PSO Algorithm

Particle swarm optimization(PSO) is a new swarm intelligence technique proposed by Eberhart and Kennedy[13], inspired by social behavior of bird flocking or fish schooling. It has been used across a wide range of applications[15].

The main idea of PSO is as follows. There is a population of random solutions. Each potential solutions, called particles, fly through the problem space by following the current optimum particles. Flying in the search space, each particle has a velocity which is dynamically adjusted according to the experiences of its own and its colleagues, this makes the swarm have an intelligent ability of flying towards the optimal position. Eventually an optimal solution can be found.

The global model equations of PSO is:

$$V_{id} = W * V_{id} + C_1 * rand() * (p_{id} - X_{id}) + C_2 * rand() * (p_{gd} - X_{id}) \tag{2}$$

and

$$X_{id} = X_{id} + V_{id} \tag{3}$$

where V_{id} and X_{id} are the velocity and the position of particle i respectively. p_{id} and p_{gd} represent the best position passed by ith particle and the swarm respectively. W is inertial weight. C_1 and C_2 are learning factors. $rand()$ is a random number between $(0,1)$.

The process of implementing the PSO algorithm is as follows:

1) Initialize a swarm of particles with random positions and velocities in the D-dimensional problem space, then evaluate their fitness function.
2) According to the equation(2), each particle begin to fly to the next position.
3) For each particle, calculate its fitness value at the current position. If the fitness value is better than the best fitness value p_{id}/p_{gd} in history, set current value as the new p_{id}/p_{gd}, and record this position. Then update particle velocity according to equation(3).
4) If maximum iterations is not attained, go to step 2), or the iteration is over, output the best result.

4.2   Encoding

A particle representation of the solution is the most important issue in applying PSO successfully to TDMA scheduling problem. Namely, a particle could be mapped to a solution of TDMA problem. Furthermore, the particle searching space also should be mapped to the problem space, in where those particles can fly stochastically, and finally find a good solution.

According to the scheduling problem description in section 3.1, a transmission task can be divided into several subtasks in sequence. Take this observation as basic, the total transmission tasks can be seen as a sequence of all the subtasks. To represent the sequence of subtasks, we firstly denote a subtask as (TaskID, Sequence-num), where TaskID points out which task the subtask belongs to, Sequence-num gives the sequence number of this subtask in the No.TaskID task. For example, subtask (0,2) means the transmission executed by the 2nd hop node of task 0. Observing this representation method, we can only take the TaskID sequence as an individual, because the appearance number of a TaskID in an individual have implied the Sequence-num of the corresponding subtask.

To sum up, the encoding rule is as follow. A particle is a sequence number which is consist of all the TaskID, the length of a particle code is $\sum_{i=min.TaskID}^{max.TaskID} N_i$, where N_i is the subtask number of the task i, $min.TaskID$ and $max.TaskID$ are the minimum ID number and maximum ID number of tasks in the system respectively.

To explain the rationality of the encoding rule, we give an example(see Fig1) and a mapping process from a particle to a feasible solution(see Fig2). In this example, there are two tasks, i.e., transmitting two packets generated by node 0 and 1 to AP. Each task contains 4 subtasks, they are $0 \rightarrow 2, 2 \rightarrow 3, 3 \rightarrow 4, 4 \rightarrow AP$, and $1 \rightarrow 2, 2 \rightarrow 3, 3 \rightarrow 4, 4 \rightarrow AP$. A random particle code is firstly generated according to the rule, then the whole mapping process is given in Fig2.

Through the mapping process, a particle can eventually result in a feasible solution of problem. While after the computation of equation(2), the positions

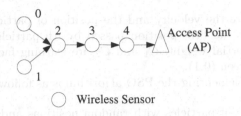

Fig. 1. Example network

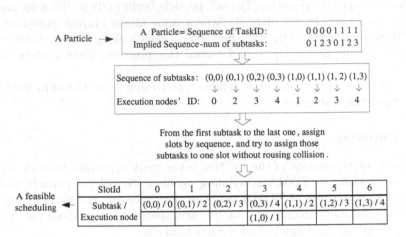

Fig. 2. Mapping process

of the particles may not be integer, such as 5.36, etc, which does not accord with the encoding rule that the TaskID must be integer. Therefore, in the algorithm, we round off the real position value to its nearest integer number if the position of a particle is not integer.

Additionally, the new position of a particle on the problem space may be an illegal solution because the number of a TaskID in a particle may not equal to its setting number of its subtasks. Under such situation, we need to adjust the number of taskID in the particle: delete the extra number of TaskID or add the absent ones in a random way. By this way, a feasible solution can be parsed from the new position of a particle.

4.3 Parameter Settings

In a PSO algorithm, there are some parameters need to be set in advance. Some of them are used to define the swarm size and its searching space, others are used to control the flying status of the swarm.

Among the former kind of parameters, the number of particles is set to 30, as the typical range is 20 ∼ 40. Dimension of particles is set to the number of the total subtasks. The border of the searching space is defined by X_{max}, which is set to the max number of TaskID. Parameter V_{max} determines the maximum change one particle can take during one iteration in case those particles fly too fast in the space. V_{max} is set as the range of $[-X_{max}, X_{max}]$.

Parameters W, C_1 and C_2 are used to control the flying status of the swarm. Parameter W proposed by Shi[14] regulates the trade-off between the global exploration and local exploitation abilities of the swarm. According to our experience, it is set to 1.5 in this paper. Parameters C_1 and C_2 are the weights of the stochastic acceleration terms that pull each particle toward the local best and global best positions, which are usually set to 2.

4.4 Fitness Function

Fitness is used as the performance evaluation of particle in the swarm. Usually the selection of fitness function depends on the optimization goals. In this paper, we directly take the objective function in formula(1) as the fitness function, i.e..

$$Fit(particle) = F(s) = \omega * MaxSlots + (1 - \omega) * EC$$

where MaxSlots and EC are the total slots and the energy consumption of the scheduling solution s respectively, which is parsed from the particle.

5 Simulation Results

To evaluate the performance of the proposed algorithm, we simulate a network with N*N sensors which are distributed randomly in a N*N grid units, one node in one unit, AP is located in the center of the area. The width of a unit is 10m, the transmission range of each sensor is set to 15m, the formed network topology is described in Table1. The capacity of the channel is set to 500kbps. A packet, whose length is 1kbit, is sent to AP by Dijsktra's shortest path algorithm. Each sensor has one data packet need to be sent. The settings concerning power are followed. The transition time between the sleep and active states is assumed to 470μsec. The power consumed in transmission and reception of a packet set to 81mW and 180mW respectively.

The experiments compare the performance of three algorithms: Max Degree First Coloring Algorithm (MDFCA, which is a common 2-distance coloring algorithm), Node Based Scheduling Algorithm (NBSA) proposed by reference[11], and the PSO-based Scheduling Algorithm (PSOSA) presented in this paper, where the results of PSOSA under two different weight factors in the objective function(1) are given. It should be pointed out that all these algorithms are used with energy-efficient modes, i.e., a node with no packet to send keeps its radio off during its allocated time slots.

The time and the energy results of the above three algorithms are given in Table2. From this table, it can be observed that the max slots of MDFCA is larger than other two algorithms, almost 3 times of the other two when the number of nodes is larger than 169. This is mainly because many slots are wasted by those nodes with the current color but without packet to send. Additionally, the energy consumption is also higher than the other two algorithms. Therefore, it can be

Table 1. Network topology description by node degree

node number	min-degree	max-degree	average-degree
49	3	8	5.46
169	3	8	5.78
225	3	8	5.91

Table 2. Comparison of three algorithms

Performance metric	Number of Nodes	MDFCA	NBSA	PSOSA $(\omega = 0)$	PSOSA $(\omega = 1)$
	49	123	62	**58**	60
MaxSlots	169	602	212	**200**	209
(slot)	225	1072	309	**296**	308
	49	1.930	1.754	1.732	**1.649**
Energy consumption	169	3.336	3.014	2.974	**2.909**
per node (mJ)	225	3.950	3.533	3.506	**3.438**

concluded that the common coloring algorithm is not suitable for time-critical sensor networks.

Although NBSA is an algorithm based on coloring idea, the data in Table2 show that NBSA can get better results on both time and energy aspects than MDFCA. This is because NBSA excludes those free slots assigned to those nodes without packets. This can help the algorithm to save time and energy.

Compare with the above two algorithms, PSOSA needs the least slots to finish a set of tasks especially when $\omega = 0$, i.e., the objective is to minimize the total slots without considering energy. Under this objective, PSOSA tries its best to maximize the parallelism of the system, hence the number of total slots is minimized. On the aspect of energy, the results of PSOSA are also less than the other two, as it has no color limitation and allow a node use the channel for several continuing slots, which can extremely save the energy consumed in state transition.

From the Table 2, it can be seen that PSOSA can flexibly get its desired results through adjusting the weight ω. In this paper, two extremeness are considered, thus the best value of the objectives can be bounded, other ω values would make a tradeoff between these two optimal bounds. In the table 2, if $\omega = 0$, PSOSA can get the minimum total slots, and if $\omega = 1$, PSOSA can get the minimum energy consumption. It can be noted that all the performance of PSO are not worse than NBSA and MDFCA. Therefore, it is concluded that PSOSA has a better performance on time and energy aspect than the other two algorithms, moreover, it is flexible on multi-objective TDMA scheduling.

6   Conclusions

Since TDMA guarantees collision-free communication hence reliability and power saving, it is believed that TDMA access method is suitable for wireless sensor networks. However, to a TDMA scheduling problem which is an NP problem, different scheduling methods will result in different performances in time and energy efficiency.

Considering the characteristics of packet transmissions in sensor networks, we presented a TDMA scheduling problem and proposed a PSO-based scheduling algorithm. Two objectives are desirable: one is to save energy by reducing the transition time between the active and sleep states at a node, the other is to reduce the total slots to finish a set of tasks. We set up a reasonable mapping between the problem and the PSO algorithm, and successfully apply the PSO algorithm to search the optimal solutions. Simulation results show that our proposed algorithm require less number of slots and less energy to finish a set of tasks. Moreover, this method can flexibly balance the tradeoff between the objectives by adjusting the weights of each objective. In future, more situations in TDMA scheduling problem are to be considered, such as bi-direction transmission, multiple access points, and more constraints in sensor networks.

References

1. Guangyu Pei and Charles Chien, Low Power TDMA in Large Wireless Sensor Networks. Proc. MILCOM, 2001, vol. 1, pp.347-351.
2. Jing Li and Georgios Y. Lazaroul. A Bit-Map-Assisted Energy-Eff icient MAC Scheme for Wireless Sensor Networks. IPSN'O4, April 26-27, 2004, Berkeley, California, USA.
3. Gaurav Jolly, Mohamed Younis. An Energy-Efficient, Scalable and Collision-Free MAC layer Protocol for Wireless Sensor Networks. Wireless Communications and Mobile Computing,2005, 5(3): pp.285-304.
4. Shuguang Cui, et al. Energy-Delay Tradeoffs for Data Collection in TDMA-based Sensor Networks, The 40th annual IEEE International Conference on Communications. Seoul, Korea, May 16-20, 2005.
5. S. Gandham, M. Dawande, R. Prakash. Link scheduling in sensor networks: distributed edge coloring revisited. INFOCOM2005.
6. Kannan Perumal, Ranjeet Kumar Patro, Balamurugan Mohan. Neighbor Based TDMA slot assignment algorithm for WSN. INFOCOM2005.
7. Florens C. and McEliece R. Packet distribution algorithms for sensor networks. In IEEE INFOCOM, 2003
8. Ju Wang, Hongsik Choi and Esther A. Hughes. Scheduling on Sensor Hybrid Network. In IEEE ICCCN, 2005.
9. Shashidhar Gandham et al. Distributed Minimal Time Convergecast Scheduling in Wireless Sensor Networks. In: The 26th International Conference on Distributed Computing Systems (ICDCS06), Lisboa, Portuga, July 4-7, 2006.
10. S. C. Ergen and P. Varaiya. Pedamacs: Power efficient and delay aware medium access protocol for sensor networks. Master Thesis, Electrical Engineering and Computer Science, GRADUATE DIVISION, University of California, Berkeley

328   J. Mao et al.

11. Sinem Coleri Ergen and Pravin Varaiya, TDMA Scheduling Algorithms for Sensor Networks, Technical Report, Department of Electrical Engineering and Computer Sciences University of California, Berkeley. July, 2005.
12. E. Shih, et al., Energy-Efficient Link Layer for Wireless Microsensor Networks. In: *Proceedings of the Workshop on VLSI 2001 WVLSI'01*, April 2001, Orlando, Florida.
13. Eberhart, R., and Kennedy, J. A new optimizer using particle swarm theory. Proceedings of the sixth international symposium on micro machine and human science, pp.39-43.
14. Shi, Y. and Eberhart, R. C. A modified particle swarm optimizer. Proceedings of the IEEE Congress on Evolutionary Computation (CEC 1998), Piscataway, NJ. pp. 69-73, 1998
15. RC Eberhart, Y. Shi, Particle Swarm Optimization: Developments, Applications and Resources, Proc. of the 2001 Congress on Evolutionary Computation, 2001, pp.81-86.

A Distributed Code Assignment Algorithm with High Code Reusability for CDMA-Based Ad Hoc Networks

Chang Wu Yu[1], Tung-Kuang Wu[2,*], Rei-Heng Cheng[3], and Chia Hu Wu[1]

[1] Department of Computer Science and Information Engineering,
Chung Hua University, Hsin-Chu, Taiwan, R.O.C
cwyu@chu.edu.tw
[2] Department of Information Management,
National Changhua University of Education, Chang-Hua, Taiwan, R.O.C
Ph.: 886-4-7232105 ext. 7615; Fax : 886-4-7211162
tkwu@mail.tkwu.net
[3] Department of Information Management,
Hsuan Chuang University, Hsin-Chu, Taiwan, R.O.C.
rhc@hcu.edu.tw

Abstract. We propose a dynamic and distributed CDMA code assignment protocol for ad hoc networks. By combining the RTS/CTS dialogue, modified busy tone signaling and power control mechanisms with our specially designed CDMA code selection rules, our protocol can not only save precious battery energy of mobile nodes, but also increase CDAM code reusability. Our simulation indicates that the proposed protocol performs better than the static code assignment method and the on-demand code assignment method (with/without using power control) in terms of successful transmission rate, code reusability and number of successful code assignment.

Keywords: CDMA, TCode Assignment, MAC, Ad Hoc NetworkT.

1 Introduction

With the widely availability of mobile devices, such as laptops, PDAs and cell phones, and the rapidly developing wireless communication technologies, ad hoc networks (MANETs) has emerged as an important part of the future ubiquitous communication. Ad hoc networks do not require infrastructure support and can be quickly deployed with low cost. Applications of ad hoc networks are emergency search-and-rescue operations, meetings or conventions in which people wish to quickly share information, data acquisition operations in inhospitable terrain, and automated battlefield ([7], [8]).

One of the most active topics with ad hoc networks is on the medium access control (MAC) protocols. Unlike their wired counterparts, several limiting factors impose significant challenges for MAC protocol design in such wireless networks.

---

* Corresponding author.

X. Cheng, W. Li, and T. Znati (Eds.): WASA 2006, LNCS 4138, pp. 329–340, 2006.
© Springer-Verlag Berlin Heidelberg 2006

Those factors include (1) limited wireless spectrum and bandwidth, (2) susceptible to path loss, fading, and interference, (3) continuously changing network topology, (4) (usually) limited in computational and battery power, (5) lack of centralized control. In other words, MAC protocols in ad hoc networks need to overcome interference problem, adapt to changing topology, coordinate and make efficient use of the limited shared wireless resource and maintain low power consumption, while achieve high data transmission throughput.

Among all MAC protocols, random medium access control protocols, such as the IEEE 802.11 MAC, have been widely studied for wireless networks due to its low cost and easy implementation. Unfortunately, the IEEE 802.11 CSMA/CA-based protocols suffer from the hidden and exposed terminal problems [6]. CDMA-based MAC protocols have also received considerable attention ([4], [9], [10], [12]). CDMA technology has long been used in cellular networks and is based on a form of transmission known as Direct Sequence Spread Spectrum (DSSS). Using this system, different users are allocated different spreading codes to provide access to the system. It can be thought of having many people standing in a room talking to each other in many different languages without interfering with the others. There are several advantages of using CDMA, with the major one being that it allows more users with a given amount of spectrum, and thus avoids problems associated with hidden/exposed terminals. It also allows adjacent base stations to operate on the same channel, allowing more efficient use of the spectrum. However, unlike cellular networks, which have base stations to coordinate the access and distribute codes to the mobile terminals, the distributed nature of ad hoc networks prohibits the codes being assigned in the same way.

Code allocation is an important part of any CDMA-based MAC protocol and it has significant impact on the performance of the protocol itself. The basic requirement of any code assignment scheme is to prevent any interference between various transmitter-receiver pairs by allocating orthogonal codes. Interference between nodes can be of two types ([1]): (1) primary interference, which occurs when two transmissions with the same code arrive at a receiver simultaneously, (2) secondary interference, occurs when transmission arrives at a terminal that is receiving a signal encoded with a different code. Although optimal code assignment has already been proven to be a NP-complete problem [4], we have noticed that some specific code conflict conditions can be ignored based on the transmission or receiving status of a mobile node. Based on such finding, we propose a distributed CDMA code assignment scheme for the mobile ad hoc networks. The protocol combines the RTS/CTS dialogue, modified busy tone and power control mechanisms ([2], [3], [5], [6]) with a specially designed CDMA code selection rule, which increases CDMA codes reusability (and channel usage, too) considerably.

The rest of the paper is organized as follows. In Section 2, we first review some related work, followed by description of our proposed protocol in Section 3. Simulations to demonstrate the performance of our protocol are shown in Section 4. Finally, Section 5 concludes the work.

2 Related Work

To alleviate the hidden and exposed terminal problem problems, a number of protocols have been proposed based on sending request-to-send (RTS) and clear-to-send (CTS) packets before the data transmission actually takes place ([4], [5], [6]). In other words, a sender-receiver pair should first "acquire the floor" before initiating a data packet transmission. While acquiring the floor to avoid collision from hidden and exposed stations is certainly a fundamental requirement for the efficient operation of wireless medium access, this method precludes multiple concurrent transmissions over the region of acquired floor [3].

To resolve the above problem, a protocol called Tintelligent medium access for mobile ad hoc networks with Tbusy tone Tand power controlT is proposed [2]. The main idea is to Tutilize the intelligent power control on top of the RTS/CTS dialogues and busy tone. Such a protocol would allow for a tighter packing of source destination pairs within a network environment, thereby improving the channel reuse. T

In the case of CDMA-based ad hoc protocols, code assignment has been one of the most addressing issues. In its extreme case, code can be assigned statically, meaning a node is assigned a fixed code during initialization phase. Although use of such static assignment scheme shortens the latency for communication, it requires a large amount of CDMA codes to accommodate more nodes. Several code assignment protocolsT that based on the on-demand channel access methodT are also proposed ([10], [11], [12]). In these on-demand channel access protocols, a terminal with a packet to transmit can start its transmission without regarding to the state of the channel. If using RTS/CTS properly, the random access protocol can be guaranteed to be free of primary interference [13].

By combining the RTS/CTS and busy tone signal, Butala and Tong propose a conflict-free dynamic channel allocation protocol [9]. In [13], Muqattash and Krunz further integrate power control mechanism with the RTS/CTS and busy tone signal. The primary concern of [13] is targeting at the MAI and the secondary interference problem. However, none of the above two protocols have their focus on the code selection procedure so as to increase the CDMA code reusability.

3 The Proposed Protocol

In this section, we illustrate how our protocol, a combination of RTS/CTS, modified busy tone signal, power control mechanisms and our proposed code selection rules, can increase CDMA codes reusability. We will first describe the basic idea of our protocol and its main operational principles briefly, and then give the formal description, followed by an example detailing how our protocol exchanges codes.

3.1 The Channel Model

In our protocol, the available bandwidth spectrum is divided into one control channel and n data channels with the assumption that control and data channels are completely orthogonal. Data channels are used to transmit data packets and acknowledgements, with each data channel having the same bandwidth. The use of the control channel is for resolving contention on data channels and assigning data channels to nodes. Control channel is further divided into common and busy tone channel. All mobile nodes send its RTS/CTS packet through the common channel, and collect CDMA code by way of the busy tone channel. Code assignment is determined through the exchange of control messages. A message contains three fields: role of the node (in transmission or receiving), transmitting code and receiving code.

The busy tone signal in our protocol is actually a very small packet that is broadcasted periodically by transmission/receiving nodes. To reduce collisions between busy tone signals and increase the probability of receiving such signals by all the neighboring nodes, we divide one busy tone cycle into eight equal sub-groups, with each sub-group further divided into eight time-slots. A node that needs to transmit busy tone signal would randomly select any three sub-groups from the eight available ones, and then choose two time-slots from each of the three selected sub-groups randomly. In other words, a node would send in six time slots in one busy tone cycle.

3.2 The Protocol

We first illustrate the basic idea of our protocol, i.e., the CDMA code reusability can be increased by distinguishing whether the neighbors of a node requesting a new CDMA code is in transmission or receiving state, with a scenario shown in Figure 1. Assume that the solid arrows represent ongoing transmissions and the dotted lines indicate that their two end nodes are neighboring to each other. In case node A needs to transmit data to node B, node A should only avoid using codes which node D and the other receiving neighbors are using. Similarly, node B needs to avoid codes that are in use by node E and the other transmitting neighbors only. In this specific case, codes that are assigned to the transmission pairs $H \rightarrow G$ and $J \rightarrow I$ can also be used by $A \rightarrow B$.

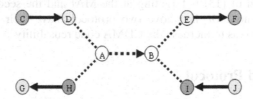

Fig. 1. Scenarios showing some specific conflict conditions can be ignored

The proposed protocol, separated into three major stages, is listed as follows.

(1) Collect CDMA codes assignment information through the busy tone channel.
   (a) A node, whether idle or not, keeps track of the CDMA codes assignment status of their neighbors by listening to the busy tone channel.
   (b) A node that is in ongoing communication has to broadcast its status (i.e. in transmission or receiving) and codes that it currently uses to its neighbors with its maximum power through busy tone packets.
(2) Exchange code assignment information and determine a CDMA code through the RTS/CTS packets.

(a) When a node demands to transmit, it initiates the CDMA code determination procedure (given later) to select an available code and the code should be released immediately after transmission finished.

(b) The transmitting node determines the available codes through monitoring the busy tone signal and sends such information to the receiving node with the RTS packet.

(c) The receiving node determines and chooses a CDMA code and informs the sender through CTS packet. The code is determined according to the information contains in the RTS packet and those collected by the receiving node through busy tone channel.

(d) In case of conflicting CDMA code, the node with lower priority, which is one that is newly assigned a code, needs to release the code and reassigned a new available CDMA code.

(3) Start transmission

(a) The sender starts transmission using the code that it receives through the CTS packet.

(b) When transmitting, the sender will properly adjust its transmission power (according to the power control assumption specified below) to save the precious battery energy and reduce co-channel interference with other neighboring nodes.

3.3 The Code Selection Procedure

One issue that needs to address is how the transmitting/receiving nodes determine which CDMA code to use. Basically, the rules are: (1) the transmitting node should avoid codes that are used by any receiving nodes within its transmitting power range, and (2) the receiving node should avoid codes that are used by any transmitting nodes within its power range. For further discussion, we make the following assumptions regarding to power control, as was illustrated in ([2], [14]).

(1) A node can choose at what power level to transmit a packet. This function should be provided by the physical layer.

(2) Upon receiving a packet, the physical layer can offer the MAC layer the power level at which the packet was received. In addition, the signal strength can be used to estimate the relative node distance.

The code selection procedure is formally described below.

(1) Refer to Figure 2, let A be the node intending to initiate transmission to the other node B. Node A learns the ongoing receiving nodes by listening at least one cycle to busy tone channel and collects CDMA codes that are used by these nodes.

(2) Node A then sends the information (codes that are occupied) to node B using a RTS packet with the maximum power.

(3) Upon receiving the RTS packet from A, node B calculates the relative distance to node A and determines the required signal power level (and range) to reach node A (the lower-right circle with solid edge in Figure 3) accordingly. Node B then collects the ongoing transmitting nodes (the three small solid filled circles in Figure 3) within its adjusted power range by listening at least one cycle to busy tone channel and collects CDMA codes that are using by these nodes.

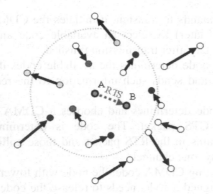

Fig. 2. The transmitting node and the ongoing transmission nodes in its vicinity

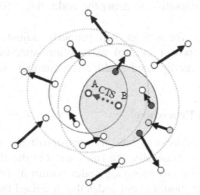

Fig. 3. The transmitting/receiving nodes and the ongoing transmission nodes in its vicinity

(4) Node *B* chooses a CDMA code by combining the information that it collects through busy tone channel and that contains in the RTS packet. Node *B* then sends the code to node *A* using the CTS packet. If there is no available code, node *B* still needs to inform node *A* the result with a CTS packet.

(5) If the above procedure does not result in a successful code assignment, the above procedure (Step 1 to Step 3) will repeat for the second time. However, this time node *A* in step 1 will use the adjusted power range (the upper-left circle with solid edge in Figure 3) instead of the maximum power range, since at this stage node *A* should be aware of the relative distance to *B*. The adjustment should allow the reuse of codes that are currently occupied by the receiving nodes located in between the adjusted and maximum power range of node *A*, and thus further improve the overall code reusability.

In the following, we further illustrate the above procedure with a sequence of examples with the assumption that both node *A* and *B* are using the adjusted power. Refer to Figure 4, in case node *A* needs to transmit data to node *B*, it has to collect the status of its neighbors that are in transmission by listening at least one cycle in busy tone channel. In this way, it can determine which CDMA codes should not be used. For example, there are two ongoing transmissions $D \rightarrow C$ and $E \rightarrow F$, with both node C and E locating within node A's adjusted transmitting power range. In this case, node A should not use the CDMA code that is used by node C to avoid interferences and collisions. On the other hand, since node A and E are both transmitting, node A can use node E's CDMA code without any conflicts. Once node A determines what codes are available, it attaches the information in RTS packet and sends it to node B.

When node B receives the RTS packet, it starts the CDMA code determination procedure. In case there are two nodes within node B's power range, with node G transmitting and node I receiving. Node B would then determine that it should not use the code that node I is using. Combining the information it collects and those that provided in RTS packet, node B can then choose a CDMA code, put it in CTS packet and send back to node A with the adjusted power. Node B will also begin radio busy tone packets on control channel with maximum power.

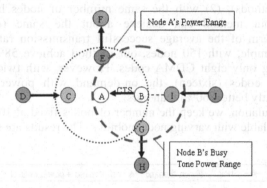

Fig. 4. Example showing how the receiving node chooses a code

Finally, when node A receives the CTS packet from node B, it adopts the CDMA code contains in CTS packet and begins data transmission. In addition, node A will also begin to transmit busy tone signal in control channel with its maximum power. Figure 6 shows the interaction between node A and B of the previous example in time domain.

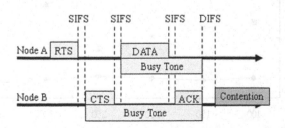

Fig. 5. Sequence of events showing how two nodes establish communication

4 Simulation Results

To demonstrate the performance of our proposed method, we run simulations with various setup environments and compare the results with those using the static code assignment and on-demand method with/without using power control. The simulation time and maximum power range (circular area) are set to 30 seconds and 150 meters respectively. Network traffic changes randomly between 5 and 10 requests/sec unless otherwise specified.

Our first simulation is fixing the node mobility (=0), but changing the CDMA codes available and the number of nodes within the 1000x1000 simulation region. Figure 6 and 7, with axis Y and X representing average rate of successful transmission and number of nodes, show the results. Based on such results, we can draw a few conclusions in the case when nodes are standing still: (1) with the same number of available CDMA codes and number of mobile nodes, our method achieves approximately 10% higher in term of the average successful transmission rate comparing to the on-demand method with power control (and much better than the other two methods), (2) with the same number of nodes but less available CDMA codes, our method can achieve about the same (or much better) performance in term of the average successful transmission rate than the other methods. For example, with 150 nodes, our method achieve 58% success rate in transmission using only eight CDMA codes. However, with twice the number of available CDMA codes (sixteen), the on-demand with power control method achieves just slightly better (60%) than ours.

In the next simulation, we keep the number of nodes fixed at 100, but change the CDMA codes available with varying node mobility. The results are shown in Figure 8

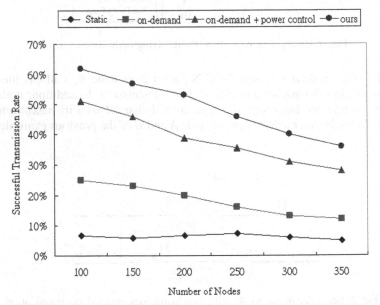

Fig. 6. Successful transmission rate with respect to node density with 8 available CDMA codes and zero node mobility

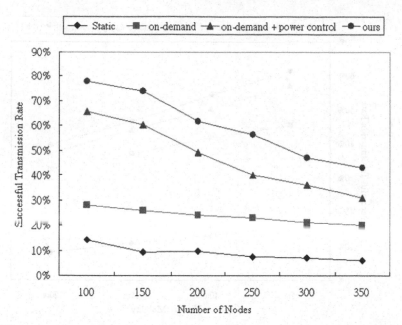

Fig. 7. Successful transmission rate with respect to node density with 16 available CDMA codes and zero node mobility

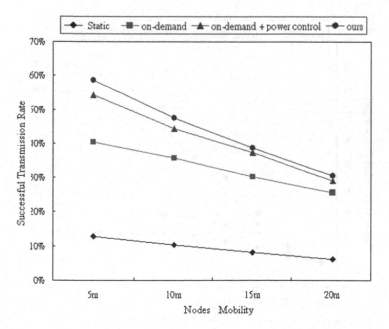

Fig. 8. Successful transmission rate with respect to node mobility with 8 available CDMA codes

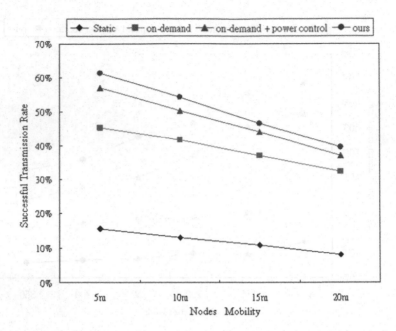

Fig. 9. Successful transmission rate with respect to node mobility with 16 available CDMA codes

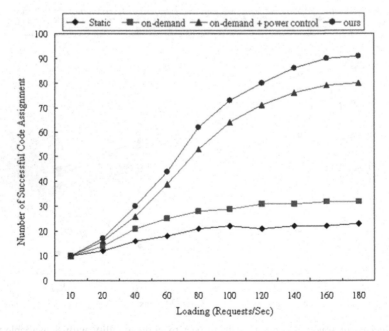

Fig. 10. Number of successful code assignment under different loading with 8 available CDMA codes

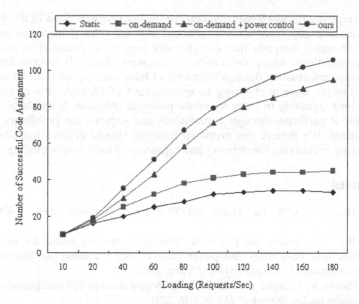

Fig. 11. Number of successful code assignment under different loading with 16 available CDMA codes

and 9, with axis X now indicating nodes mobility varying from 5 to 20 meters per second. Once again, our proposed method remains the top performer with 2% to 5% gap in successful transmission rate on top of the second best one. Note that, as the node mobility increases, two previously non-conflicting CDMA code assignments may have higher probability in interfering to each other. This explains why the margin of lead of our method is closing as the node mobility increases.

Finally, we investigate the rate of successful code assignment under varying loading. The number of nodes is set to 200, and the transmission rate is adjusted randomly every second. Figure 10 through 11 show the results. Note that axis Y and X now represent number of successful code assignment and network loading (transmission request per second), respectively.

The results show that our method achieves up to 10% more in the number of successful code assignment as compared to the on-demand with power control method, and more than twice as many than the static method.

5 Conclusion and Future Work

We develop a dynamic and distributed CDMA code assignment protocol for the Ad Hoc network. The proposed protocol combines the RTS/CTS dialog, modified busy tone signal and power control mechanisms with our specially designed code assignment rules to increase CDMA codes reusability, while saving precious battery energy of mobile nodes. Our simulation indicates that the proposed protocol performs better than the static code assignment method and the on-demand code assignment method (with/without using power control) in terms of successful transmission rate, code reusability and number of successful code assignment.

However, there remain issues that deserve further research. First of all, the fact that the performance gap (between our protocol and the others) increases as the node mobility decreases suggests that our protocol may have potential in future sensor network applications, where nodes remains stationary. Secondly, successful collection of code usage information through capturing of busy tone signal from all neighboring nodes will help a node in choosing an appropriate CDMA code. We carefully design our busy tone signaling in order to reduce potential collision. It would be interesting to see how it performs through experiments and explore the possibility of further improvements. We believe our proposed protocol should achieve even higher code reusability by optimizing the delivery and capturing of busy tone signaling.

References

1. R.Q. Huang and C.W. Yu, "Distributed OVSF code assignment scheme," *ICC 2004*, pp. 4152-4156.
2. S.L. Wu, Y.C. Tseng, and J.P. Sheu, "Intelligent medium access for mobile ad hoc networks with busy tones and power control," *IEEE Journal on Selected Areas in Communications*, 18 (9), pp. 1647-1657, Sep. 2000.
3. J. P. Monks, V. Bharghavan, and W. Hwu, "A power controlled multiple access protocol for wireless packet networks," *INFOCOM*, 2001.
4. A.A. Bertossi and M.A. Bonuccelli, "Code assignment for hidden terminal interference avoidance in multihop packet radio networks," *IEEE/ACM Transactions on Networking*, vol. 34, pp. 441-449, 1995.
5. J. Deng and Z. J. Hass, "Dual busy tone multiple access (DBTMA) - a multiple access control scheme for ad hoc networks," *IEEE Transactions on Communications*, vol. 50, no. 6, pp.975-985, June 2002.
6. F. A. Tobagi and L. Kleinrock, "Packet switching in radio channels:Part II—The hidden terminal problem in carrier sense multiple accessmodes and the busy tone solution," *IEEE Trans. Commun.*, vol. 23, pp.1417–1433, 1975.
7. E.M. Royer and C-K Toh, "A review of current routing protocols for ad hoc mobile wireless networks," *IEEE Personal Communication*, pp. 46-55, 1999.
8. Chang Wu Yu, Tung-Kuang Wu, Rei Heng Cheng, and Po Tsang Chen, "A Low Overhead Ad Hoc Routing Protocol with Route Recovery," *Lecture Notes in Computer Science*, vol. 3794, pp. 666 – 675, 2005.
9. Amit Butala and Lang Tong, "Dynamic Channel Allocation and Optimal Detection for MAC in CDMA Ad hoc Networks," *Proceedings of the Thirty-Sixth Asilomar Conference on Signals, Systems and Computers*, 2002, vol. 2, pp. 1160 – 1164.
10. K.-W. Hung and T.-S. Yum, "The coded tone sense protocol for multihop spread-spectrum packet radio networks," *Proceedings of the IEEE GLOBECOM*, 1989, vol. 2, pp. 712–716.
11. M. Joa-Ng and I.-T. Lu, "Spread spectrum medium access protocol with collision avoidance in mobile ad-hoc wireless network," *Proceedings of the IEEE INFOCOM*, 1999, vol. 2, pp. 776–783.
12. J. Garcia-Luna-Aceves and J. Raju, "Distributed assignment of codes for multihop packet-radio networks," *Proceedings of the IEEE MILCOM*, 1997. vol. 1, pp. 450–454.
13. Alaa Muqattash and Marwan Krunz, "CDMA-Based MAC Protocol for Wireless Ad Hoc Networks," *Proceedings of the MobiHoc*, 2003, pp. 153-164.
14. Xiaohu Chen, Michalis Faloutsos, and Srikanth Krishnamurthy, "Distance ADaptive (DAD) Broadcasting for Ad Hoc Networks," *IEEE International Conference on Network Protocols (ICNP)*, 2003.

A Medium Access Control Scheme for Providing Reliability in Wireless *Ad Hoc* Networks

Song-Hee Lee and Jin-Young Choi

Department of Computer Science and Engineering, Korea University
1, 5-ka, Anam-dong, Sungbuk-ku, Seoul 136-701, Korea
{shlee, choi}@formal.korea.ac.kr

Abstract. We propose a medium access control (MAC) protocol called MMPR that supports reliable medium access control in wireless *ad hoc* networks. MMPR protocol focuses on interaction between a MAC and upper layers, whereby the MAC layer indirectly influences selection of the most reliable next forwarding node set by considering link channel states. The MMPR protocol reduces the number of contention phases and control frames using transmission power control techniques, considerably reducing the time required for broadcasting. In addition, our protocol increases throughput under channel fading and interference using a modified CSMA/CA scheme. Our simulation shows that MMPR is substantially more reliable and it provides high throughput in *ad hoc* network models compared to 802.11 broadcast and BMMM*.

1 Introduction

Wireless *ad hoc* networks have recently attracted considerable interest in the field of mobile computing. These *ad hoc* networks have been deployed impromptu without any infrastructure support and most use medium access control protocols to provide somewhat dependable unicast frames [1]. When group traffic is delivered to a set of neighbor nodes, a packet can be unicast to each neighbor, but because of the medium's broadcast nature, such retransmissions are redundant. Repeated redundant retransmissions consume channel bandwidth and battery energy and reduce channel throughput [1]. A more efficient approach is to broadcast messages using a multicast address, but this broadcast paradigm is not reliable in wireless link environments. Researchers have proposed many network layer multicast protocols [e.g., 9,10], but mechanisms at the network layer cannot provide highly reliable multicast for wireless *ad hoc* networks in an efficient way. Recently, provision of multicast reliability at the medium access control (MAC) layer has received increasing attention. The MAC layer is the appropriate place to provide reliability for wireless *ad hoc* networks [2,3]. Therefore, we propose a MAC protocol called MMPR for reliable broadcasting of medium in wireless *ad hoc* networks. The MMPR protocol emphasizes interaction between MAC and upper layers, whereby the MAC layer indirectly influences selection of the next forwarding node set by adjusting the power of transmission. Researchers have strongly advocated a cross-layer design for wireless *ad hoc* networks. The MMPR protocol allows reduction in the number of contention phases and control frames, considerably reducing the time required for broadcasting using a transmission power control.

X. Cheng, W. Li, and T. Znati (Eds.): WASA 2006, LNCS 4138, pp. 341–352, 2006.

The goal of this study was not only to increase link reliability but also to increase throughput under channel fading and interference using a modified CSMA/CA scheme. Section 2 of this paper reviews related research in the CSMA/CA-based MAC protocol. Section 3 presents the MMPR protocol in detail. Section 4 examines the MMPR protocol performance with wireless *ad hoc* networks, and Section 5 presents our main conclusions.

2 Related Work

Most wireless technology uses the IEEE 802.11 Distributed Coordination Function (DCF) MAC protocol for medium access. However, IEEE 802.11 does not support reliable multicast/broadcast due to its inability to exchange RTS/CTS and ACKs with multiple recipients [2–4]. As a result, multicast/broadcast packet quality is poor, and the potential problem of packet loss during the next-hop movement detection period always threatens. Moreover, the characteristics of mobility and wireless channels make it difficult to obtain reliability in data transfer. In this paper, we modified the IEEE 802.11 based on traditional CSMA/CA, and the resulting protocol provides reliable communication with multiple receivers. Previous MAC protocols [7–10] have addressed reliable multicast protocols, but these did not include power control. A transmission power control scheme increases reuse of spatial channels, thereby increasing overall channel utilization [11]. This scheme also improves overall energy consumption in wireless networks such as wireless *ad hoc* and packet networks, prolonging network lifetimes [11]. Because nodes are usually battery powered and must operate for relatively long periods, we applied the power control scheme to increase channel utilization and reduce wasted energy in wireless *ad hoc* networks.

Researchers have recently proposed several MAC layer protocols [7–10] that provide reliable multicasts using a modified CSMA/CA. The main problem with multiple recipients is ensuring that no receiver suffers from hidden terminals. In the simple BSMA protocol [7], all receivers send CTS frames simultaneously; even though CTS frames might collide at the sender, hidden transmitters will receive them and suppress their transmissions. The sender sends a multicast RTS packet, and all multicast RTS receivers reply immediately with a CTS frame. This protocol contains a problem: close receivers could result in a collision of CTS frames at hidden terminals.

In BMW [8], every node maintains lists of its neighbors, the packets transmitted, and the sequence numbers of packets received. Neighbor lists are updated upon receiving any RTS/CTS/DATA/ACK/HELLO packets, so delivery reliability depends on neighbor list accuracy. This protocol has another problem: it is not very scalable because error recovery depends on the number of nodes in the network; if a network contains many nodes, some nodes may experience delays in recovering lost packets. Batch Mode Multicast MAC (BMMM) [9] employs control packet exchange to alleviate hidden terminal problems and achieve reliable transmission. In this protocol, the transmitter does an RTS/CTS exchange with all the next hop multicast receivers before data transmission which is followed by a round of Request For ACK (RAK) and ACK transmissions. i.e., transmission of one data packet requires n contention phases to n receivers. This process could take place repeatedly, delaying multicast transmission indefinitely. In light of these problems, we compared our contention phase numbers with these modified CSMA/CA protocols, and used experiments to demonstrate that our protocol performs better and is more reliable than IEEE 802.11 DCF unicast/broadcast.

3 Proposed Scheme

3.1 Assumptions

We made the following assumptions:
- A shared channel model in which simultaneous transmissions in neighboring receivers results in a collision at the receiver [2–5].
- All links are symmetric: if node A is the neighbor of node B, then node B is the neighbor of node A. Therefore, channel gain between two nodes is the same in both directions ($G_{ab} = G_{ba}$, where G_{ab} is a channel gain between a and b) [6,12].
- Channel gain is stationary during control and data packet transmission periods [6,12].
- Each node periodically transmits a BEACON packet (or HELLO packet) identifying itself [1].
- Nodes can control their power level for transmission [1,6].

3.2 MMPR Protocol

MMPR protocol consists of MRTS, CTS, RAK, and ACK; it shows how our protocol uses the CSMA/CA-based control packets (such as RTS, CTS, and ACK) for reliable multicast/broadcast transmission, with some modifications. First, instead of unicasting the RTS frame to a receiver, a transmitter simultaneously multicasts the RTS frame to neighboring receivers. Hereafter, we refer to the multicast RTS as the MRTS frame, which contains addresses of all neighboring receivers. A variable-length MRTS frame provides an order for multicast receivers; the four address fields in standard IEEE 802.11 DCF are the best because they are known from other 802.x LANs [5].

Procedure MMPR_at_Transmitter()

Begin
Estimate the number of ready receivers;
/* It is based on the captured beacon */
Send MRTS;
Select a next forwarding node set;
/* It is selected based on CSI fields in CTS */
Determine the power level for transmission;
/* It is the power of node which has the highest desired power value in the next forwarding node set. */
Transmit data at determined power level;
Send RAK to a selected receiver;
/* RAK refers to request for ACK */
End

Fig. 1. Pseudo-code of MMPR at the transmitter

Procedure MMPR_at_Receiver()

Begin
When MRTS intended for the receivers is received do the following
If (data channel is idle) then
Wait for data;
Set NAV of each CTS for the duration;
If (data begins to arrive before NAV expires) then
Receive the data;
Else
/* the expire time is out */
wait for data to arrive
When the data transmission is over then do the following
If (a selected receiver receives a RAK) then
Send ACK and pass it to the higher layer;
End

Fig. 2. Pseudo-code of MMPR at the receiver

This section provides a detailed description of MMPR protocol. First, we present the MMPR pseudo-code from the perspective of each node such as transmitters and receivers. Figures 1 and 2 illustrate the sequential operation from the transmitter's perspective. In MMPR, the CW and back-off timer follow generally standard wireless policy; IEEE 802.11 DCF and any node i can know set V_i of its neighbors using a Beacon (or Hello) packet. These neighboring nodes share the same wireless medium, and a local broadcast transmits each message.

MRTS/CTS Handshaking Using Transmission Power Control
If node i has a packet to transmit, it sends a MRTS frame over the control channel at minimum transmission power $P_{(i,j)}$. Transmission power $P_{(i,j)}$ must be within its parameter range, $P_{min} \leq P_{(i,j)} \leq P_{max}$. Also, transmission power $P_{(i,j)}$ is greater than $SINR_{th}$. Let P_{max} and P_{min} denote maximum and minimum transmission powers, respectively, for a transmitter on the control/data channel.

MRTS frame is similar to RTS, except it includes the addition of a variable length address for neighboring receivers. The MRTS frame contains a MAC address sequence of intended receivers; the receivers use the order of receiver appearance in this sequence to relay CTS frames to the sender. The MAC address sequence is assigned a priority order; this priority can come from routing or any lower layer. The duration field in the MRTS frame header is modified to receive CTS frames from all neighboring receivers. Upon receiving the MRTS frame, a node checks whether the MRTS frame address sequence contains its address; if so, it memorizes the corresponding index number. The transmission power between nodes i and j must be at least equal to the minimum transmission power threshold, $G_{(i,j)} \cdot P_{(i,j)} \geq SINR_{th}$. Each link must maintain the minimum required signal-to-interference noise rate (SINR) for reliable packet transmission, denoted by $SINR_{th}$. Let $G_{(i,j)}$ be the channel gain between nodes i and j (note that we assume the same gain in both, so $G_{(i,j)} = G_{(j,i)}$, $i \neq j$), and channel gain is computed as received signal power over transmitted power $P_{(j,i)}^{hello - pkt}$ advertised in the hello packet. Our protocol computes channel gain based on the Rayleigh channel-fading model; most wireless mobile networks such as wireless *ad hoc* networks use the Rayleigh channel model or multipath fading model [5][6]:

Upon receiving the MRTS frame, node j responds by sending a priority-ordered CTS frame as usual at

$$P_{(j,i)} = \max\left\{ \frac{P_{(j,i)}^{hello - pkt}}{G_{(i,j)}}, \frac{SINR_{(j,i)}}{G_{(i,j)}} \right\}. \tag{1}$$

Let $SINR_{(j,i)}$ be the SINR at node j for the desired signal from node i and $P_{(j,i)}^{hello - pkt}$ is the power that transmitted a hello packet at node j. Our protocol adds two fields, desired power and channel state information (CSI), to a CTS frame. First, $P_{desired}^{(i,j)}$ is placed in a CTS frame control to notify node i of the power level to send its data. Node j calculates $P_{desired}^{(i,j)}$ based on received power level $P_{(i,j)}$ as

$$P_{desired}^{(i,j)} = \max\left\{ \frac{P_{(i,j)}}{G_{(i,j)}}, \frac{SINR_{(i,j)}}{G_{(i,j)}} \right\}. \tag{2}$$

Second, CSI is the channel state information about an upper layer route through which a packet will fail to reach its sink node due to fading [6]. CSI is motivated to send data along the most reliable route rather than the shortest one, so our proposed protocol uses it to decide a reliable next forwarding node set (Nf_{Set}). This step is necessary because sensor networks contain wireless links and therefore experience fading, which causes transmission failure. This paper does not discuss how the CSI can be used as a metric for routing protocol at the upper layer. CSI is computed as

$$CSI_{(i,j)} = W_{(i,j)} \log_2\left(1 + G_{(i,j)} \cdot SINR_{(i,j)}\right), \tag{3}$$

where $W_{(i,j)}$ is the bandwidth between nodes i and j. In our simulations, we set bandwidth W to an equivalent value. CTS frame transmissions can be staggered in time in order of priority: the first receiver in the sequence transmits the CTS frame after an SIFS, the second after a period equal to the time to transmit CTS frame and $2 \times SIFS$, etc. All receivers set their network allocation vector (NAV) until the end the ACK period, so the NAV set from CTS frame s is

$$NAV_{CTS} = \sum_{i=1}^{n} SIFS_i + \sum_{i=1}^{n-1} CTS_i + DATA + RAK + ACK, \tag{4}$$

where n is the sequence of receivers in MRTS frame header. Because CTS frame transmissions are sequential, they do not collide.

Next Forwarding Node Set (Nf_{Set})

After a MRTS/CTS handshake, the transmitter selects a 'next forwarding node set' (Nf_{Set}) to select the set of nodes that will multicast/broadcast data; Nf_{Set} is selected based on CSI received from neighboring nodes. To avoid nodes with weak links, we can divide Nf_{Set} selection into two schemes: an absolute Nf_{Set} selection scheme and a relative Nf_{Set} selection scheme. First, absolute Nf_{Set} selection uses a set of neighbors based on a certain criteria (threshold), and then relative Nf_{Set} is selected using a few of the highest-node CSI in neighboring transmitters. In the absolute Nf_{Set} scheme, the transmitter selects neighbors with CSI values above a certain threshold; this threshold is denoted by CSI_{th}. Therefore, absolute Nf_{Set} is selected by

$$Nf_{set}^{A} = \{CSI_{th} \leq CSI_{(i,j)} \mid j \neq i, j = 1,\ldots,n\}, \tag{5}$$

where n is the number of receivers transmitting CTS frames. Relative Nf_{Set} selection depends on node ranking within a set of neighbors; there is no specific threshold value. This scheme has the advantage of avoiding disconnections that can result from the first scheme: Nf_{Set} could be an empty set (i.e., $Nf_{Set} = \phi$). Use of the absolute Nf_{Set} scheme also involves the risk that neighbors will provide no helpful information, making them worthless for consideration. Lowering the threshold makes it possible to consider more neighbors and select one with a high CSI value; higher thresholds limit choice only to neighbors with high CSI values. If the Nf_{Set} is chosen, then the transmitter multicast/broadcasts data at P_{DATA}. The node with the highest $P_{desired}^{(i,j)}$ value in the selected Nf_{Set} decides the power for data transmission P_{DATA}, which is denoted by

$$P_{DATA} = \begin{bmatrix} P_{desired}^{(i,k)} \mid P_{desired}^{(i,k)} = \max\{P_{desired}^{(i,j)},\ldots,P_{desired}^{(i,n)}\} \\ i \neq k, i \neq j, j = \{1,\ldots,n\} \in Nf_{set} \end{bmatrix} \tag{6}$$

Where $P_{desired}^{(i,k)}$ is the power of the node with the highest desired power value in the Nf_{Set}. After data transmission, node i sends a RAK to node k to require an ACK. In our protocol, an ACK for node k guarantees reliability of all others in Nf_{Set}. That is, data transmission power is the desired power of node k with the highest power in the next forwarding node set; if data transmission of node k is guaranteed, then data transmission of others should also be guaranteed.

4 Simulation Results

4.1 Numerical Analysis

We evaluated MMPR efficiency by analyzing the number of contention phases. First, we defined the number of contention phases in our simulation as the number of frame control packets transmitted by each node and measured them using numerical analysis of three protocols: BMW, BMMM, and MMPR.

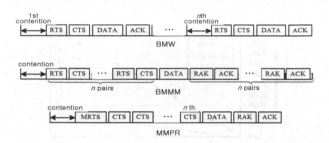

Fig. 3. Comparison of reliable multicast MAC protocols

Figure 3 shows a collision avoidance phase in the BMW protocol similar to that in IEEE 802.11. The BMMM protocol reduces the number of contention phases to one and adds a RAK frame to request an ACK frame. Because transmission of each RAK frame takes one time slot and one contention phase generally takes much more than one time slot, introduction of RAK frames considerably reduces the total time taken. Our MMPR protocol substantially decreases not only the number of contention phases but also the number of RTS frames required for multicasting. Finally, control packets such as ACK are prone to channel error and may result in unnecessary retransmission.

Table 1 lists numerical analysis of these protocols' packet transmission time. Here, n is the number of captured neighboring node, T is the amount of required time, and CW is the value of contention window. In values of theses protocols, the left parenthesis describes time taken for RTS/CTS phase and the right parenthesis describes time taken for data transfer phase.

Table 1. Numerical analysis of RTS/CTS phase and data transfer phase for packet transmission

Protocol	RTS/CTS phase	Data transfer phase
BMW	$\sum_{i=1}^{n}(CW_T^i + DIFS_T^i + RTS_T^i + SIFS_T^i + CTS_T^i)$	$\sum_{i=1}^{n}(2*SIFS_T^i + DATA_T^i + ACK_T^i)$
BMMM	$\sum_{i=1}^{n}(CW_T + DIFS_T + 2*SIFS_T^i + RTS_T^i + CTS_T^i)$	$\sum_{i=1}^{n}(2*SIFS_T^i + DATA + RAK_T^i + ACK_T^i)$
MMPR	$\sum_{i=1}^{n}(CW_T + DIFS_T + MRTS_T + SIFS_T^{n+1} + CTS_T^i)$	$(2*SIFS_T + DATA_T + RAK_T + ACK_T)$

Table 2. Parameters used to analyze the packet transmission time

Parameter type	Parameter value
SIFS Duration	10 μs
DIFS Duration	50 μs
RTS packet	160bits
MRTS packet	304bits
CTS/ACK/RAK packet	112bits
Maximum transmission range	250m
CW	31 - 1023
DATA	2KB
Data rate	1Mbps

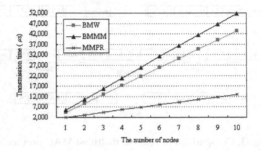

Fig. 4. The fraction of packet transmission time with different values of N

Table 2 lists the specific parameters that are used to analyze the transmission time of these protocols. This parameter follows the IEEE 802.11 standard specification [2]. Figure 4 shows the fraction of packet transmission time with different value of intended receivers for multicasting. BMW and BMMM extremely increased when the number of nodes for multicasting increased. Meanwhile, our MMPR has little effect on the number of nodes because MMPR sends a MRTS to only nodes which are selected according to link reliability such as CSI. The four nodes with a value of high CSI are selected in this analysis because the four address fields in standard IEEE 802.11 DCF are the best [5].

4.2 Simulation Performance

This section evaluates our protocol's performance and compares it to IEEE 802.11 broadcast and BMMM*. We describe a variation of BMMM denoted as BMMM* in our simulation because BMMM* is based on the assumption that there is a little difference between original BMMM [9] and our implementation of BMMM. To evaluate MMPR in both static and mobile environments, we conducted two simulations:

(a) *Stationary mode*: no node is moving.

(b) *Mobile mode*: nodes follow the random waypoint model [5], in which each node chooses a uniform destination from the simulation region, chooses a uniform speed between 0 and 20 m/s, and moves there at the chosen speed. After reaching its destination, the node pauses for an adjustable period of time before repeating the process. Degree of mobility is reflected in pause time; by default, we used a pause time of 10 s.

Our results are based on simulation experiments conducted using NS-2 [13]. For simplicity, we assumed data to be of a fixed size. We ignored overhead routing because our goal was to evaluate improved performance due to the MAC protocol. Our evaluation of MMPR focused on two aspects: reliability and throughput; we evaluated each aspect under several metrics. We used multi-hop wireless sensor networks to evaluate MMPR, IEEE 802.11 broadcast with no multicast support and BMMM*, since the RTS/CTS/DATA/ACK scheme can affect nodes within two hops of each other. Networks used in our simulations contained 20 nodes, 50 nodes, and 100 nodes randomly placed on a 1000 × 1000 plane. Radio transmission ranges for each node were a maximum of 250 m [1]. Table 3 lists the other parameters used in simulations, all of which corresponded to realistic hardware settings [1].

Table 3. Parameters used for simulations

Parameter type	Parameter value
Data packet size	2 KB
Data rate	1 Mbps
$SINR_{th}$	6 dB
Capture threshold	10 dB
Maximum transmission range	250 m
P_{max}	28.5 dBm
P_{min}	−7.5 dBm

The following sections outline the performance metrics used to evaluate protocol performance.

Reliability

To evaluate MMPR reliability, we measured data by packet drop ratio; in our simulations, we defined packet drop ratio as the fraction of packet lost per receiver. This number is equivalent to the retransmission required to recover from packet loss, so packet drop ratio has a direct relationship with reliability. A MAC protocol is reliable if it has a low packet drop ratio and a high packet delivery ratio.

Figure 5 (a, b) shows the packet drop ratios under different nodal densities; the x-axis in Figure 6 represents the packet generation of source nodes, and the y-axis indicates the packet drop ratios. As shown, the protocol packet drop ratio increased when either the number of source nodes or the density of nodes increased: the more traffic in a packet transmission, the more collisions may occur. Collisions cause many packets to time-out before they can reach their destinations; no protocols studied provided 100% reliability. However, the graph indicates that on average our protocol provided lower drop ratios than BMMM*.

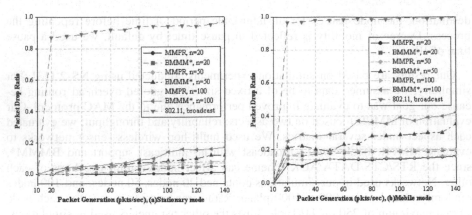

Fig. 5. Packet drop ratio in (a) the stationary mode and (b) the mobile mode

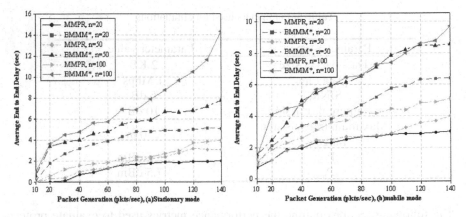

Fig. 6. Average end to end delay in (a) the stationary mode and the mobile mode

Figure 6 shows the end-to-end packet delay performance of the protocols; in our simulations, we defined packet delay as the time difference between data being generated at a source node and being correctly received at a sink node. In both protocols, end-to-end delay increased when either packet generation or node mobility increased because more packet loss may occur in moving nodes.

Throughput

Our evaluation of MMPR throughput involved measuring packet delivery ratio in figure 8 ; in our simulation, we defined packet delivery ratio as the total number of packets actually received by all nodes versus the total number of packets intended to reach all nodes. Comparison between these two numbers reveals that when nodes were stationary, the MMPR packet delivery ratio was close to 1, indicating that MMPR can achieve ideal reliability for stationary networks. When the nodes were moving, the MMPR packet delivery ratio dropped to 0.8, but it retained a value much higher than the BMMM* schemes. Therefore, it appears that protocol reliability

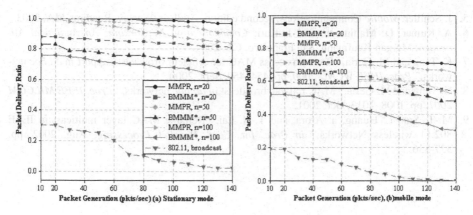

Fig. 7. Packet delivery ratio in (a) the stationary mode and (b) the mobile mode

decreases in mobile networks. In addition, packet delivery ratios for all protocols decreased when either the number of neighbors or the message generation rate increased; this resulted from more traffic in a transmission area potentially causing more collisions.

5 Conclusions

We propose a MAC protocol for wireless *ad hoc* networks called MMPR; it implements reliable multicast service at the MAC layer using channel state information and an adaptive power control mechanism. The MMPR protocol selects the most suitable next-hop link to enable efficient packet forwarding on a multi-hop route. We designed the MAC layer protocol as an extension of the IEEE 802.11 DCF and conducted an extensive performance evaluation using detailed simulation modeling. Our protocol is substantially more reliable and efficient and provides more throughput in *ad hoc* network models compared to 802.11 broadcast and BMMM*.

In summary, use of the MMPR protocol in channel conditions on various next-hop links provides improved immunity from channel errors. Our future work will focus on fine-tuning MMPR parameters, examining a number of design issues, and investigating its performance in more realistic topologies.

References

1. M. Ilyas and I. Mahgoub, *Handbook of Sensor Networks: Compact Wireless and Wired Sensing Systems*, CRC Press, New York, NY, 2004.
2. "IEEE. Part 11: Wireless LAN Medium Access Control (MAC) and Physical Layer (PHY) specifications," ANSI/IEEE Standard 802.11, 1999 edition, 1999.
3. P. Karn, "MACA: A new channel access method for packet radio," Proc. ARRL/CRRL Amat. Radio 9th Comput. Network. Conf., pp. 134–140, Sept. 1990.
4. V. Bharghavan, A. Demers, S. Shenker, and L. Zhang, "MACAW: A medium access protocol for wireless LANs," Proc. ACM SIGCOMM 1994, vol. 24, pp. 212, Oct. 1994.

5. J. Schiller, *Mobile* Communications, second edition, Addison Wesley, Reading, MA, 2003.
6. A. Kumar, D. Manjunath, and J. Kuri, *Communication Networking: An Analytical Approach*, Morgan Kaufmann, San Francisco, CA, 2004.
7. K. Tang and M. Gerla, "Random access MAC for efficient broadcast support in *ad hoc* networks," *Proc. IEEE WCNC 2000*, pp. 454–459, Sept. 2000.
8. K. Tang and M. Gerla, "MAC reliable broadcast in *ad hoc* networks," *Proc. IEEE MILCOM 2001*, pp. 1008–1013, Oct. 2001.
9. M.-T. Sun, L. Huang, a. Arora, and T.-H. Lai, "Reliable MAC layer multicast in IEEE 802.11 wireless Networks," *in Proc. Int. Conf. Parallel Processing*, Aug. 2002, pp. 527-536.

An Adaptive Latency-Energy Balance Approach of MAC Layer in Wireless Sensor Networks[*]

Jinniu Chen, Mingwei Xu, and Yong Cui

Department of Computer Science and Technology, Tsinghua University
Beijing 100084, P.R. China
{goldenbull, xmw, cy}@csnet1.cs.tsinghua.edu.cn

Abstract. CtS is a novel communication paradigm in wireless sensor networks. It's characterized by long latency and tiny energy consumption. However, the current research of CtS is under idealized assumption. In this paper, we analyse the limitation of CtS paradigm in real environment, and then introduce a new paradigm named ALEB based on CtS. In the real environment, CtS method will fail because clocks of different nodes are not synchronized perfectly, and the latency between neighbor nodes varies with an error range. To transfer data without error, we propose a Multiply-Divide method in ALEB. Further more, CtS method is restricted within a small range of applications by its long latency. We propose a mixed method to make ALEB's applicability much broader.

Keywords: Wireless Sensor Networks, MAC layer, energy-efficient protocol.

1 Introduction

The energy supply of sensor nodes in wireless sensor networks (WSNs) is generally limited and un-rechargeable. Hence the energy-efficient strategy is an important issue of system design and operation of WSNs. The primary goal of most, if not all, energy-efficient strategies are to increase the whole network lifetime. Energy-efficient strategy involves each layer of WSN nodes, including physical layer, MAC layer, networking layer, and application layer, etc.

Lots of applications do not need real-time information delivery; neither do they need wide bandwidth. Hence, one possible technique of energy saving is to increase the transfer latency and to make full utilization of the unused bandwidth[1]. CtS is a novel MAC layer communication paradigm[2]. Its most remarkable characteristic is extreme low power consumption with the expense of long latency. CtS conveys information using silent periods between two signals instead of transmit it bit by bit. Using CtS method, energy consumption of data transmission can be reduced to 10% of the traditional methods. The current research of CtS paradigm is base on the idealized assumption that the frequencies of all nodes' counters are perfectly identical and the latency between each neighbors are constant. When hardware frequency and transmission latency varies within an error range, CtS paradigm will fail because of

---

[*] This research is supported by the National Natural Science Foundation of China (No. 60373010), the Key Project of Chinese Ministry of Education.(No.106012), and National 863 project of China (No. 2005AA121510).

X. Cheng, W. Li, and T. Znati (Eds.): WASA 2006, LNCS 4138, pp. 353–362, 2006.
© Springer-Verlag Berlin Heidelberg 2006

the different silent waiting periods on each side. We analyze the real environment and deduce a deterministic limitation of CtS, and then propose a Multiply-Divide method to avoid transmission error.

WSN applications can be classified into three kinds according to their working modes: periodical data collection, event driven, and store-forward[3]. Each kind of mode has different requirement on transmission latency, thus needs different strategies to save energy. For example, periodical data collection mode does not need real-time transmission, but in event driven mode, sensor might have to deliver an urgent event to sink as quickly as possible. WSN applications are usually combined by several modes, thus one application might have different requirements of latency in different scenarios. To meet the different requirements we propose a mixed method which allows application to choose between the traditional bit-by-bit transmission method and CtS method. Thus applications can choose the balance point in the energy-latency trade-off according to their own design and requirement.

The rest of the paper is organized as follows: Section 2 introduces some related work. Section 3 analyzes systematic error and random error of the real environment in which the idealized assumptions do not come into existence, and then introduces an Adaptive Latency-Energy Balance (ALEB) approach which can transmit data without error and can also allow the upper layer to balance adaptively between energy consumption and latency. Section 4 shows the simulation result and finally Section 5 concludes the paper.

2 Related Work

Energy-efficient issue involves each layer of WSN nodes. In physical layer, using omni-directional antennas in wireless ad hoc networks can be highly inefficient in terms of power and capacity because a very small portion of the transmitted power is actually intercepted by the antenna of the intended receiver. Compared to omni-directional antenna broadcast, a directional antenna design will be more energy-efficient[4]. There are many other possible energy-efficient methods like using variable-range transmission instead of common-range transmission[5], and saving energy by coding and data combination[6,7]. However, physical layer energy-saving approaches should be deployed with consideration because they usually restrict the upper layer design and operation.

Energy-efficiency protocols in MAC layer are focused on collision, over-hearing, and idle listening problems. At present, IEEE802.11 is of the most popular MAC protocols for wireless system. But WSN applications have their particular scenarios and requirements like low data throughput, inter-nodes collaboration, data aggregation, toleration of long latency, etc. S-MAC and T-MAC protocol analyzed these particularities and then improved the IEEE802.11 protocol[8,9]. Partitioning sensor nodes into clusters can greatly improve the scalability and energy performance. For clustered WSNs, sift protocol analyzed temporal and spatial relativity within a cluster[10]. Also some TDMA-based protocols tried to use TDMA mechanism inside clusters[11]. Nevertheless, on the assumption that physical layer will spend energy E_b to transmit 1 bit data, most existing MAC layer protocols spend more then E_b to transfer 1 bit payload.

Among energy-efficient MAC protocols, CtS scheme explored the time dimension, and initiated a brand new paradigm of transmitting information between neighbor nodes. In idealized CtS scheme, transmitting a number in the form of several bits needs only two bits to be transmitted actually by physical layer - the start signal and stop signal. The waiting periods between start and stop signal equals to the number. Thus, the energy MAC layer spend to transfer 1 bit is far less than E_b. However, when idealized assumptions do not come into existence, original CtS method will not work.

3 ALEB Scheme Design

3.1 Analysis of Errors

Apparently, if the counter's frequency of sender and receiver are not perfectly identical, or the latency between sender and receiver are not constant, the receiver's counter will get a different result from the sender, making CtS transmission fail. To enable CtS scheme usage in the real environment, we first need to analyze the errors.

1. Transmission Latency Error
There are 5 delay factors in the signal transfer path between two nodes[12], each part makes a contribution to the total latency error.
- Sender processing delay: This is the time elapsed from the moment a timestamp is taken by CPU to the point it is buffered in RF device. This value is affected by CPU frequency, hardware and soft design, etc. For a well designed real-time system with low IO throughput, this time varies with a small error as the same degree as the CPU period.
- Media Access delay: This is the duration for the message stays in the RF device buffer waiting for a clear channel. This duration highly depends on the MAC protocol design. For contention-based MAC protocol, this value will become smaller when there are fewer nodes and fewer messages. For TDMA-based MAC protocol, this value is limited within a certain range. This factor is the primitive source of the error that CtS paradigm suffered.
- Transmit time: This is the time for a radio device to transmit a packet over a radio link. Since a packet's length and transmit speed for a given radio are all known, this delay can be estimated, and the error is to the degree of several nano-seconds.
- Radio propagation time: This is the duration for the message to propagate over the air to reach the receiver. The distance of neighbor sensor nodes is short and usually less then 100 meters. Compared to the radio propagation speed of 300 meters per microsecond, this duration is very short and the error can be neglected.
- Receiver processing time: This duration is similar to the sender processing delay.

2. Counter Frequency Error
The error of frequency control equipment is another source of CtS failure. Take the widely used crystal oscillator for example, even frequency of a crystal-controlled oscillator is held constant to a high degree of accuracy by the use of a quartz crystal, still the relative error can not be neglected. For commonly used crystal oscillator, the relative error can be 5PPM, 10PPM, or 20PPM, etc.

3.2 Terms

Following symbols will be used in this paper:

f • Frequency of hardware counter

Δf • Max relative error of f

F • Radio bandwidth

f_s • Frequency of sender, $\left|\dfrac{f_s - f}{f}\right| \leq \Delta f$, e.g. $f(1-\Delta f) \leq f_s \leq f(1+\Delta f)$

f_r • Frequency of receiver, $f(1-\Delta f) \leq f_r \leq f(1+\Delta f)$

T_d • Transmission delay

ΔT_d • Absolute error of transmission delay

n • The number to be transferred, supplied by upper layer

K • The primitive parameter of ALEB scheme, stands for the coefficient that n will multiply.

3.3 Multiply-Divide Method

Supposing a node is about to send number n to its neighbor using ALEB method, in order to avoid transmission error when the above errors exist, sender will wait nK counter period instead of n period before sending stop signal. In this case, if the counter of receiver records an amount of periods which is between $(n-\dfrac{1}{2})K$ and $(n+\dfrac{1}{2})K$, we can divide the result by K to get the original n.

Theorem 1. To ensure that receiver can get a counting result between $(n-\dfrac{1}{2})K$ and $(n+\dfrac{1}{2})K$, the following formulas must come into existence.

$$n < \frac{1}{4\Delta f} - \frac{1}{4} \approx \frac{1}{4\Delta f} \tag{C1}$$

$$K > \frac{2\Delta T_d (1-\Delta f^2) f}{1 - \Delta f - 4n\Delta f} \approx \frac{2\Delta T_d f}{1 - 4n\Delta f} \tag{C2}$$

Let's assume that sender waits N_s periods between sending start and stop signal. The duration on the receiver side between two signals is $\dfrac{N_s}{f_s} \pm \Delta T_d$, deducting a counting result $\dfrac{N_s}{f_s} \pm \Delta T_d$. Thus, the counting result of the receiver is

$$N_r = (\frac{N_s}{f_s} \pm \Delta T_d) f_r \tag{1}$$

Consider the extreme situation, we get

$$\max(N_r) = (\frac{N_s}{f(1-\Delta f)} + \Delta T_d)(1+\Delta f)f \tag{2}$$

$$\min(N_r) = (\frac{N_s}{f(1+\Delta f)} - \Delta T_d)(1-\Delta f)f \tag{3}$$

Because $N_s = nK$, according to ALEB requirement

$$(n-\frac{1}{2})K < \min(N_r) < \max(N_r) < (n+\frac{1}{2})K$$

namely

$$(n-\frac{1}{2})K < (\frac{nK}{f(1+\Delta f)} - \Delta T_d)(1-\Delta f)f \tag{4}$$

$$(n+\frac{1}{2})K > (\frac{nK}{f(1-\Delta f)} + \Delta T_d)(1+\Delta f)f \tag{5}$$

Solve the inequations, we get

$$\Delta T_d(1-\Delta f)f < (\frac{1}{2} - \frac{2\Delta f}{1+\Delta f}n)K \tag{6}$$

$$\Delta T_d(1+\Delta f)f < (\frac{1}{2} - \frac{2\Delta f}{1-\Delta f}n)K \tag{7}$$

Apparently $K \geq 1$, thus the coefficient of K in (6) and (7) must be positive. We get

$$n < \frac{1}{4\Delta f} - \frac{1}{4} \approx \frac{1}{4\Delta f} \tag{C1}$$

and

$$K > \frac{2\Delta T_d(1-\Delta f^2)f}{1-\Delta f - 4n\Delta f} \approx \frac{2\Delta T_d f}{1-4n\Delta f} \tag{C2}$$

Two conclusions can be derived from theorem 1. First, according to (C1), the upper extremity of n is restricted by relative error of frequency Δf. More accurate be the counter, bigger number can be transmitted by ALEB. Supposing the bit stream to be transferred is cut into frames with a fixed frame length L, the max number represented by a frame is $n_{max} = 2^L - 1$. We can deduce that

$$L_{max} = \left\lfloor \log_2 \frac{1}{4\Delta f} \right\rfloor \tag{C3}$$

For a crystal oscillator with relative error 5PPM, $L_{max} = 15$.

Second, according to (C2), lower extremity of K increases with n. Because transmission latency increases with K, K should be as small as it can be. For a given max frame length L_{max}, the minimum K in ALEB scheme is

$$K_{min} = \left\lceil \frac{2\Delta T_d f}{1 - 2^{L_{max}+2} \Delta f} \right\rceil \tag{C4}$$

3.4 Mixed Transmission Mode

In most data-collection WSN applications, requirements of latency vary by different situations and scenarios. In a typical forest temperature monitoring and fireproofing network, normal temperature collected periodically by sensors do not need to be delivered to sink quickly. But when a node gets a very high temperature from its sensor module, it should inform the sink node as quickly as possible in despite of energy-cost because this is probably indicates a forest fire. In other scenarios, when users try to query some information of a particular area or some certain nodes, the query should be transferred to the target quickly with fast forwarding on the path. To satisfy varied requirements of energy-cost and latency, ALEB allows application to choose the most suitable method for each message. We classify messages into two classes as urgent message and non-urgent message. For emergence transmission, traditional method will be faster, but costs more energy. For non-urgent messages, CtS method with Multiply-Divide can be much more energy-efficient.

Theorem 2. Transmitting number n in ALEB, the latency of urgent message is $\frac{\log_2 n}{F} + T_d$, and the latency of non-urgent message is $\frac{nK}{f} + T_d$.

The latency of CtS method is $\frac{nK}{f} + T_d$, and the latency of traditional method is $\frac{\log_2 n}{F} + T_d$. Presently the radio frequency F of WSN is much higher then the frequency f of the nodes' counter, and $\log_2 n < nK$, thus $\frac{\log_2 n}{F} + T_d < \frac{nK}{f} + T_d$.

The average latency per hop of ALEB stays inside the latencies of urgent transmission and non-urgent transmission. The latency of non-urgent transmission is expected to become lower because the frequency of hardware is growing higher and higher following the Moore's Law. Presently, the latency can be reduced to several milliseconds.

4 Simulation

In this section, we simulated a typical temperature monitoring network. Each node collects temperature data periodically and then sends to sink node as non-urgent message. When some pre-defined events occur, sensing nodes should send an urgent message to sink. The parameters are the same as typical Berkeley Motes[13].

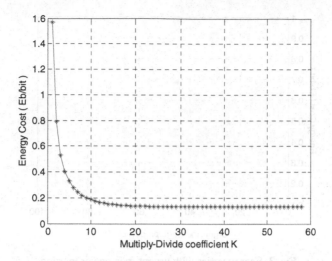

Fig. 1. Energy cost varies with Multiply-Divide coefficient K

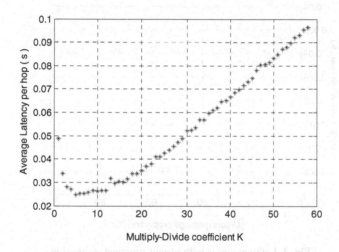

Fig. 2. Latency varies with Multiply-Divide coefficient K

4.1 Coefficient of Multiply-Divide

As analyzed in section 3.3, a minimum K is required by Multiply-Divide method. In our simulation, the calculated minimum K is 58 and the energy cost and latency performance are shown in figure 1 and figure 2. When K is smaller then 10, energy cost of each bit and latency between neighbors are both high because a big number of re-transmissions occur due to the transmission error. When K increases, the number of re-transmission decreases, making the average energy cost come to a low level. However, when K keeps increasing, the latency increases again because sender has to

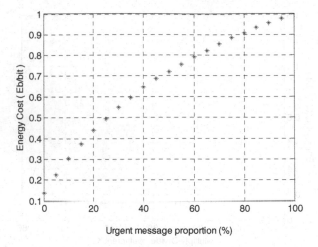

Fig. 3. Energy varies with urgent message proportion

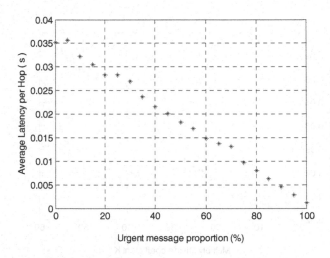

Fig. 4. Latency varies with urgent message proportion

wait more periods between two signals. It's interesting that even the calculated minimum K is 58, our simulation shows that when K once comes to 20 around, the energy cost has dropped to the same level as K is 58. That is because the formulas we derived are based on the worst situation. When errors are normally distributed, a much smaller K can be deployed in despite of a tiny amount of re-transmission.

4.2 Urgent Message Proportion

When urgent messages take different proportion of the whole messages, the energy and latency performance are shown in figure 3 and figure 4. Obviously with the increase of urgent messages, more energy is spent and shorter latency is obtained, proving the energy and latency are essential tradeoff. When all messages are urgent, ALEB degrades to traditional transmission method. Applications can choose a certain proportion of urgent messages according to their own requirements.

5 Conclusion

CtS paradigm is designed to achieve extremely low energy consumption in the cost of a long latency. This paper analyzes the real environment in which original CtS method will fail because of several errors. We propose a new scheme called ALEB based on CtS paradigm. ALEB scheme keeps the low energy consumption by increasing the latency of CtS method to even longer. Also, ALEB allow upper layer to balance adaptively in the tradeoff of energy against latency. The simulation result shows that ALEB costs more energy than idealized CtS method, but is still much more energy-efficient than traditional data transmission method. With the mixed transmission mode, ALEB is considered to be a widely applicable MAC layer energy-efficient transmission scheme.

References

1. Yang Yu, Bhaskar Krishnamachari, and Viktor K. Prasanna, Energy-latency Tradeoffs for Data Gathering in Wireless Sensor Networks, IEEE INFOCOM 2004
2. Yujie Zhu and Raghupathy Sivakumar, Challenges: Communication through Silence in Wireless Sensor Networks, MobiCom'05, August 28–September 2, 2005
3. Tod Riedel, Sokwoo Rhee, and Sheng Liu, Wireless Sensors Streamline Data Distribution, Communication Systems Design, Cover Story, July/August 2003 Issue, 9 (7) (2003) pp 10-18
4. Sabyasachi Roy, Y. Charlie Hu, Dimitrios Peroulis, Xiang-Yang Li, Minimum-Energy Broadcast Using Practical Directional Antennas in All-Wireless Networks, IEEE INFOCOM 2006
5. Javier Gomez, Andrew T. Campbell, A case for variable-range transmission power control in wireless multihop networks, IEEE INFOCOM 2004
6. M. Agarwal, JH Cho, L. Gao and J. Wu, Energy efficient broadcast. in wireless ad hoc networks with Hitch-hiking, IEEE. INFOCOM 2004
7. Christina Fragouli, Jorg Widmer, Jean-Yves Le Boudec, A Network Coding Approach to Energy Efficient Broadcasting: from Theory to Practice, IEEE INFOCOM 2006
8. Ye W, Heidemann J, Estrin D. An energy-efficient MAC protocol for wireless sensor networks. In: Proc 21st International Annual Joint Conf IEEE Computer and Communications Societies, INFOCOM 2002, New York, June 2002
9. Tijs van Dam , Koen Langendoen, An adaptive energy-efficient MAC protocol for wireless sensor networks, Proceedings of the 1st international conference on Embedded networked sensor systems, November 05-07, 2003, Los Angeles, California, USA
10. K. Jamieson, H. Balakrishnan, and Y. C. Tay, Sift: A MAC Protocol for Event-Driven Wireless Sensor Networks, MIT Laboratory for Computer Science, Tech. Rep. 894, May 2003

11. Khaled A. Arisha, Moustafa A. Youssef, Mohamed F. Younis, Energy-Aware TDMA-Based MAC for Sensor Networks, in the Proceedings of the IEEE Workshop on Integrated Management of Power Aware Communications, Computing and Networking (IMPACCT 2002)
12. Su Ping, Delay Measurement Time Synchronization for Wireless Sensor Networks, Intel Research. Berkeley Lab, 2003
13. Philip Levis, Sam Madden, David Gay, Joe Polastre, Robert Szewczyk, Alec Woo, Eric Brewer and David Culler, The Emergence of Networking Abstractions and Techniques in TinyOS, In Proceedings of the First USENIX/ACM Symposium on Networked Systems Design and Implementation (NSDI 2004).

A Convex-Hull Based Algorithm to Connect the Maximal Independent Set in Unit-Disk Graphs

Dechang Chen[1,*], Xilong Mao[2], Xia Fei[3], Kai Xing[4], Fang Liu[4], and Min Song[5]

[1] Uniformed Services University of the Health Sciences,
4301 Jones Bridge Road, Bethesda, MD 20814, USA
dchen@usuhs.mil
[2] School of Computer, National University of Defense Technology,
Changsha, Hunan 410073, P.R. China
mxilong@263.net
[3] Rizhao Geotechical Investigation and Surveying
Institute of Urban and Rural Construction,
No.269, Jinan Road, Rizhao, Shandong 276820, P.R. China
feixiarz@sohu.com
[4] Department of Computer Science, The George Washington University,
801 22nd St. NW, Washington, DC 20052, USA
{kaix, fliu}@gwu.edu
[5] Department of Electrical and Computer Engineering, Old Dominion University,
231 Kaufman Hall, Norfolk, VA 23529, USA
msong@odu.edu

Abstract. In this paper we propose and analyze a localized convex-hull based algorithm to connect a maximal independent set. The cardinality of the resultant connected dominating set is at most $76 \cdot opt + 19$, where opt is the size of a minimum connected dominating set. To our knowledge, this is a dramatic improvement compared to the best published results in the same context [1,6]. Our algorithm plays an important rule in efficiently constructing a virtual backbone for ad hoc and sensor networks.

Keywords: Ad hoc and sensor networks, maximal independent set, connected dominating set.

1 Introduction

Connected dominating set (CDS) construction is an important problem for ad hoc and sensor network research since the induced graph of the CDS can serve as a backbone for message dissemination [15,16] and QoS provisioning [13] to conserve the very limited network resource. Due to the dynamism of the network topology, localized algorithms are always favorable.

Constructing a CDS by connecting a maximal independent set (MIS) is a popular approach. In this paper, we propose and analyze a localized convex-hull based algorithm to connect a MIS. The result is a connected dominating set

---

* Dr. Chen's research is supported by the National Science Foundation grant CCR-0311252.

X. Cheng, W. Li, and T. Znati (Eds.): WASA 2006, LNCS 4138, pp. 363–370, 2006.

with a smaller cardinality compared to the other MIS based CDS construction algorithms [1,6]. This algorithm explores the geometric properties of unit-disk graphs and generates a CDS with size at most $76 \cdot opt + 19$, where opt is the size of a minimum connected dominating set.

We assume that there exists a localized algorithm to compute a MIS first. For example, the algorithms proposed in [1,6] can be applied here. We also assume that the network can be modeled by a unit-disk graph, where an edge between two nodes exist if and only if their distance is at most one unit. This assumption is reasonable as in ad hoc and sensor networks the topology is always determined by the transmission range, which is usually fixed.

This paper is organized as follows. We first outline the most related work in Section 2. Preliminaries and geometric properties of unit-disk graphs are studied in Section 3. Our convex-hull based algorithm for connecting a MIS is proposed in Section 4. We conclude our paper in Section 5.

2 Related Work

Connecting a MIS to compute a connected dominating set is a popular approach. In this section, we summarize the most related research. For a detailed literature survey, we refer the readers to [4] and the references therein.

The first MIS based CDS construction algorithm is proposed by Wan and his group [2,3,14]. A spanning tree based algorithm is first designed to compute a MIS S with the following property: the shortest distance between any subset of S and its complement is two hops. Then based on the level information in the tree, a CDS is grown from the root of the tree by inviting connectors to join the tree in order to connect all nodes in S. This is a distributed algorithm, resulting in a CDS with a size at most $8 \cdot opt + 1$. Note that in this algorithm, the procedures of constructing and connecting a MIS are detached. A similar algorithm is proposed in [7] to construct and connect a MIS simultaneously.

The previous algorithms start from a single-leader, whose election costs $O(n \log n)$ in message complexity [8]. To improve this, multiple leader based algorithms are proposed in [1,6]. The basic idea is sketched as follows. A node joins the MIS S if and only if its id becomes the smallest among all its neighbors not in S. Since no leader election is involved in this MIS construction, message complexity is dropped to $O(n)$. Note that multiple nodes may join the MIS simultaneously, and therefore the shortest distance between any subset of S and its complement is either two or three hops. To connect all nodes in S, [1] requires that each node $u \in S$ compute a shortest path to all independent neighbors (the nodes in S whose distance to u is either two or three hops) with a higher id. This connection algorithm results in a CDS with size at most $192 \cdot opt + 48$. By further exploring the geometric properties of neighboring independent nodes, [6] proposes a connection algorithm to generate a CDS with size at most $147 \cdot opt + 33$.

Note that [1] and [6] are the most related work since both propose to connect a MIS in a localized fashion. Our algorithm proposed in this paper introduces a smaller number of connecting nodes, resulting a CDS with size at most $76 \cdot opt + 19$, a dramatic improvement compared to [1] and [6].

There exist other distributed or centralized algorithms to connect a MIS. For example, a distributed spanning tree can be constructed to connect all nodes in a MIS [11]; or a Steiner tree with minimum number of Steiner points can be applied to connect a MIS [12]. For details, we refer the readers to the original papers and to the most recent survey in [4].

3 Preliminaries

3.1 Dominating Set and Independent Set

In our study, an ad hoc or sensor network is modeled by a unit-disk graph $G(V, E)$ where V represents the set of sensors and an edge $uv \in E$ if and only $u \in V$, $v \in V$, and the Euclidean distance between u and v is at most 1 unit.

Given a graph $G(V, E)$, a dominating set D of V is a subset of V such that for $\forall u \in V - D$, there exists a $v \in D$ satisfying $uv \in E$. If all nodes in D induces a connected graph, D is a connected dominating set. Among all (connected) dominating sets of V, the one with the smallest cardinality is called the minimum (connected) dominating set. Computing a minimum connected dominating set (MCDS) is an NP-Hard problem in general graphs [10] and in unit-disk graphs [10]. A PTAS for MCDS in unit-disk graphs has been found in [5].

An independent set S of V is a subset of V such that $\forall u, v \in S$, $uv \notin E$. If adding any node $w \in V$ to S breaks the independent property, S is a maximal independent set (MIS). Note that a maximal independent set of V is also a dominating set of V. Wan, Alzoubi and Frieder [14] have proved the following result that relates the size of any MIS of a unit-disk graph G to that of its MCDS.

Lemma 1. Let S be any maximal independent set and D be any MCDS of a unit-disk graph G. Then $|S| \leq 4 \cdot |D| + 1$ for $|D| > 1$.

For any vertex u in a maximal independent set S, the length of the shortest path from u to its closest vertex in S is either two hops or three hops.

3.2 Geometric Properties of Unit-Disk Graphs

Based on the definition, an edge in a unit-disk graph exists between two nodes if and only if their Euclidean distance is at most 1. We have identified the following properties:

Lemma 2. Let uv and st be two crossing edges in a unit-disk graph $G(V, E)$, as shown in Fig. 1. Then at least one of u, v, s, t has direct edges to the other three vertices in G.

Proof. Assume all the four edges in the quadrilateral $usvt$ have length greater than 1. That is, none of the four edges us, sv, vt, and tu exists in G. Since $|sv| > 1$, $|vt| > 1$, and $|st| \leq 1$, we have either $\angle stv > 60°$ or $\angle tsv > 60°$ or both. Without loss of generality, assume $\angle tsv > 60°$. Then $\angle usv > 60°$, which

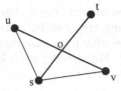

Fig. 1. uv and st are two crossing edges in a unit-disk graph G. Then at least one of u, v, s, and t can reach the other three vertices directly in G.

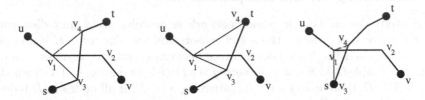

Fig. 2. P_{uv} and P_{st} are two crossing paths in a unit-disk graph G. v_1, v_2, v_3 and v_4 are the four vertices of the two crossing edges. Then u, v, s, t connect to each other by traversing only nodes in P_{uv} and P_{st}.

means either $|uv| > |sv|$ or $|uv| > |us|$. Since $|us| > 1$ and $|sv| > 1$, we have $|uv| > 1$, a contradiction. Therefore at least one of the four edges of $usvt$ must have length at most 1.

Without loss of generality, assume $|sv| \leq 1$. If $|vt| \leq 1$, then v can reach s, t, and u directly in G. Now let's assume $|vt| > 1$. Let o be the crossing point of edges uv and st. Based on the triangle inequality, we have $|ov| + |ot| > |vt|$ and $|os| + |ou| > |us|$. Therefore $|uv| + |st| > |vt| + |us|$. Since $|uv| \leq 1$, $|st| \leq 1$, and $|vt| > 1$, we have $|us| < 1$, indicating s can reach u, v, and t directly in G.

From the above analysis, we conclude that at least one of u, s, v, t can reach the other three vertices directly if uv and st intersect in a unit-disk graph G. ∎

Lemma 3. *Let u, v, s, t be four vertices in any MIS of a unit-disk graph G such that there exist a path P_{uv} with length at most three hops to connect u and v and a path P_{st} with length at most three hops to connect s and t. Let P be the set of intermediate nodes in P_{uv} and P_{st}. Then u, v, s, t can reach each other by traversing only vertices in P.*

Proof. Let v_1, v_2, v_3, v_4 be the four vertices in P_{uv} and P_{st} such that the two edges $v_1 v_2$ and $v_3 v_4$ cross. From Lemma 2, we know that one of these four vertices can reach the other three directly. Without loss of generality, assume v_1 can reach v_2, v_3, v_4 directly. Then by passing through v_1 and other vertices in P, u, v, s, t can reach each other. Three example scenarios are illustrated in Fig. 2. ∎

Note that the path length constraint of this Lemma can be relaxed. Actually in a unit-disk graph G, every pair of nodes in two crossing paths can reach each other by traversing only vertices in these two paths.

4   A Convex-Hull Based Algorithm to Connect a MIS

In this section, we propose a localized convex-hull based algorithm to connect a maximal independent set S of a unit-disk graph $G(V, E)$.

Our purpose is to compute a $C \subset V$ such that the induced graph of $C \cup S$ is connected. Let u be any vertex in S, and $N_u \subset S$ be the set of nodes in S that are at most three-hop away from u. Assume N_u is available to u. If u computes a shortest path to each node in N_u, the intermediate nodes of all the shortest paths form C. This is exactly the idea adopted by [1] and [6].

Our convex-hull based algorithm does not require u to compute a shortest path to all nodes in N_u since this introduces a large set of intermediate nodes. We compute the convex-hull of N_u first, then compute the shortest path from u to all nodes on the convex-hull only. A rigorous theoretical analysis is provided to prove the correctness of this algorithm.

Assume location information is available, and u knows the location of all nodes in N_u. The algorithm is sketched below.

Algorithm I

  – Compute the convex-hull H_u of N_u with any available algorithm (e.g. [9]).
  – Compute the shortest path in hop-count from u to any node in H_u. Break ties based on the ids of intermediate nodes[1].

Fig. 3 (a) illustrates an example for the vertex $u \in S$ and its $N_u \subset S$. The path from u to each node in N_u is either two-hop or three-hop. The convex-hull H_u of N_u is reported in Fig. 3 (b).

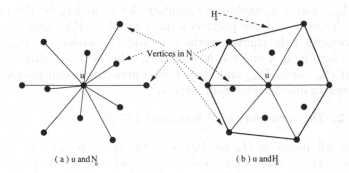

(a) u and N$_u$ (b) u and H$_u$

Fig. 3. In this example, the edges represent shortest paths from u to the corresponding node in N_u. (a) u and N_u. (b) u and H_u.

Note that Algorithm I is a localized algorithm. Each vertex in S should run a copy and all intermediate nodes computed by the algorithm form the set C to connect all vertices in S.

---

[1] If there are more than one route with the same hop-count, sort the ids of all intermediate nodes based on alphanumeric order and choose the smallest one.

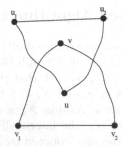

Fig. 4. u_1 and u_2 are two vertices in H_u and v_1 and v_2 are two vertices in H_v. u is enclosed in the polygon formed by P_{uu_1}, P_{uu_2}, and u_1u_2 while v is enclosed in the polygon formed by P_{vv_1}, P_{vv_2}, and v_1v_2. Since P_{uu_1} and P_{vv_1} (P_{uu_2} and P_{vv_2}) cross, u and v can reach each other by traversing only vertices in P_{uu_1} and P_{vv_1} (P_{uu_2} and P_{vv_2}).

Theorem 1. *(Connectivity)* $C \cup S$ *forms a connected dominating set if G is connected.*

Proof. For contradiction assume the induced graph of $C \cup S$, denoted by G', is not connected. Consider two neighboring components of G' with each containing a vertex from S and the shortest distance between these two vertices is at most three hops. Denote these two vertices by u and v. Since the distance between u and v is at most three hops, $u \in N_v$ and $v \in N_u$. However, $u \notin H_v$ and $v \notin H_u$ as they are in different components. Therefore u must be enclosed by H_v and v must be enclosed by H_u, as shown in Fig. 4.

Let u_1 and u_2 be the two closest vertices in H_u such that the polygon formed by P_{uu_1}, P_{uu_2}, and u_1u_2 encloses v. Similarly let v_1 and v_2 be the two closest vertices in H_v such that the polygon formed by P_{vv_1}, P_{vv_2}, and v_1v_2 encloses u. It is obvious that the shortest paths P_{uu_1} and P_{vv_1} cross, and P_{uu_2} and P_{vv_2} cross. From Lemma 3, u and v can reach each other by traversing only vertices in P_{uu_1} and P_{vv_1}, or in P_{uu_2} and P_{vv_2}. This contradicts to our assumption that u and v reside in disconnected components. ∎

Theorem 2. *The cardinality of C is at most $18 \cdot |S|$.*

Proof. Since all nodes in H_u are independent, their distance is at least one unit. In the extreme case, all vertices in H_u reside in the circle centered at u whose radius is three-unit. Therefore the maximum number of nodes in H_u is $2\pi \times 3 = 6\pi < 19$. In other words, u may be connected to at most 18 nodes in N_u through shortest paths by algorithm I. Furthermore, due to the criteria for breaking ties when selecting shortest paths, two vertices always choose the same shortest path if they reside on each other's convex hull. Since each shortest path is at most three hops, at most two intermediate nodes are introduced between u and any node in H_u. We charge one to u and the other to the vertex in H_u. Therefore each node u will be charged for at most 18 intermediate vertices. This completes the proof. ∎

Theorem 3. *The size of the connected dominating set computed by Algorithm I is at most* $76 \cdot opt + 19$, *where opt is the size of a MCDS.*

Proof. This theorem follows from Lemma 1 and Theorem 2.   ∎

Theorem 4. *The time complexity of Algorithm I is* $O(1)$.

Proof. Let u be any vertex in a MIS S. As proved by Alzoubi, Wan and Frieder in [1], the number of nodes in S that are at most three hops away from u is at most 47. Therefore Algorithm I takes $O(1)$ time.   ∎

5 Conclusion

We have proposed and analyzed a convex-hull based algorithm to connect a maximal independent set. To our knowledge, the resultant connected dominating set has the best performance compared to the published results in the same context. Constructing a CDS by connecting a MIS is a popular approach.

As a future research work, we will further explore the geometric properties of unit-disk graphs to design better algorithms for CDS construction.

References

1. K.M. Alzoubi, P.-J. Wan and O. Frieder, Message-Optimal Connected Dominating Sets in Mobile Ad Hoc Networks, *MOBIHOC*, EPFL Lausanne, Switzerland, 2002.
2. K. M. Alzoubi, P.-J. Wan, and O. Frieder, New Distributed Algorithm for Connected Dominating Set in Wireleess Ad Hoc Networks, *Proceedings of the 35th Hawaii International Conference on System Sciences*, Big Island, Hawaii, 2002.
3. K.M. Alzoubi, P.-J. Wan and O. Frieder, Distributed Heuristics for Connected Dominating Sets in Wireless Ad Hoc Networks, *Journal of Communications and Networks*, Vol. 4, No. 1, Mar. 2002.
4. J. Blum, M. Ding, A. Thaeler, and X. Cheng, Connected Dominating Sets in Sensor Networks and MANETs, in *Handbook of Combinatorial Optimization* (Eds. D.-Z. Du and P. Pardalos), pp.329-369, 2004.
5. X. Cheng, X. Huang, D. Li, W. Wu, and D.-Z.Du, Polynomial-Time Approximation Scheme for Minimum Connected Dominating Set in Ad Hoc Wireless Networks, *Networks*, Vol. 42, No. 4, pp. 202-208, 2003.
6. X. Cheng, M. Ding, D.H. Du, and X. Jia, On The Construction of Connected Dominating Set in Ad Hoc Wireless Networks, *Wireless Communications and Mobile Computing*, Vol. 6, pp. 183-190, 2006.
7. X. Cheng, Routing Issues in Ad Hoc Wireless Networks, PhD Thesis, Department of Computer Science, University of Minnesota, 2002.
8. I. Cidon and O. Mokryn, Propagation and Leader Election in Multihop Broadcast Environment, *Proc. 12th Int. Symp. Distr. Computing*, pp. 104-119, Greece, Spt. 1998.
9. T. H. Cormen, C. E. Leiserson, R. L. Rivest, and C. Stein, *Introduction to Algorithms*, 2nd Edition, Mc Graw Hill, 2001.
10. M. R. Garey and D. S. Johnson, Computers and Intractability: A guide to the theory of NP-completeness, Freeman, San Frncisco, 1978.

11. S. Guha and S. Khuller, Approximation algorithms for connected dom- inating sets, Algorithmica, 20(4), pp. 374-387, Apr. 1998.
12. M. Min, H. Du, X. Jia, C. X. Huang, S. C.-H. Huang, and W. Wu, Improving Construction for Connected Dominating Set with Steiner Tree in Wireless Sensor Networks, *Journal of Global Optimization*, Vol. 35, No. 1, pp. 111-119, May 2006.
13. R. Sivakumar, P. Sinha and V. Bharghavan, CEDAR: a core-extraction distributed ad hoc routing algorithm, *IEEE Journal on Selected Areas in Communications*, Vol. 17(8), Aug. 1999, pp. 1454 -1465.
14. P.-J. Wan, K.M. Alzoubi, and O. Frieder, Distributed Construction of Connected Dominating Set in Wireless Ad Hoc Networks, *IEEE INFOCOM*, pp. 1597-1604, 2002.
15. J. Wu, F. Dai, M. Gao, and I. Stojmenovic, On Calculating Power- Aware Connected Dominating Set for Ecient Routing in Ad Hoc Wire- less Networks, *Journal of Communications and Networks*, Vol. 5, No. 2, pp. 169-178, March 2002.
16. Y. Xu, J. Heidemann, and D. Estrin, Geography-informed energy con- servation for Ad Hoc routing, *MobiCom* 2001, pp.70-84, 2001.

A Pure Localized Algorithm for Finding Connected Dominating Set in MANETs by Classification of Neighbors

Hui Liu[1], Yi Pan[2], and Ivan Stojmenovic[3]

[1] Computer Science Department, Missouri State University, Springfield, MO 65897, USA
huiliu@missouristate.edu
[2] Computer Science Department, Georgia State University, Atlanta, GA 30303, USA
pan@cs.gsu.edu
[3] SITE, University of Ottawa, Ottawa, Ontario KIN 6N5, Canada
ivan@site.uottawa.ca

Abstract. An important problem in wireless ad hoc networks is to select a few nodes to form a virtual backbone that supports routing and other tasks such as area monitoring. Connected dominating set (CDS) has been proposed to approximate the virtual backbone. Although computing minimum CDS is known to be NP-hard, many distributed protocols have been presented to construct small CDS. However, these protocols are either too complicated, need non-local information or have slow convergence speed, are not adaptive to topology changes. In this paper, we propose a new pure localized algorithm for computing the approximate solution to the minimum CDS problem. The algorithm starts with a feasible and near-optimal CDS solution via marking process based on classification of neighbors, and removes vertices from this solution by redundancy elimination, until an approximate CDS is found. Both analytical and experimental results demonstrate that our algorithm has better performance than other distributed algorithms.

Keywords: connected dominating set, distributed algorithm, pure localized algorithm, routing, wireless ad hoc networks.

1 Introduction

The simplest way of updating routing information in wireless ad hoc and sensor networks is to send data about the neighborhood of nodes through all available links. The simple technique is called "global flooding". The main drawback of "global flooding" is the excessive amount of redundant rebroadcasts through the network, thus, degrading its available bandwidth, causing contention and collision easily, the lack of packet delivery successfully guaranteed, etc.

In order to avoid the "global flooding" problem, many researchers propose the promising idea of virtual backbones such as cluster-based routing, backbone-based routing and spine-based routing [1-4], even a mobile ad hoc network has no fixed backbone infrastructure. The basic idea behind this is to divide a mobile ad-hoc network into several small overlapping subnetworks, where each subnetwork is a clique (a complete subgraph). Each subnetwork has one or more virtual backbone

X. Cheng, W. Li, and T. Znati (Eds.): WASA 2006, LNCS 4138, pp. 371–381, 2006.
© Springer-Verlag Berlin Heidelberg 2006

hosts to connect to other parts in the network. These virtual backbone hosts form the core infrastructure of the ad-hoc mobile network. The routing process is operated over the core. As a result, any broadcasting of control packets only happens in the core, and communications between core nodes and non-core nodes are all through unicast communications. Therefore, this can substantially reduce the protocol overhead caused by global flooding. The number of hosts forming the virtual backbone must be as small as possible in order to reduce the protocol overhead, to increase the convergence speed, and to simplify the connectivity management. In this case, defining the structure of a suitable backbone is one of the subproblems that must be solved with the objective of providing optimal routing between clients.

We refer to nodes that are not selected for particular dominating set as being *covered* nodes. In case of routing, route through a covered node A may instead bypass it and traverse a connected set of its neighbors that cover it. More formally, a subset of nodes which is connected and which has the property that any node not in it is neighbor of at least one node from the subset is known as *connected dominating set (CDS)*. Currently, Minimum Connected Dominating Set (MCDS) is the main method utilized to approximate the virtual backbone in a mobile ad-hoc network.

Various algorithms that construct a CDS in ad hoc networks have been proposed in recent years. They can be divided into two categories: centralized algorithms that depend on network-wide information or coordination and decentralized that depend on local information only. Centralized algorithms usually yield a smaller CDS than decentralized algorithms, but their application is limited due to the high maintenance cost and is not practical in wireless ad hoc networks. Decentralized algorithms can be further divided into cluster-based algorithms and pure localized algorithms. Cluster-based algorithms have a constant approximation ratio in unit disk graphs, however it has relatively slow convergence ($O(N)$ in the worst case). Pure localized algorithms take constant steps to converge, produce a small CDS on average, but have no constant approximation ratio.

Wu and Li [5] introduced first fully localized dominating set definitions. Each node is marked as white initially. Let $N(v)$ be the open neighbor set of vertex v, which means $N(v)$ includes all the neighbors of vertex v. And let $N[v]$ be the closed neighbor set of vertex v, the set of all neighbors and itself. By assumption, each node has a unique ID number. This algorithm runs in two phases. In the first phase, each node broadcasts its neighbor set $N(v)$ to all its neighbors, and after collecting all adjacency information from all neighbors every node marks itself as black if there exist two unconnected neighbors. All black nodes form the initial CDS. However, considering only the first phase, there are too many nodes in the dominating set. So in the second phase, the algorithm executes extensional rules to eliminate local redundancy. Wu and Li [6] proposed several dominant pruning rules, which are rule 1, rule 2 and a generalized rule K. Thus, the second phase removes some nodes from the original dominating set and the size of a dominating set is further reduced.

Finding minimum CDS on graphs is a NP-complete problem. Authors in [7] explore the local structure of the neighborhood of a single vertex and the union of the neighborhoods of a pair of vertices, and propose a polynomial-time data reduction for dominating set. Their target is to deal with the NP-complete dominating set problem in graph theory and combinatorial optimization. However, the local structure analysis of the neighborhood of a vertex is very helpful in wireless ad hoc and sensor networks, since neighborhood information can be collected during "Hello" messages exchanged.

We propose a new pure localized heuristic algorithm for computing approximate solutions to the minimum connected dominating set problem. The algorithm starts with a feasible and near-optimal CDS solution via marking processing based on classification of neighbors, and removes vertices from this solution by redundancy elimination, until an approximate CDS is found. Using this technique, the proposed algorithm forms a feasible and small-sized CDS at the first stage; therefore, there are no setup time requirements. The approach also has the advantages of being purely localized and only exploring the local structure of a given MANET. Experimental results show that it is comparable to the best existing algorithms for finding CDS in MANETs and produces a smaller size CDS than Wu and Li's algorithm [6].

This paper is organized as follows. The following section presents the principles of classification of a vertex's neighbors, and illustrates the new marking process. The connected dominating set reduction is discussed in section 3. Section 4 presents the analysis performance evaluation. Performance evaluation by experiments is done in section 5. Finally, we conclude this paper and give an overview about future works.

2 Marking Process by Classification of Neighbors

Given a simple undirected graph $G = (V, E)$, where V is a set of vertices (hosts) and E is a set of undirected edges, an edge between u and v is denoted by an pair (u, v). A set $V' \subset V$ is a dominating set of G if every vertex $v \in V\text{-}V'$ is dominated by at least one vertex $u \in V'$. If a node $u \in V'$, we call u as a dominating node, otherwise it is a dominated node.

Neighborhood of a single vertex [7]. Consider a vertex $v \in V$ of the given graph $G = (V, E)$, let $N(v) = \{u \mid (u,v) \in E\}$ be the neighborhood of v. We partition the vertices of $N(v)$ of v into three different sets $N_1(v)$, $N_2(v)$, and $N_3(v)$ depending on what neighborhood structure these vertices have. More precisely, setting $N[v] = N(v) \cup \{v\}$, called close neighboring subset of a node v, we define

$$N_1(v) = \{u \in N(v) \cap N(u) \setminus N[v] \neq \varnothing\}$$
$$N_2(v) = \{(u \in N(v) \setminus N_1(v)) \cap (N(u) \setminus N_1(v) \neq \varnothing)\}$$
$$N_3(v) = \{N(v) \setminus (N_1(v) \cup N_2(v))\}$$

An example that illustrates the partitioning of $N(v)$ into the subsets $N_1(v)$, $N_2(v)$, and $N_3(v)$ can be seen in Fig. 1.

Note that, by definition of the three subsets, the vertices in $N_1(v)$, cannot be dominated by vertices from $N_1(v)$. A vertex in $N_3(v)$ can only be dominated by either v or by vertices in $N_2(v) \cup N_3(v)$. Since v will dominate at least as many vertices as any other vertex from $N_2(v) \cup N_3(v)$, it is safe to place v into the optimal dominating set we seek for. Based on the partitioning method of the vertex neighborhood, the following marking process can quickly find a connected dominating set in a given graph.

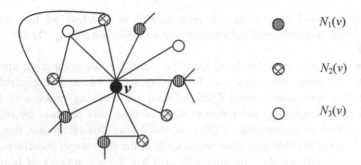

Fig. 1. The partitioning of the neighborhood of a single vertex v

---

Algorithm 1. Marking Process by Classification of Neighbors

1: Initially assign color *BLACK* to each u in V.
2: Each u exchanges its neighbor set $N(u)$ with all its neighbors.
3: Each u checks its color, if its color is WHITE already, STOP.
4: Each u partitions all its neighbors into three subsets $N_1(u)$, $N_2(u)$, and $N_3(u)$.
5: If $N_2(u) \cup N_3(v) \neq \emptyset$
       u sends a "dominating" message to all nodes in $N_2(u) \cup N_3(v)$.
7: If u receiving a "dominating" message from one neighbor v
       If $N[u] \neq N[v]$ then u changes its color $c(u)$ to WHITE
       else
          If $ID(u) < ID(v)$ then u changes its color $c(u)$ to WHITE

The marking process is a localized algorithm, where hosts only interact with others in the neighborhood. Unlike clustering algorithms, there is no "sequential propagation" of information. The marking process colors every vertex in G. $c(v)$ is a color value for vertex $v \in V$ that has two values, WHITE, and BLACK. Nodes remaining color BLACK form the initial CDS. Nodes with WHITE color are dominated by other nodes. An important issue in implementing the marking process is that during any step of this process, once a node receives a "dominating" message, it changes its color to "WHITE" from "BLACK" immediately, and then stops the marking process. Because all mobile hosts execute the marking process in a distributed manner, they do not know whether they are dominated by others and when they can stop the process except for receiving the notice messages. For each host v, its neighbor set N(v) are embedded in the beacon packet sent periodically to each neighbor. Thus, each host v has the two-hop neighboring information.

The marking process by classification of neighbors (MPCN) prefer to selecting nodes, which dominate as many as possible neighbors, into the initial CDS. While in Wu and Li's marking process [5], a node marks itself as a dominating node when it has two unconnected neighbors. We may wonder if MPCN produces a smaller CDS compared with Wu and Li's marking process [5] by intuition, especially in dense network or network of small size. Fig. 2. gives an example of MPCD and Wu and Li's marking process [5] applying to a network.

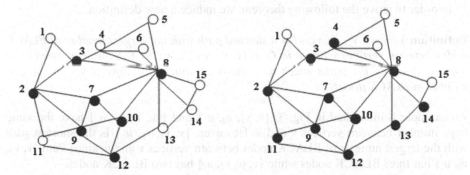

Fig. 2. Comparison of two marking processes. (a) the result applying marking process of classification of neighbors; (b) the result applying marking process by Wu and Li's marking process.

Properties. Assume V' is the set of vertices that are colored BLACK in V, i.e., V' = {v | v ∈ V, c(v) = BLACK}. The reduced graph G' is the subgraph of G induced by V', i.e., G'=G[V']. The following two theorems show that G' is a dominating set of G and it is connected.

Theorem 1. *Given a G = (V, E) that is connected, the vertex subset V' induced by BLACK nodes after the marking process by classification of neighbors, forms a dominating set of G.*

Proof. Randomly select a vertex v in G. We show that v is either in V' (a set of vertices in V that remain color BLACK) or adjacent to a vertex in V'. Assume v is colored WHITE, if there is at least one neighbor colored BLACK, the theorem is proved.

We assume v is colored WHITE and all v's neighbors $(v_1, v_2, ..., v_k)$ are colored WHITE. Based on the marking process by classification of neighbors, all nodes in graph G are initially colored as BLACK, and only if v receives a "dominating" message, it changes its color as WHITE. Let v_1 be the neighbor sending a "dominating" message to v. Then $N(v) \subset N(v_1)$. Since v_1 is also WHITE, and u is the neighbor sending a "dominating" message to v_1, u must be one of v's neighbors $(v_1, v_2, ..., v_k)$ according to MPCN, since v_1 belongs to the union of $N_2(u)$ and $N_3(u)$,. Let u be just v_2, then $N(v_1) \subset N(v_2)$, and so on, until we can conclude $N(v_1) \subset N(v_2) \subset N(v_3) \subset ...\subset N(v_k)$. Thus, at least one neighbor of v can not be dominated by others, it should remain as BLACK. When two neighboring nodes have the same close neighboring subset, MPCN only changes the one with smaller ID to WHITE. This contradicts to the assumption that all v's neighbors are WHITE.   □

Dominating sets were empty with definitions of Wu and Li's marking process [5], while this marking process by classification of neighbors selects node with lowest ID in the dominating set. Empty dominating sets in complete graphs are not an issue in broadcasting application since retransmissions are not necessary. However, in scheduling node activities it is a major issue, since it leaves such network without any active node (e.g. with no sensor to monitor given small area).

   In order to prove the following theorem, we induce a new definition.

Definition 1. *$\{v, v_1, v_2, ..., v_k, u\}$ is a shortest path with the largest number of BLACK nodes between vertices v and u in G, if $\{v, v_1, v_2, ..., v_k, u\}$ has the least number of hops, and among the paths which have the least number of hops, it has the largest number of BLACK nodes.*

An example is illustrated in Fig. 3. $\{v, v_1, v_2, u\}$ and $\{v, w, v_2, u\}$ have the same hops number between vertices v and u. However, $\{v, v_1, v_2, u\}$ is the shortest path with the largest number of BLACK nodes between vertices v and u, since Path $\{v, v_1, v_2, u\}$ has three BLACK nodes while $\{v, w, v_2, u\}$ has two BLACK nodes.

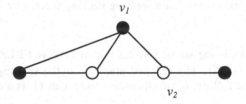

Fig. 3. An example of the shortest path with the largest number of BLACK nodes

Theorem 2. *The reduced graph $G' = G[V']$ is a connected graph.*

Proof. We prove this theorem by contradiction. Assume G' is disconnected and v and u are two disconnected vertices in G'. Assume $dis_G(v, u) = k+1 > 1$ and $\{v, v_1, v_2, ..., v_k, u\}$ is a shortest path with the largest number of BLACK nodes between vertices v and u in G. Clearly, all $v, v_1, v_2, ..., v_k$ are distinct and among them we can find at least two nodes v_{i-1} and v_i, such that $c(v_{i-1}) = $ BLACK and $c(v_i) = $ WHITE, from the node v_i this path becomes disconnected. (Otherwise, v and u are connected in G' and perhaps the node v_{i-1} is just v). On the other hand, the two adjacent vertices of v_i, v_{i-1} and v_{i+1}, are not connected in G. (otherwise, $\{v, v_1, v_2, ..., v_k, u\}$ is not a shortest path). When node v_i is colored as WHITE, we consider the following three cases: (1) node v_i receives a "dominating" message from node v_{i-1}. We can see $N(v_i) \subset N(v_{i-1})$ based on the marking process by classification of neighbors. Thus, v_{i+1} is connected to v_{i-1}. This contradicts to the assumption that the two adjacent vertices of v_i, v_{i-1} and v_{i+1}, are not connected in G. (2) node v_i receives a "dominating" message from node v_{i+1}. It is the same with case 1; nodes v_{i-1} and v_{i+1} are connected. This contradicts to the assumption that the two adjacent vertices of v_i, v_{i-1} and v_{i+1}, are not connected in G. (3) node v_i receives a "dominating" message from a BLACK node w, which is a neighbor of v_i and different from v_{i-1} and v_{i+1}, then w is connected to v_{i-1} and v_{i+1}, since $N(v_i) \subset N(w)$ according to the marking process. Thus, $\{v, v_1, v_2, ..., w, ...v_k, u\}$ has one more BLACK nodes than $\{v, v_1, v_2, ..., v_k, u\}$. This contradicts to the assumption that $\{v, v_1, v_2, ..., v_k, u\}$ is a shortest path with the largest number of BLACK nodes between vertices v and u in G.   □

Vertices in a dominating set are called dominating nodes and vertices outside a dominating set are called dominated nodes. Consider a vertex $v \in V$ such that $N_2(v) \cup N_3(v) \neq \varnothing$. The vertices in $N_2(v) \cup N_3(v)$ can only be dominated by either v or by vertices in $N_2(v) \cup N_3(v)$. But clearly $N(w) \subset N(v)$ for every $w \in N_2(v) \cup N_3(v)$. This shows that an optimal way to dominate $N_2(v) \cup N_3(v)$ is given by taking v into the dominating set. The marking process tries to select nodes, which can dominate as many as possible nodes, into the initial CDS, and it only requires constant round computations. The marking process is efficient and induces smaller initial CDS for the ad hoc wireless mobile network in average case. Our performance analysis and simulation results (to be discussed later) confirm this observation.

3 Localized Connection Dominating Set Reduction

All dominating nodes derived from marking process form the initial CDS. Consider a random vertex $v \in V$ such that $N_2(v) \cup N_3(v) \neq \varnothing$. We take v into the dominating set. For every $w \in N_2(v) \cup N_3(v)$, w can be covered by vertex v. Actually, both vertex v and vertices in $N_1(v)$, which can have connection with vertices outside the neighborhood of vertex v. Actually, our marking process already includes the case illustrated as the extended Rule 1 in Wu and Li's algorithm [105]. However, there maybe multiple connections available among vertices in $\{v\} \cup N_1(v)$, it is not necessary to keep all of them. We also adopt the extended Rule 2 in [105] to reduce the size of the connected dominating set. The idea is as following: if a vertex is covered by two connected vertices, removing this vertex from V' will not compromise its functionality as a CDS. To avoid simultaneous removal of three vertices covering by each other, a vertex is removed only if it is covered by other two vertices with higher ID's. Node ID(v) of each vertex $v \in V$ of each vertex serves as a priority. Nodes with higher priorities have high probability of becoming dominating nodes. We revise the extended Rule 2 suited to our situation as follows.

Rule 2. Assume u and w are two BLANK neighbors of BLANK vertex v in G'. If $N(v) \subseteq N(u) \cup N(w)$ in G and ID(v) = min { ID(v), ID(u), ID(w)}, then change color of v to WHITE.

It is easy to prove G' − {v} is still a connected dominating set. Obviously, an additional step needs to be added at the end of our marking process: if a host v is colored WHITE, it sends its status to all its neighbors.

4 Performance Analysis

This section discusses the efficiency and overhead of our marking process by classification of neighbors through analytical study. The performance can be measured by computation and communication complexity.

Theorem 3. The computation complexity of Algorithm 1 (the marking process by classification of neighbors) is $O(\Delta^2)$, where Δ is the maximum vertex degree in the network.

Proof. To carry out Algorithm 1, for each vertex v of the given graph G we have to determine the neighbor sets $N_1(v)$, $N_2(v)$, and $N_3(v)$. By definition of these sets, one easily observes that it is sufficient to consider the two-hop neighborhood information of the vertex v which is obtained by the beacon sent periodically. Firstly, we determine the vertices from $N_1(v)$ by comparing the neighbor sets of v and every neighbor u of vertex v. This step takes at most $O(\Delta^2)$, where Δ is the maximum degree of the given graph G. Then, it remains to determine the sets $N_2(v)$ and $N_3(v)$. To get $N_2(v)$, one basically has to go through all vertices from the one-hop neighbors of vertex v that are not already marked as being in $N_1(v)$ but have at least one neighbor in $N_1(v)$. All this can be done within $O(\Delta^2)$ time. Finally, $N_3(v)$ simply consist of vertices from the one-hop neighbors of vertex v that are neither marked being in $N_2(v)$ nor marked being in $N_3(v)$. This step can be done in $O(\Delta)$ time. After partitioning of vertex v's neighbors, vertex v sends out "dominating" messages, and a node receiving "dominating" just changes its color. These only take constant time. In summary, this shows the computation of Algorithm 1 can be executed in time $O(\Delta^2)$.   □

Theorem 4. *The communication complexity of Algorithm 1 (the marking process by classification of neighbors) is $O(n\Delta)$, where Δ is the maximum vertex degree in the network and n is the number of vertices in the network.*

Proof. The communication complexity is measured as the total number of control messages sent by the network in order to construct the approximate CDS. For each vertex $v \in V$, vertex v sends the "dominating" messages if it can cover its neighbors in $N_2(v)$ and $N_3(v)$. On the other hand, if a node $u \in V$ receives a "dominating" message, it changes its color to WHITE and sends its status change to its neighbors. We see for each vertex it sends at most $O(\Delta)$ messages. Therefore, the communication complexity of Algorithm 1 (marking process) is $O(n\Delta)$.   □

Clearly, our approach is as simple as Wu and Li's algorithm in all measurements, in particular, the number of rounds needed. Note that the number of rounds is an important metric measuring the performance of the algorithm because the topology of the ad hoc wireless network changes frequently with the movements of mobile hosts, therefore the dominating set has to be updated and recalculated frequently.

Another important measurement is the size of the dominating set generated. We can not theoretically prove that our approach generates smaller connected dominating set than Wu and Li's algorithm. However, we can show that our approach outperforms Wu and Li's algorithm on average through simulation discussed in the following section.

5 Experimental Results

In this section we conducted the simulation study which computes the average size of the CDS derived from our algorithm with those from several existing algorithms under different conditions. The smaller the size of the dominating set, the better the results.

In our simulation environments, random graphs are generated in 600×600 square units of a 2-D simulation area, by randomly inducing a certain number of mobile nodes. We assume that each mobile node has the same transmission range r, thus the generated graph is undirected. If the distance between any two nodes is less than radius r, then there is a connection link between the two nodes. If generated graph is disconnected, simply discard the graph. Otherwise continue the simulation.

Note that, for a constant r, the network density, in terms of the average vertex degree d, will increase rapidly as the network size (n) increases. Simulation is carried out by varying average degree d of the network (i.e. the average number of neighbors of a node in the network), such that the impact of network size can be observed independent of density. The transmission range can be set as a function of d, number of nodes n, and the network area using relation $r^2 = (d * 600 *600) (n-1)$. In order to observe the impact of density, each simulation is repeated on various average vertex degrees ($d = 6, 30$). All simulations are conducted in static ad hoc networks, where a simulation completes after a CDS formation algorithm converges after several rounds of information exchanges. Since the topology of ad hoc networks change very dynamically, our simulation takes snapshots on dynamic ad hoc networks. For each average vertex degree d, the number of nodes n is varied from 20 to 200. For each n, the number of running times is 500 times.

First, the performance of our approach (MPCN plus Rule 2 reduction), in terms of the size of the resultant connected dominating set, is compared with a centralized algorithm (MCDS [8]), a cluster-based algorithm (Tree [9]), and a pure localized algorithm (Wu and Li [5]). MCDS is a very good approximation to the optimal solution. We use it as a rough estimate to the real minimal connected dominating set since the brute force method to find the optimal solution is too slow to provide the result for a large size network. Tree is actually a centralized algorithm as all clusterheads are connected to a global infrastructure (i.e. the tree) controlled from a central point (i.e., the root). Our approach, named MPCN, uses the marking process by classification of neighbors to form the initial CDS, and then reduces the size of CDS further via revised Rule 2. We assume vertex ID's are used as priority values.

Fig. 4. shows the performance of these algorithms. In MCDS, the size of CDS is about 37 percent of the network size in sparse ($d = 6$) networks, and 15 percent in dense ($d = 30$) networks. This performance is much better than other algorithms. Tree has a performance of 55 percent in sparse networks and 26 percent in dense networks. Wu and Li's approach produces a dominating set that is about 12 percent larger than Tree in sparse networks, and about 35 percent larger in dense networks. The performance of MPCN is even better than Tree in sparse networks, but produces a dominating set that is about 2 percent larger than Tree in dense networks. MPCN is a pure localized algorithm and is actually more efficient than a cluster-based algorithm.

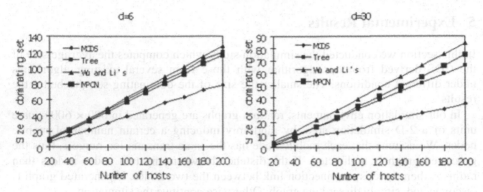

Fig. 4. Comparison with existing algorithms

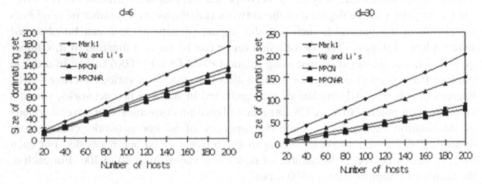

Fig. 5. Comparison of different marking processes

We can see MPCN reduces the size of the dominating set by about 10 percent more nodes in sparse networks, and about 20 percent more nodes in dense networks compared with another pure localized algorithm, Wu and Li's approach.

The second group of simulations compare performances of two marking process (MPCN and Wu and Li's) and two algorithms for computing CDS (MPCN + R). Fig. 5. shows all the situations in sparse and dense networks. Our marking process produces an initial dominating set that has almost the size of a dominating set produced by the Wu and Li's algorithm after two rounds of redundancy reductions in sparse networks. Since Wu and Li's marking process is very trivial, it produces an initial dominating set that almost has the same size with the whole network. That is, almost every host belongs to a dominating set. Our marking process is about 25 percent smaller than Wu and Li's marking process in dense networks, about 30 percent smaller than Wu and Li's marking process in sparse networks. We can also see that when the number of nodes in the network is small, only our marking approach without any redundancy reduction has a very comparable performance with Wu and Li's algorithm including two rounds of redundancy reduction. This is because our marking process prefers to select optimal hosts, which can cover as many as possible nodes, into the initial connecting dominating set. This works especially in sparse or small size networks.

Simulation results can be summarized as follows:

1. The connected dominating set produced by our marking process is about the same size as those produced by the cluster-based schemes in dense networks, and smaller than those in sparse networks. This is achieved in a pure localized way without sequential propagation.

2. Our algorithm performs better than another pure localized algorithm, Wu and Li's algorithm, with lower cost and a faster converging speed, since our algorithm has less number of rounds for computing CDS than that of Wu and Li's algorithm.

3. Only our marking process without any redundancy reduction is comparable to Wu and Li's algorithm with two rules reduction in sparse or small size networks.

6 Conclusion

In this paper, we explore the local structure of a single node in wireless ad hoc and sensor networks by exchanging beacon messages periodically. All neighboring nodes of each node are classified into three types. Based on the classification, our marking process selects nodes, which can dominate as many as possible nodes, to form the initial near-optimal CDS. Then, our algorithm decreases the size of CDS further through redundancy elimination. It is very simple, pure localized, and only requires constant round computations. The simulation results demonstrate the CDS constructed by our algorithm is comparable to those constructed by cluster-based schemes in dense networks, and smaller than those in sparse networks, while cluster-based schemes require sequential propagation. Our algorithm outperforms another pure localized algorithm, Wu and Li's, with smaller size of CDS, lower cost and faster converging speed.

References

1. B. Das, R. Sivakumar and V. Bharghavan, "Routing in ad hoc networks using a spine", in Proc. Int. Conf. Comput. and Commun. Networks, Las Vegas, NV., 1997.
2. U. C. Kozat, G. Kondylis, B. Ryu and M. K. Marina, "Virtual Dynamic Backbone for Mobile Ad Hoc Networks", in IEEE International Conference on Communications (ICC), Helsinki, Finland, 2001.
3. E. Kranakis, H. Singh and J. Urrutia, "Compass routing on geometric networks", In Proc Of 11th Canadian Conf. on Computational, Geometry, Vancouver, 1999.
4. R. Sivakumar, B. Das and V. Bharghavan, "An improved spine-based infrastructure for routing in ad hoc networks", in Proc. IEEE Symp. Comput. And Commun., Athens, Greece, 1998,
5. J. Wu and H. Li, "A dominating-set-based routing scheme in ad hoc wireless networks", Telecomm. System, special issue on wireless networks, 18 (2001), pp. 13-36.
6. F. Dai and J. Wu, "Distributed dominant pruning in ad hoc wireless networks", In Proc. Of IEEE International Conference on Communications (ICC), 2003
7. J. Alber, M. R. Fellows and R. Miedermeier, "Polynomial-time data reduction for dominating set", Journal of the ACM (JACM), 51 (2004), pp. 363-384.
8. S. Guha and S. Khuller, "Approximation algorithms for connected dominating sets", Algorithmica, 20 (1998), pp. 374-387
9. K. M. Alzoubi, P.-J. Wan and O. Frieder, "Distributed heuristics for connected dominating sets in wireless ad hoc networks", J. Comm. And Networks, 4 (2002), pp. 22-29.

Dependency-Based Dynamic Component Reconfiguration for Wireless Computing Systems*

Jung-Ho Kwon[1], Byung-Hoon Lee[1], Jai-Hoon Kim[1], and We-Duke Cho[2]

[1] Graduate School of Information and Communication
Ajou University, Korea
jungho@dmc.ajou.ac.kr, {componer, jaikim}@ajou.ac.kr
[2] Center of Excellence for Ubiquitous System
Ajou University, Korea
chowd@ajou.ac.kr

Abstract. Wireless computing system has to satisfy the changeable requirements of various users and environments. Therefore the coming wireless computing requires systems to be more available, flexible and adaptable. Dynamic reconfiguration certainly became the necessary technique because it provides adaptability and flexibility by reconstructing system components. Dynamic reconfiguration of component based wireless computing system consists of modifying the configuration of components of a system during runtime. As system can execute dynamic reconfiguration, system can have ability to easily adapt to new environment and to be more easily extensible. Therefore, the development of dynamic reconfiguration is essential for wireless computing systems. But dynamic reconfiguration has crucial problems, performance, QoS and fault tolerance. We need efficient management for dynamic reconfiguration to solve these problems. We propose an efficient method to manage dynamic component reconfiguration using the dependency relations between components for wireless computing systems. Performance analysis shows that our scheme can reduce execution time and down-time by considering dependency between components.

1 Introduction

Nowadays, many mobile users communicate each other through various wireless devices, e.g., laptop, PDA, and mobile phone. Many users and machines continuously request various kinds of the services. Furthermore, sometimes client requests service that system can not provide properly at the moment with current system state. Therefore the middleware system for wireless computing has to provide service to adapt to the changeable requirement of various users and wireless environments. We can obtain high availability, flexibility, adaptability, and easy extensibility of system such as enterprise Java-Beans, Component Object Model, and the CORBA Component can adopt dynamic reconfiguration scheme for wireless computing systems where adapta-

* This research is supported by the Ubiquitous Computing and Network (UCN) Project, the Ministry of Information and Communication (MIC) 21st Century Frontier R&D Program in Korea.

bility and flexibility are essential. Dynamic reconfiguration of component based wireless computing system will take an important role for providing high availability of future wireless computing systems.

Main issues during dynamic reconfiguration are minimizing the down-time of the system caused by the reconfiguration as well as maintaining the consistency of the system. Thus techniques are required which determine the parts of the system to be halted during reconfiguration while the other parts of the system continue execution during reconfiguration [2].

Another issue is considering dynamic dependency that provides important information for implementing fault tolerance and smooth exception handling in an environment of distributed components. Dependency of the interactions between system and application components allows system software to recognize the need of reconfiguration to support better fault tolerance, security, quality of service (QoS), and optimization. In addition, dynamic dependency lets system software reconfiguration with minimal impact on wireless computing system performance without compromising system stability and reliability [3].

Furthermore, dynamic reconfiguration is very complex because it evolves the configuration of a system during runtime. It is difficult to know exactly the interface of every component and to forecast the relationship between components accurately in the evolve system. There is a trade-off between stability and functionality. If dynamic reconfiguration that influences on the total system occurs many times, the system is difficult to guarantee stability. On the contrary if dynamic reconfiguration occurs frequently, the system can not provide stable QoS.

In this paper, we propose efficient dependency management of dynamic reconfiguration for wireless computing system to select proper reconfiguration between reconfiguration schemes according to state of dependency between components. As a result we can obtain safety and efficient reconfiguration for wireless computing system. Our dynamic reconfiguration scheme choose simple scheme when no dependency is found while complex one when many dependencies are found. Also, our dynamic reconfiguration scheme choose simple scheme when simple reconfiguration is advantageous situation.

2 Related Works

In this section, we describe the CCM(CORBA Component Model) and the basic dynamic reconfiguration. And we describe the component dependence of the dynamic reconfiguration.

2.1 CORBA Component Model

CCM components are basic building blocks in a CCM system. Component developers define the IDL interfaces that support component implementations using CCM. CCM components provide four types of mechanisms that consist of facets, receptacles, event sources/sinks and attributes. Facet is interface that component provides. Before client components request server component, it must know the reference of target object. Receptacle in the CCM is reference that object connect with client component. Receptacle provides a standard way to specify interfaces required for the component to function correctly [4]. Event source/sink is generated by components. Components can generate two forms of events. First, component publishes declaration that uses single component. Second, component emits declaration that uses an existing channel shared by multiple suppliers to broadcast events. Also, components can receive events generated by other components. Attribute is to enable component configuration. Attributes can be used by configuration tools to preset configuration values of a component.

Fig. 1 illustrates the architecture of the container programming model. The container consists of CORBA component, POA. The CORBA usage model is controlled by policies that specify distinct interaction patterns with the POA and a set of CORBA services. CORBA components rely on the automatic activation features of the POA to tailor the behavior of the components. The client's requests are routed by the ORB to the POA that created the reference and the component container. This enables the container to control activation and passivation for components, and invoke interfaces on the component as necessary [7]. Therefore, the request can not directly access to the components. The container intercepts invocation requested from the client. As a result, the client always accesses the component through passing the container.

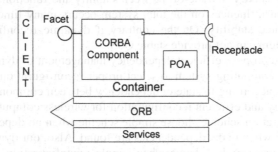

Fig. 1. The architecture of the container model

2.2 Dynamic Reconfiguration

The purpose of dynamic reconfiguration is to make a running system evolve the current configuration in the wireless computing. Dynamic reconfiguration should execute as minimal impact possible on the wireless computing system operation. Therefore, systems do not have to reboot or restart to admit changing requests. Assurance of system consistency is a major issue of reconfiguration. A system can not be useful, if the assurance of consistency is not satisfied. The reconfiguration system must assure in a "correct" state after reconfiguration. In order to support the notion of correctness of a distributed system, three aspects of consistency assurance requirements are identified. A system is said correct if the system maintains its structural integrity requirements, the components in the system satisfy mutually consistent states, and the application state invariants keep [1]. It needs the reasoning technique and the information of invocation.

As an upper's contents, dynamic reconfigurable system for wireless computing requires more accurate than static reconfiguration system. However, dynamic reconfiguration is very complex because it evolves the configuration of a system during runtime which has high variability. So, how to treat interactions between the target component and other affected components [3]. Also, developer must consider a lot of conditions to make the accurate dynamic reconfiguration system. Fig. 2 illustrates an example of reconfiguration of banking system. Fig. 2 shows changing components of Account database, Update account, and Replica component to OLTP(Online Transaction Processing) component. OLTP conduct transaction processing through computer network. In large scale wireless computing, efficient OLTP depends on transaction management software and database optimal technique to facilitate the execution of concurrent updates OLTP database. Also, OLTP can distribute transaction processing among many computers on a network. Therefore, system after reconfiguration is more efficient than previous reconfiguration system.

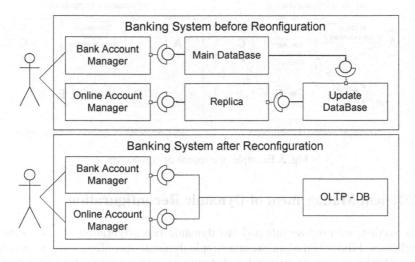

Fig. 2. Component based banking system

2.3 The Component Dependence of Dynamic Reconfiguration

The system is consistent after dynamic reconfiguration only if the system manages every dependencies relation between components. However, the component based current models do not require explicit specification of dependencies among components and do not manage the dependencies, either. However, if dependencies between components are not explicitly specified, it is difficult to build a robust component based system, especially for a dynamically reconfigurable system [3]. As a result, the component based current models can not assure that system is always consistent unless it considers dependencies of components. This is the reason why it needs dependence management.

Generally, there are four executions of dynamic reconfiguration. They are addition of a component, update of a component, removal of a component and migration of a component. Fig. 3 is an example of dependence graph of dynamic reconfiguration. It shows removal of component. At the (a), the reconfiguration occurs and component B removes. And then, the system redeploys the dependencies of components for the robust system at the (b). At the (c), system knows interfaces in the other components and dependencies of modified component. And the system can remove existing interfaces before reconfiguration. (d) is completion of dynamic reconfiguration.

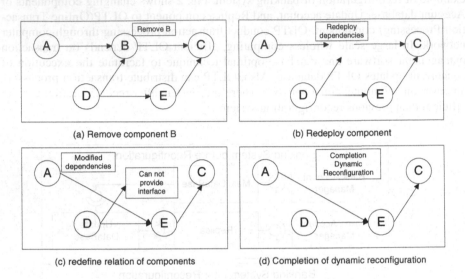

(a) Remove component B   (b) Redeploy component

(c) redefine relation of components   (d) Completion of dynamic reconfiguration

Fig. 3. Example of removal of component

3   Efficient Management of Dynamic Reconfiguration

In this section, we propose safe and fast dynamic reconfiguration of system through two schemes. First scheme can execute simple dynamic reconfiguration of the system using IIDR(Invocation inspector for dynamic reconfiguration). Second scheme is executing reconfiguration of whole system using database written by IIDR. It considers frequency about the number of components of whole systems used.

3.1   Basic Concept of Management

We divide reconfiguration schemes into simple and complex dynamic reconfiguration. Simple reconfiguration is not impact on whole system performance. Usually simple reconfiguration accomplishes alone without impact on other components. The simple reconfiguration can easily keep the consistent system without any condition during evolving system. But, our proposed system needs an execution of dynamic reconfiguration of whole system when system is not busy. So, system needs complex reconfiguration that influential with the total system. And complex reconfiguration has to minimize the down-time of the system caused by the reconfiguration. Also complex reconfiguration must keep the consistent system with various conditions during evolving system. Therefore, the complex reconfiguration is slower than simple reconfiguration. The general reconfiguration system executes complex reconfiguration always. This paper proposes system that reduces complex reconfiguration using simple reconfiguration.

3.2 IIDR (Invocation Inspector for Dynamic Reconfiguration)

Fig. 4 illustrates the location of the IIDR. The IIDR is attached in every container. As a result, the IIDR can inspect all invocation, because all invocation can only access the components through the container. The function of IIDR is divided into two parts. The first, the IIDR inspects invocation which the client sends to the server component. The second, the IIDR updates checked information of invocation at DB. IIDR inspects invocation which the client sends to the server component. Then, IIDR stores invocation information at DB.

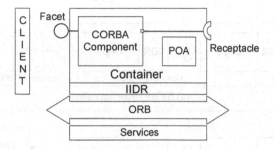

Fig. 4. The location of the IIDR

The sequence of algorithm is contents as follows.

1. IIDR inspects intercepted invocation, if container intercepts invocation requested from the client. Then, IIDR increment the dependence level of the invocation whenever client component invokes component. For an example, the dependence level of invocation is zero, if invocation executes via only one step. The dependence level of invocation is five, if invocation executes via six steps.
2. IIDR returns the value of the invocation in the component called to the last of sequential invocations to the client. IIDR updates information of invocation which the last component returns values to the client at the same time. The information of invocation consists of invocation name, last component reference(name), timestamp and dependence level.
3. The IIDR retrieves the component from stored DB, if the reconfiguration occurs. The IIDR selects the biggest dependence level of retrieved component. As a result, system easily knows dependence relation of the component.
4. The IIDR can calculate the amount of system usage by requirement of system manager. We can know system usage that IIDR calculates the number of usage, denoted as n_{usage}, from the dependence level, equation written as (1), of each invocation.

$$n_{usage} = \sum_{i=1}^{n}(l_{(i)}+1) \tag{1}$$

3.3 Advantages of the System Using IIDR

The system can directly execute reconfiguration such as addition, update, removal and migration of the component without any condition when dependence level is 0. Also, the system can execute simple reconfiguration instead of complex, if dependence level is bigger than 0. The system adds the design activity at configuration information at the same time as reference [1]. Afterwards, the system executes complex reconfiguration that redeploys all components. System manager determines the time of the system to be halted during reconfiguration refer to the amount time of system usage.

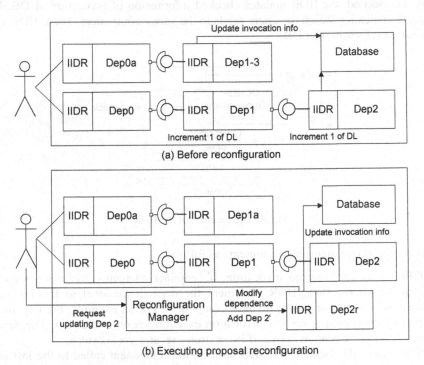

(a) Before reconfiguration

(b) Executing proposal reconfiguration

Fig. 5. The dynamic reconfiguration using the IIDR

Fig. 5 shows the adaptive+ dynamic Reconfiguration using the IIDR. At the (b), client requests reconfiguration that updates Dep2 component(dependence level of Dep2 is not zero). But the reconfiguration manager executes addition of new Dep2r component. Then the manager makes the new relation of components. Dep2r component provides service instead of Dep2 component that will update. Dep2r component has not dependency relation between other components. System satisfies new requirement through execute simple reconfiguration instead of complex reconfiguration. As a result, simple reconfiguration of system can satisfy new requirement of client.

Consequently, our proposed system has three advantages and two disadvantages. The advantages are none down-time, high consistency, and good performance. The disadvantages are requiring memory for many components, and complex dependence graph. However, our proposed system can solve two disadvantages as mentioned above. The system executes simple reconfigurations, after system executes reconfiguration of the whole system when system is not busy.

4 Analysis

In this section, we analyze the performance of regular system, complex reconfiguration and simple reconfiguration using the IIDR. The regular system is not reconfiguration system. After that we analyze performance of our dynamic reconfiguration scheme that can select schemes between simple and complex reconfiguration schemes. As mentioned in Subsection 3.3, total cost time of simple reconfiguration system using IIDR is smaller than general reconfiguration system. We will prove it. We assume that we execute very huge scientific computation. In this execution, by cost analysis we also assume parameters as follows: total executing time in the regular system(T_{total}), executed time before reconfiguration(t), multiple speedup after reconfiguration(s), required time for reconfiguration($T_{reconfig}$), probability of occurring fault reconfiguration(p_{fault}), and probability of occurring failure reconfiguration($p_{failure}$). When dynamic reconfiguration can not support the notion of correctness of a distributed system, it is necessary to perform reconfiguration again fault reconfiguration. The probability of failure reconfiguration is that the system needs to restart. When system does not know the system state exactly after reconfiguration, system must restore initial state of system. Also, when system writes incorrect value at database, system has to restore state of initial system. The total execution time of four kinds of systems is given by the following equations:

$$C(t)_{regular} = T_{total} \cdot \tag{2}$$

$$C(t)_{reconfig\_complex} = \frac{T_{total} - t}{s} + t + T_{reconf\_complex}(1 + p_{fault}) \cdot \tag{3}$$

$$C(t)_{reconfig\_complex} = \frac{T_{total} - t}{s} + t + T_{reconf\_complex}(1 + p_{fault}) + C(t)_{reconfig\_complex} \, p_{failure} \cdot$$

$$\Rightarrow C(t)_{reconfig\_complex} = \frac{1}{1 - p_{failure}} [\frac{T_{total} - t}{s} + t + T_{reconf\_complex}(1 + p_{fault})] \cdot \tag{4}$$

$$C(t)_{reconfig\_simple} = \frac{T_{total} - t}{s} + t + T_{reconf\_simple} \cdot \tag{5}$$

Equation (2) shows total executing time in regular system. Equation (3) shows in complex reconfiguration system including p_{fault}, equation (4) shows in complex reconfiguration system including $p_{failure}$ as well as p_{fault}, and equation (5) shows total execution time of simple reconfiguration system when no dependency is found. As these equations, we can know that simple reconfiguration is faster than complex reconfiguration. We assume that parameters of total executing cost of regular system, reconfiguration time, the probability of fault reconfiguration, and the probability of failure reconfiguration as shown in Table 1 which is also shown in fig. 6, 7 and 8.

Table 1. System parameters

variable	value
T_{total}	100(second)
$T_{reconfig\_complex}$	3(second)
$T_{reconfig\_simple}$	1(second)
p_{fault}	2%
$p_{failure}$	4%

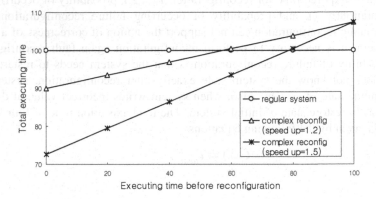

Fig. 6. Total executing time of complex reconfiguration system

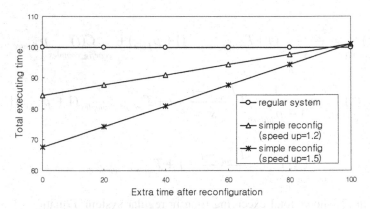

Fig. 7. Total executing time of simple reconfiguration system

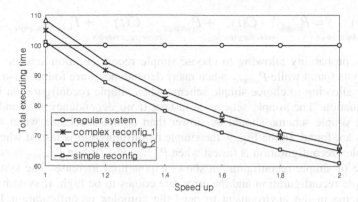

Fig. 8. Total executing time of regular system, complex reconfig_1, complex reconfig_2, and simple reconfig according to speedup (Complex reconfig_1 includes Γ_{fault} and complex reconfig_2 includes $\Gamma_{failure}$. Executing time before reconfiguration is 20s)

Total executing time of regular system is always fixed. The simple reconfiguration is faster than complex reconfiguration because simple reconfiguration does not includes $T_{reconf} \times (1 + p_{fault}) + \underset{reconfig}{C(t)} \times p_{failure}$. In the Fig. 6 and 7, if the executed time before reconfiguration (t) is smaller and speed up(s) is bigger, the reconfiguration system gets smaller cost. And, if the executed time before reconfiguration is too small, reconfiguration system is slower than regular system. In the Fig. 8, simple reconfiguration is fastest among the reconfiguration system. Therefore, proposed reconfiguration system using IIDR is faster than general reconfiguration system using complex reconfiguration if simple reconfiguration often.

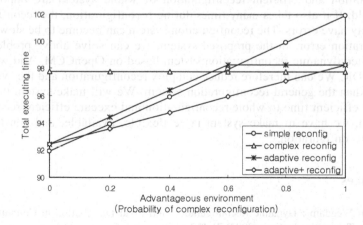

Fig. 9. Total executing time of simple, complex, adaptive, and adaptive+ reconfiguration system according to advantageous environment of probability of complex reconfiguration. Complex reconfiguration includes P_{fault} and $P_{failure}$. ($P_{simple}=1-P_{complex}$. $T_{select\_reconfig}$ is time of choosing reconfiguration scheme. It is 0.5s in adaptive reconfiguration and adaptive+ reconfiguration. Speed up is 10%).

$$C(t) \atop reconfig\_adaptive+ = P_{simple} \quad C(t) \atop reconfig\_simple + P_{complex} \quad C(t) \atop reconfig\_complex + T_{select\_reconfig} \cdot \qquad (6)$$

P_{simple} is probability allowing to choose simple reconfiguration scheme when no dependency is found while $P_{complex}$ when many dependencies are found. Also, P_{simple} is probability allowing to choice simple scheme when simple reconfiguration is advantageous situation. The simple scheme is fastest, if no dependency is found through IIDR. But, simple scheme should be slower than complex scheme when many dependencies are found. In the Fig. 9, the simple reconfiguration is fastest when $P_{complex}$ is 0. Complex reconfiguration is fastest when $P_{complex}$ is 1. When $P_{complex}$ is not 0, executing time of simple reconfiguration shows exponential increase. The system must repeat simple reconfiguration and the error rate comes to be high, if system executes simple scheme in the environment to need the complex reconfiguration. If system does not find out dependency between component relationship, complex reconfiguration should be used. However, our scheme can execute dynamic reconfiguration through IIDR. Our adaptive reconfiguration scheme shows that adaptive reconfiguration choose simple scheme when no dependency is found while complex one when dependency is found. Equation (6) shows adaptive+ reconfiguration. Our adaptive+ reconfiguration scheme can execute simple reconfiguration instead of complex reconfiguration. Adaptive and adaptiv+ scheme add $T_{select\_reconfig}$. Adaptive+ scheme is generally faster than other schemes except $P_{complex}$ is 1 or 0.

5 Conclusion and Future Works

As mentioned it, the general dynamic reconfiguration system has many weaknesses. Especially, occurrence of down-time is very important because system interrupts many requests of client during reconfiguration. Therefore, the determining time of reconfiguration and efficient reconfiguration of whole system are important research field. If it also takes many times during reconfiguration, the reconfiguration system may have errors. The reconfiguration system can become to be slow through reconfiguration error. In the proposed system, we can solve above problems. We implemented dynamic reconfiguration system based on OpenCCM. And we implemented IIDR. We can therefore reduce complex reconfiguration and the system can be faster than the general reconfiguration system. We will make system that determines the efficient time to whole reconfiguration and execute efficient reconfiguration. Also, we have to make system more flexible, available, and consistent for dynamic reconfiguration.

References

1. Maarten Wegdam : Dynamic Reconfiguration and Load Distribution in Component Middleware. Telematica Institut. (2003) 71-112
2. J. Matevska-Meyer, W. Hasselbring, R. Reussner : Exploiting Protocol Information for Speeding up Runtime Reconfiguration of Component-Based Systems. 8th International Workshop on Component-Oriented Programming(WCOP 2003), Darmstadt, Germany. (2003)

3. Xuejun Chen : Dependence management for dynamic reconfiguration of component-based distributed systems. 17th IEEE International Conference Automated Software Engineering(ASE 2002), Edinburgh UK. (2002) 279-284

4. Nanbor Wang, Douglas C. Schmidt, Carlos O'Ryan : Overview of the CORBA Component Model. Component-based software engineering: putting the pieces together. (2001) 557-571

5. Fabio Kon, Roy H.campbell : Dependence Management in Component-Based Distributed System. IEEE Concurrency, Vol. 8, Number. 1. (2000) 26-36

6. Marlon Vieria, Debra Richardson : Analyzing Dependencies in Large Component-Based System, 17th IEEE International Conference Automated Software Engineering 2002, Edinburgh UK. (2002) 241-244.

7. OMG : CORBA Component Model Specification. (2002)

Non-uniform Information Transmission for Minimum Distortion in Wireless Networks

Tongtong Li, Huahui Wang, and Jian Ren

Department of Electrical and Computer Engineering
Michigan State University, East Lansing, MI 48864-1226, USA
{tongli, wanghuah, renjian}@egr.msu.edu

Abstract. This paper considers average input-output distortion minimization through joint optimization of source index assignment and modulation design. First, we derive the general optimization criterion, and discuss the possibility of simultaneous minimization of bit-error-rate (BER) and distortion. Secondly, we propose a novel source-aware information transmission approach by exploiting the non-uniformity in Gray-coded constellations. The proposed approach makes it possible for simultaneous BER and distortion minimization and outperforms the existing schemes with big margin when the original geometric structure of the quantization codebook can not be maintained in information transmission. The simplicity and power efficiency of the proposed source-aware non-uniform information scheme make it particularly attractive for systems with tight power constraints, such as wireless sensor networks and space communications.

1 Introduction

Given a source with rate R bits/second and a channel with capacity C bits/second, Shannon's well known channel capacity theorem says that if $R < C$, then there exists a combination of source and channel coders such that the source can be communicated over the channel with fidelity arbitrarily close to perfect. This theorem essentially implies that the source coding and channel coding are fundamentally *separable* without loss of performance for the overall system.

Following the *"separation principle"*, in most modern communication systems, source coding and channel coding are treated independently. In other words, source representation is designed disjointly from information transmission. After A/D conversion of analog source signals, the bit streams are then *uniformly* encoded and mapped to symbols prior to transmission, uniform bit-error-rate (BER) has been serving as one of the most commonly used performance measures. However, for systems with analog inputs, the ultimate goal of the communication system is to minimize the overall input-output distortion. While BER plays the dominant role in distortion minimization, a communication system that minimizes the BER does not necessarily minimize the overall input-output distortion. Therefore, novel system design that can achieve simultaneous BER and distortion minimization is highly desirable.

X. Cheng, W. Li, and T. Znati (Eds.): WASA 2006, LNCS 4138, pp. 394–403, 2006.

In [1], with no specifications on the modulation schemes, Zeger proposed a locally optimal index assignment (source coding) solution for minimum input-output distortion, known as pseudo-Gray coding. Pseudo-Gray coding provided an effective approach in reducing the average distortion of a vector quantized system by rearranging the positions of code vectors in a given codebook. Various channel-optimized quantizers, multistage vector quantizers have been studied in [2,3,4]. On the other hand, assuming source index assignment has been done separately, and with the observation that the bits come out of the source encoder are generally non-uniform (i.e. have different levels of significance), Masnick, Wolf [5] and Cover [6] introduced non-uniform modulation (index mapping) schemes, known as unequal error protection codes, for which the more important bits have lower error rate than other bits. Stemmed from [5,6], unequal error protection through both symmetric and asymmetric constellations have been further developed in [7], [8] and [9]. It should be pointed out that the resulted constellation codeword design in [7,8,9] may no longer be Gray codes.

In this paper, taking a mixed analog-digital perspective, we consider average input-output distortion minimization through joint optimization of source index assignment and modulation design. *First*, we derive the general optimization criterion, and discuss the possibility of simultaneous minimization of BER and distortion, which essentially requires that the quantization codebook and the modulation constellation be of the same dimensionality. *Secondly*, based on the fact that Gray code ensures minimum BER when the channel error probability is sufficiently small, we propose a novel source-aware information transmission approach by exploiting the non-uniformity in Gray-coded constellations. The proposed approach makes it possible for simultaneous BER and distortion minimization and outperforms the existing schemes with big margin when the original geometric structure of the quantization codebook can not be maintained in information transmission. The simplicity and power efficiency of the proposed source-aware non-uniform information transmission scheme make it particularly attractive for systems with tight power constraints, such as wireless sensor networks and space communications.

2   Problem Formulation

Consider a digital communication system with analog input, as shown in Fig. 1. Let $\mathbf{x}_k$ be the discrete-time analog input vector resulted from uniform sampling of a continuous signal $x(t)$. $\mathbf{x}_k$ is first fed into a quantizer Q, which is a mapping of n-dimensional Euclidean space $\mathbf{R}^n$ to a finite set $P \subset \mathbf{R}^n$, given by $Q : \mathbf{R}^n \rightarrow P$, where $P = \{P_0, P_1, \cdots, P_{M-1}\}$ is the quantization codebook with $P_i \in \mathbf{R}^n$ for $0 \leq i \leq M - 1$. We assume that the size of P is $|P| = M = 2^m$, where $m \geq 0$ is an integer. Let $\mathbf{y}_k = Q(\mathbf{x}_k)$ denote the quantization value of $\mathbf{x}_k$, $\mathbf{y}_k$ is coded into a binary sequence through an index assignment function π, and is then fed into a source-aware digital channel encoder and a modulator, i.e., the most significant bits (MSB) and least significant bits (LSB) would be treated distinctly. Let $\hat{\mathbf{y}}_k$ denote the receiver output, which is an estimate of the quantization value $\mathbf{y}_k$, the averaged input-output distortion is then given by

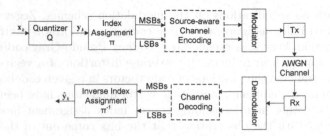

Fig. 1. System Model

$$D_0 = E\{d(\mathbf{x}_k, \hat{\mathbf{y}}_k)\}, \tag{1}$$

where $d : \mathbf{R}^n \times \mathbf{R}^n \to \mathbf{R}$ is a non-negative function that measures the distance between two vectors in $\mathbf{R}^n$.

Consider the widely used mean-square distortion function $d(\mathbf{x}, \mathbf{y}) = \|\mathbf{x} - \mathbf{y}\|^2$. In this case, the optimal quantizer satisfies the well-known nearest neighbor and centroid conditions [1,10]. The overall distortion D_0 can then be decomposed into two parts, namely, the distortion due to quantization noise, and the distortion due to channel noise [11], denoted as $\mathbf{n}_q$ and $\mathbf{n}_c$, respectively. That is,

$$\mathbf{x}_k - \hat{\mathbf{y}}_k = \underbrace{(\mathbf{x}_k - \mathbf{y}_k)}_{\mathbf{n}_q} + \underbrace{(\mathbf{y}_k - \hat{\mathbf{y}}_k)}_{\mathbf{n}_c}$$

When the quantizer satisfies the centroid condition, $E\{\mathbf{n}_q\} = 0$. Note that the quantization noise and the channel noise are independent, we have $E\{\mathbf{n}_q\mathbf{n}_c^H\} = E\{\mathbf{n}_c\mathbf{n}_q^H\} = 0$. It then follows that

$$\begin{aligned} D_0 &= E\{\|\mathbf{n}_q\|^2\} + E\{\|\mathbf{n}_c\|^2\} \\ &= E\{\|\mathbf{x}_k - \mathbf{y}_k\|^2\} + E\{\|\mathbf{y}_k - \hat{\mathbf{y}}_k\|^2\}. \end{aligned} \tag{2}$$

When the quantizer is optimal, the distortion due to quantization error is minimized. Minimization of D_0 is thus reduced to minimizing the distortion only due to the channel noise

$$D = E\{d(\mathbf{y}_k, \hat{\mathbf{y}}_k)\}. \tag{3}$$

In the sequel, we will discuss joint source index assignment and constellation codeword design for minimum distortion, as well as non-uniform transmission based on Gray-coded constellations.

3   Joint Source Index Assignment and Constellation Code Design

In this section, we consider to minimize the distortion $D = E\{\|\mathbf{y}_k - \hat{\mathbf{y}}_k\|^2\}$ through joint design of source index assignment and index mapping.

Write $\mathbf{y}_k$ as $\mathbf{y}_k = \hat{\mathbf{y}}_k + \mathbf{e}_k$, where $\mathbf{y}_k, \hat{\mathbf{y}}_k \in P = \{P_0, P_1, \cdots, P_{M-1}\}$, and $\mathbf{e}_k$ is the estimation error. For $0 \le i \le M-1$, define $E_i = \{P_i - P_j, \; 0 \le j \le M-1\}$, it then follows that

$$
\begin{aligned}
D &= E\{\|\mathbf{y}_k - \hat{\mathbf{y}}_k\|^2\} \\
&= \sum_{i=0}^{M-1} \sum_{j=0}^{M-1} \|P_i - P_j\|^2 \, p(\hat{\mathbf{y}}_k = P_j | \mathbf{y}_k = P_i) \, p(\mathbf{y}_k = P_i) \\
&= \sum_{i=0}^{M-1} p(\mathbf{y}_k = P_i) \sum_{\mathbf{e}_k \in E_i} \|\mathbf{e}_k\|^2 \, p(\mathbf{e}_k).
\end{aligned} \tag{4}
$$

Here $p(x)$ denote the probability that x occurs.

For efficient transmission, each quantizer output $\mathbf{y}_k$ is first coded to a binary sequence then mapped to a symbol in a constellation Ω. When the signal-to-noise ratio (SNR) is reasonably high, as it is for most useful communication systems, each transmitted symbol is more likely to be mistaken for one of its neighbors than for far more distant symbols. Therefore, to minimize the distortion D, the optimal index assignment and constellation codeword design should map the neighboring quantization vectors from the quantization codebook P to neighboring symbols in constellation Ω. More specifically, the optimal 1-1 mapping $S : P \to \Omega$ should satisfy the following condition:

(C1) Let $P_i, P_j, \tilde{P}_i, \tilde{P}_j \in P$, then $d(P_i, P_j) \le d(\tilde{P}_i, \tilde{P}_j)$ if and only if $d(S(P_i), S(P_j)) \le d(S(\tilde{P}_i), S(\tilde{P}_j))$.

That is, ideally, an isomorphic mapping that reserves the geometric structure should exist between the quantization codebook P and the constellation Ω. When the quantizer is optimal, and the constellation is Gray coded, condition (C1) ensures the equivalence between minimizing the BER and minimizing the average distortion D.

Next we look at the necessary conditions for the existence of S that satisfies (C1). First, assume that the size of the constellation $|\Omega| = |P| = M$, and then look at the case when $|\Omega| < |P|$.

We start with systems equipped with scalar quantizers and two-dimensional constellations. Consider a system with a 4-bit uniform scalar quantizer and a 16-QAM constellation, see Fig. 2. Since $P = \{P_0, P_1, \cdots, P_{15}\} \subset \mathbf{R}$, without loss of generality, assume $P_0 < P_1 < \cdots < P_{15}$. As can be seen, each P_i has at most two nearest neighbors, but a symbol in a 16-QAM constellation can have as many as 4 nearest neighbors. It is then impossible to find an $S : P \to \Omega$ that satisfies (C1).

In fact, assuming there is an $S : P \to \Omega$ that satisfies (C1), then we should have

$$
d(S(P_0), S(P_{15})) = \max_{x_1, x_2 \in \Omega} d(x_1, x_2), \tag{5}
$$

$$
d(S(P_0), S(P_1)) = d(S(P_{14}), S(P_{15})) = \min_{x_1, x_2 \in \Omega} d(x_1, x_2), \tag{6}
$$

$$
d(S(P_1), S(P_{14})) \ge \max_{P_i, P_j \in P} \{d(S(P_i), S(P_j))\}, \quad i, j \ne 0, 1, 14, 15. \tag{7}
$$

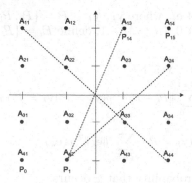

Fig. 2. Mapping of quantized values to the 16-QAM constellation

Without loss of generality, assume $S(P_0) = A_{41}$, $S(P_{15}) = A_{14}$, as illustrated in Fig. 2. Now consider the pair P_1 and P_{14}. For (6) to be satisfied, P_1 and P_{14} should be mapped to the nearest neighbors of P_0 and P_{15}, respectively. Without loss of generality, assume $S(P_1) = A_{42}$. Since $d(A_{42}, A_{13}) > d(A_{42}, A_{24})$, according to (**C1**), we should have $S(P_{14}) = A_{13}$. However, this violates (7), since $d(A_{42}, A_{13}) < d(A_{11}, A_{44})$ but A_{11}, A_{44} will correspond to points from $\{P_i, i \neq 0, 1, 14, 15\}$. This implies that, to satisfy (7), P_1 and P_{14} should be mapped to the pair A_{11} and A_{44}. Clearly, this violates (6). Therefore, an S that satisfies (**C1**) does not exist.

More generally, we have:

Lemma 1. For systems utilizing scalar quantizer with codebook P and a symmetric (two-dimensional) rectangular or square constellation Ω with $|\Omega| = |P| = 2^m$, $m > 1$, there is no 1-1 mapping $S : P \to \Omega$ that satisfies (**C1**).

For the 4-bit scalar quantizer discussed above, instead of 16-QAM, consider the one-dimensional constellation 16-AM with Gray code, see Fig. 3. Still denoting

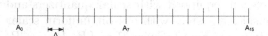

Fig. 3. Symmetric 16-AM constellation

the constellation with Ω, clearly the 1-1 mapping $S : P \to \Omega$ defined by $S(P_i) = A_i$, $0 \leq i \leq 15$, satisfies (**C1**), and it minimizes the BER and the distortion D simultaneously.

Remark 2. Our discussions in the one-dimensional case imply that simultaneous minimization of BER and distortion D essentially requires that there exists a 1-1 mapping $S : P \to \Omega_0$ which satisfies condition (**C1**), where $\Omega_0 \subseteq \Omega$ is a a real subset of Ω or Ω itself. This result provides another demonstration to the well known fact that: *the essence to obtaining larger coding gain is to design codes in* *a subspace of signal space with higher dimensionality*, as a larger minimum distance can be obtained with the same signal power. For example, two-dimensional constellation such as QAM would be a natural choice for two-dimensional vector quantizers. For multidimensional vector quantizers, multidimensional constellations would fit best [12]. In the case when $|\Omega| < |P|$, N (≥ 1) constellation symbols are needed to represent one quantization value. Again, the multidimensional signal constellation obtained from the Cartesian product Ω^N should be exploited and is currently under investigation.

Due to lack of *a priori* statistical information of the input signal, non-entropy coding is widely used for various sources in practice. That is, in each quantization codeword, some bits are more significant than other, and an error in a significant bit will result in large distortion than that in a less significant bit. This universal existence of non-uniformity in source coding calls for non-uniform information transmission, also known as unequal error protection in which the most significant bits have lower bit-error-rates than other bits. In the following, we consider source-aware non-uniform transmission design alone the line of joint source index assignment and constellation design.

4   Source-Aware Non-uniform Transmission Design

Non-uniformity exists in most constellations except BPSK and QPSK, either they are asymmetric or even if they are perfectly symmetric.

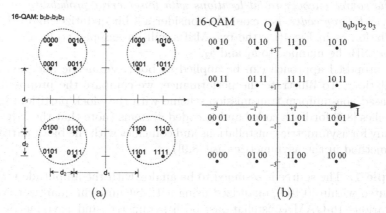

Fig. 4. (a) Asymmetric 16-QAM, $d_1 > d_2$; (b) Symmetric 16-QAM with Gray codes

Asymmetric constellations, see Fig. 4(a) for example, were originally developed for multiresolution (MR) broadcast in Digital HDTV [6,7], and further analyzed in [9]. The asymmetric constellations were designed to provide more protection to the more significant bits by grouping bits into clouds leading by the most significant bits, and the minimum distance between the clouds is larger than the minimum distance between symbols within a cloud.

For symmetric constellations, an unequal error protection scheme based on block partitioning is provided in [8], which is a generalization of the Ungerboeck's mapping by set partitioning. With block partitioning, the number of nearest neighbors is minimized for each bit level b_i. It turns out that the resulted codeword design coincide with that of the MR scheme with $d_1 = d_2$. As can be seen, constellations resulted from either block partitioning or the MR scheme may no longer be Gray-coded.

As is well known, Gray codes are developed to minimize the bit-error-rate, in which the nearest neighbors correspond to bit groups that differ by only one position. Here, we revisit the non-uniformity in constellations with Gray codes, and introduce a non-uniform transmission scheme based on Gray-coded constellations. In the following, we illustrate the idea through Gray coded 16-QAM constellation, see Fig. 4(b).

In 16-QAM, each codeword has the form $b_0b_1b_2b_3$. If we go through the 16 symbols in the constellation, there are altogether 24 nearest neighbor bit changes, among which b_0 and b_2 each changes 4 times, and b_1 and b_3 each changes 8 times. Note that when channel probability error is sufficiently small, a bit error corresponding to each bit location b_i is most likely to occur when the nearest neighbor has a different value in that specific bit location, i.e., among neighboring pairs where a change occurs. Let P_e denote the error probability, then this implies that when SNR is reasonably high, $P_e(b_0) = P_e(b_2) = \frac{1}{2}P_e(b_1) = \frac{1}{2}P_e(b_3)$. Our analysis coincides with the theoretical results in [13,14,15].

We propose to minimize the average distortion by exploiting the inherent ambiguity in Gray-coded constellations, that is, to *map the more significant bits from the source encoder to bit locations with lower error probability in constellations with Gray codes*. For example, consider a 4-bit quantizer and a 16-QAM constellation as in Fig.4(b), the two MSBs will be mapped to b_0 and b_2 while the two LSBs be mapped to b_1 and b_3.

The proposed approach can be applied to both symmetric and asymmetric constellations. To illustrate the performance, we compare the proposed Gray-code based non-uniform transmission scheme with the block partitioning based approaches [8,9] for both coded and uncoded systems (note that the MR scheme [7] is only for asymmetric constellations and coincides with the block partitioning based method in the asymmetric case [8,9]).

Example 1. The source is assumed to be analog with the amplitude uniformly distributed within [0,100], quantized using a 12-bit uniform quantizer. We consider various 16-QAM constellations, both symmetric and asymmetric. First, each 12-bit quantization output $b_0b_1\cdots b_{11}$ is partitioned into three 4-bit strings: $b_0b_1b_6b_7$, $b_2b_3b_8b_9$, $b_4b_5b_{10}b_{11}$, then mapped to both symmetric and asymmetric 16-QAM constellations based on the block partitioning (BP) scheme or the proposed Gray-code based non-uniform transmission scheme. By random index assignment, we mean that no distinction is made on MSBs and LSBs, and the strings are mapped to the Gray coded constellation based on their original bit arrangements $b_0b_1b_2b_3$, $b_4b_5b_6b_7$, $b_8b_9b_{10}b_{11}$. The result is shown in Figure 5(a).

Example 2. In this example, impact of channel coding is investigated for both systematic and non-systematic coding schemes. Using the same source as in Example 1, a 10-bit uniform quantizer is connected with a source-aware channel encoder, for which the first 4 MSBs are fed to a rate 1/3 convolutional (or Turbo) encoder and the rest 6 bits are fed to a rate 1/2 convolutional(or Turbo) encoder, respectively. The channel coding output are then mapped to 16-QAM constellations non-uniformly based on the block partitioning approach and the proposed mapping scheme. The result is shown in Figure 5(b).

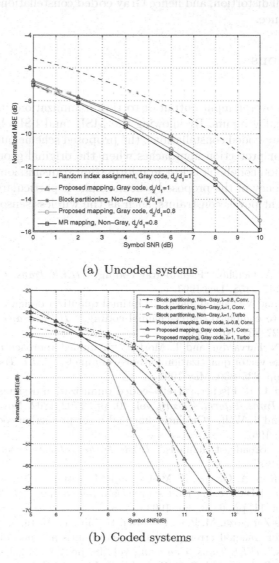

(a) Uncoded systems

(b) Coded systems

Fig. 5. MSE for different transmission schemes. (a) Example 1: Uncoded System, (b) Example 2: Coded System ($\lambda = d_2/d_1$).

Remark 3. As demonstrated by the simulation results, while the proposed approach has comparable performance with existing unequal error protection methods for uncoded systems (i.e. when there is no channel coding), the Gray-code based non-uniform transmission outperform the non-Gray-coded methods (i.e., the MR method and the block partitioning based approach) with big margins when channel coding is involved. The underlying arguments are: (i) Channel coding may change the geometric structure of the uncoded symbols; (ii) When SNR is reasonably high, BER of the MSBs vanishes, and BER of the LSBs dominates the overall distortion, and hence Gray coded constellations result in much better performance.

5   Conclusions

In this paper,we studied joint optimization of source index assignment and index mapping for overall input-output distortion minimizations in digital wireless systems with analog inputs. By allowing the MSBs and LSBs be mapped non-uniformly to Gray-coded constellations, the proposed scheme outperforms existing unequal error protection approaches when the original geometric structure of the quantization codebook is lost in information transmission. The simplicity and power efficiency of the proposed scheme make it particularly attractive for systems with tight power constraints, such as the wireless sensor networks.

References

1. K. Zeger and A. Gersho, "Pseudo-gray coding," *IEEE Trans. Commun.*, vol. 38, no. 12, pp. 2147–2158, Dec 1993.
2. N. Farvardin and V. Vaishampayan, "Optimal quantizer design for noisy channels: an approach to combined source-channel coding," *IEEE Trans. Inform. Theory*, vol. 35, pp. 827–838, Nov 1987.
3. N. Phamdo, N. Farvardin, and T. Moriya, "A unified approach to tree-structured and multistage vector quantization for noisy channels," *IEEE Trans. Inform. Theory*, vol. 39, pp. 835–850, May 1993.
4. M. Wang and T. R. Fischer, "Trellis-coded quantization designed for noisy channels," *IEEE Trans. Inform. Theory*, vol. 40, pp. 1792–1802, Nov 1994.
5. B. Masnick and J. Wolf, "On linear unequal error protection codes," vol. 13, pp. 600–607, Oct. 1967.
6. T. M. Cover, "Broadcast channels," *IEEE Trans. Inform. Theory*, vol. IT-18, pp. 2–14, Jan 1972.
7. K. Ramchandran, A. Ortega, K. M. Uz, and M. Vetterli, "Multiresolution broadcast for digital HDTV using joint source/channel coding," *IEEE J. Select Areas Commun.*, vol. 11, pp. 6–23, Jan 1993.
8. R. H. Morelos-Zaragoza, M. P. C. Fossorier, S. Lin, and H. Imai, "Multilevel coded modulation for unequal error protection and multistage decoding .i. symmetric constellations," *IEEE Trans. Commun.*, vol. 48, pp. 204–213, Feb 2000.
9. R. H. Morelos-Zaragoza, M. P. C. Fossorier, S. Lin, and H. Imai, "Multilevel coded modulation for unequal error protection and multistage decoding. ii. asymmetric constellations," *IEEE Trans. Commun.*, vol. 48, pp. 774–786, May 2000.

10. K. Zeger and A. Gersho, "Vector quantization design for memoryless noisy channels," in *Proc. IEEE Int. Conf. Commun.*, Philadelphia, PA, Jun 1988, pp. 1593–1597.
11. D. G. Messerschmitt, "Accumulation of distortion in tandem communication links," *IEEE Trans. Inform. Theory*, vol. IT-25, pp. 692–698, Nov 1979.
12. G. D. Forney and Lee-Fang Wei, "Multidimensional constellations - Part I: Introduction, figures of merit, and generalized cross constellations," *IEEE Trans. Inform. Theory*, vol. 7, pp. 877–892, Aug 1989.
13. J. Lu, K. B. Letaief, J. C-I Chuang, and M. L. Liou, "M-PSK and M-QAM BER computation using signal-space concepts," *IEEE Trans. Commun.*, vol. 47, pp. 181–184, Feb 1999.
14. L. Yang and L. Hanzo, "A recursive algorithm for the error probability evaluation of M-QAM," *IEEE Commun. Lett.*, vol. 4, pp. 304–306, Oct 2000.
15. K. Cho and D. Yoon, "On the general BER expression of one- and two-dimensional amplitude modulations," *IEEE Trans. Commun.*, vol. 50, pp. 1074–1080, Jul 2002.

A UDP-Based State-Sharing Mechanism of SIP Transaction Stateful Proxy

Luo Shi-zhang, Liao Jian-xin, and Zhu Xiao-min

State Key Laboratory of Networking and Switching Technology,
Beijing University of Posts and Telecommunications, Beijing 100876
{Luoshizhang, Liaojianxin, Zhuxiaomin}@ebupt.com

Abstract. Current IMS (IP multimedia subsystem) fault-tolerant systems only implemented state-sharing mechanism of SIP call stateful proxy. This paper proposes and implements a UDP-based state-sharing mechanism of SIP transaction stateful proxy. Based on heavy stress testing, experimental reliability figure is shown. By mathematical analysis and derivation, we proved the proposed relationship equation of T_{out} and reliability R. Experiments showed that the results of the theoretical analysis can reflect the real performance of the system, and that the theoretical and practical T_{out} breakpoint value is consistent.

Keywords: State-sharing, Fault-tolerance, Session Initiation Protocol, Reliability, UDP, transaction stateful proxy.

1 Introduction

In the 3GPP IP multimedia subsystem (IMS)[1], in order to have highly reliable Session Initiation Protocol (SIP) sessions, certain call session control function (CSCF) servers will have to support fault tolerance to improve the reliability of services. One approach is that certain CSCF servers be multipled and grouped in a pool. Within this server pool, each peer server maintains identical images of call/transaction states.

SIP contains three types of proxy servers: call stateful proxy, transaction stateful proxy and stateless proxy[2]. They extensively exist in the next generation network (NGN). Typically, Proxy-CSCF servers function as call stateful proxies, Interrogation-CSCF servers function as transaction stateful proxies; for simply and rapidly forwarding messages, stateless proxies are located in the network core.

In the process of his research, by referring to a variety of fault-resilient replication techniques[3] of distributed systems, M. Bozinovski implemented a fault-tolerant control system of call stateful proxy. In [4][5][6], he proposed a novel state-sharing algorithm. By theoretical analysis and experiments, breakpoint values on File Transfer Protocol (FTP) and Trivial File Transfer Protocol (TFTP) are obtained. Consequently, a conclusion that TFTP outperforms FTP is drawn. For ensuring the state consistency during state dissemination, a concurrency control and commitment protocol was deployed in [7][8]. A maximum availability (MA) Server Selection algorithm was proposed in [9] to dynamically choose a new server upon a failure.

M. Bozinovski implemented a fault-tolerant control system of call stateful proxy. However, he did not mention fault-tolerance of transaction stateful proxy. A typical example of transaction stateful proxy is forking proxy. To ensure all alternative

X. Cheng, W. Li, and T. Znati (Eds.): WASA 2006, LNCS 4138, pp. 404–415, 2006.

locations return final responses, a forking proxy must save the state information related to the INVITE transaction. A transaction stateful proxy concerns transaction-level states, while a call stateful proxy concerns call-level states. They differ greatly in both theory and practice. Hence, further study and implementing the transaction-level fault-tolerant system have very important and realistic significance.

In this paper, we design and implement a UDP-based multithread fault-tolerant control system of SIP transaction stateful proxy. The fault-detection and fail-over management mechanism, the format of string message packets between servers, and principles of state insertion and deletion are given and discussed subsequently. By theoretical analysis and experiments, we present the curve of reliability. Finally, the relationship equation of T_{out} and reliability R is proposed and proved. By derivation and experiments, results show that the theoretical and practical T_{out} breakpoint value is consistent.

2   State-Sharing Mechanism of Transaction Stateful Proxy

2.1   Function Model of State-Sharing Mechanism

A fault-tolerant system consists of three subsystems: state sharing, failure detection and fail-over management. The state-sharing algorithm runs at every transaction stateful proxy in a server pool, and enables servers in the pool to keep an identical image of transaction states.

The design of a state-sharing mechanism is shown in Fig.1. Host 1 and host 2 provide the same SIP functionality and run the same state-sharing mechanism. The Figure shows only two hosts, assuming two servers per pool. However, the state-sharing algorithm can be applied to larger pools.

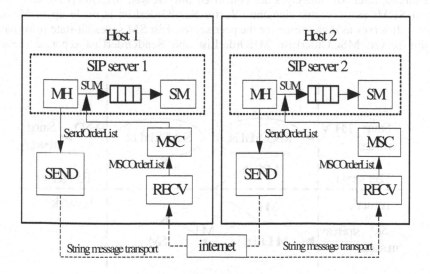

Fig. 1. Generic state-sharing block scheme

The algorithm consists of three logical components: SEND, Message-to-SUM Converter (MSC) and RECV. SEND is concerned with converting vectors, whose elements are state update message (SUM), into string messages and disseminating them to the peer server. A SUM is a data structure that consists of a number of transaction state elements. There are three mandatory elements in a SUM: caller's SIP address, callee's SIP address and call ID. The involvement of other transaction state elements depends on the specifics and requirements of the implemented state machine. RECV is concerned with receiving arrived string messages from the peer server, and converting them into vectors. MSC takes elements from vectors and adds them to state manager (SM).

We encapsulate all transaction state elements of a SUM into one string message packet. By UDP transmitting, this mechanism enables servers in a state-sharing pool to keep an identical image of ongoing calls states.

The running process of this mechanism is described as follows:

1. Message Handler (MH) creates a SUM and adds it to the input queue of SM. MH generates vector SendOrderList, which element type is SUM. SEND takes each SUM from the vector, and converts it into a string message, then sends this message to the peer server.
2. RECV listens on the peer server. On arrival of a message, it opens received message and converts it into the SUM-type vector MSCOrderList.
3. MSC takes SUM from MSCOrderList and adds them to the input queue of SM.

2.2 Implementation of State-Sharing Mechanism

Fig.2 illustrates the implementation of the multithread state-sharing mechanism. Vector MSCOrderList, whose element type is SUM, saves the output results of RECV thread. Further, it is input for MSC thread. MHOrderList is a vector too. As input of MH thread, after SIP messages are converted into SUMs, MHOrderList saves these output SUMs as its vector elements. Vector SendOrderList is made up of Message objects. It serves as data source for the peer server. List SM saves all state information of this server. MSCOrderList, MHOrderList and SendOrderList separate message

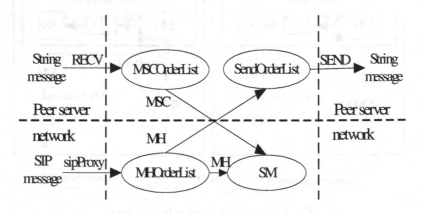

Fig. 2. Implementation of the state-sharing mechanism

reception and sending from internal data conversion, preventing data congestion and data loss caused by directly adding states to SM when heavy traffic occurs.

The state-sharing mechanism consists of 7 threads. RECV thread receives string messages from the peer server. It converts the contents of a message into a SUM. Furthermore, it adds the SUM to the vector MSCOrderList. The MSC thread takes elements from MSCOrderList and adds these SUMs to the SM (or deletes these SUMs in SM). This is referred to as remote SUM arrival. SipProxy thread receives SIP messages from network. It converts the contents of a SIP message into a SUM and pushes back the SUM at the end of the vector MHOrderList. MH thread converts MHOrderList into SendOrderList, the element type of which is Message object. Vector SendOrderList is input for the SEND. SEND thread takes Message objects from SendOrderList. It converts these objects into string messages, and sends them to the peer server using UDP. Also, after taking SUMs from MHOrderList, the MH thread queries and adds new states to the SM. It is called local SUM arrival. We distinguish between two types of SUMs, local and remote. Aside from above mentioned threads, the MONITOR thread is implemented too. By TELNET, it switches on/off the trace information of threads, realizing the monitoring function at terminals. The Main process of system generates and runs every thread after reading the configuration file.

The state-sharing mechanism is developed in UNIX environment using HP Open-Call SIP Stack v121. Threads run simultaneously, and mutex and condition variables[10] are used to organize thread synchronizations. Transaction level routines of HP Open-Call SIP Stack are called and we define SIP callback routine[11].

2.3 Format of a SUM Message

Analogously to the SC message[12], we design the format of a SUM string message shown in Fig.3. "FT" is the beginning of this message. Message Head is a 16 octet value indicating the type of operation for this SUM message. According to actual need, we can expand possible operation types. The Session Head field specifies the type of payload. If the Session Head value is "SUM", Payload field contains all elements of a SUM. If this value is "HB", this message is explained to be a heartbeat message.

Fig. 3. Format of a SUM string message between servers

2.4 Failure Detection and Fail-Over Mechanisms

Both failure detection and fail-over are initiated by user agent server (UAS). When the timer of a UAS final response (T_{out}) fires, failure is detected. Failure detection triggers the fail-over mechanism. A new server for serving the next SIP requests is chosen by applying a Server Selection Policy (SSP)[9].

According to the type of search, which is parallel or sequential, whether failure occurs in the process of searching or after successfully reaching the destination, the fail-over of forking proxy can be divided into four types. All of the four algorithms have been developed and implemented in the testbed.

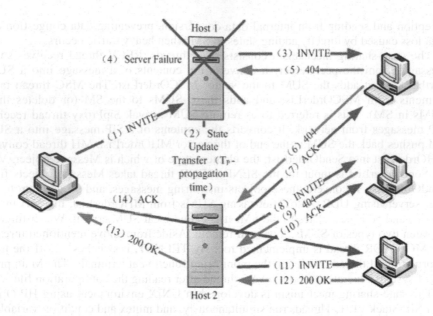

Fig. 4. A typical failure and fail-over scenario in sequential search mode

Fig.4 shows an example when failure occurs in the process of searching in the sequential search mode.

If failure occurs at step 3/8/11, the client will just retransmit this INVITE request. Hence, in this situation error processing is beyond the scope of this algorithm. When failure occurs at step 5/9, 404 final response will be retransmitted to host 1 （assuming the status code of the final response is 404）. During the time interval T_{out} if an ACK is not received, failure is detected. By applying a SSP, this final response will be retransmitted to host 2.

The fail-over algorithm pseudocode in the sequential mode is as follows:

```
If (statuscode>400)and (timeinterval>T_out)
  {//failure occurs in the process of searching
  SERVERN=SSP();//static or dynamic solution
  send (theFinalResponse,SERVERN);
   //retransmit this final response
  };
If (statuscode=200)and (timeinterval>T_out)
  {//failure occurs after reaching the target UAS
  SERVERN=SSP();
  send (200OK,SERVERN); //retransmit 200 OK
  };
```

2.5 Principles of State Insertion and Deletion

Transaction stateful proxy will not remain on the path of subsequent requests. This occurs because the endpoints have learned user's URL from the Contact header fields, thus the passing through this proxy is no longer needed. So the proxy drops out of the call flow. Transaction stateful proxy is only concerned with transaction state. When a transaction is completed, all state in this proxy will be deleted. So, in a transaction stateful proxy, we must maintain state at the transaction level.

In principle, a SIP request updates states and the final SIP response deletes these states.

INVITE: when transaction stateful proxy receives an INVITE request, transaction level states will be maintained in this proxy. Its final response (for example, 200OK) will delete these states. ACK request bypasses this proxy, so it is not need to process ACK request. Provisional responses like RING will not change states.

ACK: only forwarding. Because it can not initiate a transaction, this request will not maintain any state.

CANCEL: CANCEL request and its final response will not update any state. The explanation about INVITE and CANCEL state update principles is as follows.

When a 200(OK) are returned, its corresponding INVITE transaction is considered to complete subsequently. Hence, states should be deleted by the final response to its INVITE request. When CANCEL transaction does not complete, or CANCEL transaction complete but its INVITE transaction does not complete, states must be maintained in stateful proxy. So at this time states should not be deleted.

BYE: only forwarding. It will not maintain any states.

OPTIONS: when transaction stateful proxy receives an OPTIONS request, its transaction level states will be maintained in this proxy, and its final response will delete these states.

3 Experiment

3.1 Testbed and Experiment Condition

To evaluate performance of a UDP-based state-sharing mechanism of SIP transaction stateful proxy, we have set up an experimental testbed presented in Fig. 5. It shows a typical example when a forking proxy successfully finds the target UAS in the parallel search mode.

A server activity follows an ON/OFF process with exponential server failure and repair time distribution. The mean value of each random variable is MTTF (mean time-to-failure) and MTTR(mean time-to-repair) respectively. The UAS ring duration also follows an exponential distribution with mean $1/\mu$.

The user agent client (UAC) generates a new call request when the previous call terminates. Because the only concern of us is INVITE transactions, in experiments, the call duration was set to 0. For the purpose of simplicity, provisional responses are ignored in Fig.5.

As mentioned before, SipProxy thread receives SIP messages from network, and adds states to the end of the vector MHOrderList. Considering possible huge traffic, we adopt a batch processing method. Namely, SipProxy picks up states until collecting a fixed number of SIP messages. However, to evaluate performance, in experiments we only set the message number of each batch to the minimum 1.

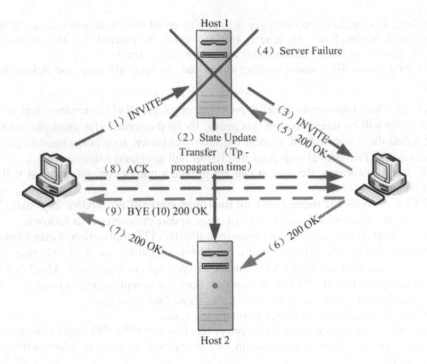

Fig. 5. Experimental testbed when finding the target UAS in the parallel search mode

In 1-proxy (without state-sharing) scenario, because SIP hop-by-hop mechanism[13] can guarantee successful session completion, reliability is 100%. When the proxy does not work, SIP messages will not reach their destinations.

In 2-proxy (with state-sharing) scenario, when the target UAS is found successfully in the parallel search, the set of fixed system parameters is shown in Table 1.

Table 1. Experiment parameters when the target UAS is found successfully in the parallel search mode

Server configuration
Processor: 2*800MHz Storage Capacity: 4Gbytes Disk Capacity: 2*72Gbyte network adaptor speed: 100Mbyte/s Operating System: HPUX11i SIP Stack development platform: HP OpenCall SIP Stack v121 Server: HP RP3410
Fixed system parameters
Call Duration: 0s   MTTR: 50s   MTTF/MTBF: 50s Collected message number of each batch: 1 UAS Mean Ring Duration: $1/\mu$=0.5s

3.2 Experimental Result

After stress testing, we achieved the delivery time of a string message between servers - T_p. Figure 6 shows the curve of T_p versus the cumulative number of propagation. The calculated reliability value is given in Table 2. Based on obtained reliability, the curve of T_{out} versus reliability is represented in Figure 7.

3.3 Result Analysis and Theoretical Derivation

The most important performance parameter is the session reliability. It is defined as the probability that an established SIP session is successfully maintained until completion.

3.3.1 Analysis of T_p Value

As shown in Fig. 6, T_p is less than 100ms at most of time. Occasionally, it will reach peak values. A peak time is several tenfold of a normal value. In this experiment, 81.9% of T_p is below 100ms, peak values beyond 200ms only account for 6.01%. That T_p peak values are excessively large is one of the main reasons for the state misread.

Table 2. System reliability values

$T_{out}(s)$	reliability(%)	$T_{out}(s)$	reliability(%)
0.2	98.2	0.4	98.51
0.6	98.73	0.8	98.98
1.0	99.32	1.2	99.62
1.4	99.79	1.6	99.86
1.8	99.89	2.0	99.9
2.2	99.92	2.4	99.925
2.6	99.925	2.8	99.93
3.0	99.93	3.2	99.93
3.4	99.93	3.6	99.935
3.8	99.935	4.0	99.935

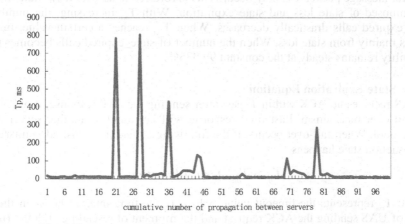

Fig. 6. T_p versus cumulative number of propagation between servers

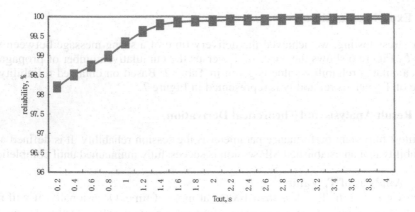

Fig. 7. T_{out} versus reliability

Experiments revealed that the main reason for the emergence of peak time is the high overhead of the multithread scheduling of operating system and long resource-waiting time.

Peak values occur in host1 and host2 during the processing of requests or string messages. T_{send}, the delay time of sending message, remains steady (between 5 and 50ms), and its average time is 15ms. Obviously, the message process time in host1- D_{proxy1}, the message process time in host2- D_{proxy2}, and the sending time T_{send} compose parameter value T_p.

3.3.2 Analysis of Reliability Value

Fig.7 illustrates the relationship between T_{out} and reliability R. As T_{out} increases, R monotonously increases. When $T_{out} \in [0.2,1.8]$, the reliability R increases significantly. When $T_{out} \in [1.8,3.2]$, it increases very slowly. If $T_{out} = 3.6$, it reaches the constant value 99.935%.

When the transport layer is UDP, during string message delivery between peer servers, message packet loss may occur. This is referred to as state loss. State misread is composed of state loss and state expiration. With T_{out} increasing, the number of state_expired calls drastically decreases. When T_{out} reaches a certain value, misread comes mainly from state loss. When the number of state_expired calls becomes 0, the reliability remains steady at the constant 99.935%.

3.3.3 State Expiration Equation

If UAS receives no ACK within T_{out} sec after sending the final response, it will trigger the fail-over mechanism. Last final response will be resent to another server in the server pool. When fail-over occurs, if the following equation is satisfied, a misread of a transaction state happens.

$$T_p > T_{out} + ringduration \quad (1)$$

Where T_{out} represents the timeout value, which is the time interval between the moment of UAS sending the ACK request and the moment of resending 200OK; ringduration denotes the ring duration value, which is the time interval between the moment of UAS receiving INVITE request and the moment of sending 200OK. (provisional responses are ignored in Fig.5); T_p denotes the time needed for propagating a SUM string message from host 1 to host 2.

Inequality (1) shows that:

①as $T_p=0$, there does not exist misread, and SIP sessions have maximum reliability1.

②as $T_{out}\downarrow$, ringduration$\downarrow$ or $T_p\uparrow$, misread probability increases.

③for given timeout value T_{out} and ringduration, as $T_p\downarrow$, SIP sessions have higher reliability. It means the higher the mechanism-efficiency or machine-performance, the shorter the propagation time of SUM string messages, and the reliability is higher.

3.3.4 Relationship Between T_{out} and Reliability

The relationship between T_{out} and reliability R is as follows: $T_{out}\uparrow$, $R\uparrow$; When T_{out} reaches a certain value, R becomes a constant value. Proof:

$$P_r(statenotfound) = P_r(T_p = \infty) + P_r(T_p > ringduration + T_{out}, T_p \neq \infty) \quad (2)$$

$$\therefore R = 1 - P_r(statenotfo und) = 1 - P_r(T_p = \infty) - P_r(T_p > ringdurati on + T_{out}, T_p \neq \infty)$$

$$= P - P_r(T_p > ringdurati on + T_{out}, T_p \neq \infty) \quad (3)$$

where P_r ($T_p=\infty$) is the state loss probability, P_r ($T_p>$ ringduration+ T_{out}, $T_p\neq\infty$) represents the state expiration probability. Obviously, P_r ($T_p =\infty$) denotes UDP packet loss rate. So, 1- P_r ($T_p =\infty$) can be denoted by the constant P.

By observing inequality Eq.1, we can find that as $T_{out}\uparrow$, P_r ($T_p >$ ringduration+ T_{out}, $T_p\neq\infty$) $\downarrow$. So that $R\uparrow$.

When $T_p\neq\infty$, because T_p- ringduration is a finite value, we can find a sufficiently large value T_{out} that will always make the inequality $T_{out} > T_p-$ ringduration satisfied. Hence, P_r ($T_p>$ ringduration+T_{out}, $T_p\neq\infty$) $=0$. By plugging this equation into Eq.1, R=P is obtained.

3.3.5 Analysis of T_{out} Breakpoint Value

T_{out} at which R first time approached constant is referred to as *breakpoint*.

$$R = P_r (statefound) = 1 - P_r(T_p > ringdurati on + T_{out}) =$$
$$P - P_r(ringdurati on < T_p - T_{out}, T_p \neq \infty) = \begin{cases} P, & T_p \leq T_{out} \\ \exp\left[-(T_p - T_{out})\mu\right] + P - 1, & T_p \geq T_{out} \end{cases} \quad (4)$$

From Eq. 4, we know: if $T_p=T_{out}$, R will reach the maximum value P; as $T_{out}\downarrow$, R monotonously decreases. When $T_{out}\in[T_p,\infty]$, R remains at the constant value P.

For the considered topology in Fig.5, and the corresponding state-sharing mechanism, the general (approximate) expression for T_p is the following:

$$T_p = D_{proxy1} + \frac{a_{message}}{B} + D_{proxy2} = na_1 + a_2 \quad (5)$$

D_{proxy1} is the INVITE message processing time in host1; the constant $a_{message}$ is interpreted as the bit number of a SUM message; B denotes the link bandwidth between servers; D_{proxy2} is the SUM string message processing time in host 2. The coefficient n is the thread number of the state-sharing mechanism; a_1 represents the mean delay of thread scheduling and waiting when peak values occur; a_2 is looked upon as the transmission delay in natural cases.

By changing the physical deployment of processes (for example, all processes including UAC and UAS run at the single host 1), we can modify the n value of Eq.3. After solving two linear matrix equations, we obtained a_1=238.6ms, a_2=88.7ms. When n=14, T_p=T_{out}=3.43s.

In practice, we did not take the breakpoint as the UAS timeout expiration value. We only set T_{out} to 1.8s. This is because at this time systemic reliability has already reached the approximate maximum- 99.89%. If reliability needs to reach constant 99.935%, it will take 1.8s more.

4 Conclusion

We proposed and implemented a UDP-based state-sharing mechanism of SIP transaction stateful proxy. Based on heavy stress testing, we represented the curve of experimental reliability values. By mathematical analysis and derivation, results showed that the theoretical and practical values are consistent.

The main contribution of this paper includes: (1) We design and implement a UDP-based multithread state-sharing mechanism of SIP transaction stateful proxy, define the format of SUM message, propose a fault-detection and fail-over management mechanism, and discuss principles of state insertion and deletion. (2) The heavy stress testing of prototype system can provide powerful data support for subsequent theoretical analysis. (3) Through mathematical analysis and experiments, we proposed relationship equation of T_{out} and reliability R. The theoretical T_{out} breakpoint value 3.43s is obtained. Results show that the theoretical value is consistent with the practical value 3.6s.

We plan to extend the experiment in two ways: (1) implementing TFTP-based transaction stateful proxy, analyzing its system performance, and comparing its performance with that of a UDP-based state-sharing mechanism. (2) Actually, using breakpoint as UAS timeout expiration value is unrealistic. We can delay a certain short time before reading states to reduce the misread rate. Devising an algorithm, which makes the read delay shortest in a certain misread rate, is an issue that could be interesting for further research.

Acknowledgments

This work is jointly supported by: (1) National Science Fund for Distinguished Young Scholars (No. 60525110); (2) Program for New Century Excellent Talents in University (No. NCET-04-0111); (3) Specialized Research Fund for the Doctoral Program of Higher Education (No. 20030013006); (4) Development Fund Project for Electronic and Information Industry (Mobile Service and Application System Based on 3G); (5) Development Fund Key Project for Electronic and Information Industry (Core Service Platform for Next Generation Network).

References

1. 3GPP TS 23.228: IP multimedia(IM) subsystem-stage 2, Technical specification, June 2001
2. Camarillo, G.: SIP Demystified. McGraw-Hill Companies, 2002
3. HELAL, A., HEDDAYA, A., and BHARGAVA, B.: Replication technique in distributed systems. Kluwer Academic Publishers, 1996
4. M. Bozinovski, L. Gavrilovska and R. Prasad.: Fault-tolerant SIP-based Call Control System. IEE Electronics Letters, Volume 39, Number 2, pp. 254-256, January 23, 2003
5. M. Bozinovski, L. Gavrilovska and R. Prasad.: A State-sharing Mechanism for Providing Reliable SIP Sessions. Telecommunications in Modern Satellite, Cable and Broadcasting Service, 2003. TELSIKS 2003. 6th International Conference on Volume 1, 1-3 Oct. 2003 Page(s): 384-387 vol.1
6. M. Bozinovski, L. Gavrilovska, R. Prasad and H.-P. Schwefel.: Evaluation of a Fault-tolerant Call Control System. Facta Universitatis Series: Electronics and Energetics, vol. 17, no. 1, pp. 33-44, April 2004.
7. Bozinovski, M., Renier, T., Schwefel, H-P., and Prasad, R.: Transaction consistency in replicated SIP call control systems. Proc. 4th Int. Conf. Information, Communications and Signal Processing, 4th IEEE Pacific-Rim Conf. On Multimedia, (ICICS-PCM), 2003, December 2003
8. M. Bozinovski, H.-P. Schwefel and R. Prasad.: Algorithm for Controlling Transaction Consistency in SIP Session Control Systems. IEE Electronics Letters, February, 2004, Vol. 40, no. 3, pp. 209-211.
9. M. Bozinovski, H.-P. Schwefel and R. Prasad.: Maximum Availability Server Selection Policy for Session Control Systems based on 3GPP SIP. In: the proceedings of Seventh International Symposium on Wireless Personal Multimedia Communications, Padova, Italy, 2004.
10. Gray, J. S.: Interprocess Communications in UNIX, Second Edition (Prentice-Hall, Inc., 1998)
11. HP OpenCall SIP stack Application Development Guide, 2003
12. Specification of Interface between BOSS and SMP, China Mobile Communications Corporation, V1.0.0, 2002
13. ROSENBER, J., et al.: SIP: session initiation protocol, RFC 3261, Internet Engineering Task Force, June 2002
14. COULOURIS, G., DOLLIMORE, J., and KINDBERG, T.: Distributed systems: concepts and design. (Addison Wesley, 2001, 3rd edn.)
15. BOZINOVSKI, M., GAVRILOVSKA, L., and PRASAD, R.: Performance evaluation of a SIP-based state-sharing mechanism. IEEE VTS 56th Vehicular Technology Conf. (VTC) 2002, Vancouver, BC, Canada, September 2002

A Novel Analog Pre-distorter of TWTA Non-linearity in High Power Satellite Transmitters

Rafik Zayani[1,2] and Ridha Bouallegue[2,3]

[1] Institut Supérieur d'Informatique / ISI
[2] Unité de recherches Systèmes de Télécommunications / 6'Tel à Sup'Com
[3] Ecole Nationale d'Ingénieur de Sousse / ENISo
rafik.zayani@laposte.net
ridha.bouallegue@supcom.rnu.tn
http://membres.lycos.f/ridhabouallegue

Abstract. OFDM systems are susceptible to HPA non-linearities in particular because of their large peak-to-average power ratios (PAPR). Several pre-distortion or post-distortion schemes for compensation these effects of nonlinearities in communications systems have been studied recently.

In this paper, we present a new analog pre-distorter to enhance the power efficiency of satellite OFDM transmitters using TWT amplifiers.

This conceptually simple technique can in linearize a HPA system quite well, if the pre-distorter and main amplifier are sufficiently well matched.

In addition, the performance of the new pre-distortion scheme for OFDM systems is evaluated in terms of spectrum and total degradation BER. Simulation results also show that our pre-distortion scheme is efficient in compensating the non-linear distortion of HPAs.

Keywords: OFDM, Pre-distorter, HPA, TWTA, SSPA.

1 Introduction

Currently, orthogonal frequency division multiplexing (OFDM) is utilized as an essential part for asymmetric digital subscriber line (ADSL) and digital audio broadcasting (DAB) [1], [2]. Moreover, OFDM is expected to be a strong candidate for wireless multimedia systems [3].

However, multicarrier systems such as OFDM show great sensitivity to nonlinear distortion. The OFDM structure requires a summation of a large number of sub-carriers for multicarrier modulation, and as a result of this summation, large signal envelope fluctuations occur. These fluctuations cause OFDM systems to be very sensitive to nonlinear distortion introduced by the high power amplifier (HPA) at the transmitter. This distortion can be mitigated by backing off the HPA from saturation; however, back off reduces the HPA output power [4] [5].

A complicated pre-distortion technique was proposed for systems using high power amplifiers (HPA) to compensate for the non-linearity.

The concept is to distort the input signals to the HPA with an inverse function of the HPA non-linearity and to generate linearly amplified signals at the HPA output.

X. Cheng, W. Li, and T. Znati (Eds.): WASA 2006, LNCS 4138, pp. 416–423, 2006.
© Springer-Verlag Berlin Heidelberg 2006

Therefore, some schemes for non-linear compensation is desirable to simultaneously reduce nonlinear distortion and the amount of back off required. Pre-distortion is one way to achieve these goals.

In this paper, we present a new analog pre-distortion scheme for compensation of nonlinear distortion in OFDM systems. The proposed pre-distortion technique connects a pre-distorting amplifier in front of the main amplifier. Compared to the compressive main amplifier, the additional has the opposite output distortion characteristic.

The results also demonstrate that our pre-distortion scheme can compensate nonlinear distortion effectively with a simple structure.

The remainder of this paper is organized as follows. In section 2, we present a description of the proposed scheme. In section 3 and 4, we describe the non-linear model for high power amplifier and pre-distorter model respectively. Section 5 presents and discusses the simulation results. The last section shows the conclusions.

2 Proposed OFDM System

The basic idea of OFDM is to transmit data on parallel QAM (Quadrature Amplitude Modulation) or QPSK (Quadrature Phase Shift Keying) modulated sub-carriers. Let N be the number of sub-carriers, $Ck, k=0...N-1$ the N complex symbols to be transmitted simultaneously, and T_s the OFDM symbol duration. The complex envelope of the ODFM base band signal is:

$$S(t) = \sum_{k=0}^{N-1} C_k e^{2i\pi k \frac{t}{Ts}}$$ (1)

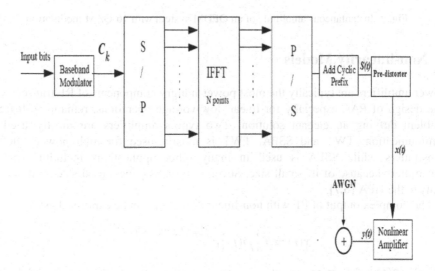

Fig. 1. Transmitter of an OFDM system with pre-distorter

The OFDM symbol can be easily generated using a IFFT algorithm, and the reception can be done with a FFT to recover the C_k symbols. The most interesting property of OFDM is that the channel equalization can be done in the frequency domain, after the FFT, and is a simple multiplication of the C_k symbols.

The OFDM system under consideration has a pre-distorter in the transmitter to compensate for nonlinear distortion of the HPA as indicated in Fig1.

The following figure presents the instantaneous amplitude of an OFDM signal (with 16-QAM modulation).

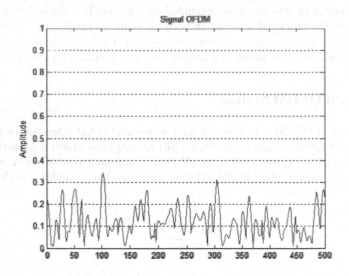

Fig. 2. Instantaneous amplitude of an OFDM system with 16-QAM modulation

3 Non-linearity Models

Power amplifiers are typically the most power-hungry components of RF transceivers. The design of PAs, especially for linear, low-voltage operations, remains a difficult problem defying an elegant solution. Two type's amplifiers are mostly used in communication: TWT and SSPA. TWT is mostly used for high power satellite transmitters while SSPA is used in many other applications including mobile transmitters because of its small size. Several previous papers used saleh's model to analyze the HPA [6,7].

The complex output of RF with non-linear distortion can be expressed as:

$$x(t) = f\left[\rho(t)\right]e^{j\left\{\varphi(t)+\phi(\rho(t))\right\}} \tag{2}$$

Where $\rho(t)$ and $\varphi(t)$ are the amplitude and phase of the input signal. The measured AM/AM and AM/PM for TWT is well presented by saleh's model [3] as:

$$\begin{cases} f(\rho(t)) = \alpha_A \rho(t) / (1 + \beta_A |\rho(t)|^2) \\ \phi(\rho(t)) = \alpha_\phi |\rho(t)|^2 / (1 + \beta_\phi |\rho(t)|^2) \end{cases} \tag{3}$$

While SSPA's AM/AM and AM/PM can be captured by [8,9]:

$$\begin{cases} f[\rho(t)] = \rho(t) / [1 + (\rho(t)/A_{max})^{2p}]^{1/2p} \\ \phi[\rho(t)] = 0 \end{cases} \tag{4}$$

Here A_{max} is the maximum output amplitude and the parameter p controls the smoothness of the transition from the linear region to the limiting region. [4]

Among the models available, here we will concentrate in describing the well-known Saleh Model for TWT memory less HPAs, which is in fact the most commonly used in the literature and thence will be applied later in our Pre-distorter model.

3.1 Saleh Model for TWT HPAs

In the expressions above, we choose to set the signal gain term to $\alpha_A = 2$, while $\beta_A = \beta_\phi = 1$ and $\alpha_\phi = \pi/3$, so that the input saturation voltage $A_s = 1/\sqrt{\beta_A}$ and the maximum output amplitude $A_{max} = \max\{f[x(t)]\} = \alpha_A A_s / 2$.

The corresponding AM/AM and AM/PM curves so scaled are depicted in the following figure.

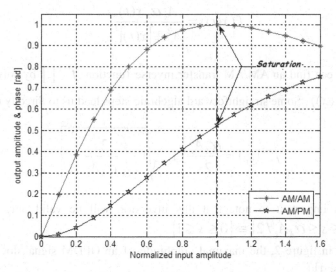

Fig. 3. AM/AM and AM/PM normalized transfer characteristics of the Saleh model for memory-less TWT HPAs

4 Analog Pre-distorter

The analog pre-distortion technique connects a pre-distorting amplifier in front of the main amplifier. Compared to the compressive main amplifier, this additional amplifier has the opposite output distortion characteristic, i.e. its nonlinearity is expansive, not compressive. These two nonlinear distortions cancel each other when summed, resulting in a linear and distortion-free output from the main RF amplifier.

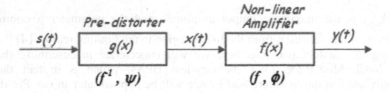

Fig. 4. Simplified pre-distorter for linearization of HPA with memory

As in figure 4, the purpose of pre-distortion is to find another pre-distortion function $g(x)$, so that the overall effect of signal output will be linear as,

$$\tilde{y}(t) = f(x(t)) = f(g(s(t)) \approx Cs(t) \tag{5}$$

The formulation of the pre-distortion, is obtained by replacing the saturation input amplitude $A_s = 1/\sqrt{\beta_A}$ in the expression (3). This gives

$$f(x(t)) = \frac{A_s^2 \alpha_A x(t)}{A_s^2 + |x(t)|^2} \tag{6}$$

Whence we can find an AM/AM transfer inverse function $f^{-1}[.]$ by solving (7) for $x = f^{-1}(f(x))$. Some straightforward algebraic steps lead us to directly obtain:

$$f^{-1}(s_t) = \frac{\alpha_A A_s^2}{2s}\left[1 - \sqrt{1 - \left(\frac{2s}{\alpha_A A_s}\right)^2}\right] \tag{7}$$

Where it is important to note that this inversion will be valid only within the interval $\{0 \leq s \leq \alpha_A A_s / 2\} \equiv \{0 \leq s \leq 1\}$.

As show in figure 2, the maximal amplitude of an OFDM signal doesn't pass 1, $\{0 \leq |s(t)| \leq 1\}$.

Wherein the AM/PM correction requires that:

$$\Psi(x) = -\Phi\left[f^{-1}(x)\right] \tag{8}$$

The corresponding AM/AM and AM/PM transfer characteristics of pre-distorter, valid for the normalized Saleh's HPA model in the interval $\{0,1\}$, is shown in the following figure.

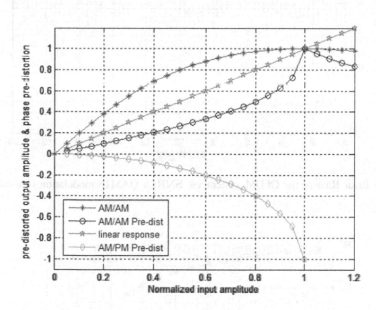

Fig. 5. AM/AM et AM/PM theoretical pre-distortion characteristics for the Saleh model

5 Simulations and Results

To simulate an OFDM system, the Matlab tool has been chosen at the level by reason of her performances of calculation and her suppleness.

The performance of the proposed pre-distorter is analyzed in an OFDM system with 48 carriers (which corresponds to the used modulation in the networks HiperLan/2) [7] and 512 carriers. We used 16-QAM modulation scheme. We also used the model in (3) with $\alpha_A = 2 \ and \ \beta_A = 1$ in the model of TWT amplifier.

The Bit Error Rate (BER) of such system vs. the Signal to Noise Ratio (SNR) is presented in the following figure, by the bend **'with corr'**. The curve by the bend **'without corr'** presents the BER of the same system without pre-distorter whereas the **'theory'** curve concerns linear systems.

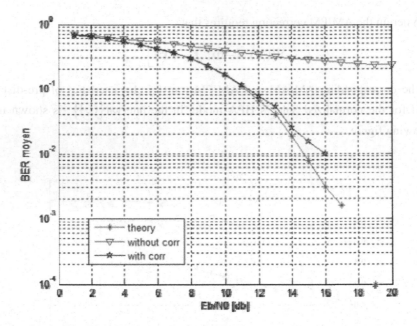

Fig. 6. Bit Error Rate of the OFDM system vs. SNR: a QAM16 modulation is used on 48 carriers

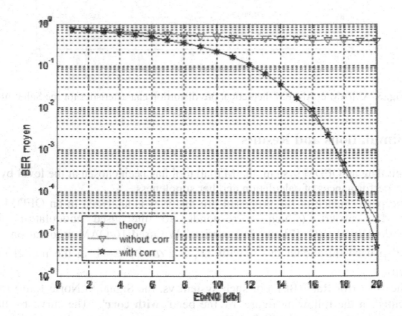

Fig. 7. Bit Error Rate of the OFDM system vs. SNR : a QAM16 modulation is used on 512 carriers

We note a real improvement of the quality of the transmission using the corrector which brings a gain of 12 dB for BER = 10^{-1}.

While increasing the number of carriers, we determine by simulation that our pre-distorter still be efficient that is for 512 carriers.

6 Conclusion

We have proposed a non-linear per-distorter to compensate non-linearity in OFDM satellite transmitters using TWT amplifier.

This conceptually simple technique can in linearize a HPA system quite well, if the pre-distorter and main amplifier are sufficiently well matched. Because of its open-loop nature, there are no stability issues and the usable bandwidth is much greater than that of closed-loop feedback systems. Because of its simplicity, this technique can be applied to microwave circuits without too great difficulties.

Simulation shows promising performance in terms of spectrum and BER.

References

[1] L. J. Cimini, «Analysis and simulation of a digital mobile channel using orthogonal frequency division multiplexing», *IEEE Trans. Communications*, vol. 33, no. 7, pp. 665–675, July 1985.

[2] S. Chang and E. J. Powers, «A simplified predistorter for Compensation of nonlinear distortion in OFDM Systems», IEEE transaction 2001.

[3] N. D'Andrea, V. Lottici and R. Reggiannin, «Nonlinear Predistortion of OFDM Signals over Frequency-Selective Fading Channels», IEEE Transactions on Communications. Vol. 49. N° 5. pp. 837-843. 2001.

[4] A. E. Jones, T. A. Wilkinson, S. K. Barton, «Block Coding Scheme for Reduction of Peak to Mean Envelop Power Ratio of Multicarrier Transmission Schemes», IEE Electronics Letters, vol. 30, no. 25, pp. 2098-2099, 1994

[5] R. zayani, S. Zid, R. Bouallegue, « Simulateur des non-linéarités HPA sur un système OFDM » OHD Conference, septembre 2005.

[6] Lei Ding, «Digital Predistortion of Power Amplifiers for Wireless Applications», a Thesis presented to the Academic Faculty, March 2005.

[7] V. Ahirwar and B. S. Rajan, « Tradeoff between PAPR Reduction and Decoding complexity in transformed OFDM System», IEEE transaction 2005.

[8] R. J. Baxley, « Analyzing Selected Mapping for Peak-to-Average Power Reduction in OFDM», a Thesis presented to the Academic Faculty, May 2005.

[9] J. G. WÄohlbier, «Nonlinear Distortion and Suppression In Traveling Wave Tubes: Insights And Methods », a Thesis presented to the Academic Faculty, 2003.

Secure Data Transmission on Multiple Paths in Mobile Ad Hoc Networks*

GeMing Xia, ZunGuo Huang, and ZhiYing Wang

School of Computer Science, National University of Defense Technology,
ChangSha, Hunan, China
victor_xgm@126.com

Abstract. In this paper, a secure data transmission scheme based on multiple paths for mobile ad hoc networks was presented. The scheme focused its attention on privacy and robustness in communication. For privacy, a coding scheme using XOR operation was established to strengthen the data confidentiality so that one can not uncover the information unless he took up all the K paths or special K-1 ones. For robustness, it educed a fault tolerant mode which combines backup with checkout, and planed a prepared distributing algorithm, by them the transmission can tolerate multiple path's dropping with moderate data redundancy, ideal path utilization, and quick data recovery.

Keywords: Mobile Ad Hoc Networks, Data Transmission, Security.

1 Introduction

Mobile ad hoc network [1] has a wide range of applications such as environment monitoring, military purposes, and field rescue. It differs from general network in many aspects such as multi-hop routing, self-organization, and dynamic topology [2]. Many fresh problems are introduced by ad hoc networks at routing, localization, synchronization, and, the security. Mobile ad hoc networks are more vulnerable in addition to common threats in wireless network [3]. The threat to MANET include passive attacking like illegitimate disclosure of information, traffic analysis, and active attacking like information injecting, messages replay, and DOS attacking.

There are four fundamental requirements of security in mobile ad hoc networks: network availability or robustness, node authenticity, data integrity, and communication confidentiality or privacy. To meet these, many researches have been developed in several issues:

Key Management. The main problems include [5]: Key Pre-distribution, Neighbor discovery, End-to-End path-key establishment, Re-keying, and Key-establishment latency. The solutions consist of Hybrid key-based protocols, Threshold cryptography [10], Certificate repository [11], and Fully Distributed Certificate Authority [12].

Secure Routing. There are many routing protocols proposed for mobile ad hoc networks, such as AODV and DSR [15]. They suffer from many vulnerabilities

---

* This research is supported by National 863 Program (Grant No. 2003AA142080).

X. Cheng, W. Li, and T. Znati (Eds.): WASA 2006, LNCS 4138, pp. 424–434, 2006.

because security features are not designed built-in [17].For secure routing in mobile ad hoc networks, the followed problems need to be solved [26]: Authentication mechanism [19], Secure route discovery and maintenance, Detecting of routing misbehavior [20], and Resisting of flooding attack [19].Many protocols have been built up for secure routing in mobile ad hoc networks: SPINS [21], Ariadne [19], etc.

Intrusion Detection. Wireless mobile ad hoc network are susceptible to many intrusions, and it requires a solution fully distributed and inexpensive in any aspect: communication, computation, and energy. Usually the use of secure groups may be an approach for decentralized intrusion detection in mobile ad hoc networks [24].

Private Data Communication. For the multi-hop routing, communication between two nodes in mobile ad hoc networks is transferred by middle node. It means that the message would be exposed to any node on the path. Further more, in a clustered MANET which applies hierarchic routing, lots of routing and management information is aggregated at cluster heads. It is matter-of-course that the location of the cluster heads to be secured, so the routing confidentiality and location privacy is required in addition [23].

Robustness to Communication. For the dynamic topology, link in mobile ad hoc networks is unstable, it require robustness to guarantee data communication. And it is necessary to address that mobile ad hoc networks is vulnerable to DOS attacks [8].ï

In this paper, we focus on private and robust data communication using multi-path. The solution consists of two parts: privacy coding and data striping & distributing. For privacy, we introduce a new method based on XOR operation, by which it be so secure that one can uncover nothing of the original data with any parts, except that he obtaining all sections transmitted separately on the multiple path. For robustness, we turn to the multiple path data forwarding [9], which is used for reliable communication in ad hoc by many research [13]. But our solution is a novel one that combines backup with checkout to meet low redundancy, quick recovery of dropped data, and need none path to act as special signaling channel.

2 Related Work

Our work relies on multi-path, which is regard as a condition in this paper. We focus on the utilizing of multi-path routing to get privacy and robustness, instead of the establishment and maintenance of it, which have been studied by many research. Reference [25] made a introduction of the multi-path in ad hoc networks. A protocol named QMPR presented by [16] use multi-path to get QOS in the ad hoc networks. The authors of [9] studied several multi-path routing schemes and proposed a new adaptive multi-path routing algorithm which is robust against Byzantine attacks. In [27], Swades De designed a meshed multi-path searching scheme suitable for mobile ad hoc networks, which reduced signaling overhead and nodal database. Especially, reference [28] did a deep research on algorithms for secure multi-path routing.

To reach robust communication on multiple paths, we use redundancy and checkout technology [4]. Backup is the most simple and strongest way to reach robustness, but the most expensive one too. To send data and its copy straightforwardly on the multiple paths will aggravate the network data load too much. Fault tolerance coding and XOR checkout is a effective method, which abroad applied on the RAID systems [14]. We referred many recent studies on multi-disk error tolerance of RAID [18, 22]. The method in [22] get the least data redundancy by graph decompositions, but the recovery cost is too expensive. Diversity Coding [6], a typical approach used for self-healing and fault tolerance in digital communication, uses multiple paths to forward the blocks of data and their checkout, so that blocks lost on some paths can be recovery from others. Diversity Coding need many path to act as special signal channel, which is not necessary in our solution.

The author of [7] introduced a new method than encryption to get privacy in ad hoc networks using multi-path, he proposed the XOR operation: message on most path is not in plain text but the XOR of data blocks, so one cannot uncover the original data by sneak message on path. But there still be one path to carry its block in plain text, and which is more serious, it may act as a key to revivify the original data. In our solution, there is no plain text on any path, and the difficulty to uncover the original data approximate holding all path and seizing all blocks. In addition, the scheme in [7] lacks robustness for any path's dropping will make it impossible to revivify the original data on the destination node. Our solution is a robust one to tolerate dropping of multiple paths.

3   The Private and Robust Data Communication

3.1   Architecture

Our network model is showed by figure1.There are two nodes, the sender S and the destination O. And there are multiple paths between both sides found by route discovery, of which we marked three ones as S-4-6-O, S-1-2-5-O, S-3-7-8-O. What we should to do is to build architecture on the multiple paths to meet privacy and robustness. In this paper, we suppose that there are K $(K>3)$ path selected to transmit the data after multiple path route discovery and some politic filtration.

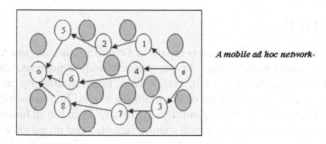

A mobile ad hoc network.

Fig. 1. An example of the network scene

Our solution consists of three parts: privacy coding phase, robust distributing phase, and reverting phase. The data for transmission has difference form in the every phase, as figured in Figure 2. In the following, we use the *italic* words to give the definitions of difference form, which will be used throughout the paper.

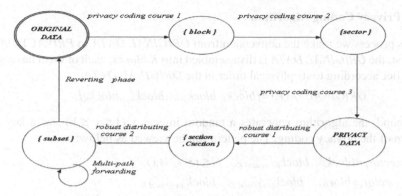

Fig. 2. The data lifecycle and its status conversion

In privacy coding phase, we disassemble the *ORIGINAL DATA* into *blocks*, put XOR operation among the blocks, get the same number of equirotal privacy coded *sectors*, and assemble them as a whole *PRIVACY DATA*. This privacy coding prevent from uncovering any part of the original data by sniffing on part of the paths.

In robust distributing phase, we strip the *PRIVACY DATA* in *sections*, combining parity and backup. We make a copy of every section named *Csection*, and distribute the *subsets* made up of sections on multi-path in so a robust matter that the destination node can build out the *PRIVACY DATA* even in case of some *sections*' false.

In reverting phase, *ORIGINAL DATA* is built out by reversion processes in turn.

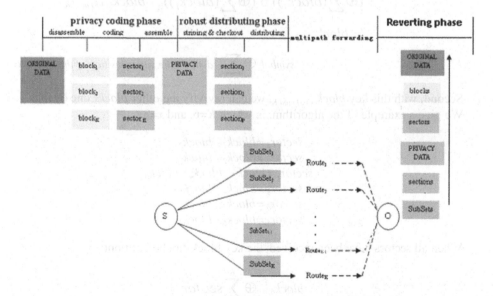

Fig. 3. The architecture of the private & robust data communication

3.2   Privacy Coding Algorithm

In this process we make the conversion from *ORIGINAL DATA* to *PRIVACY DATA*.

First, the *ORIGINAL DATA* is disassembled into *K blocks*; each of them has a unique identifier according to its physical order in the *ORIGINAL DATA*.

$$ORIGINAL\ DATA=\{block_1,\ block_2,...,block_{K-1},block_K\}. \tag{1}$$

Second, the algorithm generates a random integer x $(1 \leq x \leq k)$, as a key to the pattern of the privacy coding. The pattern can be viewed as below:

$$sector_i =block_i \square\ block_{(i+1)\ mod\ K}. \quad (1\leq i \leq k,\ i\neq x)$$
$$sector_x=block_x \square\ block_{(x+1)\ mod\ K} \square\ block_{(x+3)\ mod\ K} \tag{2}$$
It is prescribed that $block_0$ to be substituted by $block_K$ throughout the paper)

Third, the *PRIVACY DATA* can be assembled by the sectors in order.

$$PRIVACY\ DATA =\{sector_1,\ sector_2,...,\ sector_{K-1},\ sector_K\}. \tag{3}$$

Now the algorithm ends. By the privacy coding we obtain a high privacy that part of the *PRIVACY DATA* or set of some *sectors* will leak out nothing about the *ORIGINAL DATA*. This could be explained as below.

First, we build out the key *block*:

$$\oplus \sum_{i=1}^{K} sec\,tor_i =(\oplus \sum_{i=1}^{K}(block_i \oplus block_{(i+1)\bmod K}))\square\ block_{(x+3)\ mod\ K}$$

$$= (\oplus \sum_{i=1}^{K}(block_i)) \square\ (\oplus \sum_{i=1}^{K}(block_i)) \square\ block_{(x+3)\ mod\ K}$$

$$= block_{(x+3)\ mod\ K}$$

symbol $\oplus \sum$ *denotes the superposition of the all XOR*

Second, with this key $block_{(x+3)\ mod\ K}$, we can revivify the other *blocks* one by one. We give a example of the algorithm, in which $K=6$, and $x=3$

$$sector_1 =block_1 \square block_2$$
$$sector_2 =block_2 \square block_3$$
$$sector_3 =block_3 \square block_4 \square block_6$$
$$sector_4 =block_4 \square block_5$$
$$sector_5 =block_5 \square block_6$$
$$sector_6 =block_6 \square block_1$$

When all sectors have been received, the key block can be built out:

$$block_6 \square \oplus \sum_{i=1}^{6} sec\,tor_i$$

Then, we can revivify all the blocks one by one in turns:

$$block_5=sector_5 \square block_6$$
$$block_4=sector_4 \square block_5$$
$$block_3=sector_3 \square block_4 \square block_6$$
$$block_2=sector_2 \square block_3$$
$$block_1=sector_1 \square block_2$$

3.3 Striping and Distributing Algorithm

In this process we build the *subsets* from the *PRIVACY DATA*, which are to be sent on the multiple paths in fact.

First, we strip the *PRIVACY DATA* by divide it to K-1 sections:

$$PRIVACY\ DATA = \{section_1, section_2,..., section_{K-1}\}. \tag{4}$$

Second, we get the parity of the all *sections*,

$$section_P = \{section_1 \oplus section_2 \oplus,...,\oplus section_{K-1}\}. \tag{5}$$

And make each *section* a backup copy involves the *parity section*.

$$Csection1 = section1,$$
$$Csection2 = section2$$
$$,...,$$
$$Csection\ K-1 = section\ K-1,$$
$$CsectionP = sectionP, \tag{6}$$

Third, we build the subsets, following the below rules:

Rule 1. *Each subset consists of 2 sections, one original section, and the other copy one, with different order to identify each other:*

$$subset_n = \{ section_i, Csection_j\}\ (1 \leq n \leq k,\ i,j \in \{1..K-1\} \cup \{P\},\ i \neq j\ )$$

Rule 2. *the sum of any two subsets must have more than 2 different sections.*

Finally, distribute the K subsets separately on the K path.

This algorithm presents the data communication with a considerable robustness that can tolerate dropping of two paths, which means that the destination node can build the *PRIVACY DATA* even if he lost two subsets. It can be testified as below:

Definition 1. $DataSet = SubSet_1 \cup SubSet_2 \cup \cdots \cup SubSet_{k-1} \cup SubSet_P.$

Definition 2. $f(S)$=*the number of different elements in the set S*.

It is obvious that $f(DataSet)=K$,and one can easily educe the followed Theorem 1with the characteristic of the XOR operation:

Theorem 1. *If* $f(S) \geq k-1$ *then* $S => DataSet => PRIVACY\ DATA \square which\ means$ *PRIVACY DATA can be built up from S*.

The theorem needs to be proved is:

Theorem 2. *If for any* $i,j(i \neq j)$,*it be true that* $f(SubSet_i \cup SubSet_j) > 2$, *then it is conclusive that* $DataSet - SubSet_i - SubSet_j => PRIVACY\ DATA$.

The demonstrating of the Theorem 2 is followed below:

We define that :
$SubSeti=\{a_i,\ b_i\}$, $SubSetj=\{\ a_j,\ b_j\}$
$a_i,a_j \in A=\{section_1,section_2,...,section_{K-1},section_P\}$
$b_i,b_j \in$ $B=\{Csection_1,Csection_2,...,Csection_{K-1},Csection_P\}$, $a_i \neq b_i, a_j \neq b_j$

And we suppose that:
$f(SubSet_i \cup SubSet_j)>2$, *namely* $f(a_i,\ b_i,\ a_j,\ b_j)>2$

Well then
$f(a_i,b_i,a_j,b_j)>2 => (a_i \neq b_i\ \&\ a_i \neq b_j)OR(a_j \neq b_i\ \&\ a_j \neq b_j)$,

We appoint a_i, which educe that
$a_i \in B-\{b_i,b_j\}$

Then
$a_i \in B - \{b_i,b_j\} => f(DataSet-SubSet_i-SubSet_j)= f(\ (A -\{a_i,a_j\})\ \cup (B-\{b_i,b_j\})\ )$
$$\geq f(A-\{a_i,a_j\} \cup \{a_i\})=k-2+1= k-1$$

Now, employing the Theorem 1, we can conclude that :

$DataSet - SubSet_i - SubSet_j => PRIVACY\ DATA$

Theorem 2 has been proved. We can plan many algorithms to meet Rule1&Rule2, one of which was described as following:

Example of the algorithms. After the loop all SubSet are built and the distributing is prepared.

```
DataSetA={section₁,section₂,…,section_{K-1},section_K}
                              (section_K= section_P);
DataSetB={Csection₁,Csection₂,…,Csection_{K-1},Csection_K}
                              (Csection_K= Csection_P);
SubSet(S,no,forwards)={section_i .OR. Csection_i | no<i<K } ;
SubSet(S,no,backforwards)={section_i.OR.Csection_i | 1<i<no};
Random(S)=suffix of a stochastic element selected from S ;

 idA= Random(DataSetA);
 For i = 1 to K
 ① SubSet_i={};
 ② SubSet_i=SubSet_i+{ section_idA};
 ③ if Random( SubSet(DataSetB,idA,forwards)) ≠NULL
      idB= Random( SubSet(DataSetB,idA,forwards));
    else
      idB= Random( SubSet(DataSetB,idA,back wards));
    end if
 ④ SubSet_i=SubSet_i+ { section_idB};
 ⑤ DataSetA=DataSetA - {section_idA};
    DataSetB=DataSetB - { section_idB};
 ⑥ idA= idB
 Next i
```

Figure 4 show an example of our algorithm, with the function *Random (S)* always returns the first element of *S*:

$$Subset_1=\{Section_1, Csection_2\},$$
$$Subset_2=\{Section_2, Csection_3\}$$
$$,...,$$
$$Subset_K=\{Section_p, Csection_1\}$$

If route$_1$ dropped, the *subset$_1$* can be recovered by *subset$_2$* and *subset$_k$*. If route$_1$ and route$_k$ failed simultaneity, which meant both *section$_1$* and its copy C*section$_1$* have been lost, *section$_1$* can be revivified by other subsets:

$$section_1 =\{section_P \square section_2 \square,...,\square section_{K-1}\},$$
section right the equal mark are available on the other routes.

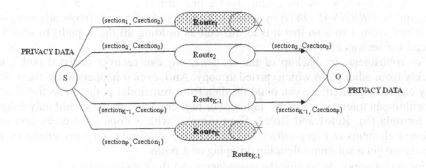

Fig. 4. A example of the striping & distributing algorithm

4 Evaluation

We evaluated our scheme on three aspects: privacy, robustness, and performance. For privacy, privacy coding makes it so confidential that one can uncover nothing of the *ORIGINAL DATA* if he gets some *sectors*. In general, the destination node should revivify the *ORIGINAL DATA* after he receive all the *sectors*. But there is an exception that a collection of K-1 *sectors* with a special block lost may built up the *ORIGINAL DATA*. The special block so-called *sector$_s$* would meet the two conditions:

Condition 1. $s \neq x$.

Condition 2. if $sectors=block_i \square block_j$, then $i=(x+3)$ mod K OR $j=(x+3)$ mod K.
Use the example presented in section 3.2, the *sector$_s$* could be either *sector$_5$* or *sector$_6$*,

$$sector5 =block5 \square block6$$
$$sector6 =block6 \square block1$$

Consider the $sector_6$, when all sectors except $sector_6$ arrived, it come into existence:

$$\oplus \sum_{i=1}^{5} \sec tor_i = \oplus \sum_{i=1}^{5} block_i \oplus \sum_{i=2}^{6} block_i \oplus block_6$$

$$= block_1 \oplus block_6 \oplus block_6$$

$$= block_1$$

Then, we can revivify all the blocks one by one in turns:

$$block2 = sector1 \square block1$$
$$block3 = sector2 \square block2$$
$$block6 = sector6 \square block1$$
$$block5 = sector5 \square block6$$
$$block4 = sector3 \sqcup block3 \sqcup block6$$

It impacts privacy to some extent. But the probability is only (2/ K-1) by which one can gain the *ORIGINAL DATA* by seized k-1 *sectors*. And we can frequently switch the key block from 1 to k so that it is as difficult as holding all the K paths to seized the special k-1 sectors every time.

For robustness, by backup of the *sections*, we can recover dropped path's data quickly from other paths which carried its copy. And, even it happened that the path the copy carried on failed; we can build the data from remainder paths. In section 3.3, the algorithm can tolerate two paths' failure. For higher criterion, we should only enhance the formula (6), Rule1 and Rule2. For example, with 3 copies for every *section*, 3 different elements in every *subset*, and more than 5 dissimilar *sections* among every 3 subsets we get a solution tolerating dropping of 3 paths.

For performance, we define the redundancy and the path utilization. as:

$$Redundancy = \frac{the\ redundant\ data}{the\ original\ data}$$

$$Path\ utilization = \frac{number\ of\ the\ paths\ carrying\ data}{sum\ of\ paths} \tag{7}$$

Table 1 make a compare of our scheme marked as * with other related works marked by the corresponding reference NO., for columns except "Path drop tolerance", we assume two paths' dropping tolerance.

Table 1. The compare of our scheme with other works

	Privacy		Robustness		Performance	
	Sectors needed to uncover		**Path drop tolerance**	**Quick recovery**	**Redundancy**	**Path utilization**
	Whole DATA	Part DATA				
[7]	K	≥1	0	null	1/(K-1)	(K-1)/K, 1 signal channel
*	K-1(special)	K-1(special)	≥2	1 copy	1+2/(K-1)	K/K 0 signal channel
[22]	≥K-2	≥1	2	K-1 XOR	2/(K-2)	(K-2)/K, 2 signal channel
[6]	≥K-2	≥1	≥2	K-1 XOR	2/(K-2)	(K-2)/K, 2 signal channel
Mirror	≥1	≥1	K-1	1 copy	K-1	K/K 0 signal channel

5 Conclusion

In this paper we introduce a solution for data transmission in the mobile ad hoc networks, which has high privacy and robustness. For privacy, we design a privacy coding, which use XOR operation to meet confidentiality. A similarity work has been found in [7], which is not as confidential as ours with a key block in plain text. For robustness, we propose a scheme combine backup with checkout. By backup we can recover data quickly from the copy, and by checkout we can revivify the data in case of the lost of both original data and its copy. With an appropriate distributing mode, the scheme may tolerate multi-paths' dropping. Work of [22] gets the least redundancy without copy, but the recovery cost is too expensive even for little data lost. Pure mirror on multiple paths may present the most robustness, but it has a big redundancy. Diversity Coding [6] need little redundancy, but it use two paths to act as special signal channel, which is not necessary in our solution.

References

1. Mobile Adhoc Networks,http://www.ietf.org/html.charters/manet-charter.html,May,2000
2. Samba,Sesay., Zongkai,Yang.,Jianhua,He.: A Survey on Mobile Ad Hoc WirelessNetwork. Information Technology Journal, 3(2004)168-175
3. Hao,Yang., Haiyun,Luo., Fan,Ye.,Songwu,Lu.,Lixia,Zhang.: Security in Mobile Ad Hoc Networks: Challenges and Solutions.IEEE Wireless Communications,2(2004)38-46
4. Mac,Williams.,F,J.,Sloane,N,J,A.:The   Theory   of   Error-correcting   Codes, Amsterdam:North Holland,1977
5. N,Asokan., P,Ginzboorg.:Key agreement in ad hoc networks. Elsevier Computer Commun ications,23(2000)1627-1637
6. E,Ayanoglu.,E,Chih-Lin.,R,D,gitlin.,J,E,Mazo.:   Diversity   Coding   for   Transparent Self-healing and Fault-tolerant. IEEE Transactions on Communications,11(1993)1677-1686
7. Souheila BOUAM, Jalel BEN-OTHMAN.:Data Security in Ad hoc Networks Using Multiple path Routing. Proceedings of the 14th IEEE PIMRC 2003,1331-1335
8. Yi,Ping.,Yiping,Zhong.,Zhang,Shiyong.:DOS Attack and Defense in Mobile Ad Hoc Networks. Journal of Computer Research and Development 4(2005)697-704
9. Mike,Burmester.,TriVan,Le.:Secure Multiple path Communication in Mobile Ad hoc Networks. Proceedings of Int'l Conference on Information Technology: Coding & Computing 2004
10. L,Zhou.,Z, J, Haas.:Securing Ad HocNetworks, IEEE Networks, 6(1999)24-30
11. J. P. Hubaux,. L. Buttyan.,S. Capkun.:The quest for security in mobile ad hoc networks.Proccedings of MobiHOC 2001, Long Beach, CA, USA, 10(2001)
12. H,Luo.,S,Lu.: Ubiquitous and Robust Authentication Services for Ad Hoc Wireless Ne tworks.Technical Report #200030, UCLA Computer Science Department 2000
13. M,Marina.,S,Das.: On-demand Multi-path Distance Vector Routing in Ad Hoc Networks. Proceedings of the International Conference for Network Procotols, Riverside, Nov. 2001
14. Hai,Jin.,Kai,Hwag.: Stripped mirroring RAID architecture. Journal of Systems Architecture 6(2000)543-550
15. Victor,O.K.Li.,Zhenxin,Lu.:Ad hoc network routing.Proceedings of the 2004 IEEE International Conference on Networking, sensing&Control Taipei,China,March,2004
16. Baolin Sun, Layuan LI:A Qos Base MultiCast Routing Protocol in Ad Hoc Networks. Chines Journal of Computers,10(2004)1402-1407

17. Panagiotis,Papadimitratos.,Zygmunt,J,Haas.:Secure Routing for Mobile Ad hoc Networks. Proceedings of the SCS Communication Networks and Distributed Systems Modeling and Simulation Conference , San Antonio, TX, January 27-31, 2002

18. Lee,NK.,Yang,S.B.,Lee,K.W.:Efficient parity placement schemes for tolerating up to two disk failures in disk arrays. Journal of Systems Architecture,15(2000)1383 -1402

19. Yih,Chun.,A,Perrig.,D,B.Johnson.:Ariadne: A secure on-demand routing protocol. Proceeding of the Mobicom 2002, Atlanda, USA, 2002

20. S,Marti.,T,Giuli.,K,Lai.,M,Baker.:Mitigating routing misbehavior in mobile ad hoc networks. Proceedings of the MOBICOM, 2000

21. Seung,Yi.,Prasad,Naldurg.,Robin,Kravets.:A Security-Aware Routing Protocol for Wireless Ad Hoc Networks. Proceedings of the 2nd ACM international symposium on Mobile ad hoc networking & computing,Long Beach, CA, USA,2001.

22. Jie,Zhou.,Gang,Wang.,Xiaoguang,Liu.,Jing,Liu.:The Study of Graph Decompositions and Placement of Parity and Data to Tolerate Two Failtures in Disk Array: Conditions and Existance.Chinese Journal of Computers,10(2003)1379-1386

23. J,Kong.,Anonymous and Untraceable Communications in Mobile Wireless Networks. PhD thesis, University of California, Los Angeles,2004

24. Amitabh,Mishr,A.,Ketan,Nadkarni.,Animesh,Patcha.: Intrusion Detection in Wireless Ad Hoc Networks. IEEE Wireless Communications,1 (2004) 48-60

25. L,Wang.,Y,Shu.,M,Dong.,L,Zhang.,O,Yang.:Adaptive Multiple path Source Routing in Ad Hoc Networks, Proceedings of the IEEE ICC 2001, Page 867 -871

26. YihChun,Hu.,Adrian,Perrig.:A Survey of Secure Wireless Ad Hoc Routing. IEEE SECURITY & PRIVACY, 5/6(2004)28-39

27. Swades,De.,Chunming,Qiao.,Hongyi,Wu.: Meshed multiple path routing with selective forwarding: an efficient strategy in wireless sensor networks. ELSEVIER Computer Networks ,43 (2003) 481–497

28. Patrick,P.C. Lee., Vishal,Misra., Dan,Rubenstein.:Distributed Algorithms for Seure Multi-path Routing. Proceedings of IEEE INFOCOM, March 2005

Accusation Resolution Using Security Metrology

Scott C.-H. Huang[1,2], Shamila Makki[2], and Niki Pissinou[2]

[1] City University of Hong Kong
shuang@cityu.edu.hk
[2] Florida International University
shamilamakki@hotmail.com, pissinou@fiu.edu

Abstract. In this paper, we design good security metrology to solve the problem when, in a network, there is a node accusing another one of misbehaving. This problem is not easy because bad nodes tend to use false accusations to disrupt the network and the result is disastrous. We set up a standard, namely the security ratings, and use it to resolve such accusations. We use approaches of negative-credit, and mixed-credit (positive-credit), respectively, to solve this problem. We exclude the use of public key infrastructure and use only symmetric ciphers and hash functions to reduce the computational overhead of the security metrology. Our results prove to be practical and robust against node compromise. The communication and computational overhead also prove to be small and suitable for real world applications.

1 Introduction

The advent of computer networks brought everybody into a new era. Since 1965, when L. Roberts connected the TX-2 computer in Massachusetts to the Q-32 in California with a low speed dial-up telephone line, computer networks have grown unbelievably fast to an extent that nobody has expected before. However, just as computer networks gave us an incredibly convenient environment to email messages across oceans, they gave us tantamount problems and inconvenience as well. Hackers have tried every means to disrupt our networks: passively dropping data, or actively modify, forge, or spam the whole network. Bad people are everywhere on the Internet just as they are everywhere in the world. A computer network or any computer system without security mechanism will bring us more agony than happiness. For this reason, researchers have tried to design security mechanism to prevent various kinds of attacks. A fundamental problem arose naturally: "who is good and who is bad?" Put it in another way: "how to determine whether a person is good or bad?" This problem is extremely difficult in a distributed environment. If a central *trusted authority* is present, then we can always go to him and ask for arbitration. If not, then there is no standard at all, which is similar to the real world. In this world, it is really difficult to find the truth, because everybody believes in different things and no obvious universal authority is present[1].

---

[1] The authors are completely neutral to all religions and philosophies.

X. Cheng, W. Li, and T. Znati (Eds.): WASA 2006, LNCS 4138, pp. 435–444, 2006.
© Springer-Verlag Berlin Heidelberg 2006

Let's consider the case of a network without a centralized authority. In such a network, due to the lack of authority, the best way to make things work is probably through democratic means. That is : *whatever reflects most people's need is good.* In other words, how to tell whether a node is good or bad? Just ask most people. If most people vote for a node and against the other one, then we can probably think the one that gets most good votes is good. We want to incorporate this idea into our system and design a certain kind of security metrology that will more or less reflect how good a node is. Our main motivation is that, in a network, if a node is accusing another node of misbehaving, which one should we believe? Oftentimes, bad nodes tend to accuse good nodes to disrupt the network. If there is no security metrology, then there will be no standards and criteria to do anything.

In the course of developing our solution, we found that designing a fully distributed scheme supporting normal security ratings turned out to be really difficult. We found that a fully distributed scheme supporting *one-sided* security ratings is feasible. We use approaches of *negative-credit, and mixed-credit* to simplify our discussion. We found that the negative-credit approach has the least overhead while mixed-credit has most functionality. Thus, in a light-weight sensor network, negative-credit seems to be most suitable.

The rest of this paper is organized as follows. In Section 2 we will introduce the negative-credit approaches. In Section 3 we will introduce the mixed-credit approach and compare it with negative-credit. We will evaluate the performance of both approaches in Section 4 and analyze their security in Section 5. In Section 6 we will present the related work, and in Section 7 we will conclude our work.

2 Negative-Credit Approach

2.1 Assumption

We assume that the network is fully-distributed, so there is no centralized entity to bookkeep the network.

2.2 Threat Model

Wireless communication is not reliable, as everybody can listen to every message sent within its communication range. The sender has no way to tell whether a message has been properly received or not (though acknowledgment can be used, it is prone to be lost or forged as well). For this reason we assume that and adversary can eavesdrop on all traffic, inject packets, replay older packets, or forge fake ones. The adversary can also take full control of compromised nodes and make them drop or alter messages. Let's consider the following example shown in Figure 1 below.

M is a malicious node and it has been misbehaving by dropping, forging, and injecting data. Now M is accusing all of its neighbors A,B,C,D,E,F of misbehaving. If M itself is believed, then the system will stop all packets from going to

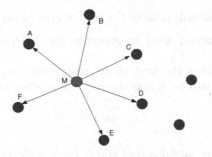

Fig. 1. Example of the threat model

A,B,C,D,E,F. The network will thus be totally disrupted. Based on this example, we are highly motivated to design a scheme using proper security metrology so that this kind of false accusations can be verified and prevented.

2.3 Design Goals

Our motivation for designing a secure rating mechanism is originated from resolving security accusations. In a network, there is no way to tell whether a node is good or bad. When a node is accusing another node of misbehaving, there is no way we can be sure the accusing node is not malicious himself, because oftentimes malicious nodes tend to accuse good nodes to disrupt the network. In the example, a malicious node can accuse many good nodes, causing the network to disfunction or even shut down. Our main design goals are:

1. Defining a good security metrology to best represent a node's behavior.
2. Each node must be evaluated by other nodes. Namely, the security ratings of a node should be independent of itself.
3. No public key infrastructure (PKI) is assumed. Asymmetric encryption or digital signature are too costly to be used on a regular basis.

We exclude the use of public key infrastructure, because this will slow down most systems. If the network is resource limited, then public key infrastructure will overwhelm the network [5]. In practice, even on the Internet, asymmetric encryption most only used to establish pairwise keys (such as TLS [4]) and digital signatures are usually used to do authentication, which only happens once per session. Our security metrology is involved in sending evaluation packet on a periodical basis. If public key infrastructure, this will be drastically detrimental to the system performance.

2.4 Notation

The following acronyms and notation are used in their usual sense.

- MAC is the message authentication code
- $MAC_K(msg)$ is the message authentication code of msg with cryptographic key K
- $E_K(msg)$ is the encrypted message of msg with cryptographic key K

The following notations will arise in the rest of this paper.

- h is the hash function used to generate the hash chain $X \rightarrow h(X) \rightarrow h^2(X) \rightarrow \cdots \rightarrow h^{n-1}(X)$
- $h^{n-1}(X)$ is the end of the hash chain, which will be pre-distributed during initialization and will be updated every time when the hash chain is used up.

2.5   The Scheme

Initialization. At the initialization stage, each node generates a hash chain and distributes it to all neighbors. Then each node also distributes the end of hash chain to everybody by flooding.

Evaluation. Each node evaluates his neighbors on a regular basis. There are only two ratings: (1) good (2) bad. Each node keeps a security rating record of every neighbor of his.

Report. When accusation arises, a security rating request of a particular node may be made. When a node receives a request, first he checks whether this is about his neighbor. If not, he simply forwards this request. If it is, he checks his record and decide whether this node is bad or not based on his previous behavior. If it is a good node, he does nothing. If it is a bad one, he does the following.

Assume node A received a request about node Z. Remember that A knows about Z's hash chain because they are neighbors. Suppose Z's hash chain is

$$X \rightarrow h_Z(X_Z) \rightarrow h_Z^2(X_Z) \rightarrow \cdots \rightarrow h_Z^{n-1}(X_Z)$$

The values on the hash chain are used in a TESLA [10] fashion. That is, the end of the hash chain $h_Z^{n-1}(X_Z)$ is distributed to everybody at the initialization stage, and $h_Z^{n-2}(X_Z)$ is disclosed at the first time. $h_Z^{n-3}(X_Z), h_Z^{n-1}(X_Z), \ldots$ are disclosed one by one. Suppose the current hash value to be disclosed is $h_Z^i(X_Z)$. Now , node A sends

$$A \rightarrow * : \langle RATING, Z, BAD, (A), (M_A) \rangle$$

$$M_A = MAC_{h_Z^i(X_Z)}(BAD, Z)$$

Suppose B is A's neighbor, then B forwards the following message

$$B \rightarrow * : \langle RATING, Z, BAD, (A, B), (M_A, M_B) \rangle$$

$$M_B = MAC_{h_A^i(X_A)}(BAD, Z, M_A)$$

Similarly, if C is B's neighbor, C forwards

$$C \rightarrow * :$$

$$\langle RATING, Z, BAD, (A, B, C), (M_A, M_B, M_C) \rangle$$

$$M_C = MAC_{h_B^i(X_B)}(BAD, Z, M_B)$$

The security rating message will thus eventually reach everybody. Since the hash values will later be disclosed to all nodes, everybody can verify the authenticity of such security rating messages. An accusation can be resolved this way based on their security ratings.

Resolving Accusation. Now the security rating message will eventually reach every node in the network. As long as there is one negative credit about the node that was being accused, everybody can get and verify it. An accusation can thus be resolved if the two nodes being questioned have different security ratings. This scheme gives us some partial information about whether a node is bad or not.

2.6 Analysis

The core of our scheme is based on the assumption that *no node will blackmail itself*. Note that every node shares the hash chain with all of its neighbors, so everybody in this neighborhood shares the same secret can thus be able to generate bad security rating messages. The node itself can definitely generate such messages as well, but it will do him no good. Our assumption means, by doing that, no node will gain anything. This property makes key distribution rather simple because all that a node has to do is set up a shared secret with all of his neighbors. This can be done locally, so the communication overhead is quite small. However, such property only exists in negative-credit schemes. In a positive-credit scheme, a node can always say good things about himself. Thus, such key-sharing mechanism will never work. Instead, in a positive-credit scheme, the key sharing should be *donut-shaped* as shown in Figure 2. Another important property of our scheme is that we can further use the end of hash chains to *relay* message authentication codes. This nice property greatly simplifies key distribution and maintenance.

2.7 Enhanced Scheme with μTESLA

We can incorporate μTESLA [10] in our scheme as another option. As other TESLA schemes, we assume it is loosely-synchronized as well as a method to set up shared secret keys between communicating nodes. Note that in our scheme, the hash values of each node are revealed at the same time. The good thing about it is that every security rating message can be verified by everybody. Remember that the security rating messages are in the following format.

$$\langle RATING, Z, BAD, (A, A_1, A_2, \ldots), (M_A, M_{A_1}, M_{A_2}, \ldots) \rangle$$

Since

$$M_{A_j} = MAC_{h^i_{A_{j-1}}(X_{A_{j-1}})}(BAD, Z, M_{A_{j-1}})$$

We know that M_{A_j} only depends on M_{A-j-1}. Therefore, each node can verify M_A and use it to verify M_{A_1}, then use M_{A_1} to verify M_{A_2}, and so on so forth. In other words, every node can verify all M_{A_j}'s, as long as they know the hash end

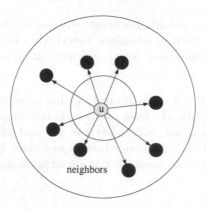

Fig. 2. Donut-shaped key-sharing in positive-credit schemes

of related nodes. This is a good feature, but every node has to store the hash end of all other nodes. Another way to solve this problem is using μTESLA. This enhanced scheme does exactly the same thing as the basic scheme in the initialization and evaluation stages. In the report stage, when other nodes forward security rating messages, they use μTESLA keys instead of their corresponding hash values, as shown below.

$$A \to * : \langle RATING, Z, BAD, (A), (M_A) \rangle$$

$$M_A = MAC_{h_Z^i(X_Z)}(BAD, Z)$$

If B is A's neighbor, B forwards the following message.

$$B \to * : \langle RATING, Z, BAD, (A, B), (M_A, M_B) \rangle$$

However,

$$M_B = MAC_{K_{AB}^i}(BAD, Z, M_A)$$

where K_{AB}^i is the i's TESLA key between A and B, which is totally independent of the hash chains

$$X \to h_Y(X_Y) \to h_Y^2(X_Y) \to \cdots \to h_Y^{n-1}(X_Y) \quad , \forall Y$$

In this enhanced scheme, nodes do not need to store the hash ends of every other node. Instead, they only have to store the hash ends of those who have been questioned.

3   Mixed-Credit Approach

The consideration of mixed-credit approach is actually the same as positive-credit approach. The major difference between positive-credit and negative-credit approaches is that in the negative-credit approach users gain nothing by sending other people bad ratings about himself. This property does not exist in positive-credit or mixed-credit approaches. As a result, a donut-shaped key distribution is needed to get around this problem. Also, in the report stage, hash ends cannot be used to relay security rating messages anymore. μTESLA (or pairwise key-sharing) is the only options available. The schemes with μTESLA is described as follows.

3.1   Mixed-Credit Approach Using μTESLA

As other TESLA schemes, we assume it is loosely-synchronized as well as a method to set up shared secret keys between communicating nodes. We also assume there is a method to set up a donut-shared secret among a node's neighbors (excluding itself).

Initialization. At the initialization stage, each node locally communicates with its neighbors and has them set up a common shared hash chain.

$$X \to h(X) \to h^2(X) \to \cdots \to h^{n-1}(X)$$

Evaluation. Each node evaluates his neighbors on a regular basis. There are only two ratings: (1) good (2) bad (3) unknown. Each node keeps a security rating record of every neighbor of his.

Report. When accusation arises, a security rating request of a particular node may be made. When a node receives a request, first he checks whether this is about his neighbor. If not, he simply forwards this request. If it is, he checks his record and look up its records based on his previous behavior. Its ratings can be represented as an integer $RVAL$ which takes values -1,0,1 to represent BAD,UNKNOWN, and GOOD respectively.

Assume node A received a request about node Z. Suppose Z's hash chain is

$$X \to h_Z(X_Z) \to h_Z^2(X_Z) \to \cdots \to h_Z^{n-1}(X_Z)$$

Note that, right now, Z does not know X_Z. Only its neighbors do. Suppose the current hash value to be disclosed is $h_Z^i(X_Z)$. Now , node A sends

$$A \to * : \langle RATING, Z, RVAL, (A), (M_A) \rangle$$

$$M_A = MAC_{h_Z^i(X_Z)}(RVAL, Z)$$

Suppose B is A's neighbor, then B forwards the following message

$$B \to * : \langle RATING, Z, RVAL, (A, B), (M_A, M_B) \rangle$$

$$M_B = MAC_{K_{AB}^i}(RVAL, Z, M_A)$$

Similarly, if C is B's neighbor, C forwards

$$C \to * : \langle RATING, Z, RVAL, (A, B, C), (M_A, M_B, M_C) \rangle$$

$$M_C = MAC_{K_{BC}^i}(RVAL, Z, M_B)$$

4   Performance Evaluation

We analyze the computational and communication overhead of our schemes.

4.1   Computational Cost

The computational cost of symmetric encryption and hash verification is low, as shown in [5]. The computation time for a Pentium II process can be as low as 1ms, that for a 16MHz Motorola processor is around 100ms. Strictly speaking, the computational overhead for a node in an Ad Hoc network is negligible, but for a sensor node is not, though not too bad.

The computational cost is involved in the following things: (1) generation of the hash chain in the initialization phase (2) generation of the MAC report. Therefore, in [5] we can see that the computation cost is negligible (3) verification of the report message

Communication Cost. The communication cost is involved in the following: (1) pre-distribution of hash chains to neighbors (2) pre-distribution of end of hash chain to the network (3) distribution of TESLA keys (4) broadcast report messages.

The pre-distribution of hash chains to neighbors does not cause too much overhead, as it can be done locally. Each node only has to communicate with his neighbors, so the communication cost is constant. The pre-distribution of end of hash chains need involves flooding, so the communication cost is linear to the size of network. The pre-distribution of hash requires one-to-one (or individual) communication at the initialization stage, which is as large as the size of the network. However, this only needs to be done once during initialization, so it actually doesn't affect the system performance much. to the number of nodes in the network. Though it is large, it only has to be done once in the initialization stage. Distribution of TESLA keys is only needed in the μTESLA enhanced scheme. This only involves neighbors' mutual communication, so its overhead is constant. Broadcast report messages obviously has overhead linear to the size of network, but this need not to be done periodically. This only needs to be done in case of a security accusation. Therefore, the overhead is negligible.

5   Security Analysis

5.1   External Attacks

In our scheme every rating message has a message authentication code that can be verified by everybody, so unauthorized node cannot inject false data without being detected. Any outside attackers cannot forge or modify these data without compromising the cryptographic keys.

5.2   Internal Attacks

Internal attacks pose more threat than external attacks. If the attack takes full control over certain nodes and compromise their cryptographic keys, then the attacker can forge, modify, or inject malicious packets to influence the security ratings. If a node is compromised and its cryptographic keys are accessible to the attacker, then our scheme will be affected because the attacker can send false security rating messages. However, there is tamper-resistant hardware that can store these cryptographic keys in a flash memory (such as SRAM), and the memory will be refreshed periodically in a very short period of time [6]. In this case, even if the node is physically capture by the attacker, its sensitive crypto-graphic keys are still not compromised. However, [3] tells us that no matter how secure the temper-resistant device is, the sensitive data (such as cryptographic keys) are still vulnerable.

In this case, we need to use *key revocation* schemes to remedy this problem Revoking the cryptographic keys can be done by [13,11,15,9,7] , though it will cause more communication or computation overhead. The use of these revocation scheme is beyond our discussion, so for now we just assume that if this situation ever arises there are ways to countermeasure it too. Compromising the end of hash chain actually causes no harm because it is used for verifying freshness of the report packets and could be open to public as well.

6   Related Work

[14] discussed the idea of security metrology and its difficulty. [1,12] evaluated computing systems and classified them by the security properties they provide. [12] provided a classification of computer systems and mandated the inclusion of various security provisions at different security levels. [1], on the other hand, provided classifications of hardware modules implementing cryptographic func-tions for use in environments where the adversary has physical access to the modules. [2] attempted to standardize the process of evaluating the evidence supporting security claims. Our work also involved in key management schemes [13,11,15,9,7]. For the sake of completeness, we list them here.

7   Conclusion and Future Work

In this paper we brought up the problem of preventing false security accusations and designed two methods to cope with it. We introduced the negative-credit approach as a major method to solve this problem. We excluded the use of public key infrastructure in order to reduce the computational and communication overhead. We also considered the mixed-credit approach for completeness. We found that negative-credit approach is very efficient, but it has considerable limitation as well. As for our future work, we will focus on enhancing our scheme to sensor networks, lessening its limitation while preserving its functionality.

References

1. U.S. National Institute of Standards and Technology. Federal information processing standards publication 140-1: Security requirements for cryptographic modules, Jan. 1994.
2. U.S. National Institute of Standards and Technology. Common criteria for information technology security evaluation, version 2.1, 1999.
3. R. Anderson and M. Kuhn. Tamper Resistance - a Cautionary Note. In *Proceedings of the Second USENIX Workshop on Electronic Commerce*, pages 1–11, Nov. 1996.
4. T. Dierks and C. Allen. The TLS protocol, version 1.0. http://www.ietf.org/rfc/rfc2246.txt, 1998.
5. W. Freeman and E. Miller. An experimental analysis of cryptographic overhead in performance-critical systems. In *The 7th International Symposium on Modeling, Analysis, and Simulation of Computer and Telecommunication Systems (MASCOTS 99)*, pages 348–357, College Park, MD, Oct. 1999.
6. P. Gutmann. Secure deletion of data from magnetic and solid-state memory. In *6th USENIX Security Symposium Proceedings*, pages 77–89, San José, California, July 1996.
7. D. Halevy and A. Shamir. The LSD broadcast encryption scheme. In *Advances in Cryptology CRYPTO'02*, pages 47–60, 2002.
8. S. C.-H. Huang, S. Makki, and N. Pissinou. On optimizing compatible security policies in wireless networks. *EURASIP Journal on Wireless Communications and Networking*.
9. D. Naor, M. Naor, and J. Lotspiech. Revocation and tracing schemes for stateless receivers. In *Advances in Cryptology- CRYPTO'01*, pages 41–62, 2001.
10. A. Perrig, R. Szewczyk, V. Wen, D. Culler, and J. D. Tygar. SPINS: Security protocols for sensor networks. *Wireless Networks*, 8(5):521–534, Sept. 2002.
11. A. T. Sherman and D. A. McGrew. Key establishment in large dynamic groups using one-way function trees. *IEEE Transactions on Software Engineering*, 29(05):444–458, 2003.
12. U.S. Department of Defense, Computer Security Center. Trusted computer system evaluation criteria, Dec. 1985.
13. C. K. Wong, M. G. Gouda, and S. S. Lam. Secure group communications using key graphs. *IEEE/ACM Transactions on Networking*, 8(1):16–30, Feb. 2000.
14. B. S. Yee. Security metrology and the monty hall problem. http://citeseer.ist.psu.edu/yee01security.html, 2001.
15. S. Zhu, S. Setia, and S. Jajodia. LEAP: Efficient security mechanisms for large-scale distributed sensor networks. In *ACM CCS'03*, 2003.

Ring Signature Based on ElGamal Signature

Jian Ren[1] and Lein Harn[2]

[1] Michigan State University, East Landing, MI 48864-1226, USA
renjian@egr.msu.edu
[2] University of Missouri-Kansas City, MO 64110-2499, USA
harnl@umkc.edu

Abstract. Ring signature was first introduced by Rivest, Shamir and Tanman in 2001. In a ring signature, instead of revealing the actual identity of the message signer, it specifies a set of possible signers. The verifier can be convinced that the signature was indeed generated by one of the ring members, however, he is unable to tell which member actually produced the signature. Ring signature provides an elegant way to leak authoritative secrets in an anonymous way, and to implement designated-verifier signature schemes which can authenticate emails without undesired side effects. In this paper, we first propose a ring signature scheme based on ElGamal signature scheme. Comparing to ring signature based on RSA algorithm, the proposed scheme has three advantages. First, all ring members can use the same prime number p and operate in the same domain. Second, the proposed ring signature is inherently a convertible ring signature and enables the actual message signer to prove to a verifier that only he is capable of generating the ring signature. Third, multi-signer ring signature schemes can be generated from ElGamal signature schemes to increase the level of confidence or enforce cross organizational joint message signing.

1 Introduction

Ring signature was first introduced by Rivest, Shamir and Tauman in 2001 [1] to provide anonymity for the message signer. In a ring signature scheme, the message signers form a ring of any set of possible signers and himself. The actual signer can then generate a ring signature entirely using only his secret key and the others' public keys without the assistance or even awareness of the other ring members. However, the generated ring signature can convince an arbitrary verifier that the message was indeed signed by one of the ring members while the real signer's identity is totally anonymous to the verifier.

The idea behind ring signature schemes is similar to that of group signatures [2], but with some variations. First of all, unlike group signature, ring signature schemes do not require a group manager to administrate the joint and revocation of the ring members. The actual message signer has the freedom to select all the ring members and sign whatever message he likes. Second, in group signature schemes, the group manager can recover the real identity of the actual message signer since group signatures only look indistinguishable to their

X. Cheng, W. Li, and T. Znati (Eds.): WASA 2006, LNCS 4138, pp. 445–456, 2006.
© Springer-Verlag Berlin Heidelberg 2006

verifiers, but not to the group manager who can even revoke the anonymity of misbehaving signers.

Since the introduction of ring signature, several related ring signature schemes have been proposed. In [3], ring signature based on Schnorr signature scheme [4] is proposed. A closely related ring signature schemes is proposed in [5]. Since both of these schemes are based on Schnorr signature scheme, the ring signature schemes are not convertible [6]. Convertibility enables the actual ring message signer to provide non-repudiation evidence such that a verifier can verify the originality of a ring signature at times of his choice. Many convertible signature schemes have been proposed in literature [7,8], however, no one is inherently convertible. They all require some extra processes for the convertibility proof.

In this paper, ring signature based on ElGamal signature scheme is proposed. The proposed ring signature scheme is secure against adaptive chosen message attacks. Comparing to ring signature schemes based on RSA, all ring members can operate in the same domain. Moreover, ring signature schemes based on ElGamal signature scheme have two *unique* advantages. First, they are intrinsic convertible ring signature schemes. The actual message signer can always prove his identity to the verifier based on the knowledge of discrete logarithm that he uses to generate the ring signature through any knowledge proof protocol [4,9]. Second, multi-signer ring signature scheme which combines multi-signature and ring signature can be produced. Though the concept of multi-signer ring signature scheme is similar to that of threshold ring signature scheme [10], multi-signer ring signature maintains the ring structure defined in [1].

The paper is organized as follows. In Section 2, an overview of the existing ring signature is given. Ring signature based on ElGamal is introduced in Section 3 along with security analysis. In Section 4, multi-signer ring signature is proposed. We conclude in Section 5.

2   Overview of Existing Work

In [1], the concept of ring signature was first proposed. Suppose that Alice wishes to generate a ring signature of a message m for a ring of n individuals $A_1, A_2, \cdots, A_n$, where the signer Alice is A_s, for some value of $s, 1 \leq s \leq n$. Each ring member A_i has a public key P_i and a corresponding private key S_i.

2.1   Definitions

Definition 1 (Ring signature). *A* ring signature *scheme consists of the following two algorithms:*

- **ring-sign** *($m, P_1, P_2, \cdots, P_n$): Given a message m and the public keys $P_1, P_2, \cdots, P_n$ of the n ring members, the actual signer A_s can produce a ring signature σ using her own private key S_s.*
- **ring-verify** *(m, σ): Given a message m and a ring signature σ, which includes the public keys of all possible signers of the ring, a verifier can determine whether (m, σ) is a valid ring signature generated by one of the ring members.*

Definition 2 (Convertible ring signature). *A ring signature is called a convertible ring signature if it also contains the following two algorithms:*

- **ring-convert:** *The real signer A_s of a ring signature σ can provide non-repudiation evidence, such that a verifier can confirm the originality of a ring signature.*
- **ring-convert-verify:** *Given a ring signature (m, σ') and a set of public keys $(P_1, P_2, \cdots, P_n)$ of a ring, the verifier can determine whether (m, σ') is a valid ring signature generated by the ring member A_s.*

The three security requirements for convertible ring signature schemes include:

- **Signer ambiguity:** The probability that a verifier successfully determines the real signer of a ring signature is exactly $1/n$, where n is the total number of ring members
- **Unforgeability:** The advantage that a non-ring-member can successfully forge a ring signature of the ring is negligible.
- **Unconvertibility against nonsigner:** The advantage that a ring member $A_i, i \neq s$, can successfully convert a ring signature into a valid ordinary signature is negligible.

Definition 3 (Combining functions). *A combining function $C_{k,v}(y_1, y_2, \cdots, y_n)$ takes as input a key k, an initialization value v, and an arbitrary values $y_1, y_2, \cdots, y_n \in \{0,1\}^b$. It outputs a value $z \in \{0,1\}^b$, such that for any given $k, v, s, 1 \leq s \leq n$ and any fixed values of $y_i, i \neq s$, the function $C_{k,v}$ is a one-to-one mapping from y_s to the output z. Moreover, this mapping is efficiently solvable. However, it should be infeasible to solve the verification equation without knowledge of the trapdoor information.*

In [1], a combining function is proposed as follows:

$$z = C_{k,v}(y_1, \cdots, y_n) = E_k(y_n \oplus E_k(y_{n-1} \oplus E_k(\cdots \oplus E_k(y_1 \oplus v)))). \quad (1)$$

For any given s, equation (1) can be rewritten as follows:

$$y_s = E_k(y_{s-1} \oplus E_k(\cdots \oplus E_k(y_1 \oplus v))) \oplus E_k^{-1}(y_{s+1} \oplus E_k(\cdots \oplus E_k^{-1}(y_n \oplus E_k^{-1}(z)))) \quad (2)$$

2.2 Ring Signatures

The ring signature proposed by Rivest, Shamir and Tauman,is based on the combining function described above. Each ring member A_i has an RSA public key $P_i = (n_i, e_i)$ which specifies the trapdoor one-way permutation f_i over $\mathbb{Z}_{n_i}$:

$$f_i(x) = x^{e_i} \bmod n_i.$$

It is assumed that only A_i knows how to compute the inverse permutation f_i^{-1} efficiently.

One of the problem that RSA algorithm faces is that the trapdoor permutations of the various ring members have domains of different size, which makes it awkward to combine the individual signatures. To solve this problem, all the trapdoor permutations are extended to a common domain $\{0,1\}^b$, where 2^b is some power of two larger than all the moduli n_i's. The extended trapdoor permutation g_i over $\{0,1\}^b$ is defined in the following way. For any b-bit input m, let $m_i = q_i n_i + r_i$, where q_i and r_i are nonnegative integers, $0 \leq r_i \leq n_i$. Then

$$g_i(m_i) = \begin{cases} q_i n_i + f_i(r_i) & \text{if } (q_i + 1)n_i \leq 2^b \\ m & \text{else.} \end{cases}$$

It is assumed the existence of a publicly defined symmetric encryption algorithm E such that for any k of length l, the function E_k is a permutation over b-bit strings. It is also assumed the existence of a publicly defined collision-resistance hash function h that maps arbitrary inputs to strings of length l, which are used as keys for E.

The ring signature scheme proposed in [1] is not designed to be a convertible ring signature. In other words, the actual signer is unable to provide non-repudiation evidence to a verifier to confirm the originality of the ring signature. In this section, we will describe the ring scheme proposed in [1], which contains the four algorithms below:

ring-sign $(m, P_1, P_2, \cdots, P_n, S_s)$: Suppose that Alice wishes to sign a message m with a ring signature for the ring of n individuals $A_1, A_2, \cdots, A_n$, where Alice is A_s for some value of $s, 1 \leq s \leq n$. Given the message m to be signed, A_s's secret key $S_s = (d_s, n_s)$, and the sequence of public keys $P_1, P_2, \cdots, P_n$ of all the ring members, A_s computes a ring signature as follows:

1. **Choose a key:** The signer A_s first computes the symmetric key k as follows:

$$k = h(m).$$

2. **Pick a random glue value:** The signer picks an initialization value $v \in \{0,1\}^b$ uniformly at random.

3. **Pick random x_i's:** A_s picks random x_i for all the other ring members $1 \leq i \leq n, i \neq s$ uniformly and independently from $\{0,1\}^b$, and computes

$$y_i = g_i(x_i).$$

4. **Solve for y_s:** A_s solves the following ring equation for y_s:

$$C_{k,v}(y_1, y_2, \cdots, y_n) = v.$$

Equivalently, y_s can be solve as follows:

$$y_s = E_k(y_{s-1} \oplus E_k(\cdots \oplus E_k(y_1 \oplus v))) \oplus E_k^{-1}(y_{s+1} \oplus E_k(\cdots \oplus E_k^{-1}(y_n \oplus E_k^{-1}(v))))$$

5. **Invert y_s using A_s's trapdoor information:** A_s uses her knowledge of the trapdoor information to invert g_s on y_s to obtain x_s:

$$x_s = g_s^{-1}(y_s).$$

6. **Output the ring signature:** The signature on the message m is defined to be the $2n + 2$-tuple:

$$S = (P_1, P_2, \cdots, P_n; v; x_1, x_2, \cdots, x_n; t).$$

ring-verify $(P_1, P_2, \cdots, P_n; v; x_1, x_2, \cdots, x_n; t)$**:** A verifier can check an alleged signature on the message m as follows.

1. **Apply the trapdoor information:** For $i = 1, 2, \cdots, n$, the verifier computes
$$y_i = g_i(x_i).$$

2. **Obtain k:** The verifier hashes the message m:
$$k = h(m).$$

3. **Verify the ring equation:** The verifier checks that the y_i's satisfy the fundamental equation
$$C_{k,v}(y_1, y_2, \cdots, y_n) = v.$$

If the ring equation is satisfied, the verifier accepts the signature as valid. Otherwise the verifier rejects.

3 Proposed Ring Signature

In this section, a ring signature based on the original ElGamal signature scheme is introduced. In ElGamal signature scheme, a large prime p and a primitive element in $\mathbb{Z}_p$ are assumed to be made publicly known. The signer can select a random $d \in \mathbb{Z}_{p-1}$ as his secret key. Then the public key is computed from $e = g^d \bmod p$. Let m be the message digest of the message to be signed. The signer randomly selects a one-time secret value $l \in \mathbb{Z}_{p-1}$ secretly and computes $\alpha = g^l \bmod p$. Then he computes $\beta = (m - d\alpha)l^{-1} \bmod p - 1$. The signature for message m is the pair (α, β). The signature can be verified $g^m = e^\alpha \alpha^\beta \bmod p$ is true.

Comparing to the original ring signature based on RSA public key scheme, for ring signature based on ElGamal signature scheme, all users can use the same prime number p and operates in the same domain. Therefore, no expansion is necessary. We can assume that the secret key of the i-th ring member A_i is $d_i \in \mathbb{Z}_p^*, i = 1, 2, \cdots, n$, the public key of the ring member is given by $e_i = g^{d_i} \bmod p$.

The construction of ring signature requires existential forgery. According to [11,12], ElGamal signature scheme is existentially forgeable with a generic message attack. In fact, there are two well-known levels of forgeries: one arbitrary parameter forgery and two arbitrary parameter forgery.

For one parameter forgery, select $c \in \mathbb{Z}_{p-1}$ arbitrarily, if we let $\alpha = g^c e \bmod p$ and $\beta = -\alpha \bmod p - 1$, then it is easy to see that (α, β) is a valid signature for the message $m = c\beta \bmod p - 1$. However, this forgery is easily detectable since $\alpha + \beta = 0 \bmod p - 1$, we will not use this method of forgery.

For the second level of forgeries [11], the actual signer selects $a_i \in \mathbb{Z}_{p-1}$ and $b_i \in \mathbb{Z}_{p-1}^*$ arbitrarily for each $i = 1, 2, \cdots, n, i \neq s$. Define

$$\alpha_i = g^{a_i} e_i^{b_i} \quad \bmod p, \tag{3}$$

$$\beta_i = -\alpha_i b_i^{-1} \quad \bmod p - 1, \tag{4}$$

$$m_i = a_i \beta_i \quad \bmod p - 1, \tag{5}$$

then it can be shown (α_i, β_i) is a valid signature of m_i.

Define

$$g_i(a_i, b_i) = (m_i, \alpha_i, \beta_i),$$

then the inverse is easy to compute. However, if we compose g_i with the project mapping p_i, where

$$p_i(m_i, \alpha_i, \beta_i) = m_i,$$

the inverse of $f_i = p_i \circ g_i$ is computationally difficult. In fact, the message signing algorithm f_i, shown in Figure 1, is a one-way trapdoor function over $\mathbb{Z}_{p-1} \times \mathbb{Z}_{p-1}^* \mapsto \mathbb{Z}_{p-1}$.

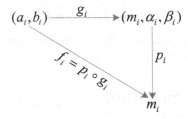

Fig. 1. Existential forgery of ElGamal signature scheme

In the proposed convertible ring signature scheme, the same combining function described in equation (2) can still be used. The assumptions for the existence of a collision-resistance hash function h remain the same. However, instead of a publicly defined ideal symmetric encryption algorithm E, we only need a hash function h, thus we can simply replace $E_{h(m)}(x)$ with $h(m, x)$ as described in [10]. We will now describe the ring-sign and ring-verify procedures below.

ring-sign $(m, e_1, e_2, \cdots, e_n, d_s, s)$***:*** Given a message m to be signed, his secret key d_s, and the sequence of public keys $e_1, e_2, \cdots, e_n$ of all the ring members, the signer computes a ring signature as follows:

1. **Choose a key:** The signer A_s first computes the symmetric key k as the hash of the message m to be signed

$$k = h(m).$$

2. **Pick a random glue value:** The signer picks an initialization value v uniformly at random from $\mathbb{Z}_p$.

3. **Create a signature forgery** (α_i, β_i) **for message** m_i**:** The purpose of this step is to forge a signature for some message m_i for each of the $n - 1$ non-signer ring members using the two arbitrary parameter forgery. To achieve this goal, the actual signer selects $a_i \in \mathbb{Z}_{p-1}$ and $b_i \in \mathbb{Z}_{p-1}^*$ arbitrarily for each $i = 1, 2, \cdots, n, i \neq s$, then (α_i, β_i) can be derived from

$$g_i(a_i, b_i) = (m_i, \alpha_i, \beta_i).$$

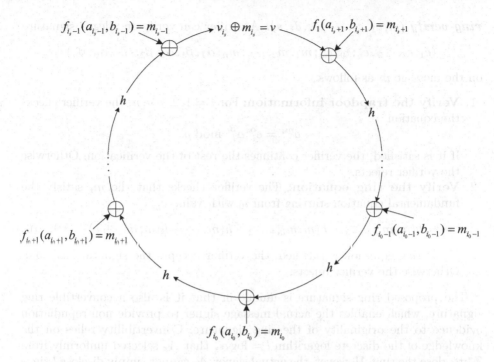

Fig. 2. Proposed ring signatures based on the ElGamal signature scheme

4. **Solve for m_{i_s}:** Suppose that the index for the signer is i_s. Let

$$v_{i_s+1} = h(m, v),$$
$$v_{i_s+2} = h(m, v_{i_s+1} + m_{i_s+1}),$$
$$\vdots$$
$$v_{i_s-1} = h(m, v_{i_s-2} + m_{i_s-2}),$$
$$v_{i_s} = h(m, v_{i_s-1} + m_{i_s-1}),$$

where the indexes are all in $\mathbb{Z}_n$. Therefore, $v_{i_s+n} = v_{i_s}$. To glue the ring, let

$$v_{i_s} + m_{i_s} = v, \quad \text{equivalently,} \quad m_{i_s} = v + v_{i_s}.$$

5. **Sign m_{i_s} using the signer's trapdoor information:** The signer uses his knowledge of the trapdoor information to sign the message m_{i_s} to obtain the signature (α_s, β_s). To do so, the actual signer A_s first selects a random l uniformly from $\mathbb{Z}_p^*$, such that $\gcd(l, p - 1) = 1$. The signature for message m_{i_s} is $(\alpha_i, \beta_i) = (g^l \bmod p, (m_{i_s} - d_i\alpha_i)l^{-1} \bmod p - 1)$.

6. **Output the ring signature:** The signature on the message m is defined to be the $4n + 2$-tuple:

$$(e_1, e_2, \cdots, e_n; i_0, v_{i_0}; m_1, m_2, \cdots, m_n; \alpha_1, \beta_1, \alpha_2, \beta_2, \cdots, \alpha_n, \beta_n),$$

where i_0 is randomly selected from $\mathbb{Z}_n$.

ring-verify $(m, e_1, e_2, \cdots, e_n, d_s, s)$: A verifier can verify an alleged signature

$$(e_1, e_2, \cdots, e_n; i_0, v_{i_0}; m_1, m_2, \cdots, m_n; \alpha_1, \beta_1, \alpha_2, \beta_2, \cdots, \alpha_n, \beta_n)$$

on the message m as follows.

1. **Verify the trapdoor information:** For $i = 1, 2, \cdots, n$, the verifier checks the equation
$$g^{m_i} = e_i^{\alpha_i} \alpha_i^{\beta_i} \bmod p.$$
If it is satisfied, the verifier continues the rest of the verification. Otherwise the verifier rejects.

2. **Verify the ring equation:** The verifier checks that the m_i satisfy the fundamental equation starting from i_0 with value v_{i_0}

$$v = h(m, m_{i_0+n-1} + h(m, m_{i_0+n-2} + h(m, \cdots + h(m, m_{i_0} + v) \cdots))). \quad (6)$$

If the ring equation is satisfied, the verifier accepts the signature as valid. Otherwise the verifier rejects.

The proposed ring signature is unique in that it is also a convertible ring signature, which enables the actual message signer to provide non-repudiation evidence to the originality of the ring signature. Convertibility relies on the knowledge of the discrete logarithm $l = \log \alpha_s$ that A_s selected uniformly from $\mathbb{Z}_p^*$ to close the ring. However, the actual signer A_s cannot simply disclose l since otherwise the secret key of A_s can be computed. In fact, the verification that A_s has in his possession the discrete logarithm α_s can rely on the knowledge proof protocols such as Schnorr's identification protocol [4] or the discrete logarithm methods described in references [9].

It should be pointed out that the actual signer can not compute $l = \log \alpha_i$ for any $i \neq s$ and falsely claim the ownership for other ring members. In fact, if he can find the discrete logarithm of α_i for some $i \neq s$, then he can solve the private key of others. This contradicts to the common assumptions.

3.1   Security Analysis

Similar to [1,10], the identity of the signer is unconditionally protected with the proposed ring signature scheme. This is because that for each k and v, regardless of the signer's identity, the ring signature has exactly p^{n-1} solutions according to equations (3)-(5), and all of them can be chosen by the signature generation procedure with equal probability without depending on any complexity-theoretic assumptions or on the randomness of the oracle.

The soundness of the ring signature scheme is computational since the ring signature cannot be stronger than the individual signature scheme used by the possible signer.

Theorem 4. *Ring signature scheme based on ElGamal signature scheme is secure against adaptive chosen message attack in the random oracle model.*

Due to page limitation, the proof of this theorem is left out.

4   Multi-signer Ring Signature

Multi-signer ring signature enables more signers to be involved in signing the message. When multiple signers work together in generating a ring signature, it may result in a higher level of confidence or broader coverage on this ring signature. As an example, a multi-signer ring signature can be generated to enforce across organizational involvement in message leaking.

In this section, we propose a multi-signer ring signature. First, let us give some definitions.

Definition 5 (Generalized ring member). *In the original ring signature scheme, each ring member is a single user. When each ring member consists of arbitrary number of message signers, then the ring member is called a generalized ring member.*

Definition 6 (Generalized multi-signer ring signature). *For a ring signature, it its ring members are all generalized ring members and the signature of each generalized ring member is a multi-signature, then this ring signature is called a generalized ring signature.*

The major difference between generalized multi-signer ring signature and threshold ring signature [10] is that for threshold ring signature, all the n possible signers are equally possible in generating the ring signature. However, for the proposed generalized multi-ring signature, this is not necessarily true. Moreover, in generalized ring signature, the "deep throat" may include members across multiple organizations such as members from financial organization and also members from management organization.

The basic idea for the generalized multi-signer ring signature is similar to the original ring signature. In the basic ring signature, there are n trapdoor one-way functions where n is the number of possible ring members. Each ring member corresponds to one trapdoor one-way function with a single secret key. In the generalized multi-signer ring signature, instead of n possible individual ring members, there are n possible generalized ring members, each generalized ring member is a multi-signature [13] consists of arbitrary number of signers that forms a generalized ring member. The union of all generalized ring members forms a generalized ring-signer group. The generalized ring members do not need to contain the same number of signers. However, we can only guarantee there exists one generalized ring member that has multi-signature generated through the genuine signers. To achieve efficiency, the multi-signature scheme proposed in [13] can be used as the trapdoor one-way function since in this scheme, when a multi-signature is generated with the knowledge of multiple secret keys, the length and verification time of the multi-signature is constant (i.e. not a linear function with respect to the number of signers involved).

Example 7. Support the possible signers' subset is A, B, C, D, E. For a 2-out-of-5 threshold ring signature, any two users could possibly be the message signers. However, for generalized ring signature, the generalized ring members could be

$\{A, B\}, \{C, D\}, \{C, D, E\}, \{A, B, E\}$. Then the generalized ring signature has either 2 or 3 signers since we are unable to determine which generalized ring member is authenticated.

It is computationally infeasible to determine the actual signer of the multi-signature, and determine the actual number of trapdoors involved in creating the ring signature if the multi-signature ring members have different number of signers. However, it should be assured that one of the multi-signature is actually generated with the knowledge of the trapdoor information. Therefore, the number of actual signers is low bounded by the ring members with the least number of signers.

The multi-signature scheme proposed in [13] is based on a variation of ElGamal signature of the following forms.

Signing. Randomly selects $k \in \mathbb{Z}_{p-1}^*$ and computes $\alpha = g^l \bmod p$, $\beta = dm - l\alpha \bmod p - 1$. (α, β) is the signature.

Verification. Check whether

$$e^m = \alpha^\alpha g^\beta \bmod p.$$

Assume that a subset consists of t signers with public keys $e_1, e_2, \cdots, e_t$ wishes to sign the same message m. The group's public key is defined as

$$e = \prod_{i=1}^{t} e_i \bmod p.$$

The generation of multi-signature can be described as following:

1. Each member randomly selects a number $l_i \in \mathbb{Z}_{p-1}$ and computes

$$\alpha_i = g^{l_i} \bmod p, \quad \text{and} \quad \alpha = \prod_{i=1}^{t} \alpha_i \bmod p.$$

2. Each member solves the equation

$$\beta_i = d_i m - l_i \alpha \bmod p - 1,$$

where d_i is his secret key, l_i is a random number that he selected from $\mathbb{Z}_{p-1}$. Define

$$\beta = \sum_{i=1}^{t} \beta_i \bmod p - 1.$$

The multi-signature (α, β) for message m can be verified if

$$e^m = g^\alpha \alpha^\beta \bmod p$$

is true.

Similar to the original ElGamal scheme, this modified ElGamal signature is also existentially forgeable with two arbitrary parameters: the actual signer selects $a \in \mathbb{Z}_{p-1}$, $b \in \mathbb{Z}_{p-1}^*$ arbitrarily and computes

$$\alpha = g^a e^b \mod p,$$
$$\beta = -a\alpha \mod p - 1,$$
$$m = b\alpha \mod p - 1,$$

then it can be shown that (α, β) signs m.

For a multi-signature subset consists of t signers with public keys $e_1, e_2, \cdots, e_t$. To forge a signature for message m, the actual signer randomly selects $a \in \mathbb{Z}_{p-1}, b \in \mathbb{Z}_{p-1}^*$ and let $\alpha = g^a (e_1 e_2 \cdots e_t)^b \mod p$, $\beta = -a\alpha \mod p - 1$ and $m = b\alpha \mod p - 1$. Then (α, β) is a valid signature of message m since (α, β) passes the verifications as

$$(e_1 e_2 \cdots e_t)^m = \alpha^\alpha g^\beta \mod p.$$

The ring-sign and ring-verify of multi-signer ring signature schemes can be defined similar to the single signer ring signature schemes described in Section 3. The detailed description will not be repeated here.

4.1   Security Analysis

The security of generalized multi-signer ring signature can be split into security of the individual generalized ring members, and security of the generalized ring signature. For the individual generalized multi-signature, the security analysis given in [13] still applies. First, it is computationally difficult for the actual generalized ring signers to impersonate any other generalized ring members and to compute discrete logarithm of $\alpha_i, i \neq s$, otherwise, he is able to solve the private key, d_i of that generalized ring member according to $\beta_i = d_i m - l_i \alpha_i \mod p - 1$, where l_i is the secret discrete logarithm of α_i. Second, it is also computationally infeasible for the other generalized ring members to impersonate the real generalized ring signers since the difficulty of this problem is equivalent to solving the discrete logarithm problem. Finally, the security analysis for generalized multi-signer ring signature is similar to the ordinary ring signature.

5   Conclusion

In this paper, ring signature based on the original ElGamal signature scheme is first introduced. Comparing to ring signature construction based on RSA scheme, in the proposed ring signature scheme, all ring members can use the same prime number and operate in the same domain. Ring signature based on ElGamal scheme is inherently a convertible ring signature which enables the actual message signer to prove to a verifier that only he is capable of generating the ring signature. Moreover, generalized multi-signer ring signature schemes can be generated from ElGamal signature schemes to increase the level of confidence or to enforce cross organizational information leaking with high efficiency.

References

1. R. L. Rivest, A. Shamir, and Y. Tauman. How to leak a secret. In *Advances in Cryptology–ASIACRYPT'01*, Lect. Notes Comput. Sci., 2248, pages 552–565, 2001.
2. D. Chaum and E. van Heyst. Group signatures. In Donald W. Davies, editor, *Advances in Cryptology - EuroCrypt '91*, pages 257–265, Berlin, 1991. Springer-Verlag. Lecture Notes in Computer Science Volume 547.
3. J. Herranz and G. Saez. Forking lemmas in the ring signatures' scenario. Technical Report 067, International Association for Cryptologic Research, http://eprint.iacr.org/2003/067.ps, 2003.
4. C. P. Schnorr. Efficient identification and signatures for smart cards. In Gilles Brassard, editor, *Advances in Cryptology - Crypto'89*, pages 239–252, Berlin, 1989. Springer-Verlag. Lecture Notes in Computer Science Volume 435.
5. M. Abe, M. Ohkubo, and K. Suzuki. 1-out-of-n signatures from a variety of keys. In *ASIACRYPT*, Lect. Notes Comput. Sci., 2501, pages 415–432, 2002.
6. S. J. Kim, S. J. Park, and D. H. Won. Convertible group signature. In *Proc. Advances in Cryptology-ASIACRYPT'96*, Lect. Notes Comput. Sci., 1163, pages 311–321, 1996.
7. K.-C. Lee, H.-A. Wen, and T. Hwang. Convertible ring signature. *IEE Proceedings - Communications*, 152(4):411–414, August 2005.
8. J. Boyar, D. Chaum, and I. Damgard. Convertible undeniable signatures. In *Proc. Advances in Cryptology-CRYPTO'90*, Lect. Notes Comput. Sci., 537, pages 189–205, 1991.
9. E. Bangerter, J. Camenisch, and U. Maurer. Efficient proofs of knowledge of discrete logarithms and representations in groups with hidden order. In *PKC 2005*, 2005.
10. E. Bresson, J. Stern, and M. Szydlo. Threshold ring signatures and applications to ad-hoc groups. In *Proc. Advances in Cryptology-CRYPTO'02*, Lect. Notes Comput. Sci., 2442, pages 465–480, 2002.
11. T. A. ElGamal. A public-key cryptosystem and a signature scheme based on discrete logarithms. *IEEE Transactions on Information Theory*, 31(4):469–472, 1985.
12. S. Goldwasser, S. Micali, and R. L. Rivest. A digital signature scheme secure against adaptive chosen-message attacks. *SIAM J. Comput.*, 17(2):281–308, April 1988.
13. L. Harn. Group-oriented (t, n) threshold digital signature scheme and digital multisignature. *IEE Proc.-Comput. Digit. Tech.*, 141(5):307–313, September 1994.

Key Management in Sensor Networks

Guorui Li[1], Jingsha He[2], and Yingfang Fu[1]

[1] College of Computer Science and Technology, Beijing University of Technology,
Beijing 100022, China
{liguorui, fmsik}@emails.bjut.edu.cn
[2] School of Software Engineering, Beijing University of Technology,
Beijing 100022, China
jhe@bjut.edu.cn

Abstract. Sensor networks are widely used in a variety of commercial and military applications due to their self organization characteristics and distributed nature. As a basic requirement for supporting security in sensor networks, key management plays an essential role in authentication and encryption. In this paper, we describe the hexagon-based key predistribution scheme and show that it can improve the effectiveness of key management in sensor networks. We show that this key management scheme can improve the probability of establishing pairwise keys between sensor nodes of up to two hops apart by more than 40% over other schemes. We also show that the security of a sensor network would decrease with the increase in sensor node deployment density or in signal propagation distance.

Keywords: sensor networks, security, key management.

1 Introduction

The development of wireless technologies has made it possible to deploy a large number of low-cost, low-power and high-performance sensor nodes in a wireless sensor network. These sensor nodes collect environmental data such as temperature, humidity and pressure and transmit the data to collection nodes through wireless links. The characteristics exhibited in a wireless sensor network, such as self-organization, self-healing, distribution and loose coupling, make such networks suitable for a variety of commercial and military applications, especially in hostile environments.

Security plays an essential role in wireless sensor networks because the confidentiality, integrity and availability of the transmitted data between sensor nodes must be preserved in a hostile environment. As a part of the basic requirement for security, key management plays a central role in encryption and authentication. However, due to resource constraints in sensor nodes, many ordinary security mechanisms such as public key-based authentication and the corresponding key management schemes are impractical, and sometimes infeasible in sensor networks.

There are currently three types of key management schemes that are commonly used in sensor networks: trusted server scheme, self-enforcing scheme, and key predistribution scheme. The trusted server scheme relies on a trusted server for key management, e.g., the Kerberos. This type of scheme is not very suitable for sensor

X. Cheng, W. Li, and T. Znati (Eds.): WASA 2006, LNCS 4138, pp. 457–466, 2006.

networks because there is usually no trusted infrastructure in sensor networks. The self-enforcing scheme relies on asymmetric cryptography, e.g., key management using public key certificates. However, limited computation and energy resources in sensor nodes often make it undesirable to use public key algorithms, such as RSA, for energy conservation. The third type of key management scheme is key predistribution, in which cryptographic keys are pre-distributed among all sensor nodes prior to deployment [1]. There have already been several key predistribution schemes in existence and we will discuss them in more detail in this paper.

Eschenauer and Gligor proposed the basic probabilistic key establishment scheme, in which each sensor node is assigned a random subset of keys from a key pool before the deployment of a network so that any two sensors will have a certain probability to share at least one key [2]. Chan et al. improved the scheme and developed the q-composite key establishment scheme and the random pairwise key scheme [3]. The q-composite key establishment scheme is based on the basic probabilistic key establishment scheme, but it requires that two sensor nodes share at least q pre-computed keys as the basis to establish a pairwise key between the two nodes. In the random pairwise key scheme, random pairwise keys are established between a specific sensor node and a random subset of other sensor nodes. Such a scheme has the property that security compromise to a sensor node doesn't lead to compromise to pairwise keys shared between uncompromised nodes. Liu and Ning developed a framework in which pairwise keys are established through using bivariate polynomials [4]. They also proposed two efficient instantiations, i.e., a random subset assignment scheme and a grid-based key predistribution scheme, to establish pairwise keys in sensor networks. They also proposed the closest pairwise key predistribution scheme and the closest polynomials predistribution scheme, which take advantage of sensor nodes' expected locations to establish appropriate keys between the sensor nodes and thus can improve the performance of key establishment [5]. However, all the schemes described above failed to take into account the information on deployment locations and signal propagation. Therefore, they could lower the probability of successful key establishment with an increase in the cost. Lately, we proposed a hexagon-based key predistribution scheme in which we take advantage of the broadcast nature of wireless communication. We showed that the new scheme can improve the probability of establishing pairwise keys between sensor nodes by more than 40% over previous schemes [6].

In this paper, we first describe the hexagon-based key predistribution scheme in sensor networks in which we use the hexagon to simulate signal propagation. We then analyze the performance and security aspects and show that the hexagon-based key predistribution scheme can greatly improve the probability of successful key establishment as well as the threshold security property. This scheme also helps to lower the cost of pairwise key establishment.

The rest of the paper is organized as follows. In the next section, we describe polynomial-based key establishment. In Section 3, we describe the hexagon-based key management scheme and analyze the performance and security properties. In Section 4, we identify some related work in sensor network security. Finally, in Section 5, we conclude this paper and discuss some future research directions.

2 Polynomial-Based Key Establishment

To establish pairwise keys, the key management server first randomly generates a number of bivariate t-degree polynomial $f(x,y) = \sum_{i,j=0}^{t} a_{ij} x^i y^j$ over a finite field F_q, where q is a prime number that is large enough to accommodate a cryptographic key. Obviously, $f(x,y)$ exhibits the property of symmetry, i.e., $f(x,y) = f(y,x)$. For each sensor node i, the key management server computes a polynomial share of $f(x,y)$, i.e., $f(i,y)$, and stores it in sensor node i. For any two sensor nodes i and j, node i can compute the pairwise key $f(i,j)$ by evaluating $f(i,y)$ at point j and node j can compute the pairwise key $f(j,i)$ by evaluating $f(j,y)$ at point i. From the property of symmetry of $f(x,y)$, $f(i,j) = f(j,i)$. So the pairwise key between nodes i and j can be established.

In this scheme, each sensor node needs to store a bivariate t-degree polynomial's coefficients, which would occupy $(t+1)log_2 q$ storage space. The proof provided in [7] ensures that this scheme is unconditionally secure and t-collision resistant. That is, the coalition of no more than t compromised sensor nodes doesn't lead to any knowledge about the pairwise keys between any two uncompromised sensor nodes.

3 Hexagon-Based Key Predistribution Scheme

3.1 The Hexagon-Based Key Predistribution Scheme

In the hexagon-based scheme, key management involves four phases: key predistribution, direct key establishment, path key establishment, sensor addition and revocation.

(1) Key predistribution phase
The key management server would partition the target deployment field into m equal-sized hexagons according to the hexagonal coordinate system [6] as shown in Fig.1. Then, it builds m different bivariate t-degree polynomials over a finite field F_q and assigns these polynomials to hexagonal coordinate system randomly in order to make sure that each hexagon has a unique bivariate polynomial. For convenience, the key management server assigns a unique ID to each polynomial.

For each sensor node i, the key management server first determines its home hexagon H_i where the sensor node is expected to locate and discover the six hexagons $\{H_{ij} \mid j = 1,...,6\}$ that are adjacent to the sensor node's home hexagon. Then it computes $P_i(ID_i, y)$ and $\{P_{ij}(ID_i, y) \mid j = 1,...,6\}$ by evaluating hexagon H_i and $\{H_{ij} \mid j = 1,...,6\}$'s corresponding polynomial P_i and $\{P_{ij} \mid j = 1,...,6\}$ at sensor node i's ID, i.e., ID_i. Finally, the key management server assigns $P_i(ID_i, y)$,

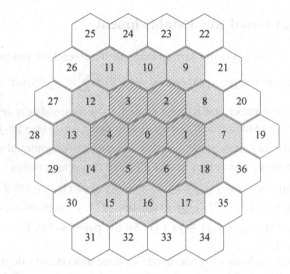

Fig. 1. The adjacent hexagons in a hexagon-based predistribution scheme

$\{P_{ij}(ID_i, y) \mid j = 1,...,6\}$ and their corresponding IDs to sensor node i and store them into the node in order to build the pairwise keys.

(2) Direct key establishment phase

After deployment, if two sensor nodes want to establish a pairwise key, they first need to identify a shared bivariate polynomial. If they can find at least one such polynomial, a common pairwise key can be established directly using the polynomial-based key establishment scheme presented in Section 2. In order to find whether the two sensor nodes hold the shared polynomial, they should exchange their polynomials' IDs. To protect information associated with their polynomials' IDs, the sensor nodes may challenge each other to solve puzzles. Sensor node i broadcasts an encryption list, α, $E_{ID_1}(\alpha)$, $E_{ID_2}(\alpha)$, ..., $E_{ID_7}(\alpha)$ where $ID_i, i = 1,...,7$ is the ID of the polynomials that sensor node i holds. If the other sensor node can correctly decrypts one of the $E_{ID_i}(\alpha)$ using one of its own polynomial ID_i, then they share the same polynomial ID_i and can proceed to establish a direct pairwise key using this shared polynomial.

(3) Path key establishment phase

If direct key establishment failed, the two sensor nodes can establish a pairwise key in the path key establishment phase. When a source sensor node broadcasts the ID of a destination sensor node, an intermediate sensor node can establish a path key for the two sensor nodes if it holds the pairwise keys with the source and the destination sensor nodes, respectively. Otherwise, the intermediate sensor node would broadcast this message continuously until it discovers a sensor node that shares a pairwise key with the previous sensor node and the destination sensor node, respectively. Then the path key can be established along the message broadcast path in the reverse direction.

(4)   Sensor node addition and revocation phase

Some sensor nodes may be destroyed or compromised after a period of time. They can't work properly or even lower the security of key management by disclosing the shared key polynomial information. We can substitute them by adding new sensor nodes and predistributing them with their own IDs and the corresponding bivariate polynomial coefficients according to their deployed location. Two sensor nodes can establish direct key as long as they share the same bivariate polynomials. So the new added node can affiliate the existing sensor network seamlessly. On the other hand, each sensor node can record the number of compromised sensor nodes that share at least one common bivariate polynomial with itself and their corresponding IDs, for the disclosure of bivariate polynomials will make the key management insecurity. If more than t sensors that share the same bivariate polynomial are compromised, it means that this polynomial is not security any more. So we should remove this polynomial and all related compromised sensor IDs to save its memory.

3.2 Analysis of the Probability of Key Establishment

(1) The probability of direct key establishment

As discussed in [6], the probability of direct key establishment for any sensor node u in

the hexagon-based key predistribution scheme is $p_u = \dfrac{n_u^s}{n_u} = \dfrac{\sum_{C_j \in S_i} p(C_j, C_i)}{\sum_{\forall j} p(C_j, C_i)}$ where

n_u^s is the average number of sensor nodes that can establish a pairwise key with node u directly, n_u is the average number of sensor nodes with which node u can directly communicate, and S_i is the set of hexagons that share at least one common polynomial with sensor node u.

As shown in Fig. 1, each sensor node takes its deployment hexagon as the center and can share polynomials with sensor nodes deployed in its 19 adjacent hexagons. Let's assume that the sensor deployment density in hexagon is ϖ and that distance of signal propagation is d_r, then the probability of direct key establishment in the

scheme is $p_u = \dfrac{n_u^s}{n_u} = \dfrac{19 \cdot \varpi \cdot \dfrac{3\sqrt{3}}{2} \cdot R^2}{\pi \cdot d_r^2 \cdot \varpi} = \dfrac{57\sqrt{3}R^2}{2\pi d_r^2}$ where R is the diameter of the

hexagon.

In contrast, the probability of direct key establishment in closest polynomial

key predistribution scheme described in [5] is $p_u' = \dfrac{n_u^s}{n_u} = \dfrac{13 \cdot \varpi \cdot L^2}{\pi \cdot d_r^2 \cdot \varpi} = \dfrac{13L^2}{\pi d_r^2}$ where

L is the side length of a square in a common rectangular coordinate system. Each sensor node can only communicate with the sensor nodes deployed in 13 adjacent squares in such a system. As shown in Fig.2, only the sensor node deployed in 13 shaded squares can establish direct pairwise keys with the sensor node u deployed at, say $C_{2,2}$.

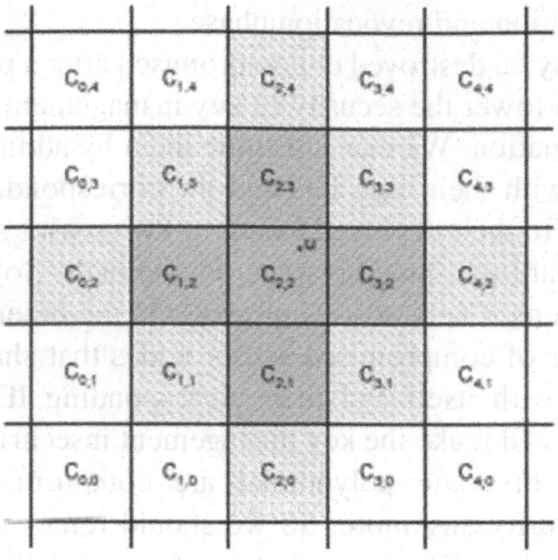

Fig. 2. The adjacent squares in a closest polynomial predistribution scheme

To simplify our analysis, we assume that the signal propagation distance in both of these schemes is the minimal distance between a sensor node and those nodes that are within the signal range of the first node that can establish a direct pairwise key with it. Consequently, in the hexagon-based key management scheme, $d_r = 3\sqrt{3}R$ whereas, in the closest polynomial predistribution scheme, $d_r = \sqrt{10}L$. Therefore, the ratio between the probabilities of the two direct key establishment schemes is:

$$\frac{p_u}{p_u'} = \frac{57\sqrt{3}}{26} \cdot (\frac{R}{L})^2 = \frac{57\sqrt{3}}{26} \cdot (\frac{\sqrt{10}}{3\sqrt{3}})^2 \approx 1.406 .$$

That is, the probability of direct key establishment in the hexagon-based key management scheme is approximately 40% higher than that in the closest polynomial predistribution scheme [5].

(2) The probability of path key establishment

Similar to the above analysis, the number of hexagons covered in the i-hop path key establishment in the hexagon-based key predistribution scheme and the number of squares covered in the i-hop path key establishment in the closest polynomial key predistribution scheme can be calculated using the following formula:

$$\begin{cases} x_0 = 1 \\ x_1 = 19 \\ x_{i+1} = 2x_i - x_{i-1} + 24 \end{cases} \quad \begin{cases} y_0 = 1 \\ y_1 = 13 \\ y_{i+1} = 2y_i - y_{i-1} + 16 \end{cases} .$$

So the ratio between the probabilities of these two path key establishment schemes is:

$$\frac{p_u}{p_u'} = \frac{\frac{3\sqrt{3}}{2}R^2 \cdot x_{i+1}}{41 \cdot L^2 \cdot y_{i+1}} = \frac{5\sqrt{3}x_{i+1}}{9y_{i+1}} .$$

For example, when we discuss the probability of path key establishment between two sensor nodes of two hops away in which only one intermediate node is reqired to help establish the path key between the source and the destination sensor nodes, the ratio between the probabilities of these two path key establishment schemes is:

$$\frac{p_u}{p_u} = \frac{\dfrac{3\sqrt{3}}{2}R^2 \cdot 61}{41 \cdot L^2} = \frac{183\sqrt{3}}{82} \cdot (\frac{\sqrt{10}}{3\sqrt{3}})^2 \approx 1.432 .$$

That is, the probability of establishing a two-hop path key in the hexagon-based key management scheme is approximately 43% higher than that in the closest polynomial predistribution scheme [5].

3.3 Analysis of Security

According to the result of the polynomial-based key predistribution scheme, unless more than t polynomial shares of a bivariate polynomial are disclosed, an attacker would not know about the uncompromised pairwise keys established using this polynomial. Thus, the security of the hexagon-based key management scheme depends on the average number of sensor nodes that share the same polynomial. Assume that there are m nodes on average in the signal range of each sensor node, the density of the sensor node deployment can be estimated to be $\varpi = \dfrac{m}{\pi d_r^2}$. Thus, the number of sensor nodes that shares at least one common polynomial in the hexagon-based key management scheme is $N_s = \dfrac{m}{\pi d_r^2} \cdot \dfrac{3\sqrt{3}}{2} R^2 \cdot 7 = \dfrac{21\sqrt{3}mR^2}{2\pi d_r^2}$. As long as $N_s \leq t$, this scheme is compromise-resistant.

Let's assume that a fraction p_c of sensor nodes in the network have been compromised. Thus, among N_s sensor nodes that hold the same polynomial shares, the probability that i sensors has been compromised can be estimated to be $P_c(i) = \dfrac{N_s!}{(N_s - i)!i!} p_c^i (1 - p_c)^{N_s - i}$. Thus, the probability that the bivariate polynomial can be compromised is $P_c = 1 - \sum_{i=0}^{t} P_c(i)$. For any pairwise key established between uncompromised sensors, the probability that it is compromised is the same as P_c .

Fig.3(a) shows the relationship between the fraction of compromised direct keys for uncompromised sensor nodes and the fraction of compromised sensor nodes under different deployment density m, given the same signal propagation distance ($d_r = 1$ measurement unit), the same hexagon size and the same key storage space ($t=39$). The result shows that the higher the deployment density, the higher the probability of keys being compromised for uncompromised sensor nodes.

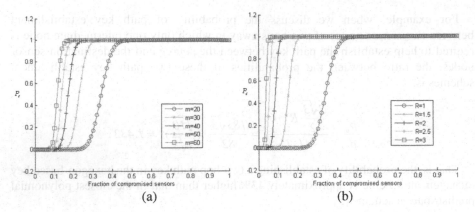

(a)   (b)

Fig. 3. (a) The security comparison of hexagon-based key predistribution scheme under different deployment density. (b) The security comparison of hexagon-based key predistribution scheme under different signal propagation distance.

Fig.3(b) shows the relationship between the fraction of compromised direct keys for uncompromised sensor nodes and the fraction of compromised nodes under different signal propagation distance R, given the same signal propagation distance (d_r =1 measurement unit), the same sensor deployment density and the same key storage space (t=39). The result shows that the longer the signal propagation distance, the higher the probability of keys being compromised for uncompromised sensors node.

The results in Fig.3(a) and Fig.4(b) can be easily understood. With an increase in sensor deployment density or in signal propagation distance, more and more sensor nodes share the same key polynomial. Consequently, the probability of the key polynomial being compromised will increase accordingly. Therefore, we can enhance the security of key management by decreasing the deployment density or by reducing the signal propagation distance.

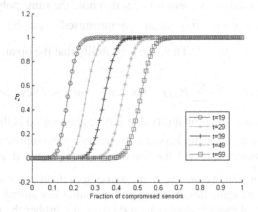

Fig. 4. The security comparison of hexagon-based key predistribution scheme under different polynomial degree

Fig.4 shows the relationship between the fraction of compromised direct keys for uncompromised sensor nodes and the fraction of compromised sensor nodes under different degree t of polynomial (as well as the key storage space), given the same signal propagation distance (d_r =1 measurement unit), the same sensor deployment density and the same hexagon size. The result shows that the higher the degree of polynomial, the lower the probability of keys being compromised for uncompromised sensor nodes.

The results in this section show a threshold security property: i.e., as long as the fraction of compromised nodes is less than the threshold, the scheme is perfectly secure. However, the fraction of compromised direct keys for uncompromised sensor nodes will increase rapidly once the fraction of compromised sensor nodes exceeds the threshold.

4 Related Work

Nowadays, there are many studies in the security of sensor networks, mostly on key management, authentication, and vulnerability analysis. In addition to the key predistribution schemes presented in [2-7], Perrig et al. proposed a security architecture for sensor networks, which included SNEP, a security primitive building block, and a broadcast authentication technique μ TESLA [8]. Liu and Ning extended this technique to a multilevel key chain scheme to prolong the time period covered by a μ TESLA instance [9]. Wood and Stankovic identified a number of DoS attacks in sensor networks [10].

5 Conclusion and Future Work

In this paper, we discussed the hexagon-based key predistribution scheme in which we took advantage of the knowledge regarding sensor nodes' expected deployment locations and establish pairwise keys between the sensor nodes by using the bivariate t-degree polynomial in a hexagonal coordinate system. We showed that this scheme could increase the probability of direct key establishment and that of 2-hop path key establishment by over 40%. We also analyzed the security of the key predistribution schemes. Our future work would focus on the development of methods and schemes that can be used to adjust the polynomial distribution by taking into consideration the difference between expected deployment locations and actual deployment locations of the sensor nodes.

References

[1] W. Du, J. Deng, Y. Han, S. Chen and P. Varshney, "A key management scheme for wireless sensor networks using deployment knowledge," in *Proc. IEEE Infocom*, March 2004, pp. 586-597.
[2] L. Eschenauer and V. D. Gligor, "A key-management scheme for distributed sensor networks," in *Proc. 9th ACM Conference on Computer and Communications Security*, November 2002, pp. 41-47.

[3] H. Chan, A. Perring, and D. Song, "Random key predistribution schemes for sensor networks," in *Proc. IEEE Symposium on Research in Security and Privacy*, 2003.

[4] D. Liu and P. Ning, "Establishing pairwise keys in distributed sensor networks," in *Proc. 10th ACM Conference on Computer and Communications Security*, October 2003, pp. 52-61.

[5] D. Liu and P. Ning, "Location-based pairwise key establishments for static sensor networks," in *Proc. 2003 ACM Workshop on Security in Ad Hoc and Sensor Networks*, 2003, pp. 72-82.

[6] G. Li, J. He and Y. Fu, "A Hexagon-based key predistribution scheme in sensor networks," to be presented at the *International Workshop on Wireless and Sensor Networks*, August 2006.

[7] C. Blundo, A. De Santis, A. Herzberg, S. Kutten, U. Vaccaro and M. Yung, "Perfectly secure key distribution for dynamic conferences," in *Advances in Cryptology-CRYPTO'92. Lecture notes in Computer Science*, Vol. 740, Springer-Verlog, New York, 1992, pp. 471-486.

[8] A. Perrig, R. Szewczyk, V. Wen, D. Culler and J. D. Tygar, "Spins: Security protocols for sensor networks," in *Proc. 7th Annual International Conference on Mobile Computing and Networks*, July 2001.

[9] D. Liu and P. Ning, "Efficient distribution of key chain commitments for broadcast authentication in distributed sensor networks," in *Proc. 10th Annual Network and Distributed System Security Symposium*, February 2003, pp. 263-276.

[10] D. Wood and J. A. Stankovic, "Denial of service in sensor networks," in *IEEE Computer*, Vol. 35, No. 10, October 2002, pp. 54-62.

Efficient Password-Based Authentication and Key Exchange Scheme Preserving User Privacy

Zhenchuan Chai, Zhenfu Cao*, and Rongxing Lu

Department of Computer Science and Engineering, Shanghai Jiaotong University,
1954 Huashan Road, Shanghai 200030, P.R. China
zcchai@gmail.com, zfcao@cs.sjtu.edu.cn

Abstract. With the flourish of applications over the wired /wireless networks, how to keep user's privacy has drawn growing concerns in recent years. Although the issue of user anonymity has been addressed in digital signature field by introducing the concepts of ring and group signatures, they are not suitable to anonymously authenticate a user in wireless mobile applications, because these signature schemes need infrastructure support and heavy computational costs which is beyond the computational ability of a smart card embedded in a hand-held device. In this paper, we propose an anonymous authentication scheme which also supports Diffie-Hellman key exchange. Our scheme is very efficient since it mainly uses hash and XOR operations. Moreover, our scheme possesses many good virtues of existing authentication schemes.

1 Introduction

Password-based remote authentication supporting key exchange has been widely used to protect resource from illegal access, due to its growing importance in the fields of computer networks, wireless networks, remote login, operation systems, and database management systems [1]. However, traditional schemes require that the identity of a user be explicitly specified to facilitate authentication and further key exchange, which may violate user's privacy in some privacy-sensitive applications, such as online drug store. To address such seemingly paradoxical issue (proving the legitimacy of a user without revealing his identity), many schemes have been proposed, such as ring signature[2], and group signature[3]. Unfortunately, signature schemes always need the support of an authorized third party, and the amount of time-consuming and computation-intensive exponential operations make these schemes impractical in some wireless mobile applications, where security operations are carried out in a resource-constrained smart card embedded in a mobile phone. Therefore, it is always desirable to design schemes that keep user's anonymity as well as low computational costs to fit into wireless mobile environment. We will address such issue and present a concrete scheme without using ring or group signature in this paper.

---

* Corresponding author.

X. Cheng, W. Li, and T. Znati (Eds.): WASA 2006, LNCS 4138, pp. 467–477, 2006.

1.1   The Anonymity Issue in Remote Authentication Scheme

As far as user privacy and anonymity is concerned, research on this topic usually focuses on two issues: anonymous communication and user anonymity [5]. Anonymous communication usually provides a communication channel that resists traffic analysis, so that the communicating parties can be anonymous against the eavesdroppers. A more complicated and seemingly paradoxical issue is user anonymity, which let the users hide their identities from the communicating peers. User anonymity in remote authentication scheme is what we discuss in this paper.

In traditional authentication schemes, a user first registers himself at a remote server by submitting his identity ID and a password PW to the server [1], and the server will store ID and PW pair in local database. When a registered user wants to login to the server, he will start by submitting authentication request first, including ID. Such scheme could not be used in privacy-sensitive applications. Suppose in an online drug store application, the administrator of the server could purposely collect all user's privacy information by matching their identities with their purchase orders, and sell these information to some interested parties. Then the leakage of these information may result in annoying drug advertizement flooding. Another example is cited as follows [4]. In a company, everyone is allowed to report her or his personal opinion on any issues to the president of the company in order to improve their performance or working environment. In the position of company, these options should only be made within the group of their own employees. However, in the position of employee, one wishes to hide her or his identify when reporting something that the president feels unpleasant. So the key issue in these applications is to authenticate oneself without revealing one's own identity.

1.2   Ways to Achieve User Anonymity

An immediate way to achieve user anonymity is to assign an alias name to each user, and a user will use his alias name to login to perform key exchange with server, instead of using his real identity. However, such idea does not work since the server could always match user's alias name with real identity.

In fact, user anonymity was first addressed in the setting of digital signature with the introduction of group signature [3]. A group signature allows each group members to sign on behalf of the whole group anonymously without revealing his own identity. So the verifier of the group signature could not tell who is the real signer in the group. User anonymity is also achieved in ring signature proposed by Rivest, Shamir and Tauman [2], where a signer takes a list of public key of other people as input to sign a message, and a signature verifier could not spot the real signer in the public key list.

Both ring and group signatures share the same idea of achieving user anonymity. The idea is to hide one's own identity among a group of identities. The difference between ring signature and group signature is that the group is formed more freely in the setting of ring signature [6]. In ring signature, the public key list which implicitly defines a group is composed by a signer himself without the help of a group manager, and the signer needs not to inform or interact with people involved in the list. While in the setting of group signature, a user must join the group first by interacting with a group manager to obtain a group membership. Therefore, it is more attractive to achieve user anonymity in a ring fashion.

However, neither ring nor group signature could readily be used in authentication schemes, since they can not work without the support of public key infrastructure. Moreover, in existing ring or group signature schemes, heavy exponential computation often grows linearly with group or ring size, which makes it impractical for implementation in wireless mobile applications, where smart cards are always used as computation devices.

1.3 Password-Based Authentication

In 1981, Lamport [12] proposed the first well-known password authentication scheme. In Lamport's scheme, a server has to maintain a password table achieve user authentication. The scheme has been criticized for suffering from the risk of stolen-verifier attack [15] and the high cost of protecting and maintaining the growing password table. To overcome the weakness, Hwang and Li [11] proposed a new smart card based remote user authentication scheme in 2000, where the remote server doesn't need to maintain password tables but only keeps a secret key. However, their scheme does not allow users to freely choose and change their passwords. Therefore, schemes that alow user to freely choose memorable passwords are more attractive in practical use. In 1999, Yang and Shieh [13] presented a timestamp-based password authentication scheme that allows users to freely choose their passwords. And examples of such user-friendly schemes are those in [8],[10], [14]. In 2005, Liao, Lee, and Hwang [1] proposed an efficient scheme that supports Diffie-Hellman key exchange.

Authentication schemes that deal with anonymous issue were proposed by Chien, Chen[7] and Viet, Yamamura, Tanaka [4] respectively. However, the former in deed deals with anonymous communications but not user anonymity. And the latter uses password tables at server side and needs lots of exponential operations.

Following above discussions, we address the user anonymity issue in authentication by presenting a concrete scheme without using ring or group signature in this paper. Our scheme acquires user anonymity by hiding a user's identity among a list of identities which is composed by the user in ring fashion. Our scheme is efficient since most of its operations are hash and XOR operation. And the scheme shares many good virtues of previous schemes, such as no password tables, freely chosen passwords, mutual authentication and supporting key exchange.

The rest of paper is organized as follows. In Section 2, we give a brief review of some basic concepts, and propose eight requirements to evaluate our scheme. In Section 3, we present our concrete scheme. Then we discuss the property and security of our scheme and analysis its efficiency in Section 4. A conclusion is draw in Section 5.

2   Preliminary

In this section, we first recall some basic concepts, and then define some requirements to evaluate our scheme.

2.1   One-Way Hash Function

An one-way hash function H is said to be secure, if the following properties are satisfied [16]:

- Given x, it is easy to compute $H(x) = y$, while inverting $H()$ is hard, that is, it is hard to compute $H^{-1}(y) = x$, when given y.
- Given x, it is computationally infeasible to find $x' \neq x$ such that $H(x') = H(x)$.
- It is computationally infeasible to find any two pair x and x' such that $x' \neq x$ and $H(x') = H(x)$.

2.2   Diffie-Hellman Key Exchange

In 1976, Diffie and Hellman proposed a well-known key exchange scheme, which allows two parties to negotiate a secret session key over insecure networks. The protocol works as follows:

1. Alice secretly chooses $x \in_R Z_p^*$, and sends $X = g^x \bmod p$ to Bob, where p is a large prime and g is a primitive element in Z_p^*.
2. Meanwhile, Bob secretly chooses $y \in_R Z_p^*$, and sends $Y = g^y \bmod p$ to Alice.
3. Alice computes $K = X^y \bmod p$. Bob computes $K' = Y^x \bmod p$.

After the protocol, Alice and Bob indeed share a secret session key $K = K' = g^{xy} \bmod p$.

2.3   Requirements to Evaluate Password-Based Authentication Scheme

We intend to design an efficient password-based authentication scheme, which is expected to inherit all the good virtues of previous schemes and support Dieffie-Hellman key exchange. Now we summarize these requirements to evaluate our scheme as follows:

R1: The scheme can resist stolen-verifier attack, namely, the password or verification tables should not be stored in a remote server.

R2: The password can be chosen and changed freely by the user.

R3: No one outside a ring (formed by a list of identities) can convince the server that he is in the ring. This property guarantees the authentication of a user's membership in a submitted ring.

R4: The scheme must resist the replay attack and parallel session attack.

R5: The scheme should achieve mutual authentication. Not only can server verify the legal users, but users can verify the legal server.

R6: The scheme should preserve user's privacy, namely, a server could not tell a user's real identity.

R7: The scheme should support Diffie-Hellman key exchange protocol, and resist man-in-middle attack.

R8: The scheme should be efficient, and the computational cost at user end should not grow as the size of ring expands.

3 Our Scheme

In this section, we present our anonymous authentication scheme. We start by listing some of the notations used in our paper, and then give the concrete scheme.

The following notations are used in our paper:

- U: a user who run the protocol to login into the remote servers.
- ID: user U's identity.
- $\mathcal{L}:= \{ID_1, \cdots, ID_n\}$, is a list of n identities, with one of which is set to be U's identity, say $ID_k = ID$ for some $k \in [1, n]$.
- PW: a password freely chosen by U.
- S: remote server.
- l: a security parameter ≥ 1024.
- p: a large prime satisfying $|p| = l$.
- g: a primitive element in Galois field $GF(p)$.
- z: a secret key maintained by S.
- $H(.), h(.):\{0,1\}^* \rightarrow \{0,1\}^l$ two collision free secure one-way hash function.

In our setting , we assume that the server S holds a secret key $z(|z| = l)$ that is used to generate user-dependent secret information, and each user U has an identity ID and a password PW. The scheme is mainly composed of two phases: registration phase and anonymous authentication and key exchange phase. In registration phase, a new user U submits his identity ID and password PW to S, and then receives a tamper-proof smart card issued by S. In anonymous authentication and key exchange phase, user U will establish an authenticated session key and achieve mutual authentication anonymously with S in three rounds.

The details are described below.

3.1 Registration Phase

When a new user U submits his identity ID and a password PW to the remote server S for registration, S first checks the validity of ID and then computes user-dependent information s_{ID} as follows, see Fig. 1:

$$s_{ID} = h(ID\|z) \oplus h(PW) \tag{1}$$

Then, server S stores the parameters $(s_{ID}, g, p, h(.), H(.))$ to a smart card. Finally, S issues the smart card to the user U via a secure channel.

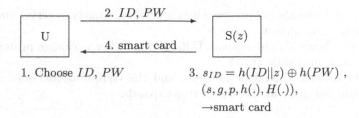

1. Choose ID, PW 3. $s_{ID} = h(ID\|z) \oplus h(PW)$,

$(s, g, p, h(.), H(.))$,

$\rightarrow$smart card

Fig. 1. Registration phase

3.2 Anonymous Authentication and Key Exchange Phase

This phase is initiated by U, and ends in three rounds, resulting in an authenticated session key between U and S. See Fig.2.

User $U(ID = ID_k)$	Server S (z)
Round 1 :$\mathcal{L} = \{ID_1, \cdots, ID_n\}$	
$r \in_R Z_p^*$ and $X = g^x$	
$C = r \oplus H(s_{ID} \oplus h(PW), T, X)$	
$\quad = r \oplus H(h(ID\|z), T, X)$	
$\xrightarrow{\quad \mathcal{L} \quad C \quad T \quad X \quad}$	
Round 2 :	$Y = g^y$
	$r_i = C \oplus H(h(ID_i\|z), T, X)$
	$\beta_i = H(h(ID_i\|z), T', X, r_i) \oplus Y$
	$K = X^y$
	$Auth = H(\mathcal{L}, T', \{\beta_i\}, X, Y, K)$
	$\xleftarrow{\{\beta_i\} \quad Auth \quad T'}$
Round 3 :$Y' = \beta_k \oplus H(s_{ID} \oplus h(PW), T', X, r)$	
$K' = Y'^x$	
$Auth' = H(\mathcal{L}, T', \{\beta_i\}, X, Y', K')$	
checks $Auth' \overset{?}{=} Auth$	
establish $K' = g^{xy}$ $\xrightarrow{\quad H(\mathcal{L}, m, K') \quad m \quad}$ checks $H(\mathcal{L}, m, K') \overset{?}{=} H(\mathcal{L}, m, K)$	establish $K = g^{xy}$

Fig. 2. Anonymous Authentication and Key Exchange Phase

Round1: When U wants to login to the remote server anonymously, he attaches his smart card to the login device and keys in his ID and PW. Then,

1. collect a group of n identities, and compose an identity list $\mathcal{L} = \{ID_1, \cdots, ID_n\}$, including U's own identity $ID = ID_k$ for some $k \in [1, n]$.
2. select a random exponent $x \in Z_p^*$, and compute $X = g^x \bmod p$.
3. select a $l-$bit random number r, and compute

$$C = r \oplus H(s_{ID} \oplus h(PW), T, X) = r \oplus H(h(ID \oplus z), T, X) \quad (2)$$

where T is the current time stamp of login device.
4. send the request message $M = (\mathcal{L}, C, T, X)$ to the remote server.

Round2: After receiving the request message M, S checks the time interval between T and receiving time, if the interval is beyond the reasonable transmission delay, the login request will be rejected. Otherwise, S will continue as follows:

1. select a random exponent $y \in Z_p^*$, and compute $Y = g^y \bmod p$.
2. for every $1 \le i \le n$, compute

$$r_i = C \oplus H(h(ID_i||z), T, X) \tag{3}$$
$$\beta_i = H(h(ID_i||z), T', X, r_i) \oplus Y \tag{4}$$

where T' is the current time stamp of server.

3. compute

$$K = X^y \bmod p \tag{5}$$
$$Auth - H(C, T', \{\beta_i\}, X, Y, K) \tag{6}$$

where $\{\beta_i\}$ is a list all of β_i for $i = 1, \cdots, n$.

4. S sends $(\{\beta_i\}, Auth, T')$ back to U.

Round3: After receiving S's reply, U checks the time interval between T' and receiving time, if the interval is beyond the reasonable transmission delay, U aborts the protocol. Otherwise, U will continue as follows:

1. compute $Y' = \beta_k \oplus H(s_{ID} \oplus h(PW), T', X, r)$.
2. compute $K' = Y'^x \bmod p$, and $Auth' = H(\mathcal{L}, T', \{\beta_i\}, X, Y', K')$,
3. checks whether $Auth' = Auth$ holds or not. If it holds, U accepts $K' = Y'^x = g^{xy} \bmod p$ as valid session key, and sends back $(H(\mathcal{L}, m, K'), m)$ for S to confirm the authenticated session key K, where m could be some message payloads. Otherwise, U aborts the protocol.

After successful execution of the protocol, U establishes a session key $K = g^{xy} \bmod p$ anonymously with S.

The correctness could easily be checked. Recall that $ID = ID_k$, $s_{ID} = s_{ID_k} = h(ID_k \oplus z) \oplus h(PW)$, then:

$$
\begin{aligned}
r_k &= C \oplus H(h(ID_k||z), T, X) \\
&\overset{equation(2)}{=} r \oplus H(h(ID||z), T, X) \oplus H(h(ID_k||z), T, X) \\
&= r
\end{aligned}
$$

$$
\begin{aligned}
Y' &= \beta_k \oplus H(s_{ID} \oplus h(PW), T', X, r) \\
&\overset{equation(4)}{=} H(h(ID_k||z), T', X, r_k) \oplus Y \oplus H(h(ID||z), T', X, r) \\
&= Y
\end{aligned}
$$

therefore

$$K' = Y'^x = Y^x = g^{xy} = K$$

$$Auth' = H(\mathcal{L}, T', \{\beta_i\}, X, Y', K')$$
$$= H(\mathcal{L}, T', \{\beta_i\}, X, Y, K)$$
$$= Auth$$

3.3 Changing Password

In our scheme, the password could be changed freely by user without registration again. That is, after receiving the current password PW and the new password PW^*, the login device will first confirm the validity of PW (e.g. by interacting with S), if PW is valid, then the login device replaces $s_{ID}(= h(ID\|z) \oplus h(PW))$ with $s_{ID} \oplus h(PW) \oplus h(PW^*)$, otherwise, the changing password request is rejected.

4 Discussion

In this section, we will first discuss the property and security of our scheme, so as to show our scheme meets all the requirements presented in section 2, and then we will analysis its performance.

4.1 Property and Security Analysis

Following the requirements presented in section 2, we examine the property and security of our scheme as follows:

R1. Traditional authentication schemes maintain a verification table at the server side to store all the registered users' passwords. Therefore, an intruder can impersonate a legal user by stealing the user's ID and PW from the verification table, or launch a successful denial of service (DOS) attack by modifying the verification table, because the server may refuse to accept all the valid login requests. In our scheme, the only value a server has to keep secret is the secret key z, and there is no password or verification table in the server. Such setting naturally makes our scheme resist stolen-verifier attack and modification attack. Therefore, our scheme meets the requirement R1.

R2. It could be easily checked that our scheme satisfies requirement R2 since a user can choose and change password as described in our scheme.

R3. No one can impersonate a legal user inside a ring to login the remote server in our scheme. In our scheme, an attacker with identity ID^* may have already possessed a registered user's secret information, that is $h(ID^*\|z)$. However, because of the hardness of inverting hash function $h(.)$, it is computationally infeasible for the attacker to calculate server's secret key z. Without z, it is hard for the attacker to forge a new registered information on any ID other than ID^*. This will further hinder the attacker from extract Y from $\beta_i = H(h(ID_i\|z), T', X, r_i) \oplus Y$, since $ID_i \neq ID^*$ and the attacker has no idea of $h(ID_i\|z)$ for $i = 1, \cdots, n$. Therefore, the attacker can not establish a session key with server to authenticate himself as a member within the submitted ring.

R4. Our scheme can defeat replay attack. The messages transmitted over the network in our scheme can not be intercepted for reuse, because of the involvement of time stamp. And the server could check the freshness of a received message by testing whether the transmission time is within legal transmission delay.

Our scheme can defeat parallel session attack. Parallel session attacks [9] occurs when an intruder first intercepts a server response message and then use the intercepted message as a login request in another parallel session to masquerade as a legal user. In our scheme, the components in the login request and response message are non symmetric, therefore a response message could not be used as login request, which defeats the parallel session attacks.

R5. Our scheme achieves mutual authentication. If an attacker wants to masquerade as a server, he should be able to compute a server response message ($\{\beta_i = H(h(ID_i||z), T', X, r_i) \oplus Y\}, Auth, T'$) to match the user login server request $C = r \oplus H(h(ID||z), T, X)$, where $r = r_k$ for some $k \in [1, n]$. However, without knowing z, it is impossible for the attacker to learn r from C, which further prevent the attack from composing a valid $\beta_k = H(h(ID_k||z), T', X, r) \oplus Y\}$ and $Auth$. Therefore, a server could authenticate itself to a user. Discussion of R3 has showed that a user could authenticate his membership in the submitted ring $\mathcal{L}$, so our scheme satisfied R5.

R6. Here, we will show that our scheme achieves user anonymity. In the first rounds of authentication and key exchange phase, a user's request message is $C = r \oplus H(h(ID||z), T, X)$, which is indeed a random string in server's view because of the randomness of r. So a server can not tell the identity of the user. After the second and third rounds, the only clue a server can get is that the user is someone among the list $\mathcal{L}$. Therefore, the real identity is hid from server.

It should be pointed out that a server in our scheme is always assumed to be honest. Indeed, a malicious server could learn whether the identity of user is the guessed identity $ID_i \in \mathcal{L}$ for some i by first choosing an unique $Y_i = g^{y_i}$ for computing r_i and β_i, and then letting $Auth = H(\mathcal{L}, T', \{\beta_i\}, X, Y_i, K = X^{y_i})$. So, the server could learn that the identity of user is ID_i if $Auth$ passes the check in Round 3. However, such a cheating could be detected by user with a probability of $\frac{n-1}{n}$, which will ruin the reputation of the server. So, it is reasonable to assume that the server is honest in our scheme.

R7. In addition, our scheme can support Diffie-Hellman key exchange as described in section 3. After execution of the protocol, there is an anonymous secret channel established between the user and the server. And due to the implicit mutual authentication, the X and Y components in the protocol can not be modified or replaced by a third party. Therefore, our scheme can resist man-in-middle attack.

R8. The detailed computational analysis is given in the next section. Here, we point out that the computational cost at user end is constant, which does not depend on the size of the ring (the length of $\mathcal{L}$).

Table 1. Performance evaluation

	Exp	Mul	Hash	XOR
Liao-Lee-Hwang's scheme	4	1	2	×
Viet-Yammura-Tanaka's scheme	6	2	4	1
Our scheme	2	×	4	4

4.2 Performance Evaluation

In a wireless mobile application, security related operations are often performed inside a tamper-proof smart card, which is characterized as lower-powered and resource-constrained devices. Therefore, computation performance at the user end is always regarded as a key criteria for a smart card based scheme. Here we mainly discuss our schemes' computation costs at user end.

The following notations are used to analyze the computation costs: Exp denotes the time for modular exponentiation; Mul is the time for modular multiplication; Hash is the time for hash operation; and XOR is the time for exclusive OR operation.

Now we compare our scheme with the one proposed by Liao-Lee-Hwang [1] and the one proposed by Viet-Yammura-Tanaka [4] respectively, since the former is an authentication scheme that meets all our requirements except for user anonymity, and the latter is a user anonymous scheme. The result is shown in Table 1.

It could be easily checked that the computational cost at smart card end in our scheme is very low compared with the other two schemes, because the computation in our scheme is mainly hash and XOR operation. Note, all the three schemes listed in the Table 1 support Diffie-Hellman key exchange, so the 2 **Exp** operations are indeed necessary to perform the key exchange protocol.

5   Conclusion

User anonymity is attached great importance in recent years to preserving user privacy in wired or wireless network environments. In this paper, we first briefly analyze the user anonymity issue in authentication schemes, and propose a concrete password-based authentication scheme that could preserve user privacy and support key exchange. Besides user anonymity, we show that our scheme is secure and possesses many other good virtues, such as no password tables, mutual authentication, user chosen password. Moreover, we give a detailed analysis on the computational performance of our scheme, which shows the scheme is efficient enough to be implemented in wireless mobile applications.

Acknowledgement

This work was supported in part by the National Natural Science Foundation of China for Distinguished Young Scholars under Grant No. 60225007, the National Research Fund for the Doctoral Program of Higher Education of China under Grant No. 20020248024, and the Science and Technology Research Project of Shanghai under Grant No. 04DZ07067, and the Special Research Funds of Huawei.

References

1. Liao,I.E., Lee,C.C., Hwang,M.S.: A password authentication scheme over insecure networks. J. Comput. System Sci. (2005).
2. Rivest,R., Shamir,A., Tauman,Y.: How to leak a secret. Advances in Cryptology ASIACRYPT' 01, LNCS, Vol. 2248,Springer-Verlag, Berlin Heidelberg New York (2001) 552-565
3. Chaum,D., Heyst,E.V.: Group signatures. Advances in Cryptology EUROCRYPT' 91, LNCS, Vol. 547,Berlin: Spring-Verlag,(1991) 257-265
4. Viet,D.Q., Yamamura,A., Tanaka.,H.: Anonymous password-based authenticated key exchange, Advances In Cryptology INDOCRYPT 2005, LNCS,Vol. 3797, Berlin: Spring-Verlag, (2005) 244-257
5. Bo,Z., Wan,Z.G., Kankanhalli,M.S., Feng,B., Deng,R.H.: Anonymous secure routing in mobile ad-hoc networks, Local Computer Networks, 2004. 29th Annual IEEE International Conference on 16-18 Nov. (2004) 102 - 108
6. Dodis,Y., Kiayias,A., Nicolosi,A., Shoup,V.: Anonymous identification in ad hoc groups. Advances in Cryptology - EUROCRYPT 2004,LNCS Vol. 3027,Berlin: Spring-Verlag, (2001) 609 -626
7. Chien,H.Y., Chen,C.H.: A remote authentication scheme preserving user anonymity, In: Proceedings of the 19th International Conference on Advanced Information Networking and Applications - AINA 2005, 245 - 248
8. Chien,H.Y., Jan,J., Tseng,Y.: An efficient and practical solution to remote authentication: smart card. Computer Security. Vol. 21(4) (2002) 372 - 375
9. Hsu,C.L.: Security of Chien et al.'s remote user authentication scheme using smart cards. Computer Standards and Inerfaces, 26(3)(2004) 167-169
10. Lu,R.X., Cao,Z.F., Su,R.W.: A self-encryption remote user anonymous authentication scheme using smart cards, Journal of Shanghai Jiaotong University, (2006)
11. Hwang,M.S., Li,L.H.: A new remote user authentication scheme using smart cards. IEEE Trans. Consum. Electron. Vol 46 (1)(2000)28 - 30
12. Lamport,L.: Password authentication with insecure communication. Communication of ACM Vol 24 (11)(1981) 770 -772
13. Yang,W.H., Shieh,S.P.: Password authentication schemes with smart card. Computer Security. Vol 18 (8)(1999) 727 - 733
14. Wu,S.T., Chieu,B.C.: A user friendly remote authentication scheme with smart cards, Computers & Security. Vol 22(6)(2003) 547-550
15. Chen,C.M., Ku,W.C., Stolen-verifier attack on two new strong-password authentication protocal. IEICE Transactions on Communications, Vol. E85-B,(11) (2002) 2519-2521
16. Damgard,I.: A design principle for hash functions. in: Advances in Cryptology, CRYPTO 89, LNCS Vol. 435 (1989) 416-427

A Trust-Based Routing Framework in
Energy-Constrained Wireless Sensor Networks*

Cheng Weifang[1], Liao Xiangke[1], Shen Changxiang[2], Li Shanshan[1],
and Peng Shaoliang[1]

[1] School of Computer Science, National University of Defense Technology,
Changsha, China, 410073
[2] First Lab, Computing Technique Institute of the Navy, Beijing, China, 100841
{wfangch, xkliao, shen, shanshanli, slpeng}@nudt.edu.cn

Abstract. As wireless sensor networks continue to grow, so does the need for effective security mechanisms. The classical mechanisms, namely authentication and encryption, can prevent some outsider attacks; however, these mechanisms are inefficient in detecting selective forwarding attacks on compromised nodes. On the basis of these observations, we build a trust model to evaluate nodes behavior. Based on the trust model, a routing framework, TRUSTEE, is further proposed for secure routing. TRUSTEE provides a flexible and feasible approach to evaluate routes' quality and chooses route that best meets the security requirements. Keeping into mind the critical resource constraint nature of sensor network, we do not adopt the energy-consuming monitoring and trust recommendations mechanisms. Simulation and analysis verify TRUSTEE's performance, it not only minimizes resource consumption but also can prevent most outsider attacks, defend selective forwarding attacks and thus significantly increase the network throughput.

1 Introduction

Wireless sensor networks have received a lot of attention recently due to their wide applications in military and civilian operations. Many sensor networks have mission-critical tasks, so it is clear that security needs to be taken into account at design time. Usually security in classical networks is achieved through authentication and encryption. These techniques could be considered as a first line of defense as they are more preventive schemes and could not provide a complete security framework for sensor networks. Indeed, the use of authentication and encryption cannot prevent a compromised node that is an authorized participant to the network to do any misbehavior, such as selective forwarding attacks.

Trust is currently a hot issue in various networks, such as P2P, ad hoc networks. Trust can solve some problems beyond the power of the traditional cryptographic security, for example, judging the behaviors of sensor nodes. We argue that it necessary to use trust management to build secure and dependable wireless sensor network applications. The trust issue is emerging as the sensor network thrives. However, it is not easy to build a comprehensive and practical trust model within a sensor network

* Supported by the National High-Tech Research and Development Program of China (Grant No. 2005AA121570, 2002AA1Z2101 and 2003AA1Z2060).

X. Cheng, W. Li, and T. Znati (Eds.): WASA 2006, LNCS 4138, pp. 478–489, 2006.

given the critical resource constraints. Furthermore, in order to keep the sensor nodes independent, we should not assume there is a trust among sensors in advance. Besides, since sensor networks pose unique challenges, existing trust models for other networks cannot be applied to sensor networks.

In this paper, we firstly propose a trust model to evaluate nodes trustworthiness based on their behaviors to detect compromised nodes. Although compromised nodes may do various misbehaviors, what we consider is selective forwarding attacks or packet dropping attacks along this paper. Taking into the account the energy constraints, we haven't considered the traditional monitoring or overhearing mechanisms. Moreover, because sensor networks are data-centric and sensor nodes only have localized interactions, popular trust recommendations can't help to evaluate trustworthiness, but cause many additional message overheads. Instead, we only record two factors at runtime: packet re-transmitting ratio and packet forwarding cooperativity, which rely on the MAC layer re-transmitting and routing acknowledgement replies techniques. Furthermore, to the authors' knowledge, little research has been done on the trust establishment in the bootstrapping phase. It is not proper for most trust mechanisms to just specify initial trust value one constant since there is no trust among sensors in advance. In our trust model, we establish initial trust relationship through node authentication. Based on the model, we further establish a trust-based routing framework where next-hop selecting is also based on the neighbor trustworthiness and the data security level.

The rest of this paper is organized as follows. Section 2 discusses related work. Section 3 provides a complete description of our trust model in detail. Based on section 3, section 4 describes our trust-based routing framework TRUSTEE. Section 5 provides performance evaluation and analysis, and section 6 concludes the paper.

2 Related Work

Because sensor networks may interact with sensitive data or operate in hostile unattended environments, it is imperative that these security concerns be addressed from the beginning of the system design [1]. Only recently researchers have studied the impact of malicious attacks on these networks [2,3,4]. There have been several proposals, mostly based on cryptography, to ensure secure communication on these resource constrained nodes such as SPINS[5], TinySec[6], INSENS[7], TinyPK[8] etc. The establishment and management of cryptographic keys [5,9,10,11] form the backbone of these schemes. Node authentication and data encryption can prevent networks from most outsider attacks. However this is still inefficient to selective forwarding attacks with respect to compromised nodes [2]. Therefore a few researchers start studying trust management in sensor networks [12,13,14]. At the same time, many literatures study trust management in ad hoc networks. Although great differences exist between ad hoc and sensor networks, some work [15,16,17,18] in ad hoc networks still enlightens me a lot.

Tanachaiwiwat et al. [12] propose a mechanism of location-centric isolation of misbehavior and establishing trust routing in sensor networks. In their trust model, the trustworthiness value is derived from the capacity of the cryptography, availability and packet forwarding. If the trust value is below a specific trust threshold, then this location is considered insecure and is avoided when forwarding packets.

Ganeriwal and Srivastava propose a reputation-based framework for high integrity sensor networks [13]. Within this framework the authors employ a beta reputation system for reputation representation, updates, and integration. A watchdog monitors the data forwarding behavior of the neighboring nodes by keeping the radio active in the promiscuous and checks for outlier detection by observing the consistency of raw sensing data among the neighboring nodes.

Abu-Ghazaleh et al. [14] consider the security of geographical forwarding. They propose a location verification algorithm avoiding misbehaving nodes falsifying their location information. They also propose approaches for route authentication and trust-based route selection to defeat attacks on the network. However they also rely on the overhearing process to perform trust management.

Marti et al. [19] detects misbehaving nodes by overhearing transmission. It maintains a buffer of recently sent packets and compares each overheard packet with the packet in the buffer to see if there is a match. If a packet remained longer than timeout, then it increases a failure tally for the responsible node or if the tally exceeds a threshold, the node is determined to be misbehaving and the source will be notified. Its advantage is that it can detect misbehavior at the forwarding level.

But as the author [12] mentioned, the packet monitoring to get evaluation information is power-wasteful and not suitable for sensor network. Firstly sensor networks may employ sleep/wakeup duty cycle to conserve energy, in which case overhearing may not be possible and may lead to excessive energy wastage. Secondly overhearing encrypted packets can't do any help to us since the link may be encrypted. Besides, trust recommendations in above work do no help but cause many message overheads since sensor nodes only interact with neighbors and base stations.

Unlike above work, our approaches do not rely on any watchdog mechanism such as monitoring or overhearing. We don't use any trust recommendation technique either. In this paper, we propose a scheme to detect both unavailability of failed nodes and selective forwarding attacks of compromised nodes with minimum energy consumption.

3 A Trust Model

For a sensor node, sensing, computation and communication are main behaviors. As far as our research goes, we define trust in this model as the reliability of packets delivery to their intended next-hop. In this section we describe the trust model in detail. The goal of the model is to establish sufficient trust relationships in sensor networks with minimum storage capacity requirements, no extra messages and negligible computational overheads on sensor nodes. Without loss of generality, we draw two basic assumptions: every node contains information in its neighborhood; neighboring nodes share secret keys between each other in order to communicate securely and the shared keys are well pre-distributed in networks through key management.

3.1 Initial Trust Establishment

Sensor networks are always deployed in hostile environments. Hostile nodes may be injected into the sensor network by an adversary at any time. Therefore, each node should authenticate its neighbors. We can establish initial trust relationship by node authentication.

In the bootstrapping phase, each sensor sends authentication messages to its neighbors. The authentication messages are encrypted with the corresponding shared key. If the neighbor denoted by node i is legal, node i should hold the corresponding shared key and can decrypt the message. Afterwards, node i sends one authentication reply to the authentication requesting sensor. Until now it can trust node i. Therefore the initial trust relationship has been established, and the initial trust value on node i is 1. Otherwise, the sensor will claim that i is an illegal node, get rid of node i from its own neighbor set, add it to its black list discussed in section 3.2, and report it to the base station. Similarly, all nodes in the network will refuse to add it to be its neighbor. Then the adversary is prevented from joining the topology of the network.

3.2 Trust Parameters

As discussed in the above section, a node's trustworthiness is defined by its behavior. Based on the unique characteristics of sensor networks, we define following important factors for evaluation.

• Black List
Black list is used for isolating hostile and compromised nodes in sensor networks. Because of not needing global routing information, every sensor maintains a black list recording which neighbor is compromised or malicious. And only the base station holds a black list of the whole network. If one neighbor's trust value is lower than a threshold η, it will be regarded as compromised one, deleted from the neighbor set and added into the black list. That is, it will be ultimately denied by the whole network.

• Packet Re-transmitting Ratio
Packet re-transmitting mechanism is used when packets are lost in many existing Medium Access Control (MAC) layer protocols for wireless sensor network [20, 21,22]. In IEEE 802.11 MAC protocol, all communication adopts active ACK mechanism (RTS/CTS). If the sender fails to get an ACK for any packet, it will re-transmit the packet until the transmission time reaches a threshold. Packet dropping is always due to malicious routing disruption, poor wireless communication quality or heavy traffic. Frequent re-transmitting means poor link quality and uncooperative node behavior. Benign nodes failures, such as battery depletion, and disabled nodes can also cause frequent re-transmitting. Thus, re-transmitting ratio is a very important factor to evaluate nodes trustworthiness.

According to the characteristic of some MAC protocols in sensor networks, it is convenient to count the corresponding re-transmitting ratio about each neighbor. The dynamic re-transmitting ratio from node i to its neighbor j, defined as $Rtran_{i,j}$, is calculated as the proportion of the number of needing re-transmitted ones with respect to the total number of packets to be forwarded from i to j during a fixed time window, as shown in equation (1).

$$Rtran_{i,j} = \frac{n}{m} \tag{1}$$

Where n represents the number of re-transmitted packets, and m represents the total number of packets to be forwarded to j.

- **Packet Forwarding Cooperativity**

It is very hard to defend from compromised nodes doing selective forwarding attacks [2]. High packet forwarding cooperativity stands for more cooperative behavior and trusted next-hop. Therefore, this factor is necessary to estimate nodes trustworthiness.

In order to evaluate the neighbors' packet forwarding cooperativity, each node holds a forwarded packets index table for recently forwarded packets. The table includes M entries for each neighbor. Each entry contains a tuple with the form: (source_node, destination_node, next-hop). For example, let's consider node i. A tuple (S, t, j) means that a packet P, which is from s to destination t, has been forwarded by i to its neighbor j. We can modify routing protocols to support acknowledgments to the source node. Then if i receives a reply from its neighbor j, (Sourced from t to s), which implies the packet P has been successfully forwarded to destination through j. In this way, the packet forwarding cooperativity can be increased. Naturally, we compute the packet forwarding cooperativity, denoted by $Pforw_{i,j}$, as proportion of received corresponding replies from j with respect to the total number of recently forwarded packets by j, as follows.

$$Pforw_{i,j} = \frac{reply_j}{M} \qquad (2)$$

Where $reply_j$ represents received corresponding replies from j in a given time window.

3.3 Trust Value Metric

Each node maintains the trust values of all neighbors that form one trust table. Considering both the packet re-transmitting ratio and the packet forwarding cooperativity, we use a simple but adaptive metric:

$$T_{i,j} = \frac{Pforw_{i,j}{}^{\alpha}}{Rtran_{i,j}{}^{\beta}} \qquad (3)$$

Here $T_{i,j}$ is the trust evaluation result conducted by node i for node j. $Pforw_{i,j}$ is normalized packet forwarding cooperativity and $Rtran_{i,j}$ is normalized packet re-transmitting ratio. Both the weighting factors α and β are positive number, which can be chosen to put emphasis upon the former or the latter. Further study needs to be done as to the best metric as it has a deep impact on the trust evaluation performance.

3.4 Trust Levels

For convenience, a logical trust level hierarchy is assigned to each node, as described and outlined in table 1. Here we simply classify various trust value into four trust levels. Each trust level is mapped to one corresponding trust value range. Indeed, this mapping can be defined differently.

Table 1. Trust levels

Value	Meaning	Trust Value Range	Description
0	Untrustworthy	$[0, \eta)$	Malicious, failed, or compromised
1	Minimum	$[\eta, 0.5)$	A low trust level
2	Good	$[0.5, 0.75)$	More trustworthy than most nodes
3	High	$[0.75, 1]$	An extremely high trust level

4 Trustee Framework

In this section, we provide a high level discussion of TRUSTEE based on our proposed trust model.

In existing routing protocols, some of them select next-hop by judging some cost metrics [23,24]. For example, EAR uses energy metric [23] and GEAR [24] uses estimated cost about the distance and consumed energy. In TRUSTEE, we regard all consideration about energy and distance as cost, and assume the minimum cost is the optimal choice of next-hop.

In data-centric sensor networks, different data always have different importance and security levels. Generally, more important data need more secure and trusted routes. Here in table 2 we simply define four security levels in accordance with trust levels. When there is packet forwarding request, a required data security level is included in the request packet. In order to route important data along more trusted paths, choosing next-hop is also based on the data security level.

Table 2. Data security levels

Value	Meaning	Description
0	General	Unimportant data
1	Secret	Important data
2	Confidential	Very important data
3	Top-secret	An extremely important data

For each node i, TRUSTEE routes the packets according to the following rules:

1. For each node j in its neighbor set, the cost $Cost_j$ and trust value $T_{i,j}$ are computed. If $T_{i,j}$ is less than trust threshold η, put node j in its black list. Then compute the ratio $T_{i,j}/Cost_j$ which we call trust-cost ratio for those trustworthy neighbors.

2. Neighbors with a very low trust-cost ratio are discarded and not added to the forwarding table. Only the neighbors with high trust-cost ratio are added to the forwarding table FT_i of i.

$$FT_i = \left\{ j \left| \frac{T_{i,j}}{Cost_j} \ge \theta * \left(\max_k \left(\frac{T_{i,k}}{Cost_k} \right) \right) \right. \right\}$$ (4)

Where θ is a ratio constant between 0 and 1.

3.   For each $j \in FT_i$, only if its corresponding trust level is not less than the data security level, it can be added to trusted forwarding set TF_i, similar to the BLP model in mandatory access control [25]. When no nodes belong to TF_i, node i reports to its upstream nodes that it can't meet their security requirement, then they will delete it from their trusted forwarding sets. If, unfortunately, one upstream node's trusted forwarding set becomes empty again, this feedback process will proceed until it reaches the source.

4.   Node i assigns a probability to each neighbor j in the trusted forwarding set TF_i, with the probability inversely proportional to the cost and directly proportional to the trust value.

$$P_{i,j} = \frac{\dfrac{T_{i,j}}{Cost_j}}{\displaystyle\sum_{j \in TF_i} \dfrac{T_{i,j}}{Cost_j}}$$ (5)

5.   Thus, node i has several candidates through which it can route packets to the destination. Which node will be selected depends on a randomly generated number μ between (0,1). The node Q will be selected as next-hop neighbor only if it meets the following conditions. Here we sort the candidates by probability.

$$P_{i,1} \le P_{i,2} \le \cdots \le P_{i,|TF_i|}$$

$$\sum_{k=1}^{Q-1} P_{i,k} < \mu \le \sum_{k=1}^{Q} P_{i,k}$$ (6)

TRUSTEE helps defend selective forwarding attacks by filtering out nodes with trust value lower than trust threshold and forwarding more packets to nodes with higher trust-cost ratio.

5   Evaluation

This section presents the evaluation for TRUSTEE. We first investigate the resource requirements, then we evaluate the security of TRUSTEE by analyzing it over selective forwarding attacks and outsider attacks described in [2]. Finally the results of our simulation are presented.

5.1 Resource Requirement

TRUSTEE only requires little resource usage additional to general routing protocols for sensor nodes. The extra memory requirements for node i are now discussed. Given N is the maximum number of neighbors. The size of the black list is less than or equal to N, so does the trusted forwarding set and trust table. The forwarded packets index table contains no more than $N*M$ tuples. Therefore the total extra memory requirements are less than $3*N+3*N*M$ bytes and are only proportional to the number of neighbors. The computational requirements of TRUSTEE are negligible as they are similar to the requirements needed to update general routing metrics. Avoiding energy-hungry recommendations and monitoring, TRUSTEE requires no additional messages in the network so the additional power requirements are also negligible.

5.2 Security Analysis

Outsider attacks: In our routing framework, trust initialization established by node authentication can refuse outside attacker without shared cryptographic keys to arbitrarily intrude the network. An adversary will never have the chance to be selected as next-hop.

Selective Forwarding: Multihop networks are often based on the assumption that participating nodes will faithfully forward messages received. In a selective forwarding attack, compromised nodes may refuse to forward certain messages and simply drop them, ensuring that they are not propagated any further. Selective forwarding is very hard to detect since compromised nodes are not completely uncooperative and are authorized participants in networks. Multipath and choosing a packet's next-hop probabilistically from a set of possible candidates only can reduce the chances of an adversary gaining complete control of a data flow [3]. This attack can be defended by using our scheme, because it records the packet forwarding cooperativity. If some packets are not really forwarded to the destination by one node, the packets' upstream node   will   detect   that   trust   evaluation   value   on   that   node

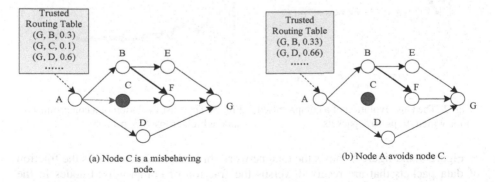

(a) Node C is a misbehaving node.

(b) Node A avoids node C.

Fig. 1. Example Scenario for detecting and isolating malicious node C

decreased as its packet forwarding cooperativity declined. Figure 1 shows a simple scenario for detecting and isolating malicious node C. Because of the selective forwarding of node C, the probability of node A's forwarding packet to node C will be very little and node C will even be excluded from the trusted routing table by node A. The worst case for node C is to be detruded into the black list. By using a forwarded packet index table to check whether the next hop node has forwarded the packet to the destination, selective forwarding nodes will be punished by declined trust evaluation. At last, TRUSTEE can detect selective forwarding attacks on compromised nodes and isolate them.

5.3 Simulation Results

Our simulation take place in a 100 by 100 meter flat space filled with a scattering of 40 wireless sensor nodes. We implement TRUSTEE combined with EAR [23], that is, the cost metric is the energy metric in EAR. Considering the simplicity and our goal to detect selective forwarding attacks, we compute trust metric only based on equation 2. During simulation, 1000 data packets are sent from one source to the sink and no data security is required.

We evaluate TRUSTEE using the following two metrics:

- Trust Evolution: the dynamic runtime trust value of one node about its neighbors.
- Throughput: the percentage of sent data packets actually received by the intended destinations.

Figure 2 and figure 3 respectively shows the runtime trust evolution of one compromised node which drops 50% and 70% packets in TRUSTEE without trust threshold. As expected, the trust values degrade quickly to 0.5 and 0.3 respectively and level off near to the two standard values.

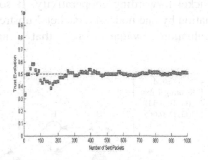
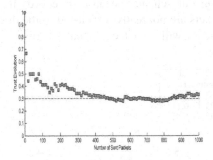
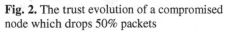

Fig. 2. The trust evolution of a compromised node which drops 50% packets

Fig. 3. The trust evolution of a compromised node which drops 70% packets

Figure 4 and figure 5 shows the total network throughput, calculated as the fraction of data packets that are received, versus the fraction of compromised nodes in the network. The channel error rate is normally distributed across the field. MAC protocol can assign a unique channel for every node to prevent possible collisions.

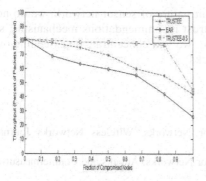   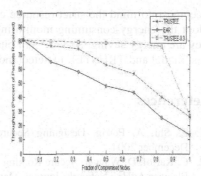

Fig. 4. Throughput with compromised nodes dropping 50% packets

Fig. 5. Throughput with compromised nodes dropping 70% packets

Thus in the case where the network contains no compromised nodes, all curves achieve around 80% throughput. After the no compromised node case, the graphs diverge. *EAR* is the basic energy aware routing protocol. *TRUSTEE* means no trust threshold mechanism and black lists. *TRUSTEE-0.5 (TRUSTEE-0.3)* means TRUSTEE with the trust threshold η equal to 0.5(0.3), where one node will be added to the black list when its trust value is less than 0.5(0.3).

As expected, TRUSTEE with threshold performs the best as compromised nodes are added to the network. Significantly, when not all nodes are compromised and we define trust threshold greater than packet dropping probability, the network throughput loses very little by avoiding the compromised nodes. TRUSTEE without trust threshold also performs much better than EAR. The mechanisms increase the throughput by up to 16% compared to EAR.

From the graphs we conclude that TRUSTEE can significantly increase the network throughput by avoiding the compromised nodes, thus it can defend selective forwarding attacks to a great extent.

6   Conclusions

With the emergence of the sensor networks paradigm, new security vulnerabilities arise. The classical mechanisms, namely authentication and encryption, can prevent some outsider attacks; however these mechanisms seem to be inefficient in detecting selective forwarding attacks. On the basis of these observations, we build a trust model to evaluate the nodes behavior and develop a community of trustworthy sensor nodes at runtime. Sensor nodes maintain trust for neighboring nodes and use it to evaluate their trustworthiness. Based on the trust model, we further propose a secure routing framework TRUSTEE. It uses trust value to guide packets forwarding. Trusted paths consist of only trusted nodes, and the most trustworthy path is used to transmit the top-secret data. TRUSTEE provides a flexible, general and feasible approach for evaluating routes and chooses the route that best meets the security requirements of the message being transmitted. Through TRUSTEE, the outsider adversaries are prevented, the selective forwarding attacks can be detected, and the compromised nodes are avoided. The proposed approaches do not require accurate synchronization.

Keeping into mind the strict resource constraint nature of sensor network, we do not adopt the energy-consuming monitoring and trust recommendations mechanisms, so they are energy saving. As part' s of our future we will concentrate on extending our trust model and TRUSTEE to detect more attacks.

References

1. E. Shi, A. Perrig. Designing Secure Sensor Networks. Wireless Networks Journal, December 2004
2. C. Karlof, D. Wagner. Secure Routing in Sensor Networks: Attacks and Countermeasures. Elsevier AdHoc Networks journal, May 2003
3. A. Perrig, J. Stankovic, D. Wagner. Security in Wireless Sensor Networks. Communications of the ACM, 2004
4. J. Newsome, E. Shi, D. Song, A. Perrig. The Sybil Attack in Sensor Networks: Analysis and Defenses. In Proceedings of IPTPS. March 2002
5. A. Perrig, R. Szewczyk, V. Wen, D. Culler, D. Tygar. SPINS: Security Protocols for Sensor Networks. Wireless Networks Journal, September 2002
6. C. Karlof, N. Sastry, D. Wagner. TinySec: Link Layer Encryption for Tiny Devices. In Proceedings of ACM SenSys, 2004
7. J. Deng, R. Han and S. Mishra. The Performance Evaluation of Intrusion-Tolerant Routing in Wireless Sensor Networks. In the Proceedings of IPSN, April, 2003
8. R. Watro, D. Kong, S. F. Cuti, C. Gardiner, C. Lynn, P. Kruus. TinyPK: Securing Sensor Networks with Public Key Technology. In second workshop on Security in Sensor and Ad-hoc Networks, 2004
9. L. Eschenauer, V. D. Gligor. A Key Management Scheme for Distributed Sensor Networks. In Proceedings of ACM CCS, November 2002
10. H. Chan, A. Perrig, D. Song. Random Key Predistribution Schemes for Sensor Networks. In Proceedings of IEEE Symposium on Security and Privacy, 2003
11. D. Liu, P. Ning. Establishing Pairwise Keys in Distributed Sensor Networks. In Proceedings of ACM CCS, October 2003
12. S. Tanachaiwiwat, P. Dave, R. Bhindwale, and A. Helmy. Location-centric Isolation of Misbehavior and Trust Routing in Energy-constrained Sensor Networks. In IEEE Workshop on Energy-Efficient Wireless Communications and Networks (EWCN04), in conjunction with IEEE IPCCC. April. 2004
13. S. Ganeriwal and M. Srivastava. Reputation-based Framework for High Integrity Sensor Networks. In Proceedings of the 2nd ACM workshop on Security of ad hoc and sensor networks, 2004
14. Nael AbuGhazaleh, KyoungDon Kang and Ke Liu. Towards Resilient Geographic Routing in WSNs. In Proceedings of the 1st ACM international workshop on Quality of service & security in wireless and mobile networks. Montreal, Quebec, Canada. Pages: 71 - 78. 2005,10
15. Z. Yan, P. Zhang, and T. Virtanen. Trust Evaluation Based Security Solution in Ad Hoc Networks. In Proceedings of the Seventh Nordic Workshop on Secure IT Systems, 2003
16. K. Ren, T. Li, Z. Wan, F. Bao, R. H. Deng, and K. Kim. Highly Reliable Trust Establishment Scheme in Ad Hoc Networks. Computer Networks: The International Journal of Computer and Telecommunications Networking 45:687–699, Aug. 2004

17. Liu Z Y, Joy A W, Thompson R A. Thompson R A. A dynamic Trust Model for Mobile Ad Hoc Networks. In: The 10th IEEE Intl.Workshop on Future Trends of Distributed Computing Systems (FTDCS'04), Suzhou, China, May 2004. 80~85

18. Yacine Rebahi, Vicente E. Mujica V, Dorgham Sisalem. A Reputation-Based Trust Mechanism for Ad Hoc Networks. Proceedings of the 10th IEEE Symposium on Computers and Communications (ISCC 2005), 27-30 June 2005

19. S. Marti, T.J. Giuli, K. Lai, M. Baker. Mitigating Routing Misbehavior in Mobile Ad Hoc Networks. ACM MobiCOM, Aug 00

20. Wei Ye, John Heidemann, Deborah Estrin. An Energy-Efficient MAC Protocol for Wireless Sensor Networks. In: Proc 21st Int'1 Annual Joint Conf IEEE Computer and Communication Societies(INFOCOM 2002), New York, NY, June 2002

21. Van Dam T, Langendoen K. An adaptive energy-efficient MAC protocol Wireless Sensor Networks. In: Proc 1st Int'1 Conf on Embedded Networked Sensor Systems (SenSys), Nov 5-7, 2003, Los Angeles, CA

22. IEEE Computer Society LAN MAN Standards Committee. IEEE Std 802.11-1999, Wireless LAN Medium Access Control (MAC) and Physical Layer (PHY) specification. 1999

23. R. C. Shah and J. Rabaey. Energy Aware Routing for Low Energy Ad Hoc Sensor Networks. In: IEEE Wireless Communications and Networking Conference (WCNC), March 17-21, 2002, Orlando, FL

24. Y. Yu, R. Govindan, and D. Estrin. Geographical and Energy Aware Routing: A recursive Data Dissemination Protocol for Wireless Sensor Networks. Technical Report UCLA/CSD-TR-01-0023, UCLA, Department of Computer Science, May 2001

25. D. Bell and L. LaPadula, Secure Computer Systems: Mathematical Foundations and Model, Technical Report MTR 2547 v2, MITRE, Nov. 1973

Minimum Multicast Time Problem in Wireless Sensor Networks*

Jianming Zhu, Xujin Chen, and Xiaodong Hu

Institute of Applied Mathematics, Chinese Academy of Sciences
P.O. Box 2734, Beijing 100080, China

Abstract. Given an undirected graph representing a network of processors, and a source node needs to broadcast a message to all other nodes in the graph, the minimum broadcast time problem is to find a scheme that accomplishes the broadcast in a minimum number of time steps under the constraint that at each time round, any node can send the message to at most one of its neighbors in the network. This NP-complete problem has been extensively studied in literature.

In this paper, we consider a generation of the minimum broadcast problem, the minimum multicast time problem, in unit disk graphs which model wireless sensor networks. The goal is to multicast a message from the source node to a set of specified sensor nodes of the network in a minimum number of time rounds. We prove that this problem is NP-complete, and give an $O(1)-$approximation algorithm for it. Our simulation results show that the practical performance of the proposed algorithm is much better than the theoretically proved approximation ratio.

1 Introduction

Due to existing and emerging applications in various situations, Wireless Sensor Networks (WSNs) have recently emerged as a premier research topic. A wireless sensor network consists of a number of small-sized sensor nodes spreading over a geographical area and a source/sink node where the end user raises a query about certain sensor area and then accesses data gathered according to the query. All nodes are equipped with capabilities of sensing, data processing, and communicating with each other by means of a wireless ad hoc network. A wide range of tasks can be performed by these tiny devices, such as condition-based maintenance and the monitoring of a large area with respect to some given physical quantity, e.g., temperature, humidity, gravity and seismic information. Usually, the end user wants to extract information from the sensor field as soon as possible, which first requires fast multicast of the query to the sensors concerned.

In WSNs, hundreds to thousands of small, low-power sensor devices (nodes) are implanted inside or beside the phenomenon, and linked by a wireless medium. With the large population of sensor nodes, it may be impractical or energy consuming to pay attention to each individual nodes in all situations; for instance,

---

* Supported in part by the National Natural Science Foundation of China under Grant No. 70221001, 60373012 and 10531070.

X. Cheng, W. Li, and T. Znati (Eds.): WASA 2006, LNCS 4138, pp. 490–501, 2006.

the user would be more interested in querying the highest temperatures in some specified areas (instead of every area in the region). To provide a quick answer to the user, these queries need to be multicasted to the destination field with low latency.

In general, a message (signal) sent by a sensor (*sender*) can reach any of its neighbors within the transmission range of this sender. But transmission collision may occur when more than one sensors send messages to the same sensor at the same time, in this case the receiver could not receive any messages from the senders (as a result, messages have to be sent again or they will be lost). In order to avoid transmission collision, sensors can be equipped with antennaes or interfaces which enable the sender to send message to exact one of its neighbors; For example, the sender and the receiver could be assigned the same frequency or channel for transmission while other neighbors of this sender do not switch to this channel. Refer to [11,15,17] for more detailed description of the techniques. In this paper we assume collision-free transmission model in WSNs, which ensures the energy-efficiency (since no messages need to be sent more than once).

Motivated by various applications of time-efficient multicast, we study in this paper the *Minimum Multicast Time* (MinMT) problem in WSNs: Given a WSN in which a distinguished source s needs to multicast a query or message to a subset D of sensors, the goal of MinMT problem is to find a sending-receiving schedule such that the message from s reaches all nodes in D in minimum time. In our consideration, the geometric nature of WSNs is emphasized, and time efficiency is used as performance metric to evaluate multicast algorithms. As usual, the WSNs under investigation are modelled as unit disk graphs. By reduction from planar 3-SAT problem we shall prove that the MinMT problem is NP-complete even when all nodes have unit transmission radius, and are positioned at integer coordinates in the Euclidean plane. When designing the algorithm for the MinMT problem, we adopt the idea of square-partition, and propose an approximation algorithm with performance ratio 41.

The remainder of this paper is organized as follows. We first introduce in Section 2 some related works, and then in Section 3 specify the MinMT problem in WSNs assuming collision-free transmission. After proving in Section 4 the NP-hardness of MinMT problem, we present in Section 5 an $O(1)-$approximation algorithm for the MinMT problem in WSNs, and the theoretical proof of this performance guarantee. Then we provide in Section 6 simulation results of our algorithm. Finally we conclude this paper in Section 7 with remarks on future research.

2 Related Work

Gandhi *et al* [8] studied the problem of minimum latency broadcasting in Ad hoc networks. In their work, the node transmission ranges do not have to be uniform, and the network is modelled as a Disk Graph; when a node broadcasts a message, all nodes within the transmission range of this node receive this message simultaneously. They considered collision-free broadcasting, and gave an $O(1)$-approximation algorithm. Pelc [13] surveyed results concerning broadcasting time under different communication scenarios and presented several fast broadcasting algorithms, emphasizing the trade-off between the time of broadcasting and the amount of knowledge of the network available to the nodes.

Ravi [14] studied the minimum broadcast time problem under the model of telephone networks: given an undirected graph representing a network of processors, and a source node containing a message to be broadcasted to all the nodes, find a scheme that accomplishes the broadcast in the minimum number of time rounds; at each time round, any processor that has received the message can communicate the message to at most one of its neighbors in the network. This problem is known NP-complete [9], and Ravi presented an $O(\frac{\log^2 n}{\log \log n})$-approximation algorithm for it by using the poise of the graph. Further researches have done in [5,6,7]. The authors studied this problem in general directed and undirected graphs, but the approximation algorithms proposed did not achieve constant ratios.

Recently, data aggregation, which appears along with WSNs, has attracted much research efforts. As a reverse of multicast, sensors need to transmit data sensed to the sink which is usually identical with the source of multicast. In this data gathering process, data aggregations are proceeded at intermediate sensors for reducing energy-cost. Lots of works have done for energy-efficiency and time-efficiency [1,18,10]. Under the collision-free constraint, Chen et al [4] studied the minimum data aggregation time problem, assuming that data sent by a sensor reaches all sensors within its transmission range simultaneously; the authors proved that this problem is NP-complete and designed a $(\Delta - 1)$-approximation algorithm, where Δ is the maximum degree of the underlying graph.

In contract to the works in [8] and [4], the assumption in present paper is that every sensor has the capability of transmitting message to exactly one of its neighbors without interfere in message being sent and received at other neighbors in the same time round. In addition, the underlying graph we consider is Unit Disk Graph, which is different from that used in [14].

3   Model Description

In view of miniature design of sensor devices, this paper considers WSNs in which all nodes are fixed and homogeneous. More specifically, the WSN under investigation consists of stationary nodes (sensor nodes and a source node) distributed in the Euclidean plane. Assuming the transmission range of any sensor node is a unit disk (circular region with unit radius) centered at the sensor, we model a WSN as a *Unit Disk Graph* (UDG) $G = (V, E)$ in which two nodes $u, v \in V$ are considered neighbors, i.e., there is an edge $(u, v) \in E$ joining u and v, if and only if the Euclidean distance $||u - v||$ between u and v is at most one. An MinMT instance $(G, \mathsf{s}, \mathsf{D})$ consists of the UDG $G = (V, E)$ modelling the WSN, the source node $\mathsf{s} \in V$ originating the multicast and the destination field $\mathsf{D} \subseteq V$ containing destination sensors of the multicast.

Now the source node s needs to send a query or message to some other nodes in the destination field D. It is assumed that communication is deterministic and proceeds in synchronous *rounds* controlled by a global clock. At each time round, any sensor that has received the message is allowed to communicate to at most one of its neighbors in the network; in other words, all other neighbors of this sensor hear nothing from this sensor. Due to collision-free constraint, two sensors can not send message to the same sensor simultaneously. The solution of (G, s, D) is a schedule $\{(S_1, R_1), (S_2, R_2), \ldots, (S_s, R_s)\}$ such that S_r (resp. R_r) is the set of senders (resp. receivers) in round r, $r = 1, 2, \ldots, s$, and all nodes in D receive the message of s within s rounds. Note that every (S_r, R_r) gives implicitly the 1-1 correspondence between S_r and R_r in a way that $v \in S_r$ corresponds to its receiver in R_r. The value s is called the *multicast time* of solution $\{(S_1, R_1), (S_2, R_2), \ldots, (S_s, R_s)\}$. The MinMT problem is to find the optimal schedule with minimum multicast time $t_{OPT(G,s,D)}$.

In way of example, consider the MinMT instance (G, s, D) depicted in Fig.1(a), where the graph G contains the source node s and destination field $D = \{v_i \mid i = 1, 2, \cdots, 7\}$. In the first round, s sends message to v_3. In the second round, s sends message to v_1, and at the same time v_3 sends message to v_6. Although v_1 is located in the transmission range of v_3, no collision occurs at v_1 since the communication between s and v_1 and the communication between v_3 and v_6 use different frequencies. In the third round, s sends message to v_2, while v_1 sends message to v_4, v_3 sends message to v_5, and v_6 sends message to v_7. Fig.1(b) shows the schedule $\{(S_1, R_1), (S_2, R_2), (S_3, R_3)\} = \{(\{s\}, \{v_3\}), (\{s, v_3\}, \{v_1, v_6\}), (\{s, v_1, v_3, v_6\}, \{v_2, v_4, v_5, v_7\})\}$ with multicast time 3.

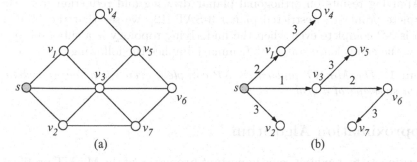

(a)   (b)

Fig. 1. An MinMT instance (G, s, D), where $D = \{v_i \mid i = 1, 2, \cdots, 7\}$

As usual (e.g. in [3]), we assume that each sensor knows its geometric position in the network, which is considered the unique ID of the sensor, and every sensor has global knowledge of all IDs in the WSN. The message will be sent from s to D following the schedule $\{(S_1, R_1), (S_2, R_2), \ldots, (S_s, R_s)\}$ determinately.

4   NP-Hardness Proof

Our NP-hardness proof is much similar to that in [4]. Let us consider a problem equivalent to the MinMT problem – the *Minimum Gathering Time* (MinGT) problem, whose definition already appeared in [14]. In an MinGT instance (G, S, d), the graph $G = (V, E)$ models the WSN, the set $S(\subseteq V)$ consists of nodes possessing messages requested by the sink node $d(\in V)$. The MinGT problem is to find a sending-receiving schedule $\{(S_1, R_1), (S_2, R_2), \ldots, (S_t, R_t)\}$ such that all messages on subset S are gathered to d in a minimum number t of time rounds, where in each round r $(r = 1, \ldots, t)$, S_r (resp. R_r) is the set of senders (resp. receivers), and

- a node can send message (be a *sender*) or receive message (be a *receiver*) but cannot do both;
- message sent by any sender *reaches* exactly one of its neighbors;
- a node receives a message only if the message is the only one that reaches it (in this round); and
- each receiver updates its message as the combination of its old message and the message received

The following lemma is obvious from the definitions of the MinMT problem and the MinGT problem.

Lemma 1. *Given a schedule of MinMT, a schedule for MinGT can be easily constructed just in the reverse order of the schedule of MinGT, and vice versa.*

Therefore the MinMT problem and the MinGT problem are equivalent, and it suffices to prove that the MinGT problem is NP-complete. The proof is very similar to the NP-hardness proof of the minimum data aggregation time problem in [4]. Applying results on orthogonal planar drawing and reduction from the NP-complete problem – restricted planar 3-SAT [12], we see that the MinGT problem is NP-complete even when the underlying topology is a subgraph of a grid. Now the equivalence stated by Lemma 1 implies the following theorem.

Theorem 1. *The MinMT problem is NP-complete even when the underlying graph is a subgraph of a grid.*

5   Approximation Algorithm

In this section we first exhibit some important properties of the MinMT problem. Then using these properties and the idea of square partition, we design an $O(1)$-approximation algorithm for the MinMT problem in WSNs.

5.1   Preliminary Results

Given an MinMT instance (G, s, D), a *shortest path tree* T of (G, s, D) is a tree in G consisting of shortest paths from s to nodes in D. The *height* of T, denoted by $h(G, s, D)$, equals to the length of the longest path in T from s to leaves of T. The following lower bound can be easily established by estimating multicasting time in a telephone network [2].

Lemma 2. $t_{OPT(G,s,D)} \geq \max\{h(G, s, D), \lceil \log_2 |\{s\} \cup D| \rceil\}$ *for any MinMT instance (G, s, D).*

Lemma 3. *If* $\{s\} \cup D$ *induces a complete subgraph graph of* G, *then* (G, s, D) *is optimally solvable in polynomial time, and* $t_{OPT(G,s,D)} = \lceil \log_2 |\{s\} \cup D| \rceil$.

Lemma 4. *If* H *is a complete subgraph of* G, *and one node of* H *has received the message, then the message can be broadcasted to all nodes in* H *along a tree* $\mathbb{T}_{V(H)}$ *of* H *within* $\lceil \log_2 |V(H)| \rceil$ *rounds.*

Note that given a tree T_s with root s, the minimum time to accomplish broadcast from s to the other nodes in T using only edges of T_s can be determined in polynomial time by using dynamic programming and working bottom-up in the rooted tree T_s [16]. Moreover, we have the following upper bound on the minimum broadcast time on T_s.

Lemma 5. *Given a tree* T_s *rooted at* s *with maximum degree* Δ *and height* h, *an optimal broadcast scheme on* T_s *starting from* s *and finishing within* Δh *rounds can be found in polynomial time.*

As an immediate corollary of Lemma 2 and Lemma 5, we have

Theorem 2. *Given an MinMT instance* (G, s, D), *if* G *is a subgraph of a grid, there exists a 4-approximation algorithm.*

Proof. Find a shortest path tree T_s of (G, s, D). Then the optimal broadcast scheme on T_s is a 4-approximation of the optimal solution of (G, s, D) since the maximum degree of T_s is at most 4.

In general unit disk graph G, if we always follow the same idea as in Theorem 2, and use the optimal broadcast scheme on a shortest path tree as an approximation of the solution to the MinMT problem on G, the approximation ratio may be very large. The worst case occurs when $G = (V, E)$ is a complete graph with a large number of nodes and $D = V$: the optimal broadcast scheme of the shortest path tree needs $|V| - 1$ rounds while the optimal broadcast time is $\lceil \log_2 |V| \rceil$.

5.2   Overview of Our Algorithm

The main concern of our algorithm is to construct an efficient multicast tree T_s so that we make use of the optimal schedule on T_s to design a good schedule for the MinMT problem. To this end, we firstly embed the graph G in a square, then divide this square into several small squares such that in each subsquare the nodes induces a complete subgraph of G. Secondly, based on this partition, we construct an auxiliary graph G' with each node representing a subsquare, then we define MinMT instance (G', s', D') for which we obtain a shortest path tree T'. Thirdly, by replacing each node with some nodes in G and some edges, we get a Steiner tree T in G so that each nonempty subsquare has at least one node contained in T. Finally we obtain T_s by joining the remaining nodes of D outside T with some nodes of T in a way that we may apply Lemma 3 later to assure a good schedule.

Our Algorithm MMT (*Minimum Multicast Time*) is composed of Algorithm CMT (*Construct Multicast Tree*) and SB(T_s) (*Schedule Broadcast on* T_s). We divide our discussion into three subsections. Subsections 5.3 and 5.4 deal with CMT, and Subsection 5.5 deals with SB(T_s).

5.3   Square Partition

In this section, we describe the details of square partition, and then generate the auxiliary graph G' together with MinMT instance (G', s', D') and its shortest path tree T'.

Recall that we are given MinMT instance (G, s, D). As aforementioned, we consider a geometric representation of $G = (V, E)$: all nodes in V are embedded in the Euclidean plane, and there is an edge $(u, v) \in E$ between two nodes $u, v \in V$ if their Euclidean distance $\|u - v\|$ is no more than 1. We choose a square such that it covers all nodes in V, and that it can be partitioned into m^2 subsquares each of size $\frac{\sqrt{2}}{2} \times \frac{\sqrt{2}}{2}$. Fig.2 shows the partition and S_{ij} denotes the subsquare, $i, j = 1, 2, \ldots, m$.

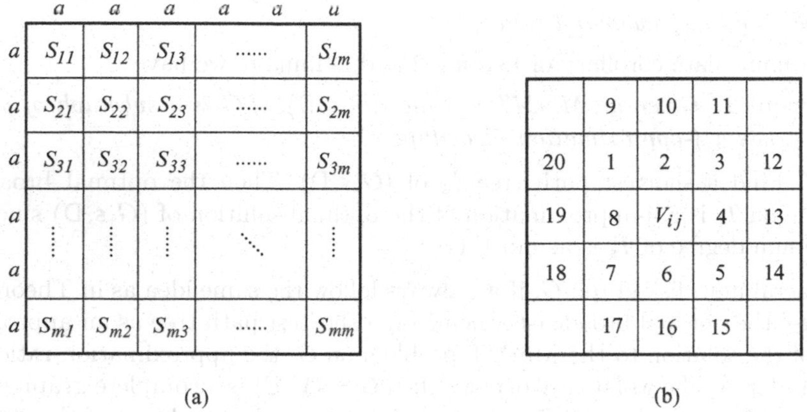

	a	a	a	a	a	u
a	S_{11}	S_{12}	S_{13}	......		S_{1m}
a	S_{21}	S_{22}	S_{23}	......		S_{2m}
a	S_{31}	S_{32}	S_{33}	......		S_{3m}
a	⋮	⋮	⋮	⋱		⋮
a						
a	S_{m1}	S_{m2}	S_{m3}	......		S_{mm}

		9	10	11
20	1	2	3	12
19	8	V_{ij}	4	13
18	7	6	5	14
	17	16	15	

(a)   (b)

Fig. 2. (a) Square partition with $a = \sqrt{2}/2$ and (b) The degree of v_{ij} is at most 20.

According to the partition, let V_{ij} denote the set of nodes in S_{ij}. We have $V = \bigcup_{i,j=1}^{m} V_{ij}$. Now we construct an auxiliary graph $G' = (V', E')$ of G. To every nonempty subset V_{ij}, we associate a vertex v_{ij} in V'.

$$V' = \{v_{ij} | V_{ij} \neq \emptyset, i, j = 1, 2, \ldots, m\}$$

And there is an edge between two different nodes v_{ij} and v_{kl}, if there exist $u \in V_{ij}$ and $v \in V_{kl}$ such that the $(u, v) \in E$.

$$E' = \{(v_{ij}, v_{kl}) | v_{ij} \neq v_{kl}, \exists u \in V_{ij}, v \in V_{kl}, s.t.(u, v) \in E\}$$

After obtaining the auxiliary graph G', we define the new source node s' to be the node v_{ij} with $s \in V_{ij}$, and the new destination field $D' = \{v_{ij} \in V' | V_{ij} \cap (\{s\} \cup D) \neq \emptyset\}$. Then we get a new MinMT instance (G', s', D'), and compute in polynomial time the shortest path tree T' of (G', s', D').

5.4   Generating T_s

After generating T' in the auxiliary graph G', let us turn back to our original problem (G, s, D). We will construct T_s in two steps. In the first step, we construct a Steiner tree T of G rooted at s, which does not necessarily contain all nodes in D. In the second step, we connect the remaining nodes in D to T to obtain T_s.

In the first step, given T' in G', now we construct T in G. Suppose $V'(T')$ (resp. $V(T)$) and $E'(T')$ (resp. $E(T)$) are the node set and edge set of T' (resp. T). For each edge $(v_{ij}, v_{kl}) \in E'(T')$, according to the definition of G', there must exist $u \in V_{ij}$ and $v \in V_{kl}$ such that $\|u, v\| \leqslant 1$. There may be many such pairs of u and v. We just take any one of them for each edge of $E'(T')$, and add vertices u, v to $V(T)$, and edge (u, v) to $E(T)$. At the same time, we construct two node sets V_{ij}^{head} and $V^{cluster}$ which stand for the *head* set of V_{ij} and set of *clusters* of all V_{ij}, respectively. Suppose v_{ij} is the parent of v_{kl} in T', we put u into V_{ij}^{head} and v into $V^{cluster}$. (We notice that each subsquare has at most one cluster.) When all edge $(v_{ij}, v_{kl}) \in E'(T')$ have been considered, we put s into both $V(T)$ and $V^{cluster}$. (Now every subsquare has exactly one cluster.) Next we connect these components in the current graph to form the tree T. For every $1 \leq k, l \leq m$, let v be the unique cluster in V_{kl}, we join v with all nodes in V_{kl}^{head} whenever $V_{kl}^{head} \neq \emptyset$. (Particularly the cluster s is joined with all nodes in the V_{ij}^{head} with $s \in V_{ij}^{head}$.) The construction of T is complete, and T is obviously a tree.

Now we consider the second step. Let $\widetilde{V}_{ij} = (D \setminus V(T)) \cap V_{ij}$. So $\widetilde{V}_{ij}$ is the set of nodes in the intersection of D and the subsquare S_{ij} but outside T. For each nonempty $\widetilde{V}_{ij}$, according to the construction, T contains at least one node in the subsquare S_{ij}, say u. Then $\{u\} \cup \widetilde{V}_{ij}$ induces a complete subgraph which possesses a broadcast tree $\mathbb{T}_{\{u\} \cup \widetilde{V}_{ij}}$ rooted at u with broadcast time $\lceil \log_2 |\{u\} \cup \widetilde{V}_{ij}| \rceil$ as stated in Lemma 4. We add $\{u\} \cup \widetilde{V}_{ij}$ to T by gluing it at u. At last, we delete all leaf nodes outside D recursively in the tree obtained, and the resulting tree is T_s as desired.

Now let's present the whole algorithm of constructing the multicast tree T_s.

Algorithm CMT. CONSTRUCT MULTICAST TREE

Input MinMT instance (G, s, D)
Output A multicast tree T_s rooted at s

1. Embed $G = (V, E)$ in the plane, and use m^2 subquares S_{ij} of size $\frac{\sqrt{2}}{2} \times \frac{\sqrt{2}}{2}$, $(i, j = 1, \ldots, m)$ to cover V.
   $V_{ij} \leftarrow V \cap S_{ij}$
2. Define auxiliary graph $G' = (V', E')$ and MinMT instance (G', s', D')
   $T' \leftarrow$ a shortest path tree of (G', s', D'), $E_0 \leftarrow E'(T')$
3. $V_{ij}^{head} \leftarrow \emptyset$, $i, j = 1, 2, \ldots, m$
   $V^{cluster} \leftarrow \{s\}$
   $V(T) \leftarrow \{s\}$, $E(T) \leftarrow \emptyset$
4. **while** $E_0 \neq \emptyset$ **do begin**
5.   Take $(v_{ij}, v_{kl}) \in E_0$ and $(u, v) \in E$ such that
           v_{ij} is the parent of v_{kl} in T' and $u \in V_{ij}$ and
           $v \in V_{kl}$

6. $V(T) \leftarrow V(T) \cup \{u, v\}$,
                $E(T) \leftarrow E(T) \cup \{(u, v)\}$
7. $V_{ij}^{head} \leftarrow V_{ij}^{head} \cup \{u\}$,
                $V^{cluster} \leftarrow V^{cluster} \cup \{v\}$
8. $E_0 \leftarrow E_0 \setminus \{(v_{ij}, v_{kl})\}$
9. **end-while**
10. **for** every $v \in V^{cluster}$ **do begin**
11. $V_{ij} \leftarrow$ the set containing v
12.   Put an edge (u, v) into $E(T)$ for every $u \in V_{ij}^{head}$
13. **end-for**
14. $T_s \leftarrow T$
15. $\tilde{V}_{ij} \leftarrow (D \setminus V(T_s)) \cap V_{ij}$, $i, j = 1, 2, \ldots, m$
16. **for** every $i, j = 1, \ldots, m$ with $\tilde{V}_{ij} \neq \emptyset$ **do begin**
17.   Take a node $u \in V_{ij} \cap V(T_s)$
18.   Add to T_s the tree $\mathbb{T}_{\{u\} \cup \tilde{V}_{ij}}$ rooted at u
19. **end-for**
20. $T_s \leftarrow$ a shortest path tree of (T_s, s, D)
21. Output T_s

5.5   Schedule Broadcast on T_s

Our algorithm MMT first runs Algorithm CMT to generate the tree T_s, and then runs the following simple implementation of an optimal broadcast algorithm on T_s, and outputs the schedule as the solution of (G, s, D).

Algorithm SB(T_s). SCHEDULE BROADCAST ON T_s

Input T_s output by CMT
Output A multicast schedule for MinMT instance (G, s, D)

1. Optimally broadcast the message on T_s according to Lemma 5
2. Output the schedule on T_s and the broadcast time t

Before proceeding, we observe that $T_s \cap T$ is a subtree of both T_s and T, where T is formed when Algorithm CMT finishes the while-loop (step 4 - 9) and T_s is the final output of CMT in step 21. To facilitate algorithm analysis in the next subsection, we mention a counterpart of SB(T_s), called SB'(T_s) in which steps 1 and 2 of SB(T_s) are replaced by the following three steps

1)' Optimally broadcast the message on T according to Lemma 5
2)' Broadcast the message simultaneously in every $\mathbb{T}_{\{u\} \cup \tilde{V}_{ij}}$ added to T_s in step 18 of CMT
3)' Output the schedule and the broadcast time t'

5.6   Algorithm Analysis

In this subsection, we prove that Algorithm MMT is an $O(1)$−approximation algorithm for the MinMT problem. The proofs of Lemma 6-8 are omitted due to space limit.

Lemma 6. $t \leq t'$.

Lemma 7. *Each* V_{ij} *induces a complete subgraph of* G.

Lemma 8. *Suppose* G' *is the auxiliary graph of* G *and* Δ' *is the maximum degree of* G', *then* $\Delta' \leqslant 20$.

Lemma 9. *Let* Δ *be the maximum degree of* T *generated in Algorithm CMT from step 3 to step 9, and* Δ *is the maximum degree of* T. *Then,*

1. T *is a tree rooted at* s.
2. $\Delta \leqslant 20$.
3. *Suppose* h' *is the height of* T', *and* h *is the height of* T. *Then,* $h \leqslant 2h' \leqslant 2h(G, \mathsf{s}, \mathsf{D})$.

Proof. 1). T is constructed in two steps. At first, all edges in T' are replaced by the corresponding edges in G. These edges may be separate since one node in T' may correspond to two or more different nodes in G. In the second step, we join every cluster with all heads in the same subsquare. Since T' is a tree, so is T.

2). Moreover, the maximum degree of T is no more than that of T'. So $\Delta \leq \Delta' \leq 20$ follows from Lemma 8.

3). By Lemma 7, in each subsquare the cluster can be joined with nodes in the head set directly. Then the length of each path in T is at most twice the length of the corresponding path in T'. Hence $h \leqslant 2h'$. By the construction of $(G', \mathsf{s}', \mathsf{D}')$, every path in G corresponds to a path in G' of equal or less length. So $h' \leq h(G, \mathsf{s}, \mathsf{D})$, establishing 3).

Lemma 10. *If* $\mathsf{D} \cap V_{ij} \neq \emptyset$, *then* $V_{ij} \cap V(T) \neq \emptyset$.

Theorem 3. *Given any MinMT instance* $(G, \mathsf{s}, \mathsf{D})$, *Algorithm MMT produces an approximation of the optimal solution within ratio 41, i.e.,* $t \leqslant 41 t_{OPT(G,\mathsf{s},\mathsf{D})}$.

Proof. Let us denote the time consumed in step 1)' and 2)' of SB'(T_s) by t_T and $t_{subsquare}$ respectively. It follows from Lemmas 6, 5, 2, 7, 3, 9, respectively, that

$$t \leq t'$$
$$\leqslant t_T + t_{subsquare}$$
$$\leqslant \Delta h + \max\{\lceil \log_2(1 + |\tilde{V}_{ij}|)\rceil\}$$
$$\leqslant 2\Delta h(G, \mathsf{s}, \mathsf{D}) + \log_2 |\mathsf{D}|$$
$$\leqslant 41 t_{OPT(G,\mathsf{s},\mathsf{D})}.$$

6   Simulation

In this section, we present simulations showing that Algorithm MMT performs much better in practice than theoretical guarantee 41. In the simulation we randomly place a large number of sensors in a 400×400 square S, and choose one of them as the source node s. WSNs are formed according to given transmission ranges of the sensors. For the simplicity, we just simulate the broadcast case, that is, D contains all nodes in S except for s.

Recalling Lemma 2, let $lowerbound = \max\{h(G, s, D), \log_2|D|\}$ be a lower bound of the minimum broadcast time. Let T(SPT) (resp. T(MMT)) be the minimum broadcast time of broadcasting on the shortest path tree (resp. on T_s. We will compare the performance of T(MMT) with the lower bound and that of T(SPT) in terms of the time efficiency.

In the first simulation, 500 nodes are randomly deployed in S. Our simulation was carried out with different transmission ranges varying from 40 to 130. As the transmission range increases, the number of edges of the UDG modelling the WSN becomes larger and larger. In the second simulation, 1000 nodes are randomly deployed in S, while transmission ranges vary from 30 to 120. We found from the obtained results, which are omitted due to space limit, that:

- The lower bound is determined by $h(G, s, D)$ and $\log_2|D|$. When the transmission range is small, $h(G, s, D)$ is much bigger than $\log_2|D|$. But as the transmission range becomes large, the lower bound tends very close to $\log_2|D|$.
- Using the shortest path tree to broadcast message may be efficient when the transmission range is small, but it becomes worse as the range increases.
- No matter how large the transmission range is, our algorithm can present an efficient broadcast schedule whose the broadcast time is very close to the lower bound.

7   Conclusion

In this paper we have studied the MinMT problem in WSNs. We prove that this problem is still NP-complete in UDGs, and present an approximation algorithm with performance ratio 41 in the worst case. Our simulation shows that the proposed algorithm is very efficient in average case. Furthermore, in our algorithm, if we use unit regular hexagons to cover the area in stead of using $\frac{\sqrt{2}}{2} \times \frac{\sqrt{2}}{2}$ subsquares, and make some more subpartitions of hexagons, we are able to reduce the approximation ratio to 21.

As future research, it is a challenge to design an approximation algorithm for the MinMT problem in WSNs with smaller performance ratio. In addition to that, it is desirable to develop new techniques to tackle interesting extension of present work to sensor networks in which sensor has different transmission range, or ability of adjusting its range. Distributed algorithms for the MinMT problem in WSNs also deserve research efforts.

References

1. V. Annamalai, S. K. S. Gupta, and L. Schwiebert. On tree-based convergecasting in wireless sensor networks. *WCNC 2003-IEEE Wireless Communication and Networking Conference*, 4(1), pp. 1942-1947, 2003.
2. A. Bar-Noy, S. Guha, J. Naor, and B. Schieber. Message multicasting in heterogeneous networks. *SIAM Journal on Computing*, 30(2), pp. 347-358, 2000.
3. N. Bulusu, J. Heidemann, and D. Estrin. GPS-less low cost outdoor localization for very small devices. *Technical Report 00-729*, Computer Science Department, University of Sourthern California, April, 2000.
4. Xujin Chen, Xiaodong Hu, and Jianming Zhu. Minimum data aggregation time problem in wireless sensor networks. *Lecture Notes in Computer Sciences*, 3794, pp. 133-142, 2005.
5. M. Elkin and G. Kortsarz. A combinatorial logarithmic approximation algorithm for the directed telephone broadcast problem. In *Proceedings of 34th ACM Annual Symposium on Theory of Computing*, pp. 438 447, 2002.
6. M. Elkin and G. Kortsarz, Sublogarithmic approximation algorithm for the undirected telephone broadcast problem: a path out of a jungle. In *Proceedings of 14th Annual ACM-SCIM Symposium on Discrete Algorithms*, pp. 76-85, 2003.
7. M. Elkin and G. Kortsarz. Approximation algorithm for directed telephone multicast problem. *Lecture Notes in Computer Science*, 2719, pp. 212-223, 2003.
8. R. Gandhi, S. Parthasarathy, and A. Mishra. Minimizing broadcasting latency and redundancy in ad hoc networks. in *Proceedings of the 4th ACM Interational Symposium on Mobile Ad Hoc Networking and Computing*, pp. 222-231, 2003.
9. M. R. Garey and D. S. Johnson. *Computers and Intractability: A Guide to the Theory of NP-completeness*. W. H. Freeman and Company, 1979.
10. C. Intanagonwiwat, D. Estrin, R. Govindan, and J. Heidemann, Impact of network density on data aggregation in wireless sensor networks, *The 22nd International Conference on Distributed Computing Systems*, Austria, July 2002.
11. P. Kyasanur and N. Vaidya. Routing and interface assignment in multi-channel wireless networks. In *Proceedings of IEEE Wireless Communications and Networking Conference*, 4, pp. 2051-2056, 2005.
12. D. Lichtenstein. Planar formulae and their uses. *SIAM Journal on Computing*, 11, pp. 329-343, 1982.
13. A. Pelc. Broadcasting in radio networks. *Handbook of Wireless Networks and Mobile Computing*, John Wiley and Sons, Inc., New York, NY, 2002.
14. R. Ravi. Rapid rumor ramification: approximating the minimum broadcast time. In *Proceedings of the IEEE Symposium on Computer Science*, pp. 202-213, 1994.
15. C. S. Raghavendra, K. M. Sivalingam, and T. Znati. *Wireless Sensor Networks*, Kluwer Academic Publishers, 2004.
16. P. J. Slater, E. J. Cockayne, and S. T. Hedetniemi. Information dissemination in trees. *SIAM Journal on Computing*, 10, pp. 692-701, 1981.
17. Leiming Xu, Yong Xiang, and Meilin Shi. On the problem of channel assignment for multi-NIC multihop wireless networks. *Lecture Notes in Computer Sciences*, 3794, pp. 633-642, 2005.
18. Yang Yu, B. Krishnamachari, and V. K. Prasanna. Energy-latency tradeoffs for data gathering in wireless sensor networks. *The 23rd Conference of IEEE Communication Society*, Hong Kong, SAR China, March, 2004.

On Broadcast Authentication in Wireless Sensor Networks

Kui Ren[1], Kai Zeng[1], Wenjing Lou[1], and Patrick J. Moran[2]

[1] Worcester Polytechnic Institute, Worcester, MA 01609
{kren, wjlou, kzeng}@ece.wpi.edu
[2] AirSprite Technologies, Inc., Marlborough, MA 01532
pmoran@airsprite.com

Abstract. Broadcast authentication is a critical security service in wireless sensor networks (WSNs), since it enables users to broadcast the WSN in an authenticated way. Symmetric key based schemes such as μTESLA and multilevel μTESLA have been proposed to provide such services for WSNs; however, these schemes all suffer from serious DoS attacks because of the delayed message authentication. This paper presents several effective public key based schemes to achieve immediate broadcast authentication and thus overcome the vulnerability presented in the μTESLA-like schemes. Several cryptographic building blocks, including Merkle hash tree and ID-based signature scheme, are adopted to minimize the scheme overhead regarding the costs in both computation and communication. A quantitative analysis on energy consumption of the proposed schemes are given in detail. We believe that this paper can serve as the start point towards fully solving the important multisender broadcast authentication problem in WSNs.

1 Introduction

Wireless sensor networks (WSNs) have enabled data gathering from a vast geographical region, and present unprecedented opportunities for a wide range of tracking and monitoring applications from both civilian and military domains [1, 2, 8, 14]. In these applications, WSNs are expected to process, store and provide the sensed data to the network users upon their demands. As the most common communication paradigm, the network users are expected to issue the queries to the network before obtaining the information of their interest. Furthermore, in wireless sensor and actuator networks (WSANs) [2], the network users may even need to issue their commands to the network (probably based on the information he received from the network). In both cases, there could be a large number of users in the WSNs, which could be either mobile or static. And the users may use their mobile clients to query or command the WSNs from anywhere in the network. Obviously, broadcast/multicast[1] operations are fundamental to the realization of these network functions. Hence, it is also highly important to ensure broadcast authentication for the security purposes.

---

[1] For our purpose, we do not distinguish multicast from broadcast in this paper.

X. Cheng, W. Li, and T. Znati (Eds.): WASA 2006, LNCS 4138, pp. 502–514, 2006.
© Springer-Verlag Berlin Heidelberg 2006

Broadcast authentication in WSNs has been first addressed by μTESLA in [3]. In μTESLA, the user of WSNs is assumed to be one or a few fixed sinks, which are always assumed to be trustworthy. The scheme adopts a one-way hash function $h()$ and uses the hash preimages as keys in a Message Authentication Code (MAC) algorithm. Initially, sensor nodes are preloaded with $K_0 = h^n(x)$, where x is the secret held by the sink. Then, $K_1 = h^{n-1}(x)$ is used to generate MACs for all the broadcast messages sent within time interval 1. At time interval 2, the sink broadcasts K_1, and sensor nodes verify $h(K_1) = K_0$. The authenticity of messages received during time interval 1 is then verified using K_1. This delayed disclosure technique is used for the entire hash chain and thus demands loosely synchronized clocks between the sink and sensor nodes. μTESLA is later enhanced in [4,5] to overcome the length limit of the hash chain. Most recently, μTESLA is also extended in [6] to support multiuser scenario at the cost of higher communication overhead per message.

It is generally held that μTESLA-like schemes have the following shortcomings even in the single-user scenario: 1) all the receivers have to buffer all the messages received within one time interval; 2) they are subject to Wormhole attacks [7], where messages could be forged due to the propagation delay of the disclosed keys. However, here we point out a serious vulnerability of μTESLA-like schemes when they are applied in multi-hop WSNs. Since sensor nodes buffer all the messages received within one time interval, an adversary can hence flood the whole network with arbitrary messages all the time and this can be easily achieved by an outsider. All he has to do is to claim that the sending messages belong to the current time interval which should be buffered for authentication until next time interval. Since wireless transmission is very expensive in WSNs[2], and WSNs are extremely energy constrained, the ability to flood the network arbitrarily could cause devastating DoS attacks. Moreover, this type of DoS attacks become even more devastating in multiuser scenario, since the adversary can easily generate more bogus messages without being detected. Obviously, all these attacks are due to authentication delay of the broadcast messages. In [7], TIK is proposed to achieve immediate key disclosure and hence immediate message authentication based on precise time synchronization between the sink and receiving nodes. However, this technique is not applicable in WSNs as pointed out by the authors. Therefore, the problem of broadcast authentication still remains wide open in WSNs.

At the time when μTESLA was proposed, sensor nodes are assumed to be extremely resource constrained, especially with respect to computation capability, bandwidth availability, and energy supply [3]. Therefore, public key cryptography (PKC) is thought to be too computationally expensive, although it could provide much simplified solutions with much stronger security strengths. However, recent studies [9, 10] showed that, contrary to widely held beliefs, PKC even with software implementations is very viable on sensor nodes. For example [9], Elliptic Curve Cryptography (ECC) signature verification takes 1.61s

---

[2] Wireless transmission of a bit can require over 1000 times more energy than a single 32-bit computation, as shown in [14].

with 160-bit keys on ATmega128 8MHz processor, a processor used for current Crossbow motes platform [11]. Hence, with the advance of fast growing technology, PKC is no longer impractical for WSNs, although still expensive for the current generation sensor nodes. And its wide acceptance is expected in the near future [10].

Having this observation and knowing that symmetric-key based solutions such as μTESLA are insufficient for broadcast authentication in WSNs, we resort to public key cryptography for effective solutions.

Organization of the paper: The remaining part of this paper is organized as follows: In Section 2, we introduce some preliminary background about the cryptography mechanisms. Section 3 presents the system assumptions, adversary model and security objectives of this paper. Then in Section 4, we introduce our proposed schemes and detail the underlying design logic. Section 5 is the scheme analysis. We conclude our paper in Section 6.

2   Preliminaries

2.1   Merkle Hash Tree Technique

We illustrate the construction and application of the Merkle hash tree [13] through an example. To authenticate data values $n_1, n_2, ..., n_w$, the data source constructs the Merkle hash tree as depicted in Fig. 1, assuming that $w = 4$. The values of the four leaf nodes are the message hashes, $h(n_i), i = 1, 2, 3, 4$, respectively, of the data values under a one-way hash function $h()$ (e.g., SHA-1 [16]). The value of each internal node is derived from its child nodes. For example, the value of node A is $h_a = h(h(n_1)|h(n_2))$. The data source completes the levels of the tree recursively from the leaf nodes to the root node. The value of the root node is $h_r = h(h_a|h_b)$, which is used to commit to the entire tree to authenticate any subset of the data values n_1, n_2, n_3, and n_4 in conjunction with a small amount of auxiliary authentication information AAI (i.e., $\log_2 N$ hash values with N as the number of leaf nodes). For example, a user, who is assumed to have the authentic root value h_r, requests for n_3 and requires the authentication of the received n_3. Besides n_3, the source sends the AAI :$< h_a, h(n4) >$ to the user. The user can then check the authenticity of the received n_3 by first computing $h(n_3)$, $h_b = h(h(n_3)|h(n4))$ and $h_r = h(h_a|h_b)$, and then checking if the calculated h_r is the same as the authentic root value h_r. Only if this check is positive, the user accepts n_3.

2.2   ID-Based Cryptography

Identity-based cryptography (IBC) is receiving extensive attention as a powerful alternative to traditional certificate-based cryptography. Its main idea is to make an entity's public key directly derivable from its publicly known identity information. Although the idea of IBC dates back to 1984 [15], only recently has its rapid development taken place due to the application of the *pairing* technique outlined below.

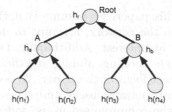

Fig. 1. An example of Merkle hash tree

Let p, q be two large primes and $\mathbb{E}/\mathbb{F}_p$ indicate an elliptic curve $y^2 = x^3 + ax + b$ over the finite field $\mathbb{F}_p$. We denote by $\mathbb{G}_1$ a q-order subgroup of the additive group of points of $\mathbb{E}/\mathbb{F}_p$, and by $\mathbb{G}_2$ a q-order subgroup of the multiplicative group of the finite field $\mathbb{F}_{p^i}^*$ ($i = 2, 3, 6$). The Discrete Logarithm Problem (DLP) is required to be hard[3] in both $\mathbb{G}_1$ and $\mathbb{G}_2$. For us, a pairing is a mapping $\hat{e} : \mathbb{G}_1 \times \mathbb{G}_1 \to \mathbb{G}_2$ with the following properties:

1. *Bilinear*: For $\forall\, P, Q, R, S \in \mathbb{G}_1$, $\hat{e}(P + Q, R + S) = \hat{e}(P, R)\hat{e}(P, S)\hat{e}(Q, R)$ $\hat{e}(Q, S)$. Consequently, for $\forall\, c, d \in \mathbb{Z}_q^*$, we have $\hat{e}(cP, dQ) = \hat{e}(cP, Q)^d = \hat{e}(P, dQ)^c = \hat{e}(P, Q)^{cd}$, etc.
2. *Non-degenerate*: If P is a generator of $\mathbb{G}_1$, then $\hat{e}(P, P) \in \mathbb{F}_{p^2}^*$ is a generator of $\mathbb{G}_2$.
3. *Computable*: There is an efficient algorithm to compute $\hat{e}(P, Q)$ for all $P, Q \in \mathbb{G}_1$.

3 System, Adversary Model, and Security Objectives

System Model: In this paper, we consider a very large spatially distributed WSN, consisting of a fixed sink and a large amount of sensor nodes. The sensor nodes are not necessarily homogenous in their functionalities and capabilities. The WSN under consideration is aimed to offer information services to a large number of network users that roam in the network, in addition to the fixed sink. These WSN users include mobile sinks, vehicles, and people with mobile clients, and they are assumed to be more powerful than sensor nodes in terms of computation and communication abilities. For example, the network users could include a number of doctors, nurses, medical equipments (acting as actuators) and so on, in the case of CodeBlue [22], where the WSN is used for emergency medical response. These network users broadcast queries/commands through sensor nodes at their vicinity, and expect the replies that reflect the latest sensed results. The network users also directly communicate with sink or the backend server if needed. We assume that the sink is always trustworthy but the sensor nodes are subject to compromise. At the same time, the users of the WSN may be dynamically revoked due to either membership changing or compromise, and the revocation pattern is not restricted. As the μTESLA-like schemes, we also assume that the WSN time is loosely synchronized.

---

[3] It is computationally infeasible to extract the integer $x \in \mathbb{Z}_q^* = \{a | 1 \le a \le q - 1\}$, given $P, Q \in \mathbb{G}_1$ (respectively, $P, Q \in \mathbb{G}_2$) such that $Q = xP$ (respectively, $Q = P^x$).

Adversary Model: In this paper, we assume that the adversary's goal is to inject bogus messages into the network, attempt to deceive sensor nodes, and obtain the information of his interest. Additionally, Deny of Service (DoS) attacks such as bogus message flooding, aiming at exhausting scarce network resources, is another important focus of the paper. We assume that the adversary is able to compromise both network users and the sensor nodes. The adversary hence could exploit the compromised users/nodes for such attacks. More specifically, we consider the following types of attacks: 1) The adversary may directly broadcast bogus messages to the WSN by itself; 2) The adversary may use one or more compromised nodes to propagate bogus messages to the WSN by pretending that the messages are initiated by legitimate network users; 3) The adversary may use one or more compromised users to broadcast messages to the WSN.

Security Objectives: Given the adversary model above, our security objective is straightforward: First, user authentication is needed so that illegitimate users will be excluded from injecting bogus messages. Second, user revocation mechanisms have to be implemented so that sensor nodes could deal with user revocations. Third, the authenticity of any message broadcast by a user should be able to be verified by every receiving node. In summary, all messages being broadcast to the WSN should be authenticated so that any bogus ones issued by the illegitimate users and/or compromised sensor nodes can be efficiently and deterministically rejected/filtered.

4   The Proposed Schemes

PKC-based solutions can realize immediate message authentication and thus overcome the delayed authentication problem present in μTESLA-like schemes. However, the straightforward solutions such as certificate-based approach can not be directly applied in WSNs due to their high scheme overhead as we analyze below. More advanced techniques have to be adopted to achieve a desirable scheme performance.

4.1   The Certificate-Based Authentication Scheme

The Scheme: Each user of the WSN is equipped with a public/private key pair (PK/SK), and signs every message he broadcasts with his SK using a digital signature scheme such as RSA or DSA [17, 18]. To prove the user's ownership over his public key, the sink[4] is also equipped with a public/private key pair and serves as the certificate authority (CA). The sink issues each user a public key certificate, and such a certificate, to its simplest form, consists of the following contents: $\text{Cert}_{U_{ID}} = U_{ID}, \text{PK}_{U_{ID}}, \text{ExpT}, \text{SIG}_{\text{SK}_{Sink}}\{h(U_{ID}||\text{ExpT}||\text{PK}_{U_{ID}})\}, \text{para},$ where U_{ID} denotes the user's ID, $\text{PK}_{U_{ID}}$ denotes its public key, ExpT denotes certificate expiration time and $\text{SIG}_{\text{SK}_{Sink}}\{h(U_{ID}||\text{ExpT}||\text{PK}_{U_{ID}})\}$ is a signature

---

[4] We assume that the sink represents the network planner.

signed over $h(U_{ID}||\text{ExpT}||\text{PK}_{U_{ID}})$ with SK_{Sink}. Hence, a broadcast message is now of the form as follows:

$$< M, tt, \text{SIG}_{\text{SK}_{U_{ID}}}\{h(U_{ID}||tt||M)\}, \text{Cert}_{U_{ID}} > \qquad (I)$$

Here, M denotes the broadcast message and tt denotes the current time. Then, sensor nodes are enabled to verify the authenticity of the received messages by preloading PK_{Sink} before the network deployment. The verification contains two steps: the certificate verification and the signature verification.

Analysis: This straightforward scheme suffers from many severe drawbacks. Firstly and most importantly, it is highly inefficient to support user revocation in this scheme. In order to support user revocation and hence certificate revocation, sensor nodes have to receive and store a certificate revocation list (CRL). Clearly, the CRL requires a storage space linear to the total number of revoked certificates over the whole network operation period at each sensor node. However, this is practically impossible due to the stringent storage limitations of sensor nodes, especially given a large number of users or a highly dynamic membership changing scenario. For example, assuming that a public key is 20-byte long, a CRL containing only 1,000 revoked certificates is at least of size 19.5 KB even in the simplest format. At the same time, resorting to the sink on-demandingly for CRL verification is obviously impossible either, because this could introduce too much communication cost. Embedding validity interval into the certificate does not really help reduce the storage overhead much, since the revocation pattern is not available priori. Secondly, to authenticate each message, it always takes two signature verification operations, instead of one. This is because the certificate should always be authenticated in the first place.

4.2   The Basic Merkle Hash Tree Based Authentication Scheme

Observing the CRL problem inherent to the first scheme, we next propose a Merkle hash tree based authentication scheme, which is highly storage efficient.

Scheme Initialization: The sink collects all the public keys of the current network users and constructs a merkel hash tree. Specifically, we construct N leaves with each leaf corresponding to a current user of the WSN. For our problem, each leaf node contains the bindings between the corresponding user ID and the public key of the user, that is, $h(U_{ID}, \text{PK}_{U_{ID}})$. The values of the internal nodes are determined with the same method as in Section 2.1. We denote the value of the final root node of the hash tree as h_r. Then, the sink preloads/broadcasts each sensor node with this value either before network deployment or during the network operation time. However, if h_r is broadcast during the network operation time, h_r should be signed by the sink to prove its authenticity. Of course, in this case, sensor nodes should be preloaded with the sink's public key. At the same time, each user should obtain its AAI according to his corresponding leaf node's location in the Merkle hash tree. Let T denote all the nodes along the path from a leaf node to the root (not including the root). Then A is defined as the set of nodes corresponding to the siblings of the nodes in T; and AAI further corresponds to the values associated with the nodes in A. Obviously, AAI is $(L * \log_2 N)$ bytes, with the hash value equal to L bytes.

Message Authentication: Now a message sent by a user U_{ID} is of form

$$< M, tt, \text{SIG}_{\text{SK}_{U_{ID}}} \{h(U_{ID}||tt||M)\}, U_{ID}, \text{PK}_{U_{ID}}, \text{AAI}_{U_{ID}} > \quad (II)$$

Each node verifies such a message in two steps. First, it verifies $\text{PK}_{U_{ID}}$ using $\text{AAI}_{U_{ID}}$ attached in the message and h_r stored by itself. The verification operation is a chain of hash operations with the final value equal to h_r as the way we demonstrated in section 2.1. A different value suggests the invalidity of the corresponding public key. Second, the sensor node verifies $\text{SIG}_{\text{SK}_{U_{ID}}} \{h(U_{ID}||M)\}$ using $\text{PK}_{U_{ID}}$. Upon user revocation and/or addition, the sink updates the Merkle hash tree and obtains a new h_r. This new h_r is then signed by the sink using SK_{Sink} and broadcast to sensor nodes immediately. Furthermore, each current user also obtains his updated $\text{AAI}_{U_{ID}}$ from the sink.

Analysis: In this scheme, a user does not need a certificate to prove the binding to his public key. Instead, a Merkle hash tree technique is used. A revoked or invalid user public key will never pass the verification, as long as the user holds the up-to-date root node value h_r. Hence, in this scheme, certificates are no longer necessary and can be eliminated. Furthermore, the user revocation problem (i.e., certificate revocation problem) is now reduced to the problem of updating sensor nodes a single hash value h_r, which requires a storage space of only L bytes. Assuming that SHA-1 [16] is used, $L = 20$ bytes. However, the scheme is communication inefficient when N becomes large. This is because the size of AAI grows logarithmically as N grows. Since $L = 20$ bytes, AAI alone is of size 200 bytes, given number of users N reaches $1,024$; and $|\text{AAI}| = 260$ bytes, when $N = 8,192$.

4.3   The Enhanced Merkle Hash Tree Based Authentication Scheme

In the above scheme, the storage overhead is only one hash value, i.e., L bytes, but the communication overhead is no less than $L * \log_2 N$ bytes. We hence, want to make a compromise between the storage and communication overheads. That is, we increase the number of stored hash values to reduce the size of AAI.

We illustrate how to do it through an example. In Fig.1, h_r is made public and stored by the authenticator. Hence, the user corresponding to leaf node n_3 must have AAI $:< h_a, h(n_4) >$. However, if both h_a and h_b are made public and stored by the authenticator, the corresponding AAI now contains $h(n_4)$ only. Therefore, by trimming down the Merkle hash tree constructed in the above scheme, we can have a set of smaller Merkle hash trees. If each sensor node is loaded with all the values of the root nodes corresponding to these smaller trees, then the size of AAI can be reduced to the height of the smaller trees multiplying L bytes. In fact, if we remove k levels of the original Merkle tree, the communication overhead is reduced by $k * L$ bytes. However, the storage cost increases to $2^k * L$ bytes. Note that if we require sensor nodes to store all the leaf values, the scheme is reduced to the trivial memorize-all-keys case, which demands $N * L$ bytes storage space.

Analysis: Since sensor nodes are storage constrained, the value of k is obviously limited. Given that $m = 2^k$ hash values can be stored by each sensor node, the size of AAI is now $(L * \log_2 \frac{N}{m})$ bytes. If $N = 1,024$ and $m = 32$, this is 100 bytes; and if N is increased to $8,192$, this is 160 bytes. If m is made to be 64, then the size of AAI will be 80 bytes, give $N = 1,024$, and 140 bytes, given $N = 8,192$. This result is much improved as compared to the above basic scheme. When $N = 8,192$, the message overhead in this optimized scheme is 120 bytes less than that of the basic Merkle hash tree based scheme. This gain comes at the cost of increased storage overhead, which is now $64 * 20 = 1,280$ bytes $= 1.25$ KB. Therefore, this scheme is still communication inefficient when N is large. However, when N is on the order of hundred, the proposed enhanced scheme can behave fairly well. We defer the detailed analysis to Section 5.

4.4 ID-Based Authentication Scheme

In this section, we propose an ID-based authentication scheme. In contrast to the Merkle hash tree based schemes, the proposed ID-Based authentication scheme requires sensor nodes to memorize the revoked user IDs only, and adopts an automatic public key update technique.

In our ID-based authentication scheme, the time is divided into consecutive time intervals, denoted by $v_1, v_2, ...,$ and we assume that sensor nodes and users are loosely synchronized. We then adopts $U_{ID} \| \overline{v_i}$ as user U_{ID}'s public key under an ID-based signature scheme [19]. In this way, before a user wants to authenticate itself to the sensor nodes, he has to firstly obtain its private key from the sink. And since each obtained private key is valid only within the current time interval, every user has to obtain a new private key from the sink at the beginning of each time interval. Now upon user revocation, the sink only needs to broadcast the corresponding user IDs to the sensor nodes. Each sensor node stores a local copy of such revoked IDs only within the current interval and dumps them afterwards. The scheme works as follows.

Scheme Initialization: Prior to network deployment, we assume that the sink does the following operations:

1. Generate the pairing parameters $(p, q, \mathbb{E}/\mathbb{F}_p, \mathbb{G}_1, \mathbb{G}_2, \hat{e})$, as described in Section 2.2. Select an arbitrary generator P of $\mathbb{G}_1$.
2. Choose two cryptographic hash functions: H, mapping strings to non-zero elements in $\mathbb{G}_1$, and h, mapping arbitrary inputs to fixed-length outputs, e.g., SHA-1 [16].
3. Pick a random $\kappa \in \mathbb{Z}_q^*$ as the network master secret and set $P_{pub} = \kappa P$.
4. Preload each sensor node with the public system parameters $(p, q, \mathbb{E}/\mathbb{F}_p, \mathbb{G}_1, \mathbb{G}_2, \hat{e}, H, h, P, P_{pub})$.
5. Preload each user U_{ID} with the private key $\mathsf{SK}_{U_{ID}} = kH(U_{ID} \| v_1)$

Message Broadcast Authentication: Assume that user U_{ID} wants to broadcast a message M. He first obtains its private key from the sink as $\mathsf{SK}_{U_{ID}} = \kappa H(U_{ID}||\overline{v_i})$, where v_i is the current time interval. U_{ID} then picks a random $\alpha \in \mathbb{Z}_q^*$ and computes $\theta = \hat{e}(P, P)^\alpha$. U_{ID} further computes $U_{x,y} = h(M \parallel tt \parallel \theta)\mathsf{SK}_{U_{ID}}$, and $\sigma_{x,y} = U_{x,y} + \alpha P$. $< \sigma_{x,y}, h(M \parallel tt \parallel \theta) >$ is the signature on message M. And the broadcast message is now of form

$$< U_{ID}, tt, M, \sigma_{x,y}, h(M \parallel tt \parallel \theta) > \quad (III)$$

Upon receiving Message (III), each sensor node verifies its authenticity in the following way: It checks the current time $\overline{tt}$ and determines whether or not the received message is fresh. Assume δ is the predefined message propagation time limit. Then, we should have $\overline{tt} - tt \leq \delta$. If so, the sensor node further computes, $\theta' = \hat{e}(\sigma_{x,y}, P)\hat{e}(H(U_{ID}||\overline{v_i}), -P_{pub})^{h(M||tt||\theta)}$, using the current time interval $\overline{v_i}$. If the message is authentic, we will have

$$
\begin{aligned}
\theta' &= \hat{e}(\sigma_{x,y}, P)\hat{e}(H(U_{ID}||\overline{v_i}), P_{pub})^{-h(M||tt||\theta)} \\
&= \hat{e}(h(M \parallel tt \parallel \theta)\mathsf{SK}_{U_{ID}} + \alpha P, P)\hat{e}(H(U_{ID}||\overline{v_i}), \kappa P)^{-h(M||tt||\theta)} \\
&= \hat{e}(h(M \parallel tt \parallel \theta)\mathsf{SK}_{U_{ID}} + \alpha P, P)\hat{e}(\kappa H(U_{ID}||\overline{v_i}), P)^{-h(M||tt||\theta)} \\
&= \hat{e}(\mathsf{SK}_{U_{ID}}, P)^{h(M||tt||\theta)}\hat{e}(P, P)^\alpha \hat{e}(\mathsf{SK}_{U_{ID}}, P)^{-h(M||tt||\theta)} = \theta.
\end{aligned} \quad (1)
$$

Therefore, if $h(M \parallel tt \parallel \theta') = h(M \parallel tt \parallel \theta)$, a sensor node considers the message authentic. If the above verification fails, a sensor node thinks of the message a fabricated or replayed one, and simply dumps it. Otherwise, it propagates the message to the next hop.

Analysis: The pros of the ID-based authentication scheme are two-fold: First, it eliminates the existence of certificate or auxiliary authentication information. Therefore, the resulted message size can be reduced. Second, it requires much smaller storage space to support user revocation, since now only the revoked user IDs have to be stored. Assuming a WSN supporting up to 65535 users, then two bytes are enough for the length of a user ID. Hence, accumulating the same 1,000 revoked users, now only 2,000 bytes = 1.95 KB storage space are needed. However, the cons of the ID-based authentication scheme are also obvious, since it has a very high computation cost due to the pairing operation involved.

5   A Quantitative Performance Comparison

Energy Consumption on Message Broadcast: In this section, we study how much are the energy consumptions to broadcast messages of different sizes to the whole WSN. We further study these energy consumptions as the function of the WSN size W. We denote by E_{tr} the hop-wise energy consumption for transmitting and receiving one byte. As reported in [9], a Chipcon CC1000 radio used in Crossbow MICA2DOT motes consumes 28.6 and 59.2 μJ to receive and transmit one byte, respectively, at an effective data rate of 12.4 kb/s. Furthermore, we assume a packet size of 41 bytes, 32 for the payload and 9 bytes

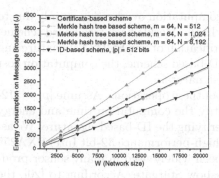
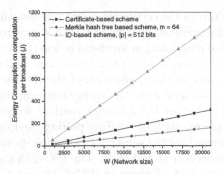

Fig. 2. Energy consumption on Message Broadcast vs. network size   **Fig. 3.** Energy consumption on computation vs. network size

for the header [9]. The header, ensuing a 8 byte preamble, consists of source, destination, length, packet ID, CRC, and a control byte [9].

For the certificate-based scheme, $\mathtt{Cert}_{UID}$ is at least 86 bytes [9], even if ECDSA-160[5] is used. The total message size of form (I) is then 148 bytes, assuming M 20 bytes, tt 2 bytes. Hence, there should be 5 packets in total, among which four of them are of size 41 bytes, and one packet is of size 29 bytes. Therefore, there should be $41 * 4 + 29 * 1 + 8 * 5 = 233$ bytes for transmission (including 8-byte preamble per packet). Hence, the hop-wise energy consumption on transmitting Message (I) equals to $233 * 59.2 \mu J = 13.79$mJ; And the energy consumption on receiving Message (I) equals to $233 * 28.6 \mu J = 6.66$mJ. To broadcast a message to the whole WSN, every sensor node should at least retransmit once and receive w' times the same message, when the simple flooding technique is used. Here, w' denotes the neighborhood density. Hence, the total energy consumption on message broadcast will be $W * (13.79 + 6.66 * w')$mJ. The energy consumption on message broadcast for the remaining scheme can also be calculated similarly.

Fig. 2 illustrates these broadcast energy consumptions as a function of network size W, assuming $w' = 20$. Clearly, we see that the ID-based scheme offers a much lower energy consumption as compared to that of the remaining two schemes. For example, when $W = 10,000$, to broadcast Message (II) to the WSN costs 1.45 KJ, give $N = 512$. And as N grows to $8,192$, the broadcast cost quickly increases to 2.17 KJ. At the same time, the energy cost on Message (III) is independent to N and is at most 1.11 KJ, which is less than 50% of the former. On the other hand, we see that the Merkle hash tree based scheme outperforms of the certificate-based scheme, when N is no more than 512.

Energy Consumption on Computation: In this subsection, we evaluate the computation overhead of the proposed schemes also in terms of energy consump-

---

[5] ECDSA is referred to Elliptic Curve Digital Signature Algorithm [23]. While RSA with 1024-bit keys (RSA-1024) provides the currently accepted security level, it is equivalent in strength to ECC with 160-bit keys (ECC-160). And hence, for the same level of security strength, ECDSA uses a much small key size and hence has a small signature size (320-bit).

tion. In the certificate-based scheme, the computation overhead is mainly due to the verification of two ECDSA signatures. In the Merkle hash tree based scheme, the computation overhead is due to the verification of one ECDSA signature and a number of hash operations. And in the ID-based scheme, the computation cost is due to the verification of the ID-based signature.

We now study the energy consumptions of these operations. Assume $|p| = 512$-bit, we use the following method to quantify the computation time and energy consumption of the Tate pairing used in verifying the ID-based signature. We assume that the sensor CPU is a low-power high-performance 32-bit Intel PXA255 processor at 400 MHz. The PXA255 has been widely used in many sensor products such as Sensoria WINS 3.0 and Crossbow Stargate. According to [20], the typical power consumption of PXA255 in active and idle modes are 411 and 121 mW, respectively. It was reported in [21] that it takes 752 ms to compute the Tate pairing with the similar parameters as ours on a 32-bit ST22 smartcard microprocessor at 33 MHz. Therefore, the computation of the Tate pairing on PXA255 roughly needs $33/400 \times 752 \approx 62.04$ ms, and the energy consumption E_p is approximately 25.5 mJ. Then, to verify the ID-based signature requires one exponentiation in $\mathbb{G}_2$, one hash function evaluation and two evaluations of the Tate pairing. As noted in [19], the pairing evaluation by far takes the most running time of a signature verification operation. Thus, for the sake of simplicity, we use energy consumed on pairing evaluations to approximate that of the signature verification, which ranges from E_p to $2E_p$. Furthermore, it was reported in [12] that it takes 92.4 ms to verify a ECDSA-160 signature with the similar parameters on a 32-bit ARM microprocessor at 80 MHz. Using the same estimation method, we can obtain the energy consumption roughly as 7.6 mJ. Similarly, we omit the energy cost on the hash operations and use 7.6 mJ as the energy cost regarding verification of an ECDSA-160 signature.

Fig. 3 illustrates the energy consumption on computation when the message is broadcast under different message forms. Several conclusions can be drawn from Fig. 3. First, for message broadcast, energy cost on propagation is much higher than that of computation. For example, when $W = 10,000$, the energy cost on computation is 510 J, while it is 1,110 J on propagation. Second, The ID-based scheme incurs a much higher computation cost as compared to the remaining schemes. When we consider energy cost on both computation and propagation, the ID-based scheme is much more energy inefficient except when N is very large. Also observe that more efficient broadcast techniques other than the simple flooding method are used for message broadcast in practice. This further obsoletes the choice of ID-based scheme. Third, when N is less than 500, the Merkle hash tree based scheme is the overall best choice, considering both communication and computation cost. Fourth, when N is large, it still remains to find a satisfying scheme when is computational and communicational efficient at the same time. We leave this as our future work.

6 Concluding Remarks

In this paper, we first identified the problem of multisender broadcast authentication in WSNs. We pointed out that symmetric-key based solutions such as μTESLA are insufficient for this problem by identifying a serious security vulnerability inherent to these schemes: the delayed authentication of the messages can lead to severe DoS attacks, due to the stringent energy and bandwidth constraints in WSNs. We then came up with several effective PKC-based schemes to address the proposed problem. Both computational and communication costs are minimized. We further analyzed both the performance and security resilience of the proposed schemes. A quantitative energy consumption analysis was given in detail. We believe that this paper can serve as the start point towards fully solving the important multisender broadcast authentication problem in WSNs.

Acknowledgement. This work was supported in part by a research grant from AirSprite Technologies, Inc., Marlborough, MA, USA.

References

1. I. Akyildiz, W. Su, Y. Sankarasubramaniam, and E. Cayirci, "A Survey on Sensor Networks, IEEE Communications Magazine," Vol. 40, No. 8, pp. 102-116, 2002.
2. I. Akyildiz and I. Kasimoglu, "Wireless sensor and actor networks: research challenges," Ad Hoc Networks 2(4): 351-367 (2004)
3. A. Perrig, R. Szewczyk, V. Wen, D. Culler, and D. Tygar, "SPINS: Security protocols for sensor networks," in Proc. of MobiCom'01, July 2001.
4. D. Liu and P. Ning, "Efficient distribution of key chain commitments for broadcast authentication in distributed sensor networks," in Proc. of NDSS'03, pp.263-276
5. D. Liu and P. Ning, "Multi-level mTESLA: Broadcast authentication for distributed sensor networks," ACM TECS, vol.3, no.4, 2004.
6. D. Liu, P. Ning, S. Zhu, and S. Jajodia, "Practical Broadcast Authentication in Sensor Networks," in Proc. of MobiQuitous 05, July 2005.
7. Y. Hu, A. Perrig, and D. Johnson, "Packet Leashes: A Defense against Wormhole Attacks in Wireless Ad Hoc Networks," In proceedings of INFOCOM, 2003.
8. K. Ren, W. Lou, and Y. Zhang, "LEDS: Providing Location-aware End-to-end Data Security in Wireless Sensor Networks," In Proc. of IEEE INFOCOM'06.
9. A. Wander, N. Gura, H. Eberle, V. Gupta, and S. Shantz. "Energy Analysis of Public-Key Cryptography on Small Wireless Devices," IEEE PerCom, March 2005.
10. W. Du, R. Wang, and P. Ning "An Efficient Scheme for Authenticating Public Keys in Sensor Networks," In Proceedings of MobiHoc, pp58-67, 2005.
11. Crossbow Technology Inc, http://www.xbow.com/, 2004.
12. M. Aydos, T. Yanik, and C. K. Koc. "An high-speed ECC-based wireless authentication protocol on an ARM microprocessor," In Proc. of ACSAC, 2000.
13. R. Merkle, "Protocols for public key cryptosystems," in Proceedings of the IEEE Symposium on Research in Security and Privacy, Apr 1980.
14. Y. Zhang, W. Liu, W. Lou, and Y. Fang, "Location based security mechanisms in wireless sensor networks," IEEE JSAC, Special Issue on Security in Wireless Ad Hoc Networks, vol. 24, no. 2, pp. 247-260, Feb. 2006.
15. A. Shamir, "Identity based cryptosystems and signature schemes," in Proc. CRYPTO'84, ser. LNCS, vol. 196. Springer-Verlag, 1984, pp. 47.53.

16. NIST, "Digital hash standard," Federal Information Processing Standards PUBlication 180-1, April 1995.
17. R. Rivest, A. Shamir, and L. Adleman, "A method for obtaining digital signatures and public-key cryptosystems," Commun. ACM 21(2), 120C126 (1978)
18. National Institure of Standards and Technology: Proposed Federal Information Processing Standard for Digital Signature Standard (DSS). Federal Register, vol. 56, no. 169, pp. 42980C42982 (1991)
19. F. Hess, "Efficient identity based signature schemes based on pairings," in Proc. SAC'02, St. John's, Newfoundland, Canada, Aug. 2002.
20. "Intel PXA255 Processor Electrical, Mechanical, and Thermal Specification," http://www.intel.com/design/pca/applicationsprocessors/manuals/278780.h
21. G. Bertoni, L. Chen, P. Fragneto, K. Harrison, and G. Pelosi1, "Computing tate pairing on smartcards," White Paper, STMicroelectronics, 2005. Available: http://www.st.com/ stonline/products/families/smartcard/ast ibe.htm
22. K. Lorincz, et al., "Sensor Networks for Emergency Response: Challenges and Opportunities," In IEEE Pervasive Computing, Special Issue on Pervasive Computing for First Response, 2004.
23. D. Hankerson, A. Menezes, S. Vanstone, "Guide to Elliptic Curve Cryptography," Springer-Verlag, ISBN 0-387-95273-X, 2004.

Tree-Based Multicast Meshes with Variable Density of Redundant Paths on Mobile Ad Hoc Networks*

Sangman Moh[1], Sang Jun Lee[1], and Chansu Yu[2]

[1] Dept. of Internet Engineering, Chosun University
375, Seoeok-dong, Dong-gu, Gwangju, 501-759 Korea
smmoh@chosun.ac.kr
[2] Dept. of Electrical and Computer Eng., Cleveland State Univ.
Stilwell Hall 340, Cleveland, OH 44115
c.yu91@csuohio.edu

Abstract. This paper proposes an *adaptive multicast* scheme for mobile ad hoc networks, called *tree-based mesh with k-hop redundant paths (TBM$_k$)*, in which path redundancy is controlled depending on the status of the network such as traffic and mobility. The proposed scheme constructs a multicast tree and adds some additional links/nodes to the multicast structure as needed to support redundancy. TBM$_k$ includes all k- or smaller-hop paths between tree nodes to provide alternative paths among the nodes. TBM$_k$ enables *tradeoffs* between multicast tree (TBM$_0$) and flooding (TBM$_\infty$) by providing *variable density* of redundant paths. When the network is unstable and node mobility is high, a large k is chosen to provide more robust delivery of multicast packets; otherwise, a small k is chosen to reduce the control overhead. Obviously, k controls the density of redundant paths in the proposed TBM$_k$ algorithm that is a *distributed algorithm* to locally discover k-hop redundant paths. According to the performance evaluation results, the *packet loss ratio* of TBM$_k$ is less than 3 percent with k of 1, 2 and 3 while that of the multicast tree is 14 ~ 18 percent at the node speed range of 0 ~ 20 *m/sec; i.e.,* the packet delivery performance is improved by a factor of up to 6.

1 Introduction

A mobile ad hoc network (MANET) [1-3] is a collection of mobile nodes without any fixed infrastructure or any form of centralized administration. In other words, it is a temporary network of mobile nodes without existing communication infrastructure such as access points or base stations. In such a network, each node plays a router for multi-hop routing as well. MANETs can be effectively applied to military battlefields, emergency disaster relief, and other applications including wireless sensor networks.

Multicasting has been extensively studied for MANETs [4-15] because its operation is fundamental to many ad hoc network applications requiring close collaboration of multiple nodes in a multicast group. A multicast packet is delivered to multiple receivers along a network structure, such as *multicast tree* or *mesh*. However,

---

* This work was supported in part by the Korea Research Foundation Grant funded by the Korean Government (MOEHRD) (KRF-2005-214-D00355).

X. Cheng, W. Li, and T. Znati (Eds.): WASA 2006, LNCS 4138, pp. 515–526, 2006.
© Springer-Verlag Berlin Heidelberg 2006

these network structures are fragile due to node mobility, and thus some members may not be able to receive the multicast packet. It has been shown that multicast meshes are more robust to mobility than multicast trees [4] due to many redundant communication paths between mobile nodes in the mesh. However, multicast meshes inherently require higher construction and maintenance cost even if those redundant paths are not critically useful. For example, when network traffic is light and node mobility is low as in many potential ad hoc network scenarios such as wireless sensor networks, multicast packets would be delivered to the receivers with a high probability. In this case, a low-overhead multicast tree is surely a better option than multicast mesh. In addition, multicast trees are much more energy efficient because they have no redundant communication path and the power-saving mechanism puts a mobile node into sleep-mode when it does not communicate [16, 17].

This paper proposes an adaptive multicast scheme, called *tree-based mesh with k-hop redundant paths* (TBM_k), in which path redundancy is controlled depending on the status of the network such as traffic and mobility. More specifically, the proposed scheme constructs a multicast tree and adds some additional links/nodes to the multicast structure as needed to support redundancy. In other words, TBM_k includes all k- or smaller-hop paths between tree nodes to provide alternative paths among the nodes. By definition, a multicast tree and network-wide flooding can be regarded as TBM_0 and TBM_∞, respectively. TBM_k enables *tradeoffs* between multicast tree (TBM_0) and flooding (TBM_∞) by providing *variable density* of redundant paths. When the network is unstable and node mobility is high, a large k is chosen to provide more robust delivery of multicast packets. On the other hand, when the network traffic as well as the mobility is low, a small k is chosen to reduce the control overhead. Obviously, k controls the density of redundant paths in the proposed TBM_k algorithm that is a *distributed algorithm* to locally discover k-hop redundant paths.

Our simulation shows that the *packet loss ratio* of TBM_k is less than 3 percent with k of 1, 2 and 3 while that of the multicast tree is 14 ~ 18 percent at the node speed range of 0 ~ 20 *m/sec*. That is, the packet delivery performance is improved by a factor of up to 6. In our simulation scenario, the acceptable value of k is 2, which is enough to achieve fairly low packet loss ratio.

The rest of the paper is organized as follows: Preliminaries of multicast trees and energy consumption model are described in the following section. In Section 3, the proposed adaptive meshes with variable density of k-hop redundant paths are presented with algorithms and examples. Section 4 discusses our simulation study, which shows the effectiveness of the proposed scheme. Finally, concluding remarks are given in Section 5.

2 Preliminaries

This section overviews the multicast trees, which are used as fundamental structure in constructing TBM_k, and the power saving and energy model for MANETs.

2.1 Multicast Trees

A *multicast tree* can be constructed using simple tree construction method based on periodic join messages. Every member node periodically (*e.g.*, every 3 seconds [4]) sends a join message to the predetermined root node that is chosen from the member nodes. The multicast tree is constructed along the paths that join messages traverse. There is only one path from the root node to each receiver node. For a multicast group, a *shared tree* can be constructed and used repeatedly, where senders forward multicast messages to the root node, or every sender constructs its own tree called *per-source tree* as needed [7]. In this paper, the per-source tree is used as a fundamental structure to derive an on-demand multicast mesh.

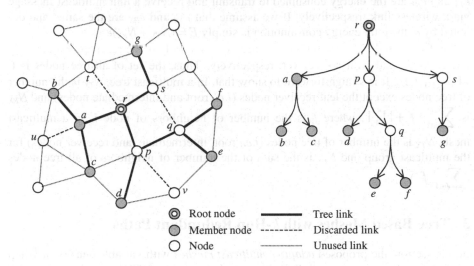

◎ Root node	—— Tree link
● Member node	------- Discarded link
○ Node	⋯⋯⋯ Unused link

Fig. 1. An example of a multicast tree

Fig. 1 shows an example of a multicast tree constructed on a MANET. Since wireless network interfaces typically accept only two packet addressing modes of unicast and broadcast, nodes *r, a, p,* and *q* must use broadcast addresses because they have more than one receiver. As a result, there are many discarded links causing the unnecessary energy consumption of packet receives.

2.2 Power Saving and Energy Model

Recent wireless network specifications usually provide power saving mechanisms for energy-constrained applications [17, 18]. In IEEE 802.11 ad hoc mode, any node requiring communication sends beacons to synchronize with nodes in its vicinity. A beacon period starts with *ATIM* (*ad hoc traffic indication map*), during which all nodes listen, and the pending traffic is advertised. Each node turns itself on or off depending on the advertised traffic [17]. Packets are buffered at the sender node and are directly transmitted to the receiver node. This power saving mechanism reduces the available channel capacity because useful traffic cannot be transmitted during the

ATIM window. In addition, it also suffers from longer packet delay because each intermediate node needs to buffer the packet until the next beacon period. The power saving mechanisms favor unicast over broadcast communication. For unicast, all other neighbors do not need to wake up and thus can save energy. However, if a sender has more than one receiver, it must resort to broadcast that results in many unnecessary receptions as well as wasted energy.

Let the total energy consumption per unit multicast packet be denoted as E, which includes the transmission energy (E_{TX}) as well as the energy required to receive the transmission (E_{RX}). This paper only considers data packets for simplicity. According to the *first-order radio model* [19], $E = E_{TX} + E_{RX} = N_{TX} \cdot e_{TX} + N_{RX} \cdot e_{RX}$, where N_{TX} and N_{RX} are the number of transmissions and the number of receives, respectively, and e_{TX} and e_{RX} are the energy consumed to transmit and receive a unit multicast message via a wireless link, respectively. If we assume that e_{TX} and e_{RX} are the same[1] and denoted by e, the total energy consumption is simply $E = (N_{TX} + N_{RX})e$.

Let Γ_+, Γ_1, and Γ_0 be the set of tree nodes with more than one receiver, with exactly one receiver, and with no receiver, respectively. Thus, the set of all tree nodes is $\Gamma = \Gamma_+ + \Gamma_1 + \Gamma_0$. It is straightforward to show that, in a multicast tree, N_{TX} is the number of tree nodes except the leaf receiver nodes (*i.e.*, root and intermediate nodes) and N_{RX} is $\sum_{i \in \Gamma_+} f_i + |\Gamma_1|$, where f_i is the number of neighbors of node i. In a multicast mesh, N_{TX} is the number of tree nodes (*i.e.*, root, intermediate, and receiver nodes) for the multicast group and N_{RX} is the sum of the number of neighbors of all tree nodes ($\sum_{i \in \Gamma} f_i$).

3   Tree-Based Meshes with k-Hop Redundant Paths

In this section, the proposed *adaptive multicast meshes* with variable density of k-hop redundant paths are presented. Definitions and examples of TBM$_k$ are described first, and the distributed algorithm to construct TBM$_k$ is discussed.

3.1   Tree-Based Meshes

A multicast tree with n nodes has exactly $n - 1$ links. If we add one or more links and zero or more nodes to a multicast tree, there are one or more cycles in the graph derived from the multicast tree. The graph is a *multicast mesh* with redundant paths and we call it *tree-based multicast mesh*. The following two definitions define a *k-hop redundant path* and a *tree-based mesh with k-hop redundant paths* (*TBM$_k$*) on a MANET:

Definition 1. A *k-hop redundant path* in a graph derived from a multicast tree on a MANET by adding one or more links and zero or more nodes is a path of length k, in which two end nodes are tree nodes and the other $k - 1$ nodes are tree or nontree nodes, where k is the number of hops (links) along the redundant path.

---

[1] In reality, e_{TX} and e_{RX} are slightly different. For example, $e_{TX} = 300$mA and $e_{RX} = 250$mA for WaveLAN-II from Lucent [20].

Definition 2. A *tree-based mesh with k-hop redundant paths* (TBM_k) is a graph derived from a multicast tree on a MANET by adding all 1-, 2-, ..., k-hop redundant paths, where k is the maximum number of hops (links) along the redundant path.

Given two nodes in a tree-based mesh, there might be a k-hop redundant path between the two nodes, where k is the number of hops (links) along the redundant path. When $k = 1$, there are only 1-hop redundant paths and no redundant nodes in the multicast mesh. When $k = 2$, there are 1- or 2-hop redundant paths with zero or more redundant nodes. That is, 1-, 2-, ..., k-hop redundant paths can exist along with 0, 1, ..., $k - 1$ redundant nodes, respectively. If k becomes larger, a more robust multicast mesh with many redundant paths is obtained. When k is infinite (*i.e.*, TBM_∞), all the nodes in the network are involved in the multicast mesh resulting in network-wide flooding. In a tree-based mesh, therefore, there might be multiple paths from the root node to each receiver node. By definition, a multicast tree can be regarded as a special case of a tree-based mesh, where $k = 0$ (*i.e.*, TBM_0).

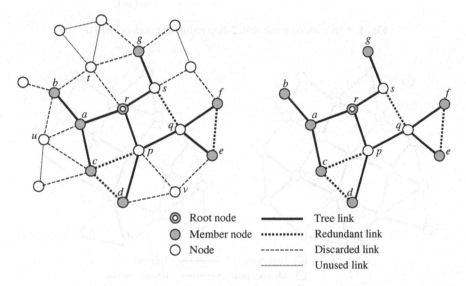

◉ Root node	—— Tree link
● Member node	·········· Redundant link
○ Node	- - - - Discarded link
	········· Unused link

Fig. 2. A tree-based mesh with 1-hop redundant paths (TBM_1)

Fig. 2 shows a tree-based mesh with 1-hop redundant paths (TBM_1). There are four 1-hop redundant paths of (s, q), (p, c), (c, d) and (e, f), which can be effectively used in case the tree links are broken. For example, when link (a, c) is broken, node c receives multicast messages from node p through redundant link (p, c). Note here that the link breakage is mainly due to the node mobility. In the figure, discarded links are due to the broadcast transmitted by tree nodes with more than one receiver.

Fig. 3 shows a tree-based mesh with 2-hop redundant paths (TBM_2). In addition to the four 1-hop redundant paths of (s, q), (p, c), (c, d) and (e, f), there are ten 2-hop redundant paths of (s, w, f), (r, t, b), (r, t, g), (b, t, g), (a, u, b), (a, u, c), (b, u, c), (p, v, d), (p, v, e) and (d, v, e), which provide more redundant paths from the root to

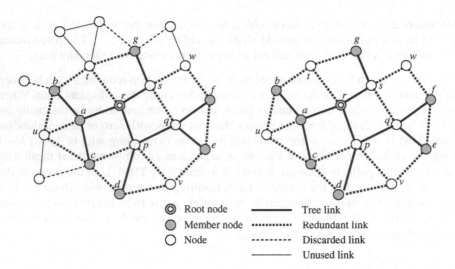

Fig. 3. A tree-based mesh with 2-hop redundant paths (TBM$_2$)

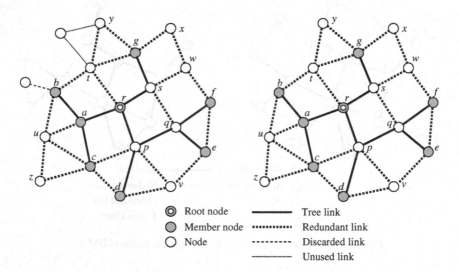

Fig. 4. A tree-based mesh with 3-hop redundant paths (TBM$_3$)

receivers resulting in more robust and reliable delivery. Note here that a path with any intermediate tree node is also a redundant path by Definition 1. For instance, path (p, c, d) is a 2-hop redundant path, which can be effectively used in case the link (p, d) is broken.

Fig. 4 shows a tree-based mesh with 3-hop redundant paths (TBM$_3$). In addition to the four 1-hop redundant paths and the ten 2-hop redundant paths, there are six 3-hop redundant paths of (g, x, w, s), (g, x, w, f), (b, t, y, g), (r, t, y, g), (b, u, z, c) and (a, u, z, c), which allow much more robust and reliable delivery of multicast packets compared to TBM$_2$.

3.2 Mesh Construction Algorithm

Algorithm 1 describes the tree construction procedure run in the root node (*i.e.*, a sender node in a per-source tree). Once join messages are collected at the root node, a multicast tree can be easily constructed by combining the $(n - 1)$ paths that the join messages traverse as described in Step 2, where n is the number of member nodes in the multicast group. Note that each join message contains an ordered list of the nodes that it traverses.

Algorithm 1. Construct_Tree(*M*, *r*, *n*)
1. Let $M = \{m_1, m_2, ..., m_{n-1}\}$ be the set of the join messages received by r from e ach receiver node, r be the root node, and n be the number of member nodes in a multicast group, where the i-th join message m_i contains an ordered list of the nodes it traverses
2. Referring to M, construct a per-source tree rooted at r by combining the $n - 1$ p aths that the join messages of $m_1, m_2, ..., m_{n-1}$ traverse.

Algorithm 2 describes the procedure to construct TBM$_k$, which is a *distributed algorithm* and thus runs locally in every node of the multicast tree in a distributed manner. The mesh is constructed by finding k-hop redundant paths in the tree constructed by Algorithm 1. Note that a node can set itself as a tree node if a join message traverses the node during the tree construction. So, a node can simply decide whether it is a tree node or not. The *k-hop broadcasting* in Step 2 is similar to the *expanding ring search* in AODV [21]. In Step 3, if multiple k-hop broadcast messages arrive successively in a short time, they can be queued in a buffer and processed one after another. Even after the local node sets itself as a forwarding node in Step 3.5, it repeatedly executes Step 3 because, if the number of hops (*i.e.*, hop count) that the message traverses is less than k, the local node must rebroadcast the received message by increasing the hop count by 1 as described in Step 3.3 in order to find as many k-hop redundant paths as possible.

Algorithm 2. Construct_TBM$_k$(*T*(*V*, *E*), *l*, *k*, *n*)
1. Let $T(V, E)$ be a multicast tree with vertex set $V(T)$ and edge set $E(T)$, l be the l ocal node, k be the maximum length of redundant paths, and n be the number o f member nodes in a multicast group.
2. If $l \in V(T)$, send a k-hop broadcast message, *i.e.*, a broadcast message with TT L (Time To Live) of k.
3. If $l \notin V(T)$ and the timeout period does not expires, wait for a k-hop broadcast message and do the following when the message arrives; otherwise, exit.
   3.1 Let S be the set of hop count values in the k-hop broadcast messages rece ived earlier and c be the number of hops (*i.e.*, hop count) that the messag e has traversed.
   3.2 If $c \geq k$, go to Step 3.

3.3   If $c \notin S$, add c to S (*i.e.*, $S \leftarrow S \cup \{c\}$) and rebroadcast the received mess
      age by increasing the hop count by 1; otherwise, go to Step 3.

3.4   If l is a forwarding node, go to Step 3.

3.5   For every $s_i \in S$, where $i = 1, 2, \ldots, |S|$, if $s_i + c \leq k$, set l as a forwarding
      node.

3.6   Go to Step 3.

In the proposed scheme, every node agrees on the same TBM_k by running a distributed algorithm. Once a TBM_k is constructed, multicast packets are forwarded along with the redundant paths in TBM_k from a sender to multiple destinations. The multicast operation is basically the same as other on-demand mash-based multicast protocols. For multicast, the unique group ID is assigned and shared among all the member nodes at the group creation time. If a node receives a multicast message and its group ID is equal to the group ID it has, it receives the multicast message and forwards it to its neighbors.

4   Performance Evaluation

In this section, the performance of the proposed TBM_k is evaluated via extensive simulation. The simulation environment is described in Section 4.1 including network model, node mobility, multicast traffic, and parameters used in the simulation. Section 4.2 discusses the simulation results.

4.1   Simulation Environment

Our performance study simulates and compares the multicast tree, the network-wide flooding, and the three tree-based meshes with 1-, 2-, and 3-hop redundant paths, respectively, in terms of packet loss ratio and per node energy consumption. Our evaluation is based on the simulation of mobile nodes moving over a square area of 1200 meters × 1200 meters for 15 minutes of simulation time. The radio transmission range is assumed to be 250 meters and a free space propagation channel is assumed with a data transmission rate of 2 Mbps. Omni-directional antennas and symmetric radio links are assumed in conjunction with the same transmission power. That is, all the nodes have the same capability over the network.

In our simulation, a constant bit rate (CBR) source and its multiple destinations are randomly selected among the mobile nodes. A CBR source sends a 512-byte multicast packet every 100 milliseconds during the simulation. For simplicity, we assume a multicast message consists of one data packet.

Mobile nodes are assumed to move randomly according to the *random waypoint model* [4, 7, 22]. Two parameters of maximum node speed and pause time determine the mobility pattern of the mobile nodes. Each node starts its journey from a randomly selected location to a target location, which is also selected randomly in the simulated area. Node speed is also randomly chosen between 0 and maximum speed (2 or 20 *m/sec*). When a node reaches the target location, it stays there for the pause time (30 *sec* in our simulation) and then repeats the mobility behavior.

For each node, energy consumption is measured during the simulation. According to the specification of IEEE 802.11-compliant WaveLAN-II [20] from Lucent, the power consumption varies from 0.045 W (9 $mA \times 5$ V) in sleep-mode to 1.25 and 1.50 W (230 and 250 $mA \times 5$ V) for receiving and transmitting modes, respectively. The instantaneous power is multiplied by time duration to obtain the energy consumed. For example, data transmission of a 512-byte packet consumes 3.1 milli-Joules (1.50 $W \times 512 \times 8$ $bits/2$ $Mbps$).

4.2 Simulation Results and Discussion

In this subsection, the simulation results of the multicast tree, the network-wide flooding, and the three tree-based meshes (*i.e.,* TBM_1, TBM_2, and TBM_3) are given and discussed in terms of packet loss ratio and per node energy consumption.

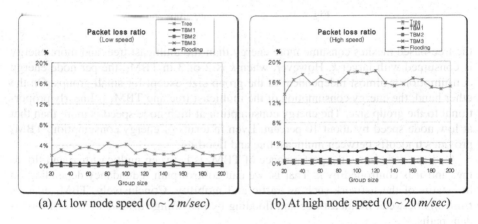

(a) At low node speed (0 ~ 2 m/sec)   (b) At high node speed (0 ~ 20 m/sec)

Fig. 5. Data packet loss ratio

Fig. 5 shows the *data packet loss ratio* of the multicast tree, the network-wide flooding, and the three tree-based meshes with 1-, 2-, and 3-hop redundant paths, respectively, with respect to the group size. Note that the group size is the number of member nodes in a multicast group. At low node speed (0 ~ 2 m/sec), the packet loss ratio of TBM_k is less than 1 percent while that of the multicast tree is 2 ~ 5 percent. At high node speed (0 ~ 20 m/sec), the former is less than 3 percent while the latter is 14 ~ 18 percent. For all the protocols at both low and high node speed, the packet loss ratio is almost uniform with the group size. As shown in the figure, the packet loss ratio of TBM_k is improved with larger k, but it is improved less and less as k increases. Obviously, in terms of packet loss ratio, TBM_k enables tradeoffs between multicast tree and flooding. In our simulation results, the acceptable value of k is 2, which is enough to achieve fairly low packet loss ratio.

Fig. 6 shows the per node energy consumption of the multicast tree, the network-wide flooding, and the three tree-based meshes with 1-, 2-, and 3-hop redundant paths, respectively, with respect to the group size. Both at low and high node speed,

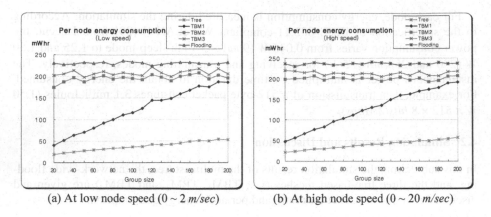

(a) At low node speed (0 ~ 2 *m/sec*)   (b) At high node speed (0 ~ 20 *m/sec*)

Fig. 6. Per node energy consumption

the tree-based meshes consume more energy than the multicast tree, and more energy is consumed with larger k. However, when k is 2 or 3 in TBM_k, the per node energy consumption is almost independent of the group size except for small groups. On the other hand, the energy consumption of the multicast tree and TBM_1 is linearly proportional to the group size. The energy consumption at high node speed is more than that at low node speed by about 10 percent. Even in terms of energy consumption, TBM_k provides tradeoffs between multicast tree and flooding.

As discussed above, the performance of TBM_k is between multicast tree and flooding, and it is controlled by k. That is, we can control path redundancy depending on the status of the network such as traffic and mobility. Conclusively, TBM_k enables *tradeoffs* between multicast tree and flooding by providing *variable density* of redundant paths.

5 Conclusions

In this paper, the novel *adaptive multicast* scheme for MANETs, called *tree-based mesh with k-hop redundant paths (TBM_k)*, has been proposed and evaluated. TBM_k provides *variable density* of redundant paths depending on the status of the network such as traffic and mobility, resulting in *tradeoffs* between multicast tree and flooding. When the network is unstable and node mobility is high, a large k is chosen to provide more robust delivery of multicast packets. On the other hand, when the network traffic as well as the mobility is low, a small k is chosen to reduce the control overhead. The k-hop redundant paths are locally obtained by running a *distributed algorithm*. According to the performance evaluation results, the *packet loss ratio* of the tree-based meshes is less than that of the multicast tree by a factor of up to 6 at node speed range of 0 ~ 20 *m/sec*. It has been also inferred that the acceptable value of k is 2, which is sufficient enough to achieve fairly low packet loss ratio.

Our future work is to apply the proposed scheme to the mixed-mode wireless sensor networks in which both static and mobile nodes exist together over the network area.

References

1. Perkins, C.E.: Ad Hoc Networking. Addison-Wesley Pub. Co., Upper Saddle River, NJ (2001)
2. Siva Ram Murthy, C., Manoj, B. S.: Ad Hoc Wireless Networks. Prentice Hall, Upper Saddle River, NJ (2004)
3. Internet Engineering Task Force (IETF) Mobile Ad Hoc Networks (MANET) Working Group Charter. http://www.ietf.org/html.charters/manet-charter.html (2006)
4. Lee, S.-J., Su, W., Hsu, J., Gerla, M., Bagrodia, R.: A Performance Comparison Study of Ad Hoc Wireless Multicast Protocols. Proc. of the IEEE Infocom 2000, Vol. 2 (2000) 565-574
5. Wieselthier, J.E., Nguyen, G.D., Ephremides, A.: On the Construction of Energy-Efficient Broadcast and Multicast Trees in Wireless Networks. Proc. of the IEEE Infocom 2000, Vol. 2 (2000) 585-594
6. Devarapalli, V., Sidhu, D.: MZR: a multicast protocol for mobile ad hoc networks. Proc. of IEEE International Conference on Communications, Vol. 3 (2001) 886-891
7. Gerla, M., Chiang, C.-C., Zhang, L.: Tree Multicast Strategies in Mobile, Multihop Wireless Networks. Baltzer/ACM Journal of Mobile Networks and Applications, Vol. 3 (1999) 193-207
8. Royer, E., Perkins, C.: Multicast Operation of the Ad-hoc On-Demand Distance Vector Routing Protocol. Proc. of the Int. Conf. on Mobile Computing and Networking (1999) 207-218
9. Lee, S., Gerla, M., Chiang, C.: On-Demand Multicast Routing Protocol. Proc. of IEEE Wireless Communications and Networking Conference (1999) 1298-1302
10. Lee, S., Kim, C.: Neighbor Supporting Ad Hoc Multicast Routing Protocol. Proc. Of the First Annual Workshop on Mobile Ad Hoc Networking and Computing (2000) 37-44
11. Moustafa, H., Laboid, H.: A Multicast On-Demand Mesh-Based Routing Protocol in Multihop Mobile Wireless Networks. Proc. of IEEE 58th Semiannual Vehicular Technology Conference (VTC 2003-Fall), Vol. 4 (2003) 2192-2196
12. Jiang, H., Cheng, S., He, Y., Sun, B.: Multicasting along Energy-Efficient Meshes in Mobile Ad Hoc Networks. Proc. of IEEE Wireless Communications and Networking Conference (WCNC 2002), Vol. 2 (2002) 807-811
13. Pandey, M., Zappala, D.: A Scenario-Based Performance Evaluation of Multicast Routing Protocols for Ad Hoc Networks. Proc. of 6th IEEE Int. Symp. on World of Wireless Mobile and Multimedia Networks (2005) 31-41
14. Dhillon, H., Ngo, H.Q.: CQMP: A Mesh-Based Multicast Routing Protocol with Consolidated Query Packets. Proc. of IEEE Wireless Communications and Networking Conference, Vol. 4 (2005) 2168-2174
15. Malaguti, M., Taddia, C., Mazzini, G., Zorzi, M.: Analysis of Performance of Multicast Routing Protocols over 802.11b. Proc. of IEEE 60th Semiannual Vehicular Technology Conference (VTC 2004-Fall), Vol. 5 (2004) 3165-3169
16. IEEE Std 802.11-1999, Local and Metropolitan Area Network, Specific Requirements, Part 11: Wireless LAN Medium Access Control (MAC) and Physical Layer (PHY) Specifications (1999)
17. Woesner, H., Ebert, J., Schlager, M., Wolisz, A.: Power-Saving Mechanisms in Emerging Standards for Wireless LANs: The MAC Level Perspective. IEEE Personal Communications, Vol. 5 (1998) 40-48

18. Frodigh, M., Johansson, P., Larsson, P.: Wireless Ad Hoc Networking – The Art of Networking without a Network. Ericsson Review, No. 4 (2000) 248-263
19. Heinzelman, W.R., Chandrakasan, A., Balakrishnan, H.: Energy-Efficient Communication Protocols for Wireless Microsensor Networks. Proc. of the Hawaii Int. Conf. on System Science (2000) 3005-3014
20. Kamerman, A., Monteban, L.: WaveLAN-II: A High-Performance Wireless LAN for the Unlicensed Band. Bell Labs Technical Journal (1997) 118-133
21. Belding-Royer, E.M., Perkins, C.E.: Evolution and Future Directions of the Ad Hoc on-Demand Distance-Vector Routing Protocol. Ad Hoc Networks, Vol. 1 (2003) 125-150
22. Cano, J.-C., Manzoni, P.: A Performance Comparison of Energy Consumption for Mobile Ad Hoc Network Routing Protocols. Proc. of Int. Symp. on Modeling, Analysis and Simulation of Computer and Telecomm. Systems (2000) 57-64

Low-Latency Broadcast Scheduling in Ad Hoc Networks

Scott C.-H. Huang[1], Peng-Jun Wan[1,2], Xiaohua Jia[1], and Hongwei Du[1]

[1] City University of Hong Kong
{shuang, pwan, jia, hongwei}@cs.cityu.edu.hk
[2] Illinois Institute of Technology
wan@cs.iit.edu

Abstract. Broadcast is a fundamental operation in wireless network, and naïve flooding is simply not practical. Previous results showed that although broadcast scheduling can achieve constant approximation ratios in respect of latency, the current state-of-the-art algorithm's ratio is still overwhelmingly large (≈ 650). In this paper we present two basic broadcast scheduling algorithms that both achieve small ratios 51 and 24, while preserving low redundancy 1 and 4 (in terms of number of retransmissions a node has to make). Moreover, we also present a highly efficient algorithm whose latency is $R + O(\sqrt{R} \log^{1.5} R)$ (where R is the network radius) and each node only has to transmit up to 5 times. This result, in a sense of approximation, is nearly optimal since $O(\sqrt{R} \log^{1.5} R)$ is negligible when R is large. Moreover, R is itself a lower bound for latency, so the approximation ratio is nearly 1 and this algorithm is nearly optimal.

1 Introduction

Among many operations of mobile ad hoc networks, broadcast is probably the most fundamental yet challenging operation since [25] tells us naïve flooding is simply not practical. Our first objective is to find a good scheduling algorithm that can mitigate the impact of potential collision and have a low broadcast latency. In addition, we also want our algorithm efficient such that nodes only have to transmit the message very few times. Redundancy is measured by how many times a node has to retransmit in order to guarantee collision-free reception. We want to balance latency and redundancy in this work.

It is known that broadcast in ad hoc networks has a constant approximation algorithm [18]. However, it is still not practical because the approximation ratio is overwhelmingly large (it was estimated to be near 648). In this paper, we present two basic broadcast scheduling algorithms that significantly reduce this ratio. One of our algorithms has ratio 51 and another has 24, and, more importantly, they do not increase redundancy much. The above two algorithms guarantee that each node only has to retransmit 1 and 4 times to guarantee proper reception, respectively. Moreover, we also present a highly efficient algorithm whose latency is $R + O(\sqrt{R} \log^{1.5} R)$ (where R is the network radius) and each node only has to transmit up to 5 times. This result, in a sense of approximation, is nearly optimal

X. Cheng, W. Li, and T. Znati (Eds.): WASA 2006, LNCS 4138, pp. 527–538, 2006.

since $O(\sqrt{R}\log^{1.5} R)$ is negligible when R is large. Moreover, R is itself a lower bound for latency, so the approximation ratio is nearly 1 and this algorithm is nearly optimal.

2   Related Work

Sheu et al [28] did empirical studies about the efficiency of broadcasting schemes in terms of collision-free delivery, number of retransmissions and latency. Basagni et al [4] presented a mobility transparent broadcast scheme for mobile multi-hop radio networks by using mobility-transparent schedule that guarantees bounded latency. Chlamtac and Kutten [8] first showed that the problem of finding an optimal deterministic broadcasting scheme for general graphs is NP-hard. Chlamtac and Weinstein [9] used undirected bipartite graphs to model this problem and gave an $O(\log^2 n)$ approximation algorithm (which gave a $O(R\log n)$ upper bound on broadcast latency where R is the radius and n is the number of nodes). Kowalski and Pelc [21] later reduced it to $O(R\log n + \log^2 n)$. Bar-Yehuda et al [3] obtained the same result earlier, but their solution was a randomized algorithm of Las Vegas type. Gaber and Mansour [17] employed clustering techniques to reduce this broadcast latency upper bound to $O(R + \log^5 n)$. Elkin and Kortsarz [16] refined this method and obtained a bound of $R + O(\sqrt{R} \cdot \log^2 n)$, thus reducing it to $O(R + \log^4 n)$. Alon et al [1] proved that there exists a family of radius-2 networks for which any broadcast schedule requires at least $\Omega(\log^2 n)$ time slots. Bruschi and Del Pinto [5] considered distributed protocols and obtained a lower bound of $\Omega(D\log n)$ with the assumption that no nodes know the identities of their neighbors. Kushilevitz and Mansour [22] proved that for any randomized broadcast protocol there exists a network whose latency is $\Omega(D\log(N/D))$. Chlebus et al [10] studied deterministic broadcasting without a-priori knowledge of the network. Elkin and Kortsarz showed in [14] that the radio broadcast problem is $\Omega(\log n)$-inapproximable unless $NP \subset BPTIME(n^{O(\log\log n)})$. Also, they showed in another work [15] that this problem can not be approximated within an additive term $c\log^2 n$ for some constant c unless $NP \subset BPTIME(n^{O(\log\log n)})$.

Gandhi et al [18] proved that constant approximation exists in disk graphs, which was impossible in general graphs according to [14]. In [18], an important technique of finding a *Connected Dominating Set* (CDS) as a virtual backbone is used. CDS plays an important role and has been used extensively in broadcast [18], routing [29] [12] [13], as well as many other areas of networking. Guha and Khuller [19] studied the minimum connected dominating set problem in general graphs and proved its NP-hardness. Clark et al [11] showed that this problem remains NP-hard even in unit disk graphs (UDGs) There are also some results on approximating this problem. Marathe et al [24] gave some heuristics for UDGs. Cheng et al [6] designed a polynomial-time approximation scheme for MCDS problem. Wan et al [30] and Alzoubi et al [2] studied the approximation of CDS, MCDS problem in terms of its size as well as time and message complexity.

3 Preliminaries

3.1 Network Model

An ad hoc network can be modelled as a unit disk graph $G = (V, E)$ along with a source node $s \in V$. Each node has transmission range 1, and two nodes u, v are neighbors if and only if their Euclidean distance is less than 1. The *radius* of G is defined as $\max_{v \in V} dist(s, v)$, where $dist(u, v)$ is the hop distance between u and v. For any node $v \in V$, its *layer* $l(v)$ is defined as the hop distance between v and s. The source node's layer $l(s)$ is 0. We can group V by layers as follows. L_i denotes the nodes whose layers are equal to i (i.e. $L_i = \{v | l(v) = i\}$). Time is assumed to be discrete and we use time slots to represent it throughout this paper.

3.2 Problem Definition

Given $G = (V, E)$ and $s \in V$, the objective is to find a *schedule* satisfying the following requirements. (1) It is represented as a function, called $TransmitTime$, from V to subsets of natural numbers. A subset of $S \subset V$ is mapped to a subset of $T \subset \mathbb{N}$ if and only if all nodes in S are scheduled to transmit in time slots indicated in T. (2) A node receives the message *collision-free* at some time if and only if exactly one of its neighbors is transmitting at this time. (3) A node cannot transmit unless it has already received the message collision-free earlier.

Latency is the first time slot such that all nodes have received the message collision-free, and *redundancy* is the maximum size of these subsets of $\mathbb{N}$ mapped by some subset in V, namely $\max_{S \subset V} |TransmitTime(S)|$. The goal this paper is to find a scheduling algorithm that minimizes this latency while having low redundancy.

3.3 Layered MIS and Virtual Backbone Construction

We will use the concept of *Maximal Independent Sets* (MIS) throughout this paper. An independent set (IS) is a subset $S \subset V$ such that no two nodes in S are adjacent to each other (i.e. all nodes are independent of each other). A maximal independent set M is an independent set with maximality, which means adding any other node will destroy the independence property. Formally, M is an MIS if it is an independent set and for all $M' \supset M$, M' is not independent. We construct MIS in a layered manner, which ensures a *2-hop separation property* as follows. Starting from the first layer L_1, we choose a MIS, denoted by $BLACK_1 \subset L_1$ first. Then we move on to L_2 and select independent nodes $BLACK_2 \subset L_2$ as well. Not only are $BLACK_2$ nodes independent of each other, they are independent of all nodes in $BLACK_1$ as well. We follow this method and select $BLACK_3, BLACK_4, \ldots$ until we finish the last layer and finally we get a layered MIS denoted by $BLACK = \cup_i BLACK_i$. Such set $BLACK$ we construct in this manner has a stronger property than arbitrarily constructed ones. Let's construct a breadth-first search tree T_{BFS} for G and pick a node $v \in BLACK_i$. Observe that v's parent $p(v)$ in T_{BFS} must be in $L_{i-1} - BLACK_{i-1}$ (since

$p(v)$ is in L_{i-1} and not independent of v), and therefore $p(v)$ must be adjacent to some node in $BLACK_{i-1}$. In short, for all i and any node in $BLACK_i$, it must have a 2-hop neighbor in $BLACK_{i-1}$. This is called the 2-hop separation property. Because of this property, if G is connected, we can construct a virtual backbone consisting of the set $BLACK$ along with another set $BLUE$ defined as $BLUE = \{v | v$ is the parent of some nodes in $BLACK$ in $T_{BFS}\}$ Obviously $BLACK \cup BLUE$ form a connected dominating set as described above. For simplicity we also use the term "black nodes" to refer to the set $BLACK$, and the term "blue nodes" to refer to $BLUE$. This virtual backbone is actually a tree T_{br} formally defined as follows. $T_{br} = (BLACK \cup BLUE, E_{br})$ where $(u, p(u)) \in E_{br}$ ($p(u)$ represents u's parent in T_{br}) if and only if

$$\begin{cases} u \in BLACK_i, p(u) \text{ is } u\text{'s parent in } T_{BFS} \\ u \in BLUE_i, p(u) \in BLACK_i \cup BLACK_{i-1}, (u, p(u)) \in E \end{cases}$$

The second condition is always valid since $BLACK$ is constructed layer by layer. Any blue node at layer i must be adjacent to a black node either at layer i or $i - 1$. However, there may be more than one black node adjacent to it. In this case, we just pick one of them arbitrarily. T_{br} has the following properties. (1) A black node's parent is always blue. (2) A blue node's parent is always black. (3) If $u \in BLACK_i$ then $p(p(u)) \in BLACK_{i-1}$ where $p(p(u))$ is the parent of u's parent (i.e. u's grandparent).

3.4   Coloring of MIS Nodes

If some black nodes get the broadcast message, then we are sure that all of their neighbor nodes will get the message from them within very few time slots. Similarly, if all black nodes get the message, then all nodes will get the message from them in a short time. We are going to show that 12,13 time slots are enough. The time required for black nodes to pass message to their neighbors depends on a *coloring* of them.

If two nodes are separated by at least 3 hops (this essentially means their Euclidean distance is greater than 2), then if they broadcast at the same time, there will be no collision at all since their transmission ranges do not overlap. In other words, two black nodes can be scheduled to transmit for the same time slot as long as they are 2-independent (not 2-hop neighbors). We can define a new graph H whose vertices are black nodes and an edge exists between two nodes if they are 2-hop neighbors, and consider the coloring of H. Nodes of the same color will be scheduled for the same time slot, and the time required for black nodes to broadcast the message to all nodes (using this scheduling method) is equal to the number of colors used. We show that 12 colors are enough if all nodes know about their locations and 13 colors are enough if not.

Lemma 3.1. *If all nodes know about their own locations, 12 colors are enough to color H (H is defined as above).*

Proof. We partition the entire plane into half-open, half-closed hexagons and give a 12-coloring, as shown in Figure 1. Each hexagon has radius 1/2 (and

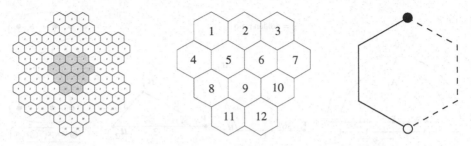

Fig. 1. Partition of the entire plane into half-open, half-closed hexagons

therefore its diameter is equal to 1). According to its location, each node belongs to exactly one hexagon and is assigned to a corresponding color. Since each hexagon has radius $1/2$, there can be at most one black node in each hexagon and the distance between any different hexagons of the same color is at least 2.   □

The above coloring takes great advantage of unit disk graphs geometrical properties. Note that this way of coloring does not need global information and can be implemented locally. If location information is not known but the global topology is known (by some server), then 13 time slots are enough. However, this is a centralized approach.

Lemma 3.2. *If the global topology is known, 13 colors are enough to color H.*

Lemma 3.3. *Given a black node v. There can be at most 12 black nodes other than v itself in any half-disk centered at v with radius 2.*

Proof. Consider a half disk shown in Figure 2(a). Since black nodes are independent, they cannot appear in the unit circle centered at v. In other words, all black nodes can only appear in the half-annulus $(A_1 \cup A_2)$. We divide this region into A_1 and A_2 (where g is the golden ratio) as shown in the figure. This lemma can be proved by showing that (1)there can be at most 5 black nodes in A_1 (2)there can be at most 7 black nodes in A_2. To prove (1), we assume there are 6 or more black nodes in A_1. If we draw a line from v to each of them, then there must be two black nodes u_1, u_2 such that $\angle u_1 v u_2$ is at most 36°. Since $1 < \overline{u_1 v}, \overline{u_2, v} < g$, we know that the distance between these two black nodes is less than 1. Figure 2(b) shows the extreme case where $\overline{u_1 v} = g$, $\overline{u_2, v} = 1$, $\angle u_1 v u_2 = 36°$, and $\overline{u_1 u_2} = 1$ but equality does not hold and $\overline{u_1, u_2}$ has to be less than 1. (2) can be proved similarly. Suppose there are 8 or more black nodes in A_2, then there must be two black nodes u_1, u_2 such that $\angle u_1 v u_2$ is at most $180/7 \doteq 25.71°$. This also implies $\overline{u_1, u_2} < 1$ since the extreme case happens when $\overline{u_1 v} = g$, $\overline{u_2, v} = 2$. $\overline{u_1, u_2} > 1$ would imply $\angle u_1 v u_2 > 29.77°$ as shown in Figure 2(b), which is impossible.   □

Proof of Lemma 3.2. Let's give an ordering of vertices as follows. Since the global topology is known, we can find the node v_1 of smallest degree in H first. Then we consider the new graph with v_1 and all its incident edges removed from

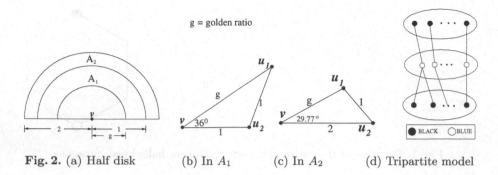

Fig. 2. (a) Half disk   (b) In A_1 (c) In A_2 (d) Tripartite model

H. We pick another node v_2 of smallest degree in this new graph, delete it, and repeat this process until all nodes have been picked and deleted. When v_i is picked, $v_1, v_1, \ldots, v_{i-1}$ have already been removed and v_i's degree in the new graph, denoted by d_i, equals $d_i = |N(v_i) \cap \{v_n, v_{n-1}, \ldots, v_{i+1}\}|$, where $N(v_i)$ is the set of v_i's neighbors in H. This gives an ordering of nodes $\{v_1, v_2, \ldots, v_n\}$. Note that $d_i \leq 12$ for all i. This is due to the fact that, at any time, there is always a vertex w that is geographically located at the leftmost position, which implies all of its neighbors in H are located in a half annulus centered at w. According to Lemma 3.3, there are at most 12 such neighbors.

We now reverse this ordering and claim that if we use first-fit coloring in the reverse order $\{v_n, v_{n-1}, \ldots, v_1\}$, 13 colors are enough. When we color a node v_i, we need to look at its neighbors in $\{v_n, v_{n-1}, \ldots, v_{i+1}\}$ and avoid using any color appeared there. Some of those neighbors may use the same color, but the worst case may happen in which none of those neighbors use the same color. In this case, $|N(v_i) \cap \{v_n, v_{n-1}, \ldots, v_{i+1}\}| = d_i$ colors have been used, and we have to use another color for v_i. Since we already know earlier that $d_i \leq 12$ for all i, 13 colors are enough to color H.   □

3.5 Tripartite Graph Model

We introduce a basic model called the *Tripartite Graph Model* for analyzing approximation ratios of broadcast latency. We focus on interactions between neighboring layers $BLACK_{i-1}$ and $BLACK_i$, for all $1 \leq i \leq R$ where R is the radius of G. Consider T_{br} again. Since we know that each black node's grandparent must be a black node of the previous layer, it suffices to consider the interaction between $BLACK_{i-1}$, $BLACK_i$ and those blue nodes in-between as connectors alone. If all black nodes have received the message, it only takes 12 or 13 more time slots to pass the message to all nodes. We know earlier that $BLACK_{i-1}$ and $BLACK_i$ are connected through blue nodes in between, so we only focus on the tripartite graph consisting of $BLACK_{i-1}, BLACK_i$, and blue nodes in between and the edges are taken directly from T_{br}, as shown in Fig 2(d). Note that it also takes 12 or 13 time slots from $BLACK_{i-1}$ to blue connectors, since $BLACK_{i-1}$ must contain all blue connectors. Broadcast latency thus depend solely on the schedule from blue connectors to $BLACK_i$, called *BLUE-to-BLACK*. Using this model, if BLUE-to-BLACK can be scheduled within ζ time slots, then we can repeat this process to pass the message to all black nodes within $(13 + \zeta)R$ time slots (where R is the network radius) and finally to all nodes within $(13 + \zeta)R$ time slots (we can regard the source s as blue and start from $BLACK_1$). We also know that R is itself a lower bound for transmission latency (since the message needs at least R time slots to reach the farthest node). This actually means that the approximation ratio of any broadcast algorithm using this model is at most $13 + \zeta$ (or $12 + \zeta$ if location is known).

4 First and Second Broadcast Algorithms

4.1 First Broadcast Algorithm - Least Redundancy

First algorithm has approximation ratio 51 and each node is only required to broadcast the message at most once. Using the tripartite graph model, we claim that applying First-Fit scheduling on BLUE-to-BLACK yields a result in which $\zeta = 39$ and the approximation ratio will be $39 + 13 = 52$ (or 51 if location is known).

Observe that for two blue nodes to be able to interfere with each other, their distance must be at most 2. Therefore, if we regard one blue node u as the origin, any potential interfering blue nodes must lie inside the circle centered at the origin with radius 2. Every interfering blue node must have at least one black child, otherwise this blue node wouldn't need to transmit and wouldn't be selected as a connector at all. The number of blue nodes lying inside a circle with radius 2 cannot exceed the number of black nodes lying inside the concentric circle with radius 3. We can apply Wegner's Theorem [31] with proper scaling to show that this number is at most 41 as follows.

Let S denote the set of black nodes that are at most three hops away from u. Then the convex hull of S is contained in the disk of radius 3.5 centered at u. Let $k = |S|$. Apply scaled Wegner Theorem, we know $k \leq 42$, and apparently 43 time slots are enough to schedule BLUE-to-BLACK. Now, we are going to show that 39 time slots are enough. First, we know that u's parent must have been counted, but u certainly does not have to transmit to its parent. Moreover, u must have a black child that it has to transmit to. This has been over-counted as an interfering blue node as well. So far, we know that 41 time slots are enough.

We will show that we only have to consider the case in which u has two or more children. The reason is that if u has only one child, we actually need way less than 39 time slots for the following reason. Assume u has only one child w, then any blue node that may interfere with u's transmission must be a neighbor of w. This essentially means the number of interfering blue nodes cannot exceed the number of black nodes inside the disk of radius 2 centered at w. Applying Wegner's Theorem and using the same argument, we can prove that the number of independent nodes lying inside a disk of radius 2 is at most 21 (the proof is omitted here for simplicity). Since w is itself a black node and has been counted already, w has at most 20 interfering blue neighbors and 39 time slots are certainly more than enough.

The above argument shows that we only have to consider the case in which u has 2 or more children. For this reason we know that we have over-counted one black node, and 40 time slots are enough so far. Finally, we are going to show that we still have over-counted one more black node and our desired result will be proved.

We look at u's parent $p(u)$ now. We claim that we only need to consider the case in which there exists some interfering blue node whose parent is not $p(u)$, otherwise it will result in an even tighter time bound. Assume the contrary that all interfering blue nodes' parent is $p(u)$, then the number of interfering blue nodes cannot exceed the number of black nodes lying inside the disk of radius 2 centered at $p(u)$. Again, by Wegner's Theorem, this results in a bound of 21 time slots and, indeed, we don't have to consider this case. Finally, since there exists some blue node whose parent is not $p(u)$, we can further subtract 1 from 40 and 39 time slots are enough to schedule BLUE-to-BLACK.

Note that all transmissions are scheduled in such a way that all possible collisions are avoided, so In the first algorithm each node needs to broadcast the message at most once.

4.2   Second Broadcast Algorithm - Tradeoff Between Latency and Redundancy

In this section we present another algorithm that achieves a better approximation ratio (24 if location is known and 26 if global topology is known) at the price of increasing redundancy by a factor of 4. Note that redundancy is measured as the maximum number of transmissions a single node has to make rather than the total number of transmissions in the entire network. We believe our metric makes the most sense in measuring redundancy, as it most precisely reflects the battery lifetime of a sensor node in sensor networks. The lifetime of a sensor network should be characterized as the lifetime of a single node rather than the number of all transmissions, since the failure of few nodes may disconnect the network and a small number of total transmissions does not guarantee network connectivity. We will study the tradeoff between latency and redundancy in detail in this subsection.

Again, we start from the tripartite graph model and schedule the part BLUE-to-BLACK. Instead of First-Fit, we now use the coloring-H method similar to the BLACK-to-BLUE part. Note that we can color H with 12 colors if location is known and with 13 colors if global topology is known. We schedule the blue nodes in the following way. Each blue nodes has at most 4 black children (since each blue node has at most 5 black neighbors and one of them must be its parent), so each blue node simply looks at its black children's colors and transmit in the corresponding time slots. For example, if a blue node has 4 children that are colored with colors #3, #5, #6, #11, this blue node simply transmit in time slots $\{3, 5, 6, 11\}$. This way of scheduling may cause collisions, but it ensures that, in any time slot, all receiving black nodes with corresponding color will receive the message collision-free. This can be proved by the following arguments. Assume that in a time slot, there is a black node w receiving from two blue nodes u, v and assume without loss of generality that u is the parent of w. Since u, v must have different black children that are their destinations, v must have a child w' other than w. Now, v is blue and w, w' are black. Then w and w' must be neighbors in H (H is defined in the tripartite graph model) since v is adjacent to both of them. Therefore, they wouldn't have been colored with the same color. On the other hand, since u, v are transmitting at the same time, w, w' must be of the same color and we finally get a contradiction.

5   Third Broadcast Algorithm - Theoretically the Best

Third algorithm achieves a highly efficient latency $R + O(\sqrt{R} \cdot \log^{1.5} R)$, where R represents the radius of the radio network. Since R is also a lower bound of the optimal solution, the above latency essentially means the approximation ratio is nearly 1, when R is large. In some sense, this means our algorithm is *nearly optimal*. This algorithm combines the first and second algorithms with the broadcast algorithm in [16] as well as some new elements to achieve this result. In addition to its high efficiency, it also has very low redundancy: Each node only needs to broadcast at most once to achieve this result if the first algorithm is used as one of its subroutines.

Phase 1: Virtual backbone construction
We construct MIS layer by layer with the 2-hop separation property and get the set $BLACK$. Then we construct the *Shortest Path Tree* (in G) of this set $BLACK$. Let $T_{sp} = (V_{sp}, E_{sp})$ denote the shortest path tree. We denote the set of non-black nodes in the shortest path tree by $GRAY$, and we also call they gray nodes as well. Note that $V_{sp} = BLACK \cup GRAY$ is a connected dominating set in G, since they form a tree and are therefore connected. V_{sp} can be regarded as a virtual backbone for G.
Phase 2: Broadcast inside virtual backbone
Let H_{vb} denote the induced subgraph of V_{sp} in G. We simply apply the broadcast algorithm in [16] to H_{vb}, s.
Phase 3: Broadcast from virtual backbone to others
Now, since all nodes in V_{sp} have already received the message, all black nodes must have received the message. By the technique of MIS coloring described in § 3.4, we know that we need 12 or 13 more time slots to pass this information to all nodes.

The latency of this algorithm is actually $R_{vb} + O(\sqrt{R_{vb}} \log^2 |V_{sp}|) + 13$ where R_{vb} is the radius of H_{vb}. Since $R_{vb} \le R$, the broadcast latency is thus $R_{vb} + O(\sqrt{R_{vb}} \log^2 |V_{sp}|)$, using asymptotic notations. The following lemma gives us an upper bound for $|V_{sp}|$.

Lemma 5.1. $|V_{sp}| = O(R^3)$ where R is the radius of G.

Proof. Since $V_{sp} = BLACK \cup GRAY$, let $m_1 = |BLACK|$ and $m_2 = |GRAY|$. Since R is the radius, the hop distance between any node and s is at most R, which essentially means the Euclidean distance between them is at most R too. If we consider a disk with radius R centered at s, then all nodes must lie within this disk. We know all black nodes are independent. If, for each black node, we draw a disk with radius $1/2$ center at it, then none of these disks will overlap since the distance between any two black nodes is at least 1. These disks altogether should lie within the disk with radius $R + 1/2$ centered at s, and the sum of their areas is bounded by the area of this big disk. Therefore, $m_1\pi(1/2)^2 \leq \pi(R + 1/2)^2$ and $m_1 = O(R^2)$. To bound m_2, we know that T_{sp} is a shortest path tree. Since the hop distance between any black node and s is at most R, there are at most $R - 2$ intermediate nodes between any shortest path from s to this black node. This means black node contributes at most $R-2$ gray nodes, and m_2 is therefore bounded by $(R - 2)m_1$. Therefore $m_2 = O(R^3)$ and $|V_{sp}| = m_1 + m_2 = O(R^3)$. Actually, $|V_{sp}| \leq 4R^3$ (This can be proved by applying Wegner's Theorem and is omitted here for simplicity.)   ⊓

This lemma tells us that by constructing a virtual backbone, the broadcast latency of unit disk graphs can be significantly improved. The latency of third algorithm is $R_{vb} + O(\sqrt{R_{vb}}\log^2 |V_{sp}|)$. Since $R_{vb} \leq R$ and $|V_{sp}| \leq 4R^3$. The latency is at most $R + O(\sqrt{R}\log^2 R)$. If we compare this bound with the latency bound of [16], which is $R + O(\sqrt{R}\log^2 n)$, although they look very similar, there is a significant difference. The latency of our third algorithm depends **solely on R**, which implies that when R is large $O(\sqrt{R}\log^2 R)$ is negligible and the latency is nearly R. Since R is a also a lower bound for broadcast latency, this essential means the approximation ratio is nearly 1 and our algorithm is **nearly optimal**. However, in [16], we still know nothing about their approximation ratio. Actually, if we modify the phase 2 of [16], we can further reduce this latency bound to $R + O(\sqrt{R}\log^{1.5} R)$. Because of the limitation of space, we omit the proof here.

6   Conclusions and Future work

In this paper we presented three broadcast scheduling algorithms in ad hoc networks modeled by unit disk graphs, and all of them have latency significantly lower than any other scheduling algorithms in the literature. In addition, they all have low redundancy as well. The first two algorithms clearly showed that there is some trade-off between latency and redundancy and we believe that we have already balanced them and achieved the maximum overall benefits.

One might think that we took great advantage in the geometrical properties of unit disk graphs, and they might be too ideal to be practical. For example, in real cases, the transmission topology and interference topology are not the same, the range a node could interfere with other nodes may be several times large than its transmission area. Actually, all three of our algorithms can be modified to suit this scenario, except that their approximation ratios may be increased. Moreover, though UDG model is ideal, it is a good place to start with. If we jump into complex models directly without know what advantages we could take in the ideal case, then we cannot get any good results.

Another important point regarding these algorithms is whether they can be implemented in a distributed manner. For first and second algorithms, if location is known, they there can be distributed implementation. However, if location is not known, we need global topology to color MIS nodes in order to get comparable results. Otherwise, the approximation ratios are not that good any more. Our third algorithm cannot be implemented in a distributed fashion either. The reason is that it involves some graph partitioning techniques which entail the knowledge of the whole topology. Although it seems to be a nearly optimal approximation algorithm, this requirement makes it excellent only from a theoretical point of view. How to find an algorithm that can avoid this strong requirement while having comparable performance is the main goal of our follow-up research topic.

References

1. N. Alon, A. Bar-Noy, N. Linial, and D. Peleg. A lower bound for radio broadcast. *Journal of Computer and System Sciences*, 43(2):290–298, 1991.
2. K. M. Alzoubi, P.-J. Wan, and O. Frieder. Message-optimal connected dominating sets in mobile ad hoc networks. In *3rd ACM international symposium on Mobile ad hoc networking & computing–MobiHoc'02*, pages 157–164, New York, NY, USA, 2002. ACM Press.
3. R. Bar-Yehuda, O. Goldreich, and A. Itai. On the time-complexity of broadcast in multi-hop radio networks: An exponential gap between determinism and randomization. *Journal of Computer and System Sciences*, 45(1):104–126, 1992.
4. S. Basagni, I. Chlamtac, and D. Bruschi. A mobility-transparent deterministic broadcast mechanism for ad hoc networks. *IEEE/ACM Transactions on Networking*, 7(6):799–807, 1999.
5. D. Bruschi and M. Del Pinto. Lower bounds for the broadcast problem in mobile radio networks. *Distributed Computing*, 10(3):129–135, 1997.
6. X. Cheng, X. Huang, D. Li, and D. Du. Polynomial time approximation scheme for minimum connected dominating set in ad hoc wireless networks. Technical Report. To appear in *Networks*.
7. I. Chlamtac and A. Faragó. Making transmission schedules immune to topology changes in multi-hop packet radio networks. *IEEE/ACM Transactions Networking*, 2(1):23–29, 1994.
8. I. Chlamtac and S. Kutten. On broadcasting in radio networks–problem analysis and protocol design. *IEEETransactions on Communications*, 33:1240–1246, 1985.
9. I. Chlamtac and O. Weinstein. The wave expansion approach to broadcasting in multihop radio networks. *IEEETransactions on Communications*, 39:426–433, 1991.
10. B. S. Chlebus, L. Gąsieniec, A. Gibbons, A. Pelc, and W. Rytter. Deterministic broadcasting in unknown radio networks. In *Symposium on Discrete Algorithms*, pages 861–870, 2000.
11. B. N. Clark, C. J. Colbourn, and D. S. Johnson. Unit disk graphs. *Discrete Math.*, 86(1-3):165–177, 1990.
12. B. Das and V. Bharghavan. Routing in ad-hoc networks using minimum connected dominating sets. In *ICC (1)*, pages 376–380, 1997.
13. B. Das and V. Bharghavan. Routing in ad-hoc networks using minimum connected dominating sets. In *ICC (1)*, pages 376–380, 1997.

14. M. Elkin and G. Kortsarz. Logarithmic inapproximability of the radio broadcast problem. *Journal of Algorithms*, 52:8–25, 2004.
15. M. Elkin and G. Kortsarz. Polylogarithmic additive inapproximability of the radio broadcast problem. In *7th Int'l Workshop on Approximation Algoorithms for Combinatorial Optimization Problems–APPROX'04*, 2004.
16. M. Elkin and G. Kortsarz. An improved algorithm for radio networks, 2005. An earlier version appeared in *SODA'05*.
17. I. Gaber and Y. Mansour. Centralized broadcast in multihop radio networks. *Journal of Algorithms*, 46(1):1–20, 2003.
18. R. Gandhi, S. Parthasarathy, and A. Mishra. Minimizing broadcast latency and redundancy in ad hoc networks. In *ACM MobiHoc'03*, pages 222–232, 2003.
19. S. Guha and S. Khuller. Approximation algorithms for connected dominating sets. In *European Symposium on Algorithms*, pages 179–193, 1996.
20. J.-H. Ju and V. O. K. Li. An optimal topology-transparent scheduling method in multihop packet radio networks. *IEEE/ACM Transactions on Networking*, 6(3):298–306, 1998.
21. D. R. Kowalski and A. Pelc. Centralized deterministic broadcasting in undirected multi-hop radio networks. In *7th International Workshop on Approximation Algorithms for Combinatorial Optimization Problems–APPROX-RANDOM'04*, pages 171–182, 2004.
22. E. Kushilevitz and Y. Mansour. An $\Omega(D \log(N/D))$ lower bound for broadcast in radio networks. *SIAM Journal on Computing*, 27:702–712, 1998.
23. N. Linial and M. Saks. Decomposing graphs into regions of small diameter. In *2nd annual ACM-SIAM symposium on Discrete algorithms–SODA'91*, pages 320–330, Philadelphia, PA, USA, 1991. Society for Industrial and Applied Mathematics.
24. M. V. Marathe, H. Breu, H. B. Hunt III, S. S. Ravi, and D. J. Rosenkrantz. Simple heuristics for unit disk graphs. *Networks*, 25:59–68, 1995.
25. S.-Y. Ni, Y.-C. Tseng, Y.-S. Chen, and J.-P. Sheu. The broadcast storm problem in a mobile ad hoc network. In *5th annual ACM/IEEE international conference on Mobile computing and networking–MobiCom'99*, pages 151–162, New York, NY, USA, 1999. ACM Press.
26. S. Ramanathan and E. L. Lloyd. Scheduling algorithms for multihop radio networks. *IEEE/ACM Transactions on Networking*, 1(2):166–177, 1993.
27. A. Sen and M. L. Huson. A new model for scheduling packet radio networks. *Wireless Networks*, 3(1):71–82, 1997.
28. J.-P. Sheu, P.-K. Hung, and C.-S. Hsu. Scheduling of broadcasts in multihop wireless networks. In *The handbook of ad hoc wireless networks*, pages 483–495. CRC Press, Inc., Boca Raton, FL, USA, 2003.
29. R. Sivakumar, B. Das, and V. Bharghavan. Spine routing in ad hoc networks. *Cluster Computing*, 1(2):237–248, 1998.
30. P.-J. Wan, K. M. Alzoubi, and O. Frieder. Distributed construction of connected dominating set in wireless ad hoc networks. *Mobile Networks and Applications*, 9(2):141–149, 2004.
31. G. Wegner. Über endliche kreispackungen in der ebene. *Studia Scientiarium Mathematicarium Hungarica*, 21:1–28, 1986.

A Study on the CI-OFDM Communication System for the High Quality and High Speed Communication System

Heui-Seop Byeon, Jin-Kook Chung, and Heung-Gyoon Ryu

Department of Electronic Engineering,
Chungbuk National University
12 Kaesin-dong, Cheongju, Chungbuk, 361-763, Korea
byuny@hanmail.net, chung198@hotmail.com, ecomm@cbu.ac.kr

Abstract. Orthogonal frequency division multiplexing (OFDM) system has been widely used for the high speed digital communication area and it is very promising for the next generation communication standard because of high data rate capability. However, OFDM system has inherent serious problem of high peak-to-average power ratio (PAPR) that makes the OFDM signal be distorted in the nonlinear HPA (high power amplifier). In this paper, CI (carrier interferometry)-OFDM system is considered to overcome this problem and is newly analyzed in the selective fading and narrow-band interference channel. CI-OFDM system distributes each parallel data to all sub-carriers in differently phase-rotated form. So, PAPR becomes lowered and it shows the frequency diversity effects. BER (bit error rate) performance is analyzed in the selective fading and narrow-band interference environment. From the simulation results, it is confirmed that CI-OFDM system calms down the high PAPR problem and CI-OFDM system is more robust than the ordinary OFDM system in the selective fading and narrow-band interference channel.

1 Introduction

Orthogonal frequency division multiplexing (OFDM) system has been used for the high speed digital communication area and it is very promising for the next generation communication standard. By distributing the very high-speed serial data symbol stream into a large number of orthogonal subchannels, it is a kind of multi-carrier suitable for the high speed and high data rate. And OFDM system has strong robustness to the multi-path interference, delay spread and frequency selective fading and has high bandwidth efficiency. So it has been adopted as the standards of European DAB/DVB-T system, Wireless LAN, Korean terrestrial DMB system.

However, OFDM system has serious drawbacks. The first is that the performance of OFDM system is degraded when it doesn't keep up the orthogonality between subcarriers. The second is that it is very difficult to convert the wide dynamic signal in the A/D and D/A converter of finite word length. The OFDM signal can have very high peak-to-average power ratio (PAPR) because of the same phase multi-carriers. The high PAPR makes the OFDM signal distorted in the nonlinear region of high power amplifier (HPA), which results in the poor performance of bit error rate (BER).

To reduce the PAPR, several methods have been proposed, such as clipping, PTS, SLM [3-9]. Clipping is another simple method for reducing the PAPR. But it causes a

X. Cheng, W. Li, and T. Znati (Eds.): WASA 2006, LNCS 4138, pp. 539–549, 2006.

serious in-band and out-of-band clipping noise that produces the adjacent channel interference (ACI). This makes BER performance degradation. Another considerable method is a phase rotation method. PTS and SLM belong to this method. PTS method divides sub-carriers into several clusters and optimizes the rotation factors to get the lowest PAPR signal. It can efficiently lower the high PAPR. However, the SI (side information) about the rotation factors is necessarily to be transmitted to the receiver for the correct data recovery. Also, the processing time is delayed by iteration to optimize the rotation factors. In SLM method, several copied OFDM data are multiplied by the different phase sequences simultaneously and the one with the lowest PAPR is selected to transmit. It can efficiently reduce the PAPR and SI (side information) is also transmitted to receiver. However, system complexity increases as the number of copy. Finally, CI-OFDM system can be classified into PAPR reduction method. CI-OFDM system distributes the same data to all sub-carriers and each phase factor called as phase code is multiplied. Therefore, each value is mixed so that peak value may be reduced. So it can solve PAPR problem. And it doesn't need the SI unlike the PTS and SLM. Also, the spread data signal is stronger than ordinary OFDM system in selective fading and narrow band interference channel [10-11].

In this paper, CI-OFDM system is considered to overcome this problem and is newly analyzed in the selective fading and narrow-band interference channel. CI-OFDM system distributes each parallel data to all sub-carriers in differently phase-rotated form. So, PAPR becomes lowered and it shows the frequency diversity effects. BER performance is analyzed in the selective fading and narrow-band interference environment. From the simulation results, it is confirmed that CI-OFDM system calms down the high PAPR problem and CI-OFDM system is more robust than the ordinary OFDM system in the selective fading and narrow-band interference channel.

2   OFDM System and PAPR

Ordinary OFDM system is used to data signals that convert serial into parallel and sends each symbol on sub carriers. It inserts guard interval between symbols. So it can remove ISI (inter-symbol interference). Fig. 1 shows block diagram of OFDM system. Input signal is transmitted after passing the mapper and IFFT, nonlinear HPA. And the receiver recovers the original signal by reverse process of transmitter. The transmitted OFDM signal is

$$x(t) = \sum_{n=0}^{N-1} X_n e^{j 2\pi n t / T}, \quad 0 \le t \le T_S, \tag{1}$$

where X_n is n^{th} complex data symbol and generally X is [X_0, X_1, $\cdots$, X_{N-1}]. N is the number of sub-carriers, T_S is OFDM symbol duration. The PAPR of the transmitted signal in (1) can be defined as

$$PAPR \equiv 10 \log_{10} \frac{P_{peak}}{P_{av}} \quad [dB]. \tag{2}$$

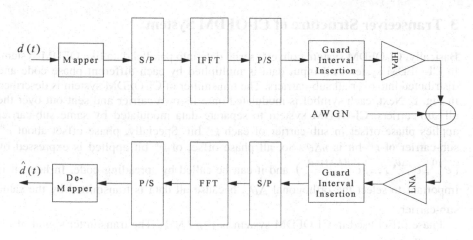

Fig. 1. Block diagram of OFDM system

where P_{peak} and P_{av} are peak power and average power, respectively. If the amplitude of all subcarrier signals are A, P_{peak} and P_{av} are computed as

$$P_{peak} = \max |x(t)|^2 = |NA|^2 ,\qquad (3)$$

$$P_{av} = \frac{1}{T} \int_0^T |x(t)|^2 \, dt = NA^2 ,\qquad (4)$$

where N is the number of subcariers. From eqs. (3) and (4), the maximum PAPR of OFDM system is written by

$$PAPR = \frac{\max_{0<t<T_s} |s(t)|^2}{\text{mean}_{0<t<T_s} |s(t)|^2} ,\qquad (5)$$

$$PAPR_{max} = 10 \log_{10} N \quad [dB] .\qquad (6)$$

The probability that PAPR does not exceed a certain level is

$$\Pr(PAPR \le PAPR_0) = (1 - \exp(-PAPR_0))^{aN} ,\qquad (7)$$

So, CCDF (complementary cumulative distribution function) is expressed as

$$\Pr(PAPR > PAPR_0) = 1 - (1 - \exp(-PAPR_0))^{aN} ,\qquad (8)$$

where $PAPR_0$ is threshold. a is usually 2.8 and OFDM signal is oversampled because Nyquist sampling is not enough to make true OFDM signals. Oversampling can be made by padding zero value into the rest part of the IFFT stage.

3 Transceiver Structure of CI-OFDM System

Basically, CI-OFDM system converts serial data into parallel data like OFDM system. In CI-OFDM system, all input data is multiplied by each different phase code and distributed into over all sub-carriers. The transmitter of CI-OFDM system is described in Fig. 2. Next, each symbol is modulated onto its own carrier and sent out over the all sub-carriers. CI-OFDM system to separate data modulated by same sub-carrier applies phase offset in sub-carrier of each kth bit. Specially, phase offset about n^{th} sub-carrier of kth bit is $n\Delta\theta$. So, all phase offset of kth bit applied is expressed by $(e^{j0}, e^{j\Delta\theta_k}, ..., e^{j(N-1)\Delta\theta_k})$ and it can be called by spreading code. In here, it is important to select the orthogonal $\Delta\theta_k$, because all data is transmitted by the same sub-carrier.

Phase offset used in CI-OFDM system is $(2\pi/N)k$. The transmitter signal of kth bit in CI-OFDM system is defined as

$$s_k(t) = \frac{1}{\sqrt{N}} \sum_{i=0}^{N-1} a_k e^{j2\pi f_c t} e^{j2\pi f_i t} e^{i\Delta\theta_k} , \qquad (9)$$

where a_k is the kth information symbol and probability of -1 and 1 is equal. f_c is the carrier frequency, f_i is the ith carrier frequency as $f_i = i\Delta f$, $\Delta f = 1/T_b$ (T_b is a bit rate) to keep the orthogonality.

$1/\sqrt{N}$ is used for the normalized bit energy. Then, the total transmitted CI-OFDM signal can be written as

$$s(t) = \frac{1}{\sqrt{N}} \sum_{k=0}^{N-1} \sum_{i=0}^{N-1} a_k e^{j2\pi f_c t} e^{j2\pi f_i t} e^{i\Delta\theta_k} . \qquad (10)$$

In the wide-band communication system and frequency selective channel, each subcarrier frequency can experience different frequency environment. So, each transmitted characteristic will be different at every each sub-carrier. However, CI-OFDM system in the receiver can get the maximum frequency diversity gain, because the same data is transmitted by all sub-carriers.

The receiver of CI-OFDM system is described in Fig. 3. The received signal passes the FFT, integrator and is multiplied by inverse phase offset to recover the data. So, the received signal is written as

$$r(t) = \frac{1}{\sqrt{N}} \sum_{k=0}^{N-1} \sum_{i=0}^{N-1} (a_i a_k e^{j2\pi f_c t} e^{j2\pi f_i t} e^{i\Delta\theta_k} e^{j\phi_i} + b_i) + n(t) , \qquad (11)$$

where a_i and ϕ_i are each fade parameter and phase offset of ith sub-carrier in the selective fading channel, b_i is narrow-band interference and n(t) is AWGN. Here, it is supposed that the received signal is perfectly synchronized and can be simply expressed. r(t) is divided by N orthogonal sub-carrier.

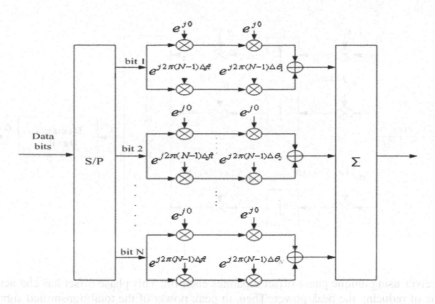

Fig. 2. Block diagram of CI-OFDM transmitter

The phase offset of kth bit is removed by each sub-carrier and r is finally (r0, r1, ... , N-1). r_i is

$$r_i = \frac{1}{\sqrt{N}}(a_i a_k + b_i) + \sum_{j=0,\, j \ne k}^{N-1} \frac{1}{\sqrt{N}}(a_i a_j \cdot e^{(i(\Delta \theta_k - \Delta \theta_j))} + b_i) + n_j \,, \quad (12)$$

where the second term is interference between bits as other bits in (12). If we select moderate $\Delta \theta_k$ and orthogonality is kept, the second term in (12) would be zero [2].

As we show (5), PAPR means peak-to-average power ratio. Let's express the PAPR of CI-OFDM system using that of OFDM system. When we use N sub-carriers, the average power of CI-OFDM system is NP_0 as $P_{mean} = NP_0$, where P_0 is effective power of one sub-carrier as $P_0 = \frac{1}{2} A_0^2$. And A_0 is maximum amplitude of given sub-carriers. OFDM system converts serial into parallel and transmitted sub-carriers have a peak power. When phase and synchronization of sub-carriers is correct, a peak power increases according to the increase of sub-carriers. So, a peak power of OFDM system is as follows.

$$P_{OFDM_{max}} = \left(\sum_{i=1}^{N} A \right)^2 = (NA)^2 = \frac{1}{2}(NA_0)^2 = N^2 P_0 \,,$$

$$PAPR_{max} = \frac{N^2 P_0}{NP_0} = N \,, \quad (13)$$

where A is effective amplitude of given sub-carrier, N is the number of sub-carriers. All bits of CI-OFDM system are transmitted to all sub-carriers at the same time, the

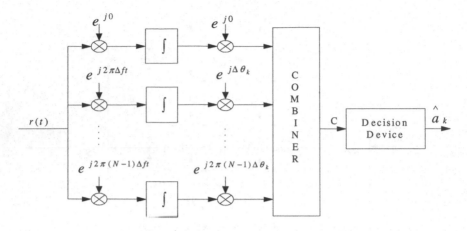

Fig. 3. Block diagram of CI-OFDM receiver

receiver using unique phase offset separates each bit. This phase offset has character-istic of reducing the peak power. Then, th peak power of the total transmitted signals in CI-OFDM system is smaller than sum of kth peak sub-carrier. Because the power of user j ($k \neq j$) is the minimum value or very small when the power of user k is maximum value. So, the peak power of CI-OFDM system is smaller than that of OFDM system. PAPR of CI-OFDM system is written as

$$PAPR_{CI-OFDM} = \frac{\frac{1}{2}(\max_{0<t<T_s} |s(t)|^2)}{NP_0} << N . \tag{14}$$

4 Simulation and Performance Evaluation

The simulation condition is basically AWGN, the selective fading and narrow-band interference channels. The nonlinear HPA is solid state power amplifier (SSPA) and parameter p is 2. The number of sub-carriers in OFDM and CI-OFDM system is 16 and modulation format is QPSK. The phase offset in CI-OFDM simulation is changed and has orthogonality according to the position of bit and transmitted sub-carrier. Namely, the multiplied phase offset of ith sub-carrier in k^{th} bit is $e^{j2\pi ki/N}$, the multiplied phase offset of ith sub-carrier in $k+1^{th}$ bit is $e^{j2\pi(k+1)i/N}$. The symbol data is multiplied by each phase offset and we measure its PAPR and CCDF of OFDM and CI-OFDM system. At first, data passes through the AWGN and transmit-ted into the receiver. Receiver recovers the original data by reverse process of trans-mitter. IBO is 0, 3 and 6dB in AWGN when we use the nonlinear HPA.

The simulations in the selective fading channel are made by using linear HPA and nonlinear HPA. In here, we establish simulation without backoff. And the attenuation rate is fixed by 1/2. The number of influenced sub-carrier is increased from 1 to 3. Narrow-band interference channel is also simulated additionally in AWGN channel.

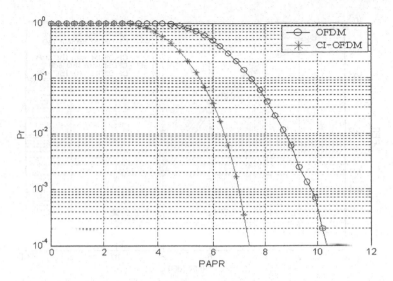

Fig. 4. CCDF of OFDM and CI-OFDM system

The simulation is divided by using linear HPA or nonlinear HPA. The number of influenced sub-carriers is increased from 1 to 3. When both selective fading and narrow-band interference channel affect the OFDM data, the number of influenced sub-carriers is from 2(selective fading 1, narrow-band interference 1) to 8(selective fading 4, narrow-band interference 4).

Figure 4 shows CCDF of OFDM and CI-OFDM system when 30000 symbols are transmitted. The probability of PAPR is found. X axis is Threshold PAPR [dB], and Y axis is the probability of PAPR. The threshold PAPR has the same probability until 3dB. However, the difference happens later. Conventional OFDM system is about 10.3dB in probability 10^{-4} of PAPR, but CI-OFDM system is about 7.3dB in probability 10^{-4} of PAPR. So we can see that PAPR reduction performance of CI-OFDM system is better than that of conventional OFDM system. This result changes the BER when transmitted signals pass the nonlinear SSPA.

Figure 5 shows BER performance in AWGN when IBO is 0, 3 and 6dB, respectively. In here, we can show better BER performance when we use linear HPA. When it uses nonlinear HPA without IBO, the BER performance of OFDM system is worst, and we can know that BER curve comes close to curve using the linear HPA when IBO increases gradually. Also the BER performance of conventional OFDM and CI-OFDM system without IBO has a difference of 1dB. But BER performance of two methods comes close to curve using the linear HPA without difference when IBO increases. However, if IBO increases gradually, it has a drawback that reduces power efficiency.

Figure 6 is BER performance of the conventional OFDM and CI-OFDM system in selective fading channel and linear HPA. Firstly, in the linear HPA without selective fading channel, simulation curves of two methods come close to theoretical curve. However, the second curves with selective fading channel show difference in two methods. The second curves are shown when two sub-channels are selectively faded.

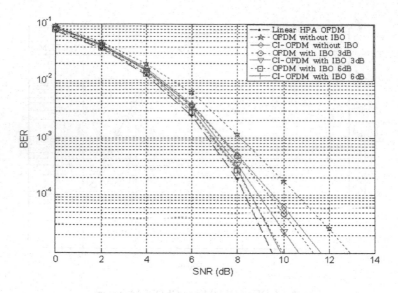

Fig. 5. BER in nonlinear HPA and AWGN

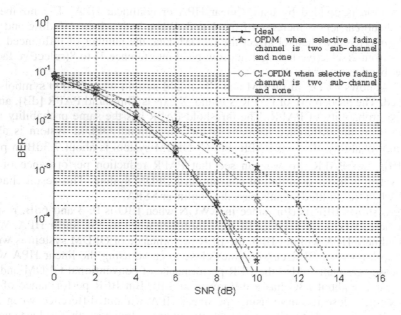

Fig. 6. BER in selective fading channel

BER performance of conventional OFDM system is 12.4dB in probability of 10^{-4}, but that of CI-OFDM system is 10.8dB. So, two methods show the SNR difference of 1.6dB at the same BER performance. This result is caused by spreading effect. We can see that spreading CI-OFDM system is stronger than conventional OFDM system in the selective fading channel.

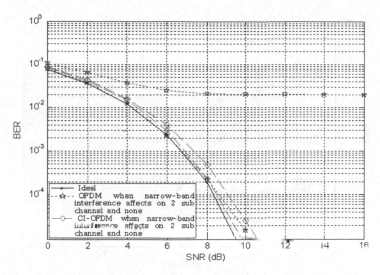

Fig. 7. BER in narrow-band interference channel

Figure 7 is BER performance using the linear HPA in narrow-band interference channel. The case using the linear HPA without narrow-band interference channel comes close to theorem curve in BER performance of two methods. However, CI-OFDM system is 9dB in the probability of 10^{-4} when narrow-band interference channel affects on 2 sub-channels. On the other hand, the conventional OFDM system is flowed. So, we can know that BER performance of CI-OFDM system is better than that of OFDM system. Also, we can know that CI-OFDM system is very robust in narrow-band interference channel because of the spreading effect.

Figure 8 is BER performance of using the linear HPA in selective fading and narrow-band interference channel. Firstly, the default using the linear HPA without selective fading and narrow-band interference channel comes close to theoretical curve of two methods. However, BER performance of CI-OFDM system is 10dB at probability of 10^{-4} when narrow-band interference and selective fading channel has an effect on each 1 sub-channel. On the other hand, that of convention OFDM system is flowed. When narrow-band interference and selective fading channel has an effect on each 2 sub-channel, BER performance of CI-OFDM system is 12.3dB in probability of 10^{-4} and that of conventional OFDM system is worse. Similarly, we can show that error probability increases more when the number of sub-channel with selective fading and narrow-band interference channel increases. Eventually, we can know that BER performance of CI-OFDM system is better than conventional OFDM system in selective fading and narrow-band interference channel.

Figure 9 is BER performance when the nonlinear HPA is used in selective fading and narrow-band interference channel. This figure is BER performance of OFDM and CI-OFDM system according to the size of selective fading and narrow-band interference channel. As results, we can show that BER performance of CI-OFDM system is better than conventional OFDM system in selective fading and narrow-band interference channel with nonlinear HPA. Additionally, figure 9 is similar to the figure 8. As results, we can know that selective fading and narrow-band interference degrade more BER performance than nonlinearity of HPA.

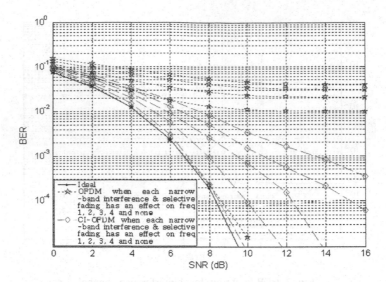

Fig. 8. BER in selective fading and narrow-band interference channel

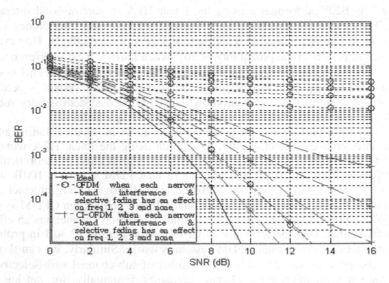

Fig. 9. BER in HPA, selective fading and narrow-band interference channel

5 Conclusion

In this paper, CI-OFDM system is studied to resolve the PAPR problem of ordinary OFDM system and it is more robust than the ordinary OFDM system in the selective fading and narrow-band interference channel. We find the PAPR reduction and the BER performance is analyzed in the frequency selective fading and narrow-band interference channel. As results, PAPR is reduced by 3.2dB than conventional OFDM system. So, BER performance is significantly improved in nonlinear SSPA. Also, it can be found that BER performance of CI-OFDM system is better than that of conventional OFDM system in selective fading and narrow-band interference channel. Finally, CI-OFDM system has a good PAPR reduction performance and strong robustness to selective fading and narrow-band interference channel.

References

1. David A. Wieganndt, Carl R. Nassar and Zhiqiang Wu : Overcoming Peak-to-Average Power Ratio Issues in OFDM via Carrier-Interferometry Codes. Vehicular Technology Conference, 2001. VTC 2001 Fall IEEE VTS 54th vol. 2, 7-11, Oct. (2001) 660-663
2. Barbosa, P.R, Zhiqiang Wu and Nassar, C.R. : High-Performance MIMO-OFDM via Carrier interfeometry. Global Telecommunications Conference, 2003. GLOBECOM '03. IEEE vol. 2, 1-5, Dec. (2003) 853-857
3. Heung-Gyoon Ryu, jus sok Park and Jin soo Park : Threshold IBO of HPA in the predistorted OFDM communication system. Broadcasting, IEEE Transactions on vol. 50, Issue 4, Dec. (2004) 425-428
4. Zhiqiang Wu, Zhijin Wu, Wiegandt, D.A and Nassar, C.R, : High-performance 64-QAM OFDM via carrier interferometry spreading codes. Vehicular Technology Conference, 2003. VTC 2003-Fall. 2003 IEEE 58th vol. 1, 6-9, Oct. (2003) 557-561
5. Wiegandt, D.A, Nassar, C.R and Wu, Z. : The elimination of peak-to-average power ratio concerns in OFDM via carrier Interferometry spreading codes: a multiple constellation analysis. System Theory. Proceedings of the Thirty-Sixth Southeastern Symposium on 2004, (2004) 323-327
6. Krongold, B.S and Jones, D.L. : A new tone reservation method for complex-baseband PAR reduction in OFDM systems. Proceedings of IEEE International Conference on Acoustics, Speech, and Signal Processing, vol. 3, 13-17, May (2002) III-2321 - III-2324
7. Seung Hee Han and Jae Hong Lee : PAPR reduction of OFDM signals using a reduced complexity PTS technique. Signal Processing Letters, IEEE vol. 11, Issue 11, Nov. (2004) 887-890
8. Xiaodong Li and Cimini, L.j. Jr. : Effects of clipping and filtering on the performance of OFDM. IEEE Communications Letters, May (1998) 131-133
9. Dae-Woon Lim, Jong-Seon No, Chi-Woo Lim and Habong Chung : A new SLM OFDM scheme with low complexity for PAPR reduction. Signal Processing Letters, IEEE vol. 12, Issue 2, Feb. (2005) 93-96
10. P. Banelli, G. Baruffa and S. Cacopardi : Effects of HPA Non Linearity on Frequency Multiplexed OFDM Signals. IEEE Trans. on Broadcasting, vol. 47, Jun. (2001) 123-136
11. Heung-Gyoon Ryu, Jae-Eun Lee and Jin-Soo Park : Dummy sequence insertion (DSI) for PAPR reduction in the OFDM communication system. IEEE Trans. on Consumer Electronics, vol. 50, Issue 1, Feb. (2004) 89-94

Design and Analysis of Side Information Embedded PTS Scheme in the OFDM Communication System

Seon-Ae Kim and Heung-Gyoon Ryu

Department of Electronic Engineering
Chungbuk National University
12 Kaesin-dong, Cheongju, Chungbuk, 361-763, Korea
i-mayo@hanmail.net, ecomm@cbu.ac.kr

Abstract. Orthogonal frequency-division multiplexing (OFDM) system is very good for the high speed communication system but the high peak-to-average power ratio (PAPR) is very serious problem. Partial transmit sequence (PTS) scheme has been widely studied to reduce the high PAPR of OFDM signal since it is flexible and efficient. However, there is an inevitable problem in the PTS scheme, which is to transmit the side information about the phase rotation factors for the correct OFDM symbol recovery. In this paper, a new side information embedded PTS scheme using the reference symbols is proposed for the PAPR reduction. Also, BER (bit error rate) performance is analyzed when the erroneous side information is received. In this proposed method, the information about the rotation factors is expressed by the phase of reference symbols. The proposed method maintains the same PAPR reduction performance as the conventional PTS scheme and OFDM symbols are correctly recovered by the side information to meet the required BER level, which is verified via the computer simulation.

1 Introduction

OFDM system is suitable for the wireless high-speed data transmission because of the robustness to the frequency selective fading channel [1]. However, the high PAPR causes the nonlinear distortion as the number of subcarriers is increased. The high PAPR signal is distorted when it passes through the non-linear devices such as high power amplifier (HPA).

Many methods have been proposed for the PAPR reduction in the OFDM communication system. The simplest solution is to clip the OFDM signal before HPA amplification [2], but this clip method results in performance degradation. Another is block coding [3] in which the desired data sequence is encoded into a larger sequence and only a special subset of the low peak power in all the possible sequences is used for OFDM symbol transmission. By this approach, 3-dB PAPR can be made with serious loss of bandwidth efficiency. Also, the size of look-up tables is exponentially enlarged as the number of subcarriers is increased.

Two kinds of the phase control schemes to reduce the PAPR of the OFDM signal were proposed: the selective mapping (SLM) [4] and partial transmit sequence (PTS) [5] approaches. In SLM, one signal of the lowest PAPR is selected in a set of several

X. Cheng, W. Li, and T. Znati (Eds.): WASA 2006, LNCS 4138, pp. 550–560, 2006.
© Springer-Verlag Berlin Heidelberg 2006

signals which all represent the same information. In PTS, the lowest PAPR signal is made by optimally combining the signal subblocks. They are very flexible and have an effective performance of the PAPR reduction without any signal degradation. PTS scheme is considered to be better than SLM. However, there are additional complexity and a little bit loss of the spectral efficiency due to the side information insertion. The side information about the phase rotation factors should be transmitted for correct OFDM symbol recovery. A side information transmission method using marking algorithm in the PTS scheme was published [6]. This can be used only for the MPSK modulation and suffers no spectral loss. However, the method cannot be applied into the M-QAM modulation, which was indicated in ref. [6] by authors. We would like to extend this basic idea into the general M-QAM modulation.

In this paper, we propose a new method on the side information transmission using reference symbols in the PTS approach. In this method, the phase of reference symbols represents the rotation factors. It has a slight spectral loss because of the supplementary subcarriers allocation for the reference symbols, but the loss is very small in case of the large subcarriers N and the small number of subblocks M. Also, the proposed method can be used for to all kinds of modulation format in OFDM system. From simulation results, this proposed method can keep up the same PAPR reduction performance as the conventional PTS and OFDM symbols are correctly recovered by the transmitted side information in order to satisfy the required BER.

2 PAPR and PTS Scheme

2.1 Peak-to-Average Power Ratio

In OFDM system, a block of N symbols, X_n, $n = 0,1,...,N-1$, is formed with each symbol modulating one of a set of N subcarriers, f_n, $n = 0,1,...,N-1$. The N subcarriers are chosen to be orthogonal, that is, $f_n = n\Delta f$, where $\Delta f = 1/NT$ and T is the OFDM symbol period. So, it can be expressed as

$$x(t) = \sum_{n=0}^{N-1} X_n e^{j2\pi f_n t}, \qquad 0 \le t \le NT . \tag{1}$$

The PAPR of the transmitted signal in Eq. (1) can be defined as

$$PAPR = \frac{\max |x(t)|^2}{E\left[|x(t)|^2\right]} . \tag{2}$$

The PAPR of the continuous-time OFDM signal cannot be precisely computed by the use of the Nyquist sampling rate, which amounts to N samples per symbol [7]. In this case, signal peaks are missed and PAPR reduction estimates are not precise. So, over-sampling is necessary and factor of 4 is sufficient for accuracy. It is performed by the simple computation of the $4N$-point zero-padded IFFT of the data frame. Hereafter, we assume the 4-times over-sampling for all calculations.

2.2 CCDF of PAPR

Theoretical results of the CCDF (complementary cumulative distribution function) of PAPR can be derived by the results in [8]. For an OFDM symbol with N subcarriers, the samples of the complex baseband signal are given by Eq.(1). From the central limit theorem, it follows that for large values of N, the real and image values of power normalized $x(t)$ become Gaussian distributed. The amplitude of the OFDM signal therefore has the Rayleigh distribution. The CDF (cumulative distribution function) of the peak power per OFDM symbol can be found based on the assumption of the uncorrelated samples. This is true for the Nyquist sampling rate. The probability that the PAPR is below the threshold level $PAPR_o$ can be written as

$$\Pr\left(PAPR \le PAPR_{o}\right) = \left(1 - \exp\left(-PAPR_{o}\right)\right)^{N}. \tag{3}$$

As Eq.(3) does not hold for the oversampling case, an approximation is presented in [8]. Adding a certain number of extra independent samples approximates the effect of oversampling. The distribution of the PAPR is given by

$$\Pr\left(PAPR \le PAPR_{o}\right) = \left(1 - \exp\left(-PAPR_{o}\right)\right)^{\alpha N}. \tag{4}$$

The CCDF of the PAPR of an OFDM signal can be expressed as

$$\Pr\left(PAPR > PAPR_{o}\right) = 1 - \left(1 - \exp\left(-PAPR_{o}\right)\right)^{\alpha N}. \tag{5}$$

When α is 2.4, the accurate results can be shown for QPSK modulation with $N=128$.

2.3 Partial Transmit Sequence (PTS)

In the PTS approach, the input data block is partitioned into disjoint clusters or subblocks that are combined to minimize the PAPR. The data block, X_n, $n = 0,1,..., N-1$ is defined as a vector, $X = \left[X_0\ X_1 ... X_{N-1}\right]^T$. Then, partition X into M disjoint sets, represented by the vectors $X^{(m)}$, $m = 1,2,..., M$ such that

$$X = \sum_{m=1}^{M} X^{(m)}. \tag{6}$$

Here, it is assumed that adjacent, interleaved and pseudo-random subblock partition scheme are used and each subblock has equal size. The objective of the PTS approach is to form a weighted combination of the M clusters

$$\hat{X} = \sum_{m=1}^{M} b^{(m)} X^{(m)}, \tag{7}$$

where $b^{(m)}$, $m = 1,2,..., M$ are weighting factors or phase factors and are assumed to be pure rotations. (i.e. $b^{(m)} = e^{j\Phi m}$).

After transforming into the time domain, Eq. (7) becomes

$$\hat{x} = \sum_{m=1}^{M} b^{(m)} x^{(m)}. \tag{8}$$

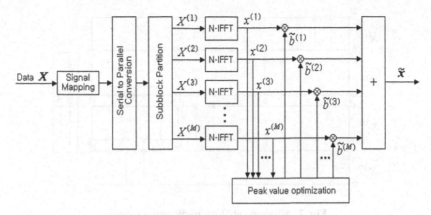

Fig. 1. OFDM transmitter of the PTS scheme

The vector $x^{(m)}$, called *partial transmit sequence*, is the IFFT of $X^{(m)}$. The weighting factors are chosen to minimize the PAPR by searching for the appropriate combination of each cluster and by corresponding weighting factors.

$$\left\{\tilde{b}^{(1)}, \tilde{b}^{(2)}, ..., \tilde{b}^{(M)}\right\} = \underset{\{b^{(1)}, b^{(2)}, ..., b^{(M)}\}}{\arg\ \min}\left(\underset{0 \le n \le N-1}{\max}\left|\sum_{m=1}^{M} b^{(m)} x_n^{(m)}\right|\right). \tag{9}$$

The combination with weighting factors is called rotation factor or combining sequence. Optimized transmit sequence is

$$\tilde{x} = \sum_{m=1}^{M} \tilde{b}^{(m)} x^{(m)}. \tag{10}$$

2.4 Side Information Transmission

To recover the data, the receiver must know the value of the rotation factors. In this paper, we present a new approach that transmits the side information. The basic strategy is to insert the reference symbols onto the transmitted data that can be used to uniquely identify the rotation factors at the receiver. Data D is partitioned into multiple disjoint subblocks. Then, reference symbol R is inserted in each cluster.

$$D = \sum_{m=1}^{M} D^{(m)}, \quad D = MPSK \quad or \quad MQAM$$

$$R = \sum_{m=1}^{M} R^{(m)}, \quad R = e^{j0°} = 1, \tag{11}$$

where D is data symbol and R is reference symbol. A new signal vector can be shown by

$$X = D + R = \sum_{m=1}^{M}\left(D^{(m)} + R^{(m)}\right) = \sum_{m=1}^{M} X^{(m)}. \tag{12}$$

X is similarly processed through the Eq. (7) ~ (10).

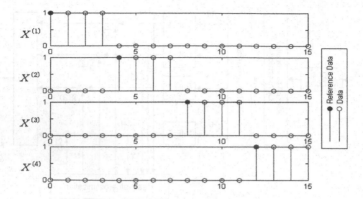

Fig. 2. Adjacent subblock partitioning scheme

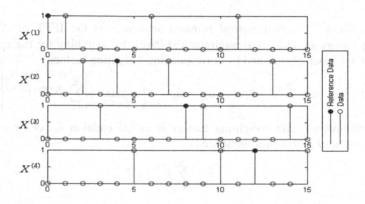

Fig. 3. Interleaved subblock partitioning scheme

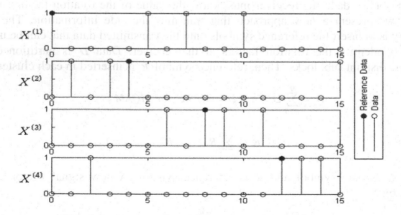

Fig. 4. Pseudo-random subblock partitioning scheme

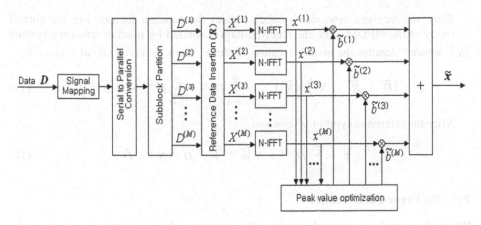

Fig. 5. Proposed side information embedded PTS scheme

As an example, adjacent, interleaved and pseudo-random subblock partitioning schemes are represented in the Fig. 2, 3 and 4. In each cluster, both data and reference symbols are not overlapped. In the Fig.2, 3 and 4, reference symbols are located in $X_0^{(1)}, X_4^{(2)}, X_8^{(3)}, X_{12}^{(4)}$.

Both detection of the reference symbol and data recovery are shown in this section. Under the AWGN channel, the received signal can be expressed as

$$y = \tilde{x} + n .\tag{13}$$

After FFT transformation,

$$Y = FFT\left\{ \tilde{x} + n \right\} = FFT\left\{ \sum_{m=1}^{M} \tilde{b}^{(m)} x^{(m)} + n \right\}$$

$$= \sum_{m=1}^{M} \tilde{b}^{(m)} FFT\left\{ x^{(m)} \right\} + N = \sum_{m=1}^{M} \tilde{b}^{(m)} X^{(m)} + N .\tag{14}$$

From Eq. (12), $X^{(m)}$ is $D^{(m)} + R^{(m)}$. Then, the received signal is given by

$$Y = \sum_{m=1}^{M} \tilde{b}^{(m)} \left(D^{(m)} + R^{(m)} \right) + N$$

$$= \sum_{m=1}^{M} \overline{D}^{(m)} + \sum_{m=1}^{M} \overline{R}^{(m)} + N = \overline{D} + \overline{R} + N ,\tag{15}$$

where $\overline{D}$ and $\overline{R}$ are received data and reference symbol. As the phase of transmitted reference symbol is $R^{(m)} = e^{j0} = 1$, the received reference symbol is

$$\overline{R} = \sum_{m=1}^{M} \overline{R}^{(m)} = \sum_{m=1}^{M} \tilde{b}^{(m)} R^{(m)} = \sum_{m=1}^{M} \tilde{b}^{(m)} .\tag{16}$$

Thus, the received reference symbols reflect the rotation factors. For the correct recovery of the OFDM data, the received data is rotated by inverse reference symbol $(\overline{R})^*$ where * denotes the inverse rotation of phase. Then, received signal is given by

$$\hat{Y} = (\overline{D} + \overline{R} + N) \cdot (\overline{R})^* = \sum_{m=1}^{M} D^{(m)} + \sum_{m=1}^{M} R^{(m)} + N (\tilde{b}^{(m)})^*. \tag{17}$$

After the reference symbol is removed,

$$\hat{Y} = \sum_{m=1}^{M} D^{(m)} + N (\tilde{b}^{(m)})^* = D + N' = \hat{D}. \tag{18}$$

2.5 Bit Error Performance

When the signal is received, receiver first recovers the side information from the received signal to detect correctly. The side information plays an important role in the overall system performance [9]. Let us derive the bit error probability considering the effect of false side information. For simplicity, we only consider in the AWGN channel, which may serve as a lower bound performance for a fading channel may be significantly changed.

P_S, the error probability of the side information, may make influence on the overall bit error probability P. So, it can be written as

$$P = P_b \cdot (1 - P_S) + P_{b|False} \cdot P_S. \tag{19}$$

P_b is the bit error probability of QPSK in the AWGN channel, which is given by

$$P_b = Q \left(\sqrt{\frac{\sigma_S^2}{\sigma_N^2}} \right) = Q \left(\sqrt{\frac{2E_b}{N_o}} \right). \tag{20}$$

$P_{b|False}$ is the conditional bit error probability given that the side information is false, and it can be shown that

$$P_{b|False} = Q \left(\sqrt{\frac{\sigma_S^2}{\sigma_N^2 + \sigma_{False}^2}} \right) = Q \left(\sqrt{\frac{2E_b}{N_o + (N-M) \cdot 2E_b}} \right), \tag{21}$$

where $\sigma_S^2 = 2E_b$ and $\sigma_{False}^2 = (N-M) \cdot 2E_b$ are signal variance and the variance of false side information, respectively.

3 Simulation Results and Discussion

Now, we show the MATLAB simulation performance of the proposed scheme when the subcarrier number is 128 (i.e., $N=128$) and the subcarriers are divided into 4 or 8 clusters (i.e., $M=4, 8$). QPSK modulation format is used for the simulation, but all kinds of digital modulation format considered in OFDM system can be easily

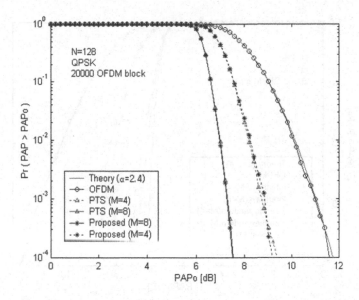

Fig. 6. Comparison of the conventional and the proposed PTS schemes

extended. The performance measures are the magnitudes of the PAPR reduction and the bit error rate (BER). Also, the oversampling factor of 4 is achieved by the $4N$-point zero-padded IFFT. Three kinds of subblock partitioning methods are used in the proposed side information embedded PTS scheme. We consider binary (i.e.,

$b^{(m)} = \pm 1$) weighting factors and optimal combining algorithm is selected for the

combining technique. So, the combination number is 2^M.

Fig. 6 shows PAPR reduction performance of the conventional and proposed PTS methods. The conventional PTS means that the OFDM receiver is assumed to know the side information about the rotation factors shown in Fig.1. The proposed PTS method is shown in Fig.5. The outer two curves are the theoretical and simulation results. Theoretical performance is given by Eq. (5) at $\alpha = 2.4$. The simulation results are obtained by the 20,000 OFDM blocks using the oversampling factor of 4. Two middle curves are the conventional PTS (M=4) and the proposed one (M=4). Two inner curves describe the conventional PTS (M=8) and the proposed one (M=8). Simulation results agree well with the theoretical results. So, PTS and proposed scheme results are reliable. The proposed PTS method shows the same PAPR reduction performance as the conventional PTS scheme.

Fig. 7 shows the CCDF performance of the adjacent, interleaved and pseudo-random subblock partitioning schemes. The outer two curves are the theoretical and simulation results like Fig.6. Three curves in the middle are the case of M=4 in which the curves of the adjacent, interleaved and pseudo-random subblock partitioning appear in order from the right. The inner three curves are the case of M=8. The pseudo-random partitioning works better than the adjacent and interleaved subblock partition schemes like the case of M=4.

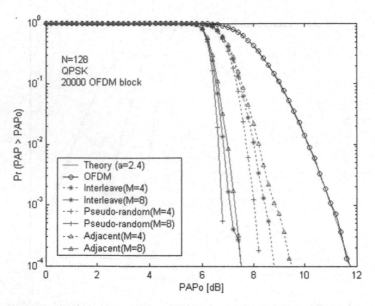

Fig. 7. Performance comparison of the three subblock partitioning schemes

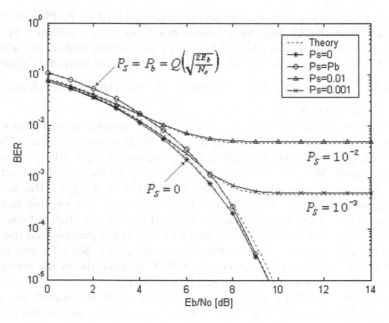

Fig. 8. BER performance in the error of the side information, P_S

Fig. 8 illustrates the bit error probability (BEP) of the proposed method and BEP can be described in Eq. (19) for the several error probabilities of the side information, P_S. Simulation results are very similar to the theoretical results. In Fig. 8, it can be seen that if there is a high error level in P_S (i.e. 10^{-2}, 10^{-3}), the serious error floor is made. However, the performance degradation due to the false side information is not a problem when $P_S = P_b$ in the most usual cases. If P_S is zero, P is only the bit error probability of QPSK in AWGN channel. We can see that there is a very small difference between the cases of $P_S = P_b$ and $P_S = 0$.

From the simulation results, the proposed scheme can correctly reconstruct the OFDM data. Also, It can be applied into all kinds of constellation unlike the results [6]. On the contrary, this method has a little spectral loss due to the side information insertion. However, the fraction of the overhead is very small for large N. For example, in case of BPSK with $N=128$ and $M=8$, the spectral loss is $8/128=0.0625$. This fraction of overhead is very small for large N so that the spectral loss is not significant but trivial.

4 Conclusion

In this paper, a new technique on the side information insertion in the PTS scheme is proposed for the PAPR reduction in the OFDM system approach and its performance is analyzed. As results of the computer simulations, the proposed scheme has the same PAPR reduction performance as the conventional PTS scheme. Whereas the conventional PTS without the side information does not meet the required BER performance, the proposed scheme can correctly recover the OFDM data and satisfy the required BER. Also, it can be easily extended into the higher-order PSK and QAM modulation formats. Therefore, the proposed scheme can be widely used for the reliable and the effective OFDM communication system.

References

1. Zihua Guo, Wenwu Zhu : Performance study of OFDMA vs. OFDM/SDMA. Vehicular Technology Conference, VTC Spring 2002, vol. 2, 6-9 May (2002) 565-569
2. R. O'Neill and L. N. Lopes : Envelope variations and spectral splatter in clipped multicarrier Signals. Proc. PIMRC '95, (1995) 71-75
3. A. E. Jones, T. A. Wilkinson, and S. K. Barton : Block coding scheme for reduction of peak to mean envelope power ratio of multicarrier transmission scheme. IEE Electronic Letters, Vol. 30, no. 25, Dec. (1994) 2098-2099,
4. H. Breiling, S. H. Müller-Weinfurtner, and J. B. Huber. : SLM Peak-Power Reduction without Explicit Side Information. IEEE Commun. Lett., vol. 5, no. 6, June (2001) 239-41.
5. S. H. Muller and J. B. Huber : OFDM with reduced peak-to-average power ratio by optimum combination of partial transmit sequences. IEE Electronic Letters, vol. 33, no.5, Feb. (1997) 368-369
6. L. J. Cimini, N. R. Sollenberger : Peak-to-Average Power Ratio Reduction of an OFDM Signal Using Partial Transmit Sequences With Embedded Side Information. GLOBECOM '00. IEEE, vol. 2, (2000) 746-750
7. Chin-Liang Wang, Yuan Ouyang : Low-complexity selected mapping schemes for peak-to-average power ratio reduction in OFDM systems. IEEE Transactions on, signal processing, vol. 53, Dec. (2005) 4652 – 4660

8. R. van Nee, OFDM wireless multimedia communication. Boston, London: Artech House, (2000)
9. H. Ochiai and H. Imai : OFDM-CDMA with peak power reduction based on the spreading sequences. IEEE International Conference on Communication, vol. 3, (1998) 1299-1303
10. K. Fazel and S.Kaiser, Multi-Carrier and Spread Spectrum Systems, John Wiley & Sons Ltd, (2003)
11. Heung-Gyoon Ryu, jus sok Park and Jin-soo Park : Threshold IBO of HPA in the predistorted OFDM communication system. Broadcasting, IEEE Transactions on vol. 50, Issue 4, Dec. (2004) 425-428
12. Heung-Gyoon Ryu, Jae-Eun Lee and Jin-Soo Park : Dummy sequence insertion (DSI) for PAPR reduction in the OFDM communication system. IEEE Trans. on Consumer Electronics, vol. 50, Issue 1, Feb. (2004) 89-94

Performance Analysis of a Framed ALOHA System with Diversity Frequency Hopping

In-Hang Chung and Ming-Ching Yen

Department of Electrical Engineering
Chung-Hua University
No. 707, Sec. 2, Wufu Rd., Hsinchu, Taiwan, R.O.C
{ihchung, mcyen}@chu.edu.tw

Abstract. In this paper, we study the performance of a framed ALOHA system that employs slow frequency hopping techniques. A new strategy that employs diversity transmission (multiple frequency-hopping) techniques to enhance the performance of a framed ALOHA system is presented. Two schemes differentiated by whether a frequency channel can be repeatedly selected by a ready user in a frame are proposed. In the first scheme, which we call diversity frequency-hopping using sampling with replacement scheme (DFH-SWIR), a frequency channel in a slot may be chosen by a user more than once. In the second scheme, which we call diversity frequency-hopping using sampling without replacement scheme (DFH-SWOR), all frequency channels in a slot selected by any user are distinct. For both of these two schemes, an exact combinatorial analysis is developed to evaluate the activity factor and throughput characteristics. Effects of parameter variations on the system performance are illustrated in the light of numerical examples.

1 Introduction

Slotted ALOHA random access techniques characterized by its low delay at light traffic, simplicity of network configuration and satisfactory coordination requirement, have frequently been employed in a telecommunication network for the transport of packetized voice or data [1]. Incorporation of a frame structure to the standard slotted ALOHA provides a number of favorable features. This includes simple synchronization, retention of time transparency for digitized voice transmission, more convenient exchanges of network control information, or higher achievable channel utilization. Moreover, since a user can transmit at most one packet per frame, the use of a frame structure reduces the retransmission rate for backlogged users that may help to maintain system stability. Consequently, numerous multiple access schemes have been developed based on this infrastructure, e.g. [2]-[5].

Spread spectrum (SS) techniques characterized by their multiple access, signal capture, and anti-interference capabilities have frequently been applied to packet radio communications networks to enhance system performance [6]. Among the two basic SS strategies, direct-sequence (DS) and frequency-hopping (FH), the latter has attracted much attention for a slotted channel. Furthermore, due to techni-

X. Cheng, W. Li, and T. Znati (Eds.): WASA 2006, LNCS 4138, pp. 561–571, 2006.
© Springer-Verlag Berlin Heidelberg 2006

cal complexity encountered in implementation and synchronization of a *fast* FH system, the *slow* FH (SFH) technique is usually adopted for wireless applications [7]. It is also found that combination of SFH with other multiple access strategies, such as TDMA [8] or DS [9], can result in efficient channel utilization and enhance system flexibility.

In this paper, a new strategy that uses Diversity FH (DFH) techniques in a framed ALOHA system is proposed. Based on this strategy, a ready user with a data packet to transmit in a frame can hop to multiple frequency channels. Then, a copy of the data packet is transmitted in each selected frequency channel. An SFH strategy in which the dwelling time of a frequency band (bin) is equal to the packet duration is assumed. Two schemes differentiated by whether a frequency channel can be selected by a user repeatedly, sample with replacement (SWIR) or without replacement (SWOR), are proposed. In the first scheme, which we call DFH using SWIR scheme (DFH-SWIR), a frequency channel in a slot may be chosen by a user more than once. The second scheme, which we call DFH using SWOR scheme (DFH-SWOR), dictates that all frequency channels selected by any user are distinct. For these two schemes, an exact mathematical analysis will be developed to evaluate the system performance.

System model and static mathematical analysis for the proposed DFH-SWIR and DFH-SWOR are described in section 2. This is followed by the dynamic analysis required for evaluating the activity factor and system throughput developed in section 3. Some numerical results for the proposed new schemes are presented in section 4 to illustrate important features. Finally, section 5 concludes this paper.

2   Static System Model of DFH-SWIR and DFH-SWOR

2.1   Model Description

Consider a packet radio communication system that uses a base station to serve a number of wireless users. Each packet is appended with a user's identification. The multiple access reverse channel (from users to the common receiver) is divided into frames in time. Let there be fixed number of slots, numbered from 1 to L, accommodated in a frame. Assume that the system consists of a finite population of M users. Each user can transmit at most one packet in a frame. All new packets generated in a frame are transmitted in the next frame. The forward channel is assumed to be reliable so that all system users can receive exact feedback information (success or failure) interpreted by the common receiver. Transmission result of each slot in a frame is assumed to be available to all system users before the start of the next frame (This corresponds to a short distance radio network, such as a wireless local area network or a wireless personal area network).

Let there be q frequency bands, numbered from 1 to q, available for the whole system. Further let the order of diversity for FH be denoted by N. Whenever a user (tagged user) gets ready to transmit a packet (either a new packet or a retransmitted one) in a frame, he first selects one of the L slots in the next frame with equal probability. Then, the tagged user makes N selections from the q frequency bands. In the DFH-SWIR, one of the q frequency bands is chosen randomly (with probability

$1/q$) for each selection so that the number of distinct frequency bands selected by the tagged user is less than or equal to N. In the DFH-SWOR, the number of distinct frequency bands selected is exactly N. Having made selections, the tagged user transmits a copy of the packet over each of the chosen distinct frequency bands during the slot interval. A frequency band during a slot interval will result in a "hit" if more than one user transmit packets over this band during the same slot. If capture effects are effective, packets transmissions that result in a hit will have some probabilities to be successful. For simplicity of analysis, we will assume that packets transmissions which cause hits are destroyed. According to this algorithm, the tagged user will succeed in packet transmission if at least one of the frequency bands chosen by him will not result in a hit. On the other hand, if all the frequency bands selected by the tagged user result in hits, the corresponding packet is not successfully transmitted and the tagged user becomes a backlogged user. A backlogged user's backlogged packet will be retransmitted following the retransmission algorithms to be described later on. We assume that a backlogged user can not generate new packets. That is, a user can generate a new packet only after his old packet has been successfully transmitted.

2.2 Static Mathematical Analysis

Assume that T users are transmitting in a frame. Each user randomly selects one of the L slots and N of the q frequency bands. Regardless of what the arrival process is, we want to determine the probability, $P_S(S = m | q, N, L, T)$, that exactly m, $0 \le m \le \min(L, T)$, users succeed in packet transmission, given q, N, L, and T.

DFH-SWIR: The conditional joint probability, $\Pr\{i_1, i_2, ..., i_T | L, T\}$, that there are i_1 slots selected by one user, i_2 slots selected by two users, . . . , i_T slots selected by T users, when T users are transmitting in a frame with L slots, can be obtained as [2]

$$\Pr\{i_1, i_2, ..., i_T | L, T\} = \frac{1}{L^T} \frac{T!}{(1!)^{i_1}(2!)^{i_2} \cdots (T!)^{i_T}} \frac{L!}{(i_1!)(i_2!) \cdots (i_T!)(L - i_1 - \cdots - i_T)!}. \quad (1)$$

Concentrating on a particular slot which is selected by w users, $1 \le w \le T$, we need the conditional probability, $P_{s|w}(S = m_w | q, N, w)$, that exactly m_w of the w users who transmit simultaneously in the same slot interval will succeed.

To simplify the analysis, let us consider the transmission results of one (the tagged user) of the w users. Let $P_{[k|w]}$ represent the conditional probability that the tagged user succeeds in some specific k, $k \le \min(N, q)$, frequency bands irrespective of the status of other frequency bands, given that w users with FH diversity order N are transmitting in this specific slot of a frame. Furthermore, let $m_i, i = 1 \sim k$, denote the number of times the i-th frequency band is selected by the tagged user. Assume that there are p distinct values for the m_i. If $\lambda_j, j = 1 \sim p$, represents the number of frequency bands (among the k frequency bands) that are chosen by the tagged user with the j-th value of times, then $P_{[k|w]}$ can be expressed as [4]

$$P_{[k|w]} = \frac{1}{q^{Nw}} \sum_{m_1=1}^{U_1} \sum_{m_2=m_1}^{U_2} \cdots \sum_{m_{k-1}=m_{k-2}}^{U_{k-1}} \sum_{m_k=m_{k-1}}^{U_k} \frac{N!}{m_1! m_2! \cdots m_k! (N - m_1 - m_2 - \cdots - m_k)!}$$

$$\cdot \frac{k!}{\lambda_1! \lambda_2! \cdots \lambda_p!} \cdot (q-k)^{Nw - \sum_{i=1}^{k} m_i}, \quad k = 1, 2, \ldots, \min(q, N), \quad (2)$$

in which $U_1 = \left\lfloor \dfrac{N}{k} \right\rfloor$, $U_2 = \left\lfloor \dfrac{N - m_1}{k-1} \right\rfloor$, $\ldots$, $U_k = \left\lfloor \dfrac{N - \sum_{i=1}^{k-1} m_i}{k - (k-1)} \right\rfloor$, and $\lfloor \ \rfloor$ denotes the

greatest integer function, i.e., $\lfloor x \rfloor$ is the greatest integer that is less than or equal to x. It is noted that $\lambda_1 + \lambda_2 + \cdots + \lambda_p = k$. Let $S_{k|w}$ represent all equal-probable arrangements for which the tagged user succeeds in k frequency bands. Then,

$$S_{k|w} = \binom{q}{k} P_{[k|w]}, \quad k = 1, \ldots, \min(q, N). \tag{3}$$

Using the principle of inclusion and exclusion [10], we can obtain the probability that the tagged user succeeds in at least one frequency band, which is also the probability that the tagged user's packet will be successfully transmitted, $P_{1|w}$, as

$$P_{1|w} = S_{1|w} - S_{2|w} + \cdots - (-1)^{\min(q, N)} \cdot S_{\min(q, N)}. \tag{4}$$

Now we want to determine the probability that r tagged users, among the w users transmitting in the same slot, succeed in packet transmission, $P_{r|w}$. Assume that each of the r tagged users is arbitrarily assigned an order from 1 to r. Further assume that the i-th tagged user succeeds in some specific $k_i, i = 1 \sim r$, frequency bands. Let $m_{i,j}, i = 1 \sim r, j = 1 \sim k_i$, denote the number of times for which the j-th frequency band, among the k_i frequency bands, has been selected by the i-th tagged user. Furthermore, let there be p_i different values among $m_{i,j}$ for $j = 1 \sim k_i$, and let $\lambda_{i,j}, i = 1 \sim r, j = 1 \sim p_i$, represents the number of frequency bands (among the k_i frequency bands) chosen by the i-th tagged user with the j-th, $j = 1 \sim p_i$, value of times. The conditional joint probability that the first tagged user succeeds in some particular k_1 frequency bands, the second tagged user succeeds in some particular k_2 of the remaining ($q - k_1$) frequency bands, $\ldots$, the r-th tagged user succeeds in some particular k_r of the remaining $(q - k_1 - \cdots - k_{r-1})$ frequency bands, given N, q, and w, $P_{[k_1, k_2, \ldots, k_r|w]}$, can be obtained as

$$P_{[k_1,k_2,\dots,k_r|w]} =$$

$$\sum_{m_{1,1}=1}^{U_{1,1}} \sum_{m_{1,2}=m_{1,1}}^{U_{1,2}} \cdots \sum_{m_{1,k_1-1}=m_{1,k_1-2}}^{U_{1,k_1-1}} \sum_{m_{1,k_1}=m_{1,k_1-1}}^{U_{1,k_1}} \frac{N!}{(m_{1,1})!(m_{1,2})!\cdots(m_{1,k_1})!(N-m_{1,1}-\cdots-m_{1,k_1})!}$$

$$\cdot \frac{k_1!}{\lambda_{1,1}!\lambda_{1,2}!\cdots\lambda_{1,p_1}!}$$

$$\sum_{m_{2,1}=1}^{U_{2,1}} \sum_{m_{2,2}=m_{2,1}}^{U_{2,2}} \cdots \sum_{m_{2,k_2-1}=m_{2,k_2-2}}^{U_{2,k_2-1}} \sum_{m_{2,k_2}=m_{2,k_2-1}}^{U_{2,k_2}} \frac{N!}{(m_{2,1})!(m_{2,2})!\cdots(m_{2,k_2})!(N-m_{2,1}-\cdots-m_{2,k_2})!}$$

$$\cdot \frac{k_2!}{(\lambda_{2,1})!(\lambda_{2,2})!\cdots(\lambda_{2,p_2})!}$$

$$\vdots$$

$$\sum_{m_{r,1}=1}^{U_{r,1}} \sum_{m_{r,2}=m_{r,1}}^{U_{r,2}} \cdots \sum_{m_{r,k_r-1}=m_{r,k_r-2}}^{U_{r,k_r-1}} \sum_{m_{r,k_r}=m_{r,k_r-1}}^{U_{r,k_r}} \frac{N!}{(m_{r,1})!(m_{r,2})!\cdots(m_{r,k_r})!(N-m_{r,1}-\cdots-m_{r,k_r})!}$$

$$\cdot \frac{k_r!}{(\lambda_{r,1})!(\lambda_{r,2})!\cdots(\lambda_{r,p_r})!} \cdot \frac{1}{q^{Nw}} \cdot (q-\sum_{i=1}^{r}k_i)^{Nw-\sum_{i=1}^{r}\sum_{j=1}^{k_i}m_{i,j}}, \quad (5)$$

in which $U_{i,1} = \left\lfloor \dfrac{N}{k_i} \right\rfloor$, $U_{i,2} = \left\lfloor \dfrac{N-m_{i,1}}{k_i-1} \right\rfloor$, ..., $U_{i,k_i} = \left\lfloor \dfrac{N-\sum_{j=1}^{k_i-1}m_{i,j}}{k_i-(k_i-1)} \right\rfloor$, $i=1\sim r$.

Let $S_{k_1,k_2,\dots,k_r|w}$ be all equal-probable arrangements for which the first tagged user succeeds in some particular k_1 slots, the second tagged user succeeds in some particular k_2 of the remaining $(q-k_1)$ slots, ..., the r-th tagged user succeeds in some particular k_r of the remaining $(q-k_1-\cdots-k_{r-1})$ slots, given N, q, and w. Then,

$$S_{k_1,k_2,\dots,k_r|w} = \binom{q}{\sum_{i=1}^{r}k_i} \frac{\left(\sum_{i=1}^{r}k_i\right)!}{\prod_{i=1}^{r}(k_i!)} \cdot P_{[k_1,k_2,\dots,k_r|w]} \cdot \quad (6)$$

Using (6) and the principle of inclusion and exclusion, we can obtain $P_{r|w}$ as

$$P_{r|w} = (-1)^r \sum_{k_1=1}^{\min[N,q-(r-1)]} (-1)^{k_1} \sum_{k_2=1}^{\min[N,q-k_1-(r-2)]} (-1)^{k_2} \cdots \sum_{k_r=1}^{\min(N,q-k_1-k_2-\cdots-k_{r-1})} (-1)^{k_r} \cdot S_{r|w}, \quad (7)$$

where

$$S_{r|w} = 0, \qquad k_1+k_2+\cdots+k_r > q$$

$$= S_{k_1,k_2,\dots,k_r|w}, \quad k_1+k_2+\cdots+k_r \leq q$$

Let $R_{1|w}, R_{2|w}, \ldots, R_{\min(w,q)|w}$ denote the probability of success for any one tagged user, any two tagged users, $\ldots$, any $\min(w,q)$ tagged users, for a slot within which w users are transmitting simultaneously. Then,

$$R_{1|w} = \binom{w}{1} \cdot P_{1|w}, \; R_{2|w} = \binom{w}{2} \cdot P_{2|w}, \ldots, R_{\min(w,q)|w} = \binom{w}{\min(w,q)} \cdot P_{\min(w,q)|w}. \tag{8}$$

By using (8), the probability of success for exactly m_w users, given q, w, and N, $P_{s|w}(S = m_w \mid q, N, w)$, can be obtained from the formula described in [10], as

$$P_{s|w}(S = m_w \mid q, N, w) =$$

$$R_{m_w|w} - \binom{m_w + 1}{m_w} R_{(m_w+1)|w} + \binom{m_w + 2}{m_w} R_{(m_w+2)|w} - \cdots \pm \binom{\min(w,q)}{m_w} R_{\min(w,q)|w}. \tag{9}$$

For the state $(i_1, i_2, \ldots, i_T)$ in a frame with L slots, q frequency bands, and T transmitting users, the conditional probability that exactly m users succeed can be obtained from the convolution of the conditional probabilities $P_{s|1}(S = m_1 \mid q, N, 1)$, $P_{s|2}(S = m_2 \mid q, N, 2), \ldots, P_{s|T}(S = m_T \mid q, N, T)$. That is,

$$P_S(S = m \mid i_1, i_2, \ldots, i_T; q, N, L, T), \text{ for } m = 1, 2, \ldots, \min(L, T)$$

$$= \underbrace{P_{s|1}(S = m_1 \mid q, N, 1) * P_{s|1}(S = m_1 \mid q, N, 1) * \cdots * P_{s|1}(S = m_1 \mid q, N, 1)}_{i_1 \text{ terms}}$$

$$* \underbrace{P_{s|2}(S = m_2 \mid q, N, 2) * P_{s|2}(S = m_2 \mid q, N, 2) * \cdots * P_{s|2}(S = m_2 \mid q, N, 2)}_{i_2 \text{ terms}}$$

$$\vdots$$

$$* \underbrace{P_{s|T}(S = m_T \mid q, N, T) * P_{s|T}(S = m_T \mid q, N, T) * \cdots * P_{s|T}(S = m_T \mid q, N, T)}_{i_T \text{ terms}}$$

$$= \left[P_{s|1}(S = m_1 \mid q, N, 1) \right]^{i_1*} * \left[P_{s|2}(S = m_2 \mid q, N, 2) \right]^{i_2*} * \cdots * \left[P_{s|T}(S = m_T \mid q, N, T) \right]^{i_T*}, \tag{10}$$

in which $*$ represent convolution and i_j*, for $1 \le j \le T$, represent convolution of i_j times. Note that $m_1 \cdot i_1 + m_2 \cdot i_2 + \cdots + m_T \cdot i_T = m$ and the largest value of i_T is 1. Consequently, for a frame with L slots, q frequency bands, and T users are transmitting, the probability that exactly m users succeed, $P_S(S = m \mid q, N, L, T)$, can be obtained from (10) and the conditional joint probability, $\Pr\{i_1, i_2, \ldots, i_T \mid L, T\}$, that there are i_1 slots selected by one user, i_2 slots selected by two users, $\ldots$, i_T slots selected by T users, when T users are transmitting in a frame, as

$$P_S(S = m \mid q, N, L, T)$$

$$= \sum_{\text{all states}} P_S(S = m \mid i_1, i_2, \ldots, i_T; q, N, L, T) \cdot \Pr\{i_1, i_2, \ldots, i_T \mid L, T\}$$

$$= \sum_{i_T=0}^{U(T)} \sum_{i_{T-1}=0}^{U(T-1)} \cdots \sum_{i_2=0}^{U(2)} \sum_{i_1=0}^{U(1)} P_S(S = m \mid i_1, i_2, \ldots, i_T; q, N, L, T)$$

$$\cdot \frac{1}{L^T} \frac{T!}{(1!)^{i_1}(2!)^{i_2}\cdots(T!)^{i_T}} \frac{L!}{(i_1!)(i_2!)\cdots(i_T!)(L - i_1 - \cdots - i_T)!}, \quad (11)$$

in which $U(T) = 1, \ldots, U(j) = \left\lfloor \dfrac{T - T \cdot i_T - (T-1) \cdot i_{T-1} - \cdots - (T - j + 1) \cdot i_{T-j+1}}{j} \right\rfloor$.

DFH-SWOR: The procedure to evaluate the performance of DFH-SWOR is the same as that which is presented above for the DFH-SWIR. What is different is the expression for the conditional joint probability that the first tagged user succeeds in some particular k_1 frequency bands, the second tagged user succeeds in some particular k_2 of the remaining $(q - k_1)$ frequency bands, $\ldots$, the r-th tagged user succeeds in some particular k_r of the remaining $(q - k_1 - \cdots - k_{r-1})$ frequency bands, given N, q, and w, $P_{[k_1, k_2, \ldots, k_r \mid w]}$. For the DFH-SWOR, $P_{[k_1, k_2, \ldots, k_r \mid w]}$ can be expressed as

$$P_{[k_1, k_2, \ldots, k_r \mid w]} = \frac{\prod_{j=1}^{r}\binom{N}{k_j}(k_j!)\prod_{v_1=W}^{W_1}(q - v_1) \cdot \prod_{v_2=W}^{W_2}(q - v_2)\cdots \prod_{v_r=W}^{W_r}(q - v_r)\cdot \prod_{u=W}^{N+W-1}(q-u)^{w-r}}{\prod_{v=0}^{N-1}(q-v)^w}, \quad (12)$$

in which $W = \sum_{i=1}^{r} k_i$, and $W_i = N - 1 + \sum_{l=1, l \neq i}^{r} k_l$.

Finally, using (12) and (6)-(11), we can determine the $P_S(S = m \mid q, N, L, T)$ for the DFH-SWOR.

3 Dynamic System Model of DFH-SWIR and DFH-SWOR

The performance of the system as it evolves from frame to frame is evaluated in this section. Specifically, we want to determine the activity factor versus throughput, F_a versus $\tilde{S}$, characteristics, in which the activity factor is defined as the average number of transmissions required for a packet to be successfully transmitted. Assume that a backlogged user in a frame will retransmit in the next frame with probability X, in which $0 < X \leq 1$. Define the following random variables:

A_i = number of new arrivals in frame i

C_i = number of backlogged users in frame i

S_i = number of users whose packets are successfully transmitted in frame i

T_i = total number of users transmitting in frame i

U_i = number of backlogged packets that are not retransmitted in frame i.

Then, the number of packets transmitted in frame i can be expressed as

$$T_i = C_{i-1} + A_i - U_i . \tag{13}$$

Since not all backlogged packets accumulated in a frame will be retransmitted in the next frame, C_i includes packets that experience collisions in frame i as well as those backlogged packets that are not retransmitted in frame i. Thus,

$$C_i = T_i - S_i + U_i . \tag{14}$$

Let $P_T(T_i \mid C_{i-1}, U_i)$ denote the conditional probability of T_i, given C_{i-1} and U_i. Further let $P_A(A_i \mid C_{i-1})$ be the conditional probability of A_i given C_{i-1}. Then, $P_A(A_i \mid C_{i-1})$ can be described by a binomial distribution, as

$$P_A(A_i \mid C_{i-1}) = \binom{M - C_{i-1}}{A_i} \phi^{A_i} (1 - \phi)^{M - C_{i-1} - A_i} , \tag{15}$$

where ϕ denotes the probability that a new user will actually transmit in a frame.

Using (14) and (15), we can obtain $P_T(T_i \mid C_{i-1}, U_i)$ as

$$P_T(T_i \mid C_{i-1}, U_i) = P_A(A_i = T_i + U_i - C_{i-1} \mid C_{i-1}, U_i)$$

$$= \binom{M - C_{i-1}}{T_i + U_i - C_{i-1}} \cdot \phi^{T_i + U_i - C_{i-1}} \cdot (1 - \phi)^{M - T_i - U_i} . \tag{16}$$

Since U_i depends only on C_{i-1}, the conditional probability of U_i given C_{i-1}, $P_U(U_i \mid C_{i-1})$, has a binomial distribution with parameters C_{i-1} and X. That is,

$$P_U(U_i \mid C_{i-1}) = \binom{C_{i-1}}{U_i} \cdot (1 - X)^{U_i} X^{C_{i-1} - U_i} . \tag{17}$$

Let $P_C(C_i \mid T_i, U_i, C_{i-1})$ denote the conditional probability of C_i, given T_i, U_i, and C_{i-1}. Note that as T_i and U_i are given, the number of backlogged packets in frame i has been specified. Thus, C_i is independent of C_{i-1}. Consequently, $P_C(C_i \mid T_i, U_i, C_{i-1}) = P_C(C_i \mid T_i, U_i)$ and (14) implies that $P_C(C_i \mid T_i, U_i) = P_S(S_i = T_i + U_i - C_i \mid q, N, L, T_i)$. Using (16) and (17), we can obtain the transition probability matrix for the backlog process, as

$$P_C(C_i \mid C_{i-1}) = \sum_{U_i=0}^{C_{i-1}} \sum_{T_i=0}^{M-U_i} P_C(C_i \mid T_i, U_i, C_{i-1}) P_T(T_i, U_i \mid C_{i-1})$$

$$= \sum_{U_i=0}^{C_{i-1}} \left[\sum_{T_i=0}^{M-U_i} P_C(C_i \mid T_i, U_i) P_T(T_i \mid U_i, C_{i-1}) \right] P_U(U_i \mid C_{i-1}) . \tag{18}$$

When the system is in equilibrium, (18) can be used to solve for the steady state distribution associated with the backlog process, $P_C(C_{i-1})$. Then, the average number of successfully transmitted packets in a frame, $E(S)$, can be expressed as

$$E(S) = \sum_{C_{i-1}=0}^{M} \left[\sum_{S_i=0}^{M} S_i \, P_C(C_i = T_i - S_i + U_i \mid C_{i-1}) \right] P_C(C_{i-1}) . \tag{19}$$

Let $P_T(T_i \mid C_{i-1})$ denote the conditional probability of T_i, given C_{i-1}. Using (16) and (17), we can obtain $P_T(T_i \mid C_{i-1})$ as

$$P_T(T_i \mid C_{i-1}) = \sum_{U_i=0}^{C_{i-1}} P_T(T_i \mid C_{i-1}, U_i) \, P_U(U_i \mid C_{i-1}) . \tag{20}$$

And the average number of packets transmitted in a frame, $E(T)$, can be evaluated by

$$E(T) = \sum_{C_{i-1}=0}^{M} \left[\sum_{T_i=0}^{M} T_i \, P_T(T_i \mid C_{i-1}) \right] P_C(C_{i-1}) . \tag{21}$$

Finally, we can evaluate the normalized throughput, $\tilde{S} = E(S)/(q \cdot L)$, and the activity factor, $F_a = E(T)/E(S)$.

4 Numerical Results and Discussion

Due to space limitation, we only illustrate some typical examples to catch essential features of the DFH-SWIR and DFH-SWOR in this paper. More numerical results can be found in [11]. For $M = 10$, $L = 3$, $q = 2$, diversity frequency hopping order $N = 2$, and various retransmission probabilities X, the throughput $\tilde{S}$ versus the probability of transmission for a new user ϕ characteristics and the activity factor F_a versus normalized throughput $\tilde{S}$ characteristics for the DFH-SWIR are plotted in Fig. 1(a) and (b), respectively. Fig. 1(a) shows that the value of X which can result in maximum throughput is a function of ϕ. Specifically, large X ($X = 0.8$, 1.0) is appropriate for small ϕ and median X ($X = 0.5$) is appropriate for large ϕ. Fig. 1(b) reveals that small to median X ($X = 0.1 \sim 0.5$) can result in better activity factor F_a versus throughput $\tilde{S}$ characteristics. For the same set of parameters as those that are used in Fig. 1, the throughput $\tilde{S}$ versus ϕ characteristics and the activity factor F_a versus normalized throughput $\tilde{S}$ characteristics for DFH-SWOR are displayed in Fig. 2(a) and (b), respectively. It is found that the DFH-SWIR and DFH-SWOR perform similarly. For $M = 10$, $N = 2$, $X = 0.5$ and 1.0, and various combination of L and q with $L \times q = 6$, Fig. 3(a) and (b) plot the throughput $\tilde{S}$ versus ϕ characteristics and the activity factor F_a versus normalized throughput $\tilde{S}$ characteristics, respectively. While Fig. 3(b) shows that for a fixed value of X, combination of larger q with smaller L can result in better delay performance, Fig. 3(a) shows that for $X = 1.0$, combination of larger L with smaller q can yield higher throughput. Moreover, for $X = 0.5$, the combination which will result in better throughput is a function of the traffic.

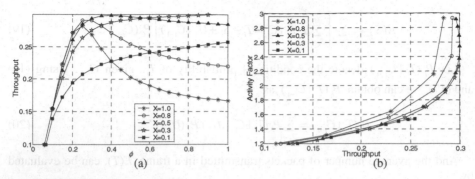

Fig. 1. DFH-SWIR scheme with $M = 10$; $L = 3$; $q = 2$; $N = 2$; $X = 0.1, 0.3, 0.5, 0.8, 1.0$: (a) the throughput $\tilde{S}$ versus the probability of transmission for a new user ϕ characteristics; (b) the activity factor F_a versus throughput $\tilde{S}$ characteristics

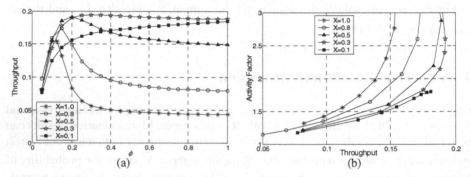

Fig. 2. DFH-SWOR scheme with $M = 10$; $L = 3$; $q = 2$; $N = 2$; $X = 0.1, 0.3, 0.5, 0.8, 1.0$: (a) the throughput $\tilde{S}$ versus the probability of transmission for a new user ϕ characteristics; (b) the activity factor F_a versus throughput $\tilde{S}$ characteristics

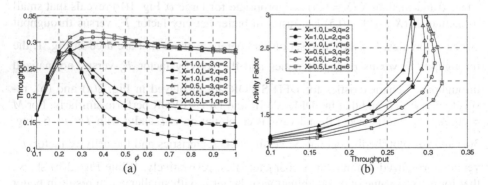

Fig. 3. DFH-SWIR scheme with $M = 10$; $N = 2$; $X = 0.5, 1.0$; $L = 3$, $q = 2$; $L = 2$, $q = 3$; $L = 1$, $q = 6$: (a) the throughput $\tilde{S}$ versus the probability of transmission for a new user ϕ characteristics; (b) the activity factor F_a versus throughput $\tilde{S}$ characteristics

5 Conclusions

In this paper, we have studied the performance of a combined framed ALOHA and SFH system. A new strategy that employs diversity transmission (multiple FH) techniques to enhance performance of this hybrid system has been presented. Two schemes which are applicable to a framed ALOHA system, DFH-SWIR and DFH-SWOR, differentiated by whether a sampling with replacement or a sampling without replacement strategy is used by a user when selecting frequency channel to perform diversity frequency hopping have been proposed. For both of these two schemes, we have developed an exact combinatorial analysis to evaluate the activity factor and throughput characteristics of this hybrid system. Numerical results based on these analyses have shown that the performance of DFH-SWIR and DFH-SWOR are similar. Furthermore, it has been shown that, under light to median traffic conditions, diversity frequency-hopping can improve the performance of the hybrid system if the number of available hopping frequencies and the number of slots accommodated in a frame are not too small. Using these numerical examples, we have also illustrated the effects of parameter variations on the system performance.

References

1. D. J. Goodman, "Cellular packet communications," *IEEE Trans. Commun.*, vol. COM-38, pp. 1272-1280, Aug. 1990.
2. J. E. Wieselthier, A. Ephremides, and L. A. Michaels, "An exact analysis and performance evaluation of framed ALOHA with capture," *IEEE Trans. Commun.*, vol. COM-37, pp. 125-137, Feb. 1989.
3. I. H. Chung and S. S. Rappaport, "Diversity reservation ALOHA," *Int. J. Satellite Commun.*, vol. 10, pp. 47-60, 1992.
4. I. H. Chung and C. A. Tsai, "Performance analysis of framed ALOHA systems with diversity transmission and erasure," in *Proc. IEEE Globecom'94*, pp. 176-180, 1994.
5. G. Benelli, G. R. Cau, and A. Radaelli, "A performance evaluation of slotted aloha multiple access algorithms with fixed and variable frames for radiomobile networks," *IEEE Trans. Veh. Technol.*, vol. VT-43, pp. 181-193, May 1994.
6. N. Abramson, "Multiple access in wireless digital networks," *Proc. IEEE*, vol. 82, pp. 1360-1370, Sep. 1994.
7. E. A. Geraniotis and M. B. Pursley, "Error probabilities for slow-frequency-hopped spread-spectrum multiple-access communications over fading channels," *IEEE Trans. Commun.*, vol. COM-30, pp. 996-1009, May 1982.
8. P. D. Rasky, G. M. Chiasson, D. E. Borth, and R. L. Peterson, "Slow frequency-hop TDMA/CDMA for macrocellular personal communications," *IEEE Personal Commun.*, pp. 26-35, Sec. Quart. 1994.
9. J. Wang and M. Moeneclaey, "Hybrid DS/SFH-SSMA with predetection diversity and coding over indoor radio multipath Rician-fading channels," *IEEE Trans. Commun.*, vol. COM-40, pp. 1654-1662, Oct. 1992.
10. W. Feller, *An Introduction to Probability Theory and its Applications*. Vol. 1, 3rd Ed., Wiley, New York, 1970.
11. I. H. Chung, "Diversity transmission and frequency-hopping techniques for a framed ALOHA wireless communication system with capture in fading environments," *Tech. Report*, Nat. Sci. Council, ROC, NSC-85-2213-E-216-022.

Optimized Channel Utilization in Multi-carrier Wireless Mobile Networks

Amrinder Arora, Fanchun Jin, and Hyeong-Ah Choi

Dept. of Computer Science, George Washington University, Washington DC 20052, USA
{amrinder, jinfc, hchoi}@gwu.edu

Abstract. This paper considers the problem of maximizing throughput in a multi-carrier wireless network that employs predictive link adaptation. The contributions of this paper are the following. We explicitly consider the time-penalty induced by the transmission-mode changes in wireless networks. We study the trade-offs between the channel-state prediction quality and the throughput. We provide sound offline problem analysis, with optimal or approximate solutions to the extent possible. We consider online version of the wireless channel scheduling problem, and provide a lower bound and propose algorithms that guarantee competitive ratios. We also extend our algorithms to accommodate the model when the actual channel capacity is different from as predicted earlier. Our results show that a modest consumption of resources for channel prediction and link adaptation may result in a significant throughput improvement, with only marginal gains through further enhancement of the prediction quality.

Keywords: Wireless networks, link adaptation, throughput maximization, offline optimal algorithm, online scheduling, competitive ratio, predictive scheduling.

1 Introduction

Channel-aware scheduling and link adaptation methods are widely considered to be crucial for realizing high data rates in wireless networks. Link Adaptation (LA), which loosely refers to changing transmission parameters, including modulation, coding rate, and power, over a link in response to changing channel conditions over time is considered to be a powerful means of achieving higher efficiency or throughput in wireless networks. The adaptation of the transmission parameters is performed according to the predicted future quality of the channel, also called as the channel-state (CS).

While it is desirable to adapt the transmission parameters according to the channel state information (CSI) to capture even small-scale variations, there are practical limitations to frequent link adaptation. Fast adaptation increases the number of mode-change messages transmitted over the channel, consuming bandwidth, and time resources [1]. While many aspects of scheduling transmissions over time-varying wireless channels have been studied (see, for example, [2,3,4] and the references therein), the penalty induced by LA has not been considered.

In this paper, we consider the scheduling problem in a multi-carrier wireless network that uses LA. The contributions of this paper are the following. We explicitly consider the time-penalty induced by the transmission-mode changes in wireless networks. We

X. Cheng, W. Li, and T. Znati (Eds.): WASA 2006, LNCS 4138, pp. 572–585, 2006.
© Springer-Verlag Berlin Heidelberg 2006

study the trade-offs between the channel-state prediction quality and the throughput. We provide sound offline problem analysis, with optimal or approximate solutions to the extent possible. We consider online version of the wireless channel scheduling problem, and provide a lower bound and propose algorithms that guarantee competitive ratios. We also extend our algorithms to accommodate the model when the actual channel capacity is different from as predicted earlier. Our results show that a modest consumption of resources for channel prediction and link adaptation may result in a significant throughput improvement, with only marginal gains through further enhancement of the prediction quality.

This paper is organized as follows. A background on link adaptation techniques is given next. System model and problem statement are given in Section 2. In Section 3, we present underlying scheduling algorithms that are used in the rest of the paper. Section 4 considers the case when multiple users share a single channel, and presents a dynamic programming algorithm for an offline optimal solution and a 2.598-competitive online algorithm. Section 5 considers the case when multiple users share multiple channels and presents an offline 2-optimal algorithm, a 4-competitive online algorithm, and an upper bound (shown to be near-optimal in simulations) to the offline optimal solution. In Section 6, we consider the model when channel estimates are imperfect (i..e, the estimate for a future channel is different from the actual one), and present our solution approach based on the results presented in Sections 4 and 5. Numerical results in imperfect channel estimates models are presented in Section 7. The paper concludes in Section 8.

1.1 Link Adaptation Techniques

Link Adaptation (LA) attempts to exploit the variations in the quality of the wireless channel by modifying a set of transmission parameters, such as the modulation, and coding modes. This is suitable for duplex communication, since the transmission parameters have to be adapted using some form of two-way transmission [5,1].

The three components of link adaptation are: (i) estimation of the channel quality (ii) transmission parameter computation, and (iii) signaling (or blind detection) of the selected parameters.

In this paper, we focus on the link adaptation for downlink transmission of data over a channel from a base-station to a mobile terminal. In this context, the adaptation of the transmission parameters is done by the transmitter at the base station.

2   System Model and Problem Statement

We assume that, at the beginning of time slot t, the base station has perfect knowledge of the channel state in time slot t, and *perfect* or *imperfect* estimates of the channel state over timeslots $t + 1, t + 2, \cdots, t + h$. We will refer to h as the *look-ahead*. Given this information at the beginning of each time slot t, the base station (BS) decides to which mobile system (MS), on what channel, and at what data rate, it is going to transmit during time slot t. If a change is required in the receiving MS or the data rate (by varying the modulation rate, coding rate, etc.), then the next downlink transmission (in time-slot t) is used to notify the receiver of the new data rate, which may be confirmed

by the MS through an ACK in the next uplink transmission. Thus, transmission at the
new data rate (possibly to a new user on the same or different channel) starts only after
a delay of a full duplex transmission cycle. Hence, the earliest time to have a new data
rate after timeslot t is $t + 2$.

We assume that there are m users, f channels, and n timeslots. The maximum rate
estimation that can be used by user i on channel j in timeslot t is denoted by $c(i, j, t)$,
and the rate assigned by the scheduler to user i on channel j in timeslot t is denoted by
$x(i, j, t)$. Clearly, $x(i, j, t) \leq c(i, j, t)$ for each $1 \leq i \leq m$, $1 \leq j \leq f$, and $1 \leq t \leq n$.

The goal is to maximize $\sum_{i=1}^{m} \sum_{j=1}^{f} \sum_{t=1}^{n} x(i, j, t)$. The decision has to satisfy the
following system constraints.

- A channel can be used for transmission to only one MS at a given time slot.
- The data transmission rate cannot exceed the time- and user-dependent maximum
  rate.
- Changing the data rate, or the intended MS, makes the next time slot useless in
  terms of data transmission.

We explore two versions of the scheduling problem in this paper: perfect and imperfect channel estimates models. At the beginning of timeslot t, the channel state over
timeslots $t, t + 1, \cdots, t + h$ are perfectly known in the perfect channel estimates model
with h look-aheads, whereas only the channel state in t is perfectly known in the imperfect channel estimates model.

2.1   Perfect Channel Estimates Model

P1: *Given a channel status matrix $C = [c(i, j, t)]$ for $1 \leq i \leq m$, $1 \leq j \leq f$,
and $1 \leq t \leq n$, the objective is to find schedule $X = [x(i, j, t)]$ that maximizes
$\sum_{i=1}^{m} \sum_{j=1}^{f} \sum_{t=1}^{n} x(i, j, t)$ such that (i) $x(i, j, t) \leq c(i, j, t)$ for each $1 \leq i \leq m$,
$1 \leq j \leq f$, and $1 \leq t \leq n$ and (ii) for any j, if $x(i, j, t) > 0$ and $x(i', j, t+1) > 0$,
then $i = i'$ and $x(i, j, t) = x(i, j, t + 1)$.*

For example, if $m = f = 1$ (i.e., single-user single-channel) and $C = [1, 3, 7, 8, 7, 15, 14]$,
then $X_1 = [0, 0, 7, 7, 7, 0, 14]$ and $X_2 = [1, 0, 7, 7, 0, 14, 14]$ are two feasible solutions,
where X_2 achieves more throughput.

2.2   Imperfect Channel Estimates Model

Let $c'_t(i, j, q)$, for $t + 1 \leq q \leq t + h$, be the *estimate* of $c(i, j, q)$ measured in time slot t.
(If $q > n$, assume $c'_t(i, j, q) = 0$.) Let $P_t^{i,j,q}(a, b)$ be the probability that $c(i, j, q) = b$,
given that $c'_t(i, j, q) = a$. Consequently, $P_t^{i,j,q}(a, a)$ denotes the prediction accuracy for
estimate a. At the beginning of each time slot t, the BS has the knowledge of $x(i, j, t -
1)$, $c(i, j, t)$, $c'_t(i, j, q)$, and $P_t^{i,j,q}(a, b)$ for each user i.

P2: *Given a channel status matrices $C = [c(i, j, t)]$ and $C' = [c'_t(i, j, q)]$, and estimation error probability $P_t^{i,j,q}(a, b)$, for $1 \leq i \leq m$, $1 \leq j \leq f$, $1 \leq t \leq n$, and
$t + 1 \leq q \leq t + h$, the objective is to maximize $\sum_{i=1}^{m} \sum_{j=1}^{f} \sum_{t=1}^{n} x(i, j, t)$ such
that (i) $x(i, j, t) \leq c(i, j, t)$ for each $1 \leq i \leq m$, $1 \leq j \leq f$, and $1 \leq t \leq n$,
and (ii) for any j, if $x(i, j, t) > 0$ and $x(i', j, t + 1) > 0$, then $i = i'$ and
$x(i, j, t) = x(i, j, t + 1)$.*

2.3   Notations

Following notations are used consistently in this paper:

- m: Total number of users
- f: Total number of channels
- n: Total number of timeslots
- h: Lookahead for the online algorithm
- $c(i, j, t)$: Capacity for i-th user on j-th channel, during t-th timeslot
- $c'_t(i, j, q)$: Estimate of $c(i, j, q)$ done in timeslot t.
- $P_t^{i,j,q}(a, b)$: Prob. that actual capacity $c(i, j, q) = b$ given estimate $c'_t(i, j, q) = a$
- $P_t^{i,j,q}(a, a)$: Prob. that actual capacity $c(i, j, q) = a$ given estimate $c'_t(i, j, q) = a$
- $x(i, j, t)$: Allocation for i-th user on j-th channel, during t-th timeslot
- i, j, t: Indices for user, channel and timeslot respectively

3   Theoretical Foundations

To prepare solid theoretical foundations, we first of all consider the single-user single-channel version of the problem. Throughout this section, the notation $c(t)$ and $x(t)$ will be used instead of $c(i, j, t)$ and $x(i, j, t)$ for simplicity.

Firstly, we focus on finding a lower bound for the competitive ratio for a one-lookahead online algorithm for problem **P1**. Note that if the performance of an online algorithm $\mathcal{A}$ is c-times worse than the performance of an optimal offline algorithm, then algorithm $\mathcal{A}$ is said to be c-competitive.

3.1   Lower Bound

Theorem 1. *For the single-user single-channel version of problem* **P1***, no one-look-ahead algorithm can be better than $3/2$-competitive.*

Proof. Consider a deterministic 1-lookahead online algorithm $\mathcal{A}$ for single-user single-channel version of problem **P1**. Let $a(t)$ denote the output selected by algorithm $\mathcal{A}$ during timeslot t and let $x(t)$ denote the output of the constructed offline solution.

Consider input of $1, 2, c(3)$, where value of $c(3)$ is controlled by an adaptive online adversary. If algorithm $\mathcal{A}$ chooses $a(1) > 0$ in the first slot, adversary sets the value of $c(3) = a(1) - \epsilon$. In this case, the algorithm can only achieve a total allocation of $2a(1)$, while optimal total allocation is $3a(1) - 3\epsilon$. If algorithm chooses $a(1) = 0$ in the first slot, adversary sets the value of $c(3) = 1$. In this case, the algorithm can only achieve a total allocation of 2, while optimal total allocation is 3. Thus, no 1-lookahead online algorithm can achieve a total allocation of more than $2/3$ times that of optimal.   ∎

3.2   Wait-Dominate-Hold Algorithm

We use the Wait-Dominate-Hold Algorithm presented in [6]. It uses the usage of the previous time slot $x(t-1)$, the current capacity $c(t)$, and the next capacity $c(t+1)$. Let $m(t)$ denote the maximum possible current usage given $x(t-1)$ and $c(t)$ defined as: (a) $m(t) = 0$ if $x(t-1) > 0$ and $c(t) < x(t-1)$, (b) $m(t) = c(t)$ if $x(t-1) = 0$, and (c) $m(t) = x(t-1)$ if $c(t) \geq x(t-1) > 0$. An example usage of the Wait-Dominate-Hold algorithm is shown in Table 1. The precise set of rules for choosing $x(t)$ is as follows:

($\mathcal{R}$1) If $c(t+1) > 2m(t)$, set $x(t) = 0$.

($\mathcal{R}$2) If $m(t) \geq 2c(t+1)$, set $x(t) = m(t)$ (we note that $x(t+1) = 0$ will be assigned in the next slot schedule).

($\mathcal{R}$3) If $c(t+1)/2 \leq m(t) < 2c(t+1)$ and $x(t-1) > 0$, set $x(t) = m(t)$.

($\mathcal{R}$4) If $c(t+1)/2 \leq m(t) < 2c(t+1)$ and $x(t-1) = 0$, set $x(t) = \min\{m(t), c(t+1)\}$.

3.3 Wait-Dominate Algorithm

We generalize the WD algorithm presented in [6], by introducing a parameter ψ and modifying the algorithm definition as follows. We refer to the modified algorithm as WD(ψ). The modified WD algorithm uses the usage of the previous time slot $x(t-1)$, the current capacity $c(t)$, and the next capacity $c(t+1)$. Let $m(t)$ denote the maximum possible current usage given $x(t-1)$ and $c(t)$ defined as: (a) $m(t) = 0$ if $x(t-1) > 0$ and $c(t) < x(t-1)$, (b) $m(t) = c(t)$ if $x(t-1) = 0$, and (c) $m(t) = x(t-1)$ if $c(t) \geq x(t-1) > 0$.

The precise set of rules for choosing $x(t)$ is as follows:

($\mathcal{R}$1) If $c(t+1) > \psi\, m(t)$, set $x(t) = 0$.

($\mathcal{R}$2) If $\psi\, m(t) \geq c(t+1)$, set $x(t) = m(t)$ (we note that $x(t+1) = 0$ will be assigned in the next slot schedule).

An example usage of the Wait-Dominate algorithm using $\psi = 2$ is shown in Table 1. We observe that every non-zero usage from the WD algorithm is surrounded by 0 in preceding and succeeding timeslots.

Competitive Analysis

Theorem 2. *Wait-Dominate algorithm WD(ψ) is $\frac{\psi^3}{\psi^2-1}$-competitive.*

Proof. Define a block B_i as $[c(1), c(2), \ldots, c(k), c(k+1)]$, s.t.

$$c(i) > \psi\, c(i-1) \quad 1 < i \leq k$$
$$c(k+1) \leq \psi\, c(k)$$

Say we define a new capacity array C' as: $c'(i) = c(i)$ for all $1 \leq i \leq k$, and $c'(k+1) = \psi\, c(k)$. We observe that the array C' as defined is strictly larger than the original capacity array C. Thus, $\text{OPT}(C) \leq \text{OPT}(C')$.

Table 1. Example usage of Wait-Dominate-Hold and Wait-Dominate algorithms, using $\psi = 2$

C:	23	23	7	5	15	31	62	3	7	7	15	17
X(WDH):	23	23	0	0	0	31	31	0	7	0	15	15
X(WD,$\psi = 2$):	23	0	7	0	0	31	0	0	7	0	15	0

By using a simple geometric progression on alternate timeslots, we observe that $\text{OPT}(C') \leq c'(k+1)\psi^2/(\psi^2-1)$. Let $|X|$ denote the allocation achieved by WD algorithm. Then, to summarize:

$$|X| = c(k)$$
$$\text{OPT}(C) \leq \text{OPT}(C')$$
$$\text{OPT}(C') \leq c'(k+1)\,\psi^2/(\psi^2-1)$$
$$= c(k)\,\psi^3/(\psi^2-1)$$
$$\Rightarrow \text{OPT}(C) \leq \psi^3/(\psi^2-1)|X|$$

Since the allocation for the last timeslot of each block is always 0, the analysis for each block is independent. Thus, the result follows by extrapolating the result over the sum of all blocks. ∎

Theorem 3. *Wait-Dominate algorithm* $WD(\psi)$ *always achieves at least* $\frac{\psi-1}{\psi^2}$ *fraction of the total throughput.*

Proof. Proof is similar to that of Theorem 2 and is omitted for space constraints. ∎

Using the theorems presented above, we can easily reach the following results.

Corollary 1. *WD algorithm can be tuned to yield competitive ratio of* $3\sqrt{3}/2$, *that is,* 2.598.
Proof. Using a value of $\psi = \sqrt{3}$ in Theorem 2 yields the desired result. ∎

Corollary 2. *WD algorithm can be tuned to achieve* $1/4$ *of total capacity.*

Proof. Using a Value of $\psi = 2$ in Theorem 3 yields the desired result. ∎

4   Multiple User Single Channel

In this section, we consider the special case of problem **P1** in which there is only one channel. That is, multiple users share the same channel. We call that channel 1, and so, all capacity variables used in this section are of the form $c(i, 1, t)$. We begin by considering the offline version of the problem.

4.1   Dynamic Programming Optimal Algorithm

We propose the following algorithm $\mathcal{MUSC\text{-}OPT}$ for multiple user, single channel offline version of the problem. The algorithm works as follows:

Let $A(t_1, t_2)$ $(t_1 < t_2)$ denote the optimal solution from timeslot t_1 to t_2 both inclusive. The algorithm is based upon the observation that optimal solution must belong in one of two cases:

Case I: Only one user uses the channel from timeslot t_1 to t_2 without changing transmission rate.
Case II: There exists timeslot k between timeslots t_1 and t_2 which has 0 transmission rate (this is the timeslot for which the users and/or transmission rates were changed).

$A(t_1, t_2)$ is the maximum of the solutions obtained from both cases. We can solve this problem with dynamic programming algorithm, and the formulation is:

$$A(t_1, t_2) = \max \begin{cases} (t_2 - t_1 + 1) * \max_{1 \leq i \leq m} \{\min_{t_1 \leq k \leq t_2} c(i, 1, k)\} & \text{(Case I)} \\ \max_{t_1 \leq k \leq t_2} \{A(t_1, k - 1) + A(k + 1, t_2)\} & \text{(Case II)} \end{cases} \quad (1)$$

For the special case, where $t_1 = t_2$, $A(t_1, t_2)$ is equal to the maximum capacity for the channel possible from all users at timeslot t_1. That is, $A(t_1, t_1) = \max_{1 \leq i \leq m} c(i, 1, t_1)$ for each i, $1 \leq i \leq m$, Also, for the sake of completeness of above recurrence, we define: $A(t, t - 1) \overset{\text{def}}{=} 0$.

Theorem 4. *Algorithm $\mathcal{MUSC\text{-}OPT}$ is optimal.*

Proof. (By induction on the length of time interval $t_2 - t_1 + 1$).

Base Step: If the length of time interval is 1, then the optimum solution is simply by choosing the user that has the maximum capacity for that timeslot. This is the solution returned by $\mathcal{MUSC\text{-}OPT}$ in Case I.

Inductive Hypothesis: $\mathcal{MUSC\text{-}OPT}$ is optimal for all time intervals of size up to n.

Induction Step: Say the optimum solution for a problem where length of time interval is n is OPT. As noted in the above observation, OPT contains either one time interval where capacity is 0, or it consists of a user using the channel capacity uniformly for all timeslots. $\mathcal{MUSC\text{-}OPT}$ considers both the cases and returns the maximum. ■

4.2 Time Complexity Analysis

Theorem 5. *Algorithm $\mathcal{MUSC\text{-}OPT}$ runs in $O(mn^3)$ time.*

Proof. The proof is immediate from the analysis of the algorithm and is omitted here due to space constraints. ■

4.3 2.598-Competitive Online Algorithm

In the online version, we assume that all the channel capacities are not known ahead of time, and only a very limited lookahead is given. This version is a more practical approach, and we extend the results obtained from the offline version both for obtaining online algorithms and for competitive analysis.

Next we formally specify algorithm $\mathcal{MUSC\text{-}ON}$ for online variation of multiple user single channel problem. The algorithm $\mathcal{MUSC\text{-}ON}$ is a 1-lookahead algorithm based on the WD algorithm discussed in section 3.3. The precise definition for choosing $x(i, 1, t)$ is as follows:

1. For each timeslot, compute the maximum capacity over all users. Thus from the matrix $c(i, 1, t)$, we compute a one-dimensional matrix $C = [c_{max}(t)]$, where $c_{max}(t) = \max_{1 \leq i \leq m} c(i, 1, t)$.
2. Use the WD algorithm, to allocate based upon the one-dimensional matrix $C = [c_{max}(t)]$.

We remind the reader that WD algorithm has the property that each non-zero allocation is surrounded by 0 allocation in preceding and succeeding timeslots. Next we present the competitive analysis of the $\mathcal{MUSC\text{-}ON}$ algorithm by comparing it to the performance of the optimal offline algorithm.

Theorem 6. *Algorithm $\mathcal{MUSC\text{-}ON}$ is 2.598-competitive.*

Proof. Proof is largely based upon the known result for WD algorithm which is known to be 2.598-competitive. Say the optimal channel allocation matrix is given by X, and the total throughput is OPT. Since only one user can be active at one time,

$$OPT \leq \sum_{1 \leq t \leq n} \max_{1 \leq i \leq m} c(i, 1, t) \tag{2}$$

Say the solution returned by $\mathcal{MUSC\text{-}ON}$ is β. Since WD is 2.598-competitive, it implies that

$$\beta \geq \frac{1}{2.598} \sum_{1 \leq t \leq n} c_{max}(t) \tag{3}$$

From equations (2) and (3), we obtain that $\beta \geq OPT/2.598$. ∎

Time Complexity for $\mathcal{MUSC\text{-}ON}$. The optimal solution for each time slot can be computed $O(m)$ time, where m is the number of users. After that, decision of whether or not to use that timeslot can be made in constant time. The overall running time is thus $O(m)$ for each timeslot, and $O(mn)$ total for all timeslots.

5 Multiple User Multiple Channel

In this section, we consider the most general form of the problem that is presented in Section 2.1. We observe that in this case the we are given a total of fmn entries (one entry per user-channel combination for each of the n timeslots). Our goal is to find out the allocation for each of the entries such that the solution is feasible, and the total throughput is maximized.

We assume that each user is only allowed to use at most one channel in any given timeslot. Hence, for each of the timeslots, only $\min\{f, m\}$ entries can be non-zero, and from the total data set, at most $n \cdot \min\{f, m\}$ entries can be non-zero. Note that such a constraint can be due to a user's hardware constraint (e.g., each user is equipped with only one transceiver).

5.1 Maximum Throughput for One Timeslot

In this section, we consider the special case when there is only one timeslot and this provides a base step that is used repetitively in the remainder of this section.

If there is only one timeslot, then the problem is defined as: Given m users and f channels, with $c(i, j, 1)$ being the capacity for i-th user and j-th channel, we want to

Table 2. Example capacity matrix for 6 users and 6 channels for 1 timeslot, with maximum matching solution for maximum throughput. An optimal solution is shown in bold.

	U1	U2	U3	U4	U5	U6
C1	3	8	3	7	4	**8**
C2	**11**	7	3	9	0	2
C3	3	2	7	1	**9**	7
C4	3	**9**	3	9	8	2
C5	7	5	**8**	3	4	8
C6	8	5	3	**12**	11	4

find an assignment that maximizes the throughput. An example capacity matrix for 6 users and 6 channels is shown in Table 2.

For a single timeslot, the problem of finding the maximum throughput is identical to finding the maximum weighted matching in the user-channel bipartite graph. Maximum weighted matching in a bipartite graph is a very well studied problem, and an optimal solution can be found in $O(m^{2.5})$ time [7]. (Here, we assume that $m \geq f$ without loss of any generality in our system model.)

5.2   2-Approximation Offline Algorithm

We propose the following algorithm $\mathcal{MUMC}$-2 for multiple user, multiple channel offline version of the problem. The algorithm works in two stages:

- **Step 1:** Use maximum matching to calculate the optimal user-channel assignment for each timeslot, independent of preceding and succeeding timeslot. Say the output of 1st step is an array: $\alpha = [\alpha(1), \alpha(2), \alpha(3), \ldots, \alpha(n)]$.
- **Step 2:** Optimally select timeslots such that the total value is maximized and no adjacent timeslots are chosen. This can be done using a single pass dynamic programming algorithm, that is based upon the following recurrence. $\beta(k) = \max\{\beta(k-2) + \alpha(k), \beta(k-1)\}$.

We observe that the step 2 of this problem is different from the single user single channel offline problem. In the single user single channel problem, it is permissible for two adjacent timeslots to be both nonzero provided they are equal. However, for the step 2 of this problem, even if $\alpha(i) = \alpha(i+1)$, we still cannot allocate both of the slots, as the overall solution may not be feasible.

Lemma 1. $\beta(n)$ is at least half of sum of $\alpha(t)$, i.e., $\beta(n) \geq \frac{1}{2} \sum_{t=1}^{n} \alpha(i)$.

Proof. Consider two specific feasible solutions: (i) feasible solution in which only odd timeslots are chosen, and (ii) feasible solution in which only even timeslots are chosen. Since $\beta(n)$ is optimal solution, it must be greater than both these feasible solutions. That is, $\beta(n) \geq \sum_{i \text{ is odd}} \alpha(i)$ and $\beta(n) \geq \sum_{i \text{ is even}} \alpha(i)$. Taking the sum of these two equations, we obtain that $\beta(n) \geq \sum_{i=1}^{n} \alpha(i)/2$.

Theorem 7. Algorithm $\mathcal{MUMC}$-2 is 2-Approximation.

Proof. Say the optimum solution for the multiple user multiple channel is OPT. In that case, the OPT must be less than the sum of the optimum solutions obtained for each time slot. That is, $OPT \leq \sum_1^n \alpha(i)$. Using Lemma 1, $\beta(n) \geq \frac{1}{2} \sum_1^n \alpha(i)$. Hence, $\beta(n) \geq \frac{1}{2}OPT$. ∎

Time Complexity Analysis. In the first stage, we use maximum weighted matching algorithm which runs in $O(m^{2.5})$ time, for each timeslot. Thus, the total time of execution for the first stage is $O(nm^{2.5})$. The second stage runs in $O(n)$, resulting in an overall time complexity of $O(nm^{2.5}) + O(n)$, i.e., $O(nm^{2.5})$.

5.3 4-Competitive Online Algorithm

In this section, we study a 1-lookahead algorithm for scheduling in multiple user multiple channel network. This version is a more practical approach compared to the offline version, and we extend the results obtained from the offline version both for obtaining online algorithms and for competitive analysis.

The algorithm $\mathcal{MUMC\text{-}ON}$ is specified as follows:

- **Step 1:** Calculate the maximum matching for each time slot independently. This step is the same as Step 1 for the offline 2-approximation algorithm $\mathcal{MUMC}$-2 . Again, we assume that the value of the maximum matching for the timeslot t is given by $\alpha(t)$.
- **Step 2:** Choose the timeslots to use using the Wait-Dominate (WD) algorithm, using the parameter $\psi = 2$. We observe that WD algorithm has the property that each non-empty allocation is surrounded by 0 allocation in preceding and succeeding timeslots.

Theorem 8. *Algorithm* $\mathcal{MUMC\text{-}ON}$ *is 4-competitive.*

Proof. The proof is based on the proof for WD algorithm that is used in Step 2. Let the value of an optimal offline algorithm be given by OPT. Since the optimum value cannot exceed the sum of optimum values obtained independently for each timeslot, we have $OPT \leq \sum_{t=1}^n \alpha(t)$. Let the total throughput using the $\mathcal{MUMC\text{-}ON}$ be β. Then using the fact that when using $\psi = 2$, WD algorithm always achieves at least $1/4$ of the total capacity, we have $\beta \geq \frac{1}{4} \sum_{t=1}^n \alpha(t)$. Combining these two equations, we obtain that $\beta \geq \frac{1}{4}OPT$. ∎

5.4 Upper Bound for Performance Analysis

In section 5.3, we presented a 4-competitive online algorithm. However, the ratio is against the sum of maximum usage in each time slot taken separately, which provides a loose upper bound on the optimal. In fact, the sum of maximum possible usage in each time slot taken separately may be twice as much as the optimal. We denote that upper bound by U_1, where $U_1 = \sum_{t=1}^n \alpha(t)$.

From the analysis in Section 4.1, we observe that optimal throughput for multiple channels is no more than the sum of optimal solution $\mathcal{MUSC\text{-}OPT}$ for each channel considered separately. We use that to propose the following alternate upper bound in which $OPT_{MUSC}(j)$ denotes the optimal throughput for channel j obtained using the $\mathcal{MUSC\text{-}OPT}$ algorithm. We denote this upper bound by U_2, where $U_2 = \sum_{j=1}^{f} OPT_{MUSC}(j)$.

The overall upper bound is now given by $U = \min\{U_1, U_2\}$.

In our numerical analysis we observed that the channel based optimal upper bound (U_2) is almost always tighter than the upper bound achieved using the maximum matchings (U_1). In fact, simulation results in Section 7 show that U_2 is near-optimal.

6   Imperfect Channel Estimates

Both the online and offline versions of the problems considered before assume that the channel state is known deterministically. In reality, however the channel state for even the next timeslot may have a certain error probability due to the user's movements, or other network parameters, In this section, we consider 1-lookahead for multiple user single channel and multiple user multiple channel versions of the problem, assuming imperfect channel estimation. Thus our 1-lookahead online algorithm uses the true capacity $c(i, j, t)$ for the current timeslot and the estimated capacity $c'(i, j, t + 1)$ for the next timeslot.

6.1   Multiple User Single Channel

For incorporating the case of imperfect estimates for multiple user single channel, we modify WDH discussed in Section 3.2 as follows.

The modified algorithm is called *Weighted-Wait-Dominate-Hold* (WWDH) and accepts weight parameter (w), where w is the weight that the algorithm uses when considering the projected allocation in the next time slot ($t + 1$). The algorithm is defined as follows (We note that for single channel case, j is always equal to 1).

1. For each user i, first form a tentative two-slot schedule using the same rules as WDH. That is, calculate $x(i, 1, t)$ and $x'(i, 1, t + 1)$ using $x(i, 1, t - 1)$, $c(i, 1, t)$ and $c'(i, 1, t + 1)$. Again, we note that $x'(i, 1, t + 1)$ is the projected allocation for the i-th user during the $(t + 1)$-th timeslot.
2. Compute $x(i, 1, t) + wx'(i, 1, t + 1)$.
3. Say the user i^* has the maximum value of $x(i, 1, t) + wx'(i, 1, t + 1)$, i.e.,
   $i^* = \arg\max_{1 \le i \le m}\{x(i, 1, t) + wx'(i, 1, t + 1)\}$.
4. Set $x(i', 1, t) = 0$, where $i' \ne i^*$, and keep $x(i^*, 1, t)$ to be as calculated.

As noted earlier, the WDH algorithm, designed for single user single channel version of problem, allocates usage for the current timeslot keeping into consideration the "projected" allocation for the next timeslot. In the next timeslot, it may or may not use that projected allocation. The situation is even more marked for the multiple user single channel case, since there are m possible combinations that may change the anticipated decision. We interpret this increased likelihood of change to suggest that the next timeslot should have lesser weightage than the current timeslot.

6.2 Multiple User Multiple Channel

For the case of multiple user multiple channel, we propose best-fit heuristic algorithm based on WWDH for multiple user single channel. The essential idea of the algorithm is to iterate over channels from 1 to f, and use WWDH for each channel. All users allocated over a particular channel are considered to be unavailable over other channels.

At each timeslot t, we use the following algorithm to allocate usage with the sequence of channels 1 to f.

- For the first channel, i.e., if $j = 1$, we proceed by using WWDH for multiple user single channel.
- For the case of $j > 1$, if $x(i, k, t - 1) > 0$ or $x(i, k, t) > 0$ for $1 \leq k \leq j - 1$, $c(i, j, t)$ is forced to be 0. Then apply the algorithm WWDH for multiple user single channel to get $x(i, j, t)$.

7 Numerical Results

In this section, we present the empirical results for the algorithms presented in the preceding sections. Our goal here is to evaluate the algorithms by varying the number of users, channels and the prediction accuracy.

For calculating empirical results, we assume $1,000$ timeslots and channel capacity is randomly chosen from one of the 9 levels. We use the MCS capacity levels: $[8.8, 11.2, 14.8, 17.6, 22.4, 29.6, 44.8, 54.5, 59.2]$ (in kb/s) as outlined in [1].

For the case of algorithms for imperfect channel estimates, the following procedure is used to calculate the estimated capacity and true capacity values. The prediction accuracy is used to calculate the values $p(a, b)$ for all values of $b \neq a$, where $p(a, b)$ is the probability that actual capacity $c(i, j, t + 1)$ turns out to be equal to b, given the estimated value $c'(i, j, t + 1)$ was equal to a.

1. We assume that for any rate a, the prediction accuracy in capacity estimation for each user, each channel, and each time slot is the same, and is given by $p(a, a)$.
2. We first generate the value a by choosing a random value from the MCS list.
3. We assume that the $p(a, b)$ is inversely proportional to the "distance" between a and b, considering their indices in the MCS List.

We note that many results for the case of perfect estimation can be subsumed under the results for imperfect estimation, by setting the prediction accuracy probability to 1.

Next we plot throughput for different number of users, number of channels and different values of weight $w > 0$ (an input parameter to the WWDH algorithm), as well as different values of prediction accuracy. The throughput when $w = 0$ is obtained using a simple greedy algorithm without using the estimate $c'(i, j, t + 1)$ (i.e., 0-lookahead). The upper bound U used in all these figures is obtained by taking the sum of upper bound taken over each channel considered separately, as noted in Section 5.4.

In Figure 1, the throughput is plotted against the weight w used by WWDH, for 5 users and 5 channels, and for prediction accuracy varying from 0.5 to 1.0. The plot suggests that the weight of 0.5 maximizes the throughput for all values of accuracy. We observe that even for 1-lookahead with only 50% accuracy, we can still obtain a throughput that exceeds 75% of the upper bound. The results also confirm that the throughput is higher if the prediction accuracy for the channel is higher. This is also consistent for results shown in Figures 2, 3 and 4. Note that for a wide range of w values, the WWDH algorithm performs well, but for two extreme values (i.e., $w = 0$ or $w = 1$), the performance is lower. Again, this is also consistent for results shown in Figures 2, 3 and 4.

In Figures 2 and 3, the throughput is plotted against the weight w used by WWDH, for 5 channels where the number of users is 20 and 40 respectively. The prediction accuracy varies from 0.5 to 1.0. The plot suggests that the optimal weight tends to decrease when the ratio m/f increases, though the throughput values are quite close for all weight values between 0.1 and 0.7. For $m = 20$, the optimal weight is observed to be 0.3, while for $m = 40$, the weight of 0.2 maximizes the throughput. We observe that for the case of $m = 20$, even with a 1-lookahead with only 50% accuracy, we can still obtain a throughput that exceeds 88% of the upper bound. Similar observations are made for $m = 40$.

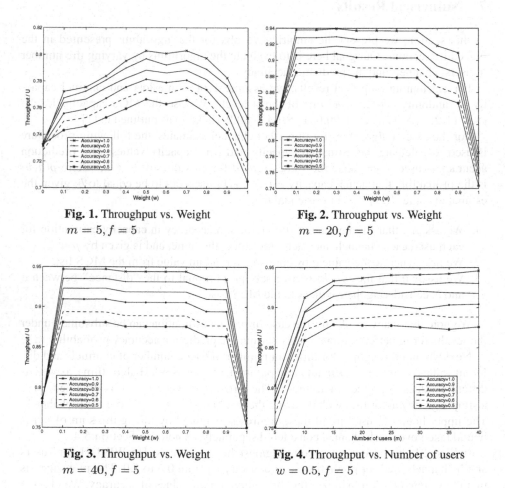

Fig. 1. Throughput vs. Weight $m = 5, f = 5$

Fig. 2. Throughput vs. Weight $m = 20, f = 5$

Fig. 3. Throughput vs. Weight $m = 40, f = 5$

Fig. 4. Throughput vs. Number of users $w = 0.5, f = 5$

In Figure 4, we summarize our results. Even in case of single lookahead with only 50% prediction accuracy for 5 users, a throughput of 75% can be achieved by properly setting the weight parameter in WWDH algorithm algorithm. The achieved throughput for single lookahead with 50% prediction accuracy can be as high as 87% if the number of users is increased to 10.

8 Conclusions and Future Work

In this paper, we have considered the problem of maximizing throughput in a multi-carrier wireless network that employs predictive link adaptation. The contributions are two-folds. Firstly, the time-penalty induced by the transmission mode change is incorporated in the scheduling. Secondly, the trade-offs between the channel state prediction quality and the throughput are studied.

We first considered the deterministic model in which the estimate for a future channel state is assumed to be accurate and developed several algorithms (offline and online) with provable bounds. We then extended the model to include the case when the channel estimates are imperfect and developed algorithms based on our deterministic solutions. Our simulation results show that a modest consumption of resources for channel prediction and link adaptation may result in a significant throughput improvement, with only marginal gains through further enhancement of the prediction quality. The results presented in this paper can provide meaningful guidelines in deciding what level of system resource consumption is justified for channel quality estimation and link adaptation.

We have not considered the quality of service requirements for different users in the scheduling problem. A natural extension of this work would be to study the effects of the channel prediction quality on the QoS requirements.

References

1. S. Catreux, V. Erceg, D. Gesbert, and R.W. Heath, "Adaptive modulation and MIMO coding for broadband wireless data networks," *IEEE Communications Magazine*, vol. 40, pp. 108–115, June 2002.
2. V. Tsibonis, L. Georgiadis, and L. Tassiulas, "Exploiting wireless channel state information for throughput maximization," in *Proceedings of IEEE Infocom '03*, April 2003, pp. 301–310.
3. S. Kulkarni and C. Rosenberg, "Opportunistic scheduling policies for wireless systems with short term fairness constraints," in *Proceedings of Globecom 2003*, December 1992, pp. 533–537.
4. X. Liu, E.K.P. Chong, and N. Shroff, "Opportunistic transmission scheduling with resource-sharing constraints in wireless networks," *IEEE JSAC*, vol. 19, no. 10, pp. 2053–2064, Oct. 2001.
5. T. Keller and L. Hanzo, "Adaptive multicarrier modulation: a convenient framework for time-frequency processing in wireless communications," *Proceedings of the IEEE*, vol. 88, pp. 1369–1394, August 1990.
6. A. Arora and H. A. Choi, "Channel aware scheduling in wireless networks," Tech. Rep. 002, The George Washington University, 2006.
7. J. E. Hopcroft and R. M. Karp., "An n 5/2 algorithm for maximum matchings in bipartite graphs," *SIAM Journal on Computing*, vol. 2, no. 4, pp. 225–231, 1973.

An Energy-Aware Quality of Services Routing Protocol in Mobile Ad Hoc Networks

Yun-Sheng Yen[1], Chih-Shan Liao, Ruay-Shiung Chang, Han-Chieh Chao[2], and Wei-Ming Chen[3]

Department of Computer Science and Information Engineering,
[1] Department of Electrical Engineering, [3] Department of Information Management
National Dong Hwa University
[2] Department of Electronic Engineering
National Ilan University
Taiwan, Republic of China
d9223008@em92.ndhu.edu.tw, toptom@tccn.edu.tw,
rschang@mail.ndhu.edu.tw, hcc@niu.edu.tw,
wmchen@mail.ndhu.edu.tw

Abstract. The paper proposes a QoS guaranteed on-demand routing protocol on the MANET, named an Energy-Aware Quality of Services Routing Protocol (EAQSRP). This protocol addresses how to find a feasible path to satisfy some QoS parameters such as delay, bandwidth and power consumption. Simulation results show our protocol provides better performances than other protocols, especially in end-to-end delay, throughput and packet loss.

Keywords: Quality of Services (QoS), Mobile Ad Hoc Network (MANET).

1 Introduction

The Internet has already become indispensable to human life. There are two kinds of transmission media for Internet. One is wireless and the other is wired. Many limitations exist in wireless networks. Hence many wired services are difficult to implement in wireless networks, especially when Quality of Service (QoS) is needed for real time applications (such as video and voice).

The MANET is composed of a set of mobile hosts with wireless transceivers. It does not rely on any infrastructure or centralized management. Wireless mobile hosts communicate with each other through multiple-hop wireless path. The data transmission of a mobile host is limited by the transmission range and therefore it needs the assistance of intermediate mobile hosts. Many papers [2, 3, 7, 15, 19] discussed the MANET routing protocols in the past. The Internet Engineering Task Force (IETF) has a working group focusing on problems arising from MANET and it encourages research in this area. In this paper, we will propose a QoS guaranteed routing protocol for MANET.

To guarantee QoS, we have to consider the end-to-end delay, the path bandwidth and the battery power of mobile hosts. Therefore, the QoS parameters considered should include delay time, bandwidth and power consumption. We propose an on-

X. Cheng, W. Li, and T. Znati (Eds.): WASA 2006, LNCS 4138, pp. 586–596, 2006.

demand routing algorithm, named an Energy-Aware Quality of Services Routing Protocol (EAQSRP). This novel protocol addresses how to find a feasible path to satisfy QoS conditions (i.e. bandwidth, end-to-end delay, and power consumption).

EAQSRP uses a limited flooding mechanism to broadcast route request (RREQ) packets to find a suitable routing path. The destination will reply with the route reply (RREP) packet to form a reverse path back to the source. Whenever a wireless link connection breaks, the route maintenance procedure will be initiated for route recovery. We adopt a detection mechanism called "acting against the QoS mechanism" [22]. It can trigger the route recovery immediately. The destination node will send an unsolicited RREP packet back to the source node for repairing the path.

The limited flooding approach addresses a QoS functionality to deal with limited available resources in a dynamic environment. We add the QoS requirements of flows to our proposal. The solution is based on decomposition of a routing area and the restriction on the exchange of routing information. It reduces the size of the control messages, restricts the amount of routing information, minimizes the overhead from the flooding of control traffic, and decreases the complexity of path selection.

2 Related Works

2.1 Routing Protocol

Basically, we classify the routing protocol into two categories in the MANET. The first one is proactive routing protocol and the other is reactive routing protocol. Proactive routing protocols need to exchange packets between mobile hosts frequently and to continuously update their routing databases. Each mobile host must maintain all of the network status at real time. This makes mobile hosts overloaded, network crowded and requires lots of memory space. The advantage is that each mobile host has correct and up-to-date data. So, when we need a path, we can find it directly in the memory and establish links quickly. Example routing protocols are CGSR [6], DSDV [16], etc. The main topic of these protocols is "How to reduce the frequency of broadcast and at the same time maintain the correct information of routing table".

The reactive routing protocol searches for a path to the destination only when it is needed. The advantage is that they don't update routing table in the memory continuously. They don't need more memory space to record network information. But, the disadvantage is that they can't establish connections at real time. The common routing protocols are AODV [8, 15], DSR [9, 10], TORA [14], etc. So, the main topic of these protocols is "How to save time in searching of routing paths and prevent delay in maintenance".

2.2 Power-Aware and QoS-Aware Routing

In an ad hoc network, some papers [1, 4, 11, 13, 17] proposed power-aware (energy-aware) protocols to reduce power consumption. They considered the power information when the maintenance and transmission of routing is designed. In order to reach better power utilization rate and promote longer vitality, a power-aware routing is necessary. The MTPR (Minimum Total Transmission Power Routing) [18, 21] is an on-demand routing technology which considers power. It tries to minimize the total transmission power consumption of nodes participating in an acquired route. The RREQ packet contains the information of power consumed so far. The destinations elect the route lowest with power consumption.

There are many QoS routing methods in the MANET at present. First in [22], Qi Xue's research proposes a quality of service on-demand routing protocol, which provides per-flow end-to-end QoS support. Seoung-Bum Lee proposes and implements the INSIGNIA structure in [12]. They use "In-band Signaling" and "Soft-state resource management" to achieve end-to-end QoS support in the MANET. Prasun Sinha proposes the CEDAR algorithm in [15]. They use "Core" and "Increase/Decrease waves" method to achieve efficiency and robustness in the dynamic network topology. Their algorithm has lower overhead. Chenxi Zhu improves an AODV on-demand QoS routing protocol in [5]. They integrate AODV routing protocol and TDMA-based mobile hosts to increase the throughput and reduce the delay.

3 The EAQSRP Mechanism

When a mobile host wants to communicate with another host on the MANET, the communication needs to satisfy QoS (e.g. minimum requested bandwidth, maximum allowable delay, etc.) requests if it were real-time. Hence, we will propose a routing protocol to satisfy the QoS requests. We also add power constraints to make our protocol more robust and reliable. The Energy-Aware Quality of Services Routing Protocol (EQARP) mechanism can be divided into two parts basically: one is route establishment, and the other is route maintenance. The route establishment contains the procedures of route discovery and data transmission. As shown in Fig. 1, a source node S wants to send data to the destination node D. First, the source node S will initiate the procedure of QoS route discovery. Once the destination node D is found, the source starts the data transmission. Whenever any wireless link in the communication path breaks, the protocol will initiate the procedure of route recovery. Details will be explained later.

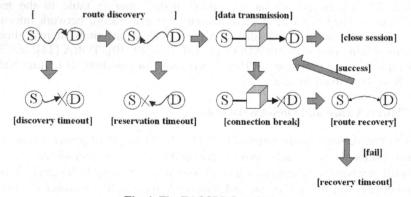

Fig. 1. The EAQSRP flowchart

3.1 QoS Constraints

Assume that a network is represented as a weighted graph $G = (V, E)$, where V denotes the set of vertices as nodes, and E denotes the set of edges as communication links connecting the nodes. $|V|$ and $|E|$ denote the number of nodes and links on the MANET, respectively. Associated with each link are parameters that describe the current status of the link. Let $s \in V$ be the source node, and $d \in V$ be the destination node. In a delivery tree T ($T \subseteq G$) rooted at s and spanning all of the nodes in V, a path from source S to destination D is denoted by $p(s, d)$. Let R^+ be the set of real positive numbers. For any link $e \in E$, we can define the some QoS metrics: bandwidth function $bandwidth$ (e): $E \rightarrow R^+$; delay function $delay$ (e): $E \rightarrow R^+$; Similarly, for any node $n \in V$, we can also define a metric: power function $power$ (n): $V \rightarrow R^+$. Then for a path $p(s,d)$, we define the following QoS parameters:

$$bandwidth_{min} (p(s,d)) = \min\{ bandwidth (e) \}, \in p(s,d) \tag{1}$$

$$delay_{max} (p(s,d)) = \min_{p(s,d)} \sum_{e \in P(s,d)} delay(e) \tag{2}$$

$$power_{min} (p(s,d)) = \min\{ power (n) \}, n \in p(s,d) \tag{3}$$

A QoS-based routing algorithm should satisfy some QoS constraints. Our EAQSRP algorithm considers the following three parameters of QoS:

$$\text{bandwidth constraint: } bandwidth_{min} (p(s,d)) \geqq Bc \tag{4}$$

$$\text{delay constraint: } delay_{max} (p(s,d)) \leqq Dc \tag{5}$$

$$\text{power constraint: } power_{min} (p(s,d)) \geqq Pc \tag{6}$$

where Bc is the bandwidth constraint; Dc is the end-to-end delay constraint and its value is defined by the source node before initiating, and would be reduced by $delay(e)$ every time passing an edge e; Pc is the power constraint. It can be described by a triple (Bc, Dc, Pc). Before initiating, the value of triple (Bc, Dc, Pc) are defined by the source node. The functions $bandwidth$ (e), $delay$ (e), and $power$ (n) represent the real value of bandwidth, delay, and power on each edge and node. The path from the source to destination has a measured value $bandwidth_{min}$, $delay_{max}$, and $power_{min}$ that should be limited by the QoS constraint Bc, Dc, and Pc (Eq. (4), (5), and (6)).

The source node S sends data to the destination node D (see Fig. 1). In the beginning, the source node S should initiate the route discovery. We use a limited flooding mechanism to broadcast RREQ packets to find a suitable routing path. When the source node S broadcasts the RREQ packet, all its neighbors will receive the RREQ packet and check the delay, bandwidth and power energy for conforming to the QoS constraints (Bc, Dc, Pc). If the request is accepted, a node n will add a route entry in its route cache with status explored and rebroadcast the request to the next hop. The node n will only remain in explored status for a period of $2(Dc - \sum_{e \in P(s,n)} delay(e))$, $\sum_{e \in P(s,n)} delay(e)$ denotes the total delay from the source S to node n ; If no reply arrives at the explored node in time, the route entry will be deleted at the node and late coming reply packets will be ignored.

This flooding mechanism guarantees that we will be able to generate a route that meets a specified set of constraints. Only a few paths can successfully pass the QoS constraints test. After that, EAQSRP algorithm uses another two QoS parameters: the total delay time and the delivery rate to decide which path is the best one. The total delay time means the summation of the end-to-end delay from source to the destination. The total delay is a defined as

$$delay_{total}(p(s,d)) = \sum_{e \in P(s,d)} delay(e) \tag{7}$$

The delivery rate shows the rate of transmitted packets from one node to another. In general, if the *packet loss rate* is defined as $[(packet_{sent} - packet_{received}) / packet_{sent}]$, then the delivery rate of each link can be calculated as follows:

$$delivery\_rate = 1 - packet\ loss\ rate = 1 - \frac{packet_{sent} - packet_{received}}{packet_{sent}} = \frac{packet_{received}}{packet_{sent}} \tag{8}$$

The *delivery_rate(p(s,d))* can be defined as

$$delivery\_rate(p(s,d)) = \prod_{e \in p(s,d)} delivery\_rate(e) \tag{9}$$

If the route is longer, obviously the delivery rate will be smaller. Then *cost(p(s,d))* is calculated as:

$$cost(p(s,d)) = \frac{delay_{total}(p(s,d))}{delivery\_rate(p(s,d))}$$

$$= \frac{\sum_{e \in p(s,d)} delay(e)}{\prod_{e \in p(s,d)} delivery\_rate(e)} \tag{10}$$

Besides satisfying the conditions in Eq. (4), (5), and (6), the route selection in EAQSRP is based on *cost()* value, which is the ratio of total delay time over delivery rate. Cost function *cost()* is used as a fitness function to select the best route. By minimizing the *cost()* value (Eq. (10)), we try to minimize the delay time value and maximize the delivery rate. This means that a packet from source to destination is transmitted with a small delay and a high transmission rate.

3.2 Route Cache

Each mobile host implementing EAQSRP needs to maintain a route cache for routing information. A mobile host adds information to its route cache as it learns of new links between hosts in the ad hoc network by receiving packets carrying a route request or route reply. Likewise, a mobile node removes information from its route cache as it learns that existing links in the ad hoc network have broken when link-layer retransmission mechanism reporting a failure in forwarding a packet to its next-hop destination. In searching the route cache for a route to some destination node, the route cache is indexed by destination node address. When a mobile host has a packet to send, it first consults its route cache. If there is an unexpired route, then it will use it. Otherwise, a route discovery will be performed. The source node will add its address to the entry. On receipt of the route request packet, a host will add its address to the "route record" and rebroadcast the packet if it satisfies the QoS constraints. To limit the number of RREQ packets, each mobile host only rebroadcasts the packet at most once. A RREP packet is generated when the route request packet reaches the destination or an intermediate mobile host that has an unexpired route to the destination. On route maintenance, all routes which contain broken links or hops have to be removed from the route cache. Although the connecting path may change in an arbitrary way, the transmission characteristics of the path tend to remain approximately constant over a time period longer than a single typical host-host transport connection. Therefore, a route cache entry is a natural place to cache the properties of a path.

3.3 Route Establishment

Assume S is the source and D is the destination. In the beginning, S should activate the route discovery using a limited flooding mechanism to broadcast RREQ packet to find a suitable routing path. When S broadcasts the RREQ packet, all its neighbors will receive the RREQ packet and check whether the bandwidth (*bandwidth()*), delay (*delay()*) and power energy (*power()*) constraints are satisfied (*Bc*, minimum bandwidth; *Dc*, maximum end-to-end delay; *Pc*, minimum power level). As shown in Fig. 3(a), source node S broadcasts RREQ packet to all its neighbors E, J and F. The neighbors E, J and F receive the RREQ packet and check whether it matched the QoS constraints or not respectively. The example is shown in Fig. 3(b). In Fig. 3(b), the triple on each edge denotes the edge bandwidth, edge delay, and the next node power level respectively. Nodes E and F do not satisfy *bandwidth()* constraint because their bandwidth *Bc* is not enough (smaller than 500Kbps/s). So nodes E and F will drop this RREQ packet. On the contrary, node J receives this RREQ and satisfies the QoS constraint (*Bc* ≤ *bandwidth()*; *Dc* ≥ *Σdelay()*s; *Pc* ≤ *power()*). Node J will add the last upstream neighbor address to its route cache, set route status to explored, and forward this RREQ packet to all its downstream neighbors. Continuing, J forwards RREQ packet to its next neighbors K and G, until this RREQ packet reaches the destination node D. Destination node D receives the RREQ packet coming from node M. So the route is J, K, L and M. Finally, the routing path built is S-J-K-L-M-D. Node D will reply a RREP packet to the source node S.

The intermediate nodes may receive more than one RREQ packets from different upstream neighbors in the route discovery. We choose the first arrived RREQ packet since it has the minimum delay. Others are discarded. Certainly, the destination node D also will receive more than one RREQ packet from different route paths. The first arrived will trigger the RREP response. For each arriving path, the *cost()* (Eq.12) is calculated. If the cost() decreases, a new RREQ is sent. When an intermediate node *n* whose route state was explored received the RREP packet, it will check whether it has exceed the $2(Dc - \sum_{e \in P(s,n)} delay(e))$ time limit. If not, the route state is set as registered. Otherwise it is rejected. At last, the source node S will receive the RREP packets. The source can begin sending real data flow. But, if the source node S does not receive any RREP packet during 2Dc time, it means this discovery procedure fails. The source node S rejects this request and can wait for a moment to begin rediscovery.

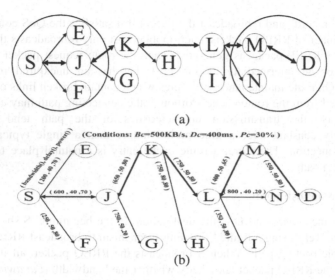

(a)

(b)

Fig. 2. The limited flooding mechanism

3.4 Route Maintenance

In general, there are three situations that can cause the routing path breaking. One is the electric power exhaustion, another is the route disconnection by ambulation, and the last is the radio outage. We adopt a detection mechanism called "acting against the QoS" mechanism. If the destination node D does not receive the next data during Dc time, the situation is "acting against the QoS" and it will trigger the route repair mechanism immediately. Thus, the destination node will send an unsolicited RREP packet back to the source node. Once the interrupted node receives this message, it will trigger the route recovery immediately.

As shown in Fig. 2(a), assume the connection breakage is between nodes J and K. Node J's upstream interface will shut down and receive an unsolicited RREP packet from the destination node D. At present, we regard this node J as a source node to broadcast a new RREQ packet to look for another node and set the R-bit to repair the route.

The repair procedure will continue as far as necessary. Similarly, the mobile hosts H, M, and N in the new route still need to satisfy the QoS constraints (Bc, Dc, Pc). If the QoS constraints are satisfied, they will directly add the last upstream neighbor address to the route cache, set route status to registered, and forward the new RREQ and to all its neighbors (such as the dash line shown in Fig. 3). If the searched mobile host (e.g., L node engage with the repaired link) is found, it will choose the path of the first RREQ packet arrived back to the source node, and update its route cache. Others RREQ packet are discarded. This is for speeding up to repair the route. After the path reestablishment, the repaired link L-N-M-J will be built. Finally, S will deliver the data according to the new path S-P-L-N-M-J-D.

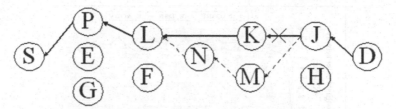

Fig. 3. The process of route recovery

4 Simulation Results

In this paper, we use the simulation tool OPNET to simulate our proposed routing algorithm. We compare the performances of AODV+MTPR (Minimum Total Transmission Power Routing) [18, 21] scheme (E_AODV), DSR+MTPR scheme (E_DSR) and EAQSRP algorithm. The simulation assumption and environment is an area of 4Km*4Km. The number of mobile hosts is 200. The bandwidth of wireless links is 1.5Mbps/sec. Each mobile host obeys 802.11 media access specifications. The power is classified into 3 classes. In this simulation environment, assume a mobile host with only 30% power left is unusable. The initial power level for a node is chosen randomly. Finally, the source and destination nodes are randomly chosen.

In Fig 4, the comparison of average end-to-end delay is shown. This delay is collected only from the packets that have been successfully received by the destination nodes. Each simulation is processed for a long term period and an average value is collected every 1 minute. Obviously, our proposed protocol results in shorter end-to-end delay compared to E_DSR and E_AODV. The MTPR prefers routes with hops having short transmission ranges. Thus it will increase the path length and delay. By using the cost function, our proposal improves the delay by considering both the delay the delivery rate.

Fig. 5 shows the throughput performances. This throughput is calculated only from the packets that have been successfully received by every node. According to the results, the E_DSR has the worst cost performance. Our proposal has the best throughput performance than the others, because it chosen the most suitable route with QoS constraint.

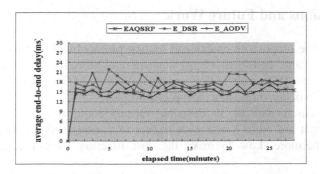

Fig. 4. Average end-to-end delay v.s. elapsed time

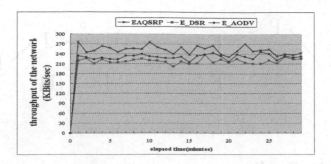

Fig. 5. Throughput of the network v.s. elapsed time

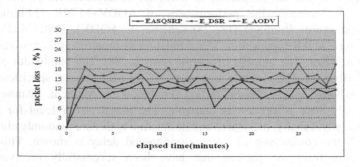

Fig. 6. Packet loss v.s. elapsed time

Fig. 6 shows the comparisons of packet losses. We can see that our proposed performances are better than others, because we use power and bandwidth constraints to reduce packet loss rate. Bandwidth constraint guarantees that a route has guaranteed minimum bandwidth. Power constraint prevents a node from deceasing before completing the transmission. In addition, since the MTPR does not consider the remaining power of nodes, it fails to prolong the lifetime of each node.

5 Conclusions and Future Work

In this paper, we propose an on-demand routing protocol called EAQSRP that have service quality and considers energy constraints. Moreover, compared to other protocols such as DSR with MTRP and AODV with MTRP, EAQSRP has better performances in delay, throughput, and packet losses.

Further research will lie in devising various route discovery and recovery mechanisms that are more robust with respect to various network fluctuations and failures. Furthermore, how to make the cost function more precise also needs studying.

References

[1] Bahl, P., Li, L., Wang, Y.-M., and Wattenhofer, R., "Distributed topology control for power efficient operation in multihop wireless ad hoc networks," *Proceedings of IEEE Twentieth Annual Joint Conference of the IEEE Computer and Communications Societies*, Vol. 3, pp. 1388–1397, 2001.

[2] Chakrabarti, S. and Mishra, A., "QoS issues in ad hoc wireless networks", *IEEE Communication Magazine*, 39(2), 142-148, 2001.

[3] Chan, Y.-S., Tseng, Y.-C., Sheu, J.-P. and Kuo, P.-H., "An on-demand, link-state, multi-path QoS routing in a wireless mobile ad hoc network", *Computer Communications*, 27(1), 27-40, 2004.

[4] Chen, B., Jamieson, K., Balakrishnan, H., and Morris, R., "Span: an energy-efficient coordination algorithm for topology maintenance in ad hoc wireless networks," *Wireless Networks*, Vol. 8 No. 5 , Sep. 2002.

[5] Chenxi, Z. and Corson, M. S., "QoS Routing for mobile ad hoc networks", *Twenty-First Annual Joint Conference of the IEEE Computer and Communications Societies (INFOCOM 2002)*, 2, 958-967, 2002.

[6] Chiang, C.-C., "Routing in clustered multi-hop mobile wireless networks with fading channel", *Proceedings of the IEEE Singapore International Conference on Network (SICON)* , 197-211, 1997.

[7] Corson, M. S. and Macker, J., "Mobile Ad hoc Networking (MANET): Routing Protocol Performance Issues and Evaluation Considerations", *RFC 2501*, 1999.

[8] Johnson, D. B., Maltz, D. A. and Hu, Y.-C. "The Dynamic Source Routing Protocol for Mobile Ad Hoc Networks", *Internet-Draft, draft-ietf-manet-dsr-10.txt*, 2004.

[9] Hunag, C.-F., Tseng, Y.-C., Wu, S.-L., and Sheu, J.-P., "Increasing the Throughput of Multihop Packet Radio Networks with Power Adjustment," *Int'l Conf. on Computer Communication and Networks (ICCCN)*, pp. 220-225, 2001.

[10] Lee, S.-B., Ahn, G.-S., Zhang, X. and Campbell, A. T., "INSIGNIA: An IP-Based Quality of Service Framework for Mobile ad Hoc Networks", *Journal of Parallel and Distributed Computing*, 60, 374-406, 2000.

[11] Liu, Y. and Lau, J., "A power-based source routing for wireless mobile ad hoc communications," *Proceedings of the 4th International Workshop on Mobile and Wireless Communications Network*, pp. 363 -367, 2002.

[12] Park, V. D. and Corson, M. S., "Temporally-Ordered Routing Algorithm (TORA) Version 1 Functional Specification", *INTERNET-DRAFT, draft-ietf-manet-tora-spec-04.txt*, 2001.

[13] Perkins, C. E., Belding-Royer, E. M. and Das, S. R., "Ad hoc On-Demand Distance Vector (AODV) Routing", *RFC 3561*, 2003.

[14] Perkins, C. E. and P. Bhagwat., "Highly Dynamic Destination-Sequenced Distance Vector routing (DSDV) for mobile computers", *Proceedings of SIGCOMM'94*, 234-244, 1994.

[15] Ramanathan, R. and Rosales-Hain, R., "Topology control of multihop wireless networks using transmit power adjustment," *Proceedings of IEEE Nineteenth Annual Joint Conference of the IEEE Computer and Communications Societies*,Vol. 2, pp. 404 –413, 2000.

[16] Scott, K. and Bambosm N., "Routing and channel assignment for low power transmission in PCS," ICUPC '96, Oct., 1996.

[17] Sheltami, T. and Mouftah, H., "A Comparative Study of On-demand and Cluster-based Routing Protocols in MANETs", *Performance, Computing, and Communications Conference*, 291-295, 2003.

[18] Sinha, P., Sivakumar, R. and Bharghavan, V., "CEDAR: a Core-Extraction Distributed Ad hoc Routing algorithm", *Eighteenth Annual Joint Conference of the IEEE Computer and Communications Societies (INFOCOM 1999)*, 1, 202-209, 1999.

[19] Toh, C.-K., Cobb, H., and Scott, D. A., "Performance evaluation of battery-lifeaware routing schemes for wireless ad hoc networks," *IEEE International Conference on Communications*, Vol. 9, pp. 2824-2829, 2001.

[20] Xue, Q. and Ganz, A., "Ad hoc QoS on-demand routing (AQOR) in mobile ad hoc networks", *Journal of Parallel and Distributed Computing*, 63, 154-165, 2003.

Bandwidth Guaranteed Routing
in Wireless Mesh Networks

Hongju Cheng[1,2], Nuo Yu[2], Qin Liu[1,2], and Xiaohua Jia[2]

[1] School of Computing, Wuhan University,
Wuhan, P.R. China
{hjcheng, qinliu}@cityu.edu.hk
[2] Department of Computer Science, City University of Hong Kong,
83 Tat Chee Ave, Kowloon, Hong Kong
csjia@cityu.edu.hk

Abstract. Interference can make significant impact on the performance of wireless networks. Wireless mesh networks (WMNs) allow multiple orthogonal channels to be used simultaneously in the system and the throughput can be greatly improved because transmissions on different orthogonal channels do not interfere with each other. However, due to the limited number of available orthogonal channels, interference is still a factor in WMNs. In this paper an H-hop interference model in WMNs is proposed, where the transmission is successfully received if no other nodes that are within H hops from the receiver are transmitting on the same channel simultaneously. Based on this model, the interference-free property in the TDMA WMNs is analyzed. A heuristic algorithm with max-min time slots reservation strategy is developed to get the maximum bandwidth of a given path. And it is used in the bandwidth guaranteed routing protocol to find the shortest path for a connection with bandwidth requirement. Extensive simulations show that our routing protocol decreases the blocking ratios significantly compared with the shortest path routing.

1 Introduction

Wireless mesh network (WMN) [1] is a new broadband Internet access technology drawing increasing attention these days. The mesh routers are equipped with a gateway capability through which they connect with the wired network. The network of mesh routers forms the backbone of WMNs to provide network access for both mesh and conventional clients which brings many advantages such as minimal upfront investments, easy network maintenance, robustness, and reliable network coverage.

One of the major problems facing the wireless networks is the capacity reduction due to the interference among multiple simultaneous transmissions. The WMNs equip mesh routers with multiple network interface cards (NICs) operating on different channels. Using multiple orthogonal channels instead of a single channel has been shown to be able to improve the network throughput because transmissions on different orthogonal channels do not interfere with each other [2], [3], [4]. However, since the number of orthogonal channels is limited, interference is still a factor in WMNs.

The WMNs are expected to support various kinds of broadband applications in many scenarios [1]. It is conceivable, and in fact quite desirable, that quality of ser-

X. Cheng, W. Li, and T. Znati (Eds.): WASA 2006, LNCS 4138, pp. 597–608, 2006.
© Springer-Verlag Berlin Heidelberg 2006

vice (QoS) can be offered to the users. QoS routing requires not only a route from the source to the destination, but a route that satisfies the end-to-end QoS requirement. When a connection request arrives at the network with a QoS requirement, the routing protocol needs to setup a path satisfying this requirement. If no such a path can be found, this connection request shall be blocked. If there are multiple paths satisfying the bandwidth requirement, the shortest (minimum hop-count) path is preferred since it uses the least resources. In this paper, we consider the bandwidth as the QoS requirement. We assume the network employs Time Division Multiple Access (TDMA) MAC layer. The available bandwidth in the TDMA networks can be measured in terms of the number of free time slots in the frame that can be used for the transmission or reception.

The rest of this paper is organized as follows. In section 2, we discuss the related works. In section 3 we give the system model and problem formulation. In section 4 we propose the multi-channel Path Bandwidth Reservation Algorithm (PBRA). In section 5 we develop a Bandwidth Guaranteed Routing protocol (BGRP). Simulation results are presented in section 6. And in section 7 are concluding remarks.

2 Related Works

Recent researches have shown that interference can make significant impact on the performance of a wireless network. Jain et al. [5] studied the impact of interference and modeled the influence of interference by using the conflict graph. They presented methods to compute the upper and lower bounds on the optimal throughput.

Zhai et al. [6] characterized the congestion of traffic flows as intra-flow contention and inter-flow contention and illustrated their severe impact on the performance of ad hoc networks. Then they proposed a distributed scheme combining both flow control and media access control to alleviate these two kinds of contentions.

Tang et al. [7] presented a definition of co-channel interference to capture the interference in WMNs. They developed a centralized algorithm to optimally solve the bandwidth guaranteed routing problem under the assumption that the traffic demands are splittable. For the non-splittable traffic, they proposed a maximum bottleneck capacity path routing heuristic.

Zhu [8], [9] showed that in a TDMA ad hoc network to find out the maximum available bandwidth along a given path is NP-complete, and it is conceivably more difficult to find a path with the maximum available bandwidth connecting two nodes in the entire network. They also proposed a heuristic algorithm to calculate the end-to-end bandwidth on a path used together with the route discovery mechanism of AODV. Shao et al. [10] pointed out the shortcut collision problem existing in Zhu's algorithm, and proposed an algorithm to solve this problem.

Georgiadis et al. [11] assumed that in ad hoc networks two transmissions interferes if the transmitter or receiver of one transmission is within a number of hops from the transmitter or receiver of another. They showed the problem of selecting a path satisfying the bandwidth requirement is NP-complete.

3 System Model and Problem Formulation

3.1 System Model

We assume there are K orthogonal channels available in the WMN numbered from 0 to $(K - 1)$ and each mesh router is equipped with I Network Interface Cards (NICs). The backbone of the WMN is modeled by a graph $G = (V, E)$, where V is a set of nodes representing the mesh routers and E is a set of bi-directional links. There is a link $(n_i, n_j; k)$ between nodes n_i and n_j on channel k if both n_i and n_j have one NIC attached to channel k and $d(i, j) \leq r$, where $d(i, j)$ is the Euclidean distance between n_i and n_j, and r is the transmission range. For simplicity, we assume that all nodes have the same transmission range.

In a TDMA system all nodes are synchronized and a frame is partitioned into a set of time slots $S = \{s_1, s_2,..., s_{LEN}\}$. There may be some traffic load existing in the network and thus some of the time slots in the frame are already used. Let $T_i(k)$ and $R_i(k)$ be the set of time slots used for sending and receiving by n_i on channel k, respectively.

3.2 H-Hop Interference Model

We propose an H-hop interference model to describe when a transmission is *received* successfully by its intended receiver. Supposing node n_i transmits over channel k to node n_j, this transmission is successfully received by node n_j if no other node n_w within H hops from n_j is transmitting over channel k simultaneously. This H-hop interference model describes the situation where a zone (within H hops from the receiver) is specified to prevent a nearby node from transmitting on the same channel at the same time. The parameter H is a constant depending on the system signal-to-interference ratio (SIR) required for a correct reception.

Let $NB_i(h)$ be the set of nodes that are within h hops from n_i (including n_i itself), i.e., $NB_i(1)$ contains n_i and the set of nodes that connect with n_i in the graph G. In general, for a successful transmission from n_i to n_j on channel k, it should be guaranteed that no other node $n_w \in NB_j(H)$ is transmitting on channel k simultaneously. Moreover, in order to ensure that the sending of n_i does not interfere with the other ongoing transmissions, it should also be guaranteed that no other node $n_w \in NB_i(H)$ is receiving packets on channel k simultaneously. The sets of the *available* time slots of n_i on channel k for sending and receiving without interference are denoted by $TS_i^t(k)$ and $TS_i^r(k)$, respectively. Since a node can not receive and send packets simultaneously on the same time slot, we get

$$TS_i^t(k) = S - T_i(k) - \bigcup_{j \in NB_i(H)} R_j(k), 0 \leq k < K . \tag{1}$$

$$TS_i^r(k) = S - R_i(k) - \bigcup_{j \in NB_i(H)} T_j(k), 0 \leq k < K . \tag{2}$$

Let $TS_{i,j}(k)$ be the set of time slots that n_i can use to send data to a neighbor n_j over channel k and n_j can use to receive data from n_i. Obviously, $TS_{i,j}(k)$ is the set of shared time slots between $TS_i^t(k)$ and $TS_j^r(k)$, i.e.,

$$TS_{i,j}(k) = TS_i^t(k) \cap TS_j^r(k), 0 \leq k < K . \tag{3}$$

Note that our interference model is different from the CSMA/CA mechanism in the IEEE 802.11 MAC which uses RTS/CTS handshake to avoid collision on both sides of the sender and the receiver. Since in the TDMA system, the time slots are carefully scheduled to avoid any collision, we only need to consider the interference to make sure that the reception is successful.

3.3 Problem Formulation

Given a path $P = \{(n_i, n_{i+1}; k_i) \mid 0 \le i < M\}$ in the graph $G = (V, E)$, let $TS_i(k_i)$ be the set of time slots reserved on channel k_i for node n_i to transmit data to node n_{i+1} and also the time slots reserved for node n_{i+1} to receive data from node n_i on the path P. To ensure that the transmission of node n_i does not influence the existing transmissions in the network, we get

$$TS_i(k_i) \subseteq TS_{i,i+1}(k_i), 0 \le i < M. \tag{4}$$

Now consider the interference among these simultaneous transmissions along the path P. The transmission of node n_i will influence the reception of any node $n_{j+1} \in NB_i(H)$ $(j \ne i)$ if they use the same channel k_i. It implies that node n_i cannot send data on the time slots that are to be used by node n_{j+1} for reception. The set of time slots used by node n_{j+1} for reception is $TS_j(k_j)$, then we have $TS_i(k_i) \cap TS_j(k_j) = \varnothing$, which is shown in (5). Similarly, any node within H hops from n_{i+1}, i.e., $n_j \in NB_{i+1}(H)$, can not transmit on channel k when n_{i+1} is receiving data from n_i to avoid interference if they use the same channel, as shown in (6).

$$TS_i(k_i) \cap TS_j(k_j) = \varnothing, \forall n_j \in \{n_p \mid (n_p, n_{p+1}; k_p) \in P,$$
$$n_{p+1} \in NB_i(H), k_p = k_i, n_p \ne n_i\}, 0 \le i < M. \tag{5}$$

$$TS_i(k_i) \cap TS_j(k_j) = \varnothing, \forall n_j \in \{n_p \mid (n_p, n_{p+1}; k_p) \in P,$$
$$n_p \in NB_{i+1}(H), k_p = k_i, n_p \ne n_i\}, 0 \le i < M. \tag{6}$$

Equations (4) ~ (6) give the constraints for the interference-free transmission on path P, where (4) specifies that there is no interference between the transmission on path P and the other ongoing transmissions in the network, and (5) ~ (6) specify that there is no interference among the transmissions along path P. The end-to-end bandwidth $BW(P)$ of the path P is determined by the bandwidth of the bottleneck link, i.e.,

$$BW(P) = \min\{\mid TS_i(k_i) \mid\}, 0 \le i < M. \tag{7}$$

We formalize the problems in the following.

Definition 1 (PBR Problem). Given a path $P = \{(n_i, n_{i+1}; k_i) \mid 0 \le i < M\}$ in the graph $G = (V, E)$ and the sets of available time slots for one-hop communications $TS_{i,i+1}(k_i)$, the **Path Bandwidth Reservation (PBR)** problem is to find the sets of time slots $TS_i(k_i)$ $(0 \le i < M)$ reserved for the transmission of node n_i (also the reception of node n_{i+1}) on channel k_i such that the end-to-end bandwidth $BW(P)$ is maximized while transmissions on path P are free of interference.

Definition 2 (BGR Problem). Given a graph $G = (V, E)$ and the sets of time slots $T_i(k)$ and $R_i(k)$ that have been used for transmission and reception by each node $n_i \in V$ on each channel k ($0 \le k < K$), for a connection request (s, d, B), the **Bandwidth Guaranteed Routing (BGR)** problem is to find the shortest (minimum hop-count) path P from the source node s to the destination node d with $BW(P) \ge B$.

4   Algorithm for the PBR Problem

The path bandwidth reservation (PBR) problem is a max-min scheduling problem. Zhu [8] proved that it is NP-complete in the ad hoc networks when $H = 1$. Since ad hoc networks can be considered as a special case of WMNs with only one channel and one NIC on each node, the problem PBR is also NP-complete. We propose a heuristic multi-channel Path Bandwidth Reservation Algorithm (PBRA) to solve this problem

Consider a path $P = \{(n_i, n_{i+1}; k_i) \mid 0 \le i < M\}$ and the sets of available time slots for one-hop communication $TS_{i,i+1}(k_i)$. To calculate the sets $TS_i(k_i)$ that satisfy the constraints (4) ~ (6), we initialize $TS_i(k_i)$ as $TS_{i,i+1}(k_i)$ and build a series of subpaths:

$$P_0 = \{(n_0, n_1; k_0)\};$$
$$P_1 = \{(n_0, n_1; k_0), (n_1, n_2; k_1)\};$$
$$\dots$$
$$P_{M-1} = P = \{(n_0, n_1; k_0), (n_1, n_2; k_1), \dots, (n_{M-1}, n_M; k_{M-1})\}.$$

The path bandwidth reservation process is as follows. First we consider the PBR problem on subpath P_0. Obviously $TS_0(k_0)$ is the set of time slots for this one-hop transmission without interference. Then we consider the PBR problem on subpath P_1. If $k_1 \ne k_0$, the time slots in $TS_1(k_1)$ are all reserved since there is no interference between the transmissions on $(n_0, n_1; k_0)$ and $(n_1, n_2; k_1)$. If $k_1 = k_0$, it implies and the sets $TS_0(k_0)$ and $TS_1(k_1)$ need to be rescheduled to avoid interference. With the max-min strategy which is described in details later, we obtain two sets $TS_0(k_0)$ and $TS_1(k_1)$ sharing no time slots, and the bandwidth of P_1 is maximized. Then we consider the next subpath and so on until the path P_{M-1} is calculated. Note that P_{M-1} is equal to P. In each step, we eliminate interference between the transmission on the last hop and the previous ones. Finally we reserve time slots for every hop transmission along path P_{M-1} to make them free of interference.

Assume that the sets of time slots $TS_i(k_i)$, $0 \le i < m$, have been reserved for subpath P_{m-1}. Let's consider the PBR problem on subpath $P_m = P_{m-1} \cup \{(n_m, n_{m+1}; k_m)\}$. Generally, we pick up the links on subpath P_m that interfere with link $(n_m, n_{m+1}; k_m)$, and reschedule the time slots of those links and $(n_m, n_{m+1}; k_m)$ to eliminate interference. In the algorithm PBRA, we divide the links interfered with $(n_m, n_{m+1}; k_m)$ on subpath P_m into two sets to make rescheduling efficient. Consider the links $(n_j, n_{j+1}; k_j)$, $m - H \le j + 1 \le m$, which are the $(H + 1)$ links immediately previous to $(n_m, n_{m+1}; k_m)$ on subpath P_m. If $k_j = k_m$, the transmission on $(n_m, n_{m+1}; k_m)$ affects the reception of $(n_j, n_{j+1}; k_j)$ because $n_{j+1} \in NB_m(H)$. Let X denote these interfering links such as

$$X = \{(n_j, n_{j+1}; k_j) \mid (n_j, n_{j+1}; k_j) \in P_{m-1}, m - H \le j+1 \le m, k_j = k_m\}. \tag{8}$$

For any two links $(n_j, n_{j+1}; k_j)$ and $(n_{j'}, n_{j'+1}; k_{j'})$ in X, without loss of generality we assume that $j < j'$. Since $0 \leq j' - (j + 1) \leq H - 1$, i.e., $n_{j+1} \in NB_{j'}(H)$, it indicates that links $(n_j, n_{j+1}; k_j)$ and $(n_{j'}, n_{j'+1}; k_{j'})$ interfere with each other. Since we have already eliminate interference along subpath P_{m-1}, the reserved time slots for links in X do not overlap, i.e., $TS_j(k_j) \cap TS_{j'}(k_{j'}) = \varnothing$.

Let Y denote the remaining links interfering with $(n_m, n_{m+1}; k_m)$ on subpath P_m that are not in X, i.e.,

$$Y = \{(n_j, n_{j+1}; k_j) \mid (n_j, n_{j+1}; k_j) \in P_{m-1},$$
$$0 \leq j < m - H - 1, k_j = k_m, n_{j+1} \in NB_m(H) \text{ or } n_j \in NB_{m+1}(H)\}. \tag{9}$$

Note that links in Y do not necessarily interfere with each other.

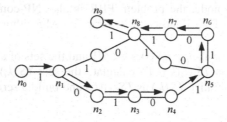

Fig. 1. An example of interference along a path

Figure 1 shows an example of the interfering links. The number besides each link represents the corresponding channel. A path is given as $P = \{(n_0, n_1; 1), (n_1, n_2; 0),$ $(n_2, n_3; 1), (n_3, n_4; 0), (n_4, n_5; 1), (n_5, n_6; 1), (n_6, n_7; 0), (n_7, n_8; 1), (n_8, n_9; 1)\}$. In the case where $H = 2$, the transmission on $(n_8, n_9; 1)$ interferes with those on links $(n_0, n_1;$ $1), (n_4, n_5; 1), (n_5, n_6; 1),$ and $(n_7, n_8; 1)$. These interfering links are divided into two sets: $X = \{(n_5, n_6; 1), (n_6, n_7; 1)\}$ and $Y = \{(n_0, n_1; 1), (n_4, n_5; 1)\}$. It's clear that $(n_5, n_6;$ $1)$ and $(n_5, n_6; 1)$ interfere with each other while $(n_0, n_1; 1)$ and $(n_4, n_5; 1)$ do not interfere with each other.

Algorithm PBRA( )

Input: subpath $P_m = \{(n_i, n_{i+1}; k_i) \mid 0 \leq i \leq m\}$
       reserved time slots $TS_i(k_i), 0 \leq i \leq m$
Output: rescheduled time slots $TS_i(k_i), 0 \leq i \leq m$
1: find the sets X and Y for link $(n_m, n_{m+1}; k_m)$;
2: **for each** $(n_j, n_{j+1}; k_j) \in Y$
3:    $NTS = \{TS_j(k_j)\}$;
4:    MaxMinRsv($NTS, TS_m(k_m)$);
5: **endfor**
6: $NTS = \varnothing$;
7: **for each** $(n_j, n_{j+1}; k_j) \in X$
8:    $NTS = NTS \cup \{TS_j(k_j)\}$;
9: **endfor**
10: MaxMinRsv($NTS, TS_m(k_m)$);

Fig. 2. The algorithm of PBRA

Algorithm MaxMinRsv( )

Input: a collection of non-overlapping sets of time slots $NTS = \{ts_1, ts_2,...\}$
a new set of time slots ts_0

Output: rescheduled NTS and ts_0

1: **if** $(NTS = \varnothing)$ **exit**;
2: $E_0 = ts_0$; $U = ts_0$;
3: **for each** $ts_i \in NTS$
4:     $I_i = ts_i \cap \overline{ts_0}$; $E_i = ts_i \cap ts_0$;
5:     $E_0 = E_0 \cap ts_i$; $U = U \cup ts_i$;
6: **endfor**
7: $avg = \lfloor |U|/(|NTS|+1) \rfloor$;
8: **if** $(|E_0| \geq avg)$
9:     $ts_0 = E_0$; // NTS is not changed
10: **else**
11:    $num = avg - |E_0|$;
12:    $done = \textbf{false}$;
13:    **while** $(num > 0 \textbf{ and not } done)$
14:       choose j : $ts_j \in NTS$, $|I_j| > 0$ and $(|E_j| + |I_j|)$ is the largest;
15:       **if** $(j$ is not found **or** $|E_j| + |I_j| - 1 \leq |E_0| + 1)$
16:          $done = \textbf{true}$;
17:       **else**
18:          randomly select a time slot s from I_j;
19:          $E_0 = E_0 \cap \{s\}$; $I_j = I_j \cap \overline{\{s\}}$;
20:          $num = num - 1$;
21:       **endif**
22:    **endwhile**
23:    $ts_0 = E_0$;
24:    **for each** $ts_i \in NTS$
25:       $ts_i = ts_i \cap \overline{ts_0}$;
26:    **endfor**
27: **endif**

Fig. 3. The algorithm of MaxMinRsv

The main idea of PBRA is to employ the max-min reservation strategy to reschedule time slots for the interfering links. Specifically, for a number of non-overlapping time slots sets, denoted by $NTS =\{ts_1, ts_2,...\}$, and a new time slot set ts_0, the function MaxMinRsv is used to reserve time slots for the sets in NTS and ts_0 again such that each time slots set $ts_i \in NTS$ is a subset of its initial value and does not overlap ts_0, and $\min_{ts_i \in NTS \cup \{ts_0\}} \{|ts_i|\}$ is maximized. When considering subpath P_m, we first execute MaxMinRsv for some times, each of which reschedules the time slots of a link in Y and link $(n_m, n_{m+1}; k_m)$. Then we execute MaxMinRsv again to reserve time slots for the links in X and link $(n_m, n_{m+1}; k_m)$. In this way, transmissions on subpath P_m are free of interference. The algorithms of PBRA and MaxMinRsv are shown in Figure 2 and

Figure 3. When P_m is processed, we move on to P_{m+1} by using the same algorithm. This procedure is repeated until the last subpath P_{M-1} has been computed. Finally, the maximum bandwidth of path P is got by (7).

5 Bandwidth Guaranteed Routing Protocol (BGRP)

The Bandwidth Guaranteed Routing (BGR) problem is to find a path that guarantees the bandwidth requested by the incoming connection. In this section, we propose a distributed routing protocol BGRP for the BGR problem.

5.1 Local Information Exchange and Collection

As we have mentioned, the current traffic load in the network is represented by $T_i(k)$ and $R_i(k)$ ($n_i \in V$, $0 \le k < K$). For node n_i, as shown in (1) and (2), the computation of the available time slots on channel k for transmission and reception, i.e., $TS_i^t(k)$ and $TS_i^r(k)$, requires $T_j(k)$ and $R_j(k)$ of nodes that are within H hops. Accordingly, each node maintains a neighbor table. There are four fields in the table: node-id, channel-id, T, and R, where node-id and channel-id represent the node identity and the channel number, and T and R represent the sets of used time slots for transmission and reception on this specific channel.

Periodically, each node n_i creates a HELLO message with the information $T_i(k)$ and $R_i(k)$ of all channels included in the message, and floods this HELLO message out through all its NICs to the nodes within H hops. When a node receives a HELLO message, it drops it if this HELLO message is heard before; if not, it adds a new item or updates the corresponding item in the neighbor table and forwards this HELLO message out through all its NICs. This local flooding can be realized by setting the TTL field in the header of the HELLO message as H. A node will decreases the value of the TTL field by one before it forwards the received HELLO message. When the TTL value reaches zero, this HELLO message is discarded.

5.2 Route Discovery

The routing discovery process is similar to the mechanism of AODV [14]. AODV is an on-demand routing protocol used to find a path from a source node to a destination node. Since the routing discovery process is carried out hop-by-hop, our PBRA is suitable to be carried out together with the routing discovery process to find a path with bandwidth guaranteed.

Assume a new connection arrives at the network with the source node as s, the destination node as d, and the bandwidth requirement as B (in the number of time slots). For each channel k that is assigned to one of its NIC, node s calculates the $TS_s^t(k)$ with (1) and creates a RREQ message with the corresponding $TS_s^t(k)$ information appended and broadcasts this RREQ on channel k.

When a node n_i receives RREQ message from node s on channel k, it calculates $TS_i^r(k)$ and $TS_{s,i}(k)$ with (2) ~ (3), where $TS_s^t(k)$ is obtained from the message. A path is built as $P = \{(s, n_i; k)\}$, the path bandwidth is calculated with PBRA and the corresponding set $TS_s(k)$ is obtained. If $BW(P) < B$, this RREQ is dropped; otherwise, this

RREQ needs to be forwarded. For each channel k' that is assigned to one of its NIC, node n_i calculates $TS_i^t(k')$ with (1), puts the information $P = \{(s, n_i; k)\}$, $TS_s(k')$ and $TS_i^t(k')$ into the RREQ message and forwards it on channel k'.

Generally, assume a node n_{m+1} receives a RREQ message from a node n_m through channel k_m with the current path information in RREQ as $P_{m-1} = \{(n_i, n_{i+1}; k_i) \mid 0 \le i < m\}$, reserved time slots $TS_i(k_i)$ ($0 \le i < m$) and $TS_m^t(k_m)$. First, node n_{m+1} checks if it is already on the path P_{m-1}, and discards this RREQ if so. Otherwise node n_{m+1} calculates the $TS_{m+1}^t(k_m)$, $TS_{m+1}^r(k_m)$ and $TS_{m,m+1}(k_m)$ with (1) ~ (3), builds a new path as $P_m = P_{m-1} \cup \{(n_m, n_{m+1}; k_m)\}$ and runs PBRA on this path P_m. If $BW(P) < B$, this RREQ is dropped; If $BW(P) \ge B$ and node n_{m+1} is the destination node d, a routing path satisfying the bandwidth requirement has been found, and the reserved time slots $TS_i(k_i)$ ($0 \le i \le m$) along the path are also obtained as the result of the PBRA. If node n_{m+1} is not the destination node, this RREQ is forwarded on each of its channel k', with the path information P_m, $TS_i(k_i)$ ($0 \le i \le m$) and $TS_{m+1}^t(k')$ included in the message.

If a node drops the RREQ on a specific channel k, it will process the next RREQ packet received on this channel since this new RREQ may come from a different path with more bandwidth. However, the next RREQ on the same channel k is dropped if a RREQ satisfying the bandwidth requirement has been processed and forwarded. In this way, RREQ is forwarded hop by hop in the network.

It is worth pointing out that to reduce the overhead during the routing discovery process, in our routing protocol a node will drop the rest RREQ messages if it has already received and forwarded a RREQ on this channel. It is possible that the first RREQ forwarded by this node does not reach the destination eventually, while another RREQ arriving later will reach the destination node if not dropped. Our scheme is suboptimal but helps to control the routing overhead.

5.3 Shortest Path Finding

The destination node may receive several RREQ message with the path bandwidth satisfying the connection requirement, meaning that there are multiple candidate paths from the source node to the destination node with bandwidth guaranteed. Generally the destination node is willing to select the shortest (minimum hop-count) path for the incoming connection request to reserve resource in the network. This can be done in two methods: 1) the destination node waits for a while for the rest RREQ messages to arrive after it receives the first RREQ that satisfies the bandwidth requirement. When the timer expires, all the rest RREQ messages are discarded and the destination node selects the RREQ with $BW(P) \ge B$ and the minimum hop count; or 2) the destination node replies the first RREQ that satisfies the requirement with a RREP message, and may RELEASE it and resends a new RREP when a shorter path is found. In this work, we use the first method to obtain the shortest path.

5.4 Time Slots Reservation

When the shortest path P that satisfies the bandwidth requirement B is found, the resource must be reserved for this new connection. The destination node replies a RREP when the shortest path P is found. The TS information in the RREP about the reserved time slots for per-hop transmission is copied from the results of the PBRA with the selected RREQ. And this RREP is sent back to the source node in the reverse direction of the path. The node n_i that receives the RREP from the downstream node n_{i+1} will randomly select B time slots from $TS_i(k_i)$ and reserve them for this new connection. Let T be the set of B time slots selected from $TS_i(k_i)$. Node n_i and n_{i+1} recalculate their $TS_i^t(k_i)$ and $TS_{i+1}^r(k_i)$ with (10) and flood a new HELLO message out immediately with the modified information to the nodes within H hops.

$$\begin{cases} TS_i^t(k_i) = TS_i^t(k_i) \cup T \\ TS_{i+1}^r(k_i) = TS_{i+1}^r(k_i) \cup T \end{cases} \quad (10)$$

6   Simulation Results

In this section, we evaluate the performance of Bandwidth Guaranteed Routing Protocol (BGRP) via simulations. We consider a simple mesh network in a 1000m× 1000m grid topology of 25 nodes. The distance between two adjacent grid points is 250m, and nodes are placed in the grid points. Each node has a fixed transmission range as 250m and the interference hop H is assumed as 2. In the simulation, we vary the number of the available channels and the number of NICs on each node. We also simulate the cases of different existing traffic loads. In each case, the simulation is carried out 100 times and the average performance is analyzed.

There are 3 and 12 orthogonal channels in 802.11b/a standard respectively. In the simulation, we set the number of available channels in the system to 3 in some scenarios and 12 in others, and the number of NICs on each node is set to 2 in some cases and 3 in others. We adopt the topology control algorithm in [7] to assign channels to each NIC and build a connected graph by making minor modification to reflect the H-hop interference model.

In the simulation, we assume there are 40 time slots in a frame. The availability of each slot for sending or reception of each NIC is modeled as Bernoulli random variable with probability $p \in (p_a, p_b)$, and $0 \le p_a \le p_b \le 1$. We consider the two typical traffic loads in the network: uniform and random. In the random case, the percent of the available time slots for transmission and reception of the link is a random value $p \in (p_a, p_b)$. In the uniform case, the probability p for the percent of the available time slots on all links in the graph is identical.

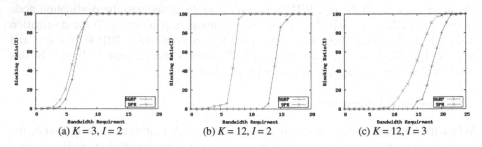

(a) $K = 3, I = 2$ (b) $K = 12, I = 2$ (c) $K = 12, I = 3$

Fig. 4. Random traffic loads with $p_a = 0.6$ and $p_b = 0.9$

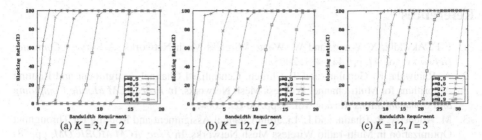

(a) $K = 3, I = 2$ (b) $K = 12, I = 2$ (c) $K = 12, I = 3$

Fig. 5. Uniform traffic loads

We compare our solution with the shortest (minimum hop-count) path routing which is labeled as SPR for brevity. The blocking ratio is the ratio between the number of blocked connections and the total connections. Figure 4 shows the performance of our solution in random traffic load where $p_a = 0.6$ and $p_b = 0.9$. In the case where $K = 3$ and $I = 2$, the performance of our algorithm is a little better than that of the SPR. In the other two cases there is great blocking ratio reduction with our solution. This is because BGRS is aware of interference, while SPR takes no interference into account. So BGRS is more likely to find a path satisfying the requirement.

We also analyze the impact of traffic load on the blocking ratios with different slot requirements. In the uniform case, we vary the probability p from 0.5 to 0.9. Figure 5 shows the simulation results. As we can see, the blocking ratios increase rapidly during certain slot requirement range, i.e. in Figure 5(a) with $p = 0.7$, the blocking ratio increases from 0.03 to 0.98 when the slot requirement increases from 3 to 7. This is because the traffic load in the network is uniform and the number of available slots on each link is similar with identical probability p. However, for a given bandwidth requirement, with the increase of p, the number of available time slots increase too, and thus the blocking ratio decreases, as we can observe from Figure 5.

Under the same probability p and the bandwidth requirement, the blocking ratio decreases when the number of available channels increases from 3 to 12. This is because with the increase of available channels, the nodes in the neighbors are more likely assigned to different channels so that the influence of interference is reduced. This increases the chance for a new request to be admitted.

7 Conclusions

In this work we consider the influence of interference in the multi-channel WMNs and propose an H-hop interference model in which a guard zone (within H hops from the receiver) is specified to guarantee the successful reception. Based on this model, we analyze the interference-free property in the TDMA WMNs. Then we present a heuristic algorithm with max-min time slots reservation strategy to solve the path bandwidth reservation problem, and propose a multi-channel routing protocol to find the shortest path for a connection with bandwidth requirement. Simulation results show that our routing protocol decreases the blocking ratios significantly compared with the shortest path routing protocol.

References

1. I. F. Akyildiz, X. Wang, and W. Wang. Wireless Mesh Networks: A Survey. *Computer Networks*, vol. 47, pp. 445-487, 2005.
2. A. Raniwala, K. Gopalan, and T. Chruch. Centralized Channel Assignment and Routing Algorithms for Multi-channel Wireless Mesh Networks. In *Proc. ACM Mobile Computing and Communcations Review*, vol. 8, pp. 50-65, 2004.
3. M. Alicherry, R. Bhatia, and L. Li. Joint Channel Assignment and Routing for Throughput Optimization in Multi-radio Wireless Mesh Networks. In *Proc. ACM MOBICOM*, pp. 58-72, 2005.
4. P. Gupta and P. R. Kumar. The Capacity of Wireless Networks. *IEEE Transactions on Information Theory*, vol. 2, pp. 338-404, 2000.
5. K. Jain, J. Padhye, V. Padmanabhan, and L. Qiu. Impact of Interference on Multi-hop Wireless Network Performance. In *Proc. ACM MOBICOM*, pp. 66-80, 2003.
6. H. Zhai, J. Wang, and Y. Fang. Distributed Packet Scheduling for Multihop Flows in Ad hoc Networks. In *Proc. Wireless Communications and Networking Conference*, pp. 1081-1086, 2004.
7. J. Tang, G. Xue, and W. Zhang. Interference-Aware Topology Control and QoS Routing in Multi-Channel Wireless Mesh Networks. In *Proc. ACM MOBIHOC*, pp. 68-77, 2005
8. C. Zhu. Medium Access Control and Quality-of-Service Routing for Mobile Ad hoc Networks. PhD thesis, Department of Electrical and Computer Engineering, University of Maryland, College Park, MD 20906, 2001.
9. C. Zhu and M. S. Corson. QoS Routing for Mobile Ad hoc Networks. In *Proc. IEEE INFOCOM*, pp. 958-967, 2002.
10. W. Shao, V. Li, and K. Chan. A Distributed Bandwidth Reservation Algorithm for QoS Routing in TDMA-based Mobile Ad hoc Networks. In *Proc. Workshop on High Performance Switching and Routing*, pp. 317-321, 2005.
11. L. Georgiadis, P. Jacquet, and B. Mans. Bandwidth Reservation in Multihop Wireless Networks: Complexity and Mechanisms. In *Proc. Distributed Computing Systems Workshops*, pp. 762-767, 2004.
12. C. Perkins, E. M. Royer, and S. R. Das. Ad-Hoc On-Demand Distance Vector Routing. In internet-draft, draft-ietf-manet-aodv-06.txt, 2000.

An Altitude Based Dynamic Routing Scheme for Ad Hoc Networks

Rei-Heng Cheng[1], Tung-Kuang Wu[2,*], Chang Wu Yu[3], and Chun-Hung Kuo[1]

[1] Department of Information Management,
Hsuan Chuang University, Hsin-Chu, Taiwan, R. O. C
rhc@hcu.edu.tw
[2] Department of Information Management,
National Changhua University of Education, Chang-Hua, Taiwan, R. O. C
Tel.: 886-4-7232105 ext. 7615; Fax: 886-4-7211162
tkwu@mail.tkwu.net
[3] Department of Computer Science and Information Engineering,
Chung Hua University, Hsin-Chu, Taiwan, R. O. C
cwyu@chu.edu.tw

Abstract. Ad-hoc On-Demand Distance Vector Routing (AODV) is a famous routing protocol for mobile ad hoc networks. Routing path established with AODV remains unchanged during data transmission unless the link fails. Due to the mobile nature of nodes in an ad hoc network, the network topology changes frequently. As a result, some intermediate nodes of an earlier established path may later become redundant and results in packet routing through longer link. In addition, a path established at one time may later be broken due to some intermediate nodes of the path move out of the range. In this paper, we propose an ad hoc network routing protocol with both dynamic link shortening and broken avoidance features. Each node only needs to turn on its overhearing function and keeps minimal extra information. The simulation results show that the proposed protocol does improve the performance of the AODV protocol in terms of data delivery ratio, average delay time, and the network overhead.

Keywords: Ad hoc network, Path shortening, Link broken avoidance, AODV.

1 Introduction

Mobile ad hoc networks are wireless networks with no fixed infrastructure. They can be characterized by dynamic topology due to node mobility, limited battery power and limited bandwidth. Each mobile node in ad hoc networks may move arbitrarily and acts as both a router and a host.

Many routing protocols for ad hoc networks have been developed, such as AODV ([7]), DSR ([4], [5]), TORA ([1]) and DSDV ([6]). These routing protocols are usually categorized into two types: table-driven and source-initiated on-demand protocols ([8]). The table-driven protocols, such as DSDV, always try to maintain the routes in

---

* Corresponding author.

X. Cheng, W. Li, and T. Znati (Eds.): WASA 2006, LNCS 4138, pp. 609–619, 2006.
© Springer-Verlag Berlin Heidelberg 2006

the network, so that the transmission route can be established immediately for data packets delivery. However, protocols in this category suffer from heavy overhead result from frequent routing table update. On the other hand, the source-initiated on-demand protocols initiate a route request only when they need a route for transmission. They save the overhead due to periodic routing information refresh, but suffer from longer latency before the actual data delivery can start.

Among all the routing protocols, AODV has been known for its outstanding performance. Routing path established with AODV remains unchanged during data transmission unless the link fails. However, due to the frequently changing network topology of an ad hoc network, two possible situations may very likely occur with the ADOV routing protocol. First of all, a path established at one time may later be broken due to some intermediate nodes of the path moving out of the range. Secondly, some intermediate nodes of an earlier established path may later become redundant and results in packet routing through unnecessarily longer link. However, with proper arrangement, we can shorten a link by identifying and removing the redundant nodes from the transmission link. Similarly, it is also possible to keep a link from breaking by replacing some of the intermediate nodes that are moving away from the path with nodes that are moving around the neighborhood.

In this paper, we propose an ad hoc networks routing scheme with both dynamic link shortening and broken avoidance features. The protocol uses the AODV as the basis and makes a few slight modifications. With our protocol, each node needs to turn on its overhearing function and maintains very minimal extra information. The simulation results show that the proposed protocol does improve the performance of the AODV protocol in terms of data delivery ratio, average delay time, and network overhead.

The rest of this paper is organized as follows. In Section 2, we describe previous researches that are related to our work. Section 3 presents the details of the proposed scheme with the simulation results shown in Section 4. Finally, we conclude our work and list possible future work in Section 5.

2   Related Work

Some researches that do path shortening in mobile ad hoc networks will be discussed in this section.

Dynamic Source Routing (DSR) is an on-demand routing protocol. The full routing path is stored in the source node. When a node overhears a packet carrying a source route, it examines the unexpended portion of that source route. If this node is not the intended next-hop destination for the packet, it is named in the later unexpended portion of the packet's source route, and then it can infer that the intermediate nodes before itself in the source route are no longer needed in the route ([2], [5]). This mechanism is based on the extra routing path information piggybacked in the transmitted packets, and the node has to reply a so called *gratuitous* route to the original sender of the packet for shortening routes. It is not efficient since the reply may take many hops to reach the source node.

Saito *et al.* ([10]) presents a proximity-based dynamic path shortening scheme. In this scheme, each node in the active route monitors its local link quality and estimates whether to enter the proximity of its neighboring node to shorten the active route.

Both of the methods mentioned above only concern whether some of the intermediate nodes should be removed from the active route so as to reduce the number of routing hops. However, they do not consider the possibility of replacing two (or more) intermediate nodes with a node that happens to be in the right position.

Roy ([9]) presents the source-tree on-demand adaptive routing protocol (SOAR). In SOAR, wireless routers exchange minimal source trees consisting of the state of the links that are in the path used by the router to reach active destinations ([9]). Based on this information, SOAR can find the shorter route to replace the active paths. Just like the source route information in DSR, the minimal source trees information in SOAR puts extra transmission burden on the network.

Note that shortening the routing path implies that distance between two neighboring routing hops increases, which also results in a link that is more vulnerable to being broken. As a result, it is desirable that a link broken avoidance scheme exists to compensate this side effect.

3 The Proposed Scheme

The details of our proposed scheme will be presented in this section. We first introduce the basic idea, with further implementation details explained in subsequent sub-sections.

The proposed protocol is implemented as an extension to the AODV protocol. In AODV, the hop counts to the destinations are kept in every mobile node in the active

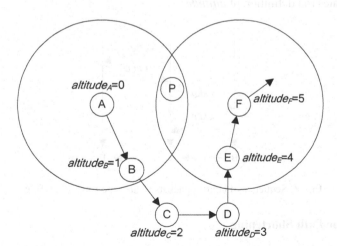

Fig. 1. An illustration of the definition of *altitude* (with node *A* and *F* representing the source and destination, respectively)

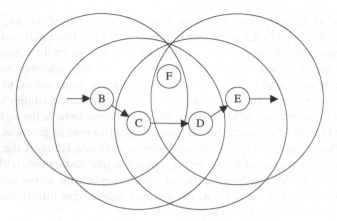

Fig. 2. Node *F* overhears the data packets sent out by node *B*, *C*, *D* and *E*

routes. Since a mobile node located around the data transmission path can overhear the delivering data packets, it should be able to determine if it can act as a detouring node for the original link and create a shorter one by piggybacking the hop count information within the data packets. In case a node does find itself a suitable detouring node, it can contact the related nodes, its potential upstream and downstream nodes, to direct traffic to it.

To reduce the number of control packets (to be discussed later in Section 3.2), hop counts in our protocol is defined as the distance from the source, as opposed to AODV. And to avoid any confusion, we name our so called hop counts the *altitude* hereafter. Accordingly, $altitude_X$ represents the *altitude* of node X, which also means that the node X is the $altitude_X$–*th* node from the source (without counting the source). Fig. 1 illustrates the definition of *altitude*.

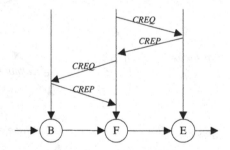

Fig. 3. Sequence of control packets to arrange route detouring

3.1 Dynamic Path Shortening

When a mobile node moves closer toward a data transmission link, it may overhear data packets from various nodes in the route. For example, suppose that node *F* in Fig. 2 can overhear data packets sent by node *B*, *C*, *D* and *E*. Since the difference between $altitude_B$ and $altitude_E$ is greater than 2, node *F* knows that a detour of the traffic through nodes *B-F-E* would make a shorter path. In this case, node *F* informs node *E* by a *CREQ* (Changing route REQuest) control packet to make sure that node *E* is still within its power range. After receiving the *CREP* (Changing route REPly))packet from node *E*, node *F* makes node *E* its next hop in the routing table. Node *F* then proceeds by sending a *CREQ* control packet to node *B* to suggest a new route. Node *B* will then change its routing table by making node *F* its next hop and reply a *CREP* packet to node *F*. The detouring process is complete with a new shorter path. Fig. 3 demonstrates the above process.

3.2 Hop Count Information Maintenance

The path shortening may be done by removing some redundant nodes from route (Fig. 4a) or replacing two or more nodes in the active route with a node (Fig. 4b). In both cases, the *altitude* information of all affected nodes in the route has to be recalculated. In our proposed protocol, a node changes its *altitude* according to the *altitude* information piggybacked in the received data packets originated from its upstream node. Take Fig. 5 for example, node *B* will send data packets to node *F* after the path being re-organized and shortened. Once node *F* finds out the *altitude* of *B*, which is 2 in this case, from the received data packets, it knows 3 would be its new *altitude*. The *altitude* of node *E*, and all the downstream nodes, will adjust their *altitude* accordingly. As we can see, this process is simple and straightforward. On the other

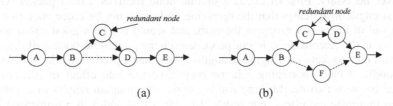

(a)   (b)

Fig. 4. Two types of path shortening (a) removing redundant nodes from an active route (b) replacing nodes in the active route with a node

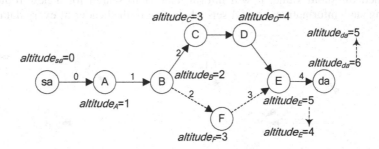

Fig. 5. The dash lines indicate the altitude information update sequence after route *B-C-D-E* is changed to *B-F-E*

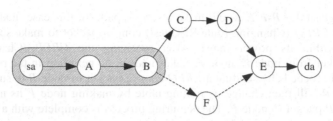

Fig. 6. If the hop count is defined to the destination instead of from the source, the hop counts of upstream nodes sa, A and B have to be re-assigned

hand, if the information we keep were hop counts to the destination as AODV does, the adjusted hop-count information of the nodes in a newly established path can not be determined until the reply control packets sent back from the destination node. This can be easily seen in Fig. 6, where edge *B-C-D-E* is replaced with *B-F-E* and the hop counts (to the destination) of all the upstream nodes (node *sa*, *A* and *B*) of node *F* have to be determined and re-assigned according to the reply messages from node *da*.

3.3 Link Broken Avoidance

Link quality is the major concern when we determine whether a route should be detoured. We deal with such quality issue by (1) carefully choosing the detouring nodes, and (2) monitoring the stability of an active link and take proper measure whenever necessary. First of all, if a mobile node receives a data packet with low signal strength, it indicates that the receiving node may not be close enough to or be getting out of the power range of the path, and would not be a good candidate for a detouring node. Accordingly, in our proposed scheme, a mobile node will discard the overheard data packets with signal strengths lower than a predefined threshold value.

Secondly, a path shortening scheme may have the side effect in increasing the distance between two neighboring routing hops, which again results in a vulnerable link. To minimize the effect, our protocol requires that nodes in a transmission path check the signal strength of the data packets received from their upstream nodes. Fig. 7 illustrates how this operates. For example, in case node *B* receives a data packet from its upstream node *A* and notices that the signal strength is lower than the predefined threshold value, it will inform node *A* to search for a new route. Upon receiving such information, node *A* sets a help flag in the header of every data packets

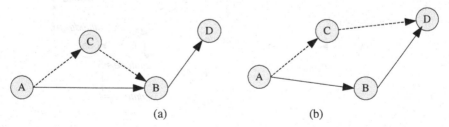

(a)   (b)

Fig. 7. Two types of link broken avoidance (a) $altitude_B - altitude_A = 1$; inserting a new node into a link (b) $altitude_B - altitude_A = 2$; replacing a node in the active route with another node

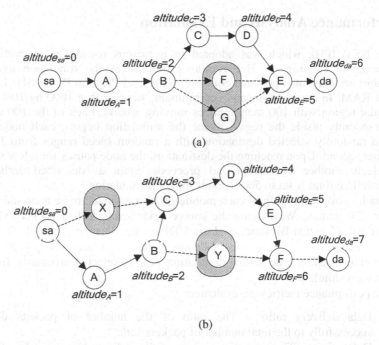

(a)

(b)

Fig. 8. Illustrations of the two kinds of race conditions. (a) Two nodes inform one upstream node to detour. (b) Two nodes inform two different upstream nodes to detour.

it sends hereafter. Suppose a node C receives packets with help flag set from node A and finds itself a good detouring candidate for the link, it will execute the dynamic route shortening procedure as described in Section 3.1 even though the difference between $altitude_A$ and $altitude_B$ is less than 3.

3.4 Race Condition

The other concern that one may have is the effect of race condition, which occurs when two mobile nodes find new shorter paths almost at the same time and ask their upstream nodes to detour simultaneously. There can be two types of race conditions as shown in Fig. 8. The first type of race condition occurs when two potential downstream nodes ask the same upstream node for a detour. Fig. 8a illustrates such case, in which both node F and E ask node B to detour. Depending on which node initiates the request first, the final route would either be B-G-E or B-F-E. In either case, a shortened path is established. The other type of race condition occurs when two potential downstream nodes ask two different upstream nodes for detouring. This is depicted in Fig. 8b, where node X asks node sa and node Y asks node B to detour respectively. It is true that the detour which goes through node Y has no effect, however, the newly established route, sa-X-C-D-E-F-da, is still a valid one. In other words, even under the race conditions, our proposed path shortening scheme would still operate properly.

4 Performance Analysis and Evaluation

We use NS-2 ([3]), which was adopted in numerous researches to evaluate the performance of existing Ad Hoc routing protocols, as the simulation tools. The simulations are done on a personal computer with Intel Pentium IV 2.4GHz CPU and 512 MB RAM. In our experimental environment, we specify a 1000 by 1000 meters rectangular region with 100 mobile nodes moving around. Each of the 100 nodes is placed randomly inside the region. Once the simulation begins, each node moves toward a randomly selected destination with a random speed ranges from 10 to 50 meters per second. Upon reaching the destination, the node pauses for a few seconds, then selects another destination and proceeds again as described earlier. The simulation time limit is set to 500 seconds for each simulation.

The radio coverage region of each mobile node is assumed to be a circular area of diameter 250 meters. We assume the source node sends a data packet every half second (CBR: Constant Bit Rate), and use UDP as the transport protocol. The size of data packet is set to 512 bytes. Each node has a queue that can hold up to 50 packets awaiting transmission. One source-destination pair is selected arbitrarily from 100 nodes in each simulation.

Three performance metrics are evaluated:

- Data delivery ratio – The ratio of the number of packets delivered successfully to the total number of packets sent.
- Delay time – The time that a successfully delivered packet takes from the source to the destination.
- Network overhead – The total number of packets sent out by all nodes during a simulation.

Path shortening and link broken avoidance are the two main features of the proposed dynamic routing scheme. Our simulation compares results with four different setups, include AODV, AODV with path shortening (denoted by *shortening* in the following figures), AODV with link broken avoidance (denoted by *LBA* in the following figures), and AODV with both path shortening and link broken avoidance (denoted by *LBA+shotening* in the following figures).

Fig. 9 shows simulation result in data delivery ratio. It indicates that the proposed link broken avoidance scheme can achieve higher data delivery ratio than the original AODV does. This is well within our expectation since the probability of link broken decreases with application of the *LBA* scheme, and the number of lost packets can also be reduced. On the other hand, the link shortening scheme performs nearly the same as AODV does in this aspect. Though the delivery ratio gain is only around 2%, however, the combination of link broken and shortening schemes achieves the best data delivery ratio, and in some cases, it can almost reach the 100% mark.

In Figure 10, the simulated average delay time is illustrated. As expected, each of our proposed schemes performs better than AODV does. This is no surprise since our schemes take into account the link quality and adjust the route accordingly, which reduces the probability of link broken. The less in link broken implies that less time is taken to wait for routes rebuilding. This explains why the average delay time of *LBA* is also less than that of AODV, even though it has consistently the longer link as indicated by Fig. 11. Furthermore, once the dynamic path shortening scheme is applied, the average delay time would be further reduced since shorter paths are now used to deliver data packets.

Fig. 11 shows the average number of hops that a data packet has to go through in order to reach its destination. Apparently, link shortening does reduce the average hop counts, although only marginally. On the other hand, the application of link broken avoidance seems to increase the average hop counts quite significantly. This is due to the fact that nodes are kept inserting in-between links with low signal strength to prevent link from being broken, which results in longer route. However, as we already know, the higher delivery ratio and reduced latency still make it a worthy option. Finally, combining the link shortening with the *LBA* scheme closes the margin of difference with AODV.

Fig. 12 presents the simulation result in term of overhead. It seems that the *LBA* scheme performs not so well in this aspect, either. However, this is the direct consequence of its averagely longer path, which causes more packets to be sent in each successful data delivery. On the other hand, in the case of AODV, the overhead is mainly caused by high number of control packets in order to reconstructs a new route after link-broken. Once again, the combination of *LBA* and link shortening schemes achieve the least overhead.

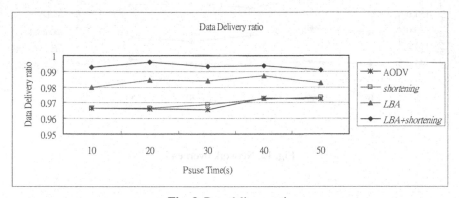

Fig. 9. Data delivery ratio

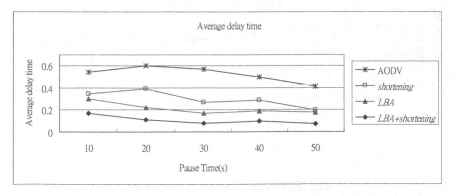

Fig. 10. Average delay time

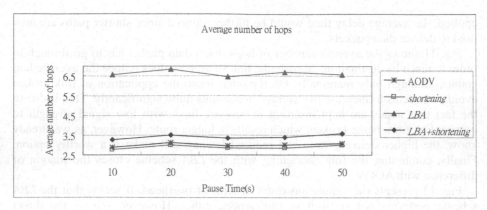

Fig. 11. Average numbers of hops

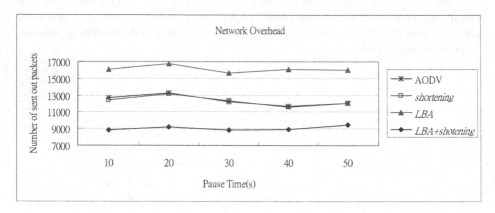

Fig. 12. Network overhead

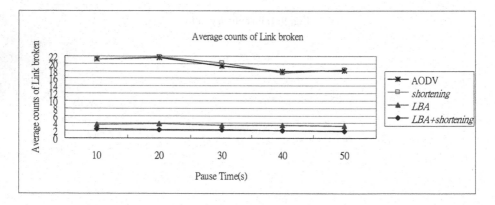

Fig. 13. Average frequency of link broken

Fig. 13 shows the average frequency in link broken. The link shortening scheme performs about the same as AODV does. However, both the *LBA* and combination of LBA and link shortening schemes perform a lot better than AODV does in this aspect. In the best case, the frequency of link broken is only one tenth of that of AODV.

In summary, the combination of *LBA* and link shortening scheme performs best in terms of data delivery ratio, average delay time, network overhead and link quality, while on par with the AODV in term of average number of hop counts of a routing path.

5 Conclusions

In this paper, we present a new dynamic path scheme that is a simple extension of the famous AODV protocol. By requiring mobile nodes store a few data records and adding two extra fields (the *altitude* information and the help flag) in the data packets, we can significantly improve the performance of AODV routing protocol. Our analysis and simulation results show that we can achieve higher delivery ratio, lesser average delay time, higher link quality and with less network overhead.

However, our proposed path shortening scheme consider only the case that a node is used to replace two or more nodes in an established path. How to use more than one node to form a new shorter route is the major research direction of our future work.

References

1. M. S. Corson and V. D. Park,"Temporally Ordered Routing Algorithm (TORA) version 1: Functional specification" Internet-Draft, draft-ietf-manet-tora-spec- 00.txt, 1997.
2. S. R. Das, C. E. Perkins, and E. M. Royer, "Performance Comparison of Two On-demand Routing Protocols for Ad Hoc Networks," *IEEE INFOCOM*, 2000, pp. 3-12.
3. Kevin Fall and Kannan Varadhan, editors. Ns notes and documentation, The VINT Project, UC Berkeley, LBL, USC/ISI, and Xerox PARC, November 1999. Available from http://www.isi.edu/nsnam/ns/.
4. D.B. Johnson and D.A. Maltz, "Dynamic Source Routing in Ad-Hoc wireless networks", *Mobile Computing*, 1996, pp. 153-181.
5. D.B. Johnson, D.A. Maltz, and Y.C. Hu, "The Dynamic Source Routing Protocol for Mobile Ad Hoc Networks (DSR)", IETF Internet-Draft, draft-ietf-manet-dsr-10.txt, 2004.
6. Charles E.Perkins and P.Bhagwat, "Highly Dynamic Destination Sequenced Distance Vector Routing (DSDV) for Mobile Computers", *ACM SIGCOMM*, 1994, pp.234-244. Comp Communication Rev, 1994.
7. C. Perkins and E. Royer, "Ad-hoc On-Demand Distance Vector Routing", *Proceeding of IEEE WMCSA*.
8. E.M. Royer and C.K. Toh, "A review of current routing protocols for ad hoc mobile wireless networks", *IEEE Personal Communications*, pp. 46-55, 1999.
9. S. Roy and J.J. Garcia-Luna-Aceves, "Using Minimal Source Trees for On-Demand Routing in Ad Hoc Networks," *IEEE INFOCOM*, 2001, vol. 2, pp. 1172-1181..
10. Masato Saito, Yoshito Tobe, and Hideyuki Tokuda, "A Proximity-Based Dynamic Path Shortening Scheme for Ubiquitous Ad Hoc Networks", *24th International Conference on Distributed Computing Systems (ICDCS'04)*, 2004.

PREG: A Practical Power Control Algorithm Based on a Novel Proximity Graph for Heterogeneous Wireless Sensor Networks*

Xue Zhang[1,2], Sanglu Lu[1], Daoxu Chen[1], and Li Xie[1]

[1] State Key Laboratory for Novel Software Technology
Department of Computer Science and Technology
Nanjing University, Nanjing 210093, P.R.China
zhangxue@dislab.nju.edu.cn, sanglu@nju.edu.cn,
cdx@nju.edu.cn, xieli@nju.edu.cn
http://cs.nju.edu.cn
[2] Department of Electrical Engineering, School of Engineering
Nanjing Agricultural University, Nanjing 210031, P.R. China
http://www.njau.edu.cn

Abstract. Power control is one of the most important techniques used in wireless sensor networks. However, most power control algorithms proposed so far are impractical, because previous work usually makes such perfect assumptions as uniform transmission ranges, location-awareness, and so on. In this paper, we propose REG (Relative Energy-cost Graph), an algorithm to derive a novel proximity graph, which is optimal in the sense of sparseness while preserving the least energy consumption path between any two nodes. And based on REG, we further put forward a new practical power control algorithm PREG (Practicalized REG) for heterogeneous networks. Our theoretical analyses and simulation results show that PREG has a better performance than other power control algorithms thanks to its high practicality and energy efficiency.

1 Introduction

Wireless sensor networks have a wide variety of potential applications in many fields. However, there are many issues that need to be addressed for efficient operation of real sensor network systems. Energy efficiency and network capacity are perhaps two of the most important issues. Many topology control algorithms have been proposed to maintain network connectivity while reducing energy consumption and improving network capacity. There are two primary mechanisms for topology control in sensor networks: power control and sleep scheduling [1]. Power control is effective for sparse networks, and sleep scheduling, which is not covered in this paper, is only suitable for over-deployed networks.

---

* This work is partially supported by the National Basic Research Program of China (973) under Grant No.2002CB312002; the National Natural Science Foundation of China under Grant No.60402027; Jiangsu Natural Science Foundation under Grant No.BK2005411.

X. Cheng, W. Li, and T. Znati (Eds.): WASA 2006, LNCS 4138, pp. 620–631, 2006.

The key idea of power control is that, instead of transmitting using the maximal power, nodes in a wireless multi-hop network collaboratively determine their transmission power while preserving some required properties. Power control is of great importance to saving energy (and hence prolonging network lifetime), improving spatial reuse (and hence improving network capacity), reducing radio interference (and hence mitigating MAC contention).

Over the past several years, power control has drawn a significant amount of research interests, and various algorithms have been proposed to create energy-efficient topology in wireless sensor networks, which are summarized in Section 3. However, most of them are impractical. In this paper, we propose the REG (Relative Energy-cost Graph) algorithm followed by a full-scale analysis. The network topology derived under REG holds good properties. It is the best proximity graph in the sense of sparseness while preserving the least energy consumption path between any two nodes. We do know that REG is impractical because it is proposed for homogeneous networks and also because it depends upon location information. Therefore, based on REG, we further propose PREG (Practicalized REG), which works locally and asynchronously at each node for heterogeneous networks without any knowledge of locations. Our theoretical analyses and simulation results show that PREG is better than other power control algorithms for its high practicality and energy efficiency.

The rest of the paper is organized as follows. In Section 2, we give some concepts for the understanding of this paper. In Section 3, we summarize related work on power control. Following that, we propose REG together with an analysis in Section 4. Based on that , we further develop the PREG power control algorithm for heterogeneous networks in Section 5, and evaluate the performance of REG and PREG by simulation in Section 6. Finally we conclude this paper in Section 7.

2   Preliminaries

This section provides formal definitions of basic concepts essential for the understanding of this paper.

2.1   Network Model

Most work on power control assumes that wireless sensor networks are deployed in the two-dimensional plane and each node has the knowledge of its location. A homogeneous network is usually modeled as a UDG (Unit Disk Graph), i.e., two nodes can communicate as long as their Euclidean distance is no more than a threshold. However, a real network cannot be perfectly modeled as a UDG, because the maximum transmission ranges of wireless devices may be extremely different for electrical, mechanical, environmental or else reasons. More realistic are heterogeneous networks, which can be modeled by MG (Mutual inclusion Graph). In a MG, two nodes can communicate directly only if they are within the transmission range of each other. We assume that any link of UDG or MG is symmetric, since uni-directed links in wireless sensor networks are shown to be costly.

The topology of a network can be modeled as $G = (V(G), E(G))$, where V is the set of sensor nodes, and E is the set of communication links. Let $r(u)$ denote the maximal transmission radius of node u, and $d(u, v)$ denote the Euclidean distance between node u and node v. Note that (u, v) is an ordered pair representing an edge from node u to node v. Then the neighbor set of node u can be expressed as $N(u) = \{v \in V(G) : d(u, v) \leq r(u)\}$.

In a weighted graph G, every edge $(u, v) \in E(G)$ is attributed a weight $w(u, v)$. When referring to a weighted graph, if without other particular declarations, we assume that the weights are symmetric, i.e., $w(u, v) = w(v, u)$. Given two edges $(u_1, v_1), (u_2, v_2) \in E$, weight function $w : E \rightarrow R$ satisfies: $w(u_1, v_1) > w(u_2, v_2) \iff d(u_1, v_1) > d(u_2, v_2)$.

2.2   Design Objectives

When creating the network topology, the following properties are desirable:

(1) Connectivity: A network is connected if and only if there exist both a path from u to v and a path from v to u for any two nodes u and v contained in the network. Connectivity is extremely desirable to be guaranteed. We assume that the deployed network, modeled by UDG or MG, is static and strongly connected. To guarantee connectivity of UDG or MG is not this paper's interest.

(2) Symmetricity: The resulting network topology should also be symmetric, i.e., node u is a neighbor of node v if and only if node v is a neighbor of node u. Asymmetric communication graphs are impractical, because many communication primitives become unacceptably complicated. A simple ACK message confirming the receipt of a message, for example, is already a nightmare in an asymmetric graph [2,3].

(3) Planarity: Sometimes we need to discuss the planarity of a graph, for example, in order to run a geometric routing algorithm. In this paper, graph G is said to be planar if and only if it contains no two intersecting edges. It is well known that a planar graph is also sparse.

(4) Sparseness: Sparseness refers to that the number of links is in the order of number of nodes. Sparseness is desirable because it means low interference, which saves energy and improves spatial reuse.

(5) Degree boundedness: Degree boundedness means that the maximum degree in the graph is bounded from above by a constant. Degree boundedness results in sparseness, while sparseness may not result in degree boundedness.

(6) Spanner property: The distance in graph G between two nodes $u, v \in V(G)$ is the cost of the minimum cost path between u and v, and it is denoted by $D_G(u, v)$. A subgraph H, derived from G, is a k-spanner of G if for every $u, v \in V(G)$, $D_H(u, v) \leq k \cdot D_G(u, v)$. The value of k is called the stretch factor or spanning ratio. In this paper, the weight of an edge (u, v) is defined as the power to support the communication of (u, v). Therefore k is called the power stretch factor and H is called an energy spanner of G.

3   Related Work

Kirousis et al reduced the power control problem to the RA (Range Assignment) problem, which is the problem of assigning a transmitting range to nodes in such a way that the resulting communication graph is strongly connected and the energy cost is minimum. The computational complexity of RA has been analyzed in Kirousis et al [4] and Clementi et al [5]. The conclusion is that the RA problem is solvable in polynomial time in one-dimensional case, whereas is NP-hard in two-dimensional case or three-dimensional case. The real power control problem is more complicated.

Narayanaswamy et al proposed COMPOW [6]. The basic idea is that all the nodes use the same transmission power, which is minimized without destroying network connectivity. The drawback is that a relatively separate node may lead to a high transmission power. Kawadia and Kumar proposed CLUSTERPOW [7], which solves the problem existing in COMPOW. But CLUSTERPOW is too costly.

Kubisch et al proposed LMA and LMN [8], which are based on node degrees. The main idea of all the degree-based algorithms is that the transmission power of a node is adjusted so that the degree is between a lower bound and an upper bound. The common drawback of those algorithms is that it cannot (or cannot effectively) preserve network connectivity. Bahramgiri et al proposed connectivity-preserved CBTC [9], which is based on direction. But CBTC is also impractical for it requires that the arrival angle problem be well solved and nodes be equipped with directional antennas.

Another wave of power control algorithms advocated the employment of classic computational geometry, and in this direction, Hou and Li can be considered originators [3]. Those algorithms are based on proximity graphs, such as RNG (Relative Neighborhood Graph) [10], GG (Gabriel Graph) [11], DG (Delaunay triangulation Graph) [12], YG (Yao Graph) [13] and MST (Minimum Spanning Tree) [14]. The RNG derived from a given graph G, denoted by $RNG(G)$, consists of all edges (u, v) such that the intersection of two circular areas (called disks), centered at u and v and with radius $d(u, v)$ do not contain any node w from $V(G)$. The GG, denoted by $GG(G)$, contains edge (u, v) if and only if $disk(u, v)$ contains no other nodes of $V(G)$, where $disk(u, v)$ is the disk with edge (u, v) as its diameter. DG and MST cannot be computed locally, therefore they lack of practicality. Because of that, some work has been done based on localized DG [12] and localized MST [14]. YG is something like CBTC, and of course there is some difference. Because these structures are only applicable for UDG, researchers have made great effort to modify them in order to deal with heterogeneous networks [13,15,16,17]. The main defect of algorithms based on those structures is that they require exact position information of sensor nodes. Wattenhofer et al adopted the essential idea of RNG, and proposed simple and exotic XTC [3], which works without knowing locations. To the best of our knowledge, XTC is relatively more practical than other power control algorithms for heterogeneous networks. In this paper, we make efforts to go further in the same direction as XTC.

4   REG

In this section, we present our REG, an algorithm to derive a new proximity graph, for homogeneous networks under such a perfect assumption that the network can be modeled as a UDG with exact location information. Following that, we make an analysis of properties of the topology derived under REG.

4.1   The REG Algorithm

It is well known that the received signal power averaged over large-scale variations has been found to have a distance dependence, which is well modeled by $1/d^\alpha, \alpha \geq 2$, where d denotes the distance between the transmitter and receiver antennas, and α, the path loss exponent, is determined from field measurements for the particular system at hand. Therefore, relaying information between nodes may result in lower energy consumption than communicating over large distances. The main idea of REG is to minimize the number of links while preserving the least energy consumption path between any two nodes.

According to the path loss model, the power consumption of communicating over a link of distance d can be measured by kd^α, where k is a positive constant. We attribute the weight function $w(u, v) = kd^\alpha$ to each edge (u, v) in the UDG. The topology derived from a given UDG graph G is denoted by $REG_\alpha(G)$, where α is the path loss exponent. $REG_\alpha(G)$ contains edge $(u, v) \in E(G)$ if and only if there does not exist x, $(u, x) \in E(G)$ and $(x, v) \in E(G)$, such that $d^\alpha(u, x) + d^\alpha(x, v) < d^\alpha(u, v)$, i.e., $w(u, x) + w(x, v) < w(u, v)$.

4.2   Analysis of REG

For simplicity, we also use REG to denote the topology derived under the REG algorithm. According to the definitions of RNG, GG, and our REG, it is easy to draw the conclusion on REG's relationship to RNG and GG, which is visualized in Figure 1 and formalized by the following theorem.

Theorem 1. $RNG(G) \subseteq REG_{\alpha \geq 2}(G) \subseteq GG(G)$, and particularly, $REG_2(G) = GG(G)$.

We omit the proof of theorem 1 since it is intuitively true.

Theorem 2 (Properties of REG). (1)REG(G) is strongly connected if G is strongly connected; (2)REG(G) is symmetric if every edge in the given graph G is symmetric; (3)The energy stretch factor of REG is 1; (4)$REG_{\alpha \geq 2}(G)$ is planar and sparse.

Proof. (1),(2) and (3) are obvious. As for (4), $REG_{\alpha \geq 2}(G)$ features planarity and sparseness because $REG_{\alpha \geq 2} \subseteq GG(G)$ and $GG(G)$ is already known to be planar and sparse (virtually,$|GG(G)| \leq 3n - 8$, where n is the number of nodes [18]).

It is easy to know that $REG_\alpha(G)$ is sparser and sparser when α is increasing. But we can prove this: for any α, the node degree is not bounded. In spite of that, sparseness implies the average node degree is bounded by a constant.

5   PREG

It is obvious that, as other location-based algorithms, REG is impractical. Therefore, in this section, based on REG, we further propose PREG, a practical power control algorithm for heterogeneous networks, followed by a full-scale analysis.

5.1   The PREG Algorithm

The PREG algorithm is executed at all nodes. The following description assumes the point of view of a node u. The pseudocode is shown in the box.

PREG consists three main steps:

(1) Information collection (Lines 1 to 3),
(2) Neighbor ordering (Line 4), and
(3) Topology creation (Lines 5 to 7).

PREG Algorithm:

1. Make the set of power levels $P = \{p_1, p_2, ..., p_k\}$;
2. $N_0(u) = \phi$;
3. For $i = 1$ to k
   compute $N_i(u)$ and $N_{i-1}^i(u) = N_i(u) - N_{i-1}(u)$;
   compute P_{min}: if $v \in N_{i-1}^i(u)$, then $P_{min}(u, v) = p_i$;
4. Establish a total order $\prec_u$ over $N(u)$ according to P_{min} with respect to increasing communication cost.
5. Broadcast and receive P_{min} to and from each neighbor;
6. Traverse $\prec_u$. For each node $v \in N(u)$, if there does not exist some x, $x \prec_u v$, such that $P_{min}(u, x) + P_{min}(x, v) < P_{min}(u, v)$, then node u sends a REQUEST message to node v;
7. An edge (u, v) is selected by u if and only if node u both sends and receives a REQUEST message to and from v;

In the first step, each node u computes the minimum power that it requires to communicate with each one of its neighbors in the network graph G. Let $P_{min}(u, v)$ be the minimum power required for node u to communicate with its neighbor node v. Note that $P_{min}(u, v)$ may not be equal to $P_{min}(v, u)$. Suppose $P = \{p_1, p_2, ..., p_k\}$ is the set of discrete power levels, where $p_1 < p_2 < ... < p_k$. Let $N_i(u)$ be the set of nodes with which node u can communicate using power p_i, and let $N_{i-1}^i(u) = N_i(u) - N_{i-1}(u)$. For each node $v \in N(u)$, if $v \in N_{i-1}^i$, then $P_{min}(u, v) = p_i$. If transmission is possible only at a small number of discrete power levels, node u is able to acquire the knowledge of all the minimum powers by exchanging HELLO messages with its neighbors at each power level. This is usually true of the current off-the-shelf wireless network interface cards capable of transmit power control. For example, the Cisco Aironet 350 series cards (IEEE 802.11b) allow the transmit power level to be set to one of 1, 5,

20, 30, 50, and 100mW [19]. Even so, PREG is developed to be independent of that assumption. No matter how many possible power levels there are, node u may always exchange HELLO messages with its neighbors at a small number of discrete power levels. By this means, the overhead during this step can be bounded by a constant.

In the second step, each node u computes a total order over all its neighbors based on P_{min} with respect to increasing communication cost. For those neighbors with whom the same power is required for u to directly communicate, node u may order them according to other factors, such as packet arrival rate or the signal to noise ratio, etc. Furthermore, we can also make P_{min} more accurate by this means. But how to do it still requires further research. After the second step, a total order is obtained at each node. Let $\prec_u$ be the total order at node u. A neighbor s appearing before t in order $\prec_u$ is denoted by $s \prec_u t$, which means that $P_{min}(u, s) \leq P_{min}(u, t)$, in other words, link (u, s) is better than (u, t).

In the third step, after broadcasting and receiving P_{min} functions to and from all its neighbors, node u traverses $\prec_u$. Good neighbors are considered first, worse ones later. For each neighbor of u, say v, if there does not exist some x, $x \prec_u v$, such that $P_{min}(u, x) + P_{min}(x, v) < P_{min}(u, v)$, then node u sends a REQUEST message to node v. An edge (u, v) is selected by u if and only if node u both sends and receives a REQUEST message to and from v.

5.2   Analysis of PREG

Here we make an analysis of PREG. Mostly, PREG refers to the PREG algorithm, whereas for simplicity, sometimes we also use PREG to denote the network topology derived under the PREG algorithm. We do not explain what each PREG means if without confusion.

If the given graph is a UDG, PREG features all the properties that REG features, because for this case, PREG is reduced to REG. Note that since PREG is hoped to be practical, the following analysis does not depend on the UDG model, which REG very much depends on.

Theorem 3 (Properties of PREG). *(1) PREG(G) is connected if and only if G is connected; (2) PREG(G) is symmetric if every edge in the given graph G is symmetric; (3) The energy stretch factor of PREG is 1.*

The proof of theorem 3 is omitted since those properties are obvious. Planarity is another property often discussed in research on topology control. Unfortunately, the following theorem shows that planarity cannot be guaranteed for heterogeneous networks.

Theorem 4. *Connectivity and planarity cannot be simultaneously guaranteed for all MGs.*

Proof. To prove that, we need only an example as shown in Figure 2. Suppose $r(u) = r(v) = d(u, v)$, $r(s) = d(s, u)$, $r(t) = d(t, s)$, $d(s, t) < d(s, u) < d(s, v)$,

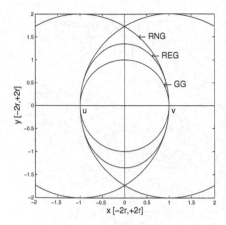

Fig. 1. Comparision of definitions of RNG, REG_4, and GG

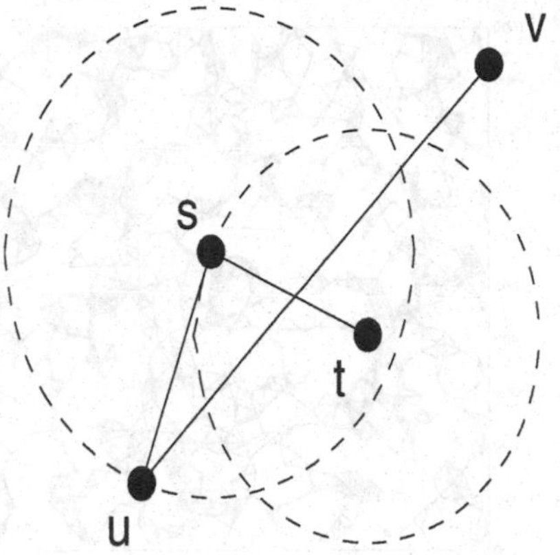

Fig. 2. Connectivity and Planarity cannot be simultaneously guaranteed

$d(s,t) < d(t,u)$, $d(s,t) < d(t,v)$. In order to achieve planarity, either edge (u,v) or (s,t) need to be taken away, which results in disconnectivity. That is to say, connectivity and planarity cannot be simultaneously guaranteed for all MGs.

So far, it is unknown whether PREG is sparse or not. But we can conclude an upper bound of the number of edges contained in PREG. If G is a MG, then $PREG(G)$ has at most $O(n^{8/5}log\gamma)$ edges, where $\gamma = r_{max}/r_{min}$ (r_{max} is the maximal transmit radius, and r_{min} is the minimal transmit radius). The conclusion depends on the previous work presented in [15,16]. Kapoor and Li have proved that $LGG_2(G)$ has at most $O(n^{8/5}log\gamma)$ edges [15]. The definition of $LGG_2(G)$ is this: An edge (u,v) is contained in $LGG_2(G)$ if and only if there is no another node x inside $disk(u,v)$ and both edge (u,x) and (x,v) are contained in G. Since it is obvious that $PREG(G) \subseteq LGG_2(G)$, $PREG(G)$ has at most $O(n^{8/5}log\gamma)$ edges.

That PREG does not feature planarity or even does not feature sparseness should not be regarded as a defect of PREG, since connectivity and planarity cannot be simultaneously guaranteed as shown by theorem 4. In fact, in real wireless sensor networks, connectivity is more important than planarity and sparseness.

The PREG algorithm is distributed. Each node in the network needs only to exchange information with its immediate neighbors. It is easily to conclude that, at each node, the time complexity of PREG is $O(N^2)$, and the space complexity is $O(N)$, where N is the number of its neighbors in the given graph. It runs without synchronization and localization. It works correctly for three-dimensional heterogeneous wireless sensor networks. It is practical, because it does not depend on any perfect assumption that most previous work highly depends on.

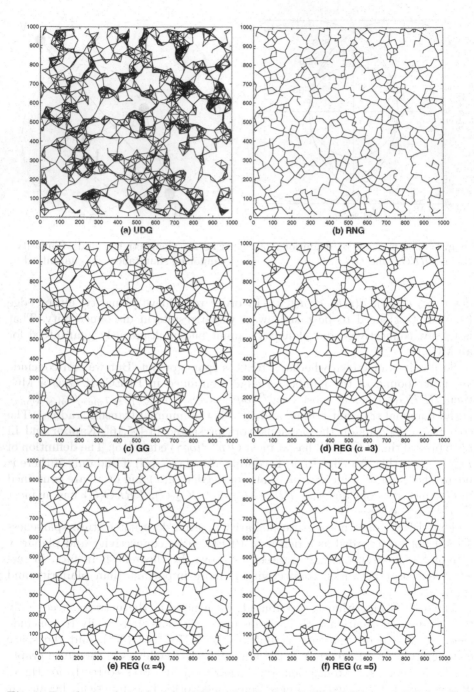

Fig. 3. Topologies derived under UDG, RNG, GG, REG_3, REG_4 and REG_5, there being 1000 nodes randomly deployed in a $1000m \times 1000m$ region, with a common transmission radius of 50m

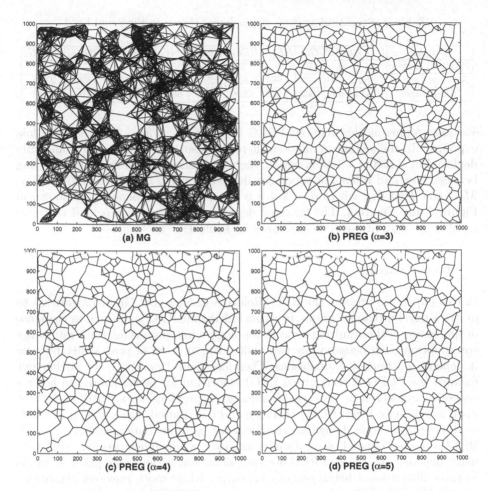

Fig. 4. Topologies derived under MG, $PREG_3$, $PREG_4$ and $PREG_5$, there being 1000 nodes randomly deployed in a $1000m \times 1000m$ region, their transmission radii varying between $50m$ and $100m$

6   Simulation Study

In this section, we evaluate the performance of RNG, GG, REG and PREG by simulation. It is shown that the simulation results coincide very well with the theoretical conclusions.

The first simulation is for REG. The network being homogeneous, there are 1000 location-aware nodes randomly deployed in a $1000m \times 1000m$ planar region with a common transmission radius of 50 meters. The second simulation is for PREG. Note that since PREG is designed to be practical, it works without any perfect assumptions. However, it is too difficult to simulate PREG in that sense. Therefore, for simplicity, we assume PREG is location-aware, and use the path loss model to compute the communication cost over a link, as we do for REG.

Table 1. Statistical analysis of topologies shown in Fig.3 and Fig.4

Graphs	UDG	RNG	GG	REG_3	REG_4	REG_5	MG	$PREG_3$	$PREG_4$	$PREG_5$
Maximal Degree	18	4	7	6	5	5	32	7	7	6
Average Degree	7.482	2.370	3.326	2.864	2.656	2.558	13.274	3.050	2.832	2.706
Total Edges	3741	1185	1663	1432	1328	1279	6637	1525	1416	1353

We may represent this reduced PREG as $PREG_\alpha$, where α is the path loss exponent. In the second simulation, there are also 1000 sensor nodes randomly deployed in a $1000m \times 1000m$ region, their transmission radii randomly varying between $50m$ and $100m$. The topologies derived under UDG, RNG, GG, REG_α, MG, and $PREG_\alpha$, where $\alpha = 3, 4, 5$ is the path loss exponent, are shown in Figure 3 and Figure 4. The maximal degree, the average degree and the total number of edges of each one are shown in Table 1.

7 Conclusions

In this paper, we propose the REG (Relative Energy-cost Graph) algorithm to derive a novel proximity graph. It is concluded that REG is optimal in the sense of sparseness of the resulting network topology while preserving the least energy consumption path between any two nodes. But it lacks of practicality because it depends on perfect assumptions. Therefore, based on REG, we further put forward the PREG (Practicalized REG) algorithm for power control in heterogeneous wireless sensor networks. Compared to previous work, PREG has three main advantages. First, PREG is simple and distributed. Each node in the network needs only to exchange information with its immediate neighbors. Second, PREG does not depend on position information, which much previous work very much depends on. Third, PREG does not make any strict assumption. It works in three-dimensional heterogeneous networks, while most previous algorithms do not. We make full-scale theoretical analyses of PREG followed by simulation study. It is concluded that PREG is better than other power control algorithms thanks to its high practicality and energy efficiency.

References

1. Poduri S, Pattem S, Krishnamachari B, Sukhatme G. A unifying framework for tunable topology control in sensor networks. Technical Report, CRES-05-004, Center for Robotics and Embedded Systems, University of Southern California, 2005.
2. Prakash R. Unidirectional links prove costly in wireless ad-hoc networks. In Proceedings of International Workshop on Discrete Algorithms and Methods for Mobile Computing and Communications, 1999.
3. Wattenhofer R, Zollinger A. XTC: A practical topology control algorithm for ad-hoc networks. In: Proceedings of International Parallel and Distributed Processing Symposium (IPDPS), 2004. 216-223.
4. Kirousis L.M, Kranakis E, Krizanc D, Pelc A. Power consumption in packet radio networks. Theoretical Computer Science, 2000, 243(1-2): 289-305.

5. Clementi A, Penna P, Silvestri R. Hardness results for the power range assignment problem in packet radio networks. In: Proceedings of the 2nd International Workshop on Approximation Algorithms for Combinatorial Optimization Problems (RANDOM/APPROX), 1999. 197-208.
6. Narayanaswamy S, Kawadia V, Sreenivas R.S, Kumar P.R. Power control in ad-hoc networks: theory, architecture, algorithm and implementation of the COMPOW protocol. In: Proceedings of European Wireless Conference, 2002. 156-162.
7. Kawadia V, Kumar P.R. Power control and clustering in ad-hoc networks. In: Proceedings of the IEEE Conference on Computer Communications (INFOCOM), 2003. 459-469.
8. Kubisch M, Karl H, Wolisz A, Zhong L.C, Rabaey J. Distributed algorithms for transmission power control in wireless sensor networks. In: Proceedings of IEEE Wireless Communications and Networking Conference (WCNC), 2003.
9. Li L, Halpern J.Y, Bahl P, Wang Y.M, Wattenhofer R. A cone-based distributed topology control algorithm for wireless multi-hop networks. IEEE/ACM Transactions on Networking, 2005, 13(1): 147-159.
10. Borbash S.A, and JenningsE.H. Distributed topology control algorithm for multi hop wireless networks. In: Proceedings of World Congress on Computational Intelligence (WCCI), Hawaii, 2002.
11. Bose P, Devroye L, Evans W, and Kirkpatrick D. On the spanning ratio of Gabriel graphs and beta-skeletons. In: Proceedings of the Latin American Theoretical Informatics (LATIN), 2002.
12. Li X.Y, Calinescu G, and Wan P. J. Distributed construction of planar spanner and routing for ad hoc networks. In: Proceedings of the IEEE Conference on Computer Communications (INFOCOM), 2002.
13. Li X.Y, Song W.Z, and Wang Y. Efficient topology control for wireless ad hoc networks with non-uniform transmission ranges. ACM Wireless Network (WINET), 2005,11(3): 255-264, 2005.
14. Li N, Hou J.C, and Sha L. Design and analysis of an MST-based topology control algorithm. In: Proceedings of the IEEE Conference on Computer Communications (INFOCOM), 2003.
15. Li N, Hou J.C. Topology control in heterogeneous wireless networks: problems and solutions. In: Proceedings of the IEEE Conference on Computer Communications (INFOCOM), 2004.
16. Kapoor S, and Li X.Y. Proximity structures for geometric graphs. International Journal of Computational Geometry and Applications, July, 2004.
17. Li X.Y, Song W.Z, Wang Y. Localized topology control for heterogeneous wireless sensor networks. ACM Transactions on Sensor Networks, to be published.
18. Li X.Y, Wan P. J, and Wang Y. Power efficient and sparse spanner for wireless ad hoc networks. In: Proceedings of the IEEE International Conference on Computer Communications and Networks, 2001, 564-567.
19. Kawadia V. Protocols and architecture for wireless ad hoc networks [PhD Dissertation]. Department of Electrical and Computer Engineering, University of Illinois at Urbana-Champaign, 2004.

Algorithms for Delay Constrained and Energy Efficiently Routing in Wireless Sensor Network*

Yuanli Wang[1], Xianghui Liu[1,2], Jing Ning[2], Jianping Yin[1], and Yongan Wu[1]

[1] School of Computer Science, National University of Defense Technology,
Changsha City, Hunan Province, 410073, PRC
[2] School of Electronic Science & Technology, National University of Defense Technology,
Changsha City, Hunan Province, 410073, PRC
LiuXH@tom.com

Abstract. The growing popularity of wireless sensor network applications has stimulated strong interest in extending quality of service support to existing routing protocols. Conventional wireless sensor network routing protocols usually concentrate on the constrained condition of 'shortest path' with minimum used energy. However, the path with minimum used energy can't provide the minimum end to end delay guarantee. Moreover, wireless sensor network is required to support the delay-sensitive traffic. So the reduction of the end to end delay is a new challenge for wireless sensor network. To this point, this paper mainly focuses on the node delay constrained energy efficiently routing algorithm.

1 Introduction

Recent advances in micro-electro-mechanical systems (MEMS) and low power and highly integrated digital electronics have led to the development of micro sensors [1~4]. Such sensors are generally equipped with data processing and communication capabilities and can send collected data, usually via radio transmitter, to a command center (sink) either directly or through a data concentration center (a gateway). The decrease in the size and cost of sensors, resulting from such technological advances, has fueled interest in the possible use of large set of disposable unattended sensors.

However, sensor nodes are constrained by transmission power, on-board energy, processing capacity and storage, and thus require careful resource management. Such constraints combined with a typical deployment of large number of sensor nodes have posed many challenges to the design and management of sensor networks. At the network layer, the challenges had lead researchers to find ways for energy efficiently routing algorithm. Yet it is not possible for us to build a global addressing scheme for the deployment of sheer number of sensor nodes. Therefore, classical IP-based protocols cannot be applied to sensor networks.

Due to such differences, many algorithms have been proposed for the problem of route in sensor networks. These routing mechanisms have considered the characteristics of sensor nodes along with the various architecture requirements.

Almost all of the routing protocols can be classified as data-centric, hierarchical or location-based protocols. Data-centric protocols are query-based and depend on the

---

* Supported by the National Natural Science Foundation of China under Grant No.60373023.

X. Cheng, W. Li, and T. Znati (Eds.): WASA 2006, LNCS 4138, pp. 632–642, 2006.

naming of desired data, which helps in eliminating many redundant transmissions. Hierarchical protocols aim at clustering the nodes so that cluster heads can do some aggregation and reduction of data in order to save energy. Location-based protocols utilize the position information to relay the data to the desired regions rather than the whole network. Among most proposed routing algorithm, the conventional way of routing in sensor networks is to route packets on the minimum-cost path from the source to the destination. The minimum-cost shortest path tree (rooted at the source) connecting all nodes can be constructed to identify the minimum-cost paths from source to base sink. In particular, the most recently works addresses the problem of minimizing the energy to transmit the data [4~8]. The limits of those rest with their sole consideration of energy. In addition to energy constraint, the data querying procedures in wireless sensor network have different demands in terms of bandwidth, reliability, delay and jitter. To our known, although many routing methods have been proposed, this previous work focused on how to find the correct route with energy used efficiently, but did not consider delay effect while sending messages and no much research has developed a sound strategy for route within its delay bound, thereby allows a tradeoff between delay and cost. The work presented in this paper is different from these previous results in that we develop distributed algorithms for delay constrained and energy efficiently routing in wireless sensor network.

The rest of this paper is structured as follows. In the remaining of this section, at first we present the network model and an algorithmic statement of the routing problem. Next we present algorithm for delay-constrained energy efficiently path selection. And at last we analyze the correctness of presented algorithm.

2 Network Model and Problem Formulation

Before outlining the system model, we introduce some necessary notation illustrated as table 1.

Table 1. Notation in the paper

Symbol	Semantics
$G(V,E)$	We consider multi-hop wireless networks. The network is modeled as a directed graph $G(V,E)$. The nodes of the graph correspond to individual transceivers and a directed edge (u,v) denotes that u can transmit to v directly
$C(e)$	Each link $e((u,v)\in E)$ is associated with an energy used value $E(e)$
$D(S)$	Each link $e((u,v)\in E)$ is associated with a delay value $D(e)$
$Path(u,v)$	$Path(u,v)$ denotes an unique path from sensor node u and v, where $u\in V \wedge v\in V$.
$E(Path(u,v))$	Represent the relative links (edges) of $Path(u,v)$

We assume that vertices V are embedded in the plane R^2. Each vertex (transceiver) u has an associated range denoted by $range(u)$. A necessary (but not sufficient) condition for a transceiver v to hear u is that v is within a distance $range(u)$ of u. Specifically, if transmission is not feasible from u to v either because v is outside the range of u or because of other reasons (such as the presence of an obstruction between u and v), then the edge $e(u,v)$ is not present in the graph $G(V,E)$.

The goal of delay constrained and energy efficiently routing, in general, is to find a resource efficient path that satisfies the constraint on the maximum packet delay and can be stated as follows:

Definition 1. Delay Constrained Energy Efficiently (DCE2) Problem: Consider a network that is represented by a directed graph $G(V,E)$, where V is the set of sensor nodes and E is the set of possibly asymmetric links. Each link $e((u,v)\in E)$ is associated with binary value $(C(e),D(e))$. With given a delay constraint δ, the problem is to find a path P from a source node u to a destination node v satisfied the delay constraint $D(P(u,v)) = \sum_{e\in P(u,v)} D(e) < \delta$ with the objective (cost function) $C(P(u,v)) = \sum_{e\in P(u,v)} C(e)$ is minimized over all paths satisfying delay constraint.

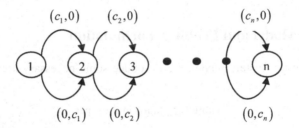

$$(c_1,0) \quad (c_2,0) \qquad\qquad (c_n,0)$$

$$(0,c_1) \quad (0,c_2) \qquad\qquad (0,c_n)$$

Fig. 1. Graph to show the reduction from the knapsack problem

Theorem 1. The DCE2 problem is NP-hard.

Proof. Given a path p and energy constraint C and delay constraint D. We say p is a feasible path if delay and cost constraint of path p is satisfied where the delay constraint of path is $D(p) = \sum_{e\in p} D(e) < D$ and cost constraint of path is $C(p) = \sum_{e\in p} C(e) < C$. And find a feasible path from u to v is to decide that whether such path exists.

From the theorem of computer complexity, if we can prove that finding a feasible path satisfying energy constraint and delay constraint is NP-Compete, then The DCE2 problem is NP-hard. Now we show the finding a feasible path with delay and cost constraints is NP-Complete.

We will provide a reduction from the knapsack problem. Recall that in the knapsack problem, we are given positive integers $c_1, c_2, \cdots, c_n$ and N, and the objective is to find a subset $S \subset \{1, 2, \cdots, n\}$ such that $\sum_{i \in S} c_i = N$.

From the knapsack problem, we construct a graph with vertices $\{1, 2, \cdots, n\}$. There are two edges from vertex i to $i+1$ with different binary value $(c_i, 0)$ and $(0, c_i)$. Figure 1 shows this scenario. Our objective is to find a path from vertex 1 to vertex n with cost constraint N and delay constraint $\sum_{i \in S} c_i = N$. It is easy to check that there is a path that satisfies the constraints if and only if there is a solution to knapsack problem. So the DCE2 problem is NP-hard.   ∎

The DCE2 problem has been widely considered by QoS path selection research in traditional IP network. Several computationally efficient heuristics have been proposed and the author proposed an algorithm that performs a breadth-first search to find the optimal solution for the DCE2 problem [9, 10]. However, the running time of this algorithm grows exponentially with the network size. Fully polynomial approximation schemes (FPAS) are already known for many NP-complete problems that can be solved by pseudo-polynomial algorithms. An efficiently ϵ-optimal approximation algorithms were proposed by Hassin [9], where algorithm produces a path with a energy that is at most ϵ-factor from the optimal one. Despite the algorithmic elegance of these algorithms, they are still too complex to be applied in sensor networks because this is source based.

In this paper at first we propose centralized algorithm and its distributed implementation for the delay constraint energy efficiently routing in wireless sensor network based on way presented by Baoxian Zhang   and Marwan Krunz [10]. At last our simulations indicate that routes obtained using our algorithm have much better performance in most instances than the routes obtained using the path algorithm by hop-count based shortest.

3 Routing Algorithms

The following assumptions are made about the system model. (1) Sensor nodes are deployed in an ad-hoc basis for unattended operation and they are static. And (2) each node in the network maintains a delay table and an energy table.

Without losing generality, let $P_{u,v}$ represent the set of path between the node u and v, where u and v are any two nodes in V. Let $p_{\min E}^{u,v}$ denotes the minimum energy path in set $P_{u,v}$ and $p_{\min D}^{u,v}$ denotes the minimum delay path in set $P_{u,v}$, where

$$C(p) = \sum_{e \in E(p)} C(e) \left(p \in P_{u,v} \right) \text{ and } D(p) = \sum_{e \in E(p)} D(e) \left(p \in P_{u,v} \right).$$

Consider the DCE2 problem with delay constraint δ and the algorithm is to find the path between the source node s and destination node d. The centralized algorithm is stated as figure 2.

```
Path function () //Centralized algorithm
{
For all every node v, compute the minimum delay path
from S to v. (1)
```

If $D\left(p_{\min D}^{s,d}\right) \geq \delta$ return null /* There is no feasible path */

```
Else
{
    For all every node v, compute the minimum energy path
    from S to v. (2)
```

If $D\left(p_{\min E}^{s,d}\right) < \delta$ return path $p_{\min E}^{s,d}$ /* minimum energy path
from S to d satisfies the delay constraint */

```
    Else
    {
        For every node v, compute the minimum delay path
        from v to d. (3)
        For every node v, compute the minimum energy path
        from v to d. (4)
        From the resulting 4|V| paths choose the one with
    the smallest energy which satisfies the delay
    constraint. (5)
    }
}
}
```

Fig. 2. Centralized Algorithm for DCE2 problem

For each node $v \in V$, the algorithm considers the four possible paths: $p_{\min E}^{s,v} \cup p_{\min E}^{v,d}$,
$p_{\min D}^{s,v} \cup p_{\min D}^{v,d}$, $p_{\min D}^{s,v} \cup p_{\min E}^{v,d}$ and $p_{\min E}^{s,v} \cup p_{\min D}^{v,d}$. Of the $4|V|$ possible paths, the
algorithm selects the one with the minimum energy provided that this path satisfies
the delay constraint. Steps 1 and 2 require two runs of Dijkstra's algorithm, while
Steps 3 and 4 require two runs of Reverse Dijkstra's. The running time of Step 5
is $O(|V|)$. Therefore, the overall complexity of Algorithm is $O(|V|^2)$.

Next we will analysis the performance of Algorithm. Let $Path^*$ and $Path^a$ denote
the optimal path and the path returned by Algorithm, respectively.

Lemma 1. For a node $v \in Path^*$, if $p_{\min E}^{s,v} \cup p_{\min E}^{v,d}$ is a feasible path,
then $C\left(Path^*\right) = C\left(Path^a\right)$.

Lemma 1 is to say if minimum energy path source node s and destination node d satisfies the delay constraint the path and returned by Algorithm, then it is optimal and the proof is trivial.

Lemma 2. For any node $v \in V$, if both $p_{\min D}^{s,v} \cup p_{\min E}^{v,d}$ and $p_{\min E}^{s,v} \cup p_{\min D}^{v,d}$ are feasible, then $D\left(p_{\min E}^{s,v} \cup p_{\min E}^{v,d} \right) < 2\delta - D(p_{\min D}^{s,d})$.

Proof. As $D\left(p_{\min D}^{s,v} \cup p_{\min D}^{v,d} \right) + D\left(p_{\min E}^{s,v} \cup p_{\min E}^{v,d} \right) < 2\delta$, so that

$$D\left(p_{\min E}^{s,v} \cup p_{\min E}^{v,d} \right) < 2\delta - D\left(p_{\min D}^{s,v} \cup p_{\min D}^{v,d} \right) \le 2\delta - D(p_{\min D}^{s,d}).$$

From the lemma above, the algorithm has below property.

Theorem 2. If $p_{\min E}^{s,v} \cup p_{\min E}^{v,d}$ is a feasible path with energy that is larger than the energy of the path returned by Algorithm, then it must be that $v \notin Path^*$.

If both $p_{\min D}^{s,v} \cup p_{\min E}^{v,d}$ and $p_{\min E}^{s,v} \cup p_{\min D}^{v,d}$ are feasible, where $v \in Path^*$, then $C(Path^a)(2\delta - D(p_{\min D}^{s,d})) \le C(Path^*)$.

It is obvious that the algorithm always returns a feasible path, if one exists. And the paper [10] shows the returned path by algorithm is loop-free.

4 Distributed Implement of Algorithm

As we know, the centralized algorithm introduced above is source based. In source-based routing algorithm, the source node performs the path computation and determines the full path in the connection request before sending the real data to the next hop. Source routing algorithm is rarely used in wireless sensor network because it needs lots extra communication effort to request other nodes to join the sending task. Instead, the vast majority of IP implementations rely on hop-by-hop (distributed) routing, in which all nodes along the path participate in the path computation task. To maintain compatibility with the current IP infrastructure, we present a distributed implementation of our delay constrained energy efficiently routing approach, which is based on hop-by-hop packet forwarding.

The reservation message travels along the minimum delay path until reaching a node from which the delay of its minimum energy path satisfies the delay constraint. From that node and on, the message travels along the Minimum energy path all the way to the destination. The distributed implement of algorithm is presented by paper [10] with replacing the path construction process by a path probing process and extend the probing direction to include both the minimum energy and minimum delay directions.

In general each node in the network maintains a delay table and an energy table. These tables entry for the node to a destination is replaced by the next hop along the minimum delay (minimum energy) path. Note that the nodes need not maintain the network topology and link-state information, as in source-based routing algorithms. The information in the delay and energy tables can be distributed to nodes using distance vector protocols [11] or based on a 'minimum prediction of delay (energy)' mechanism. The distance vector protocols act as to invoke the sensor discovery mechanisms to find the path to the destination, when a source wants to send to a destination.

Initially, the algorithm checks the feasibility of the minimum energy path from source s to destination d. If $D\left(p_{\min E}^{s,d}\right) < \delta$, the algorithm returns this path. Otherwise, the algorithm checks if a feasible path is available (by verifying that $D\left(p_{\min D}^{s,d}\right) < \delta$). If so, the algorithm tries to discover an appropriate relay node that results in a low-energy feasible path.

Before outlining distributed implement of algorithm, we introduce some necessary notation illustrated as table 2.

Table 2. Notation for distributed implement of algorithm

Symbol	Semantics
sum_D	Accumulated delay of path traversed by the probe message from the source node up to the current node.
sum_E	Accumulated energy of path traversed by the probe message from the source node up to the current node.
$Energy^*$	Energy of the best-known feasible path which initially set to $C\left(p_{\min D}^{s,d}\right)$. Once a relay node is discovered, the value in this field is adjusted (reduced) to reflect the energy of the new path.

In algorithm the probe reply message contains the identity of the relay node and the total energy of the discovered path. Without losing generality, the probe message that is sent along the minimum delay path direction, a probe reply is generated by the first relay node named v that satisfies $D\left(p_{\min D}^{s,v}\right) + D\left(p_{\min E}^{v,d}\right) < \delta$. This is because it is not possible to obtain a lower-energy path than $p_{\min D}^{s,v} \cup p_{\min E}^{v,d}$ by selecting another relay node on the minimum delay path from v to d. So there is no point is continuing the search beyond node v. This does not apply to the probe message sent along the minimum energy path, where in this case the search continues for a possibly better relay node. However, in this case, the search terminates unsuccessfully if the probe message sent along the minimum energy path encounters a node v for which $D\left(p_{\min E}^{s,v}\right) + D\left(p_{\min D}^{v,d}\right) \geq \delta$. This is because for any subsequent node w on the path $p_{\min E}^{s,d}$, the path $p_{\min E}^{s,w} \cup p_{\min E}^{w,d}$ cannot be feasible since

$$
\begin{aligned}
D&\left(p_{\min D}^{s,w} \cup p_{\min E}^{w,d}\right) \\
&= D\left(p_{\min D}^{s,w}\right) + D\left(p_{\min E}^{w,d}\right) \\
&= D\left(p_{\min D}^{s,v}\right) + D\left(p_{\min D}^{v,w}\right) + D\left(p_{\min E}^{w,d}\right) \\
&\geq D(p_{\min D}^{s,v}) + D(p_{\min E}^{v,d}) \\
&> \delta
\end{aligned}
$$

So there is no use in continuing to search for a relay node along the minimum energy path from v to d.

```
Void function () /*compute for individual node v*/
{
   if direction is to find minimum delay path
   {
      if  sum_D + D(p_{minE}^{v,d}) < δ /* node v is a relay node */{

         if  sum_E + C(p_{minE}^{v,d}) < Energy* /* path is better than the
current selected path */{

            V is a relay node and  Energy* = sum_E + C(p_{minE}^{v,d})

         }

      Send a probe reply message to source
      } else /* node v is not a relay node */
      {
         Search the next hop node named u in delay table with
sum_D = sum_D + D(v,u)  and sum_E = sum_E + C(v,u) ,  and Forward probe
query message.
      }
   else      /*   direction is to find minimum energy path */
   {
      if  sum_D + D(p_{minD}^{v,d}) < δ /* node v is a relay node */{

         if  sum_E + C(p_{minD}^{v,d}) < Energy* /* path is better than current
selected path */{

            V is a relay node and  Energy* = sum_E + C(p_{minD}^{v,d})

         }
      Send a probe reply message to source
   }
}
```

Fig. 3. Distributed Implement of Algorithm for DCE2 problem

When node s receives the two probe reply messages, it selects the path with the lower energy (if both messages contain empty relay node, then node source selects the minimum delay path from it to destination). A probe query message may visit up to $|V|-1$ nodes. Hence, the worst-case message complexity of algorithm is $O(|V|)$.

5 Simulation

At first we simulate the workload of network to maintain the energy table and delay table. As we know, the vector distance protocols use traditional routing tables, one entry per destination. Without source routing, they rely on routing table entries to propagate a reply message back to the source and, subsequently, to route data packets to the destination. An important feature of vector distance protocols is the maintenance of timer-based states in each node, regarding utilization of individual routing table entries. A routing table entry is expired if not used recently. We care about the number of routing packets transmitted to maintain table. Each hop-wise transmission of a routing packet is counted as one transmission.

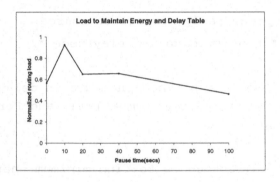

Fig. 4. Load to Maintain Energy and Delay Table

The algorithm described in the previous section was simulated over a network of 100 nodes randomly distributed over a square of side 15 units. Each node was assumed to have a maximum communication radius of 3 units. The energy consumption for sending a packet from node u to node v was taken to be $e_{u,v} = c_1 + c_2 d^4$, with $c_2 = 0.1 * c_1$. This corresponds to a deterministic path loss model over an AWGN channel, where the received power decays as $1/d^4$, over a distance d. The constant c_1 corresponds to the fixed energy cost of transmitting a unit of information between any two nodes. All the nodes were assumed to have equal initial energy. Recall $Path^*$ and $Path^a$ denote the optimal path and the path returned by Algorithm, respectively. And more precisely, with definition the inefficiency of algorithm as:

$$inefficiency = \frac{C(Path^a) - C(Path^*)}{C(Path^*)}$$

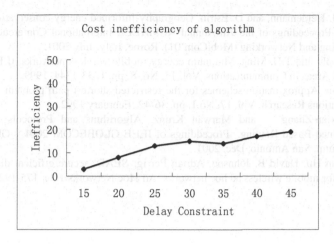

Fig. 5. Cost inefficiency of algorithm compare with optimal

It seems the algorithm can achieve good average cost performance.

6 Conclusions

In this paper, we presented an approach for delay constrained energy efficiently routing in Wireless sensor networks. The approach is based on simple heuristics for finding a low-energy delay-constrained path in a network. In addition, however, we are interested in examining the performance, such as the experimental results including the metrics of the end-to-end delay, energy consumptions, and path selection overheads. This is our effort to do more experiments by simulation next.

References

1. I. F. Akyildiz et al. Wireless sensor networks: a survey. Computer Networks, Vol. 38, pp. 393-422, March 2002.
2. K. Sohrabi, et al. Protocols for self-organization of a wireless sensor network. IEEE Personal Communications, Vol. 7, No. 5, pp. 16-27, October 2000.
3. J.M. Rabaey, et al. PicoRadio supports ad hoc ultra low power wireless networking. IEEE Computer, Vol. 33, pp. 42-48, July 2000.
4. R. H. Katz, J. M. Kahn and K. S. J. Pister. Mobile Networking for Smart Dust. Proceedings of the 5th Annual ACM/IEEE International Conference on Mobile Computing and Networking (MobiCom'99), Seattle, WA, August 1999.
5. M. Youssef, M. Younis and K. Arisha. A constrained shortest-path energy-aware routing algorithm for wireless sensor networks. Proceedings of the IEEE Wireless Communication and Networks Conference (WCNC 2002), Orlando, FL, March 2002.
6. M. Younis, P. Munshi and E. Al-Shaer. Architecture for Efficient Monitoring and Management of Sensor Networks. Proceedings of the IFIP/IEEE Workshop on End-to-End Monitoring Techniques and Services (E2EMON'03), Belfast, Northern Ireland, September 2003.

7. Y. Xu, J. Heidemann, and D. Estrin. Geography-informed energy conservation for ad hoc routing. Proceedings of the 7th Annual ACM/IEEE International Conference on Mobile Computing and Networking (MobiCom'01), Rome, Italy, July 2001.
8. V. Rodoplu and T.H. Ming. Minimum energy mobile wireless networks. IEEE Journal of Selected Areas in Communications, Vol. 17, No. 8, pp. 1333-1344, 1999.
9. R. Hassin. Approximation schemes for the restricted shortest path problem. Mathematics of Operations Research, Vol. 17, No.1, pp. 36-42, February 1992.
10. 10. Baoxian Zhang   and Marwan Krunz. Algorithms and Protocols for Stateless Constrained-Based Routing. Proceddings of IEEE GLOBECOM 2001 – Global Internet Symposium, San Antonio, Dec. 2001.
11. Yih-Chun Hu, David B. Johnson, Adrian Perrig. SEAD: secure efficient distance vector routing for mobile wireless ad hoc networks. Ad Hoc Networks 1(1): 175-192 (2003)

The Effective Radius Model for Multi-hop Wireless Networks

Liran Ma[1], Weidong Jiang[2], Kai Xing[1], and E.K. Park[3,*]

[1] Department of Computer Science, The George Washington University,
Washington D.C.20052, U.S.A
[2] Institute of Electronic Science and Engineering,
The National University of Defense Technology, P.R. China
[3] Computer Science and Electrical Engineering Department, School of Computing and
Engineering, University of Missouri at Kansas City, Kansas City, MO 64110, U.S.A

Abstract. In this paper, we introduce a novel model, termed as *Effective Radius* (ER), to calculate the expected number of t-hop neighbors in a multi-hop wireless network with a uniform node distribution on the average. This ER model is an analytical tool that recursively computes a t-hop effective radius for $t = 2, 3, \cdots$. The total number of nodes covered by the disk with a t-hop effective radius equals to the expected number of nodes reachable through at most t hops in the original physical topology. We conduct extensive simulation studies to validate our model and the results demonstrate that the ER model is accurate and can be adaptive to different deployment scenarios. Our findings have interesting applications to the design and evaluation of multi-hop wireless networks.

Keywords: Multi-hop Wireless networks, Effective Radius model, t-hop neighborhood.

1 Introduction

A group of wireless nodes that wish to communicate may self-organize into a multi-hop wireless network, i.e., an ad hoc network, a sensor network, or a mesh network. Each node has a limited transmission range that covers a disk centered at the node. Node u can receive the signal from node v if it is within the transmission range of the sender v. Otherwise, two nodes communicate through multi-hop wireless links by employing intermediate nodes as relay points.

The expected number of one-hop neighbors[1] per node, also known as the node degree, is a fundamental property of a multi-hop wireless network. It is usually associated with the connectivity of the network. This is particularly true for random graphs where the graph is almost certainly connected if its average node degree is above some threshold [1]. The indications of the node degree have been extensively studied in [2, 3, 4]. However, knowing such information is not enough to explore other important characteristics of multi-hop wireless networks. The expected number of t-hop neighbors, where $t > 1$, plays an equally important role in many application scenarios.

---

* This material is based upon work supported by (while serving at) the National Science Foundation.
[1] Nodes that can be reached via one hop.

X. Cheng, W. Li, and T. Znati (Eds.): WASA 2006, LNCS 4138, pp. 643–651, 2006.

For example, when estimating the control message overheads of routing protocols such as AODV [5] and DSR [6], which mainly utilize flooding with a bounded TTL (Time-To-Live) value to perform route discoveries, it is helpful to have the knowledge of the number of reachable t-hop neighbors, where $t = 2, 3, 4, \cdots$. In addition, other classical problems like fault tolerant node deployment [7], topology control [8, 9], and multi-path routing [10], can be better explored with the information of t-hop neighbors.

Recently, security provisioning in multi-hop networks has become a central concern. It is indicated that the number of t-hop neighbors plays an important role in assisting security protocol design and analysis. For instance, in order to enhance data confidentiality, Lou, Liu, and Fang [11] propose to deliver secret messages via multiple paths. As a result, precise information about t-hop neighbors is required. In [12], *multi-hop path reinforcement* technique is employed to strengthen the security of an established link key. Moreover, for authentication schemes using en-route filtering methods [13, 14] to filter out injected packets, pairwise keys need to be setup among nodes that are some t-hop away. Clearly, all these mechanisms require the estimated number of t-hop neighbors.

Nevertheless, calculating the expected number of t-hop neighbors, denoted as d_t, is a non-trivial problem due to the randomness of the node positions (as we shall see in Section 2). Chan, Perrig, and Song [12] claims that $d_t = \pi * (t^2 - (t-1)^2) * \phi$, where ϕ is the node density on the average. Intuitively, this result only gives the upper bound of d_t.

As a matter of fact, lacking a sound method to calculate d_t often becomes a barrier in the design and actual deployment of multi-hop wireless networks. Indeed, it is such a concern that has motivated our work. In this paper, we propose a novel *Effective Radius (ER)* model to calculate d_t, the expected number of t-hop neighbors under a uniform random node distribution.

We explore the problem of determining the number of t-hop neighbors using a probabilistic approach. Assuming all nodes have a fixed transmission range R. Given the node density ϕ, we derive a series of equations to calculate d_t and the t-hop effective radius R_t^e that can cover $\sum_{i=1}^{t} d_t$ number of nodes. The effective radius model is an analytical tool that can recursively compute R_t^e and therefore derive d_t for $t = 2, 3, \cdots$. This ER model is evaluated through extensive simulation studies. Our results indicate that the ER model is efficient and accurate for moderate and high density multi-hop networks. To the best of our knowledge, this is a pioneer work in deriving the expected number of t-hop neighbors. Our major contributions are two-fold.

1. We propose a novel analytical model, termed as *Effective Radius*, for calculating the expected number of t-hop neighbors in a multi-hop wireless network.
2. Extensive simulation studies on different network deployment models are presented in detail, demonstrating that the ER model can accurately estimate d_t with simple calculations.

The remaining parts of this paper are organized as follows. The ER model is proposed in Section 2 and evaluated through simulation studies in Section 3. We conclude our paper in Section 4.

2   Effective Radius Model

In this section, we present our *Effective Radius* (ER) model to identify the expected number of t-hop neighbors[2] (d_t) a wireless node may have, where $t = 2, 3, \cdots$, in a uniformly randomly deployed large-scale multi-hop wireless network. The notations listed in Table 1 are utilized throughout the whole model derivation procedure.

Table 1. Notations

N	The total number of nodes
A	The area of the deployment region
R	Transmission range
r	The Euclidian distance between two arbitrary nodes
t	Hop count
R_t^e	The effective radius of the tth-hop
d_t	The number of t-hop neighbors
P_t^a	The conditional probability of a node being a t-hop neighbor

2.1   Network Model and Assumptions

Consider a multi-hop wireless network with (i) a uniform random node distribution on an average spatial sense, (ii) no inter-node interference (INI), and (iii) omnidirectional transmission from each node. For simplicity, we assume that the wireless nodes are distributed in a vast terrain (e.g., square or disk) such that boundary effects can be ignored.

Each node is assumed to transmit with a fixed radio power. Two nodes can communicate directly with each other if and only if they are separated at most R apart.

2.2   Model Derivation

We assume that there are N nodes uniformly distributed in the deployment region with an area of A. Thus, an arbitrary node u can cover $d_1 = \pi R^2 \frac{N}{A} - 1$ nodes within one hop on the average. Now, how to derive d_t, where $t = 2, 3, \cdots$, the expected number of t-hop neighbors that an arbitrary node may have? In the next, we introduce our ER model to recursively compute these values.

In the first place, we consider the case of $t = 2$. Let v be another arbitrary node whose Euclidian distance to u is denoted by r. If $r \le R$, v is a one-hop neighbor of u; if $r > 2R$, v can not be reached by u via two hops. Therefore, v is a two-hop neighbor of u if and only if (i) $R < r \le 2R$ and (ii) u and v share at least one immediate neighbor[3].

Let E_1 be the event that the distance $r \in (R, 2R]$. Let E_2 be the event that u and v have at least one common immediate neighbor. Given $R < r \le 2R$, $Pr[E_2|E_1]$ equals to the probability that at least one of the d_1 immediate neighbors of u falls into the region covered by both u and v. This overlapping area is denoted by A_1^o, as shown in Fig. 1(a). Thus, we have

---

[2] In shortest path.
[3] A one-hop neighbor can also be called an immediate neighbor.

$$Pr[E_2|E_1] = 1 - (1 - \frac{A_1^o}{\pi R^2})^{d_1}, \tag{1}$$

where A_1^o is defined as Eq. (2).

$$A_1^o = 2R^2 \arccos(\frac{r}{2R}) - \frac{r}{2}\sqrt{4R^2 - r^2}. \tag{2}$$

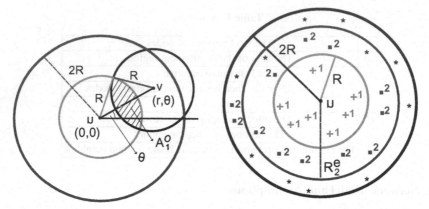

(a) v is a two-hop neighbor of u.   (b) The effective two-hop radius R_2^e of u.

Fig. 1. The two-hop neighborhood and the effective two-hop neighborhood of a node u

Based on Eq. (1), the expected value of $Pr[E_2|E_1]$ throughout the annulus region from R to $2R$ (see Fig. 1(a)), denoted by P_2^a, can be represented by

$$P_2^a = \frac{\int_0^{2\pi} d\theta \int_R^{2R}(1 - (1 - \frac{A_1^o}{\pi R^2})^{d_1})rdr}{\pi((2R)^2 - R^2)}. \tag{3}$$

As a result, the number of u's two-hop neighbors, denoted by d_2, follows

$$d_2 = (3\pi R^2)\frac{N}{A}P_2^a. \tag{4}$$

Directly computing the exact number of t-hop neighbors is a difficult problem when t is larger than two. Therefore, we introduce the ER model to facilitate this computation. Let D_t be the expected number of neighbors that are at most t-hop away. In our ER model, the effective radius of the t-hop coverage of a node is defined as the radius of a virtual disk centered at the node that can cover D_t number of nodes.

For example, Fig. 1(b) depicts the effective radius for the case of two hops. In this figure, the virtual disk centered at u with a radius of R_2^e covers $d_1 + d_2$ number of nodes in total. These covered nodes include all the one-hop neighbors (labelled with plus signs), a number of two-hop neighbors (labelled with dots), and a few other nodes (labelled with star signs). Note that the number of two-hop neighbors that fall out of the virtual disk equals to the number of nodes that can't be reached from u within two hops but fall into this virtual disk.

Accordingly, the effective radius R_2^e for the two-hop case can be calculated as follows.

$$\pi(R_2^e)^2\frac{N}{A} = d_1 + d_2 + 1. \tag{5}$$

Plug $d_1 = \pi R^2 \frac{N}{A} - 1$ and Eq. (4) into Eq. (5), we obtain

$$R_2^e = \sqrt{R^2 + 3R^2 P_2^a}. \tag{6}$$

Now we are ready to derive the number of three-hop neighbors of u. In our ER model, v's transmission range remains to be R while u's transmission range is set to be R_2^e. In other words, the virtual disk with a radius R_2^e centered at u represents u's two-hop coverage. In this case, v is a three-hop neighbor of u if and only if (i) $R_2^e < r \le R_2^e + R$ and (ii) u's virtual disk covers at least one of v's immediate neighbors.

Let P_3^a be the probability that v is a three-hop neighbor of u given that the distance between u and v is in the range of $(R_2^e, R_2^e + R]$. With a similar analysis, we obtain

$$P_3^a = \frac{\int_0^{2\pi} d\theta \int_{R_2^e}^{(R_2^e+R)}(1 - (1 - \frac{A_2^o}{\pi R^2})^{d_1})r dr}{\pi((R_2^e + R)^2 - (R_2^e)^2)}, \tag{7}$$

where A_2^o, the overlapping area covered by both u and v as shown in Fig 2(a), is regulated by Eq. (8).

$$A_2^o = R^2 \arccos(\frac{r^2 + R^2 - (R_2^e)^2}{2rR})$$
$$+ (R_2^e)^2 \arccos(\frac{r^2 + (R_2^e)^2 - R^2}{2rR_2^e})$$
$$- \frac{1}{2}\sqrt{4r^2(R_2^e)^2 - (r^2 - R^2 + (R_2^e)^2)^2}. \tag{8}$$

Thus, the number of u's three-hop neighbors can be approximated by

$$d_3 = \pi((R_2^e + R)^2 - (R_2^e)^2)\frac{N}{A}P_3^a. \tag{9}$$

And the equivalent radius for three hops is

$$R_3^e = \sqrt{(R_2^e)^2 + ((R_2^e + R)^2 - (R_2^e)^2)P_3^a}. \tag{10}$$

By recursively applying this procedure, we get the probability P_t^a of v being u's t-hop neighbor given that the Euclidean distance r between u and v satisfies $R_{t-1}^e < r \le R_{t-1}^e + R$, the expected number of u's t-hop neighbors d_t, and the equivalent radius R_t^e as follows.

$$P_t^a = \frac{\int_0^{2\pi} d\theta \int_{R_{t-1}^e}^{(R_{t-1}^e+R)}(1 - (1 - \frac{A_{t-1}^o}{\pi R^2})^{d_1})r dr}{\pi((R_{t-1}^e + R)^2 - (R_{t-1}^e)^2)}, \tag{11}$$

$$d_t = \pi((R_{t-1}^e + R)^2 - (R_{t-1}^e)^2)\frac{N}{A}P_t^a, \tag{12}$$

and

$$R_t^e = \sqrt{(R_{t-1}^e)^2 + ((R_{t-1}^e + R)^2 - (R_{t-1}^e)^2)P_t^a}. \tag{13}$$

Our ER model will be validated through simulation studies in the following section.

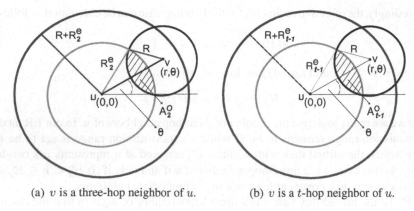

(a) v is a three-hop neighbor of u.   (b) v is a t-hop neighbor of u.

Fig. 2. Effective radius for t-hop neighbors

3   Evaluation of Effective Radius Model

In this section, we evaluate the performance of our ER model through simulation studies that complement our analysis.

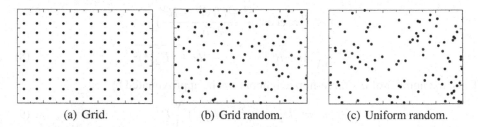

(a) Grid.   (b) Grid random.   (c) Uniform random.

Fig. 3. Deployment models

Network Model. We consider a square terrain in which nodes are deployed according to the following three models (shown in Fig. 3):

- **Gird:** In a $\sqrt{N} \times \sqrt{N}$ grid deployment, each of the N nodes is located in the intersection of a grid. This is a deterministic placement.
- **Grid random:** Grid random deployment is similar to the grid deployment except that every node is placed in a uniform random manner within a grid instead of the intersection.
- **Uniform random:** In a uniform random deployment, each sensor falls at any location in the deployment area with an equal likelihood, independent of the other sensors.

The reason that we choose these three models is to examine the adaptivity of the ER model to different deployment scenarios given equal node density on the average.

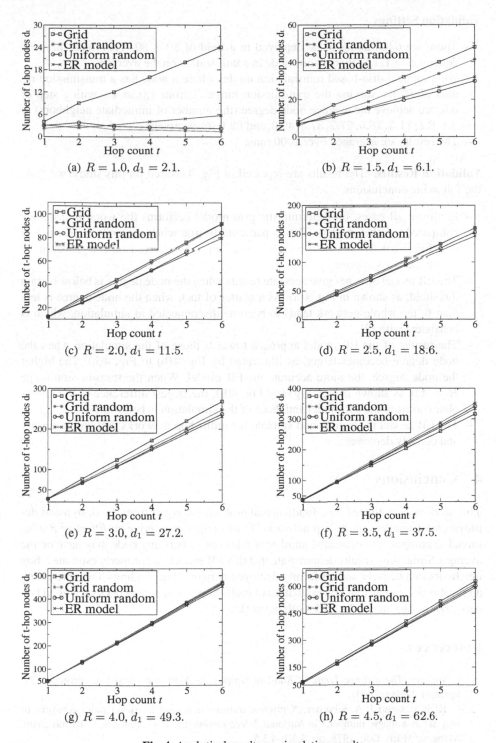

(a) $R = 1.0$, $d_1 = 2.1$.

(b) $R = 1.5$, $d_1 = 6.1$.

(c) $R = 2.0$, $d_1 = 11.5$.

(d) $R = 2.5$, $d_1 = 18.6$.

(e) $R = 3.0$, $d_1 = 27.2$.

(f) $R = 3.5$, $d_1 = 37.5$.

(g) $R = 4.0$, $d_1 = 49.3$.

(h) $R = 4.5$, $d_1 = 62.6$.

Fig. 4. Analytical results *vs.* simulation results

Validation Settings

- There are 6400 nodes to be deployed in a field of 80×80. Therefore, the node density $\phi = 1$, i.e., there is one node in a unit square on the average.
- We assume a disc-based transmission model where a node has a transmission radius of R. By varying the transmission range R from 1.0 to 4.5 with a step of 0.5, we achieve the average node degree (the number of immediate neighbors) of 2.1, 6.1, 11.5, 18.6, 27.2, 37.5, 49.3, and 62.6, respectively.
- The results are averaged over 1000 runs.

Validation Results. The results are reported in Fig. 4. Based on this study, we draw the following conclusions.

- In almost all cases, the deterministic grid model performs the worst in accuracy compared to other models. This is particularly true when the node degree is low (e.g. Fig. 4(a)). The reason is because our ER model is derived under a probabilistic deployment assumption.
- The ER model does not give accurate results when the node degree is below certain threshold, as shown in Fig. 4(a). As a matter of fact, when the node degree is less than 6, the whole network tends to become disconnected in simulation, which is consistent with [2].
- The results of the ER model approach towards those of the simulation when the node degree becomes larger, as illustrated by Fig. 4(b) to Fig. 4(h). The higher the node degree, the more accurate the ER model. When the transmission range $R \geq 4.0$, as shown in Fig. 4(g) and Fig. 4(h), the largest difference of the results obtained from the ER model and those of the simulation is below 3.5%.
- The ER model is accurate and suitable for multi-hop networks that are uniformly and densely deployed.

4   Conclusions

This work was motivated by a fundamental problem emerged from the design and deployment of wireless multi-hop networks. In this paper, we derive an *Effective Radius* model to compute the estimated number of t-hop neighbors any node may have on the average. Simulation results demonstrate that this ER model can properly estimate t-hop neighbors in a densely and uniformly deployed network. Our findings have interesting applications in the design and evaluation of multi-hop wireless networks such as ad hoc networks, sensor networks, and mesh networks.

References

1. J. Spencer, *The Strange Logic of Random Graphs.*   Algorithms and Combinatorics 22, Springer-Verlag, 2001.
2. L. Kleinrock and J. A. Silvester, "Optimum transmission radii in packet radio networks or why six is a magic number," in *National Telecommunications Conference.*   Birmingham, Alabama: IEEE, Dec. 1978, pp. 4.3.1–4.3.5.

3. C. Bettstetter, "On the Minimum Node Degree and Connectivity of a Wireless Multihop Network," in *The ACM Symposium on Mobile Adhoc Networking and Computing (MOBIHOC 2002)*, Lausanne, Switzerland, June 9–11 2002, pp. 80–91.

4. F. Xue and P. Kumar, "The number of neighbors needed for connectivity of wireless networks," *Wireless Networks*, vol. 10, no. 2, pp. 169–181, March 2004.

5. C. E. Perkins and E. M. Royer, "Ad-hoc on-demand distance vector routing," in *Proceedings of the Second IEEE Workshop on Mobile Computer Systems and Applications*. IEEE Computer Society, 1999, p. 90.

6. D. B. Johnson, D. A. Maltz, and J. Broch, "DSR: The dynamic source routing protocol for multihop wireless ad hoc networks," in *Ad Hoc Networking*, C. Perkins, Ed. Addison-Wesley, 2001, ch. 5, pp. 139–172. [Online]. Available: http://monarch.cs.rice.edu/monarch-papers/dsr-chapter00.ps

7. X.-Y. Li, P.-J. Wan, Y. Wang, and C.-W. Yi, "Fault tolerant deployment and topology control in wireless networks," in *MobiHoc '03: Proceedings of the 4th ACM international symposium on Mobile ad hoc networking & computing*. New York, NY, USA: ACM Press, 2003, pp. 117–128.

8. C. Schurgers, V. Tsiatsis, S. Ganeriwal, and M. Srivastava, "Topology Management for Sensor Networks: Exploiting Latency and Density," in *The ACM Symposium on Mobile Adhoc Networking and Computing (MOBIHOC 2002)*, Lausanne, Switzerland, June 9–11 2002, pp. 135–145.

9. J. Pan, Y. T. Hou, L. Cai, Y. Shi, and S. X. Shen, "Topology control for wireless sensor networks," in *MobiCom '03: Proceedings of the 9th annual international conference on Mobile computing and networking*. New York, NY, USA: ACM Press, 2003, pp. 286–299.

10. A. Nasipuri, R. Castaneda, and S. R. Das, "Performance of multipath routing for on-demand protocols in mobile ad hoc networks," *Mob. Netw. Appl.*, vol. 6, no. 4, pp. 339–349, 2001.

11. W. Lou, W. Liu, and Y. Fang, "Spread: Enhancing data confidentiality in mobile ad hoc networks." in *INFOCOM*, 2004, pp. 2404–2413.

12. H. Chan, A. Perrig, and D. Song, "Random key predistribution schemes for sensor networks," in *SP '03: Proceedings of the 2003 IEEE Symposium on Security and Privacy*. IEEE Computer Society, 2003, p. 197.

13. S. Zhu, S. Setia, S. Jajodia, and P. Ning, "An interleaved hop-by-hop authentication scheme for filtering of injected false data in sensor networks." in *IEEE Symposium on Security and Privacy*, 2004, pp. 259–271.

14. H. Yang, F. Ye, Y. Yuan, S. Lu, and W. Arbaugh, "Toward resilient security in wireless sensor networks," in *MobiHoc '05: Proceedings of the 6th ACM international symposium on Mobile ad hoc networking and computing*. New York, NY, USA: ACM Press, 2005, pp. 34–45.

Modeling and Analysis for an Enhanced Three-Tier Dynamic Location Management in 3G*

Jiachun Wu, Hao Zhang, Jianxin Liao, Xiaomin Zhu, and Bo Yang

State Key Laboratory of Networking and Switching Technology,
Beijing University of Posts and Telecommunications, Beijing 100876, China
wujiachun@ebupt.com

Abstract. Location management is a key function in mobile communication systems to guarantee the mobile terminals to continuously receive services. In this paper, we study an enhanced movement-based location management scheme for 3G cellular networks where the home location registers, gateway location registers and visitor location registers form a three-tier hierarchical mobility database structure. Furthermore, we formulate analytically the cost model of location update and paging for the proposed scheme and compare the proposed scheme with the basic movement-based location management scheme. The outcomes show that the enhanced movement-based location management scheme outperforms the other scheme.

1 Introduction

Location management is a key function in mobile network. The location management of GSM [1] and ANSI-41 [2] is based on two-tier mobility databases: HLR (Home Location Register) and VLR (Visitor Location Register). Location update is performed when mobile terminal crosses LA (Location Area): mobile terminal sends register request to VLR and the VLR sends register request to HLR. HLR updates its VLR address and notifies the old VLR to delete user profile. When a caller calls for the callee, the MSC (Mobile Switch Center) queries the HLR of the callee. And the HLR queries VLR serving the callee. VLR returns the address to HLR and HLR forwards it to the MSC. The number of HLR is few in 2G networks, so the HLR self and the signal traffic load between the HLR and VLR will be the bottleneck.

In 3G networks, in order to decrease the signaling traffic load between HLR and VLR, GLR (Gateway Location Register) is proposed in specification 3GPP 23.119 [3]. The GLR is a node between the VLR and HLR, and located in the visited network. It handles location management of roaming subscribers in visited network without involving the HLR in every change of LA. Therefore, the signaling traffic between the

* This work is jointly supported by: (1) National Science Fund for Distinguished Young Scholars (No. 60525110); (2) Program for New Century Excellent Talents in University (No. NCET-04-0111); (3) Specialized Research Fund for the Doctoral Program of Higher Education (No. 20030013006); (4) Development Fund Project for Electronic and Information Industry (Mobile Service and Application System Based on 3G); (5) Development Fund Key Project for Electronic and Information Industry (Core Service Platform for Next Generation Network).

visited mobile system and the home mobile system will be reduced and the location updating and the handling of user profile data across network boundaries are optimized.

Two basic operations are involved in mobility management: location update and paging. Location update is the process through which system tracks the location of mobile users that are not in conversation. The up-to-date location information of a mobile user is reported by the mobile terminal dynamically. Paging is the process that system searches for the mobile user by sending polling signals to cells in the location area. There are two kinds of location update schemes: static location update schemes and dynamic location update schemes. In the static location update schemes, the size of a LA and PA is fixed. Every cell in a LA is paged each time when a call arrives for any mobile terminal currently registered in the LA. Location update is performed when the mobile terminal crosses the boundary of LA. The existing 2G mobile networks adopt the static location management scheme. In the dynamic location update schemes, the location area size is determined dynamically according the changes of mobility and calling patterns of mobile terminal. Three kinds of dynamic location update schemes [4-10]: distance-based, time-based, movement-based, have been proposed. In distance-based location update schemes [4, 5], location update is performed whenever the distance between the current cell and the last cell where the update is performed is d. For time-based location update schemes [6, 7], the location update is performed every t units of time. In movement-based location update schemes [8-10], the location update is performed whenever the mobile completes d boundary crossings between cells. The value d is the threshold.

Most existing movement-based schemes only consider that a VLR location update occurs when the mobile terminal completes d movements between cells, and fail to consider the case that a VLR location update also occurs when the mobile terminal crosses an LA boundary. And most existing movement-based schemes only take 2G mobile networks into consideration. Ref [11] considers the both two cases. But the movement-based scheme in Ref [11] only counts the movement number and does not take locality into account. In many situations, mobile terminal roams zigzag between a few adjacent cells and when the cell boundary crossings exceeds the threshold, location update is performed. It is apparent that the location update is not necessary. This paper, based on hexagonal cell configuration, carefully analyzes the state model for enhanced movement-based location update scheme in which the threshold is the distance between rings and presents the cost for location update and paging. The contrast of our dynamic location update scheme with Ref [11] dynamic location update is taken.

The rest of the article is structured as follows. In section 2, we briefly introduce the hexagonal cell configuration in location management for 3G network. Section 3 presents the cost modeling of location update and paging for the enhanced movement-based dynamic location management for three-tier location management in 3G. In section 4, Experiments were carried out to contrast the model with the basic movement-based location dynamic management scheme. At last, the conclusion is presented.

2   Location Management for 3G Networks

Fig. 1 shows the three-tier location management architecture in 3G [3]. The service area in 3G is partitioned into many GLAs (Gateway Location Area) and a GLA is further partitioned into many LAs. A HLR location update is performed when a mobile terminal crosses the boundary of a GLA. A GLR location update is performed when a mobile terminal crosses the boundary of an LA. When a mobile terminal roams in a GLA, only the GLR location update is performed and the HLR location update is not performed. So the signaling traffic load between the Home Network and Visited Network is reduced. GLR keeps the profile information of a mobile terminal until a *Cancel Location* message is received from the HLR.

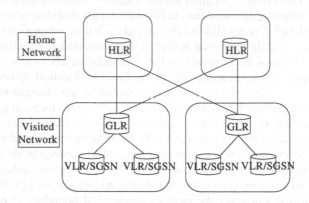

Fig. 1. Location management database architecture in 3G

The relationship between the GLR and the HLR in 3G wireless systems is the same as that between the VLR and the HLR in 2G wireless systems in terms of the signaling traffic for location management. From the viewpoint of the VLR at the visited network, the GLR can be treated as the roaming user's HLR. From the viewpoint of the HLR at the home network, the GLR can be treated as the VLR.

For the convenience of analysis, suppose that cells in 3G network are isomorphic and each cell has the same size. Each cell is surrounded by rings of cells. The innermost ring (ring 0 in Fig. 2) consists of only one cell and we call it is the center cell. Ring 0 is surrounded by ring 1 which in turn is surrounded by ring 2, and so on.

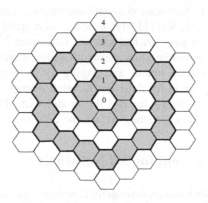

Fig. 2. Hexagonal cell configuration

In this paper, enhanced movement-based dynamic location management is considered. The location update scheme is: the cell where the mobile terminal performs the location update is set Ring-0; when mobile terminal moves from Ring-0 to Ring-K, the location update is performed. When the mobile terminal crosses the boundary of LA, the location update is performed. The paging scheme is: when a call for a terminal arrives, cells in the area from Ring-0 to Ring-(k-1) are all paged.

3 Analysis Model for Three-Tier Dynamic Location Management

3.1 The Model for Location Update Probability

For the hexagonal cell configuration given in Fig. 2, we suppose that each mobile terminal resides in a cell for a time period then moves to one of its neighbors with equal probability. So the mobility of the mobile terminal is a random walk model in a one-dimensional hexagonal plan [12] as Fig. 3 shows. For the state diagram given in Fig. 3, the state presents the distance between the cell where the mobile terminal currently resides and the cell where the mobile terminal updates its location.

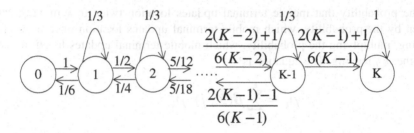

Fig. 3. State transition diagram

Fig. 3 shows that when the distance between two layers exceeds K, the mobile terminal should update location once again. So stake K is an absorbing state and state 0 is a barrier state. The one step transition matrix P_k is

$$
P_k =
\begin{bmatrix}
0 & 1 & 0 & 0 & 0 & \cdots & 0 & 0 & 0 \\
1/6 & 1/3 & 1/2 & 0 & 0 & \cdots & 0 & 0 & 0 \\
0 & 1/4 & 1/3 & 5/12 & 0 & \cdots & 0 & 0 & 0 \\
0 & 0 & 5/18 & 1/3 & 7/18 & \cdots & 0 & 0 & 0 \\
M & M & M & M & M & \cdots & M & M & M \\
0 & 0 & 0 & 0 & 0 & \cdots & \dfrac{2(K-1)-1}{6(K-1)} & 1/3 & \dfrac{2(K-1)+1}{6(K-1)} \\
0 & 0 & 0 & 0 & 0 & \cdots & 0 & 0 & 1
\end{bmatrix}
\tag{1}
$$

An element $P_{i,j}$ in P_k is the probability the mobile terminal moves from layer i-1 to layer j-1 in one step. The n steps transaction matrix is

$$P_k^n = \begin{cases} P_k & n=1 \\ P_k \times P_k^{n-1} & n>1 \end{cases} \tag{2}$$

And an element $P_{i,j}^n$ in P_k^n is the probability the mobile terminal moves from layer i-1 to layer j-1 in n steps. Let $\beta(d,k)$ denote the probability that mobile terminal moves from state 0 to state d in k steps. It is

$$\beta(d,k) = P_{1,d+1}^k \tag{3}$$

Suppose that mobile terminal moves across k cells during two incoming calls. So if the mobile terminal updates its location once during the period, the probability is

$$\rho_k^1 = \sum_{m=K}^{k} \left\{ \beta(K,m) \cdot \left[\sum_{n=0}^{K-1} \beta(n,k-m) \right] \right\} \tag{4}$$

The probability that mobile terminal updates location twice in k moving can be gotten by the probability, which mobile terminal updates location once in the first j moving, multiplying the probability, which mobile terminal updates location once in the other k-j moving. The equation is

$$\rho_k^2 = \sum_{j=K}^{k} \beta(K,j) \cdot \rho_{k-j}^1 \tag{5}$$

So on, the probability which mobile terminal updates location n times in k movings can be written as

$$\rho_k^n = \sum_{j=K}^{k} \beta(K,j) \cdot \rho_{k-j}^{n-1} \tag{6}$$

3.2 Total Cost for Location Update and Paging

To conveniently carry out our analysis, we provide three lemmas in this section from Ref [11].

Lemma 1. Let $\{N_1(t), t \geq 0\}$ and $\{N_2(t), t \geq 0\}$ be two independent Poisson processes with rate λ_1 and λ_2 respectively. Let t1 and t2 denote the times of the first event of the first process and the second process respectively. The probability of one event occurs in the first process before one event occurs in the second process is given as follows:

$$P(t1 < t2) = \delta(\lambda_1, \lambda_2) = \frac{\lambda_1}{\lambda_2 + \lambda_1} \qquad (7)$$

Lemma 2. Let $\{N_1(t), t \geq 0\}$ and $\{N_2(t), t \geq 0\}$ be two independent Poisson processes with rate λ_1 and λ_2 respectively. Let $\alpha(\lambda_1, \lambda_2, n)$ denote the probability that exactly n events occur in the first process between two events which occur in the second process. We have

$$\alpha(\lambda_1, \lambda_2, n) = \delta(\lambda_2, \lambda_1)[\delta(\lambda_1, \lambda_2)]^n \qquad (8)$$

Lemma 3. Let $\{N_1(t), t \geq 0\}$ and $\{N_2(t), t \geq 0\}$ be two independent Poisson processes with rate λ_1 and λ_2 respectively. Let N denote the mean number of events occu-rring in the first process between two events in the second process. We have $N = \lambda_1 / \lambda_2$.

Several parameters are introduced as Table.1 shows in this paper.

Table 1. Parameters Explain

Expression	Meaning
$1/\eta_{GLA}$	mobile terminal's mean residence time in GLA
$1/\eta_{LA}$	mobile terminal's mean residence time in LA
$1/\eta_{cell}$	mobile terminal's mean residence time in CELL
λ	call arrive rate which follow Poisson process
R_{poll}	cost for polling a cell
R_{HLR}	cost for each HLR location update
R_{GLR}	cost for each GLR location update
R_{VLR}	cost for each VLR location update
C_{HLR}	HLR location update cost between two incoming calls
C_{GLR}	GLR location update cost between two incoming calls
C_{VLR}	VLR location update cost between two incoming calls
C_{Page}	paging cost for second call
C_{TOTAL}	total cost

An HLR location updates is performed when a mobile terminal first enters a new GLA. Therefore, wherever a mobile crosses the boundary of a GLA, an HLR location update action is executed and it is requested by the GLR. By Lemma3, the average number of HLR location updates between two call arrivals is η_{GLA}/λ. A GLR location update is performed when a mobile terminal crosses a boundary of an LA. By Lemma3, the average number of GLR location updates between two all arrivals is η_{LA}/λ. Therefore, we have

$$C_{TOTAL} = C_{HLR} + C_{GLR} + C_{VLR} + C_{Page} \tag{9}$$

$$C_{HLR} = R_{HLR} \cdot \frac{\eta_{GLA}}{\lambda} \tag{10}$$

$$C_{GLR} = R_{GLR} \cdot \frac{\eta_{LA}}{\lambda} \tag{11}$$

$$C_{Page} = R_{Poll}(3K^2 - 3K + 1) \tag{12}$$

To derive the C_{VLR}, we have to consider the movement of mobile terminal among PA, LA and GLA. Note that the sizes of an LA and a GLA are fixed and the size of a PA is variable. By lemma 2, the probabilities that there are i GLAs, j LAs and k cells boundary crossings between two call arrivals are $\alpha(\eta_{GLA}, \lambda, i)$, $\alpha(\eta_{LA}, \lambda, j)$ and $\alpha(\eta_{cell}, \lambda, k)$ respectively. Without loss of generality, assume that when the previous phone call arrives, the mobile terminal resides in the GLA_0 and the $LA_{0,0}$. Let N_{VLR} denote the average number of VLR location updates between two call arrivals, $N_{VLR,i}$ denote the average number of location updates in VLR with our movement-based location update scheme when the mobile terminal receives the next phone call in the ith GLA, and $N_{VLR,i,j}$ denote the average number of location updates in VLR with our movement-based location update scheme when the mobile terminal receives the next phone call in the jth LA. Therefore, we obtain:

$$N_{VLR} = \sum_{i=0}^{\infty} N_{VLR,i} \cdot \alpha(\eta_{GLA}, \lambda, i) \tag{13}$$

$$N_{VLR,i} = \sum_{j=0}^{\infty} N_{VLR,i,j} \cdot \alpha(\eta_{LA}, \lambda, j) \tag{14}$$

There are two cases to get the $N_{VLR,i,j}$.

Case 1: i=0

1) If the mobile terminal is still in $LA_{0,0}$, when the next call arrives, the probability that there are k cell boundary crossings with $LA_{0,0}$ when the next call arrives is $\alpha(\eta_{cell}, \lambda, k)$ by Lemma2.

2) If the mobile terminal is in $LA_{0,1}$, when the next call arrives, the probability that there are k cell boundary crossings with LA0,0 is $\alpha(\eta_{cell}, \eta_{LA}, k)$ by Lemma2.

3) The probability that there are k cell boundary crossings with $LA_{0,m}$ (0<m<j) during the time period within LA0,m is $\alpha(\eta_{cell}, \eta_{LA}, k)$

4) The probability that there are k cell boundary crossings after entering the last $LA_{0,j}$ until the next phone call arrival is $\alpha(\eta_{cell}, \lambda, k)$ by Lemma2.

So, we have

$$
N_{VLR0,j} = \begin{cases}
\sum_{x=1}^{\infty} x \sum_{k=1}^{\infty} \alpha(\eta_{cell}, \lambda, k) \rho_k^x & j=0 \\
\sum_{x=1}^{\infty} x \sum_{k=1}^{\infty} \alpha(\eta_{cell}, \eta_{LA}, k) \rho_k^x & \\
+ (j-1)\sum_{x=1}^{\infty} x \sum_{k=1}^{\infty} \alpha(\eta_{cell}, \eta_{LA}, k) \rho_k^x & \\
+ \sum_{x=1}^{\infty} x \sum_{k=1}^{\infty} \alpha(\eta_{cell}, \lambda, k) \rho_k^x & j>0
\end{cases}
\tag{15}
$$

Case 2: i>0

1) If the mobile terminal is still in $LA_{1,0}$ when the next call arrives, the probability that after entering GLA_1, there are k cell boundary crossings within $LA_{i,0}$ when the next call arrives is $\alpha(\eta_{cell}, \lambda, k)$ by Lemma2.

2) If the mobile terminal is still in $LA_{1,1}$ when the next call arrives, the probability that after entering GLA_1, there are k cell boundary crossing within $LA_{1,0}$ is $\alpha(\eta_{cell}, \eta_{LA}, k)$ by Lemma2.

3) The probability, that after entering GLA_1, there are k cell boundary crossing within $LA_{1,m}$(0<m<j) is $\alpha(\eta_{cell}, \eta_{LA}, k)$ by Lemma2.

4) The probability, that after entering GLA_1, there are k cell boundary crossing after entering the last $LA_{1,j}$ until the next phone call arrives is $\alpha(\eta_{cell}, \lambda, k)$ by Lemma2.

5) Before entering GLA_1, the mobile terminal passes i GLA_s. By Lemm3, the average number of LA boundary crossings in a GLA is η_{GLA}/η_{LA}.

So, we have

$$
N_{VLR,i,j} = \begin{cases}
i\dfrac{\eta_{GLA}}{\eta_{LA}}\sum_{x=1}^{\infty} x\sum_{k=1}^{\infty}\alpha(\eta_{cell},\eta_{LA},k)\rho_k^x \\[2mm]
+\sum_{x=1}^{\infty} x\sum_{k=1}^{\infty}\alpha(\eta_{cell},\lambda,k)\rho_k^x & j=0 \\[4mm]
i\dfrac{\eta_{GLA}}{\eta_{LA}}\sum_{x=1}^{\infty} x\sum_{k=1}^{\infty}\alpha(\eta_{cell},\eta_{LA},k)\rho_k^x \\[2mm]
+\sum_{x=1}^{\infty} x\sum_{k=1}^{\infty}\alpha(\eta_{cell},\eta_{LA},k)\rho_k^x \\[2mm]
+(j-1)\sum_{x=1}^{\infty} x\sum_{k=1}^{\infty}\alpha(\eta_{cell},\eta_{LA},k)\rho_k^x \\[2mm]
+\sum_{x=1}^{\infty} x\sum_{k=1}^{\infty}\alpha(\eta_{cell},\lambda,k)\rho_k^x & j>0
\end{cases}
\tag{16}
$$

Note that (15) is a special case of (16) when i=0. We have

$$
\begin{aligned}
N_{VLR,i,j} &= i\frac{\eta_{GLA}}{\eta_{LA}}\sum_{x=1}^{\infty} x\sum_{k=1}^{\infty}\alpha(\eta_{cell},\eta_{LA},k)\rho_k^x \\
&+ j\sum_{x=1}^{\infty} x\sum_{k=1}^{\infty}\alpha(\eta_{cell},\eta_{LA},k)\rho_k^x \\
&+ \sum_{x=1}^{\infty} x\sum_{k=1}^{\infty}\alpha(\eta_{cell},\lambda,k)\rho_k^x
\end{aligned}
\tag{17}
$$

From (6), (17), (9), (10), (11), (12), we have

$$
N_{VLR} = \sum_{i=0}^{\infty}\sum_{j=0}^{\infty} N_{VLR,i,j}\,\alpha(\eta_{LA},\lambda,j)\alpha(\eta_{GLA},\lambda,i)
\tag{18}
$$

$$
C_{TOTAL} = R_{HLR}\frac{\eta_{GLA}}{\lambda} + R_{GLR}\frac{\eta_{LA}}{\lambda} + R_{VLR}N_{VLR} + R_{Pol}(3K^2-3K+1)
\tag{19}
$$

4 Performance Evaluation

From the total cost formula, we can get that the total cost is affected by many elements including paging cost, location update cost, size of PA, mean residence time in cell/LA/GLA, call arrival rates.

For the purpose of comparing with Ref [11], we adopt the following parameters as Ref [11] for this section: $1/\eta_{GLA} = 18000$ seconds, $1/\eta_{LA} = 1800$ seconds, $1/\eta_{cell} = 120$ seconds, $R_{HLR} = 60$, $R_{GLR} = 20$, $R_{VLR} = 15$, $R_{poll} = 6$. The value of $1/\lambda$ is variable.

4.1 Comparison of Dynamic and Static Schemes in 3G

In this section, we compare the two schemes: static 3G location management and dynamic 3G location management proposed in this paper. For the static scheme, the LA includes 61 cells. Fig. 4 compares dynamic and static scheme under different $R_{Poll} = 20$, 10, 5 and 1. As illustrated in the figures, the cost difference between dynamic and static schemes is large when the page cost R_{Poll} is big. But if the page cost R_{Poll} is small, the cost difference between dynamic and static schemes is small. So the cost of dynamic scheme is smaller than the cost of static scheme and dynamic scheme is better than the static scheme.

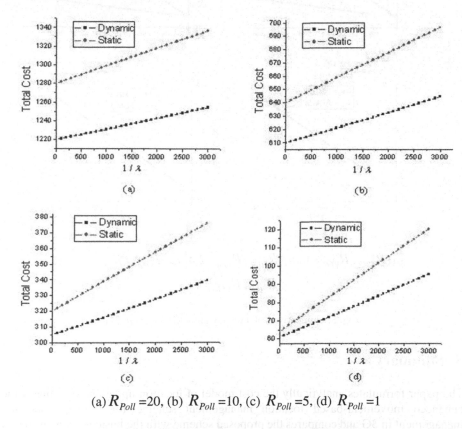

(a) $R_{Poll} = 20$, (b) $R_{Poll} = 10$, (c) $R_{Poll} = 5$, (d) $R_{Poll} = 1$

Fig. 4. Comparison of dynamic and static schemes in 3G

4.2 Comparison of Two Dynamic Schemes in 3G

In this section, the difference between scheme proposed in this paper and the scheme provided in Ref [11] is discussed. For briefness, the scheme proposed in Ref [11] is denoted as DMBLM (Dynamic Movement-Based Location Management); the scheme proposed in this paper is denoted as ADMBLM (Advanced Dynamic Movement-Based Location Management). Fig. 5 compares these two schemes under different $R_{HLR} : R_{VLR}$ =4, 2.5, 1.5 and 1.1. As illustrated in the figures, the scheme proposed in this paper has less cost than the DMB. Therefore, the scheme proposed in this paper is better than the scheme proposed in Ref [11].

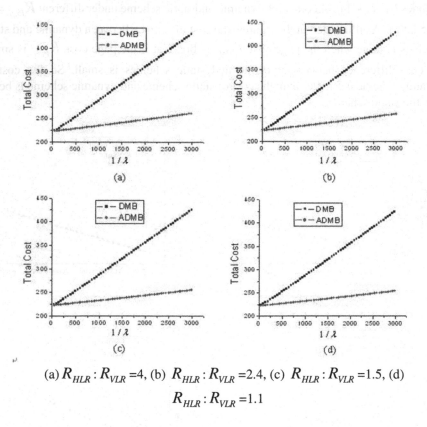

(a) $R_{HLR} : R_{VLR}$ =4, (b) $R_{HLR} : R_{VLR}$ =2.4, (c) $R_{HLR} : R_{VLR}$ =1.5, (d) $R_{HLR} : R_{VLR}$ =1.1

Fig. 5. Comparison of Two Dynamic Schemes in 3G

5 Summary

The paper formulates analytically the cost model of location update and paging of the enhanced movement-based location management scheme for three-tier location management in 3G and compares the proposed scheme with the basic movement-based location management scheme.

The main contribution of this paper is that: (1) formulates analytically the cost model of location update and paging for the enhanced movement-based location management scheme for three-tier location management in 3G; (2) compares the proposed scheme with the basic movement-based location management scheme. The end shows that the enhanced movement-based location management scheme is better than basic movement-based location management scheme.

References

1. Mobile Application Part (MAP) Specification, Version 4.8.0, ETSI/TC, Technical Report, Recommendation GSM 09.02, 1994
2. Cellular Intersystem Operations, EIA/TIA, Technical Report IS-4, 1995
3. Gateway Location Register (GLR)-Stage2, 3G TS 23.119 V3.0.0, Mar 2000
4. Vimal Bhat, Digvijav Singh Khati. Timer Based Dynamic Location Management. Wireless Telecommunications Symposium. (2004) 55-60
5. Yong Lee, Goo Yeon Lee. Optimal Time-Interval for Time-based Location Update in Mobile Communications. Global Telecommunications Conference. (2002) 2079-2083
6. Vincent W.-S.Wong, Victor C.M.Leung. An Adaptive Distance-Based Location Update Algorithm for PCS Networks. IEEE International Conference on Communications. (2001) 2001-2005
7. Daisuke Senzaki, Goutam Chakraborty. Distance based location management in cellular PCS network –a critical study. The 18th International Conference on Advanced Information Networking and Application. (2004) 95-98
8. Ian F.Akyildiz, Joseph S.M.Ho, Yi-Bing Lin. Movement-Based Location Update and Selective Paging for PCS Networks. IEEE/ACM Transaction on Networking, Vol 4, No.4. (1996) 629-638
9. Lei Li, Yi Pan, Jie Li. An Improved Movement-Based Location Management Scheme for PCS Network. IEEE 58th Vehicular Technology Conference. (2003) 757-760
10. Y.Fang, I. Chlamtac, Y Lin. Portable Movement Modeling for PCS Networks. IEEE Transaction on Vehicular Technology. Vol 49, No.4. (2000) 1356-1363
11. Yang Xiao, Yi Pan, Jie Li. Design and Analysis of Location Management for 3G Cellular Networks. IEEE Transactions on Parallel and Distributed Systems. Vol 15, No.4. (2004) 339-349
12. Cheng Rong, Yuan Senmiao, Zhu Jinquan. A Dynamic Location Management Method of Personal Communication System. IEEE E-Tech. (2004) 1-9

MTSP: Multi-hop Time Synchronization Protocol for IEEE 802.11 Wireless Ad Hoc Network

Guan-Nan Chen[1], Chiung-Ying Wang[2], and Ren-Hung Hwang[2]

[1] Dept. of Communication Engineering
[2] Dept. of Computer Science & Information Engineering,
National Chung-Cheng University, Taiwan
[1]horowitz@exodus.cs.ccu.edu.tw, [2]{wjy, rhhwang}@cs.ccu.edu.tw

Abstract. Clock synchronization is very important for power management protocol in a multi-hop MANET. However, since MANET is a network temporarily formed by a collection of mobile nodes without the aid of any centralized coordinator, clock synchronization is very difficult to achieve. Therefore, most of previous works on power efficiency assumed asynchronous clock. As a consequence, a mobile node will waste a lot of power and time waiting for forwarding a packet to its neighbors, due to the lack of information of wakeup times of its neighbors. In this paper, we propose a multi-hop time synchronization protocol, referred to as MTSP, for multi-hop MANETs based on IEEE 802.11 ad hoc mode. The MTSP consists of two phases: beacon window (BW) phase and synchronization (SYN) phase. In BW phase, several devices, which can directly communicate with each others, form a synchronization group. And each group selects the device with fastest timer as the leader node of the group. In SYN phase, leader nodes then synchronize with each other. Our simulation results show that MTSP is a distributed and effective multi-hop time synchronization protocol, especially for dense networks.

Keywords: IEEE 802.11, mobile ad hoc network (MANET), multi-hop, time synchronization.

1 Introduction

In recent years, wireless networks have become prevail in our surroundings. The most popular wireless technique is from the set of IEEE 802.11 standards. The IEEE 802.11 supports Infrastructure mode and Ad Hoc mode. In infrastructure mode, mobile nodes communicate through an access point (AP), which usually connects to the Internet. In the ad hoc mode, mobile nodes dynamically form an ad hoc network and communicate with each others through multi-hop routing. Although infrastructure mode is more commonly adopted, ad hoc mode may be the only solution in some special applications, such as battlefields, disaster areas, and outdoor activities. No matter in which mode, the power of mobile nodes is a limited resource. Without power, any wireless device will become useless. Therefore, power saving becomes a critical issue in wireless networks.

X. Cheng, W. Li, and T. Znati (Eds.): WASA 2006, LNCS 4138, pp. 664–675, 2006.

In recent years, several power saving protocols have been proposed for IEEE 802.11 wireless LANs. They can be classified in to two groups: synchronous wake up and asynchronous wake up. In the synchronous wake up approach, all nodes wake up at the same time in order to send or receive packets from its neighbors. Thus, time synchronization becomes the most important part of this kind of protocols. Examples of synchronous wake up protocols are IEEE 802.11 Power saving protocol [1], and p-MANET [2]. On the other hand, asynchronous wake up protocols do not synchronize wake up time of mobile nodes. Nodes asynchronously wake up a period of time for receiving packets from its neighbors. Examples of asynchronous wake up power saving protocols are [3-5]. Concerns of asynchronous wake up protocols are less power efficiency, longer transmission delay, and difficult to perform broadcast. In this paper, we focus on the design of synchronous wake up power saving protocols.

However, to synchronize mobile nodes in MANET is very difficult, since there is no base station to perform centralized control. The IEEE 802.11 Standard has defined a Timing Synchronization Function (IEEE 802.11 TSF) for single-hop ad hoc networks. Mobile nodes generate a beacon with its system time and periodically send a beacon. Nodes can be synchronized by the time information in the beacon. However, IEEE 802.11 TSF may encounter the "beacon contention problem" in dense networks where the fastest node cannot send out its beacon due to beacon contention. As a consequence, the network becomes out of synchronization. In [10], "Adaptive Timing Synchronization Procedure" (ATSP) has been proposed to solve beacon contention problem where the fastest node cannot send out its beacon due to beacon contention. Lai *et al.* [11] proposed the "Tiered Adaptive Time Synchronization Procedure" (TATSP) to improve synchronization accuracy of ATSP and reduce the convergence time of synchronization. They also proposed to prioritize the beacon-generation timer such that faster nodes get shorter timers to send beacons in [12]. Extension of this protocol for multi-hop ad hoc networks can be found in the literature [15], however synchronization accuracy is still an issue.

In IEEE 802.11, if the synchronization accuracy, i.e., the time difference between the clock of the fastest node and that of the slowest node, is larger than 224µs, which is equivalent to the time to change from one operating channel frequency [1], the network is called "out of synchronization." Sometimes small clock skew and the defects of IEEE 802.11 TSF may cause the problem of out of synchronization. In [10], Huang and Lai proposed that let faster node have higher priority to send a beacon can improve the synchronization accuracy on single hop ad hoc networks.

In the last few years, several papers have been devoted to the study of time synchronization. For example, [6-7] have proposed time synchronization mechanisms for sensor networks. [8] proposed how to synchronize mobile devices in Bluetooth networks. In [10-13], researchers pointed out that network density may affect the synchronization accuracy in IEEE 802.11 ad hoc networks. [14] showed that time synchronization mechanism for single hop ad hoc networks is not suitable for multi-hop ad hoc networks. All of the aforementioned works consider only the single-hop ad hoc environment. Only few attempts so far have been made for time synchronization in multi-hop networks. Sheu *et al.* [15] proposed a time synchronization scheme, called Automatic Self-time-correcting Procedure (ASP), for multi-hop networks. In ASP, mobile nodes adjust their clocks according to the beacon information among neighbors. However, the convergence time of synchronization is too long and out of synchronization still may occur. In this paper, we proposed a new time synchronization mechanism based on IEEE 802.11 TSF, called Multi-hop Time Synchronization Protocol (MTSP). IEEE 802.11 Standard only defines how to synchronize clocks in single hop networks. Extending TSF to multi-hop networks will cause out of synchronization problem. Our MTSP adapts to both single hop and multi-hop ad hoc networks and improves the synchronization accuracy.

MTSP consists of two phases: Beacon Window (BW) Phase and Synchronization (SYN) Phase. The BW phase tackles the synchronization accuracy problem in high density single-hop networks while the SYN phase solves the time partition problem in multi-hop networks. In BW phase, similar to [14], faster node has higher priority to send beacon. After BW phase, several one-hop synchronization groups will be formed, and the fastest node in each group is selected as the group leader node. At this time, clock skew between different groups may be significant, referred to as the time partition problem. The SYN phase solves this problem by synchronizing all of the leader nodes. Our simulation results show that MTSP can achieve very good synchronization accuracy.

This paper is organized as follows: Session 2 describes the proposed multi-hop time synchronization protocol. Performance analysis of MTSP is given in session 3. Simulation results of MTSP are presented in session 4. Session 5 concludes this paper.

2 Multi-hop Time Synchronization Protocol

In this section, we present our multi-hop time synchronization protocol (MTSP) for the IEEE 802.11 multi-hop ad hoc network. The main design goals are:

(1)   Improve synchronization accuracy, especially in high density networks.
(2)   Avoid the out of synchronization problem.
(3)   Solve the time partition problem.

2.1 System Architecture

As shown in Fig. 1, MTSP operates under the network layer and above the physical layer; it provides the synchronization information for power management protocols.

In MTSP, time is synchronized and divided into beacon intervals. Each beacon interval is composed of four windows:

(1)   Beacon Window: nodes generate a random timer to contend to send beacons in the beacon window.
(2)   Synchronization Window (sync window): leader nodes synchronize with each others in the synchronization window; other nodes stay at idle state.
(3)   ATIM Window: ATIM window is the same as the IEEE 802.11 Standard. Data Window: Data window is used for transmitting and receiving data frames.

Fig. 2 shows the beacon interval of MTSP. The length of a beacon interval is 100 ms, as suggested by the IEEE 802.11 standard [2]. MTSP adds a 4-ms beacon window and a 6-ms sync window. The length of beacon window is the same as that of IEEE 802.11 standard. The length of sync window is 1.5 times more than that of beacon window. The length of ATIM window is 20 ms, same as that of IEEE 802.11 standard.

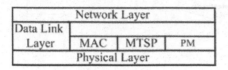

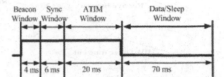

Fig. 1. Multi-hop time synchronization protocol   Fig. 2. Beacon interval of MTSP

2.2 Beacon Window Phase

Beacon window phase is designed based on IEEE 802.11 TSF. Nodes use random timers to contend for wireless medium to send beacons with 64-bit timestamp. By following the fastest node, nodes can be synchronized. The length of beacon packet is 50 bytes, same as defined in the IEEE 802.11 standard.

The beacon-generation timer, BWTimer, is managed as follows such that faster nodes have higher priority to transmit beacons. First of all, nodes are either in high priority (HI) state or low priority (LO) state. Nodes in HI state will randomly generate BWTimer within the range of (0, 1/2 beacon window length) while nodes in LO state generate BWTimer within the range of (1/2 beacon window length, beacon window length). The design goal is to have the fastest node of a synchronization group to stay in HI state while the rest of nodes to stay in LO state such that the fastest node can send out its beacon without contention. However, if a node in LO state becomes faster, it still has the chance to announce its beacon.

The flow chart of the BW phase operation is shown in Fig. 3. Nodes are grouped into synchronization groups in a self-organizing way. A synchronization group is centered at a node with the fastest system time among all nodes in the same group.

Let us consider an example of the BW phase. Assume there are four nodes in the network. The clock rate of these nodes are C>D>B>A. Initially, all nodes are in HI state and randomly generate their BWTimer timers within the range of [0, 1/2 beacon window length]. As shown in Fig. 4(a), let us assume that node B generates the smallest BWTimer. Node B then transmits its beacon. Upon receiving the beacon, node A will update its clock, cancel its BWTimer, and enter the LO state. On the other hand, since C and D are faster than B, so they will continue to count down their BWTimer. Later on, as shown in Fig. 4(b), BWTimer of node C expires. Node C then transmits a beacon. Since node C is the fastest node, all other nodes will synchronize their clocks with C and node D will cancel its timer and enter LO state. At the same time, node B will also enter LO state. Therefore, after the BW phase, node C is the only node in HI State and all other nodes stay into LO State. We called node C as the "leader node".

Nodes that outside the transmission range of node C will not able to receive node C's beacon, therefore, more than one synchronization group will be formed. Each group will have a leader node which is the fastest node within the group. Nodes in the same group will be synchronized after the BW phase. Synchronization between different groups will be done in the SYN phase.

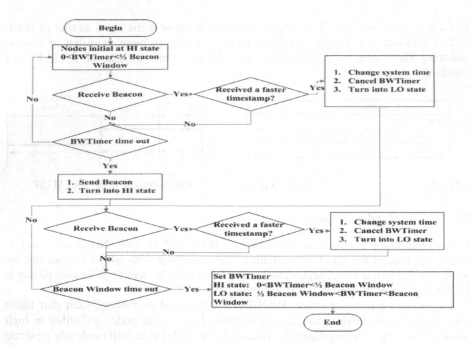

Fig. 3. Flow chart of Beacon Window Phase

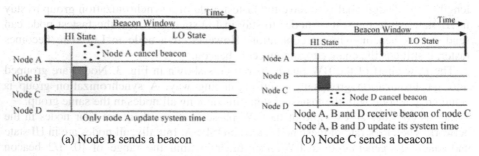

(a) Node B sends a beacon   (b) Node C sends a beacon

Fig. 4. An example of BW phase

2.3 Synchronization Phase

The purpose of synchronization phase is to solve the time partition problem [16]. In multi-hop ad hoc networks, nodes can only receive beacon from its neighbors. Therefore, the beacon of the fastest node cannot be received by nodes that are not within the fastest node's transmission range. A mechanism thus is required to broadcast the beacon of the fastest node to all nodes in the ad hoc network.

The basic idea of the synchronization phase is to synchronize leader nodes which in turn synchronize nodes in their group. Let us consider the example shown in Fig. 5 where there are four leader nodes A, B, R, and S. The clock rates in decreasing order are A>R>S>B. Power level will be increased for communication between leader nodes, which will be described in more detail later. If node A sends a synchronization packet with its timestamp to node R, and node R relays to node S, and then to node B, these four leader nodes can then be synchronized.

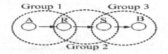

Fig. 5. Basic idea of synchronization phase

Before describing the algorithm of the synchronization phase, let us define the synchronization packet format first. The synchronization (SYN) packets are classified into three types:

(1) SYNC-Query: SYNC-Query packet is used by a leader node to query if there are other faster leader nodes within SYN packet transmission range. Each leader node sends a SYNC-Query, which carries its 64-bit timestamp, in the synchronization phase.

(2) SYNC-ACK: a SYNC-ACK packet is used to respond a SYN-Query packet with slower timestamp.

(3) SYNC-RACK: when a leader node receives a SYNC-Query with a faster timestamp, it will update its system time and send a SYNC-RACK to notify its neighbor leader nodes.

Recall that more than one synchronization groups may be formed after the BW phase. Nodes that are in HI-state will become the leader nodes of synchronization groups. Only leader nodes will involve in the SYN phase. Similar to BWTimer, each leader node maintains a randomly generated MTSF timer and will send a SYNC-Query packet when this timer expires. The flow chart of SYN phase is shown in Fig. 6.

Fig. 7 shows the SYN phase during the first beacon interval. Without loss of generality, let us assume that the order of randomly generated MTSF timer is A>B>C>D. Firstly, node D sends a SYNC-Query packet to node C. Upon receiving this packet, node C replies a SYNC-ACK to node D since node C is faster than node D. Node D will synchronize its clock to that of node C, denoted by Tc. Later on, node C sends out a SYNC-Query when its MTSF timer expires. Similarly, node B replies a SYNC-ACK to node C since it is faster. As a consequence, node C updates its clock to Tb, the system timestamp of node B. Later on, node B sends out a SYNC-Query. Node C updates its clock again upon receiving this packet. Node C also sends a SYNC-RACK to notify its neighbor leader nodes such that node D also synchronizes its clock to that of node B. Finally, node A sends out its SYNC-Query when its MTSF timer expires. This time, node B synchronizes its clock with node A and sends a SYNC-RACK to notify node C. When the SYNC window ends, node A, B, and C have synchronized their clocks, while node D needs another round of SYN phase in order to synchronize its clock with the fastest node, node A. After the first beacon interval, node B, C, and D have received faster timestamp from other nodes, so they will increase their MTSFmax by one slot time at next beacon interval in order to decrease the priority of sending SYNC-Query packets. On the other hand, node A decreases its MTSFmax by one.

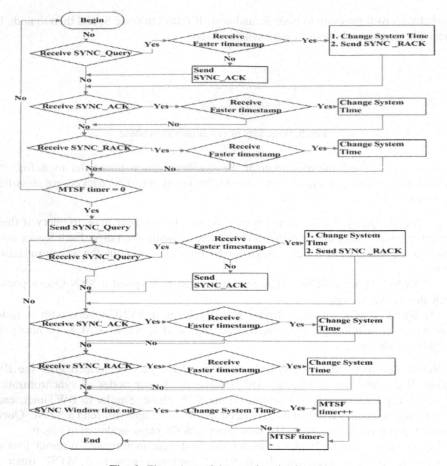

Fig. 6. Flow chart of the synchronization phase

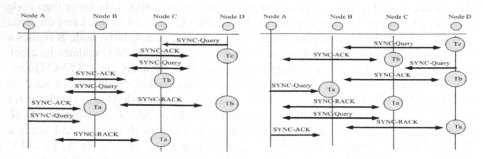

Fig. 7. SYN phase of the first beacon interval   **Fig. 8.** SYN phase of the second beacon interval

Fig.8 shows the SYN phase of the second beacon interval. Here, we assume the order of the randomly generated MTSF timers is C>D>A>B. So, node C sends a SYNC-Query first. Upon receiving this packet, node D updates its clock while node B replies a SYNC-ACK which updates node C's clock. Later on, node D sends a SYNC-Query and node C replies with a SYNC-ACK which synchronizes node D's clock to Tb. The fastest leader node A sends SYNC-Query next. Upon receiving this packet, node B updates its clock and sends out a SYNC-RACK to notify node C. Node B and node C now synchronize with node A. Finally, node B sends a SYNC-Query which causes node C to send a SYNC-RACK to node D. After node D receives this SYNC-RACK, all nodes synchronize with node A.

3 Design Issues and Performance of MTSP

In this section, we will discuss some design issues and performance of MTSP.

3.1 Transmission Range

The purpose of beacon is to synchronize nodes in a synchronization group, which can be considered as local synchronization. For power saving and transmission efficiency, we propose to have different power levels when transmitting beacon and synchronization packets. That is, the transmission range of beacon is smaller than that of synchronization packet.

Let the transmission range of beacon be R. We show that in an ideal environment, the distance between two leader nodes, D, is bounded by (R, 3R). We shall only consider the case that the network is not partitioned. The proof is given as follows:

Theorem. The distance between two leader nodes, D, is bounded by $R<D<=3R$.

Proof

R<D: This is trivial since if the distance is less than D, they would hear each other's beacon packets, and the slower should be synchronized to the faster, not becoming the leader node.

D<=3R: Fig.9 shows the worst case where node A and D are leader nodes, and node B and C are normal nodes. $\overline{AB}$ and $\overline{CD}$ cannot be larger than R. So, if $\overline{AD} > 3R$, then $\overline{BC}$ must greater than R. However, in that case, the network becomes partitioned which violates our assumption that network is not partitioned. Therefore, the distance between two leader nodes must be less than 3R. In our simulation, we will show the results of setting the transmission range to 2R as well as 3R.

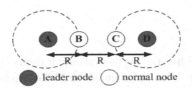

Fig. 9. Transmission range between leader nodes

3.2 BW Phase Synchronization

In this section, we discuss the stability problem of the BW phase. In particular, we discuss how different synchronization groups can be formed distributedly. The major concern is that all nodes should either be a leader node or a group member of a leader node. Consider the topology shown in Fig. 10, where the order of the clock rate is A<B<C. Without loss of generality, assume that in the first beacon interval, node B sends a beacon first. Node A will set node B as its leader node and turn into LO State. Node C ignores beacon from node B. Node C sends a beacon when its BWTimer times out. After node B received the beacon from node C, node B considers node C as its leader node and turn into LO State. In the second beacon interval, node C stays in HI State and sends a beacon first. Node B cancels its BWTimer and keeps quiet. Therefore, node A will not receive any beacon before its BWTimer times out. Node A then sends out its beacon and returns to HI State. As a consequence, two synchronization groups, with leader nodes A and C, will be formed in the third beacon interval.

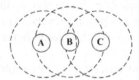

Fig. 10. Example of forming different SYN groups

Next, we discuss the maximum clock skew within a synchronization group. Let the maximum difference of the clock rates of the leader node and a member node is d per time slot. Let the length of the beacon interval be BI slots and that of beacon window be BWL slots. The leader node will send out a beacon every beacon interval at the first 1/2 beacon window. Therefore, the maximum clock skew is given by $d*(BI+0.5*BWL)$.

3.3 SYN Phase Synchronization

Now we discuss the maximum clock skew among leader nodes. Assume the network diameter is K, i.e., the maximum distance between any two leader nodes is K-1 hops. In the worst case, it takes K-1 rounds (beacon intervals) to have the timestamp of the fastest node be transmitted to the lowest node. Therefore, the maximum clock skew between any two leader nodes is given by $d*(BI*(K-1)+BWL+SYNL)$, where $SYNL$ is the length of SYN phase.

4 Simulations

Effectiveness of the multi-hop time synchronization protocol (MTSP) is evaluated by simulations in this section. We implemented the MTSP simulator in C language.

Most of the system parameters in our simulations are set according to IEEE 802.11 standard. Direct Sequence Spread Spectrum (DSSS) modulation scheme is adopted. The beacon interval is set to 0.1 second. The clock accuracy of nodes is uniformly distributed in the range of [-0.01%, +0.01%]. The maximum tolerable clock skew is 224µs. 50 to 300 nodes are simulated, which are randomly placed in a 1000m x 1000m area. The transmission range of beacons is 125m and that of synchronization packets is 250m. All nodes move according to the random way-point model [16], with a maximum speed of 20m/s and pause time of 20 seconds. Simulation results of other performance metrics are presented in the following:

4.1 Out of Synchronization Percentage

Intuitively, out of synchronization percentage, which defined as the ratio of out of synchronization time to the total simulation time, is affected by node density. Therefore, we evaluate the impact of node density on the performance of MTSP. Table 1 shows the out of synchronization percentage of MTSP and IEEE TSF under various node densities. We can observe from Table 1 that out of synchronization percentage of IEEE TSF is significantly higher than that of MTSP and increases tremendously as the network becomes denser. Noticeably, the out of synchronization percentage of MTSP remains less than 0.1% in all simulation cases. Synchronization accuracy of MTSP is also significantly better than that of TSF. The average maximum clock skew of MTSP is less than 40µs in all cases, which is far less than the out of synchronization threshold, 224µs. On the other hand, the average maximum clock skew of TSF exceeds this threshold when the network has more than 40 nodes.

Table 1. Out of synchronization percentage and synchronization accuracy

# of node		20	30	40	50	60
% of out of synchronization	TSF	5.79%	29.76%	41.6%	67.02%	100%
	MTSP	0.07%	0.07%	0.07%	0.07%	0.1%
Average max. clock skew	TSF	124.5µs	203.4µs	246.2µs	274.9µs	500.2µs
	MTSP	22.4µs	25.1µs	29.3µs	31.1µs	39.1µs

4.2 Synchronization Accuracy

Fig. 11 compares the synchronization accuracy (max. clock skew) at each beacon interval of MTSP and TSF. Cause the limited space, only 50 and 200 nodes are shown in Fig. 11. From results of Table 1, the clock skew is much higher in TSF, and as the number of nodes increases, the clock skew becomes worse. For a network with more than 50 nodes, more than 50% of beacon intervals has clock skew more than 224µs, thus become out of synchronization. Fig. 11 also shows that nodes become synchronized quickly in MTSP. The rationale for this observation is that faster node has higher priority to send beacon is very important and synchronization packets among leader nodes are effective.

4.2.1 Synchronization Overhead
Synchronization overhead is measured by the beacon and synchronization packets transmitted by the synchronization protocol. Fig. 12 compares the averaged total

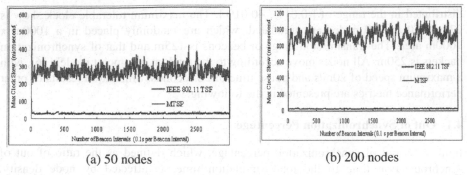

(a) 50 nodes   (b) 200 nodes

Fig. 11. Max. clock skew at each beacon interval

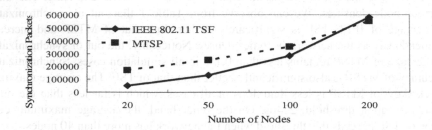

Fig. 12. Synchronization overhead under various network densities

number of beacons and synchronization packets transmitted by TSF and MTSP in a 300-second simulation run. As we can see that, MTSP has higher overhead than TSF when the network is sparse. As the network becomes denser, MTSP requires more synchronization overhead because the synchronization packets sent in the SYN phase.

5   Conclusions

In this paper, we presented a time synchronization protocol, MTSP, for multi-hop ad hoc networks. Based on two synchronization phases, MTSP has been shown to have high synchronization accuracy. MTSP is especially suitable for high density networks as it not only provide high synchronization accuracy but also yield competitive overhead as compare to IEEE TSF.

Power saving and time synchronization are both important issues for wireless and sensor networks. Therefore, we are currently designing a power saving protocol based on MTSP. We are also investigating the time synchronization issue in sensor networks.

Acknowledgments

This research is partially supported by National Science Council of Taiwan under grant number NSC 94-2213-E-194-001.

References

1. IEEE Std 802.11-1999, Wireless LAN Medium Access Control (MAC) and Physical Layer (PHY) Specifications. LAN MAN Standards Committee of the IEEE Computer Society (1999)

2. Wang C.-Y., Wu C.-J., Chen G.-N., and Hwang R.-H.: p-MANET: Efficient Power Saving Protocol for Multi-Hop Mobile Ad Hoc Networks. The third IEEE International Conference on Information Technology and Applications (2005) 271–276

3. Tseng Y.-C., Hsu C.-S., and Hsieh T.-Y.: Power Saving Protocols for IEEE 802.11-Based Multi-Hop Ad Hoc Network. Computer Networks: The International Journal of Computer and Telecommunications Networking (2003) 271–276

4. Jiang J.-R., Tseng Y.-C., Hsu C.-S. and Lai T.-H.: Quorum-Based Asynchronous Power-Saving Protocols for IEEE 802.11 Ad Hoc Networks. IEEE International Conference on Parallel Processing (2003) 257–264

5. Zheng R., Hou J. C., and Sha L.: Asynchronous wakeup for ad hoc networks. MobiHoc (2003) 35–45

6. Sichitiu M. L. and Veerarittiphan C.: Simple, accurate time synchronization for wireless sensor networks. IEEE Wireless Communications and Networking (WCNC) (2003) 1266–1273

7. Kumar R., Srivastava M. B., and Ganeriwal S.: Timing-sync Protocol for Sensor Networks. ACM SenSys (2003) 138–149

8. Sairam K. V. S. S. S. S., Gunasekaran N., and Reddy S. R.: Bluetooth in wireless communication. IEEE Communications Magazine (2002) 90–96

9. Awerbuch B., Holmer D., and Rubens H.: The Pulse Protocol: Energy Efficient Infrastructure Access. IEEE INFOCOM (2004) 1467–1478

10. Huang L. and Lai T.-H.: On the scalability of IEEE 802.11 ad hoc networks. MobiHoc (2002) 173–182

11. Lai T.-H. and Zhou D.: Efficient and scalable IEEE 802.11 Ad Hoc Mode Timing Synchronization Function. IEEE International Conference on Advanced Information Networking and Applications (2003) 318–323

12. Zhou D. and Lai T.-H.: Analysis and Implementation of Scalable Clock Synchronization Protocols in IEEE 802.11 Ad Hoc Networks. Mobile Ad Hoc and Sensor Systems (MASS) (2004)

13. Ye M.-H., Lau C.-T. and Premkumar A. B.: A modified time synchronization function in IEEE 802.11 using differentiated contention window. IEEE International Conference on Information and Communication Security (2003) 1076–1080

14. Rauschert P., Honarbacht A., and Kummert A.: On the IEEE 802.11 IBSS and its Timer Synchronization Function in Multi-Hop Ad Hoc Networks. IEEE International Symposium on Wireless Communication Systems (2004) 304–308

15. Sheu J.-P., Chao C.-M., and Sun C.-W.: A clock synchronization algorithm for multi-hop wireless ad hoc networks. IEEE International Conference on Distributed Computing Systems (2004) 574-581

16. Broch J., Maltz D., Johnson D., Hu Y., and Jetcheva J.: A Performance Comparison of Multi-Hop Wireless Ad Hoc Network Routing Protocols. In Proceedings of the Fourth Annual ACM/IEEE International Conference on Mobile Computing and Networking (1998) 85–97

Upperbounding End-to-End Throughput of Multihop Wireless Networks

Hong Lu and Steve Liu

Department of Computer Science
Texas A&M University
{hongl, liu}@cs.tamu.edu

Abstract. End-to-end throughput θ_{sd} is the maximum amount of data that can be successfully delivered from source s to sink d across a given network in unit time. Determining θ_{sd} is essential to understanding the network limit and is of important value to network design and evaluation. In the past few years, the problem of computing θ_{sd} in multihop wireless networks has been extensively studied in the literature. It has been shown that this problem is NP-hard in general and various approaches have been proposed to compute approximate solutions. In this paper, we study one side of the problem, computing the upperbound of θ_{sd}. We present a general solution framework based on linear program $\mathrm{LP}(\mathcal{F})$, where $\mathcal{F}$ is an arbitrary set of link sets. We show each choice of $\mathcal{F}$ corresponds to an upperbound of θ_{sd} and identify several good choice of $\mathcal{F}$ based on the notions of clique and congestion. The tightness of these clique and congestion based upperbounds are evaluated by simulation.

1 Introduction

We consider a multihop wireless network consisting a set of nodes communicating with each other. The problem studied in this paper, THROUGHPUT, is to find the maximum amount of data that can be successfully delivered across the network from a source node to a sink in a given period of time. End-to-end throughput is one of the most fundamental network parameters that is essential to understanding the network limit. Knowing the throughput of a network can help to identify potential bottleneck, coordinate network traffic, plan and evaluate network design, etc.

Problem THROUGHPUT in wired networks, also known as the MAXFLOW problem, is one of the best solved problems in computer science. The situation in wireless networks, however, is more complicated due to the effect of radio interference. In recent years, this problem has attracted considerable research attention. Jain et. al. first showed this problem is NP-hard in general[1], thus making exact solutions intractable assuming P $\neq$ NP. After that, many results came out[2,3,4,5] aiming at achieving reasonably good approximate solutions. In this paper, we focus on one side of the problem: computing the upperbound of end-to-end throughput. Motivated by the work in [1] and [2], our main contributions are:

X. Cheng, W. Li, and T. Znati (Eds.): WASA 2006, LNCS 4138, pp. 676–687, 2006.
© Springer-Verlag Berlin Heidelberg 2006

– We propose a general solution framework based on a linear program LP($\mathcal{F}$), where $\mathcal{F}$ is an arbitrary set of link sets. We show each choice of $\mathcal{F}$ corresponds to an upperbound of the end-to-end throughput.
– We improve [1]'s clique based upperbounding approach by showing that a reasonably tight upperbound can be achieved by a small set of carefully chosen cliques.
– We derive a congestion based upperbound from the results in [2]. A unique characteristic of this upperbound is that it is guaranteed to be within a constant factor of the exact throughput.

2   Network Model

The multihop wireless network under consideration is a four tuple $(V, E, \nmid, c)$, where V is the set of wireless nodes, $E \subseteq V \times V$ is the set of communication links. The effect of radio interference is modeled by a relation $\nmid \subseteq E \times E$. Vector c on E specifies the capacity of each link $e \in E$, that is, c_e is the maximum amount of data that can be transmitted by link e in unit time.

Graph (V, E), called communication graph, specifies the topology of a multihop wireless network. The communication graph considered in this paper falls into the class of graphs called disk graphs, where all the nodes reside in a two dimensional Euclidean plane. Each node is equipped with an omni-directional radio with a fixed transmission range. There is a one-way link e from $u \in V$ to $v \in V$ if and only if v is within u's transmission range. If $uv \in E$, u is called v's predecessor and v is u's successor. Figure 1 shows the communication graph of an example wireless network, where each double-arrow line represents two one-way links.

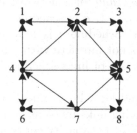

Fig. 1. The communication graph of an example network

A transmission is a link level communication between a node and one of its successors. A set of wireless transmissions scheduled to happen at the same time may interfere with each other resulting in transmission failures. We adopt the protocol interference model[6] in this paper: a transmission from u to v is successful if all the other nodes whose transmission range v is within are not transmitting. Protocol interference model can also be stated in terms of links as follows: transmission on link $e = uv$ interferes with transmission on link $e' = wh$ at node v, denoted as $e \nmid e'$(a convenient form of $ee' \in \nmid$), if $wv \in E$, $h = v$, or $w = v$, see Figure 2(a), (b), and (c); transmission on e is successful if all the links that e interferes with are not in transmission. In addition to the above three interference patterns, transmissions on link e and e' shown in Figure 2(d) are also considered to interfere with each other, since a wireless node, equipped with one radio, can only transmit to one of its successors at a time. Traditionally, the interference pattern in Figure 2(a) is called secondary interference[7], while the patterns in Figure 2(b), (c) and (d) are called primary interference. Graph $(E, \nparallel)$ is called the interference graph.

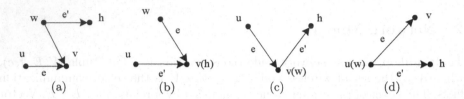

Fig. 2. The four patterns of interference

Take Figure 1 as an example, $25 \nparallel 47$ at node 5, $41 \nparallel 46$, $14 \nparallel 42$ and $14 \nparallel 64$ at node 4.

3   Problem Formulation

Before formally defining the notion of end-to-end throughput, we first introduce the concept of schedule, which specifies the actions of every network link during one time unit. Formally, a *schedule* of a network is a 0-1 vector z indexed by $e \in E$ and $0 \le t \le 1$. If $z_{e,t} = 1$, e is scheduled to be active at t, otherwise e is scheduled to be inactive. Schedule z is *feasible* if $\forall e, e' \in E$, $0 \le t \le 1$, $z_{e,t} = z_{e',t} = 1$ implies e does not interfere with e'. In other words, z is feasible if at any time $0 \le t \le 1$, the set of links scheduled to be active is interference free .

Let s be a source node, and let d be a sink. Let $E_{in}(v)$ and $E_{out}(v)$ denote the set of incoming and outgoing links incident on v. An $s - d$ *flow* x is a vector indexed by $e \in E$ that satisfies the capacity constraints

$$0 \le x_e \le c_e, \forall e \in E. \tag{1}$$

and the flow conservation constraints

$$x(v) = 0, \forall v \in V \backslash \{s, d\}, \tag{2}$$

where $x(v) = \sum_{e \in E_{out}(v)} x_e - \sum_{e \in E_{in}(v)} x_e$. The capacity constraints (1) simply say that the amount of data that link e carries cannot exceed its capacity. By flow conservation constraints (2), the amount of data that flows into each node(except s and d) is equal to the amount of data that flows out of it. The *value* of an $s - d$

flow x is defined to be $x(s)$, the net amount of data that flows out of source s. Flow x is *schedulable* if there exists a feasible schedule z such that

$$x_e/c_e = \int_0^1 z_{e,t} dt, \forall e \in E.$$

If the above equation holds, then x is said to be realized to z. The term $\int_0^1 z_{e,t} dt$ here is the fraction of time that e is scheduled to be active.

Problem 1 (Throughput). Given wireless network $(V, E, \not\mid, c)$, and two nodes $s, d \in V$, problem THROUGHPUT is to find a schedulable $s - d$ flow x with maximum value. This value, denoted as θ_{sd}, is called the $s - d$ *throughput*.

Each schedulable $s-d$ flow is a feasible solution to THROUGHPUT. All the schedulable $s - d$ flows form the feasible solution space. The above formulation of problem THROUGHPUT in wireless networks is similar to problem MAXFLOW in wired networks. The only difference is, THROUGHPUT has an extra constraint that flow x must be schedulable while MAXFLOW does not. Due to this extra constraint, the feasible solution space of THROUGHPUT has a much more complicated combinatorial structure. More specifically, it may not be possible to describe the feasible solution space of THROUGHPUT by a small set of linear constraints. The key idea of the upperbounding approaches to be presented in the following discussion is to use a polynomial number of linear constraints to characterize a superset of the feasible solution space of THROUGHPUT.

4 Upperbounding End-to-End Throughput

An *independent set* is a set of mutually non-interfering links. The *independence number* $\alpha(F)$ of a set of links $F \subseteq E$ is the size of the maximum independent set in F. The following lemma gives a necessary condition for a flow to be schedulable.

Lemma 1. *If flow x is schedulable, then it must satisfy the following independence constraints, where each $F \in \mathcal{F}$ is a subset of E, and 2^E is the set of all subsets of E:*

$$\sum_{e \in F} x_e/c_e \leq \alpha(F), \forall F \in \mathcal{F} \subseteq 2^E. \tag{3}$$

Proof. Let z be a feasible schedule that realizes x. Consider an arbitrary link set $F \in \mathcal{F}$. By definition of schedulability, $\forall e \in E$, $x_e/c_e = \int_0^1 z_{e,t} dt$. Thus,

$$\sum_{e \in F} x_e/c_e = \sum_{e \in F} \int_0^1 z_{e,t} dt = \int_0^1 \sum_{e \in F} z_{e,t} dt. \tag{4}$$

By the feasibility of z, the set of active links at time t is interference free. In other words, the set of active links at time t forms an independent set. Since $\alpha(F)$ is the size of the maximum independent set of F, $\sum_{e \in F} z_{e,t} \leq \alpha(F)$. Plug it into equation (4), we have (3).

Each constraint of form (3) is called an independence constraint on F. Since every schedulable flow satisfy (3), constraints (3) together with the flow conservation constraints (2) and capacity constraints (1) specify a superset of the feasible solution space of THROUGHPUT. Let $\bar{\theta}_{sd}(\mathcal{F})$ be the optimal objective value of the following linear program LP($\mathcal{F}$), where $\mathcal{F} \subseteq 2^E$ is a set of subsets of E.

$$\text{maximize} \qquad x(s)$$

$$\text{subject to} \quad \sum_{e \in F} x_e/c_e \leq \alpha(F), \qquad \forall F \in \mathcal{F}$$

$$x(v) = 0, \quad \forall v \in V \backslash \{s, d\}$$

$$0 \leq x_e \leq c_e, \qquad \forall e \in E$$

Theorem 1. $\forall \mathcal{F} \subseteq 2^E$, $\theta_{sd} \leq \bar{\theta}_{sd}(\mathcal{F})$. That is, $\bar{\theta}_{sd}(\mathcal{F})$ is an upperbound of θ_{sd}.

Proof. By Lemma 1, every feasible solution of THROUGHPUT is also a feasible solution of LP($\mathcal{F}$), therefore, the optimal objective value of LP($\mathcal{F}$) must be an upperbound of the $s - d$ throughput, that is, $\theta_{sd} \leq \bar{\theta}_{sd}(\mathcal{F})$.

Theorem 1 tells us that each $\mathcal{F} \subseteq 2^E$ corresponds to an upperbound $\bar{\theta}_{sd}(\mathcal{F})$ of θ_{sd}, however, it does not tell which choice of $\mathcal{F}$ is good in the sense that the corresponding $\bar{\theta}_{sd}(\mathcal{F})$ is close to θ_{sd} and is easy to compute. In general, the more link sets $\mathcal{F}$ contains, the tighter $\bar{\theta}_{sd}(\mathcal{F})$ will be. The tightest $\bar{\theta}_{sd}(\mathcal{F})$ is achieved when $\mathcal{F} = 2^E$. $\bar{\theta}_{sd}(2^E)$, however, is obviously too expensive to compute since there are exponential number of elements in 2^E. In the following, we propose several choice of good $\mathcal{F}$ based on the concepts of clique and congestion.

4.1 Clique Based Upperbounds

In the above discussion, we argued that any link set F corresponds to an independence constraint, which can be used to establish an upperbound of θ_{sd}. In this subsection, we restrict our attention to those link sets called cliques. A *clique* is a set mutually interfering links. Dealing with cliques instead of arbitrary link sets has several advantages. First, given an arbitrary clique F, the term $\alpha(F)$ in LP($\mathcal{F}$) can be immediately substitued with 1 since the links in F mutually interfere with each other. Note that, it is often expensive to compute $\alpha(F)$ if F is an arbitrary link set. Second, given two class of cliques $\mathcal{F}_1$ and $\mathcal{F}_2$, sometimes we can know which one of $\bar{\theta}_{sd}(\mathcal{F}_1)$ and $\bar{\theta}_{sd}(\mathcal{F}_2)$ is tighter without solving LP($\mathcal{F}_1$) and LP($\mathcal{F}_2$). Specifically, if for every clique $F_2 \in \mathcal{F}_2$, there is a clique $F_1 \in \mathcal{F}_1$ such that $F_2 \subseteq F_1$, then we say $\mathcal{F}_1$ is *stronger* than $\mathcal{F}_2$. If $\mathcal{F}_1$ is stronger than $\mathcal{F}_2$, then the independence constraints on $\mathcal{F}_2$ must be implied by the independence constraints on $\mathcal{F}_1$, and as a result $\bar{\theta}_{sd}(\mathcal{F}_1)$ must be closer to θ_{sd} than $\bar{\theta}_{sd}(\mathcal{F}_2)$. Therefore, in order to obtain a relatively tight upperbound $\bar{\theta}_{sd}(\mathcal{F})$ within a reasonable amount of time, we would want to pick a small set $\mathcal{F}$ of strong cliques .

We start our discussion of searching a good set of cliques by considering the following class of cliques call star cliques:

$$\mathcal{Q}_s = \{E_{in}(v) \cup E_{out}(v), \forall v \in V\}. \tag{5}$$

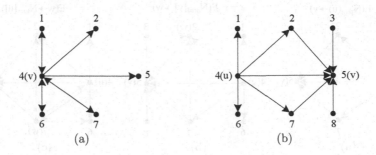

Fig. 3. Star and bell clique

By primary interference, any two links in $E_{in}(v) \cup E_{out}(v)$ interfere with each other at node v, thus each member of Q_s is indeed a clique. Figure 3(a) shows the star clique on node 4 of the network in Figure 1, which contains link 14, 41, 42, 45, 46, 64, 47, and 74. Star cliques are actually used in [3] to derive an approximate upperbound for wireless networks free of secondary interference.

Another class of cliques, called bell cliques, has the following form:

$$Q_b = \{E_{out}(u) \cup E_{in}(v), \forall uv \in E\}. \tag{6}$$

We say $E_1 \subseteq E$ interferes with $E_2 \subseteq E$, if $\forall e_1 \in E_1$ and $\forall e_2 \in E_2$, e_1 interferes with e_2. Each member of Q_b is indeed a clique since $E_{out}(u)$ and $E_{in}(v)$ are both cliques by primary interference and $E_{out}(u)$ interferes with $E_{in}(v)$ at node v by secondary interference. The bell clique on link 45 of the network in Figure 1 is depicted in Figure 3(b).

By (5) and (6), there are only $|V|$ and $|E|$ number of star and bell cliques respectively for a given wireless network, thus all of them can be enumerated efficiently. Starting from star and bell cliques, we propose three classes of stronger cliques in the following discussion. To ease the description of these cliques, we introduce the following additional notations. The set of predecessors and successors of v are denoted as $N_{pred}(v)$ and $N_{succ}(v)$. Define $N_{pred}[v] = N_{pred}(v) \cup \{v\}$ and $N_{succ}[v] = N_{succ}(v) \cup \{v\}$. Let U be a set of nodes, and v be a single node. The set of all links $e = uv$ such that $u \in U$ is denoted as $E(U \rightarrow v)$. Similarly, $E(v \rightarrow U)$ denotes the set of all links $e = vu$ such that $u \in U$.

First, consider the following class of cliques called class one cliques:

$$Q_1 = \{E_{in}(u) \cup E_{out}(u) \cup E(N_{pred}(u) \rightarrow v), \forall uv \in E\} \tag{7}$$

It is straightforward to verify that $E(N_{pred}(u) \rightarrow v)$ interferes with $E_{in}(u)$ either at u or v, and $E(N_{pred}(u) \rightarrow v)$ interferes with $E_{out}(u)$ at v. We have already known $E_{in}(u) \cup E_{out}(u)$ forms a star clique, therefore, $E_{in}(u) \cup E_{out}(u) \cup E(N_{pred}(u) \rightarrow v)$ is indeed a clique. Figure 4(a) shows the class one clique on node 4 and 5 of the network in Figure 1. Q_1 is stronger than Q_s since it is obtained by augmenting each star clique $E_{in}(u) \cup E_{out}(u)$ with $E(N_{pred}(u) \rightarrow v)$.

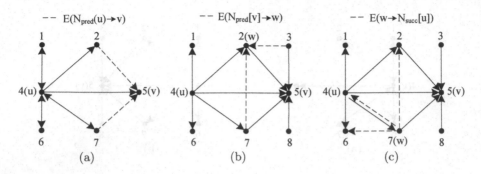

Fig. 4. Class one, two, and three clique

Second, let u, v and w be three nodes such that $uv \in E$ and $uw \in E$. Consider class two cliques as follows:

$$Q_2 = \{E_{out}(u) \cup E_{in}(v) \cup E(N_{pred}[v] \rightarrow w), \forall uv, uw \in E\} \qquad (8)$$

It is straightforward to verify that $E(V_{pred}[v] \rightarrow w)$ interferes with $E_{out}(u)$ at w, and it also interferes with $E_{in}(v)$ at v. We have already known $E_{out}(u) \cup E_{in}(v)$ is a bell clique, so $E_{out}(u) \cup E_{in}(v) \cup E(N_{pred}[v] \rightarrow w)$ is indeed a clique. Figure 4(b) shows the class two clique on node 4, 5 and 2 of the network in Figure 1. Q_2 is stronger than Q_b since it is obtained by augmenting each bell clique $E_{in}(u) \cup E_{out}(v)$ with $E(N_{pred}[v] \rightarrow w)$.

Finally, let u, v and w be three nodes such that $uv \in E$ and $wv \in E$. Consider class three cliques as follows:

$$Q_3 = \{E_{out}(u) \cup E_{in}(v) \cup E(w \rightarrow N_{succ}[u]), \forall uv, wv \in E\} \qquad (9)$$

By similar analysis we can show that, each member of Q_3 is indeed a clique too. As an example, Figure 4(c) shows the class three clique on node 4, 5 and 7 of the network in Figure 1.

The asymmetricity in the form of Q_1, Q_2 and Q_3 stems from the fact that protocol interference model is essentially a receiver oriented model, which precludes all the predecessors of the receiver but not the sender of a communication from transmitting. By (7), (8), and (9), there are at most $|E|$ cliques in Q_1, and $|E| \cdot |V|$ cliques in Q_2 and Q_3 respectively. Thus, Q_1, Q_2 and Q_3 can all be enumerated in polynomial time, which means that the corresponding upperbounds $\bar{\theta}_{sd}(Q_1)$, $\bar{\theta}_{sd}(Q_2)$, $\bar{\theta}_{sd}(Q_3)$, or even $\bar{\theta}_{sd}(Q_1 \cup Q_2 \cup Q_3)$ can be computed efficiently. Later we will show by simulation that these upperbounds are fairly tight in practice.

4.2   Congestion Based Upperbounds

In this section, we discuss congestion based upperbound. A unique characteristic of this upperbound is that it is guaranteed to be within a constant factor of the exact throughput.

Define $I_\geq(e)$ as the set of links that e interferes with and whose Euclidean length is larger than e. Define $I_\geq[e] = I_\geq(e) \cup \{e\}$. $I_\geq[e]$ is called the congestion set of e. Let $\mathcal{C}$ be the set of all congestion sets, i.e.,

$$\mathcal{C} = \{I_\geq[e] : \forall e \in E\} \tag{10}$$

The following two lemmas are given in [2]:

Lemma 2. *If flow x satisfies the following constraints, then it must be schedulable:*

$$\sum_{e' \in I_\geq[e]} x_{e'}/c_{e'} \leq 1, \forall e \in E \tag{11}$$

Lemma 3. *For any $e \in E$, $\alpha(I[e]) \leq q$, where q is a constant number.*

By Theorem 1, the optimal objective value $\bar{\theta}_{sd}(\mathcal{C})$ of LP($\mathcal{C}$) is an upperbound of θ_{sd}. The following theorem shows that this upperbound is guaranteed to be a within constant factor of θ_{sd}.

Theorem 2. $\bar{\theta}_{sd}(\mathcal{C})/\theta_{sd} \leq q$, *where q is the constant in Lemma 3.*

Proof. Let $\underline{\theta}_{sd}$ be the optimal objective value of the following linear program LP1:

$$\text{maximize} \qquad x(s)$$
$$\text{subject to} \sum_{e' \in I_\geq[e]} x_{e'}/c_{e'} \leq 1, \qquad \forall e \in E$$
$$x(v) = 0, \quad \forall v \in V \backslash \{s, d\}$$
$$0 \leq x_e \leq c_e, \qquad \forall e \in E$$

By Lemma 2, every feasible solution of LP1 is a feasible solution of THROUGH-PUT, thus $\underline{\theta}_{sd}$ must be a lowerbound of θ_{sd}, that is,

$$\underline{\theta}_{sd} \leq \theta_{sd}. \tag{12}$$

Let $\hat{\theta}_{sd}$ be the optimal objective value of the following linear program LP2:

$$\text{maximize} \qquad x(s)$$
$$\text{subject to} \sum_{e' \in I_\geq[e]} x_{e'}/c_{e'} \leq q, \qquad \forall e \in E$$
$$x(v) = 0, \quad \forall v \in V \backslash \{s, d\}$$
$$0 \leq x_e \leq c_e, \qquad \forall e \in E$$

By Lemma 3, $\alpha(I[e]) \leq q, \forall e \in E$. Therefore, every feasible solution of LP($\mathcal{C}$) is also a feasible solution of LP2. So,

$$\bar{\theta}_{sd}(\mathcal{C}) \leq \hat{\theta}_{sd}. \tag{13}$$

Furthermore, for any feasible solution x of LP1, $q \cdot x$ is a feasible solution of LP2. And, for any feasible solution x of LP2, x/q is a feasible solution of LP1. As a result, the optimal objective value of LP1 and LP2 must satisfy:

$$\hat{\theta}_{sd} = q \cdot \underline{\theta}_{sd}. \qquad (14)$$

Finally, by (12), (13), and (14), $\bar{\theta}_{sd}(\mathcal{C}) \leq q \cdot \theta_{sd}$.

5   Simulation Evaluation

In this section, we evaluate the clique and congestion based upperbounds on grid networks and random networks respectively. In our simulations, linear programs are solved by Lp_solve[9], and the following simple recursive algorithm is used to compute the independence number α. The algorithm is based on the fact that $\alpha(F) = max\{\alpha(F\backslash\{e\}), \alpha(F\backslash I[e]) + 1\}$ where e is a link in F, $I[e] = I(e) \cup \{e\}$ and $I(e)$ is the set of links that e interferes with.

Algorithm 1. Independence number α

Input: interference graph $(E, \mathcal{I})$, a set of links $F \subseteq E$
Output: independence number $\alpha(F)$

1. if $|F| = 0$ return 0
2. pick a link $e \in F$
3. recursively compute $\alpha(F\backslash\{e\})$ and $\alpha(F\backslash I[e])$
4. return $max\{\alpha(F\backslash\{e\}), \alpha(F\backslash I[e]) + 1\}$

5.1   Grid Network

We create a 10x10 grid network as shown in Figure 5(a). All the nodes have the same transmission range. Each line in Figure 5(a) represents two one-way links. We assign to each link a random capacity with uniform distribution from 0 to 100. We randomly pick 10 pairs of nodes, and compute their $s - d$ throughputs. The upperbounds $\bar{\theta}_{sd}(\mathcal{Q}_1)$, $\bar{\theta}_{sd}(\mathcal{Q}_2)$, $\bar{\theta}_{sd}(\mathcal{Q}_3)$ and $\bar{\theta}_{sd}(\mathcal{C})$ are listed under column $\bar{\theta}_1$, $\bar{\theta}_2$, $\bar{\theta}_3$ and $\bar{\theta}_c$ in Table 1. Column $\bar{\theta}_{123}$ and $\bar{\theta}_{123c}$ are upperbounds $\bar{\theta}_{sd}(\mathcal{Q}_1 \cup \mathcal{Q}_2 \cup \mathcal{Q}_3)$ and $\bar{\theta}_{sd}(\mathcal{Q}_1 \cup \mathcal{Q}_2 \cup \mathcal{Q}_3 \cup \mathcal{C})$ respectively. Column $\underline{\theta}$ lists the lowerbounds computed by the maximal independent sets enumeration method in [1].

From the results we can see that, first, $\bar{\theta}_1$, $\bar{\theta}_2$ and $\bar{\theta}_3$ are consistently closer to $\underline{\theta}$ than $\bar{\theta}_c$. It always holds that $\bar{\theta}_1 > \bar{\theta}_2 = \bar{\theta}_3 = \bar{\theta}_{123}$, and the numbers in column $\bar{\theta}_{123}$ are very close to the numbers in column $\underline{\theta}$. Furthermore, $\bar{\theta}_{123c}$ always coincides with $\bar{\theta}_{123}$. That is to say, adding congestion constraints does not further lower the upperbound computed by clique constraints. These evidences suggest that $\bar{\theta}_{123}$ is a practically good upperbound. In this regards, we computed $\bar{\theta}_{123}$ for all pairs of nodes in this network and compare them with $\underline{\theta}$. We found that more than 90% of the time, $\bar{\theta}_{123}$ is within $1.05\underline{\theta}$, and never goes above $1.25\underline{\theta}$.

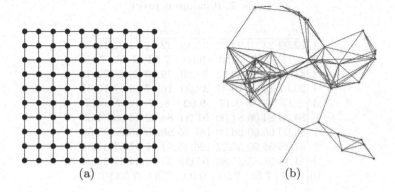

(a)   (b)

Fig. 5. Grid and random network

Table 1. Grid network

	$\bar{\theta}_1$	$\bar{\theta}_2$	$\bar{\theta}_3$	$\bar{\theta}_c$	$\bar{\theta}_{123}$	$\bar{\theta}_{123c}$	$\underline{\theta}$
1	60.04	53.06	53.06	101.68	53.06	53.06	51.33
2	53.41	51.62	51.62	115.96	51.62	51.62	51.41
3	86.00	86.00	86.00	158.90	86.00	86.00	86.00
4	73.79	64.71	64.71	149.52	64.71	64.71	56.62
5	63.84	60.14	60.14	121.11	60.14	60.14	51.89
6	62.79	54.70	54.70	103.83	54.70	54.70	54.70
7	60.62	47.70	47.70	95.06	47.70	47.70	41.17
8	44.13	41.57	41.57	82.20	41.57	41.57	34.67
9	33.20	31.36	31.36	77.44	31.36	31.36	31.07
10	33.20	31.36	31.36	75.46	31.36	31.36	31.28

5.2 Random Network

We create a set of 40 nodes on a 500x500 Euclidean plane as shown in Figure 5(b). Each node is equipped with one radio with a random transmission range of mean 100 and variance 20. Each link in the network is assigned a random capacity with uniform distribution from 0 to 100. We randomly pick 10 pairs of nodes, and compute their $s - d$ throughputs. The results are listed in Table 2.

From the results we can see that, $\bar{\theta}_1$, $\bar{\theta}_2$ and $\bar{\theta}_3$ are still consistently closer to $\underline{\theta}$ than $\bar{\theta}_c$. $\bar{\theta}_{123}$ is always smaller than $\bar{\theta}_1$, $\bar{\theta}_2$ and $\bar{\theta}_3$. Most of the times except for the first and third run, $\bar{\theta}_{123c}$ coincides with $\bar{\theta}_{123}$. Even though $\bar{\theta}_{123c}$ is a little bit tighter than $\bar{\theta}_{123}$ for the first and third run, the difference between them is small. Again, these results suggest that $\bar{\theta}_{123}$ is a practically good upperbound. After that, we computed $\bar{\theta}_{123}$ and $\underline{\theta}$ for all pairs of nodes in this network, and found that more than 90% of the time, $\bar{\theta}_{123}$ is within $1.35\underline{\theta}$, and never goes above $2\underline{\theta}$. Notice that, $\underline{\theta}$ is only a lowerbound of θ, thus, the gap between $\bar{\theta}_{123}$ and θ could be even smaller than that between $\bar{\theta}_{123}$ and $\underline{\theta}$.

Table 2. Random network

	$\bar{\theta}_1$	$\bar{\theta}_2$	$\bar{\theta}_3$	$\bar{\theta}_c$	$\bar{\theta}_{123}$	$\bar{\theta}_{123c}$	θ
1	22.99	23.10	22.72	32.45	22.71	22.22	17.66
2	8.17	7.53	7.53	9.00	7.53	7.53	7.53
3	41.18	39.90	40.81	59.59	39.90	39.86	27.91
4	20.67	16.47	16.47	38.00	16.47	16.47	16.47
5	8.17	8.17	8.17	9.00	8.17	8.17	8.17
6	84.00	84.00	84.00	91.00	84.00	84.00	84.00
7	96.00	96.00	96.00	181.75	96.00	96.00	96.00
8	67.38	61.90	55.77	126.45	54.57	54.57	44.96
9	51.58	38.85	37.82	63.00	35.42	34.47	32.00
10	8.17	7.53	7.53	9.00	7.53	7.53	7.53

6 Related Work

The problem of computing end-to-end throughput for multihop wireless networks was first studied in [10], where the system under study is assumed to be free of secondary interference. The author gave a polynomial time algorithm based on the famous ellipsoid method. The exact time complexity of their algorithm, however, is unknown. Following [10]'s work, [3] proposed a more practical algorithm that computes approximate throughput based on Shannon's coloring theorem. Both [10] and [3] neglect the existence of secondary interference. [1] proposed a maximal independent set based lowerbounding and a clique based upperbounding technique. Their approach is general enough to be applied to a wide class of networks. However, it does not take fully advantage of the special topology and interference pattern of wireless networks. [2] first established a lowerbound that is within a constant factor of the throughput in wireless networks with secondary interference. Based on their results, we developed a complementary upperbound. Finally, [4,5] considered throughput estimation in multi-radio multi-channel wireless networks by extending results for the single-radio single-channel case.

7 Conclusion

In this paper, we studied the problem of computing end-to-end throughput upperbounds in multi-hop wireless networks. We proposed a general linear program $LP(\mathcal{F})$ based solution framework, and show each choice of $\mathcal{F}$ corresponds to an upperbound $\bar{\theta}_{sd}(\mathcal{F})$ of the end-to-end throughput θ_{sd}. We identify several good choice of $\mathcal{F}$: $\mathcal{Q}_1$, $\mathcal{Q}_2$, $\mathcal{Q}_3$, and $\mathcal{C}$, where $\mathcal{Q}_1$, $\mathcal{Q}_2$, and $\mathcal{Q}_3$ are class one, two, and three cliques and $\mathcal{C}$ is the set of all congestion sets. We prove that $\bar{\theta}_{sd}(\mathcal{C})$ is within constant factor of θ_{sd}, and show by simulation that $\bar{\theta}_{sd}(\mathcal{Q}_1 \cup \mathcal{Q}_2 \cup \mathcal{Q}_3)$ is close to θ_{sd} in practice.

References

1. K. Jain, J. Padhye, V. Padmanabhan, and L. Qiu, "Impact of interference on multi-hop wireless network performance," in *Proceedings of the 9th annual international conference on Mobile computing and networking(Mobicom)*, 2003, pp. 66–80.
2. V. A. Kumar, M. V. Marathey, S. Parthasarathyz, and A. Srinivasan, "Algorithmic aspects of capacity in wireless networks," in *International Conference on Measurement and Modeling of Computer Systems(Sigmetrics)*, 2005.
3. M. Kodialam and T. Nandagopal, "Characterizing achievable rates in multi-hop wireless networks: the joint routing and scheduling problem," in *Proceedings of the 9th annual international conference on Mobile computing and networking(Mobicom)*. ACM Press, 2003, pp. 42–54.
4. ——, "Characterizing the capacity region in multi-radio multi-channel wireless mesh networks," in *Proceedings of the 11th annual international conference on Mobile computing and networking(Mobicom)*, 2005, pp. 73–87.
5. M. Alicherry, R. Bhatia, and I. F. Li, "Joint channel assignment and routing for throughput optimization in multi-radio wireless mesh networks," in *Proceedings of the 11th annual international conference on Mobile computing and networking(Mobicom)*, 2005, pp. 58–72.
6. P. Gupta and P. R. Kumar, "The capacity of wireless networks," *IEEE Transactions on Information Theory*, no. 2, pp. 388–404, 2000.
7. S. Ramanathan and E. L. Lloyd, "Scheduling algorithms for multihop radio networks," *IEEE/ACM Transaction on Networking*, vol. 1, no. 2, pp. 166–177, 1993.
8. A. Wagler, "Rank-perfect and weakly rank-perfect graphs," *Mathematical Methods of operations research*, 2002.
9. [Online]. Available: http://groups.yahoo.com/group/lp_solve
10. B. Hajek and G. Sasaki, "Link scheduling in polynomial time," *ACM/IEEE Transactions on Information Theory*, vol. 34, no. 5, 1988.

Dynamicity Aware Graph Relabeling Systems and the Constraint Based Synchronization: A Unifying Approach to Deal with Dynamic Networks

Arnaud Casteigts and Serge Chaumette

LaBRI, Université Bordeaux 1,
351 Cours de la Libération, F-33405 Talence, France
{arnaud.casteigts, serge.chaumette}@labri.fr
http://www.labri.fr/

Abstract. Many research projects are being done in the domain of wireless mobile and/or ad-hoc networks to provide tools, algorithms and applications that make it possible to handle or use their dynamic characteristics. The purpose of most of these projects is to solve a specific problem, in a specific context. Most often, the models and formalisms that are used are also specific and the results are therefore difficult both to understand and to use in another context. We believe that what is needed is a general model offering a very high level of abstraction, in order to define and characterize what is feasable or not feasable in a dynamic network, depending upon some of its characteristics. In this paper we define such a model and its associated formalism. They are adapted to the study of dynamic networks and to the modeling of algorithms in a dynamic context at a high level of abstraction. The proposed model (Dynamicity Aware Graph Relabeling Systems) derives from what has been achieved in the area of local computations, and that produced useful results in the context of static networks. Our contribution comprises a model and the associated formalism, plus an original synchronization mode between nodes that allows to seemlessly adapt an algorithm to different mobility contexts. All the concepts are illustrated and discussed through the example of a document propagation algorithm, with a resume feature.

1 Introduction

The research activity in the area of wireless and pervasive networks keeps on growing. The emergence of numerous broadband wireless standards such as 802.11/16, bluetooth or 3G/UMTS that offer many new possibilities enforces the trend.

While many research projects focus on routing layers [9], or on a specific problem in a given network, we study these different kinds of networks from a theoretical point of view in terms of what basically makes them similar or different, and what can be done (or not) in each of them. This requires a well adapted model, which makes it possible to take into account the dynamicity

X. Cheng, W. Li, and T. Znati (Eds.): WASA 2006, LNCS 4138, pp. 688–697, 2006.

of the network, and the `locality` of the communications. To understand this last point, let us examine more precisely one single device in such a network. The only thing this device can basically be aware of is its own state, and the state of its direct neighbors. The only thing it can be sure of is that, `at a given instant`, it can communicate with these neighbors, and that this communication link can have disappeared at the next instant, because one of the devices has moved or has been turned off.

Another property of the desired model (in addition to locality and dynamicity) is to be at a high level of abstraction. It should be possible to ignore physical implementation details when designing an algorithm.

Our first contribution is the **DA-GRS model** (Dynamicity Aware Graph Relabeling Systems). It has been inspired by the area of local computations, in which most of the desired properties described above were considered, even though it addresses distributed algorithms in the context of static networks.

Our second contribution is what we call the **constraint based synchronization**. While local computations traditionally synchronize the nodes by using a rendezvous algorithm[8], we propose in this paper a new approach that allows to seamlessly adapt an algorithm to different contexts.

The rest of this paper is organized as follows. In section 2 we present local computations and the GRS formalism. In section 3 we present our contributions. We first explain the DA-GRS model, the grounds of which have been introduced in [4]. We then describe the rendez-vous synchronization algorithm used by local computations and the new synchronization mode that we propose, stressing the fact that it is well adapted to DA-GRS. In section 4 we illustrate the model and the synchronization mode by means of an example that consists in propagating a document within a dynamic ad-hoc network. This propagation supports a resume feature, so it can be used for the diffusion of a large, for instance multimedia, file. We eventualy conclude, present futur work and some other possible applications in section 5.

2   Related Work

The model that we propose in this paper (the DA-GRS model), is an extension of local computations to dynamic networks. This section briefly presents the area of local computations, and the precise model we derive from. The formalism that is used is that of the well known Graph Relabeling Systems.

Model. Local computations have been introduced as a technique to express and evaluate distributed algorithms on a network of communicating processors. The physical network is seen as a graph, the edges of which represent the communication links, and the vertices (or nodes) represent the computing resources. Local computation models are very "powerful" theoretical models in the sense that a problem that has no solution with local computations has no solution with any other model (the opposite being false). This property is due to the fact that the communication model (message passing, mail boxes, shared memory, etc..) is abstracted. A basic computation step is defined by a couple (pre-condition,

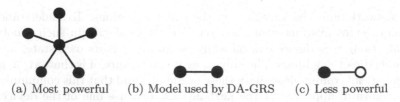

(a) Most powerful   (b) Model used by DA-GRS   (c) Less powerful

Fig. 1. Local computation models

post-condition) that modifies the states of the involved nodes and/or edges according to their previous states, and without considerations about the way they actually do it.

Local computation models do not require any assumption about the network such as the existence of unique identities for nodes, topology knowledge, etc. On the contrary it is often used to characterize which assumptions have to be done in order to solve a given problem. Local computations also provide a way to express distributed algorithms in an elegant way, and help to prove their correctness.

Regarding the properties that we stated to be important in the introduction, the most interesting one for dynamic networks is **locality**, that matches the reality of the network. Local computations only consider communications between nodes that are direct neighbors.

Many local computation models exist, from the most powerful - where the evolution of a node in one step depends on the states of its neighboring ball of radius 1, and can impact on the state of the whole ball (figure 1(a)) - to the weakest - where the evolution of a node in one step depends on its state and on the state of one of its neighbors, and impacts only its own state (figure 1(c)). We have chosen to use the model illustrated on figure 1(b), which we believe is the most realistic in a dynamic context, because of the difficulty to synchronize more than two nodes that can move at any time.

The reader is further referred to [2], [6] and [10] for the grounding work on local computation, respectively by Angluin and by Yamashita and Kameda. A classification of local computation models can be found in [5].

Formalism. Graph Relabeling Systems (GRS) are one of the formalisms that can be used to represent local computations. With this formalism, the states of vertices and edges are represented by labels, and a computation step is represented by a relabeling rule.

A basic and intuitive example, as described in [7], is the modelization of a spanning tree algorithm. In this example, each node has its label in $\{I, N\}$ that represents the fact that it is *Integrated* in the tree or *Not*. An edge belongs to the tree if it is labeled 1. Initially, all edges are labeled 0 and all nodes are labeled N except one, the root, which is labeled I. The tree is then built by repeatedly appling the following simple rule:

$$R1: \quad \overset{I}{\bullet} \underset{0}{\!-\!-\!-\!} \overset{N}{\bullet} \quad \longrightarrow \quad \overset{I}{\bullet} \underset{1}{\!-\!-\!-\!} \overset{I}{\bullet}$$

Such an execution will stop when no rule is applicable anymore. Figure 2 shows an execution example of this algorithm in an arbitrary network.

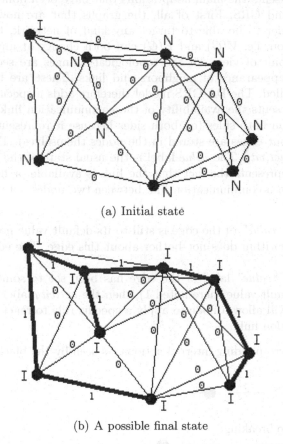

(a) Initial state

(b) A possible final state

Fig. 2. Spanning tree algorithm (multiple applications of rule R1)

Note that the tree is computed in a finite number of relabeling steps (depending on the diameter of the graph), and all the computation steps are done locally.

3   The DA-GRS Model and Its Synchronization Mode

The local computation model presented in the previous section deals with static graphs, where $V(G)$ and $E(G)$ do not change during computation. In order to use a similar approach in a dynamic context, this model has to be adapted. This is what we have done by defining the DA-GRS model. In addition, while a rendez-vous is used to synchronize two nodes before they work together in a static network, we propose another synchronization mode that we call *constraint based synchronization* that enables to adapt an algorithm to different target networks, without modifying the algorithm itself.

3.1 The DA-GRS Model

This section presents the main adaptations that have been done based on local computations and GRS. First of all, the graphs that are now delt with are dynamic. In order to be able to target any kind of network, this dynamicity has no restriction, i.e. $V(G)$ and $E(G)$ can both change at any time. From a strictly local point of view, all the topological changes are seen by nodes as appearance/disappearance of neighbors and links. These are the events that have to be handled. The DA-GRS model therefore adds a special label on each edge, that represents the availability of the communication link. Now, an edge has two labels on both sides (on both sides because it represents the fact that information about edges are stored in the nodes themselves). These two labels are: *value* and *activity*. The *value* label is the usual state of the edge, while the *activity* label represents the fact that the link is available or has been broken (on/off). When a communication link between two nodes is broken, two cases are considered:

- if the label "*value*" of the edge is still to its default value noted 0, it means that the algorithm does not bother about this edge. The edge thus simply disappears.
- if the label "*value*" label of the edge has been set to something different from its default value (here noted 1), then the *activity* label takes the value off, what will allow a node to apply a specific rule to react to the loss of a communication link.

Here are the corresponding internal actions, as seen by the black node:

- New edge:

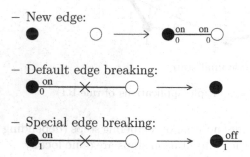

- Default edge breaking:

- Special edge breaking:

Note that these operations are not part of any algorithm. They are intrinsic reactions of the model to topology changes and make it possible for an algorithm to handle dynamicity.

3.2 The Rendezvous Algorithm

The rendezvous algorithm used in a static context, ensures a fair distribution of the computation steps between the nodes. In this synchronization algorithm, each node iterates through the following actions:

- *select one of my neighbors $c(v)$ at random*
- *send 1 to $c(v)$*

– *send 0 to the other neighbors*
– *receive a message from each of my neighbors*
– *there is a rendezvous with c(v)*
        if I receive 1 from it.

When there is a rendezvous between two nodes, they try to apply a rule if possible. More information about the rendezvous algorithm can be found in [8].

3.3 The Constraint Based Synchronization

Intuitive Idea. In many cases, the management of dynamicity must be adapted to the context (pedestrians, vehicles on the road, researchers in a conference room, sensors with weak mobility, etc.) and to the type of application that is being considered (propagation of information, construction of a global structure for topology control, music sharing, etc). From a purely local point of view, this adaptation can be carried out by giving a higher priority to the interactions satisfying certain criteria, which we call *constraints*. We propose to manage these constraints at the synchronization level, replacing the rendezvous algorithm presented above in order to relieve the algorithm from these considerations.

Architecture. The resulting global model is shown figure 3.

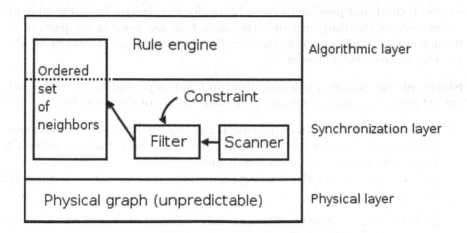

Fig. 3. The multi-layer model

Explanation. At regular intervals, the network *scanner* of each node builds a set of reachable neighbors that are detected. This set is then ordered by the *filter*, according to a given constraint (see below). Once the set of neighbors has been ordered, the top level layer, i.e. the DA-GRS rule engine, uses it as a replacement for the rendezvous algorithm. Instead of choosing a neighbor at random, the rule engine tries to apply a rule with each neighbor in the order given by the constructed set until success. This mechanism ensures that the communication links that match the constraint are favored.

Discussion About the Constraint. The pieces of information that a node can have about a communication link with a neighbor can be of different natures. This could be for example the time since it is available, the strength or the variation of the (radio) signal. These pieces of information, possibly combined, make it possible to give priority to a communication that would for instance be *stable, weak, near-to-break, with a good bandwidth*, etc...

4   Illustration

The example presented in this section illustrates the formalism, the model and the use of the constraint based synchronization. We first present the algorithm and give explanation about DA-GRS. We then discuss it and show how it can be adapted to different target networks without any modification.

4.1   The DA-GRS Propagation Algorithm

The example that we use is an algorithm the aim of which is to propagate a possibly large document in a dynamic network. To receive the document, a node selects a source in its neighbourhood and tries to keep on working with this source. If this is not possible (because of topological changes for instance) it will go on working (resume) with any other node that has some of the parts of the document that it misses, and so on. Note that all parts of the document are thus received in an ordered manner.

States of the Nodes. Each node has two labels representing its state (*main* and *offset*). The possible values of the state *main* are the following:

 − F: The node has the whole document, and does not try to get it anymore.
 − N: The node does not have the whole document, and it wants to connect to another node to get the parts that it misses.
 − R: The node is currently receiving parts of the document from a connected neighbor.

The value of the state *offset* is the number of the last part of the document that the node has received. The document is split into n pieces.

States of the Edges. Two connected nodes have their common edge locally labeled 1. The other edges are labeled 0.

The Algorithm
When a node labeled F meets a node labeled N, a connection start between them:

When a node labeled N meets another node labeled N, and their *offset* are different, a connection starts between them:

R2: $\overset{N,\,j}{\underset{0}{\bullet}} \overset{on}{} \overset{on}{\underset{0}{\bullet}} \overset{N,\,i<j}{} \longrightarrow \overset{N,\,j}{\underset{1}{\bullet}} \overset{on}{} \overset{on}{\underset{1}{\bullet}} \overset{R,\,i}{}$

The following rule models the transfer of a block between two nodes. (F/N means that the rule applies the same way for nodes labeled F or N):

R3: $\overset{F/N,\,j}{\underset{1}{\bullet}} \overset{on}{} \overset{on}{\underset{1}{\bullet}} \overset{R,\,i<j}{} \longrightarrow \overset{F/N,\,j}{\underset{1}{\bullet}} \overset{on}{} \overset{on}{\underset{1}{\bullet}} \overset{R,\,i+1}{}$

During the connection, if the node labeled R has received the last block of the document then the transfer is finished, it becomes labeled F and the connection is closed:

R4: $\overset{F,\,n}{\underset{1}{\bullet}} \overset{on}{} \overset{on}{\underset{1}{\bullet}} \overset{R,\,i=n}{} \longrightarrow \overset{F,\,n}{\underset{0}{\bullet}} \overset{on}{} \overset{on}{\underset{0}{\bullet}} \overset{F,\,n}{}$

During the connection, if the node labeled R has received the last block the node labeled N can give, then the connection is closed, and it returns in the waiting state:

R5: $\overset{N,\,j}{\underset{1}{\bullet}} \overset{on}{} \overset{on}{\underset{1}{\bullet}} \overset{R,\,i=j}{} \longrightarrow \overset{N,\,j}{\underset{0}{\bullet}} \overset{on}{} \overset{on}{\underset{0}{\bullet}} \overset{N,\,j}{}$

If the link between two connected nodes breaks, then the receiving node returns to the waiting state:

R6: $\overset{R,\,i}{\underset{1}{\bullet}} \overset{off}{} \longrightarrow \overset{N,\,i}{\bullet}$

and the sending node cleans its state by removing the edge:

R7: $\overset{F/N,\,j}{\underset{1}{\bullet}} \overset{off}{} \longrightarrow \overset{F/N,\,j}{\bullet}$

Note that the algorithm is able to react to topological changes thanks to the dynamicity management that we have introduced in the DA-GRS model.

4.2   Adaptation to Different Target Networks

As explained above, we use a constraint to order the neighbors of a node. The chosen constraint impacts on which neighbor nodes will preferably work together. This enables to take into account some characteristics of the context in which the algorithm is executed. For the example of document propagation presented above, we can distinguish several contexts to which we would like to adapt the algorithm.

First context: *little mobility and large messages.* If the nodes are hardly mobile and the data to transfer are large (e.g. people in a room who exchange multimedia files), then we would like to give priority to the most stable communication links. The chosen constraint is then the *Minimum signal variation.*

Second context: *strong mobility and short messages.* If the nodes are very mobile and the messages are short (e.g. cars on a road that propagate information relative to an accident), it may be worth giving priority to the communication links that are the more volatile, in order to inform a maximum number of nodes (cars that are going away). The chosen constraint is then the *Maximum signal variation.*

Third context: *big covering and short messages.* If the aim of the propagation is to inform the farthest node or to cover the largest area in the smallest amount of time, the constraint would be the *Less powerful signal.*

Fourth context: *big bandwidth.* If the application needs the biggest available bandwidth, the favored communications would be those which offer the strongest signal. The constraint is then the *Most powerful signal.*

An algorithm can thus be studied and possibly simulated in various contexts, without being modified.

5   Conclusion

In this paper, we have presented our contribution to the study of wireless, dynamic and mobile network algorithms. We have introduced the DA-GRS model and the constraint based rendezvous. The DA-GRS model, allows to work on general issues of dynamic networks, while keeping control of dynamicity. Its main advantages are its ability to take into account the locality of the communication, the dynamicity of the topology in an innate way, and to provide an abstraction of the communication layer.

The example that we have shown has been designed to illustrate the model and the fact that an algorithm could be quite easily described with this formalism. We have focused on how the *constraint based synchronization* mechanism makes it possible to take into account different contexts of dynamicity, each using a set of constraints to impact the behavior of the algorithm. We have shown that the adaptation from one context to another is straightforward and is done without any modification of the algorithm itself. Concerning the practical validation of the model, we have developed a free software simulator (under the terms of the GPL) that allows to run algorithms designed with the DA-GRS formalism. This simulator can be found at [1].

The research on the DA-GRS model are quite recent, and it has opened many potential directions. First of all, we plan to use it to classify dynamic networks, in terms of what kinds of problems can be solved, in which network classes, and with which asumptions. The problems we plan to study in a first step are classical theoretical problems, such as election, naming or enumeration. From a more practical point of view, we are also studying the model driven capabilities of the DA-GRS [3] in terms of code and interface generations from rules. This will be used along with an embedded rule engine.

Acknowledgements. The work presented in this paper is carried out at LaBRI (Laboratoire Bordelais de Recherche en Informatique) and more precisely in the SOD (Distributed Systems and Objects) team. It is partly achieved within the framework of the Sarah (Asynchronous services for mobile ad-hoc networks) project supported by the ANR (Agence Nationale de la Recherche).

References

1. SimuDAGRS, a Dynamic Network simulator for algorithms modeled by DA-GRS. available at http://www.labri.fr/~casteigt/simulator.html, 2005.
2. D. Angluin. Local and global properties in networks of processors. In *Proceedings of the 12th Symposium on theory of computing*, pages 82–93, 1980.
3. A. Casteigts. Model driven capabilities of the da-grs model. In *Proceedings of the 1st IEEE workshop on self-adaptability and self-management of context-aware systems (SELF'06)*.
4. A. Casteigts and S. Chaumette. Dynamicity Aware Graph Relabeling Systems - a model to describe MANet algorithms. In *Proceedings of the 17th IASTED International Conference on Parallel and Distributed Computing and Systems*, 2005.
5. J. Chalopin, Y. Metivier, and W. Zielonka. Election, naming and cellular edge local computations. In *second international conference on graph transformation*, pages 242–256. Lectures Notes in Computer Science, 2004.
6. T. Kameda and M. Yamashita. Characterizing the solvable cases. In *Computing on anonymous networks*, pages 69–89. IEEE Transactions on parallel and distributed systems, 7, 1996.
7. I. Litovsky, Y. Metivier, and E. Sopena. Graph relabelling systems and distributed algorithms. In World Scientific Publishing, editor, *Handbook of graph grammars and computing by graph transformation,*, volume Vol. III, Eds. H. Ehrig, H.J. Kreowski, U. Montanari and G. Rozenberg,., pages 1–56, 1999.
8. Y. Metivier, N. Saheb, and A. Zemmari. Analysis of a randomized rendezvous algorithm. *Inf. Comput.*, 184(1):109–128, 2003.
9. E.M. Royer and C.K. Toh. A review of current routing protocols for ad-hoc mobile wireless networks. In *Personnal Communications, IEEE*, pages 46–55, 1999.
10. T. Kameda and M. Yamashita. Decision and membership problems. In *Computing on anonymous networks*, pages 90–96. IEEE Transactions on parallel and distributed systems, 7, 1996.

Studying Rational User Behavior in WCDMA Network and Its Effect on Network Revenue*

Yufeng Wang[1] and Wendong Wang[2]

[1] Communications Engineering Department, Nanjing University of Posts and Telecommunications (NUPT), Nanjing 210000, China
[2] State Key Laboratory of Networking & Switching Technology, Beijing University of Posts and Telecommunications (BUPT),Beijing 100876, China

Abstract. In WCDMA networks, most economic-based resource management algorithms only assumed that network users were obedient, that is, users only accepted the price declared by network, which is called as price acceptance mechanism. Many research issues argued that it is necessary to accommodate, if possible, to use self-interest behaviours of users to strengthen the technical architecture of network engineering. Thus, this paper explicitly considered the selfishness of users, investigated the price anticipation mechanism in WCDMA networks, in which users acted as price anticipators. By price anticipator it meant users anticipated the effect of their behaviours on the network resource allocation, and adopted strategy correspondingly. From the view point of game theory, we investigated equilibrium properties of the price anticipation mechanism in WCDMA networks, and, through two scenarios, illustrated the relationship between price anticipation mechanism and price acceptance mechanism from the viewpoint of network revenue. Finally, we drew the conclusion that, the network revenue generated in price anticipation mechanism was less than revenue generated in price acceptance mechanism, (the difference between those two mechanisms is called as "price as anarchy"), and the network revenue generated in those two mechanisms tends to be consistent, when the effect of individual user is negligible.

Keywords: WCDMA networks, price acceptance mechanism, price anticipation mechanism, game theory, Nash equilibrium.

1 Introduction

The economic patterns of information systems and networks not only take into account the distributed implementation of those systems, but also provide incentive to regulate users' behaviors. So a great deal of research efforts focus on network resource allocation schemes based on economic models. In general, those approaches can be classified into two types: 1) Market-Based Approach: In this approach, utility

* Research supported by the NSFC Grants 60472067, JiangSu education bureau (5KJB510091) and State Key Laboratory of Networking and Switching Technology, Beijing University of Posts and Telecommunications.

X. Cheng, W. Li, and T. Znati (Eds.): WASA 2006, LNCS 4138, pp. 698–706, 2006.
© Springer-Verlag Berlin Heidelberg 2006

function is used to characterize the service requirements of an individual user. It is assumed that the utility function of individual user is unknown to the network, but users know their own utility function. The goal of the network is to allocate resources to maximize an objective function that depends on the users utilities. For example, the goal of the network could be to allocate resources to maximize the total utility over all users (called the social welfare). To achieve this goal, the network uses pricing to obtain (implicit) information about the users' utility functions and to allocate resources accordingly; 2) Control-Based Approach: In this approach, the utility functions are assigned to users (applications) by the network to characterize their service requirements. The users' utility functions can then be interpreted as a control variable, which is used by the network to achieve a desired resource allocation goal.

Markets are important not only because they are the mechanisms for the exchange of many traditional goods but they have also emerged as a new paradigm for managing and allocating resources in complex systems. Among the many features that make them attractive is the establishment of currency, which allows for a common valuation of heterogeneous resources. This gives managers or agents the ability to specify preferences or establish priority. Markets are appropriate for decentralized systems because once a currency exchange protocol is established, negotiations can occur simultaneously at various nodes without the necessity of a central authority. Scalability is another advantage as new resources and new resource users can be added simply by establishing the ability to receive or give currency. Also, prices serve as useful low-dimensional feedback for control. So in this paper, we pursue a market-based approach to model the effect of user's rationality on WCDMA network revenue.

In general, the performance perceived by each user is affect by other users which visit the same network resource. So the service level offered to all users will be the equilibrium negotiated among users to maximize their utility, and the goal of negotiation is to find out the stable operation points among competing entities, which is the very application of game theory.

In research field, there exists a lot of congestion pricing models, which provide the economic-based solution to heterogeneous resource requirement of users, that is, the network resources are treated as market, and priced correspondingly [1~10]. In Ref. [1], F.P. Kelly provides a market approach for network resource allocation, in which individual user offers bid value (or willingness-to-pay) to network in each time slot, and network determines prices of network links. The resource obtained by each user is proportional to its bid value, and inversely proportional to the price of links used by the user. Ref. [1] indicates that this approach can maximize the aggregated users' utility (social welfare), but the fundamental assumption in Ref. [1] is that each user acts as price taker, in other words, this paper didn't consider the rationality of users, that is, user can anticipate the effect of their behaviors on networks, and correspondingly declare the bid value for network resource. Ref. [2,3] investigated the resource usage based on economic models of uplink and downlink in WCDMA networks, and provided a service differentiation mechanism in Ref. [11], which designs a novel weight parameter to reflect the usage of congestion resource, and can achieve weighted proportional fairness in resource allocation. Similar to approach offered in Ref. [1], this paper didn't consider the users' rationality, furthermore, it also didn't analyze the equilibrium property of the game-based resource allocation mechanism. It is well-known that users in networks are rational (self-interest), so it is necessary to explicitly take into account the rational behaviors of users, and models their effects on networks revenue. Based on the above idea, the contributions of this paper lied in that: A price anticipation mechanism in WCDMA networks was proposed, in which users explicitly anticipated the effect of their behaviours on the network resource allocation, and adopted strategy correspondingly; Then, the equilibrium properties of the price anticipation was investigated, finally the network revenue in price acceptation mechanism and price anticipation mechanism was compared.

The paper was organized as follows: in section 2, we briefly introduced resource model of uplink in WCDMA network. The price acceptation mechanism provided in related papers was briefly discussed in section 3. The price anticipation mechanism which explicitly considered the users' rationality was investigated in section 4, in which a theorem was provided to verify the equilibrium property of this mechanism, and two numerical examples were offered to illustrate the difference between price acceptation mechanism and price anticipation mechanism. Finally, in section 5, we briefly conclude this paper.

2 Resource Model in WCDMA Networks

In this paper, we considered the uplink of single CDMA cell. Let W be the chip rate, which is fixed and equal to 3.84 Mcps for WCDMA. The SIR (Signal-to-Interference Ratio) of mobile i in uplink is given by:

$$SIR_i = \frac{W}{r_i} \frac{g_i pw_i}{\sum_{j \neq i} g_j pw_j + \eta} = G_i \alpha_i \qquad (1)$$

where r_i is the transmission rate, pw_i is the transmission power, g_i is the path gain between the base station and mobile i, η is the power of the background noise (assuming all users experience same background noise power). The G_i and α_i are the spreading factor or processing gain and CIR (Carrier-to-Interference Ratio) for mobile i respectively, which correspond to transmission rate and channel quality of mobile i. SIR_i corresponds to the signal quality, since it determines the BER (Bit Error Rate). Under the realistic assumption of additive white Gaussian noise, BER is a non-decreasing function of SIR_i, which depends on the multipath characteristics, the modulation and FEC (Forward Error Correction) algorithms. Assuming γ_i is the target SIR required to achieve specific BER (equivalent, specific FSF, Frame Successful Function). Solving the set of equations given by (1) for each mobile i, we get

$$g_i pw_i = \frac{\eta \rho_i^{UL}}{1 - \sum_j \rho_j^{UL}} \qquad (2)$$

where the load factor ρ_i^{UL} is given by $\rho_i^{UL} = 1 \bigg/ \left(\dfrac{W}{r_i \gamma_i} + 1 \right)$ \hfill (3)

For the uplink of single CDMA cell, the load factor of mobile i is given in (3). Since the each user's power can take only positive values, from (3), we get $\sum_i \rho_i^{UL} < 1$.

When there are a large number of mobile users, each using a small portion of the available resource, we have $\dfrac{W}{r_i \gamma_i} \gg 1$, hence $\rho_i^{UL} \approx \dfrac{r_i \gamma_i}{W}$, and the resource constraint can be approximated by $\sum_i r_i \gamma_i < W$.

3 Price Acceptation Mechanism

In practice, due to the limited transmission power of the mobile users, imperfect power control, shadow, etc, the total load of uplink must be well below 1, and let it L^U. Based on microeconomic theory and congestion pricing, V.A. Siris etc. provided the following service differentiation mechanism [11], in contrast to our price anticipation mechanism, which is called price acceptation mechanism.

$$r_i \gamma_i = \frac{\omega_i}{\sum_j \omega_j} L^U W \hfill (4)$$

where vector $\omega = (\omega_1, \ldots, \omega_N)$ denotes the users' willingness-to-pay in certain time slot. Assume the network treats all users identically, that is, each user is charged with the price of unit resource: $\mu = \sum_j \omega_j$. In Ref. [3], Siris verify that when users evaluate network service with the parameter of throughput (the transmission rate times frame successful function), then SIR is independent of transmission rate, and determined by frame successful function. So for given SIR, Equation (4) can be used to compute the user's transmission rate. When service class requires fixed transmission rate, but the SIR is adaptive, then Equation (4) can be used to calculate user's SIR.

In the downlink, the resource constraint is related to the total transmission power. The power can be allocated according to each user's weight correspondingly, which can also implement the service differentiation with proportional fairness.

The above service differentiation mechanism can be implemented in two approaches: one way is to communicate the price from RNC (Radio Network Controller) to mobile users, then mobile users select transmission rate to maximize their utility, which is shown in figure 1 (a); the alternative way is to send the bid values from mobile users to RNC, and then the later allocates transmission rate for users, which is shown in figure 1 (b).

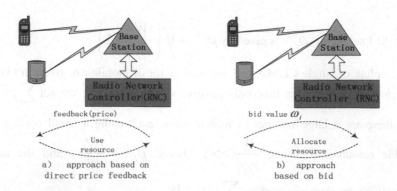

Fig. 1. Economic model-based service differentiation mechanism in WCDMA networks

Note that the goal of closed-loop power control between users and base station is to achieve the specific SIR, which operates in relatively fast time-scale (in comparison with adjustment of transmission rate). WCDMA supports fast (1500Hz) closed-loop power control in both the uplink and the downlink. While, the transmission in WCDMA occurs in fixed-size frames, the minimum duration of which is 10 milliseconds, and the rate can change between frames, but must remain the same within a single frame. So if the first approach is adopted, the extra channel from RNC to mobile users is added.

The approach based on bid is attractive for the following reasons: 1) WCDMA supports negotiation of bearer service properties both at call setup, and during a call; 2) the RNC already has intelligence for supporting flexible packet scheduling; 3) radio network are single hop networks, hence the approach satisfies desirable fairness properties, namely proportional fairness; 4) the approach is less demanding for mobile users, which do not need to adjust their rate in the (relatively fast) timescale over which the congestion price changes, but rather adjust their willingness-to-pay on a slower timescale.

In theory, it is provable that the price acceptance mechanism corresponds to the proportional fairness approach in which user i has the following utility function forms: $\omega_i \log(x_i)$ (x_i represents the user i's load factor in uplink, power in downlink). Ref. [8] offers that this utility function form can achieve the weighted proportional fairness property in resource allocation, that is the obtained resource of user i, x_i^*, satisfies:

$$\sum_{i=1}^{N} \omega_i \frac{x_i - x_i^*}{x_i} \leq 0 \tag{5}$$

For the general form of utility function $U_i(x_i)$, the user i can offer the bid according to the following principle:

$$\omega_i(t) = U_i'(x_i(t))x_i(t) \tag{6}$$

But the fundamental assumption in above approaches is that users only act as price taker, that is, those approaches didn't consider the rationality of users, and model their effects on networks. For this problem, in section 4, the price anticipation mechanism is provided, which explicitly takes into account the rational behaviors of users.

4 Price Anticipation Mechanism

In general, utility function represents users' (consumers or producers) evaluation for obtained service or resource, which can be viewed as the value of service x_i to users (for consumers), or the revenue from sale of service x_i (for producers). Utility function converts the evaluation to the equivalent value (generally measured in money). Let $\omega_{-i} = \sum_{j \neq i} \omega_j$ denote the sum of all users' bid without user i. without loss of generality, assume the amount of total resource in network is 1. User tries to maximize its net utility $V_i(\omega)$ (that is, the utility gained from obtaining network resource minus the cost paid for the resource). Then, according to the resource allocation approach introduced in section 3, the net utility of user i is given as follows:

$$V_i(\omega) = V_i(\omega_i; \omega_{-i}) = U_i\left(\frac{\omega_i}{\omega_i + \omega_{-i}}\right) - \omega_i \tag{7}$$

By the first order necessary condition, we have:

$$U_i'\left(\frac{\omega_i}{\omega_i + \omega_{-i}}\right) = \frac{(\omega_i + \omega_{-i})^2}{\omega_{-i}} \tag{8}$$

In order to discuss the effects of users' rational behaviors on network revenue, we define the price function and demand function related to net utility function.

Definition 1. Price function $p_i(x_i) : \mathfrak{R} \to \mathfrak{R}$ is defined as the price at which the user would choose an allocation of x_i. The price function represents the set of cost-allocation pairs, which are the unique response of a given user over a range of bids of other users. From (8), we get

$$p_i(x_i) = \omega_i + \omega_{-i} = U_i'\left(\frac{\omega_i}{\omega_i + \omega_{-i}}\right)\frac{\omega_{-i}}{\omega_i + \omega_{-i}} = U_i'(x_i)\left(1 - \frac{\omega_i}{\omega_i + \omega_{-i}}\right) = U_i'(x_i)(1 - x_i) \tag{9}$$

From (9), we get $p_i(0) = U_i'(0)$, which denotes that, if price is larger than marginal utility of user i, user i will choose not to join the network. The optimal bid strategy of user i is given as follows:

$$\omega_i = p_i(x_i)x_i = U_i'(x_i)(1 - x_i)x_i \tag{10}$$

So, at equilibrium, the price per unit resource that the user would be paying is less than its marginal utility by a factor of $(1 - x_i)$. This is the benefit gained by the agent for knowing its own effect on the price of the resource. Users with larger allocations at equilibrium are able to scale their costs away from their marginal utility to a larger degree. In the case where there are many users and each user receives a small portion of the resource, i.e, $x_i \ll 1$, the prices being paid will be very close to the marginal utility.

Definition 2. Demand function $d_i(p): \mathfrak{R} \to \mathfrak{R}$ is the inverse of the price function, which is defined as the quantity of resource that the user would desire if the price is p.

The above model describes N users to bid for a portion of network resource. If the resulting allocation does not lie on the user's optimal demand curve, the user will change their bid. An immediate question is whether there exist a set of bids that is Nash equilibrium, i.e., a set of bids such that no single user wishes to deviate from its bid given the bides of all the other users remains the same. That is, no user can improve its net utility through unilaterally changing bid strategy, i.e,

$$\omega_i^* = \arg\max_{\omega_i} V_i(\omega_i; \omega_{-i}^*) \quad \forall i \in \{1, \cdots, N\}.$$ Because each user's optimal

response can be characterized by its demand function, the above question is equivalent to whether there exists a value for the sum of total bids p, such that $\sum_{i=1}^N d_i(p) = 1$.

Theorem 1. Let $d_i(p)$ represent demand function of user i, $i=1,\ldots,N$, in which $d_i(0) = 1$, $d_i(p) = 0 \ \forall p > \overline{p}_i$, and $d_i(p_1) > d_i(p_2) \ p_1 < p_2 < \overline{p}_i$ (that is, $\overline{p}_i$ is the price upper bound that user i can accept. When price exceeds the upper bound, user i thinks that it is not worth joining the network). Then there exists a unique value p^*, such that $\sum_{i=1}^N d_i(p^*) = 1$.

Proof. Let $\overline{d}(p) = \sum_{i=1}^N d_i(p)$. Then $\overline{d}(p)$ is a continuously decreasing function whose maximum is $\overline{d}(0) = N > 1$. Let $\overline{p}_{\max} = \max_i \overline{p}_i$, then $\overline{d}(\overline{p}_{\max}) = 0$. According to the Intermediate Value Theorem, we get there exists a unique value p^*, such that $\sum_{i=1}^N d_i(p^*) = 1$.

In the approach above, parameter p not only denotes the price and measurement of congestion, but represents the network revenue generated by resource. The following remark intuitively demonstrates the means of p^*.

Remark 1. Let demand function $d_i(p)$ have the properties described in Theorem 1, $i=1,\ldots,N$. Those demand functions are indexed such that $\overline{p}_1 \geq \overline{p}_2 \geq \cdots \geq \overline{p}_N$, then the value of p^* that solves $\sum_{i=1}^N d_i(p) = 1$ has the following property:

$$p^* \in [\overline{p}_n, \overline{p}_{n-1}], \ 1 < n \leq N, \text{ where } \overline{p}_n \text{ and } \overline{p}_{n-1} \text{ satisfies: } \sum_{i=1}^{n-1} d_i(\overline{p}_{n-1}) \leq 1$$

and $\sum_{i=1}^{n-1} d_i(\overline{p}_n) \geq 1$.

Remark 1 stated that, if the resource were able to pick the set of users with the highest price limits, the Nash equilibrium point allocation is also the allocation that would maximize the revenue generated. Obviously, the network revenue generated by the price anticipation mechanism is less than the network revenue generated by price acceptation mechanism. The difference between those two approaches is known as the "price of anarchy" [8]. As the number of number of users increase gradually, each user shares less resource. To certain degree, individual effect on network resource price can be neglected, and, those two mechanisms achieve the same network revenue. The following two examples demonstrate the result more clearly.

Let $U_i(x_i) = \overline{p}_i x_i$ utility function of user i, where parameter $\overline{p}_i$ denotes the price upper bound accepted by user i. then, from (9), the demand function of user i is given: $d_i(p) = \max\{0, 1 - \dfrac{p}{\overline{p}_i}\}$. At equilibrium, we have: $\displaystyle\sum_{i=1}^{n} d_i(p_n^*) = 1$, then

$$p_n^* = (n-1)\left(\sum_{i=1}^{n} \frac{1}{\overline{p}_i}\right)^{-1} \tag{11}$$

The maximal network revenue generated at equilibrium is given as follows: $p^* = \max p_n^*$.

Considering the following two cases:

Case 1. There are two users access to single cell in WCDMA network, where $U_1(x_1) = x_1$, $U_2(x_2) = \varepsilon x_2$. When users act as price taker, in terms of network revenue, the optimal resource allocation is given as follows: $x_1=1$, $x_2=0$. So the optimal revenue is 1, which is also the price of unit resource, $\mu = 1$ (in this paper above, we assume the total resource amount in single WCDMA cell is 1); when users act as price anticipator, the price of unit network resource at equilibrium is

$p^* = \dfrac{\varepsilon}{1+\varepsilon}$. So we can infer that the optimal network revenue gradually tends to zero, when $\varepsilon \to 0$,

Case 2. There exists N users, each user with utility function $U_i(x_i) = x_i$, $i=1,\ldots,N$. Then the optimal revenue in price acceptation mechanism is 1; from (11), the optimal revenue in price anticipation mechanism is $p^* = \dfrac{N-1}{N}$. When $N \to \infty$,

$p^* \to \mu$, which means that those tow mechanisms achieve same network revenue, under the condition that individual user's effect on network is negligible.

5   Conclusion

David D. Clark said that it is necessary to accommodate, if possible, to use self-interest behaviors of users to strengthen the technical architecture [14]. In WCDMA networks, most researches based on economic models of resource control assumed that network users only accepted the price declared by network (we named it as price acceptance mechanism), but didn't take into account user's rationality (self-interest behaviors). In this paper, we explicitly considered users' rationality, and provided the price anticipation mechanism, in which users anticipated their effect on network revenue, and adopted corresponding strategy, then offered the comparison between price acceptance mechanism and price anticipation mechanism. We drew the conclusion that, the network revenue generated in price anticipation mechanism was less than revenue generated in price acceptance mechanism, (the difference between those two mechanisms was called as "price as anarchy"), and the network revenue generated in those two mechanisms tends to be consistent, when the effect of individual user is negligible, i.e, each user only occupied a very small portion of system resource.

References

[1] F.P. Kelly, "Charging and rate control for elastic traffic", European Transactions on Telecommunications, vol. 8, pp. 33-37, 1997.
[2] V.A. Siris, B. Briscoe, D. Songhurst, "Economic models for resource control in wireless networks", In Proc. of IEEE PIMRC, 2002.
[3] V.A. Siris, "Resource control for elastic traffic in CDMA networks", In Proc. of ACM MOBICOM, 2002.
[4] P. Marbach, "Priority service and Max-Min fairness", In Proc. of INFOCOM 2002, pp. 266–275.
[5] R.-F. Liao, R.H. Wouhaybi, A.T. Campbell, "Wireless Incentive Engineering", IEEE Journal of Selected Areas in Communications (JSAC), Special Issue on Recent Advances in Multimedia Wireless, (to be published), 4th Quarter 2003.
[6] M. Dramitinos, C. Courcoubetis, G.D. Stamoulis, "Auction-based Resource Reservation in 2.5/3G Networks, Kluwer/ACM Mobile Networks and Applications" ACM MONET, 2003.
[7] E.W. Fulp, D.S. Reeves, "QoS rewards and risks: A multi-market approach to resource allocation", In Proceedings of the IFIP-TC6 Networking 2000, Paris France, 2000.
[8] R. Johari, J. N. Tsitsiklis, "Network Resource Allocation and a Congestion Game", Mathematics of Operations Research, 2003.
[9] P. Marbach, R. Berry, "Downlink resource allocation and pricing for wireless networks", In Proc. of IEEE INFOCOM, 2002.
[10] J.W. Lee, R.R. Mazumdar, N.B. Shroff, "Downlink power allocation for multiclass CDMA wireless networks", IEEE INFOCOM 2002.
[11] V.A. Siris, B. Briscoe, D. Songhurst, "Service differentiation in third generation mobile networks", In Proc. of 3rd International workshop on quality of future Internet services (QofIS'02), Zurich, Switzerland, October, 2002.
[12] R.T. Maheswaran, T. Basar, "Decentralized network resource allocation as a repeated game", Proc. 40th IEEE Conf. Decision and Control, pp. 4565-4570, Orlando, Florida, December 4-7, 2001
[13] R.T. Maheswaran, T. Basar, "Nash equilibrium and decentralized negotiation in auctioning divisible resources", J. Group Decision and Negotiation (GDN), May 2003.
[14] David D. Clark etc., "Tussle in cyberspace: defining tomorrow's Internet", SIGCOMM'02.

Author Index

Lecture Notes in Computer Science

For information about Vols. 1–4020

please contact your bookseller or Springer

Vol. 4066: A. Rensink, J. Warmer (Eds.), Model Driven Architecture – Foundations and Applications. XII, 392 pages. 2006.

Vol. 4065: P. Perner (Ed.), Advances in Data Mining. XI, 592 pages. 2006. (Sublibrary LNAI).

Vol. 4064: R. Büschkes, P. Laskov (Eds.), Detection of Intrusions and Malware & Vulnerability Assessment. X, 195 pages. 2006.

Vol. 4063: I. Gorton, G.T. Heineman, I. Crnkovic, H.W. Schmidt, J.A. Stafford, C.A. Szyperski, K. Wallnau (Eds.), Component-Based Software Engineering. XI, 394 pages. 2006.

Vol. 4062: G. Wang, J.F. Peters, A. Skowron, Y. Yao (Eds.), Rough Sets and Knowledge Technology. XX, 810 pages. 2006. (Sublibrary LNAI).

Vol. 4061: K. Miesenberger, J. Klaus, W. Zagler, A. Karshmer (Eds.), Computers Helping People with Special Needs. XXIX, 1356 pages. 2006.

Vol. 4060: K. Futatsugi, J.-P. Jouannaud, J. Meseguer (Eds.), Algebra, Meaning, and Computation. XXXVIII, 643 pages. 2006.

Vol. 4059: L. Arge, R. Freivalds (Eds.), Algorithm Theory – SWAT 2006. XII, 436 pages. 2006.

Vol. 4058: L.M. Batten, R. Safavi-Naini (Eds.), Information Security and Privacy. XII, 446 pages. 2006.

Vol. 4057: J.P.W. Pluim, B. Likar, F.A. Gerritsen (Eds.), Biomedical Image Registration. XII, 324 pages. 2006.

Vol. 4056: P. Flocchini, L. Gąsieniec (Eds.), Structural Information and Communication Complexity. X, 357 pages. 2006.

Vol. 4055: J. Lee, J. Shim, S.-g. Lee, C. Bussler, S. Shim (Eds.), Data Engineering Issues in E-Commerce and Services. IX, 290 pages. 2006.

Vol. 4054: A. Horváth, M. Telek (Eds.), Formal Methods and Stochastic Models for Performance Evaluation. VIII, 239 pages. 2006.

Vol. 4053: M. Ikeda, K.D. Ashley, T.-W. Chan (Eds.), Intelligent Tutoring Systems. XXVI, 821 pages. 2006.

Vol. 4052: M. Bugliesi, B. Preneel, V. Sassone, I. Wegener (Eds.), Automata, Languages and Programming, Part II. XXIV, 603 pages. 2006.

Vol. 4051: M. Bugliesi, B. Preneel, V. Sassone, I. Wegener (Eds.), Automata, Languages and Programming, Part I. XXIII, 729 pages. 2006.

Vol. 4049: S. Parsons, N. Maudet, P. Moraitis, I. Rahwan (Eds.), Argumentation in Multi-Agent Systems. XIV, 313 pages. 2006. (Sublibrary LNAI).

Vol. 4048: L. Goble, J.-J.C.. Meyer (Eds.), Deontic Logic and Artificial Normative Systems. X, 273 pages. 2006. (Sublibrary LNAI).

Vol. 4047: M. Robshaw (Ed.), Fast Software Encryption. XI, 434 pages. 2006.

Vol. 4046: S.M. Astley, M. Brady, C. Rose, R. Zwiggelaar (Eds.), Digital Mammography. XVI, 654 pages. 2006.

Vol. 4045: D. Barker-Plummer, R. Cox, N. Swoboda (Eds.), Diagrammatic Representation and Inference. XII, 301 pages. 2006. (Sublibrary LNAI).

Vol. 4044: P. Abrahamsson, M. Marchesi, G. Succi (Eds.), Extreme Programming and Agile Processes in Software Engineering. XII, 230 pages. 2006.

Vol. 4043: A.S. Atzeni, A. Lioy (Eds.), Public Key Infrastructure. XI, 261 pages. 2006.

Vol. 4042: D. Bell, J. Hong (Eds.), Flexible and Efficient Information Handling. XVI, 296 pages. 2006.

Vol. 4041: S.-W. Cheng, C.K. Poon (Eds.), Algorithmic Aspects in Information and Management. XI, 395 pages. 2006.

Vol. 4040: R. Reulke, U. Eckardt, B. Flach, U. Knauer, K. Polthier (Eds.), Combinatorial Image Analysis. XII, 482 pages. 2006.

Vol. 4039: M. Morisio (Ed.), Reuse of Off-the-Shelf Components. XIII, 444 pages. 2006.

Vol. 4038: P. Ciancarini, H. Wiklicky (Eds.), Coordination Models and Languages. VIII, 299 pages. 2006.

Vol. 4037: R. Gorrieri, H. Wehrheim (Eds.), Formal Methods for Open Object-Based Distributed Systems. XVII, 474 pages. 2006.

Vol. 4036: O. H. Ibarra, Z. Dang (Eds.), Developments in Language Theory. XII, 456 pages. 2006.

Vol. 4035: T. Nishita, Q. Peng, H.-P. Seidel (Eds.), Advances in Computer Graphics. XX, 771 pages. 2006.

Vol. 4034: J. Münch, M. Vierimaa (Eds.), Product-Focused Software Process Improvement. XVII, 474 pages. 2006.

Vol. 4033: B. Stiller, P. Reichl, B. Tuffin (Eds.), Performability Has its Price. X, 103 pages. 2006.

Vol. 4032: O. Etzion, T. Kuflik, A. Motro (Eds.), Next Generation Information Technologies and Systems. XIII, 365 pages. 2006.

Vol. 4031: M. Ali, R. Dapoigny (Eds.), Advances in Applied Artificial Intelligence. XXIII, 1353 pages. 2006. (Sublibrary LNAI).

Vol. 4029: L. Rutkowski, R. Tadeusiewicz, L.A. Zadeh, J.M. Zurada (Eds.), Artificial Intelligence and Soft Computing – ICAISC 2006. XXI, 1235 pages. 2006. (Sublibrary LNAI).

Vol. 4028: J. Kohlas, B. Meyer, A. Schiper (Eds.), Dependable Systems: Software, Computing, Networks. XII, 295 pages. 2006.

Vol. 4027: H.L. Larsen, G. Pasi, D. Ortiz-Arroyo, T. Andreasen, H. Christiansen (Eds.), Flexible Query Answering Systems. XVIII, 714 pages. 2006. (Sublibrary LNAI).

Vol. 4026: P.B. Gibbons, T. Abdelzaher, J. Aspnes, R. Rao (Eds.), Distributed Computing in Sensor Systems. XIV, 566 pages. 2006.

Vol. 4025: F. Eliassen, A. Montresor (Eds.), Distributed Applications and Interoperable Systems. XI, 355 pages. 2006.

Vol. 4024: S. Donatelli, P.S. Thiagarajan (Eds.), Petri Nets and Other Models of Concurrency - ICATPN 2006. XI, 441 pages. 2006.

Vol. 4021: E. André, L. Dybkjær, W. Minker, H. Neumann, M. Weber (Eds.), Perception and Interactive Technologies. XI, 217 pages. 2006. (Sublibrary LNAI).